COSTA

015.

WELCOME TO COSTA RICA

Costa Rica has it all: nowhere else can you gaze upon an active volcano while soaking in a hot spring one day, hike deep into a rain forest the next, and end your trip learning to surf at a luxurious seaside resort. Miles of pristine beaches on the Pacific and Caribbean coasts, fabulous national parks with plentiful opportunities for wildlife viewing, and world-renowned eco-lodges have made this one of the hottest destinations around. The welcoming people of Costa Rica, and their mellow *pura vida* lifestyle, add warmth to every visit.

TOP REASONS TO GO

★ **Active Volcanoes:** Five imposing behemoths exude, fume, seethe, and smolder.

★ **Beaches:** From pristine secluded hideaways to palm-fringed resort strands.

★ **Eco-friendly Hotels:** Wilderness lodges set the standard for green tourism with style.

★ **Outdoor Adventure:** Zip lining, canopy tours, hiking, and surfing are all top notch.

★ **Wildlife Galore:** Monkeys, sloths, and turtles abound, and the birding is superb.

★ **Coffee:** A plantation tour shows you what makes the country tick.

Fodor's COSTA RICA 2015

Publisher: Amanda D'Acierno, *Senior Vice President*

Editorial: Arabella Bowen, *Editor in Chief*; Linda Cabasin, *Editorial Director*

Design: Fabrizio La Rocca, *Vice President, Creative Director*; Tina Malaney, *Associate Art Director*; Chie Ushio, *Senior Designer*; Ann McBride, *Production Designer*

Photography: Melanie Marin, *Associate Director of Photography*; Jessica Parkhill and Jennifer Romains, *Researchers*

Maps: Rebecca Baer, *Senior Map Editor*; David Lindroth, Mark Stroud (Moon Street Cartography) *Cartographers*

Production: Linda Schmidt, *Managing Editor*; Evangelos Vasilakis, *Associate Managing Editor*; Angela L. McLean, *Senior Production Manager*

Sales: Jacqueline Lebow, *Sales Director*

Marketing & Publicity: Heather Dalton, *Marketing Director*; Katherine Punia, *Senior Publicist*

Business & Operations: Susan Livingston, *Vice President, Strategic Business Planning*; Sue Daulton, *Vice President, Operations*

Fodors.com: Megan Bell, *Executive Director, Revenue & Business Development*; Yasmin Marinaro, *Senior Director, Marketing & Partnerships*

Copyright © 2015 by Fodor's Travel, a division of Random House LLC

Writers: Jeffrey Van Fleet, Dorothy MacKinnon, Marlise Kast-Myers

Editor: Salwa Jabado
Editorial Contributors: Amanda Theunissen, Linda Cabasin
Production Editor: Elyse Rozelle

ISBN 978-0-8041-4268-7

ISSN 1522–6131

All details in this book are based on information supplied to us at press time. Always confirm information when it matters, especially if you're making a detour to visit a specific place. Fodor's expressly disclaims any liability, loss, or risk, personal or otherwise, that is incurred as a consequence of the use of any of the contents of this book.

SPECIAL SALES

This book is available at special discounts for bulk purchases for sales promotions or premiums. For more information, e-mail specialmarkets@randomhouse.com

PRINTED IN THE UNITED STATES OF AMERICA

10 9 8 7 6 5 4 3 2 1

CONTENTS

Fodor's Features

ABOUT
THIS GUIDE

Fodor's Recommendations

Everything in this guide is worth doing—we don't cover what isn't—but exceptional sights, hotels, and restaurants are recognized with additional accolades. Fodor'sChoice★ indicates our top recommendations; and **Best Bets** call attention to notable hotels and restaurants in various categories. Care to nominate a new place? Visit Fodors.com/contact-us.

Trip Costs

We list prices wherever possible to help you budget well. Hotel and restaurant price categories from **$** to **$$$$** are noted alongside each recommendation. For hotels, we include the lowest cost of a standard double room in high season. For restaurants, we cite the average price of a main course at dinner or, if dinner isn't served, at lunch. For attractions, we always list adult admission fees; discounts are usually available for children, students, and senior citizens.

Hotels

Our local writers vet every hotel to recommend the best overnights in each price category, from budget to expensive. Unless otherwise specified, you can expect private bath, phone, and TV in your room. For expanded hotel reviews, facilities, and deals visit Fodors.com.

Top Picks
★ Fodor'sChoice

Listings
⊠ Address
⊠ Branch address
☎ Telephone
🖷 Fax
⊕ Website
✉ E-mail
✒ Admission fee
🕓 Open/closed times
Ⓜ Subway
⊹ Directions or Map coordinates

Hotels & Restaurants
🏨 Hotel
🛏 Number of rooms
🍴 Meal plans
✗ Restaurant
🍸 Reservations
👔 Dress code
🚫 No credit cards
$ Price

Other
⇨ See also
☞ Take note
⛳ Golf facilities

Restaurants

Unless we state otherwise, restaurants are open for lunch and dinner daily. We mention dress code only when there's a specific requirement and reservations only when they're essential or not accepted. To make restaurant reservations, visit Fodors.com.

Credit Cards

The hotels and restaurants in this guide typically accept credit cards. If not, we'll say so.

EXPERIENCE
COSTA RICA

1

WHAT'S WHERE

Numbers correspond to chapters.

3 San José. Do you know the way to San José? You will soon enough. Almost everyone passes through on their way to the beach or the mountains. This capital city isn't much to look at, but it has great restaurants and nightlife, and fascinating museums dedicated to gold and jade.

4 The Central Valley. You likely won't linger long in the Central Valley, as it lacks any of the country's big-name attractions. But there are quite a few day-trip possibilities, including exploring mountain villages, rafting through white-water rapids, and gaping into the mouths of some of the country's most accessible active volcanoes.

5 Arenal, Monteverde, and the Northern Lowlands. This part of Costa Rica attracts those who don't like sitting still. After zipping along cables through the misty jungle of Monteverde Cloud Forest, windsurfing on glittering Lake Arenal, or taking in the majesty of the Arenal Volcano, you can reward yourself with a dip in the bubbly waters of Tabacón Hot Springs.

6 Guanacaste and the Nicoya Peninsula. If you came for beaches, this area is for you. Each has a unique personality: Flamingo's

Elevation	
12,500	3,810
10,000	3,048
7,500	2,286
5,000	1,525
4,000	1,220
3,000	915
2,500	762
2,000	610
1,500	457
1,000	305
750	230
500	152
250	75
100	30
feet	meters

Map labels: Largo de Nicaragua, NICARAGUA, Peñas Blancas, Los Chiles, La Cruz, Bahía Salinas, Golfo de Santa Elena, Orosí, Guanacaste National Park, Upala, Caño Negro National Wildlife Refuge, Cacao, Rincón, Caño Negro, SANTA ELENA PENINSULA, Rincón de la Vieja, Rincón de la Vieja National Park, Santa Rosa National Park, Golfo de Papagayo, Liberia, Lake Arenal, Arenal Volcano National Park, Juan Castro Blanco National Park, Comunidad, Bagaces, Tilarán, Arenal, La Fortuna, El Coro, Palo Verde National Park, Cañas, CORDILLERA DE TILARÁN, Platanar, Filadelfia, Flamingo, Belén, Zarcero, Huacas, Barra Honda National Park, San Ramón, Tamarindo, Santa Cruz, Nicoya, Puntarenas, Atenas, NICOYA PENINSULA, Jicaral, Caldera, Orotina, Nosara, Carmona, Paquera, Tárcoles, Sámara, Carrillo, Tambor, Gulf of Nicoya, Mal País, Cobano, Jacó, Montezuma, Pacific, CORDILLERA DE GUANACASTE

endless stretch of sand draws sun worshippers; Tamarindo's nightlife is legendary; Avellanas's strong swells challenge surfers; Ostional's nesting sea turtles bring nature lovers; and the Papagayo Peninsula's all-inclusive resorts provide every creature comfort.

7 **Manuel Antonio and the Central Pacific Coast.** The area's not just for spring breakers (although it helps in funky surf towns like Jacó). Drive down the coast to the cluster of small hotels and restaurants at Manuel Antonio. The national park, on a peninsula jutting into the ocean, has the easiest wildlife viewing on the planet and the country's most-visited attraction.

8 **The Osa Peninsula and the South Pacific.** Rustic lodges in the Osa Peninsula sit on the edge of the country's wildest region, consisting almost entirely of Corcovado National Park. Hikes reveal toucans and scarlet macaws in the treetops, and boating trips often include swimming with whales and dolphins.

9 **Tortuguero and the Caribbean Coast.** Come here for the spirited music, the tasty food, the chance to mix with the Afro-Caribbean population, and the turtle-watching at Tortuguero National Park.

COSTA RICA PLANNER

When to Go

High Season: Mid-December to April
The sunniest, driest season in most of the country occurs from mid-December through April, with Christmas and Easter bracketing the busiest tourist season. March and April get downright sweltering in lowland areas, with temperatures in the arid North Pacific, Costa Rica's hottest region, frequently exceeding 33°C (90°F).

Low Season: May to mid-December
In a stroke of marketing genius, Costa Rica promotes the rainy season as the "green season," touting lush vegetation, smaller crowds, and lower prices. Afternoon showers kick in by May and last through November most everywhere, with a brief drier season in June and July. Rain or not, North American and European summer vacations do increase the influx of visitors from June through August. Rains become more prolonged and heavy in September and October.

Shoulder Season: May, mid-November to mid-December
The transition periods between rainy and dry seasons and back again make a marvelous time to visit Costa Rica. Visitor numbers are smaller and the threat of rain does exist but is minimal.

Getting Here

San José's Aeropuerto Internacional Juan Santamaría is in the center of the country, so it's especially convenient for destinations in the Central Valley and along the Central Pacific. The closest destinations are less than an hour away. The only other international gateway is Liberia's Aeropuerto Internacional Daniel Oduber Quirós in the western part of the country. Flying here makes sense if you're planning to spend most of your time in Guanacaste and the northern Nicoya Peninsula region.

A relatively small number of travelers arrive in Costa Rica by road, especially with the difficulties taking rental cars between countries. Long-distance buses travel directly to San José from the larger cities in Nicaragua and Panama, but these are arduous journeys. The Managua–to–San José route takes between 8 and 10 hours.

Getting Around

To save time, many people take domestic flights to their ultimate destination. SANSA and Nature Air fly to various destinations from San José's Aeropuerto Internacional Juan Santamaría and Liberia's Aeropuerto Internacional Daniel Oduber Quirós. Both offer flights to resort areas, especially those near the beaches. Regional airports are very small, sometimes with no terminal at all and staff that arrives at about the same time as the plane.

Costa Rican towns are connected by regular bus service. Buses between major destinations have comfortable seats and air-conditioning. If you have to transfer along the way, you may get a converted school bus cooled only by the tropical breezes. If you're traveling a long distance, make sure to request a *directo* (express) bus. Otherwise you may stop in every small town along the way.

The country's improving highway system means renting a car is a great way to get around. You can travel on your own schedule, stopping where you like. San José and Liberia have rental desks; at smaller airports a representative will meet you and drive you to the nearby office.

Festivals and Celebrations

Every day is a patron saint's day somewhere in Costa Rica, so you may very well see some community's annual *festejo patronal* (patron-saint festival). Listen for the loud firecracker explosion at dawn that kicks off the festivities.

The festivals mirror Costa Rica: devoutly Catholic but increasingly secularized. The festival is a religious tradition and an important part of the day is a Mass and parade where the saint's figure is carried through the streets. That said, there's also bingo games, rickety carnival rides—a certain amount of luck and prayer is in order here—horse parades, and amateurish bullfights.

Año Nuevo (*New Year's Day*). New Year's Day is a time that most Costa Ricans spend with family and friends.

Fiestas de Santa Cruz. Mid-January brings the Santa Cruz Fiestas, with bullfights, rodeos, folk dancing, and marimba music.

Semana Santa (*Holy Week*). Lasting from Palm Sunday through Easter Sunday, Holy Week is a major observance in Costa Rica, especially on Good Friday, when there are religious processions all over the country. Little is open Thursday and Friday, and the country legally goes dry. Make hotel reservations far in advance.

Día de Juan Santamaría. This public holiday, on April 11, commemorates Costa Rica's national hero.

Día del Trabajo (*Labor Day*). On May 1, Costa Rica celebrates Labor Day.

Día de la Virgen de los Angeles. Costa Rica's patron saint is celebrated on August 2, with religious processions from San José to the Basílica de Nuestra Señora de Los Angeles in Cartago.

Día de las Madres (*Mother's Day*). Costa Rica's reverence for motherhood means that Mother's Day on August 15 is a legal holiday here.

Día de la Independencia (*Independence Day*). Lantern-lighted parades the night before and marching bands throughout the country during the day mark the Independence Day holiday on September 15.

Inmaculada Concepción de la Virgen María (*Immaculate Conception*). On December 8, Masses honor the Virgin Mary.

Navidad (*Christmas*). The celebration of Christmas goes on throughout December, and extends into the last week of the month, with year-end festivals including bullfights around San José.

Money Matters

The local currency is the *colón*. Don't bother getting *colones* before your trip; it's difficult, and the exchange rate outside Costa Rica is abysmal. There are currency exchange booths in the international arrivals terminal of San José's Aeropuerto Internacional Juan Santamaría and Liberia's Aeropuerto Internacaional Daniel Oduber Quirós. Both airports also have ATMs that dispense both dollars and colones.

Most ATMs (*cajero automático*) are linked to the Cirrus and the Plus networks; they can be used by holders of most U.S.-issued debit and credit cards. Make sure that your PIN has four numbers; most machines don't accept longer ones.

Credit cards are accepted by almost all businesses catering to tourists. Because businesses are charged a hefty fee for credit-card purchases, some will add a small surcharge or impose a minimum purchase amount if you use plastic. Ask beforehand.

The tourism industry prices its offerings in dollars—but you can pay in colones at the current exchange rate if you wish. Other large businesses do accept dollars as payment, but will use an exchange rate less favorable to you. Small mom-and-pop places won't be set up to handle dollars. If paying in dollars, make sure the bills are in good condition and in smaller denominations.

COSTA RICA
TOP ATTRACTIONS

Arenal Volcano

(A) Costa Rica has five active volcanoes, with Arenal being its most visited. The behemoth has settled into a less-active phase these days—likely temporary—but its sinister, majestic, perfectly shaped cone never fails to impress, if the clouds part long enough for you to get a view.

Selvatura Park

(B) Soaring over the treetops on a zip line is a thrilling experience. But canopy tours aren't just for adrenaline junkies. Many rain forests have hanging bridges and elevated platforms to give you a bird's-eye view of the rain forest. Many of the best, like Selvetura, are around Monteverde Cloud Forest Biological Reserve and the Santa Elena Reserve, but others are clustered around Lake Arenal and Manuel Antonio.

Manuel Antonio National Park

(C) Some of the country's most thrilling views can be seen from the trails through Manuel Antonio National Park. As you emerge from the rain forest, don't be surprised to find yourself alone on a palm-shaded beach. Make sure to look up—sloths and three types of monkey make their home in the canopy, and on a good day you might see them all.

Corcovado National Park

(D) Bird-watchers come to this vast and pristine rain forest with hopes of catching a glimpse of the endangered harpy eagle. It's notoriously difficult to see, but other feathered friends—like the scarlet macaw, the orange-bellied trogon, and the golden-hooded tanager—practically pose for pictures. No need to head off into the rain forest with your binoculars; dozens of hummingbirds are likely to dart around you as you relax by the pool.

Playa Carrillo

(E) This long, picturesque beach, backed by a line of swaying palms and protective cliffs, is certainly one of the most beautiful stretches of sand in the country. Perfect for swimming, snorkeling, or just walking, the beach isn't marred by a single building. Visit on a weekday and it's possible that you may have the entire shore to yourself.

Nicoya Peninsula

(F) Popular with the sun-and-fun crowd, the peninsula still has a yet-to-be-discovered feel. Maybe that's because its sandy shores are never covered with a checkerboard of beach blankets. Drive a few miles in any direction and you can find one all to yourself. But civilization isn't far away—some of the country's best restaurants are within reach.

Turrialba

(G) Heavy rainfall, steep mountains, and rocky terrain make this region a magnet for white-water rafters, and there's a river to match anyone's level of expertise. Not far from San José, the Central Valley has outfitters who offer everything from easy day trips to challenging multiday excursions. Many of these companies congregate around Turrialba, the country's white-water capital and close to the Rio Pacuare and Rio Reventazón.

Monteverde Cloud Forest Biological Reserve

(H) The roads leading here are terrible, but you won't mind once you see the mist-covered reserve. Because of the constant moisture, this private park is unbelievably lush. It's gorgeous during the day, but many prefer night hikes, when you can see colorful birds asleep in the branches, hairy tarantulas in search of prey, and nocturnal mammals like the wide-eyed kinkajou.

FAQS

Do I need any special documents to get into the country?

Aside from a passport that's valid for at least three months after date of entry and a round-trip/outbound ticket, you don't need anything else to enter the country. You'll be given a 90-day tourist visa as you pass through immigration. You're no longer required to have your passport with you at all times during your trip, but you must carry a photocopy while you're out and about.

How difficult is it to travel around the country?

It's extremely easy. Thanks to the domestic airlines, getting to your ultimate destination takes far less time than just a few years ago; almost every worthwhile spot is within an hour of San José. Long-distance buses and vans are usually very comfortable, so don't overlook these as a way to get to far-flung destinations. Renting a car is a great way to get around, because you're not tied to somebody else's schedule. Alas, roads are not always well marked. It's good to have a detailed map if you're driving in rural areas, as it's easy to miss a turn.

Are the roads as bad as they say?

Yes and no. You'll still find potholes the size of bathtubs on the road leading to Monteverde Cloud Forest Biological Reserve, and the gravel roads on the Nicoya Peninsula are often so grooved by the rain that they feel like an endless series of speed bumps. But roads are improving. The most dramatic improvements have been made near the resort area of Lake Arenal. Repairs to the road between Nuevo Arenal and La Fortuna have cut your travel time almost in half. During and immediately after the rainy season is the worst time for driving. The constant deluge takes its toll on the pavement.

Should I rent a four-wheel-drive vehicle?

Probably. If your trip will take you mostly to the beaches, you won't necessarily need a 4WD vehicle. If you're headed to more-mountainous areas, such as any destination in the Northern Plains, you'll definitely want one. But even on the most badly maintained roads through the mountains, you'll see locals getting around just fine in their beat-up sedans. There's usually only a minor difference in the cost, so there's no reason not to go for the 4WD. Keep in mind, though, manual transmission cars are standard, so if you have to drive an automatic, you'll pay a good bit extra for it.

Should I get insurance on the rental car?

Even if your own insurance covers rental cars, go ahead and take full insurance. The cost is often less than $10 a day. For that you get the peace of mind of knowing that you're not going to be hassled for a scratch on the fender or a crack in the windshield. One traveler reported returning a rental car with a front bumper completely detached, and because he had full insurance the clerk just smiled and wished him a good trip home.

Should I consider a package tour?

If you're terrified of traveling on your own, sign up for a tour. But Costa Rica is such an easy place to get around that there's really no need. Part of the fun is the exploring—finding a secluded beach, hiking down to a hidden waterfall, discovering a great craft shop—and that's just not going to happen on a tour. If you're more comfortable with a package tour, pick one with a specific focus, like bird-watching or boating, so that you're less likely to get a generic tour.

Do I need a local guide?

Guides are a great idea for the first-time visitor in search of wildlife. A good guide will know where to find the animals, and will bring along a telescope so that you can get an up-close look at that sloth high in the trees or the howler monkeys across the clearing. After the first day, however, you'll probably grab your binoculars and head out on your own. It's much more gratifying to tell the folks back home that you discovered that banded anteater all by yourself.

Will I have trouble if I don't speak Spanish?

No problema. Most people in businesses catering to tourists speak at least a little English. If you encounter someone who doesn't speak English, they'll probably point you to a coworker who does. Even if you're in a far-flung destination, locals will go out of their way to find somebody who speaks your language.

Can I drink the water?

Costa Rica is the only Central American country where you don't have to get stressed out about drinking the water. The water is potable in all but the most remote regions. That said, many people don't like the taste of the tap water and prefer bottled water.

Are there any worries about the food?

None whatsoever. Even the humblest roadside establishment is likely to be scrupulously clean. If you have any doubts about a place, just move on to the next one. There's no problem enjoying fruit, cheese, bread, or other local products sold from the stands set up along the roads.

Do I need to get any shots?

You probably don't have to get any vaccinations or take any special medications. The U.S. Centers for Disease Control and Prevention warns that there is some concern about malaria, especially in remote areas along the Caribbean coast. If you plan to spend any amount of time there, you may want to talk with your doctor about antimalarial medications well before your trip.

Should I bring any medications?

Other than your prescription and habitual over-the-counter medications, the only thing we recommend is using an insect repellent containing the active ingredient DEET. Ordinary repellents, even those labeled "extra strength," aren't going to do the trick against the mosquitoes of the tropics. A formulation with 10% to 25% DEET will be fine; those with more are likely to irritate your skin.

Can I use my ATM card?

Most ATMs are on both the Cirrus and Plus networks, so they accept debit and credit cards issued by U.S. banks. Some might accept cards with just the MasterCard or just the Visa logo; if that's the case, try a machine at a different bank. Know the exchange rate before you use an ATM for the first time so that you know about how much local currency you want to withdraw.

Do most places take credit cards?

Almost all tourist-oriented businesses accept credit cards. Smaller restaurants and hotels may not accept them at all. Some businesses don't like to accept credit cards because their banks charge them exorbitant fees for credit-card transactions. They will usually relent and charge you a small fee for the privilege.

Do I need a plug adaptor?

Outlets in Costa Rica are 110 volts, with standard U.S. two-prong plugs, three prongs if grounded, so U.S. appliances will work without adaptors.

COSTA RICA TODAY

Government

Costa Rica is a democratic republic whose structure will be familiar to any citizen of the United States. The 1949 constitution divides the government into independent executive, legislative, and judicial branches. All citizens are guaranteed equality before the law, the right to own property, freedom of speech, and freedom of religion.

Costa Rica elected its first female president for a four-year term in 2010, the fifth of, now, six Latin American countries to take such a step. Now a former occupant of the office, Laura Chinchilla became the first person here to hold the title "La Presidenta."

The country is famous for lacking an army, which was abolished when the constitution was ratified in 1949. The country's stable government and economy have made this possible, even as its neighbors were embroiled in civil war. Costa Rica does maintain a small national guard.

Economy

By the mid-1990s, Costa Rica had diversified its economy beyond agriculture, and tourism was bringing in more money than its three major cash crops: coffee, bananas, and pineapples. High-tech companies such as Intel, Hewlett-Packard, and Motorola; Internet purveyor Amazon; and pharmaceutical companies like Procter & Gamble and GlaxoSmithKline have now opened plants and service centers in Costa Rica, providing well-paid jobs for educated professionals. The U.S. chains and big-box stores have arrived, too, most notably Walmart, which operates eight supercenters here.

Costa Rica and its Central American neighbors have staked hopes on international free-trade agreements in recent years, most notably with the United States in 2008 and the European Union in 2010. Opponents of the treaties are wary of how much benefit they provide for the country, however.

The economy continues to bedevil Costa Rica. Although economic growth is on the rise, it still has a $4.1 billion trade deficit and annual inflation just under 5%. Unemployment stands at 7.9%.

Tourism

Today Costa Rica faces the challenge of conserving its natural resources while still permitting modern development. The government has been unable or unwilling to control illegal logging, an industry that threatens to destroy the country's old-growth forests. Urban sprawl in the communities surrounding San José and the development of mega-resorts along the Pacific coast threaten forests, wildlife, and the slow pace of life that makes Costa Rica so desirable.

Although tourism injects much-needed foreign cash into the economy, the government has not fully decided the best way to promote its natural wonders. The buzzwords now are not just eco-tourism and sustainable development, but also adventure tourism and extreme sports. The two sides do not always see eye to eye.

Religion

Because it was a Spanish colony, Costa Rica continues to have a close relationship to the Catholic Church. Catholicism was made the country's official religion in the constitution. Because of this, priests are the only type of clergy authorized to perform civil marriages. (Others require the assistance of a legal official.)

More than 70% of Costa Ricans consider themselves Catholics. But even among this group, most people do not have a strong identification with the church or with its teachings. The live-and-let-live attitude of most Costa Ricans does not mesh well with religious doctrine. That's also probably why the evangelical churches that have made huge inroads in neighboring countries are not as prevalent here.

Every village has a church on its main square, always hopping once a year—when the town's patron saint is honored. These are times for food, music, and dancing in the streets. If the celebrations lack much religious fervor—well, that's Costa Rica for you.

Sports

Like everyone else on this soccer-mad isthmus, Costa Ricans take their game seriously, and passions bubble over when it comes to their beloved national team.

On the national level, the big local rivalry is between LD Alajuelense (*La Liga*, or The League) and Deportivo Saprissa (*El Monstruo Morado*, or The Purple Monster). They have won the Costa Rican championship 26 and 29 times, respectively, which makes the rivalry particularly intense. You can tell how important the sport is when you fly into the country. As your plane flies across the Central Valley, you'll notice that every village, no matter how small, has a soccer field.

Cash Crops

If nearby Honduras was the original "Banana Republic," 19th-century Costa Rica was a "Coffee Republic." Coffee remains inexorably entwined with the country, with economists paying close attention to world prices and kids in rural areas still taking class time off to help with the harvest.

The irony is that it's hard to get a decent cup of the stuff here. True to economic realities of developing countries, the high-quality product gets exported, with the inferior coffee staying behind for the local market. (The same is true of bananas, Costa Rica's other signature agricultural product.) The best places to get a cup of high-quality Costa Rican coffee are upscale restaurants and hotels. Owners understand foreign tastes and have export-quality coffee on hand. Gift shops sell the superior product as well.

The Central Valley is where you'll find many of the coffee plantations. You'll recognize them immediately by the rows of brilliant green plants covered in red berries. Because many of these plants are sensitive to light, they are often shaded by tall trees or even by canopies of fabric. Tours of the plantations are a great way to get to know the local cash crop.

In recent years, the producers of coffee have focused on quality rather than quantity. That's why bananas are now the top agricultural export, followed by pineapples. Both grow in sunny lowland areas, which are abundant on both the Atlantic and Pacific coasts. These crops are treated with just as much care as coffee. You're likely to see bunches of bananas wrapped in plastic bags—while still on the tree. This prevents blemishes that make them less appealing to foreign consumers.

ECOTOURISM, COSTA RICA STYLE

Perhaps more than anyone else, the two men who wrote a field guide about tropical birds were responsible for the ecotourism movement in Costa Rica.

Environmental officials frequently identify the 1989 publication of *A Guide to the Birds of Costa Rica* by F. Gary Stiles and Alexander Skutch as drawing the first flock of bird-watchers to the country. The rest, as they say, is history.

The country's leaders, seeing so many of its primary growth forests being felled at an alarming rate by loggers and farmers, established its national park system in 1970. But it wasn't until nearly two decades later, when the birding guide was published, that they realized that the land they had set aside could help transform the tiny country's economy. (Lasting peace finally coming to neighboring countries was key to overcoming visitors' apprehensions about travel to Central America, too.)

Of the 2.2 million people who travel each year to Costa Rica, many are bird-watchers who come in search of the keel-billed toucan, the scarlet-rumped tanager, or any of the 850 other species of birds. Other travelers are in search of animals, such as two types of sloth, three types of anteater, and four species of monkey, all of them surprisingly easy to spot in the country's national parks and private reserves.

But other people come to Costa Rica to go white-water rafting on the rivers, soar through the treetops attached to zip lines, or take a spin in a motorboat. And many people combine a little bit of everything into their itineraries.

Which raises a couple of questions: Is the person coming to see the wildlife practicing ecotourism? Is the adventure traveler? And exactly what is the definition of ecotourism, anyway?

Defining Ecotourism

The word *ecotourism* is believed to have been coined by Mexican environmentalist Héctor Ceballos-Lascuráin in 1983. According to him, ecotourism "involves traveling to relatively undisturbed natural areas with the specific object of studying, admiring, and enjoying the scenery and its wild plants and animals."

His original definition seemed a bit too general, so in 1993 he amended it with a line that stressed that "ecotourism is environmentally responsible travel."

Ceballos-Lascuráin said he is pleased that ecotourism has gained such acceptance around the world. But he is also concerned that the term has been "variously abused and misused in many places."

The trouble, he said, is a misunderstanding about what is meant by the term *ecotourism*. In Costa Rica, for example, it has been used to describe everything from hiking through the rain forest to rumbling over the hillsides in all-terrain vehicles, and from paddling in a kayak to dancing to disco music on a diesel-powered yacht.

"I am sad to see," Ceballos-Lascuráin told a reporter for EcoClub, "that 'ecotourism' is seen mainly as adventure tourism and carrying out extreme sports in a more or less natural environment, with little concern for conservation or sustainable development issues."

That is not to say that adventure sports can't be part of a green vacation. It all depends what impact they have on the environment and the local community.

Going Green

Over the past decade, the concept of ecotourism has made a strong impression on the average traveler. Many people now realize that mass tourism can be damaging to environmentally sensitive places like Costa Rica but that much can be done to alleviate the negative effects. At the same time, *ecotourism* has become a marketing term used to attract customers who have the best intentions. But is there really such a thing as an eco-friendly car-rental company or a green airline?

In addition to giving travelers the chance to observe and learn about wildlife, ecotourism should accomplish three things: refrain from damaging the environment, strengthen conservation efforts, and improve the lives of local people.

The last part might seem a bit beside the point, but environmentalists point out that much of the deforestation in Costa Rica and other countries is by poor people trying to eke out a living through sustenance farming. Providing them with other ways to make a living is the best way to prevent this.

What can you do? Make sure the hotel you choose is eco-friendly. A great place to start is the Costa Rican Tourism Board (⊕ *www.turismo-sostenible.co.cr*). It has a rating system for hotels and lodges called the Certification for Sustainable Tourism. The New York–based Rainforest Alliance (⊕ *www.rainforest-alliance.org*) has a convenient searchable database of sustainable lodges. The International Ecotourism Society (⊕ *www.ecotourism.org*) has a database of tour companies, hotels, and other travel services that are committed to sustainable practices.

Other Things You Can Do

What else can help? Make sure your tour company follows sustainable policies, including contributing to conservation efforts, hiring and training locals for most jobs, educating visitors about the local ecology and culture, and taking steps to mitigate negative impacts on the environment.

Here are a few other things you can do:

Use locally owned lodges, car-rental agencies, or tour companies. Eat in local restaurants, shop in local markets, and attend local events. Enrich your experience and support the community by hiring local guides.

Stray from the beaten path—by visiting areas where few tourists go, you can avoid adding to the stress on hot spots and enjoy a more authentic Costa Rican experience.

Support conservation by paying entrance fees to parks and protected sites and contributing to local environmental groups.

Don't be overly aggressive if you bargain for souvenirs, and don't shortchange local people on payments or tips for services.

The point here is that you can't assume that companies have environmentally friendly practices, even if they have pictures of animals on their website or terms like *eco-lodge* in their name. Do business only with companies that promote sustainable tourism, and you'll be helping to preserve this country's natural wonders for future generations.

WEDDINGS AND HONEYMOONS

Ever dreamed of getting married on a sandy beach shaded by palm trees? Many people who envision such a scene immediately think of the Caribbean. But Costa Rica is fast becoming a favored destination for tropical nuptials.

Compared with the complicated procedures in many other destinations, getting married in Costa Rica is easy. There are no residency restrictions or blood-test requirements. At least a month in advance, couples of the opposite sex who are over 18 should provide their local wedding planner with a copy of their birth certificates and passports so they can be submitted to the local authorities. Same-sex unions have no legal status in Costa Rica—the matter is under consideration—but wedding planners here have arranged commitment ceremonies.

Any previous marriage complicates things a bit. The couple needs to provide documentation that the marriage was terminated. Divorce papers or death certificate of a previous spouse must be translated into Spanish and notarized.

The Big Day

Judges, attorneys, and Catholic priests have legal authority to certify a marriage in Costa Rica. (Most foreign couples avoid the latter because a Catholic wedding requires months of preparation.) The official ceremony is simple, but couples are free to add their own vows or anything else they would like. The officiant will register the marriage with the civil registry and the couple's embassy.

At the wedding, the couple needs to have at least two witnesses who are not family members. Many couples choose their best man and maid of honor. If necessary, the wedding planner can provide witnesses.

The license itself takes three months to issue and is sent to the couple's home address. For an extra fee, couples can ask for the process to be expedited. Virtually all Western countries recognize the legality of a Costa Rican marriage.

Beautiful Backdrops

Although Costa Rica offers no shortage of impressive backdrops for a ceremony, the Central Pacific coast sees the most tourist weddings and honeymoons. May and June are the most popular months for foreigners, but many people choose January or February because you are virtually guaranteed sunny skies. (Costa Ricans favor December weddings.) Manuel Antonio's Makanda by the Sea, La Mariposa, Si Como No, and Punta Leona's Villa Caletas are among the many lodgings here with events staffs well versed in planning ceremonies and tending to the legalities.

There are many details to attend to: flowers, music, and photography. Most large hotels have on-staff wedding planners to walk you through the process. Couples can also hire their own wedding planner, which is often less expensive. Either way, wedding planners have a wide range of services available, and couples can pick and choose.

Honeymoons

As far as honeymoons go, no place in Costa Rica is inappropriate. Although honeymoons on the beach, especially along the Northern Pacific and Central Pacific coasts, are popular, many couples opt for treks to the mountains or the rain forests. Dozens of newlyweds choose offbeat adventures, such as spotting sea turtles along the Caribbean coast or swimming with pilot whales off the Osa Peninsula.

THE PEOPLE OF COSTA RICA

Unlike many of its neighbors, Costa Rica never had a dominant indigenous population. When Christopher Columbus arrived in the early 16th century, he didn't encounter empires like those in present-day Mexico and Peru. Instead, a small contingent of indigenous Caribs rowed out in canoes to meet his ship. The heavy gold bands the indigenous peoples wore led to Columbus mistakenly calling the land Costa Rica, or "Rich Coast."

On the mainland, the Spanish encountered disparate peoples like the Chorotega, Bribri, Cabécar, and Boruca peoples. Archaeological evidence shows that they had lived in the region for thousands of years. But that would change with breathtaking speed. European diseases felled many of their members, and the brutality of slavery imposed by the colonial power drove most of those remaining into the mountains.

Some of these peoples still exist, although in relatively small communities. Several thousand Bribri, Kekoldi, and other peoples live in villages scattered around Talamanca, a mountainous region close to the border of Panama. Although many traditions have been lost over the years, some have managed to retain their own languages and religions. If you're interested in seeing the local culture, tour companies in the coastal communities of Limón and Puerto Viejo de Talamanca can arrange visits to these villages.

That isn't to say that there's no local culture. More than 90% of the country's residents are mestizos, or mixed-race descendants of the Spanish. But few people express any pride in their Spanish heritage. Perhaps that is because Spain had little interest in Costa Rica, the smallest and poorest of its Central American colonies. Instead, the people here created a unique culture that mixes parts of Europe, Latin America, and the Caribbean. There's a strong emphasis on education, and the 95% literacy rate is by far the highest in the region. There's a laid-back attitude toward life, typified by the common greeting of *pura vida*, which translates literally as "pure life" but means something between "no worries" and "don't sweat the small stuff."

It sounds like a cliché, but Costa Ricans are an incredibly welcoming people. Anyone who has visited other Central American countries will be surprised at how Ticos seem genuinely happy to greet newcomers. If you ever find yourself lost in a town or village, you may find locals more than willing to not only point you in the right direction but walk you all the way to your destination.

Others cultures have added their own spice to Costa Rica. On the Caribbean coast you'll find Afro-Caribbean peoples, descendants of Jamaicans who arrived in the late 19th century to build the railroad and remained to work on banana and cacao plantations. In the seaside town of Limón, cruise ships frequently call, and the passengers who hurry down the gangplank encounter steel-drum music, braided hair, and rickety houses painted every color of the rainbow. They may think that they have discovered the "real" Costa Rica, and they have, in a way. But they also have barely scratched the surface.

FLAVORS OF COSTA RICA

A common misconception among first-time visitors to Costa Rica is that all south-of-the-U.S.-border cuisine is the same. This is absolutely not the case—the only place you'll dine on tacos and fajitas is in a Mexican restaurant. Although Costa Rican food is not spicy, you'll frequently find homemade *chilero* sauces—cauliflower, carrots, onions, and hot peppers pickled in vinegar—in a jar on tables in local restaurants to spoon onto your food for more of a kick. It's always optional, of course. Costa Rican cuisine is hearty and mild, but certainly not the country's biggest draw. *Comida típica,* or typical food, consists primarily of chicken, pork, beans, and rice, although kitchens around the country serve sophisticated Thai, Indian, Italian, and Lebanese cuisine.

Start with the Staples

The cilantro-and-onion-flavored pot of black beans cooked with yesterday's rice, known as *gallo pinto* (literally "spotted rooster"), is synonymous with all things Costa Rican—"As Tico as gallo pinto" is a common expression here. Mounds of this hearty dish—served with scrambled eggs, tortillas, and sour cream—can be had in all of the quintessential local eateries called *sodas.* (Costa Rican Spanish calls a carbonated beverage a *gaseosa.*) Gallo pinto usually serves as a breakfast staple—even McDonald's and Burger King have embraced the dish on their morning menus—but it shows up for lunch and dinner in Costa Rican homes, too.

Lunch is typically the biggest meal of the day here. If you're watching your budget, follow that lead; you'll find omnipresent midday restaurant specials. *Casado* (married) is a plate that "marries" rice with cabbage salad, fried plantains, and a main entrée of beef, chicken, pork, or fish; it's always the lunchtime bargain. Hearty dishes of *olla de carne* (a beef and vegetable stew) and *sopa negra* (a black-bean soup with a poached egg) will fortify you for an afternoon of sightseeing, too. The mildly seasoned *arroz con pollo* (chicken with rice) makes a good choice if you're not feeling too adventurous. Few visitors develop of taste for the ubiquitous *chicharrones,* fried pork rinds.

Add the Bounty of the Land

You've never seen so many fruits and vegetables. The usual suspects like bananas, oranges, pineapples, lemons, mangoes, potatoes, and cabbage are all ubiquitous, but a walk through any Costa Rican market turns up new products you won't find back home. Most visitors develop a fondness for *carambola,* or star fruit, a mildly sweet treat that's perfect on a warm day.

Don't try eating plantains raw—*plátanos* should always be cooked. They end up as a side dish in casados around the country. The Caribbean coast always marches to its own drummer, of course, and cooks there mash them, fry them, and serve them as *patacones* with a touch of salt. Plátanos, along with breadfruit and yams, also get mixed in with fish or meat to make *rondón,* a hearty Caribbean stew. Coconut (*coco*) infuses Caribbean cuisine, most notably the long-simmering rice and beans—the name is always in English—that bears no resemblance to the gallo pinto you've been eating elsewhere in Costa Rica. Roadside vendors around the country will whack a coconut in half with a machete, insert a straw, and, *voilà,* a refreshing drink.

Costa Rica is one of the world's top exporters of *palmito*, the heart of palm that is a staple in salads here. The starchy palm fruit *pejibaye* is cooked and served with a dollop of mayonnaise. *Ensalada rusa*, the so-called Russian salad, mixes beets with potatoes, eggs, and mayonnaise, and is a must-have in the arsenal of any Costa Rican cook. *Elote*, or roasted corn on the cob, is a favorite at any small-town Costa Rican celebration. The hearty, gourd-like *chayote* and the starchy cassava root *yuca* taste bland on their own, but as ingredients in other dishes, assume a variety of flavors.

Wash It Down

Café con leche mixes strongly brewed coffee with milk and lots of sugar for breakfast. (Your best bet for a decent cup of coffee is always an upscale restaurant that's attuned to foreign tastes.) Costa Rica's signature beverage takes center stage again mid-afternoon when seemingly the entire country takes a coffee break. Natural fruit juices, called *frescos,* also come with teeth-shattering amounts of sugar, but the variety of flavors is astounding. If you're watching your own or your child's intake, request one with only a little sugar (*con poco azúcar*); chances are it will be sweet enough, but you can always top it off if need be.

Cervecería Costa Rica, the country's sole large brewery, has a virtual monopoly on beer production, but makes some respectable lagers that pair well with beach lounging. Iconic Imperial (known by the red, black, and yellow eagle logo that adorns bar signs and tourist T-shirts) is everybody's favorite. The slightly bitter Pilsen is a close runner-up, followed by the gold, dark, and light variations of Bavaria. Feeling brave? *Guaro*, the locally distilled sugarcane firewater, really packs a punch. House wines are typically a low-end Chilean choice (this simply isn't wine-drinking country). Our advice? Go tropical! The country's abundant tropical fruit juices mix refreshingly well with local rums or, in a pinch, with a dash of guaro.

Leave Room for Dessert

You'll soon realize that Costa Ricans like things sweet; the country has one of the world's highest rates of sugar consumption—and, alas, also a high incidence of Type II diabetes. *Tres leches* mixes three milks (evaporated, condensed, and whole)—the name means "three milks"—into a very sweet sponge cake. As an alternative, *cajeta de coco* makes for a tasty coconut fudge. *Pan de maíz* translates literally as "corn bread," but all the sugar in the recipe makes it more like a corn cake instead.

GREAT ITINERARIES

Costa Rica looks disarmingly small on the map. This country the size of Vermont and New Hampshire combined *should* be easy to take in, right? Arrive here and you'll see that a mountainous spine transects the country and off the beaten path the roads turn downright abysmal. Ambitious plans to see the entire country never materialize. Rather than rushing around—and rushing is something you can't easily do here—pick and choose a couple of destinations and get to know them well.

Lay of the Land

San José and the Central Valley. Costa Rica's congested capital sits smack-dab in the center of the country. It being the country's transportation hub, you'll likely pass through, even if only on your first and last days here. Coming to Costa Rica on business? You'll probably get to know the city well. San José gives way to bustling suburbs, then smaller towns, then pastoral countryside ringing the capital in a mountain valley (3,000–5,000 feet). Take in the valley as day trips from the city or base yourself out here. San Jose's Aeropuerto Internacional Juan Santamaría sits in the Central Valley, too.

The North. Transportation is straightforward in the vast, mostly flat northern one-third of the country that makes up the Northern Lowlands—this area has two of Costa Rica's biggest attractions, Arenal Volcano and Monteverde Cloud Forest. Roads are decent here with the exception of the notoriously awful route to Monteverde—and, even here, paving is scheduled to begin at this writing. You'd think a highway, north to south, would line the northern Pacific coast, making it easy to bop among this region's famed beaches and down through the

Nicoya Peninsula. You frequently have to head back inland to get to the next strand of sand down the coast, though. If this area is your sole destination, book your flights to Liberia's Aeropuerto Internacional Daniel Oduber Quirós, rather than down in San José.

Manuel Antonio and the Central Pacific Coast. A spiffy highway puts San José an hour or two from the beaches along this sector of coast. Great news for the tourism industry here but you should book space for holidays and high-season weekends in advance; Costa Ricans love to take mini-breaks to this region, too.

The Osa Peninsula and the South Pacific. The south is rarely first-timer's territory—even most Costa Ricans have never ventured to the southern third of their country, a land of remote beaches, mountains, and wilderness eco-lodges. Transportation is improving to and within this splendid region, but can still be a chore. Sample it, though, and you might count yourself among the growing number of fans.

Tortuguero and the Caribbean Coast. Once you get over the hump of the mountains north of San José, a good road puts you directly en route to the sultry, tropical, southern Caribbean coast, still largely the province of European visitors and less known in American circles. The northern Caribbean coast near Tortuguero National Park is a different story entirely: no roads exist up here, making boat or plane your only travel options.

Timing

Costa Rican Tourist Board surveys show that U.S. visitors spend an average of nine days on a trip here. That's ample occasion to take in destinations in a couple of regions, and it accounts for

NICARAGUA

Caribbean Sea

The North
◆

**Tortuguero and the
Caribbean Coast**
◆

San José
✪
**San José and the
Central Valley**
◆

**Manuel Antonio
and the
Central Pacific Coast**
◆

**Osa Peninsula and the
South Pacific**
◆

PANAMA

PACIFIC OCEAN

time to get from one place to the other. (Depending on places you choose, that last part can be more of a chore than you may realize.) Rather than packing too much in, keep repeating that most Costa Rican of expressions: "*Si Dios lo quiere.*" If God is willing, you'll get back here to partake of what you didn't see the first time around.

Itineraries

We proffer four possible itineraries, each taking in a small slice of the country and showcasing some of the crowd-pleasing destinations for which Costa Rica is known. The third of these leans more toward the "leave the driving to them" end of the spectrum; the fourth incorporates domestic air travel. If you have time, these itineraries can be combined or broken apart and reassembled to suit your needs. If you are doing the driving,

remember the sun sets here around 5:30 pm all year long, give or take about 15 minutes. Always plan to arrive at your destination before dark.

Peak Season: December to April

The Christmas-to-Easter period essentially defines Costa Rica's high season. With little rain and temperatures in the 80s and higher, the country makes an ideal escape for North Americans and Europeans fleeing those frigid winters.

GREAT ITINERARIES

BEST OF COSTA RICA

ARENAL VOLCANO, MANUEL ANTONIO, AND BEACHES, 7 DAYS

Volcanoes and beaches are two of the things Costa Rica does best, so the classic first-timer's itinerary to Costa Rica takes in two of its most popular destinations: the impressive Arenal Volcano and the beaches of the Central Pacific coast's lovely Manuel Antonio.

Day 1: San José

Arrive in **San José's Aeropuerto Internacional Juan Santamaría** (most arrivals are in the evening) and head straight to one of the small hotels north of the city in the **Central Valley**. The airport lies northwest of the capital, so staying in San José requires a bit of backtracking. The **Hampton Inn** just across from the airport lets you ease into your Costa Rican experience in familiar surroundings; the **Xandari Resort & Spa** offers a far more local, and pricier, first night here. Brace yourself for lines at immigration if you arrive in the evening along with several other large flights from North America. Try to get a seat near the front of the plane, and don't dawdle when disembarking.

Day 2: Poás Volcano and Tabacón Hot Springs

(45 minutes by paved road from airport to Poás Volcano; 2½ hours by paved road from airport to La Fortuna)

If you have the time, set out early for **Poás Volcano**, where you can peer over the edge of the crater. It makes an interesting start to your first full day in Costa Rica. Fortify yourself with the fruits, jellies, and chocolates sold by vendors on the road up to the summit. Otherwise, get going to the

Arenal area right away. Set out on the scenic drive—turn north at San Ramón—to **La Fortuna**, which sits at the foot of **Arenal Volcano** and is its hub. (Portions of the route twist and turn and fog over by noon.) Drop your luggage at one of many fantastic hotels, and partake of the myriad activities here. Take a zip-line or hanging-bridges tour through the forest canopy north of the volcano with amazing views of the mountain itself. Follow up with a visit to the **Tabacón Hot Springs & Resort** to pamper yourself with a spa treatment. Finish the day by sinking into a volcanically heated mineral bath with a cocktail at your side as the sun sets behind Volcán Arenal.

Shuttle vans have hotel-to-hotel service, usually from the Hampton Inn to many Arenal-area hotels. You can stay right at Tabacón and have access to facilities there not open to day or evening visitors. **Nayara Hotel & Spa** also offers terrific views of Arenal Volcano.

Day 3: Caño Negro Wildlife Refuge
(90 minutes by paved road from La Fortuna)

Spend your entire day in the **Caño Negro Wildlife Refuge**, a lowland forest reserve replete with waterfowl near the Nicaraguan border. Book your trip the night before; tour operators in La Fortuna keep evening hours for exactly that reason. All transport is included, and it's far easier than trying to visit the refuge on your own.

Day 4: Scenic Drive to the Central Pacific
(4–4½ hours by paved road from La Fortuna)

Today's a traveling day—a chance to really see the country's famous landscape. Four hours' drive from Arenal takes you to fabled **Manuel Antonio** on the Central

Los Chiles

Caño Negro Wildlife Refuge

NICARAGUA

Caribbean Sea

Tabacón Hot Springs & Resort Nayara Hotel & Spa

Arenal Volcano La Fortuna

Poás Volcano

San Ramón Alajuela Central Valley

Atenas

Juan Santamaria International Airport

⭐ **San José**

PACIFIC OCEAN

Jacó

Quepos

Manuel Antonio National Park/ Beaches

Pacific coast. Beyond-beautiful hotels are the norm here, and you have your choice of seaside luxury—we like the **Arenas del Mar Beachfront and Nature Resort**—or tree-shrouded lodges like **Villas Nicolás.**

Hotel-to-hotel shuttle-van services can get you from Arenal to Manuel Antonio. If you drive instead, start out as early as possible. You'll pass again through the mountainous stretch between La Fortuna and San Ramón—that's the way you came—to get back to the main highway heading east. Exit at **Atenas**, a pleasant town that makes a good lunch stop. South of Atenas, hook up with the Pacific Highway—follow the signs directing you to Caldera. The Jacó exit takes you on the fairly good road to Manuel Antonio.

Day 5: Manuel Antonio National Park
(10–20 minutes from most area lodgings)

Manuel Antonio is Costa Rica's most famous national park for a reason: it has beaches, lush rain forest, mangrove swamps, and rocky coves with abundant marine life. You can—and should—spend an entire day exploring the park, home to capuchin monkeys, sloths, agoutis, and 200 species of birds. It's also one of two locales in the country where you'll see squirrel monkeys. Almost all Manuel Antonio hotels have transport to the park.

If yours doesn't, taxis are plentiful and cheap. Don't forget: the park is closed on Monday, so schedule carefully.

Day 6: Beaches
(10–20 minutes from most area lodgings)

Days 1 through 5 were on-the-go days. Reward yourself today with lots of relaxation. One of Costa Rica's most popular strands of sand, **Playa Espadilla** hums with activity on weekends and holidays. Alas, riptides can make swimming risky here. Within the national park, **Playa Manuel Antonio** and **Playa Espadilla Sur** offer more seclusion, but no real facilities. Manuel Antonio and its neighboring town, **Quepos**, have the best selection of restaurants of any beach community in the country.

Day 7: San José
(2–2½ hours by paved road from Manuel Antonio)

An easy morning drive back to San José gives you time to spend the afternoon in the city. Visit the **Teatro Nacional** and the **Museo de Oro Precolombino**, and save time for late-afternoon shopping. An evening dinner caps off your trip before you turn in early to get ready for tomorrow morning's departure. We recommend that you check in three hours before your flight.

GREAT ITINERARIES

THE NORTH

DAY TRIPS FROM PLAYA HERMOSA BASE, 6 DAYS

The province of Guanacaste and the Nicoya Peninsula is known as Costa Rica's "fun in the sun" destination. Kids and adults alike enjoy the region's huge variety of land- and water-based activities.

Days 1 and 2: Playa Hermosa

(30 minutes by paved road from Liberia airport)

Most arrivals to **Liberia's Aeropuerto Internacional Daniel Oduber Quirós**, Costa Rica's second international airport, are in early afternoon. You can't go wrong with any North Pacific beach, but we like **Playa Hermosa** for its location—it lies about 30 minutes from the airport—one that lets you use it as a base for visiting area attractions. The smaller lodgings here make the perfect antidote to the megaresorts that lie not too far away. They can arrange to have transport waiting at the airport, with advance notice. **Hotel La Finisterra** perches above the ocean; the pricier **Hotel Playa Hermosa Bosque del Mar** hugs the beach itself. The big all-inclusives up here have their own minivans to whisk you in air-conditioned comfort from airport to resort. Otherwise, the airport contains the full selection of car-rental counters.

Start Day 2 off lazing on the beach. Morning is a great time of day to hit the beach in this part of Costa Rica—the breezes are refreshingly cool and the sun hasn't started to beat down yet. After lunch, explore Playa Hermosa's "metropolis," the small town of **Playas del Coco**. Quite frankly Coco is our least favorite beach up here. But we like the town for its little souvenir shops, restaurants, and local color.

Taxis are the easiest way to travel between Playa Hermosa and Coco, about 10 minutes away. Have your hotel call one, and flag one down on the street in town when it's time to return.

Day 3: Rincón de la Vieja Volcano

(1½-hour drive from Playa Hermosa, the last 45 minutes by dirt and stone road)

The top of **Rincón de la Vieja Volcano** with its steaming, bubbling, oozing fumaroles lies about 90 minutes from Hermosa. Lather on the sunscreen and head for the **Hacienda Guachipelín**—tours are open to non-hotel guests, too—and its volcano-viewing hikes, canopy tours, rappelling, horseback riding, mountain biking, and river tubing. Cap off the day with a spa treatment, complete with thermal mud bath.

If you don't have a rental car, book a private driver for the day, which can usually be arranged through your hotel. The region has seen an increase in tour operators who can take you to area attractions, too, which your hotel can arrange.

If you are driving yourself, you may wish to spend the night up here and not trek back down to the coast the same day. Hacienda Guachipelín itself is a solid lodging value.

Day 4: Golf or Diving

(30 minutes by paved road from Playa Hermosa to Papagayo Golf & Country Club; 10 minutes by paved road from Playa Hermosa to Playas del Coco)

Golf is big up here. The 18-hole **Papagayo Golf & Country Club** is just southeast of Playas del Coco. The other popular, slightly pricey, sport here is scuba diving. Dive

PACIFIC
OCEAN

operators are based in nearby Playas del Coco—we like **Rich Coast Diving**—or Playa Panamá. A daylong diving course won't certify you, but gives you a taste of the deep. A taxi can transport you to and from the golf course, and dive operators will pick you up from and return you to your hotel.

Day 5: Palo Verde National Park
(1½ hours by paved road from Playa Hermosa to Palo Verde, the last 45 minutes by dirt road)

We like the morning guided tours at **Palo Verde National Park,** one of the last remaining dry tropical forests in Central America. The **Organization for Tropical Studies,** which operates the biological station here, has terrific guides. Spend the afternoon observing nature in a more relaxed fashion with a float (easy Class I and II rapids) down the nearby Río Corobicí. The aptly named **Safaris Corobicí,** near Cañas on the Pan-American Highway, specializes in the floating trips. This excursion is a bit roundabout, so this is the day your own vehicle would come in handiest. But you can also hire a private driver or get a tour operator to fix you up (arranged through your hotel). Bring water to drink: it gets hot here.

Day 6: Departure
(30 minutes by paved road from Playa Hermosa)

Grab a last dip in the ocean this morning, because your flight departs from Liberia in the early afternoon. The airport terminal is modern and spacious, but allow yourself plenty of time for check-in in any case.

GREAT ITINERARIES

SAN JOSÉ, CENTRAL VALLEY, AND TORTUGUERO

DISCOVERING SAN JOSÉ, ITS ENVIRONS, AND THE REMOTE CARIBBEAN COAST, 7 DAYS

It's entirely possible to take in a mix of urban, suburban, and remote Costa Rica without having to rent a car with this let-someone-else-do-the-driving itinerary. Tortuguero, on the Caribbean coast, is accessible only by boat.

Day 1: Arrival

Following your evening arrival in **San José**, head to one of the many in-town lodgings. **Hotel Grano de Oro**, west of Downtown, or **Hôtel Le Bergerac**, east of Downtown, are good options. Your hotel can arrange for transport with advance notice. The big players have their own hotel shuttle vans, but smaller lodgings can arrange for a taxi. Otherwise, grab one of the official orange airport cabs at the customs exit. Plan on spending $25–$30 for a taxi ride into the city.

Day 2: San José

A full day in the city gives you time to spend the morning visiting the **Teatro Nacional** and the **Museo de Oro Precolombino**—they're on the same block. Duck into the **Museo del Jade** in the afternoon, especially if it's raining, or partake of some late-afternoon crafts shopping. An evening dinner at one of San José's fine restaurants caps off the day. Asian restaurant **Tin Jo** is one of the country's top dining experiences.

Day 3: Day Tours to the Central Valley

San José's location makes it the perfect place from which to fan out to the Central Valley's many sights. The list of things to see and do in the valley is impressive: learn all about coffee at the installations of **Café Britt**, near Heredia, or the **Doka Estate**, near Alajuela; peer over the rim into bubbling cauldrons of the **Poás** or **Irazú** volcanoes; wander among fluttering butterflies at the **Butterfly Farm** in Alajuela; step back into history in the **Orosi Valley**; learn what makes nature tick at **INBioparque**, in Santo Domingo; or shop for crafts in **Sarchí**, the country's signature artisan town. Hitting all the attractions in one day is next to impossible, of course—Café Britt and INBioparque lie 30 minutes or less from the capital, but plan on up to an hour to reach the others. San José's several tour operators offer half- or full-day excursions that incorporate various Central Valley's attractions, or can tailor one that fits your interests. Plan to be picked up from your hotel between 7 and 8 in the morning and return after midday for a half-day tour, or around 5 for a daylong excursion.

Days 4 and 5: Tortuguero

(2 hours by paved road plus 2–2½ hours by boat from San José)

An early-morning pickup at your San José hotel and you are off to one of Costa Rica's most remote destinations. Once you traverse **Braulio Carrillo National Park** north of the capital, you switch from van to boat at a put-in point in the Caribbean lowlands. The final stretch to **Tortuguero** takes place by boat; this is a roadless part of Costa Rica. Arrive at your lodge by mid-afternoon. Rest and get cleaned up for a sumptuous buffet dinner.

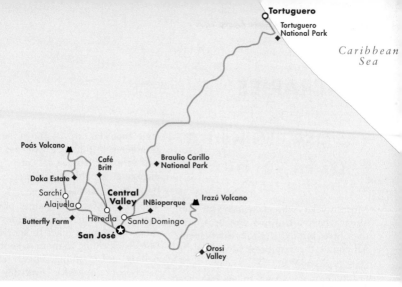

Although you can do Tortuguero on your own, most visitors opt for an all-inclusive tour. **Pachira Lodge,** along the main canal, or the more-secluded **Evergreen Lodge** are good options.

The knock at the door comes early in the morning of day five as you are roused out of bed to go on a pre-breakfast bird-watching excursion in **Tortuguero National Park.** (Remember: there are no roads, so transport is by boat.) The day entails a guided hike in the national park and a stroll through the tiny village of the same name. Evenings give way to turtle-watching during the nesting season (July through October).

Tortuguero is the rainiest spot in Costa Rica, and the rains spread evenly throughout the year. Plan to get wet (it's half the fun). Most of the lodges here provide ponchos and rain boots.

Day 6: Back to San José
(60–90 minutes by boat plus 2 hours by paved road from Tortuguero)

Day six is your fourth day in reverse. After a hearty breakfast at your lodge, you board the launches back to civilization. The boat travels faster than it did on the way up here. You transfer to a waiting van at the put-in point and head back to your city hotel, arriving in the afternoon.

TIPS

■ Tortuguero has no roads. Forget the car and let someone else take care of your transportation needs.

■ Many San José hotels will allow you to leave your things while you're touring outside the city, a particular boon when you're headed to Tortuguero. Space inside the small boats is limited.

■ July through October is prime turtle-nesting season in Tortuguero.

■ If you have more money than time, the Tortuguero lodges can arrange for you to fly to and from San José on domestic airline Nature Air.

Tortuguero lodges do offer two-day/one-night excursions, but go for the extra day if your schedule permits.

Day 7: Departure
(30–45 minutes from San José)

Most international flights depart Aeropuerto Juan Santamaría in the morning. Recommended check-in time is always three hours in advance of departure.

GREAT ITINERARIES

THE OSA PENINSULA

COSTA RICA AT ITS WILDEST, 8 DAYS

Most travelers who make it this far south already have a trip to Costa Rica under their belts, but feel free to break that rule. All you need is a spirit of adventure.

Day 1: Arrival

Following your arrival in **San José**, head to one of the several lodgings near the airport. We recommend staying out here rather than heading into San José itself, about 30 minutes away. You need to be back at the airport the next morning for your flight to the Osa Peninsula, and you'll appreciate the extra time. You cannot get closer to the airport than the **Hampton Inn**; it's just across the highway. Wherever you stay, your hotel can arrange for transport with advance notice, whether its own shuttle vans or sending a taxi for you. Otherwise, grab one of the official orange airport cabs as you exit customs.

Day 2: San José to Puerto Jiménez to Cabo Matapalo

(60 minutes by air to Puerto Jiménez and 1 hour by gravel road)

You're back at the airport for your hour-long flight to Puerto Jiménez on either of the country's two domestic airlines: Nature Air is inside the international terminal; SANSA has its own building. Check-in is a leisurely affair, but you should arrive at the airport at least 45 minutes before departure. Arrival at the airstrip in Puerto Jiménez, Osa's "metropolis," is even more low-key. Our recommended lodgings in Cabo Matapalo, 21 km (14 miles) south, can arrange for transfers. Each has its own

style: **Lapa Ríos** rates as one of the world's premier eco-lodges; **El Remanso** is quiet and intimate; **Bosque del Cabo** draws an engaging, sociable clientele.

Days 3 and 4: Nature Excursions

The Cabo Matapalo lodges offer their own nature-themed activities. They range from quiet hikes to snorkeling to horseback riding to more strenuous rappelling and climbing. Highly regarded local tour operator **Everyday Adventures** takes you on excursions that skew toward the adrenaline-rushing end of the spectrum. The end of the day puts you back at your lodge, chatting with other guests about what you saw that day well into the evening.

Day 5: Cabo Matapalo to Carate

(1 hour by road)

Carate is literally Osa's end of the road. The lodges here can arrange for an overland transfer from Cabo Matapalo or all the way from Puerto Jiménez if you're skipping Matapalo entirely. On the topic of where to stay, accommodation here has its own personality, too: **Finca Exótica** caters to nature lovers; **Luna Lodge** is for the yoga or wellness lover. A trip to the beach rounds out your day. Alas, as is the case elsewhere in Costa Rica, riptides are dangerous here.

Day 6: Corcovado National Park

(45-minute hike to La Leona park entrance from Carate; half day or full day of hiking in park)

If you've come this far, Costa Rica's famed **Corcovado National Park** should be on your agenda. The lodges here can arrange for guided walks to the park— it's the only way to approach Corcovado from this direction. No one ever tires of repeating the platitudes about Corcovado, most often citing National

Geographic's description of the park as "the most biologically intense place on earth in terms of biodiversity."

Day 7 and 8: Carate to Puerto Jiménez to San José

(2 hours by road and 60 minutes by air to San José)

The lodges here can arrange for an overland transfer back to Puerto Jiménez, or you can take the colectivo, the public transport here. Carate does have its own tiny airstrip with charter planes making the quick jaunt back to Puerto Jiménez. If timing does not coincide with Nature Air or SANSA's schedules, a night in Puerto Jiménez gives you a dose of civilization again in the style of a tropical frontier town. You can catch a flight back to San José the next morning, from where you can depart for other destinations in Costa Rica.

TIPS

■ Opt for morning flights during the rainy season.

■ Same-day international-to-domestic and domestic-to-international air connections are risky; both Nature Air and SANSA advise against them.

■ Domestic airlines limit your luggage to anywhere from 15 to 40 pounds, depending on your fare. Pack lightly, or make advance arrangements with your hotel.

■ September and October are the wettest months of the rainy season and Osa roads occasionally become impassable.

■ You *can* do this trip overland with your own 4WD vehicle or by public bus, but it's a long slog down here. If you choose the land option, add an extra full day at the beginning and end of this itinerary.

KIDS AND FAMILIES

With so much to keep them interested and occupied, Costa Rica is a blast with kids. The activities here are things the whole family can do together: discovering a waterfall in a rain forest, snorkeling with sea turtles, or white-water rafting down a roaring river. There are also activities for kids that will allow parents time to stroll hand-in-hand down a deserted beach.

Choosing a Destination

Basing yourself in one place for several days is a great idea. Climbing into the car every day or two not only makes the kids miserable but means that the best part of the day is spent traveling. (Winding, twisting roads, like the road to Monteverde Cloud Forest, don't go well with kids who are prone to carsickness either.) The good news is that there are many destinations where you could stay for a week and still not do and see everything.

Headed to the beach? Remember that for families, not all beaches are created equal. Choose a destination with a range of activities. Manuel Antonio, on the Central Pacific coast, is your best bet. The proximity to the national park is the main selling point, but you're also close to other nature preserves. As for activities, there's everything from snorkeling and surfing lessons to kayaking excursions to zip-line adventures. And the range of kid-friendly restaurants is unmatched anywhere in the country. On the Nicoya Peninsula, Playas del Coco and Playa Tamarindo have a decent amount of activities for the small fry.

Santa Elena, the closest town to Monteverde Cloud Forest Biological Reserve, is another great base. There are several nature preserves in the area, and they offer both day and night hikes. If skies are cloudy—as they often are—there are indoor attractions like the display of slithering snakes. The town is compact and walkable, and has many eateries with children's menus. La Fortuna, the gateway to the Lake Arenal area, has activities from waterfall hikes to canopy tours. The town itself isn't attractive, so you'll want to choose a place nearby.

Believe it or not, the San José area is not a bad base. Activities like white-water rafting are nearby, and on rainy days you can visit the city's excellent museums dedicated to gold and jade. The hotels in the surrounding countryside are often a long drive from good restaurants. We prefer the hotels in the city, as dozens of restaurants line the pedestrian-only streets.

Kid-Friendly Activities

You can't beat the beach in Costa Rica. Avoid those without lifeguards, and take warning signs about rip currents very seriously. Snorkeling and surfing lessons are great for older kids, but stick with a licensed company rather than that enthusiastic young person who approaches you on the beach.

Canopy tours are good for kids of all ages. Ask the staff about how long a tour will take, because once you set out on a hike over a series of hanging bridges, you often have no choice but to continue on to the end. Zip lines are appropriate for older teens, but they should always be accompanied by an adult.

For the smallest of the small fry, the butterfly enclosures and hummingbird gardens that you find near many resort areas are wonderful diversions. Indoor activities, like the display of frogs at Santa Elena, fascinate youngsters. And don't avoid the easier hikes in the national parks. Seeing animals in the wild is likely to start a lifelong love of animals.

BIODIVERSITY

Costa Rica's forests hold an array of flora and fauna so vast and diverse that scientists haven't even named thousands of the species found here. The country covers less than 0.03% of Earth's surface, yet it contains nearly 5% of the planet's plant and animal species. Costa Rica has at least 9,000 plant species, including more than 1,200 types of orchids, some 2,000 kinds of butterflies, and 876 bird species.

Costa Rica acts as a natural land bridge between North and South America, so there is a lot of intercontinental exchange. But the country's flora and fauna add up to more than what has passed between the continents. Costa Rica's biological diversity is the result of its tropical location, its varied topography, and the many microclimates resulting from the combination of mountains, valleys, and lowlands. The isthmus also acts as a hospitable haven to many species that couldn't complete the journey from one hemisphere to the other. The rain forests of Costa Rica's Caribbean and southwestern lowlands are the most northerly home of such southern species as the crab-eating raccoon. The tropical dry forests of the northern Pacific slope are the southern limit for such North American species as the Virginia opossum. And then there are the dozens of northern bird species that spend their winter holidays here.

Research and planning go a long way in a place like Costa Rica. A short trip around the country can put you in one landscape after another, each with its own array of plants and animals. The country's renowned national park system holds examples of all of its major ecosystems, and some of its most impressive sights. In terms of activities, there's more interesting stuff to do here than could possibly ever fit into one vacation. But keep in mind that somewhere around three-fourths of the country has been urbanized or converted to agriculture, so if you want to see the spectacular nature that we describe in this book, you need to know where to go. *In addition to this section on biodiversity, you'll find regional planning information, national park highlights, and a list of our favorite eco-lodges at the front of each chapter.*

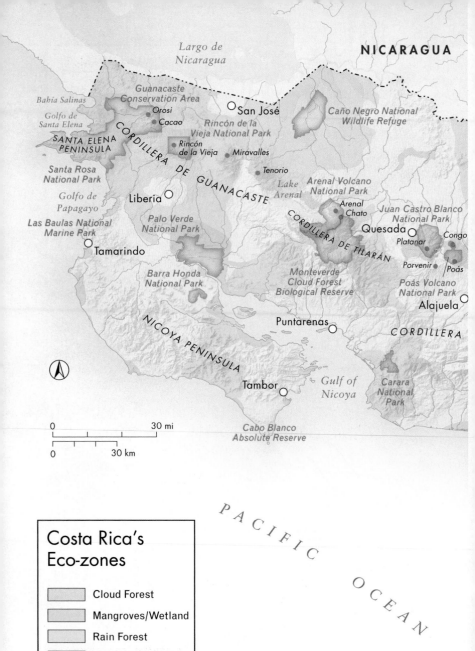

NICARAGUA

Largo de
Nicaragua

Bahía Salinas

Golfo de
Santa Elena

Guanacaste
Conservation Area

Orosi
Cacao

San José

Caño Negro National
Wildlife Refuge

SANTA ELENA
PENINSULA

Rincón de la
Vieja National Park

Rincón
de la Vieja

Miravalles

CORDILLERA DE GUANACASTE

Santa Rosa
National Park

Tenorio

Arenal Volcano
National Park

Golfo de
Papagayo

Lake
Arenal

Liberia

Arenal
Chato

Juan Castro Blanco
National Park

Las Baulas National
Marine Park

Palo Verde
National Park

Quesada

Congo

CORDILLERA DE TILARÁN

Platanar

Tamarindo

Porvenir

Poás

Barra Honda
National Park

Monteverde
Cloud Forest
Biological Reserve

Poás Volcano
National Park

Alajuela

NICOYA PENINSULA

Puntarenas

CORDILLERA

Gulf of
Nicoya

Carara
National
Park

Tambor

Cabo Blanco
Absolute Reserve

0   30 mi

0   30 km

PACIFIC OCEAN

Costa Rica's Eco-zones

Cloud Forest

Mangroves/Wetland

Rain Forest

Tropical Dry Forest

Cultivated Land
and Urban Areas

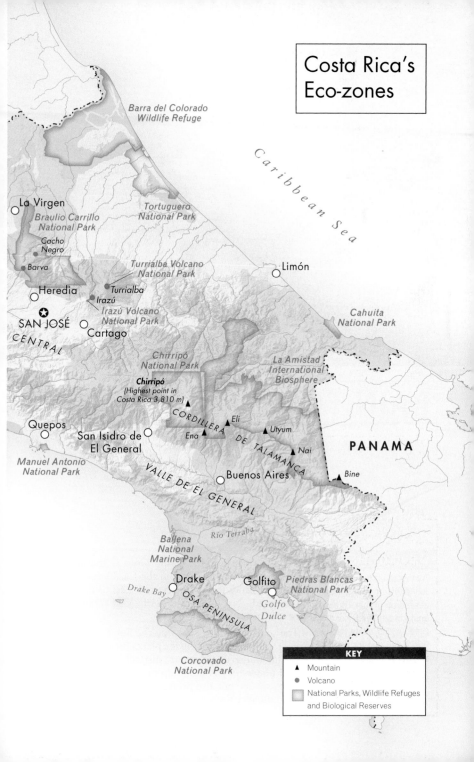

Costa Rica's Eco-zones

Barra del Colorado
Wildlife Refuge

Caribbean Sea

La Virgen

Braulio Carrillo
National Park

Cacho
Negro

Barva

Tortuguero
National Park

Turrialba Volcano
National Park

Limón

Heredia

Turrialba

Cahuita
National Park

SAN JOSÉ

Irazú

Irazú Volcano
National Park

CENTRAL

Cartago

Chirripó
National Park

La Amistad
International
Biosphere

Chirripó
(Highest point in
Costa Rica 3,810 m)

Quepos

San Isidro de
El General

CORDILLERA

Eli

Ena

DE

Utyum

TALAMANCA

Nai

PANAMA

Manuel Antonio
National Park

VALLE DE EL GENERAL

Buenos Aires

Bine

Ballena
National
Marine Park

Río Terraba

Drake

Drake Bay

Golfito

OSA PENINSULA

Piedras Blancas
National Park

Golfo
Dulce

Corcovado
National Park

KEY	
▲	Mountain
●	Volcano
▢	National Parks, Wildlife Refuges and Biological Reserves

RAIN FOREST

Warm and wet, Costa Rica's rain forest is the quintessential dripping, squawking, chirping, buzzing jungle. In this sultry landscape of green on green, birds flap and screech overhead and twigs snap under the steps of unseen creatures. All the ingredients for life—water, sunlight, and more water—drench these areas.

The amount of rain in a rain forest is stunning. The enormous swath of forest in the Caribbean lowlands averages more than 4 meters (13 feet) of rain a year. Corcovado National Park, on the Osa Peninsula, can get 5½ meters (18 feet).

The soaring canopy soaks up the lion's share of sunlight, seriously depriving the plants below. Underneath the highest trees are several distinct layers of growth. The understory is made up of smaller and younger trees, shaded but also protected from harsh winds and rainfall. Shrubby species and even younger trees stand

farther below, and small plants, fungus, dead trees, and fallen leaves cover the constantly decomposing forest floor.

Light rarely passes through these layers and layers of growth. At the forest floor, plants lie poised, in a stasis of sorts, waiting for one of the giants above to fall and open a patch of sky. When this does happen, an incredible spectacle occurs as the waiting plants unveil an arsenal of evolutionary tricks. Vines twist out, looking for other trees to pull themselves up along, shoots explode from hidden bulbs, and ferns and lianas battle for height and access to the sun.

But as competitive as the jungle sounds, it is essentially a series of ecosystems based on interdependence and cooperation. Trees depend on the animals that eat their fruit to disperse their seeds. Fungi feed off the nutrients produced by the decomposing forest floor. From death comes life—an abundance of life.

Costa Rica's rain forests have suffered from incursions by agriculture, logging, and cattle farming, but they're still home to the majority of the nation's biodiversity, with more species per square mile than anywhere else.

ADVENTURE HIGHLIGHTS

■ Novice bird-watchers can enroll in La Selva's Birding 101 class. It's taught by some of the finest naturalists in the country.

■ Join the folks at Brisas del Nara, 32 km (20 miles) outside Manuel Antonio, for an all-day horseback-riding excursion through the protected Cerro Nara mountain zone. It ends with a swim in a natural pool with a 107-meter (350-foot) waterfall.

■ Stray way off the beaten path on a multiday hike through Corcovado National Park with tropical biologist Mike Boston from Osa Aventura.

TOP DESTINATIONS

Most of Costa Rica's rain forest can be found across the Caribbean lowlands and on the South Pacific coast.

CORCOVADO NATIONAL PARK

At the other end of the spectrum is Corcovado National Park, the remote, untamed jewel of Costa Rica's biodiversity crown. Covering one-third of the Osa Peninsula, Corcovado National Park holds about one-quarter of all tree species in Costa Rica and at least 140 identified species of mammals. Covering 445 square km (172 square miles), the park includes Central America's largest tract of lowland Pacific rain forest, including some old-growth areas. Corcovado is home to the largest concentration of jaguars left in the country, and the biggest population of scarlet macaw. There are at least 116 species of amphibians and reptiles, and about 370 bird species. Ranger stations and campsites are available for the more adventurous, and luxurious eco-lodges surround the park for those who don't like to rough it. *(See Chapter 8.)*

LA SELVA

If anybody knows anything about the rain forest, it is the researchers at La Selva biological station, situated in the midst of 3,900 acres of protected forest in northern Costa Rica. The station,

A green and black poison frog, La Selva

run by the Organization for Tropical Studies, was founded by famed biologist Leslie Holdridge in 1954 and is one of the most important sites worldwide for research on tropical rain forest. The research station can sleep up to 80 people in dormitory-style rooms and two-room family cabins, and feed as many as 100 in the dining hall. More than 50 km (31 miles) of trails provide access to a variety of ecosystems. *(See Chapter 9.)*

MANUEL ANTONIO NATIONAL PARK

For a tame, up-close glimpse of the rain forest and some of its more photogenic inhabitants, Manuel Antonio National Park is a favorite. Located on the Central Pacific coast, Manuel Antonio is one of Costa Rica's most visited—and smallest—national parks. Capuchin monkeys are used to humans to the point of practically ignoring them, unless a snack is poking out from an unattended backpack. The highly endangered squirrel monkeys are less bold, but can be seen at the park or from nearby hotels. Sloths are a common sight along the trail, as are a host of exotic birds and other creatures. But despite the apparent vibrancy of life found here, Manuel Antonio is isolated, with no biological bridges to other forests, and threatened by encroaching development. *(See Chapter 7.)*

Squirrel Monkey; danmike, Fodors.com member

EXPERIENCING A RAIN FOREST

Photographing a spiderweb

For an ecosystem as diverse as the rain forest, it is fitting that there is a variety of ways to explore and experience it.

CANOPY TOURS
Canopy tours are a wonderful way to get a bird's-eye—or sloth's—view of the rain forest. Suspension bridges and zip lines, originally used for canopy research, offer a fantastic glimpse into the upper reaches of the forest. If you're not very mobile or don't feel like walking, go on a rain-forest tram; it's a small, slow-moving gondola that carries passengers gently through the jungle canopy.

HIKING
Hiking or walking through any one of Costa Rica's numerous national parks is an easy way to fully experience the vibrancy of the life found there. And we can't say this too many times: guided hikes are the way to go for anyone who hopes to catch a glimpse of the more exotic and hard-to-find species or better understand the complexity of the surrounding ecosystems.

MOUNTAIN BIKING
During the dry season, some parks open up trails for mountain bikers. But once the rains begin, a bike trip can turn into a long slog through the mud. Before you rent a bike, ask about the conditions of the trails.

RAFTING
Gentle, slow-moving rivers beg to be explored by canoe or kayak. It's a wonderful way to experience the deep calm of the jungle, and stealthy enough to increase your chances of seeing wildlife. If you're more of a thrill seeker, choose from any of the white-water rafting tours that pass through rain forests.

FLORA

To enter into a Costa Rican rain forest is to be overwhelmed by the diversity and intensity of life. A single hectare (2½ acres) contains almost 100 species of trees, and many of the more than 1,000 species of orchids are nested in their branches.

FALSE BIRD OF PARADISE
No avid photographer will return from Costa Rica without snapping a few shots of a heliconia, one of the most vibrant families of plants in the rain forest. This genus of flowering plant, containing between 100 and 200 species, includes the false bird of paradise (*Heliconia rostrata*), a dangling, impossibly colorful flower of alternating bulbous protrusions, colored red and tipped with green and yellow. Its vibrant colors and nectar make it a favorite for hummingbirds.

False Bird of Paradise

GUARIA MORADA
Almost every tree here plays host to lichens, woody vines called lianas, and rootless epiphytes, including the national flower, *guaria morada* (*Guarianthe skinneri*). Because this is an orchid species, you'll find it in several different shapes and colors: the flowers can be from pure white to deep magenta, and the base of its lip can range from yellow to white. There can be anywhere from 4 to 14 flowers per stem.

Guaria morada

SILK COTTON TREE
The silk cotton tree (*Ceiba pentandra*), known locally as *ceiba,* is one of the most easily recognizable of the rain-forest giants. Growing nearly 60 meters (200 feet) tall, it can be identified close to the ground by its tall, winding, and narrow roots, which act as buttresses to support the enormous trunk.

STRANGLER FIG
Aptly called *matapalo* in Spanish, meaning "tree killer," the strangler fig begins its life as an epiphyte, living high in the branches of another tree. Over several years, it grows dangling roots to the forest floor that capture nutrients from the soil, thicken, and slowly meld onto the host tree. Eventually—it might take as long as 100 years—the strangler completely engulfs its host. In time the "strangled" tree decomposes and disintegrates, leaving the strangler fig—replete with branches, leaves, flowers, and fruit—standing hollow but victorious.

The Silk Cotton Tree

Strangler Fig

FAUNA

Keep an eye out for three-wattled bellbirds, chestnut-mandibled toucans, or the secretive Baird's tapir. A host of wildcats, include the ocelot, jaguarundi, puma, margay, and rarely seen jaguar.

Harpy Eagle

HARPY EAGLE

The endangered harpy eagle, nearly extinct from Costa Rica, is the country's largest and most powerful raptor. It's named for the Greek spirits that carried the dead to the underworld of Hades, who are said to have the faces of humans but the bodies of eagles. Harpy eagles are huge—females are more than 0.6 meter (2 feet) in length and have a 1.8-meter (6-foot) wingspan. They hunt above the canopy, searching for large mammals or, occasionally, for large birds like the macaw.

MORPHO BUTTERFLY

The bright blue morpho butterfly bounces through the jungle like a small piece of sky on a string. The entire life cycle, from egg to death, is approximately 137 days, and the adult butterflies live for only about a month. Once they emerge from the cocoon, morphos have few predators, thanks to the poisonous compounds that they retain from feeding habits back in their caterpillar days. In fact, the hairy brown tufts on the morpho caterpillar have been known to irritate human skin.

Blue Morpho

SCARLET MACAWS

Every bit the pirate's crimson parrot, these large and noisy birds mate for life, travel in pairs or large groups, and can often be found gathered in almond trees in low-elevation forests of the central and southern Pacific coast. Their cousin, the critically endangered great green macaw, travels across the Caribbean lowlands, following the ripening of the mountain almond.

Scarlet Macaw

THREE-TOED OR TWO-TOED SLOTH

Though difficult for us to spot, the barely moving three-toed sloth and two-toed sloth are principal meals for the harpy eagle. This animal's fur is a small self-sustaining ecosystem unto itself: because the forest is so wet and the sloth so inert, two species of blue-green algae thrive on its fur and provide it with needed camouflage. Non-parasitic insects also live here, feeding off the algae and keeping the growth under control.

■TIP→ **The vibrantly colored red-eyed tree frog, like the white tent bat, sometimes rests on the underside of large jungle leaves. If you're lucky, your guide may be able to coax one out for you to see.**

Three-toed-sloth

VOLCANOES

As part of the Pacific Ring of Fire, the country has three volcanic mountain ranges: Guanacaste, Central, and Tilarán. There are around 300 volcanic points in Costa Rica, but only 5 have formed volcanoes that have erupted in recent memory: Turrialba, Irazú, Poás, Rincón de la Vieja, and Arenal.

Costa Rica's volcanoes are the result of friction between two enormous tectonic plates—the Cocos plate and the Caribbean plate. As these plates rub against each other, the friction partially melts rock. Although everyone uses the term "lava," pyroclastic flow, or hot gas and rock, more accurately describes the product spewed from the volcanoes here. The flow is forced toward the surface, leaking through cracks or weak spots in the crust along with volcanic gas. In Rincón de la Vieja, gas escapes through craters high on the volcano, as well as seeping up through the surrounding ground, creating bubbling mud pits, hot springs, and fumaroles.

The volcanic mountain ranges divide the country's Pacific and Caribbean slopes and are responsible for the differences in climate between each side. Rain-laden trade winds blowing westward can't pass over these ranges without shedding their precipitation and rising. This creates Guanacaste's rain shadow: the dry plains and tropical dry forest that lie leeward, or west of the mountains. The mountains block the rain-producing weather system and cast a "shadow" of dryness.

Costa Rica's volcanic lakes occur when there is no natural drainage from a crater. The chemicals, minerals, and gases from below the earth's crust infuse the water and vibrantly color it. Irazú's lake is neon green; the baby-blue lagoon in Poás is extremely acidic and gives off toxic sulfur clouds and massive amounts of carbon dioxide.

The surface ecology of a volcano varies. Rincón de la Vieja is skirted by Guanacaste's signature grasslands and tropical dry forest. Poás Volcano is blanketed with rain forest and tipped with cloud forest. Some of the country's best coffee is grown on the slopes of Poás.

ADVENTURE HIGHLIGHTS

■ A hike through lush cloud forest will take you to the five magnificent waterfalls at La Paz Waterfall Gardens near Poás Volcano National Park.

■ Anglers love the guapote, tilapia, and machaca pulled from Lake Arenal.

■ The Arenal area is the jumping-off point for Class II–IV white-water rafting trips on the Blancas, Arenal, Toro, and San Carlos rivers.

■ Take the tough hike to La Fortuna Waterfall, near Arenal. Swimming under the waterfall is a slice of paradise.

TOP DESTINATIONS

Costa Rica's volcanoes are often the centerpieces of large national parks.

ARENAL VOLCANO

At 1,680 meters (5,512 feet), Arenal Volcano, rising on the northwestern plains of San Carlos, is every bit an awesome sight. Tall and perfectly conical, its sides are scarred by a history of violent eruptions and textured by decades of pyroclastic flow. Located at the northern end of the Tilarán Mountain Range, northwest of the capital, it is Costa Rica's best-known volcano. Arenal has settled into a less active phase these days. It's likely temporary: research suggests that Arenal has a 400-year cycle of major eruptions, and the activity since the 1968 explosion is small in comparison with what it's capable of. *(See Chapter 5.)*

On the Road to Arenal; piper35w, Fodors.com member

Note: The most recent active volcano of note is Turrialba Volcano, which is letting off a lot of sulfuric steam. Authorities currently prohibit entry to the national park.

POÁS VOLCANO

Poás Volcano is Costa Rica's most visited national park, in part because it is the closest active volcano to the capital of San José and the Aeropuerto Internacional Juan Santamaría. Located in the Cordillera Volcánica Central Mountain Range, Poás is topped by three craters, the tallest reaching 2,708 meters (8,885 feet) above sea level. Only the main cone has shown any volcanic eruptions in the last 200 years. You can get a good look at the crater from the viewing deck. *(See Chapter 4.)*

Gaudy Leaf Frog; Marco13, Fodors.com member.

RINCÓN DE LA VIEJA

A mass of slopes, craters, and biodiversity that bridges the Continental Divide, Rincón de la Vieja is in Costa Rica's arid northwest. It's not the classic conical volcano, but rather a ridge made of a series of craters that include bare, rocky bowls with brilliantly colored lakes, and velvety cones covered in rain forest. Scientists believe Rincón de la Vieja was born of simultaneous volcanic activity at nine different eruption points. The Rincón de la Vieja National Park covers nearly 35,000 acres and is a wonderland of volcanic activity that includes bubbling mud pits, hot springs, and geysers, as well as refreshing lagoons and spectacular waterfalls. *(See Chapter 6.)*

EXPERIENCING THE VOLCANOES

Horseback riding in Arenal

The Guatuso people believed that the fire god lived inside the Arenal Volcano . . . and in 1968, the gods were not happy. After 500 years of dormancy, Arenal erupted savagely, burying three small villages and killing 87 people. Today, thousands live at its base in the thriving town of La Fortuna, which is literally in Arenal's shadow.

HIKING
Volcano tourism is a major draw for international visitors, but given the dangers at the active sites, activities at the top are limited. There are no zip lines across open craters, and there's no snorkeling in acidic volcano lakes. At the peak, activities are limited to viewing, hiking, and photography. But the otherworldly look and feel of these sights is reason enough to visit. Arenal is in a temporarily less active state these days, but the sight is still impressive. The Turrialba Volcano, in the southeastern

Central Valley, has become more active in recent years. Hiking and horseback ascents to the summit, once staples of local tourism, are prohibited these days.

HORSEBACK RIDING
Many of Costa Rica's volcanoes are the centerpieces to broad national parks. Depending on the park, the infrastructure can be outstanding or nonexistent. Arenal and Poás have good horseback-riding trails and outfitters.

STANDING IN AWE
Volcanic activity is not, however, limited to a volcano's peak. The underground heat that fuels these giants also results in hot springs, bubbling mud pits, and geysers, among other geological wonders. Minerals from the dormant Tenorio Volcano create a fascinating effect in one of the rivers running down its side, the Río Celeste, giving it a baby-blue tint.

FLORA

The habitat and ecology of these geologic giants is influenced mostly by their surrounding ecology zones and elevation. Conditions around the crater of an active volcano are intensely harsh, but some tougher species do manage to survive.

FERN

Contrary to popular stereotypes, ferns don't necessarily grow in shady, moist environments. The tongue fern (*Elaphoglossum lingua*) extends long, rubbery, tongue-shape leaves and has evolved to grow around volcanic rock and hardened ash. You'll find it around the top of the Poás Volcano. Farther down, you'll find other types of ferns adapted to friendlier conditions.

Ferns

MYRTLE

Myrtle (*Myrtaceae*) and other low-lying shrubs survive this environment thanks to their slow growth rate. Myrtle, poor man's umbrella (*Gunnera insignis*), papelillo (*Senecio oerstedianus*), and other shrubs and ferns cover the higher bluffs around Irazú's crater. Mistletoe (*Psittacanthus*) can be found near the major volcanoes in the Central Valley. These flowering plants are interesting because they attach to trees by haustoria, special structures that penetrate the host plant and absorb its water and nutrients. When the mistletoe dies, it leaves a mark on the tree, a woodrose or *rosa de palo*.

Myrtle

OAK

Forests in Costa Rica's higher mountain areas share some plant species with cloud forests. However, the plants here have adapted to live in cold temperatures and, if the volcano is active, in compacted ash. Surrounding the Botos Lagoon, on the south side of the principal Poás crater, is high-elevation cloud forest of oak (*Quercus costaricensis and Q. copeyensis*), small cedar (*Brunellia costaricensis*), and the flowering cypress (*Escallonia poasana*)—trees that are typically crowded with epiphytes, bromeliads, and mosses.

Great Roble Oak

WILD BALSAM

Wild balsam, oak, and poor man's umbrella carpet the inactive cones around Rincón de la Vieja. Tropical dry forest species grow farther down. Look for the guanacaste tree (*Enterolobium cyclocarpum*), Spanish cedar (*Cedrela odorata*), oak (*Q. oocarpa*), and the country's largest wild population of the guardia morada orchid, Costa Rica's national flower.

Wild Balsam aka
Touch-me-not Balsam

FAUNA

Like the flora around a volcano, the wildlife diversity of this region is dictated by the ecology around the mountain. Also, the more humans there are, the fewer animals you'll see.

FIERY-THROATED HUMMINGBIRD

Birds are one of the most populous types of creature to live on the flanks of Poás and many more of Costa Rica's volcanoes. The fiery-throated hummingbird, the summer tanager, the sooty robin, and the emerald toucanet are among the 79 bird species that have been recorded at Poás. The fiery-throated hummingbird is recognizable by its forecrown, throat, and breast colors, as well as its bluish hump and blue-black tail.

Fiery-Throated Hummingbird

NINE-BANDED ARMADILLO

Irazú is home to smaller creatures such as the nine-banded armadillo, the eastern cottontail, and the little spotted cat. The nine-banded armadillo has a long snout and fantastic sense of smell. It can hold its breath for up to six minutes. This helps it keep dirt out of its nostrils while digging. Under stressful conditions, a female armadillo can prolong her pregnancy for up to three years by delaying the implantation of the fertilized egg into the uterus wall.

Nine-banded armadillo

NORTH AMERICAN PORCUPINE

The much drier region of Rincón de la Vieja has a distinctly different—and broader—set of animal inhabitants, including the North American porcupine and the agouti (a large, short-legged relative of the guinea pig). Pumas, ocelots, raccoons, and three species of monkeys (the howler, the white-faced capuchin, and the Central American spider monkey) are among the larger mammals. More than 300 bird species have been recorded there, including the collared aracari, the bare-necked umbrella bird, and the three-wattled bellbird.

North American Porcupine

PUMA

In the Barva region, pumas (also called mountain lions and cougars), and even jaguars still stalk the more remote forests, searching for the tapir or an unlucky spider monkey. The puma is an excellent climber and can jump to branches 5 meters (16 feet) off the ground, essentially giving monkeys nowhere to hide. Pumas have never been hunted for their pelts, but are suffering from habitat destruction. In Costa Rica, they are rarely found outside protected areas.

Puma

CLOUD FOREST

The four mountain ranges that make up Costa Rica's own piece of the Continental Divide split the country into its Caribbean and Pacific regions. At these higher altitudes, temperatures cool, clouds settle, and rainfall increases. The forests found here are shrouded in mist and rich in biodiversity. Welcome to Costa Rica's famed cloud forests.

Like its lowland rain-forest cousins, cloud forests are packed with plant and animal species, thanks largely to their water-drenched conditions. There's an average of 5 meters (16 feet) of rainfall a year, but that number doubles when you factor in the amount of moisture gleaned from the clouds and fog that drift through every day. Like rain forests, giant hardwoods reaching as high as almost 60 meters (200 feet) set the ceiling for this ecology zone, while a variety of smaller trees, ferns, shrubs, and other plants fill the understories. Epiphytes flourish here, as do mosses, lichens, and

liverwort. These plants cling to passing moisture and capture it like sponges. As a result, cloud forests are constantly soaking wet even when there is no rain.

Because conditions in a cloud forest can be harsh, many of the tougher and more adaptable rain-forest species make their home here. The relentless, heavy cloud cover can block sunlight even from the highest reaches of the forest, and deeper inside, light is rare. Photosynthesis and growth are slower, so the plants tend to be smaller with thicker trunks and stems. These unique conditions also produce an unusually high number of endemic and rare species.

The Monteverde Cloud Forest Preserve, one of the world's most famous protected cloud forests, shelters innumerable life-forms. There are more than 100 mammal species; 400 bird species, including at least 30 species of hummingbird; 500-plus species of butterfly; and more than 2,500 plant species, including 420 types of orchids. There is only a handful of protected cloud forests here and worldwide, and this type of ecozone is increasingly threatened by human encroachment.

ADVENTURE HIGHLIGHTS

■ Leave the car at home and travel on horseback to or from the Arenal Volcano area and Monteverde Cloud Forest. Contact Desafío Adventures, the only guides we recommend for this journey.

■ The good folks at the Savegre Hotel will give you an education on one of their daylong natural-history hikes around San Gerardo de Dota cloud forest.

■ Selvatura, right next to Monteverde, is the only canopy tour in the area with a zip line built entirely inside the cloud forest.

TOP DESTINATIONS

Regardless of which cloud forest you visit, bring a raincoat and go with a guide if you want to see wildlife. You'll marvel at their ability to spot a sloth at a hundred paces.

BRAULIO CARRILLO NATIONAL PARK

Descending from the Cordillera Volcánica Central Mountain Range, Braulio Carrillo National Park is an awesome, intimidating, and rugged landscape of dense cloud forest that stretches toward the rain forests of the Caribbean lowlands. The enormous park encompasses 117,580 acres of untamed jungle and is less than an hour's drive from San José. The country's principal eastbound highway cuts a path straight through it. Elusive (and endangered) jaguars and pumas are among the many animal species here, and scenic viewpoints are plentiful along the highway. A handful of trails, including the easy-to-access loop trails at the Quebrada González station, can be taken a short distance into the park's interior. *(See Chapter 9.)*

MONTEVERDE CLOUD FOREST BIO-LOGICAL RESERVE

Costa Rica's most famous cloud forest reserve is packed with an astonishing variety of life: 2,500 plant species, 400 species of birds, 500 types of

Banded Anteater; maddytem, Fodors.com member

butterflies, and more than 100 different mammals—many of them bats—have been catalogued so far. The reserve reaches 1,535 meters (5,032 feet) above sea level, spans the Tilarán Mountain Range, and encompasses 9,885 acres of cloud forest and rain forest. There are 13 km (8 miles) of well-marked trails, zip-line tours, and suspended bridges for canopy viewing, bird tours, guided night walks, and a field research station with an amphibian aquarium. Allow a generous slice of time for leisurely hiking; longer hikes are made possible by some strategically placed overnight refuges along the way. *(See Chapter 5.)*

SAN GERARDO DE DOTA

One of Costa Rica's premier nature destinations, San Gerardo de Dota is a damp, epiphyte-laden forest of giant oak trees and an astonishing number of resplendent quetzals. Outdoor enthusiasts may never want to leave these parts—some of the country's best hiking is in this valley, and it's popular with bird-watchers. It's also great for horseback riding and trout fly-fishing. *(See Chapter 8.)*

Braulio Carrillo National Park

EXPERIENCING A CLOUD FOREST

Zipline tour in Selvature just outside of Monteverde Cloud Forest

You may need to get down and dirty—well, more like wet and muddy—to experience a cloud forest's natural wonders, but then, that's half the fun.

BIRD-WATCHING

Bird-watching is rewarding in the cloud forest, where some of the most vibrant and peculiar of nature's winged creatures can be found. Rise early, enjoy some locally grown coffee, and check the aguacatillo trees for quetzals. If you opt to go without a guide, bring along waterproof binoculars and a good guidebook (we recommend *The Birds of Costa Rica*, by Richard Garrigues and Robert Dean) for spotting and identifying birds.

CANOPY TOURS

Canopy tours and suspended bridges run right through the upper reaches of the cloud forest—an ecosystem in its own right. Spot birds, monkeys, and exotic orchids from a viewpoint that was once nearly impossible to reach. Get even closer to butterflies, amphibians, snakes, and insects at various exhibits in the parks' research centers.

FISHING

If freshwater fishing in spectacular surroundings is right up your alley, check out the Savegre River, in the San Gerardo de Dota Valley. It's been stocked with rainbow trout since the 1950s.

HIKING

Well-guided hikes through this eerie landscape, draped with moss and vines, make it easier to spot the less obvious features of this complex ecosystem. Compared with the barren tropical dry forest and colorful rain forest, cloud forests don't easily offer up their secrets. Binoculars and a good guide will go a long way toward making your hike and wildlife-spotting richer experiences.

FLORA

A typical hectare (2½ acres) of cloud forest might be home to nearly 100 species of trees. Contrast that with a mere 30 in the richest forests of North America.

EPIPHYTES

Epiphytes thrive in cloud and rain forests, thanks to all the moisture and nutrients in the air. The *stanhopea* orchid is interesting because of its clever pollination tricks. The blossoms' sweet smell attracts bees, but the flower's waxy surface is slippery so they slide down inside. As they slowly work their way out, they brush up against the flower's column and collect pollen. This pollen is then transferred to the sticky stigma of other flowers.

Epiphyte Stanhopea

Bromeliads, another family of flowering plants, compete with epiphytes for space on the branches and trunks of the forest's trees. The spiraling leaves form caches for water, falling plant material, and insect excretion. These are mineral-rich little ponds for insects and amphibians, and drinking and bathing water for birds and other animals.

POOR MAN'S UMBRELLA

If you're caught in the rain, take cover under a poor man's umbrella (*Gunnera insignis* and *Gunnera talamancana*), whose broad and sturdy leaves sometimes grow large enough to shelter an entire family. These shrubby plants love the dark, moist interior of the cloud forest.

Poor Man's Umbrella

ROBLE TREE

Majestic roble, or oak—principally the white oak (*Quercus copeyensis*) and black oak (*Quercus costarricensis*)—is the dominant tree of Costa Rica's cloud forests and grows to 60 meters (200 feet). The deciduous hardwood *cedro dulce*, or Spanish cedar (*Cedrela tonduzii*), is also a giant at 40 meters (147 feet). These two are joined by evergreens like the *jaúl*, or alder, and the *aguacatillo*, a name meaning "little avocado" that's given to a variety of trees from the *lauracea* family.

White Oak Tree

STAR ORCHID

The star orchid (*Epidendrum radicans*) is one of the few orchids that is not an epiphyte. It grows on land and mimics in color and shape other nectar-filled flowers in order to attract butterflies who unwittingly become pollinators.

Star Orchid

FAUNA

The resplendent quetzal, the blue-crowned motmot, the orange-bellied trogon, and the emerald toucanet are just some of the hundreds of species that can be logged in a cloud forest.

COLLARED TROGON

The collared trogon and the orange-bellied trogon are in the same family as the quetzal. They all share square black-and-white tail plumage and bright orange or yellow chest feathers. The collared trogon perches very quietly and is easy to miss. Luckily, it doesn't fly far, so its flight is easy to follow.

Collared Trogon

GLASS FROGS

One of the more bizarre amphibians is the tiny, transparent glass frog of the *Centrolenellu* genus, whose internal organs can be seen through its skin. It lives in trees and bushes and can often be heard at night near the rivers and streams. Cloud forests have fewer amphibian species than rain forests, but amphibian populations worldwide have plummeted in recent decades. No one knows the cause yet. Some blame acid rain and pesticides; others believe it is yet another sign of coming ecological disaster.

Glass Frogs

HOWLER MONKEYS

One of the largest New World monkeys, howlers are named for their loud, barking roar that can be heard for miles. If you want to spot a howler, be sure to scan the treetops; their diet consists mainly of canopy leaves, and they rarely leave the protection of the trees. Other cloud forest mammals include the white-faced capuchin monkey, white-nosed coatis, porcupines, red brocket deer, and Alston's singing mouse.

Howler Monkey

RESPLENDENT QUETZAL

Perhaps the most famed resident of Costa Rica's cloud forests is the illustrious resplendent quetzal. Every year, bird-watchers come to Costa Rica hoping to spot the green, red, and turquoise plumage of this elusive trogon. Considered a sacred creature by the Maya and the namesake of Guatemala's currency, the quetzal spends much of its time perched in its favorite tree, the *aguacatillo*.

Resplendent Quetzal

TROPICAL DRY FOREST

The most endangered biome in the world, these seasonal forests swing between two climate extremes—from drenching wet to bone dry. To survive, plants undergo a drastic physical transformation: forests burst into life during the rainy months, and are brown, leafless, and seemingly dead during the dry season.

For about half the year, northwestern Costa Rica is as wet as the rest of the country. The weather blows in from the Pacific, and it can rain every day. During the dry season, from January to April, weather patterns change, winds shift, and the land becomes parched.

Tall deciduous hardwoods are the giants in this ecology zone, with spindly branches creating a seasonal canopy as high as 30 meters (100 feet). A thorny and rambling understory of smaller trees and bushes thrives thanks to the plentiful light permitted once the canopy leaves fall to the forest floor. The challenges of

the dry months have forced plants to specialize. The hardwoods are solitary and diffuse, their seeds spread far and wide by animals and insects. Some even flower progressively through the dry season, depending on the plant species and the particular bees and birds that have evolved to pollinate them.

Dry season is perfect for bird- and animal-watching since the lack of foliage makes wildlife spotting easy. Keep your eyes peeled for monkeys, parrots, lizards, coyotes, rabbits, snakes, and even jaguars.

There was once one great, uninterrupted swath of dry forest that began in southern Mexico, rolled across Mesoamerica, and ended in northwest Costa Rica. Today, less than 2% of the Central American tropical dry forest remains, the majority of it in Costa Rica. But even here, the forest is fractured into biologically isolated islands, thanks to decades of logging and agriculture. The Guanacaste Conservation Area has managed to corral off large chunks of land for preservation, and private and government efforts are under way to create biological corridors between isolated dry forests so that animals and plants can roam farther and deepen their gene pools, so critical to their survival.

ADVENTURE HIGHLIGHTS

■ Adrenalin-spiked tours with Hacienda Guachipelín (bordering Rincón de la Vieja National Park) include river tubing, rappelling, zip lines, and a Tarzan swing.

■ Let the knowledgeable folks from the Organization for Tropical Studies (OTS) take you on a guided bird-watching tour through Palo Verde National Park. Boat rides float you past hundreds of waterfowl.

■ Take the kids on a bird- and monkey-watching journey down the Río Corobicí, in Palo Verde National Park.

TOP DESTINATIONS

Most of Costa Rica's remaining tropical dry forests are located in the northwest of the country, not too far from the Nicaragua border.

GUANACASTE CONSERVATION AREA

Santa Rosa is part of the larger Guanacaste Conservation Area, which is composed of some tropical dry forest and former farmland that's being regenerated to its natural state. The park is intended to serve as a much-needed biological corridor from Santa Rosa up to the cloud forests of the Orosi and Cacao volcanoes, to the east. Park infrastructure is generally lacking, though three biological stations offer some accommodations to student groups and researchers. *(See Chapter 6.)*

PALO VERDE NATIONAL PARK

Farther south, Palo Verde National Park skirts the northeastern side of the Río Tempisque, straddling some of the country's most spectacular wetlands and tropical dry forest. Thanks to these two very different ecology zones, Palo Verde is packed with very diverse bird, plant, and animal species—bird-watchers love this park. The Organization for Tropical Studies has a biological station at Palo Verde and offers tours and accommodations. Park guards also maintain a ranger station with rustic overnight accommodations. *(See Chapter 6.)*

Hummingbird Nesting; reedjoella, Fodors.com member

RINCÓN DE LA VIEJA NATIONAL PARK

More tropical dry forest can be found inside the Rincón de la Vieja National Park, ringing the base of the two volcanoes of this protected area—Santa María and Rincón de la Vieja. *(See Chapter 6.)*

SANTA ROSA NATIONAL PARK

The largest piece of tropical dry forest under government protection in Central America spreads out over Santa Rosa National Park, about 35 km (22 miles) north of Guanacaste's capital, Liberia. The park, which covers 380 square km (146 square miles), also includes two beaches and coastal mangrove forest. Thanks to trails and equipped campsites, you can venture deep into the park. During the dry season, visibility is excellent and chances are good in terms of spotting some of the hundreds of bird and animal species there. Playa Nancite, Santa Rosa's northern beach, is also one of the world's most important and most protected beaches for the nesting of olive ridley sea turtles. They come ashore by the hundreds of thousands between May and October in a phenomenon called the *arribada*. Access is limited to researchers. *(See Chapter 6.)*

Canopy Tour at Rincón de la Vieja National Park

EXPERIENCING A DRY TROPICAL FOREST

Rincón de la Vieja National Park

Many of Costa Rica's roads are rough at best, and tropical forests are often remote. We recommend renting a four-wheel-drive vehicle for getting around.

BIKING

Some parks allow biking, but again, this is certainly something you don't want to do during the rains. Contact the park that you'll be visiting ahead of time for trail and rental information.

BIRD- AND WILDLIFE-WATCHING

Most people come to these areas for bird-watching and wildlife spotting, but it's best done during the dry season, when all the foliage drops from the trees. Bring a good bird or wildlife guide, binoculars, lots of water (we can't stress this enough), and plenty of patience. It's a good idea to find a watering hole and just hunker down and let the animals come to you. If you don't want to explore the forest alone, tours can be arranged through hotels, ranger stations, and private research centers inside the parks. In terms of bird and wildlife guides, we recommend *The Birds of Costa Rica* by Richard Garrigues and Robert Dean and *The Mammals of Costa Rica* by Mark Wainwright. If you'd like to know more about plants, pick up *Tropical Plants of Costa Rica* by Willow Zuchowski.

HIKING

The best way to experience these endangered woods is to strap on your hiking boots, grab a hat and lots of water, and get out and walk. Most of the dry forests are protected lands and found in Guanacaste's national parks. Some have road access, making it possible to drive through the park, but most are accessible only by hiking trails. During the rainy season, roads become mud pits and hiking trails are almost impassable.

FLORA

Among other types of flora, tropical forests are filled with deciduous hardwoods, such as mahogany (*Swietenia macrophylla*), black laurel (*Cordia gerascanthus*), ronrón (*Astronium graveolens*), and *cocobolo* (*Dalbergia retusa*). Much of the wood is highly prized for furniture and houses, so many of these trees are facing extinction outside national parks and protected areas.

Cornizuelo

CORNIZUELO
The spiky, *cornizuelo* (*Acacia collinsii*) is an intriguing resident of the lower levels because of its symbiotic relationship with ants. This small evergreen tree puts out large thorns that serve as a home for a certain ant species. In exchange for food and shelter, the ants provide the tree protection from other leaf-munching insects or vines. Sometimes the ants will even cut down encroaching vegetation on the forest floor, allowing the tree to thrive.

Frangipani; plumboy, Fodors.com member

FRANGIPANI TREE
The frangipani tree (*Plumeria rubra*) can grow up to 8 meters (26 feet) and has meaty pink, white, or yellow blossoms. The flowers are most fragrant at night to lure sphinx moths. Unfortunately for the moth, the blooms don't produce nectar. The plant simply dupes their pollinators into hopping from bloom to bloom and tree to tree in a fruitless search for food.

GUANACASTE
Perhaps the most striking and easy-to-spot resident of Costa Rica's tropical dry forest is the *guanacaste* (*Enterolobium cyclocarpum*), an imposing tree with an enormous, spherical canopy that seems straight out of the African savanna. The guanacaste is the northwest province's namesake and Costa Rica's national tree. It is most easily identified standing alone in pastures. Without the competition of the forest, a pasture guanacaste sends massive branches out low from its trunk, creating an arching crown of foliage close to the ground. The ear-shaped seedpods are also a distinct marker; the hard seeds inside are popular with local artisan jewelers.

Guanacaste

GUMBO-LIMBO
Costa Ricans call the gumbo-limbo tree (*Bursera simaruba*) *indio desnudo* (naked Indian) because of its red, peeling bark. This tree is also found in Florida, and the wood has historically been used for making carousel horses in the United States.

Gumbo-limbo

FAUNA

Tropical dry forests are literally crawling with life. Bark scorpions, giant cockroaches, and tarantulas scuttle along the forest floor, and the buzz from wasps and cicadas gives the air an almost electric feel. A careful eye may be able to pick out walking sticks frozen still among the twigs. The jaguar, and one if its favorite prey, the endangered tapir, also stalk these forests.

Black-headed Trogon

BLACK-HEADED TROGON

With an open canopy for much of the year, and plentiful ground rodents and reptiles, these forests are great hunting grounds for birds of prey like the roadside hawk and the spectacled owl. The white-throated magpie jay travels in noisy mobs, while the scissor-tailed flycatcher migrates from as far north as the southern United States. The rufous-naped wren builds its nest in the spiky acacia trees. The black-headed trogon, with its bright yellow breast, and the elegant trogon both nest exclusively in Costa Rica's tropical dry forest.

COYOTE

Nearly unique to the dry tropical forest is the coyote, which feeds on rodents, lizards, and an assortment of small mammals, as well as sea turtle eggs (when near the beach) and other improvised meals. Like the Virginia opossum and the white-tailed deer, the coyote is believed to have traveled south from North America through the once-interconnected tropical dry forest of Mesoamerica.

Coyote

NEOTROPICAL RATTLESNAKE

The venomous neotropical rattlesnake and the exquisite painted wood turtle are among the reptiles that exclusively call this region home. Salvin's spiny pocket mouse, the eastern cottontail rabbit, and both the spotted and hooded skunk are also unique to Costa Rica's dry forests.

Neotropical Rattlesnake

WHITE-FACED CAPUCHIN

Monkeys are common all over Costa Rica, and the dry forests are home to three species: the howler monkeys, with their leathery black faces and deep barking call, are the loudest of the forest's mammals; the white-faced capuchin travel in playful packs; and the endangered spider monkey requires large, undisturbed tracts of forest for a healthy population to survive. This last group is in steep decline—another indicator of the overall health of this eco-region.

White-faced capuchin

WETLANDS AND MANGROVES

Wetlands are any low-lying areas that are perpetually saturated with water. Their complex ecosystems support a variety of living things—both endemic species unique to the area and visitors who travel half-way around the hemisphere to get here. Here, land species have evolved to live much of their lives in water.

One common type of wetland in Costa Rica is a flood-plain, created when a river or stream regularly over-flows its banks, either because of heavy rains or ocean tides. Thanks to huge deposits of sediment that are left as the floodwaters recede, the ground is extremely fer-tile and plants thrive, as do the animals that feed here.

Mangroves are a unique type of wetland and cover 1% of the country. They are found at the edges of tidal areas, such as ocean inlets, estuaries, and canals where saltwater mixes with fresh. Mangrove forests are made

up of a small variety of plants, principally mangrove trees, but attract a huge variety of animals.

Mangrove trees are able to survive in this stressful habitat because they have developed the ability to cope with constant flooding, tolerate a lack of oxygen, and thrive in a mix of salt- and freshwater thanks to uniquely adapted roots and leaves. The nutrient-rich sediment and mud that build up around these trees and between their prop roots create habitat for plankton, algae, crabs, oysters, and shrimp. These, in turn, attract larger and larger animals that come to feed, giving mangrove forests a remarkable level of biodiversity.

These thick coastal forests are protective barriers for inland ecosystems; they dissipate the force of storm winds and sudden surges in tides or floods triggered by coastal storms or tsunamis.

Sadly, coastal development is a big threat to mangroves. It is illegal to clear mangrove forests, but enforcement is weak, and beachfront developers have been caught doing it. Wetlands are also threatened by the diversion of water for agriculture.

ADVENTURE HIGHLIGHTS

■ Witness the spectacle of nesting turtles at Tortuguero National Park. Turtle-watching excursions require a certified guide and take place only between the February and November nesting season.

■ Anglers can hook mackerel, tarpoon, snook, calba, and snapper in the canals and along the coast of Tortuguero and Barra Colorado.

■ Take a kayaking tour through the mangrove estuary of Isla Damas, near Manuel Antonio. You'll probably see monkeys, crocodiles, and numerous birds.

TOP DESTINATIONS

The Ramsar Convention on Wetlands is an intergovernmental treaty to provide a framework for the conservation of the world's wetlands. There are 11 Ramsar wetlands in Costa Rica: all are impressive, but we've listed only our top 3.

CAÑO NEGRO NATIONAL WILDLIFE REFUGE

One Ramsar wetland is found in the Caño Negro National Wildlife Refuge, in the more remote northern plains close to the border with Nicaragua. Caño Negro has a seasonal lake that can cover as many as 1,975 acres and grow as deep as 3 meters (10 feet). The lake is actually a pool created by the Frio River that dries up to nearly nothing between February and May. The park also has marshes, semipermanently flooded old-growth forest, and other wetland habitats. *(See Chapter 5.)*

PALO VERDE NATIONAL PARK

Within the Palo Verde National Park is perhaps Costa Rica's best-known wetland—a system that includes shallow, permanent freshwater lagoons, marshes, mangroves, and woodlands that are seasonally flooded by the Tempisque River. A good portion of this 45,511-acre park is covered by tropical dry forest. In fact, this park has 12 different habitats, creating one of the most diverse collections

Alpha Howler Monkey; Liz Stuart, Fodors.com member

of life in the country. At least 55 aquatic plants and 150 tree species have been identified here, and the largest number of aquatic and wading birds in all of Mesoamerica can be found at Palo Verde wetlands. A total of 279 bird species have been recorded within Palo Verde, so little surprise that it's listed by the Ramsar Convention as a wetland of international importance. The Organization of Tropical Studies maintains a research station at the park with limited accommodations but great views of the marshes, as well as extremely knowledgeable guides. *(See Chapter 6.)*

TORTUGUERO NATIONAL PARK

Ninety-nine percent of mangrove forests are found on Costa Rica's Pacific coast. But the best place to see some of the remaining 1% on the Caribbean side is Tortuguero National Park. Like Palo Verde, Tortuguero is home to a wide variety of life—11 distinct habitats in total, including extensive wetlands and mangrove forests. Beach-nesting turtles (*tortugas*) are the main attraction here, but the park is included in the Ramsar list of internationally important wetlands. Many of the species listed here can be spotted along the banks of Tortuguero's famous canals. *(See Chapter 9.)*

Tortuguero; StupFD, Fodors.com member

EXPERIENCING THE WETLANDS AND MANGROVES

Paddling through Tortuguero at dawn; Thornton Cohen, Fodors.com member

Wildlife viewing in general can be very rewarding in these areas, because a wide variety of creatures comes together and shares the habitat.

BIRD-WATCHING

The most populous and diverse of the creatures that live in and depend on wetlands and mangroves are birds, so bring some binoculars and your field guide, and prepare to check off some species. For good photos, take a long lens and tripod, and get an early start—midday sun reflecting off the ubiquitous water can make your photos washed out or create some challenging reflections.

BOATING

The best way to see Costa Rica's remaining mangrove forests is by boat—we recommend using a kayak or canoe. These vessels allow you to slip along canals and protected coastlines in near silence, increasing your chance of creeping up on many of the more impressive creatures that call this habitat home. A guided boat tour is also recommended—a good naturalist or biologist, or even a knowledgeable local, will know where creatures habitually hang out and will be able to distinguish between thick branches and a knotted boa at the top of a shoreside tree.

FISHING

Canals that are not part of protected areas can be ripe for fishing—another, tastier way to get a close-up look at some of the local fauna. Make sure to ask about what's biting, as well as local fishing regulations.

VIEWING PLATFORMS

Hiking can be more difficult in these areas because wetlands are by definition largely underwater. But some areas have elevated platforms that make for great up-close viewing of the interior parts of marshes and shallow lagoons.

FLORA

Wetland and mangrove plants share an ability to live in soggy conditions. However, not all wetland plants are able to survive brackish water in the way coastal mangrove flora can.

BLACK MANGROVE
The black mangrove can grow as tall as 12 meters (40 feet) and has adapted to survive in its habitat by excreting salt through special glands in its leaves. It grows on the banks above the high-tide line and has evolved to breathe through small roots it sends up vertically in case of flooding.

Black Mangrove

RED MANGROVE
Costa Rica has seven species of mangrove trees, including red mangrove (*Rhizophora mangle*), black mangrove (*Avicennia germinans*), white mangrove (*Laguncularia racemosa*), and the rarer tea mangrove (*Pelliciera rhizophorae*). Red mangrove is easily identified by its tall arching prop roots that give it a firm foothold against wind and waves. The tidal land is also unstable, so all mangroves need a lot of root just to keep upright. As a result, many have more living matter underwater than above ground. They also depend on their prop roots for extra nutrients and oxygen; the red mangrove filters salt at its roots.

Red Mangrove

THORNY SENSITIVE PLANT
Aquatic grasses and herbs grow along the shallower edges of swamps and marshlands where they can take root underwater and still reach the air above. The curious dormilona, or thorny sensitive plant (*Mimosa pigra*) is another invasive wetland shrub and can be identified by the way its fernlike leaves wilt shyly to the touch, only to straighten out a little later.

Thorny sensitive plant

WATER HYACINTH
The succulent, floating water hyacinth (*Eichornia crassipes*) is recognizable by its lavender-pink flowers that are sometimes bundled at 8 to 15 per single stalk. The stems rise from a bed of thick, floating green leaves, whereas the plant's feathery roots hang free in the still freshwater. The water hyacinth is prolific and invasive; they've even been known to clog the canals of Tortuguero.

Water Hyacinth

FAUNA

Though the diversity of plant life in mangrove swamps and wetlands is small compared with other ecozones, this habitat attracts an extremely wide variety of fauna.

BLACK-BELLIED WHISTLING DUCK

Bird-watchers love the wide-open wetlands and marshes, with flocks of thousands of migrating and resident species. In these tropical floodplains pink-tinged roseate spoonbills will be found stalking the shallow water alongside the majestic great egret and the bizarre and endangered jabiru stork. Keep an eye out for the black-bellied whistling duck, which actually perches and nests in trees. These migrant ducks can also be found in some Southern U.S. states.

Black-Bellied Whistling Duck

BLACK-CROWNED NIGHT HERON

Mangroves are critical nesting habitats for a number of birds, including the endangered mangrove hummingbird, the yellow-billed continga, the Amazon kingfisher, and the black-crowned night heron. Interestingly, black-crowned night herons don't distinguish between their own young and those from other nests, so they willingly brood strange chicks.

Black-Crowned Night Heron

CRAB-EATING RACCOON

Bigger creatures are attracted to these mangroves precisely because of the veritable buffet of sea snacks. The crab-eating raccoon will prowl the canopy of the mangrove forests as well as the floor, feeding on crabs and mollusks. The endangered American crocodile and the spectacled caiman can be found lurking in still waters or sunning themselves on the banks of mangrove habitat.

RAINBOW PARROT FISH

Rainbow parrot fish, in addition to many other fish species, spend time as juveniles in mangrove areas, feeding in the relative safety of the roots until they're big enough to venture out into more open water. Parrot fish have a few unusual abilities: they are hermaphroditic and can change sex in response to population density; at night they wrap themselves in a protective mucus cocoon; and they eat coral and excrete a fine white sand. One parrot fish can create a ton of sand per year, which ultimately washes ashore. Think about it the next time you're lying on the beach.

Crab-eating Raccoon

Rainbow Parrot Fish

SHORELINE

Costa Rica has a whopping 1,290-km-long (799-mile-long) coastline that varies from expansive beaches, tranquil bays, muddy estuaries, and rocky outcroppings. They're backed by mangrove, rain, transitional, and tropical dry forests.

Each of Costa Rica's coastal environments, as well as the currents and the wind, has its own distinct impact on the ecology of the beach.

Costa Rica's sand beaches come in different shades and textures: pulverized black volcanic rock (Playa Negra), crushed white shells (Playa Conchal), finely ground white coral and quartz (Playa Carrillo), and gray rock sediment (many stretches along both coasts). These strips of sand may seem devoid of life, but they're actually ecological hotbeds, where mammals, birds, and amphibians live, feed, or reproduce. The hardiest

of creatures can be found in the tidal pools that form on rockier beaches; keep an eye out for colorful fish, starfish, and sea urchins, all of which endure pounding waves, powerful tides, broiling sun, and predator attacks from the air, land, or sea.

By law, all of Costa Rica's beaches are public, but beaches near population centers get strewn with trash quite quickly. It's one of the great ironies of Costa Rica that a country renowned for its environmental achievements litters with such laissez-faire. Limited access tends to make for more scenic beaches. If you're worried about pollution, keep an eye out for Blue Flag beaches (marked on our maps with blue flags), an ecological rating system that evaluates water quality—both ocean and drinking water—trash cleanup, waste management, security, signage, and environmental education. Blue flags are awarded to communities rather than to individual hotels, which feeds a sense of cooperation. In 2002, the competition was opened to inland communities. Out of 182 that applied, 147 communities—107 beaches and 40 inland towns—won flags at the 2014 ceremonies.

ADVENTURE HIGHLIGHTS

■ From October 15 to February 15, Playa Grande sees lumbering, huge leatherback turtles come ashore to nest. Sixty days later, the hatchlings will scramble toward the water.

■ Gentle, consistent waves and a couple of good surfing schools make Sámara, on the North Pacific coast, a good choice for first-timers hoping to catch a wave.

■ Snorkeling is phenomenal near Cahuita's coral reef and at Punta Uva on the Caribbean coast. Look for colorful blue parrot fish, angelfish, sponges, and seaweeds.

TOP DESTINATIONS

Costa Rica's beach scenes are wildly diverse, so a little planning can go a long way.

BALLENA NATIONAL MARINE PARK

This unique park is along one of the more remote stretches of coastline, on the southern end of the Central Pacific region, and encompasses several beaches. *Ballena*, which is Spanish for "whale," gets its name from the humpback whales who feed here, and for a peculiar sandbar formation at Playa Uvita that goes straight out toward the ocean before splitting and curving in two directions, much like a whale's tail. *(See Chapter 8.)*

Uvita Beach; Toronto Jeff, Fodors.com member

THE CARIBBEAN

This coast has an entirely different feel from the Pacific. North of Limón, there are miles of undeveloped, protected beaches where green sea turtles come in July to October to lay eggs. There have also been sightings of the loggerhead, hawksbill, and leatherback turtles. The currents here are strong, so don't plan on swimming.

To the south of Limón, beaches are bordered by dense green vegetation all year long, and the quality of the sand can change dramatically as you wander from cove to cove. Some of the country's healthiest living coral reefs are offshore, so snorkeling is worthwhile. Beaches of note are Cahuita's Playa Negra and Playa Blanca, and Puerto Viejo de Talamanca's Punta Uva. *(See Chapter 9.)*

MANUEL ANTONIO NATIONAL PARK

On the northern end of the Pacific, Manuel Antonio National Park shelters some of the country's more precious beaches. A series of half-moon bays with sparkling sands are fronted by transitional forest—a combination of flora and fauna from the tropical dry forests farther north and the tropical rain forests that stretch south. Wildlife is abundant at Manuel Antonio, and the towering jungle at the beach's edge can give the area a wild and paradisiacal feel. *(See Chapter 7.)*

THE NICOYA PENINSULA

A succession of incredible beaches are scattered along this region of the Pacific coast, from Playa Panama in the north all the way south to Montezuma, including Avellanas, Guiones, and Sámara. Ostional, just north of Guiones, offers something none of the others can: the turtle arribada. The beach is part of the Ostional Wildlife Refuge, granting an extra level of protection to the area. *(See Chapter 6.)*

Montezuma; Justin Hubbell, Fodors.com member

EXPERIENCING THE SHORELINE

Nesting Olive Ridley Turtles at Ostional Wildlife Refuge

Costa Rica's beaches have tons of activities. If you like getting wet, the ocean is bathwater warm and there are water-sports outfitters just about everywhere. There are also plenty of hammocks and cafés.

HORSEBACK RIDING

Horseback riding on the beach is great fun, but you can't do it everywhere. Many of the most popular beaches have outlawed it for health reasons, especially if it's where a lot of people swim.

SURFING

Costa Rica is a world-class surfing destination, and the Pacific coast in particular has enough surf spots to satisfy both pros and novices. You can arrange lessons in most beach towns. Surfing is an activity that involves a lot of floating, so it allows for plenty of wildlife watching: keep a weather eye for jumping fish, stingrays, dolphins, and squads of brown pelicans.

TURTLE TOURS

Witnessing the nesting ritual of Costa Rica's visiting sea turtles is a truly unforgettable experience. Various organizations oversee the nesting beaches and arrange tours. The onslaught of mother turtles is most intense throughout the night, so setting out just before dawn is the best way to see and take pictures of the phenomenon in progress at first light.

⚠ Take great care at beaches that drop off steeply as you enter the water. This is an indicator not only of large waves that crash straight onto the shore but also of strong currents.

FLORA

The plants along the coast play an important role in maintaining the dunes and preventing erosion in the face of heavy winds and other forces.

COCONUT PALMS

Coconut palm trees are the most distinctive plants in any tropical setting. No postcard photo of a white-sand beach would be complete without at least one palm tilting precariously over the shore. Palm trees (from the *Arecaceae* family) require a lot of sunlight and, thanks to their strong root system, will often grow at nearly horizontal angles to escape the shade of beachside forests. The coconut palm is also the proud parent of the world's largest seed—the delicious coconut—which can float long distances across the ocean, washing up on a foreign shore and sprouting a new tree from the sand.

Coconut Palms

MANGROVE

Mangrove swamps are rich, murky forests that thrive in brackish waters up and down Costa Rica's coasts. They grow in what's known as the intertidal zone, the part of the coast that's above sea level at low tide and submerged at high tide. Mangrove trees (*rhizophora*) are just one of the species that live in these coastal swamps—you can recognize them by their stilt roots, the long tendril-like roots that allow the tree to breathe even when it's partially submerged. These forests are vibrant and complex ecosystems in their own right.

Mangrove tree

MANZANILLO DE PLAYA

Steer clear of the poisonous manchineel, or *manzanillo de playa* (*Hippomane mancinella*), the most toxic tree in Costa Rica. Its fruit and bark secrete a white latex that's highly irritable to the touch and poisonous—even fatal—if ingested. Don't burn it either, because the smoke can also cause allergic reactions. The tree can be identified by its small, yellowish apples and bright green leaves. It's found along the North Pacific coast, stretches of the Nicoya Peninsula, the Central Pacific's Manuel Antonio National Park, and on the Osa Peninsula.

Manzaniillo de playa

SEAGRAPE

Seagrape (*Coccoloba uvifera*) and similar types of shrubby, ground-hugging vegetation grow closer to the water, around the edges of the beach. These plants play a part in keeping the beach stable and preventing erosion.

Seagrape

FAUNA

Beaches are tough environments where few animals actually make their home. But as we all know, you don't have to live on the beach to enjoy it.

Brown Pelican

BROWN PELICAN

Brown pelicans fly in tight formation, dropping low over the sea and running parallel with the swells in search of shoals of fish. Browns are unique in that they're the only pelican species that plunge from the air to catch their food. After a successful dive, they have to guard against gulls, who will actually try to pluck the freshly caught fish from their pouch.

IGUANAS

A common sight on Costa Rica's sandy shores are iguanas. The green iguana (*Iguana iguana*) and the black spiny-tailed iguana, or black iguana (*Ctenosaura simi*), are often found sunning themselves on rocks or a few feet from the shade (and protection) of trees. Interestingly, the green iguana has been known to lay eggs and share nests with American crocodiles and spectacled caimans.

Iguanas

OLIVE RIDLEY TURTLE

At 34 to 45 kilos (75 to 100 pounds) the olive ridley (*Lepidochelys olivacea*) is the smallest of the five marine turtles that nest in Costa Rica. During mass nesting times (arribada), anywhere from tens to hundreds of thousands of females drag themselves ashore, gasping audibly, to lay their eggs. Between dusk and dawn, the prehistoric creatures crawl over the beach, sometimes even over one another, on their way between the ocean and their nests. People who are lucky enough to witness the event never forget it. Costa Rica's shores are also visited by the green turtle, the hawksbill, the loggerhead, and the leatherback turtle.

Olive Ridley Turtle

PAINTED GHOST CRAB

These intriguingly named crabs are called "ghosts" because they move so quickly that they seem to disappear. They're also one of the few creatures that actually live full time on the beach. Sun beats down, wind is strong, danger lurks everywhere, and there's little to no cover, but painted ghost crabs (*Ocypode cuadrata*) survive all this by burrowing deep under the sand where the temperature and humidity are more constant and there's safe protection from surface threats like the black iguana.

Painted Ghost Crab

SAN JOSÉ

WELCOME TO SAN JOSÉ

TOP REASONS TO GO

★ **Eating out:** After traveling around Costa Rica eating mostly rice and beans and chicken, San José's varied restaurants offer a welcome change of pace.

★ **Gold and Jade museums:** For a sense of indigenous Costa Rica, frequently forgotten during the nation's march to modernity, the country's two best museums are must-sees.

★ **Historic Barrios Amón and Otoya:** These northern neighborhoods abutting and sometimes overlapping downtown have tree-lined streets and century-old houses turned trendy hotels and restaurants.

★ **Location, location, location:** From the capital's pivotal position, you can be on a coffee tour, at the base of a giant volcano, or riding river rapids in an hour or less.

★ **Shopping:** San José is the best place to stock up on both essentials and souvenirs. Look for leather-and-wood rocking chairs, ceramics, textiles, and, of course, wonderful coffee.

1 Downtown. This area holds San José's historic and commercial districts and many top attractions: the Museo del Jade (Jade Museum), Museo del Oro Precolombino (Gold Museum), Mercado Central (Central Market), and Teatro Nacional (National Theater).

2 West of Downtown. The mostly residential neighborhoods here are anchored by large Parque Metropolitano La Sabana (La Sabana Park) and the Museo de Arte Costarricense (Museum of Costa Rican Art).

GETTING ORIENTED

The metropolitan area holds around 2 million residents, but the city proper is small, with some 288,000 people living in its 44 square km (17 square miles). Most sights are concentrated in three downtown neighborhoods, La Soledad, La Merced, and El Carmen, named for their anchor churches. Borders are fuzzy: one *barrio* (neighborhood) flows into the next, districts overlap, and the city itself melts into its suburbs with nary a sign to denote where one community ends and another begins.

3 North of Downtown. Historic barrios Amón and Otoya and the Museo de los Niños (Children's Museum) are a few of the attractions to the north.

4 East of Downtown. Several good restaurants and hotels and the Universidad de Costa Rica (University of Costa Rica) are ensconced in the San Pedro suburb.

ECO-LODGES IN SAN JOSÉ

Clean? Green? Pristine? San José is none of these, but even in Costa Rica's congested capital, you can count on a handful of pioneers who keep the environmental spirit alive.

The capital's few pockets of greenery are its parks, and, in this regard, the city does itself proud. The grandiose monuments so common in other Latin America countries are not very prominent. Small is the watchword in Costa Rica, so parks are places to enjoy mini eco-refuges rather than shrines to past heroes and glories. A trio of parks—Morazán, España, and Nacional—graces the area just northeast of downtown and provides a mostly contiguous several blocks of peace and quiet. La Sabana Park on San José's west side once served as the country's international airport. Its lush greenery and ample space for recreation get our vote as being one of the most pleasing uses of urban space. The capital's parks have one big downside: after dark, a small cast of unsavory characters replaces the throngs of day-trippers. Make a point to vacate city parks before the sun goes down.

GREEN PRACTICES

Use public transportation whenever possible. Buses travel everywhere in San José, and suburbs, and taxis are relatively easy to find. In addition to reducing your carbon footprint, it also saves you the hassle of driving and parking in an already congested city.

Ask whether your hotel recycles glass, plastic, and aluminum. A few lodgings—and, unfortunately, "few" is the operative term here—do. Take advantage if you can.

Don't litter—the city has a burdensome trash problem—although you'll swear no one else here follows this advice.

TOP ECO-LODGES IN SAN JOSÉ

To ensure that your hotel really is eco-friendly, do a bit of research or ask a few questions. Check on the property's lighting—does it use compact fluorescent bulbs? What about sensors or timers? Is any form of alternative energy, like solar or wind power, employed? Are there low-flow faucets, showers, and toilets? What sort of recycling programs are in place for guests *and* staff? Answers to such questions give you a sense of whether a property is green. Here are a couple of San José properties that do more than pay lip service to the environmental movement.

HOTEL ARANJUEZ

This popular lodging talks the talk and walks the walk with its use of solar-heated water and biodegradable products. These folks are avid recyclers, too. Any unused organic material gets composted as fertilizer for the hotel's garden, which, in turn, nourishes some of the food you eat in its restaurant. *(Full hotel review on page 112.)*

HOTEL PRESIDENTE

Costa Rica's first "carbon neutral" hotel has taken major steps to reduce its carbon footprint. What is left over is offset by a tree-planting project the lodging supports. The Presidente has organized a small but growing consortium of San José hotels to take up recycling. All in all, not bad for a place located smack-dab in the center of the city. *(Full hotel review on page 112.)*

HOTEL RINCÓN DE SAN JOSÉ

Your hot water in this small Barrio Otoya hotel will be solar heated, and the place makes maximum use of natural light in its public areas. The Rincón de San José uses only biodegradable products whenever possible, it also engages in an active recycling program. Even captured rainwater finds its way into your room's toilet basin. *(Full hotel review on page 113.)*

3

PEDESTRIANS ONLY

The government is forever announcing some grandiose plan to make San José more livable. Few, however, make it off the ground, mostly due to a chronic lack of funds. Two have come to fruition, though, and you will notice the benefit.

For years, the city government has been turning downtown streets into pedestrian-only thoroughfares. Some 39 blocks in the center city—sections of Avenidas Central and 4, and Calles 2, 3, 9, and 17—now have *bulevar* (boulevard) status, with more on the drawing board. Thank China and the European Union for much of the funding.

Weekday driving restrictions cover all of San José and parts of neighboring San Pedro. The last digit of your license plate dictates the day of the week when you may not bring a car into the large restricted zone from 6 am to 7 pm. The city still hosts far too many cars, but the 20% reduction in vehicles each weekday has made a noticeable difference.

By Jeffrey Van Fleet

San José is the center of all that is Costa Rica, and, to the Tico in the countryside, it glitters every bit as much as New York City does. True to developing-country patterns, every-thing—politics, business, art, cuisine, nightlife, and cul-ture—converges here. The capital may not be the center of your trip to Costa Rica, though—those rain forests and volcanoes have your name written on them—but the city is worth a day or two as a way to ease into Costa Rica at the start of a visit or to wrap things up with a well-deserved dose of civilization.

Amid the noise and traffic, shady parks, well-maintained museums, lively plazas, terrific restaurants, and great hotels do exist. Further, the city makes a great base for day trips: from downtown it's a mere 30- to 40-minute drive to the tranquil countryside and myriad outdoor activities of the surrounding Central Valley.

You'd never know San José is as old as it is—given the complete absence of colonial architecture—but settlers migrating from then-provincial-capital Cartago founded the city in 1737. After independence in 1821, San José cemented its position as the new nation's capital after struggles and a brief civil war with fellow Central Valley cities Cartago, Alajuela, and Heredia. Revenues from the coffee and banana industries financed the construction of stately homes, theaters, and a trolley system (later abandoned and now visible only in old sepia photographs).

As recently as the mid-1900s, San José was no larger than the present-day downtown area; old-timers remember the vast coffee and cane plantations that extended beyond its borders. The city began to mush-room only after World War II, when old buildings were razed to make room for concrete monstrosities. The sprawl eventually connected the capital with nearby cities.

It has attracted people from all over Costa Rica, yet it remains, in many ways, a collection of distinct neighborhoods where residents maintain friendly small-town ways. For you, this might mean the driver you're following will decide to abruptly stop his vehicle to buy a lottery ticket or chat with a friend on the street. Or it might mean you have to navigate a maze of fruit-vendor stands on a crowded sidewalk. But this is part of what keeps San José a big small town.

PLANNING

WHEN TO GO
HIGH SEASON: MID-DECEMBER TO APRIL
San José's altitude keeps temperatures pleasant and springlike year-round. The capital's status as a business-travel destination means lodging rates rarely vary throughout the year. The dry season literally blows in with a change in wind patterns that make December and January brisk, but sunny. February warms up; by March and April, the heat and dust pick up considerably.

LOW SEASON: MAY TO MID-NOVEMBER
The wet season moves in gradually, with manageable brief afternoon showers from May through July. August becomes wetter. September and October might mean constant rain for days at a time, and navigating a traffic-clogged city in a torrential rush-hour downpour is little fun.

SHOULDER SEASON: MID-NOVEMBER TO MID-DECEMBER
Rains wind down by mid-November and you'll even experience a bit of a nip in the air—it's still the tropics, though—as the city decks itself out for the holidays. The big influx of tourists won't arrive until just before Christmas itself, so this is the time to enjoy the capital at its best.

PLANNING YOUR TIME
SAN JOSÉ IN A DAY
If you have only a day to spend in San José, the must-see stops are the Teatro Nacional (National Theater)—we recommend the guided tour—and the Museo del Oro Precolombino (Pre-Columbian Gold Museum). That's easy to accomplish because they sit on the same block.

With more time, take in the Museo del Jade (Jade Museum) and Museo Nacional (National Museum). The Museo de los Niños (Children's Museum), north of downtown, is a kid pleaser. It's in a dicey part of the barrio El Carmen, more north of downtown than actually in downtown; take a taxi.

BYPASS SAN JOSÉ?
San José isn't necessarily the Costa Rica you came to see. Those beaches and rain forests beckon, after all. If that is, indeed, the case, you can avoid the city altogether.

The international airport actually lies just outside the city of Alajuela, about 30 minutes northwest of the capital. Look for lodgings in Alajuela, San Antonio de Belén, Escazú, or Santa Ana—all within striking distance of the airport. Or head west. *For information about lodgings near Aeropuerto Internacional Juan Santamaría, see Chapter 4.*

Few international flights arrive in the morning, but they do exist, especially via Miami. Get here early and you can head out of town immediately.

A third option is to join the growing number of visitors flying into Daniel Oduber International Airport in Liberia, where Costa Rica's northern and western reaches (including the North Pacific) are nearby.

DAY TRIPS FROM THE CAPITAL

The capital sits smack-dab in the middle of the country and in the middle of the fertile Central Valley. Although a day trip to either coast would be grueling—despite Costa Rica's small size, it takes longer than you think to get from place to place—you can easily pop out to the Central Valley's major sights and be back in the city in time for dinner. Several of these attractions provide pickup service in San José, some for a nominal additional cost. Alternatively, tour operators include many of these attractions on their itineraries.

DESTINATION	FROM SAN JOSÉ (BY CAR)	
Basílica de Nuestra Señora de los Ángeles	30 mins southeast	⇨ p. 181
Café Britt	30 mins north	⇨ p. 174
Carara National Park	2 hrs southwest	⇨ p. 157
Doka Coffee Estate	1 hr west	⇨ p. 160
Guayabo National Monument	2 hrs southeast, 4WD necessary	⇨ p. 191
INBioparque	15 mins north	⇨ p. 166
Irazú Volcano	60 mins east	⇨ p. 183
La Paz Waterfall Gardens	2 hrs north	⇨ p. 177
Orosi Valley	60 mins southeast	⇨ p. 184
Poás Volcano	60 mins northwest	⇨ p. 178
Rainforest Adventures	45 mins north	⇨ pp. 384, 519
River Rafting	2–2½ hrs southeast or north	⇨ p. 190
Sarchí	60 mins northwest	⇨ p. 153
Tortuga Island	3 hrs west	⇨ p. 353
Tropical Bungee	60 mins west	⇨ p. 152
World of Snakes	60 mins west	⇨ p. 152
Zoo Ave	45 mins west	⇨ p. 162

GETTING HERE AND AROUND

AIR TRAVEL

Aeropuerto Internacional Juan Santamaría, 16 km (10 miles) northwest of downtown, receives international flights and those of domestic airlines SANSA and Nature Air.

BUS TRAVEL

San José's public bus stations are all in sketchy neighborhoods. Always take a taxi to and from them. Even better: use air-conditioned minivan shuttles instead of buses to travel into and out of the capital.

City buses are cheap (40¢–60¢) and easy to use. For Paseo Colón and La Sabana, take buses marked "Sabana–Cementerio" from stops at Avenida 2 between Calles 5 and 7 or Avenida 3 next to the post office. For Los Yoses and San Pedro, take the "San Pedro" bus from Avenida Central between Calles 9 and 11.

Bus Terminals Gran Terminal del Caribe ⊠ *C. Ctl. and Avda. 13, Barrio Tournón.* **Terminal Atlántico Norte** ⊠ *C. 12 and Avda. 9, Barrio La Merced.* **Terminal Coca-Cola** ⊠ *Av. 1 and C. 16, Barrio La Merced.* **Terminal San Ramón** ⊠ *C. 16 and Avda. 12, Barrio La Merced.* **Terminal Tracopa** ⊠ *C. 5 and Avda. 20, Barrio El Pacífico* ☎ *2221–4214.*

Shuttle Companies Grayline ☎ *2220–2126, 800/719–3905 in North America* ⊕ *www.graylinecostarica.com.* **Interbus** ☎ *2283–5573* ⊕ *www.interbusonline.com.*

CAR TRAVEL

Paved roads fan out from Paseo Colón west to Escazú and northwest to the airport and Heredia. For the Pacific coast, Guanacaste, and on to Nicaragua, take the Pan-American Highway north (CA1). Calle 3 runs north into the highway to Guápiles, Limón, and the Atlantic coast through Braulio Carrillo National Park, with a turnoff to Sarapiquí. Follow Avenida Central or 2 east through San Pedro to enter the Pan-American Highway south (CA2), which has a turnoff for Cartago, Volcán Irazú, and Turrialba before it heads toward Panama.

Avoid driving in the city if you can help it. Streets are narrow, rush hour (7 to 9 am and 5 to 7 pm) traffic is horrible, and drivers can be reckless. What's more, San José and neighboring San Pedro enforce rigid weekday driving restrictions (6 am–7 pm) for all private vehicles, including your rental car. The last digit of your license plate determines your no-driving day: Monday (1 and 2), Tuesday (3 and 4), Wednesday (5 and 6), Thursday (7 and 8), and Friday (9 and 0).

TAXI

You can hail cabs on the street or call for one. Licensed cabs are red with a gold triangle on the front doors. Taxis Unidos Aeropuerto—which go to the airport—are orange. A 3-km (2-mile) ride costs around $3; tipping isn't customary. By law cabbies must use *marías* (meters) within the metropolitan area. (The meter starts at $1.20.) Cab drivers hate it if you slam the door; close the door gently.

Taxis Alfaro ☎ *2223–3373.* **Coopetaxi** ☎ *2235–9966.* **San Jorge** ☎ *2221–3434.* **Taxis Unidos Aeropuerto** ☎ *2221–6865* ⊕ *www.taxiaeropuerto.com.*

TUNE IN: COSTA RICAN RADIO

Take Costa Rican radio along if you're driving to your adventures out of San José. The airwaves here are filled with the hottest Latin hits or a hefty dose of religion, be it Catholic or evangelical. Below are a few of our favorite stations, a couple of which break that mold:

Radio Sinfonola (90.3 FM): vintage Spanish romantic music of the *Bésame Mucho* type.

Radio Puntarenas (91.1 FM): merengue, cumbia, and salsa, and all your favorite Latin sounds.

Radio Universidad (96.7 FM): Bach, Beethoven, Brahms, and more, with commentary in Spanish.

Radio Dos (99.5 FM): American and British pop hits of the '70s, '80s, and '90s, with Spanish-speaking DJs. (English-speaking jocks handle 6 to 9 am and 5 to 7 pm drive times.)

HEALTH AND SAFETY

San José is safer than other Latin American capitals. Violent crime is rare; the greatest threat you're likely to face is petty theft. Standard big-city precautions apply:

Exchange money only at banks. Street money changers slip counterfeit bills into their stash, or doctor their calculators to compute unfavorable rates. In the extreme, they might grab your cash and run off.

Select ATMs in well-lighted areas. Better still, use a bank's ATM during opening hours, when a guard will likely be present. Go with a buddy, and conceal cash immediately.

Use only licensed red taxis with yellow triangles on the front doors. The license plate of an official taxi begins with TSJ ("Taxi San José").

Park in guarded, well-lighted lots ($1.50 to $2 an hour). If you must park on the street, make sure informal *guachimen* (watchmen) are present. Usually this is someone with a big stick who will expect payment of about $1 per hour. Never leave anything valuable in your parked vehicle.

Medical Assistance Clínica Bíblica ✉ *Avda. 14, Cs. Ctl.–1, Barrio El Pacífico* ☎ *2522–1000* ⊕ *www.clinicabiblica.com.* **Hospital La Católica** ✉ *C. Esquivel Bonilla, Guadalupe* ☎ *2246–3000* ⊕ *www.hospitallacatolica.com.*

MONEY MATTERS

It's a bad sign when San José banks have televisions to watch while you pass the time in the horrendous lines. Bypass that process and get cash with your ATM card instead. Cash machines inside a bank, during the day while a guard keeps watch, are your safest bet.

Bank/ATM BAC San José ✉ *Avda. 2, Cs. Ctl.–1, Barrio El Carmen* ☎ *2295–9797* ⊕ *www.bac.net.* **Banco Nacional** ✉ *Avda. 1, Cs. 2–4, Barrio La Merced* ☎ *2212–2000* ⊕ *www.bncr.fi.cr.* **Scotiabank** ✉ *C. 5, Avdas. Ctl.–2, behind Teatro Nacional, Barrio La Soledad* ☎ *2521–5680* ⊕ *www.scotiabankcr.com.*

TOURS

Grayline Costa Rica operates sightseeing and shopping tours, as well as excursions to the surrounding Central Valley. City walking tours are usually daytime affairs, but Nocturbano offers guided, police-escorted tours of nighttime San José. Tours are in Spanish, but guides will conduct tours in English with advance notice for groups of eight or more.

Grayline Costa Rica ☎ 2220–2106 *in Costa Rica, 800/719–3905 in North America* ⊕ *www.graylinecostarica.com.*

Nocturbano ☎ *2222–7548* ⊕ *www.chepecletas.com* ⊠ *$30.*

VISITOR INFORMATION

The ubiquitous "Tourist Information" signs you see around downtown are really private travel agencies looking to sell you tours rather than provide unbiased information. The Instituto Costarricense de Turismo, the official tourist office, operates an office on Avenida Central and a booth in the arrivals area of the international airport.

Visitor Information Instituto Costarricense de Turismo (*ICT*). ⊠ *Avda. Ctl., Cs. 1–3* ☎ *2222–1090* ⊕ *www.visitcostarica.com* ⊙ *Weekdays 9–5.*

EXPLORING

The Irish group U-2 could have written its song "Where the Streets Have No Name" about San José. Admittedly, some of its streets have names, but no one seems to know or use them. Streets in the center of the capital are laid out in a grid, with *avenidas* (avenues) running east and west, and *calles* (streets), north and south. Odd-number avenues increase in number north of Avenida Central; even-number avenues, south. Streets east of Calle Central have odd numbers; those to the west are even.

Costa Ricans rely instead on a charming and exasperating system of designating addresses by the distance from landmarks, as in "100 meters north and 50 meters west of the school." Another quirk: "100 meters" always refers to one city block, regardless of how long it actually is. Likewise, "200 meters" is two blocks, and so on. (As you can imagine, getting a pizza delivered here is quite a challenge.)

Historically, the reference point was the church, but these days it might be a bar, Burger King, or even a quirky landmark: the eastern suburb of San Pedro uses the *higuerón*, a prominent fig tree. The city has embarked on an ambitious project to name all its streets once and for all. Even after it's completed, we still don't expect anybody will know or use the names. Your best bet is to follow the time-honored practice of *ir y preguntar* (keep walking and keep asking). *See the Vocabulary section in Understanding Costa Rica for help asking for directions in Spanish.*

DOWNTOWN

It's a trend seen the world over: businesses and residents flee city centers for the space, blissful quiet, and lower-priced real estate of the burbs. Although Costa Rica's capital is experiencing this phenomenon, downtown still remains the city's historic and vibrant (if noisy and congested) heart. Government offices have largely stayed put here, as have most attractions. It's impossible to sightsee here without finding yourself downtown.

Boundaries are fuzzy. For example, the neighborhoods of El Carmen, La Merced, and La Soledad are anchored in downtown but sprawl outward from the center city. And, in an effort to seem trendier, several establishments in downtown's northern fringes prefer to say that they're in the more fashionable barrios of Amón or Otoya.

TOP ATTRACTIONS

Fodor's Choice ★ **Museo del Jade** (*Jade Museum*). Long ensconced in cramped quarters in a downtown office building, San José's Jade Museum moved to spacious new digs on the west side of the Plaza de la Democracia in 2014. For the first time ever, it has room to display its entire collection of American jade—that's "American" in the hemispheric sense—the world's largest collection of the green gemstone at 5,000-plus pieces. Nearly all the items on display were produced in pre-Columbian times, and most of the jade (pronounced *hah*-day in Spanish) dates from 300 BC to AD 700. A series of drawings explains how this extremely hard stone was cut using string saws with quartz-and-sand abrasive. Jade was sometimes used in jewelry designs, but it was most often carved into oblong pendants. The museum also has other pre-Columbian artifacts, such as polychrome vases and three-legged *metates* (small stone tables for grinding corn), as well as a gallery of modern art. Also included on the tour is a startling display of ceramic fertility symbols. A glossy, photo-filled English-language guide to the museum sells for $15; the Spanish version is only $3. ☒ *Avda. Ctl., C. 13, Barrio Amón* ☏ *2287–6034* 💲 *$9* ⊙ *Weekdays 8:30–3:30, Sat. 11–2.*

Fodor's Choice ★ **Museo del Oro Precolombino** (*Pre-Columbian Gold Museum*). This dazzling, modern museum in a three-story underground structure beneath the Plaza de la Cultura, contains Central America's largest collection of pre-Columbian gold jewelry—20,000 troy ounces in more than 1,600 individual pieces—all owned by the Banco Central (the country's central bank) and displayed attractively in bilingual exhibits. Many pieces are in the form of frogs and eagles, two animals perceived by the region's early cultures to have great spiritual significance. A spiffy illumination system makes the pieces sparkle. All that glitters here is not gold: most spectacular are the various shaman figurines, which represent the human connection to animal deities. One of the halls houses the Museo Numismática (Coin Museum), a repository of historic coins and bills and other objects used as legal tender throughout the country's history. Rotating art exhibitions happen on another level. For an extra $7, you can take a guided tour via an app you download at the museum on your smartphone. However, the exhibits are well marked, both in English and Spanish, so there's little need for the app. ☒ *C. 5, Avdas. Ctl.–2, eastern end of Plaza de la Cultura, Barrio La Soledad* ☏ *2243–4202* ⊕ *www.museosdelbancocentral.org* 💲 *$11, includes Museo Numismática* ⊙ *Daily 9–5.*

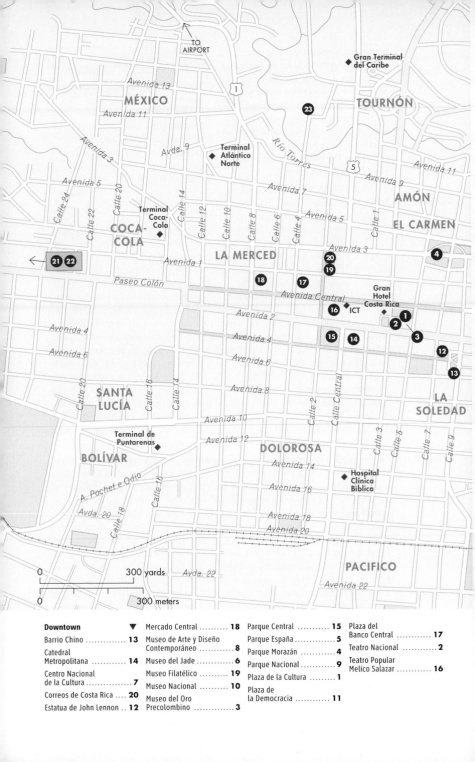

TO AIRPORT

Gran Terminal del Caribe

MÉXICO

TOURNÓN

Avenida 13

Avenida 11

23

Avenida 3

Avda. 9

Terminal Atlántico Norte

Río Torres

AMÓN

Avenida 5

Avenida 7

EL CARMEN

Calle 24

Calle 22

Calle 20

Terminal Coca-Cola

Calle 14

Calle 12

Calle 10

Calle 8

Calle 6

Calle 4

Avenida 9

Avenida 5

Avenida 11

Avenida 3

COCA-COLA

LA MERCED

20

19

21 22

Avenida 1

18

17

Paseo Colón

Gran Hotel Costa Rica

Avenida Central

16

ICT

1

2

Avenida 4

Avenida 2

15

14

3

Avenida 4

Avenida 6

12

Avenida 6

13

Avenida 8

SANTA LUCÍA

Calle 20

Calle 16

Calle 14

Avenida 8

LA SOLEDAD

Avenida 10

Calle 2

Calle Central

Terminal de Puntarenas

Avenida 12

Calle 3

Calle 5

Calle 7

Calle 9

BOLÍVAR

DOLOROSA

Avenida 14

A. Pochet e Odio

Calle 16

Hospital Clínica Bíblica

Avenida 16

Avda. 20

Calle 18

Avenida 18

Avenida 20

PACÍFICO

0   300 yards   Avda. 22

0   300 meters

Avenida 22

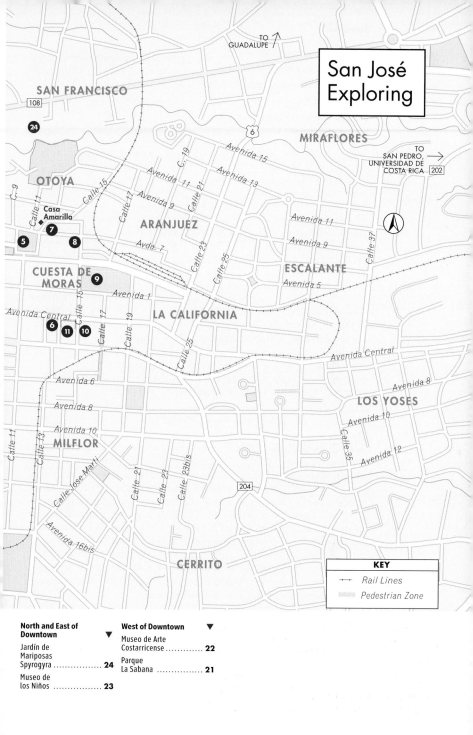

San José
Exploring

TO
GUADALUPE

SAN FRANCISCO
108
24

MIRAFLORES

TO
SAN PEDRO,
UNIVERSIDAD DE
COSTA RICA 202

OTOYA

C. 9

Calle 11

Calle 15

Casa
Amarilla
7

5   8

ARANJUEZ

Avenida 15

C. 19

Avenida 11

Avenida 13

Calle 17

Avenida 9

Calle 21

Avenida 11

Avenida 9

Calle 37

Avda. 7

Calle 23

Calle 25

ESCALANTE

Avenida 5

CUESTA DE
MORAS   9

Avenida 1

LA CALIFORNIA

Avenida Central

6   11   10

Calle 15

Calle 17

Calle 19

Calle 25

Avenida Central

Avenida 6

Avenida 8

LOS YOSES

Avenida 8

Calle 11

Calle 13

Avenida 8

Avenida 10

MILFLOR

Avenida 10

Avenida 12

Calle 35

Calle José Martí

Calle 21

Calle 23

Calle 23bis

204

Avenida 16bis

CERRITO

KEY

Rail Lines

Pedestrian Zone

NEED A BREAK?

A slew of unnamed *sodas*—that's the Costa Rican term for a mom-and-pop eatery—populate the heart of the Mercado Central. Grab a quick bite while you explore. It's all very informal.

Fodor's Choice ★

Teatro Nacional. The National Theater is Costa Rica at its most enchanting. Chagrined that touring prima donna Adelina Patti bypassed San José in 1890 for lack of a suitable venue, wealthy coffee merchants raised import taxes and hired Belgian architects to design this building, lavish with cast iron and Italian marble. The theater was inaugurated in 1897 with a performance of Gounod's *Faust,* featuring an international cast. The sandstone exterior is marked by Italianate arched windows, marble columns with bronze capitals, and statues of strange bedfellows Ludwig van Beethoven (1770–1827) and 17th-century Spanish Golden Age playwright Pedro Calderón de la Barca (1600–81). The Muses of Dance, Music, and Fame are silhouetted in front of an iron cupola. French designer Alain Guilhot created the building's nighttime external illumination system. (He did the same for the Eiffel Tower.) The soft coppers, golds, and whites highlight the theater's exterior nightly from 6 pm to 5 am. A project funded by the German government has restored the theater's cupola to its original red color.

The sumptuous neo-baroque interior is of interest, too. Given the provenance of the building funds, it's not surprising that frescoes on the stairway inside depict coffee and banana production. Note Italian painter Aleardo Villa's famous ceiling mural *Alegoría del Café y Banano* (*Allegory of Coffee and Bananas*), a joyful harvest scene that appeared on Costa Rica's old 5-colón note. (The now-defunct bill is prized by collectors and by visitors as a souvenir, and is often sold by vendors in the plaza between the theater and the Gran Hotel Costa Rica next door.) You can see the theater's interior by attending one of the performances that take place several nights a week (tickets are reasonably priced); intermission gives you a chance to nose around. Stop at the *boletería* (box office) in the lobby and see what strikes your fancy. (Don't worry if you left your tuxedo or evening gown back home; as long as you don't show up for a performance wearing shorts, jeans, or a T-shirt, no one will care.)

For a nominal admission fee you can also move beyond the lobby; a 40-minute guided tour is included. Call a day in advance if you'd like a guided tour in English; it's included in your admission price. (The theater is sometimes closed for rehearsals, so call before you go.) If you're downtown on a Tuesday between February and Christmas, take in one of the Teatro al Mediodía (Theater at Midday) performances that begin at noon. It might be a chamber-music recital or a one-act play in Spanish. A similar program called Música al Atardecer (Music at Dusk) takes place each Thursday at 5 pm. Admission for either

DID YOU KNOW?

What's an old theater without its resident ghost? Patrons have claimed to see figures moving in the Teatro Nacional's second-floor paintings. Sightings were common during the theater's early days, although none have been reported in years.

is $2, and both are presented in the second-floor foyer. ⊠ *Plaza de la Cultura, Barrio La Soledad* ☎ *2221–5341* ⊕ *www.teatronacional. go.cr* ⌦ *$7* ⊙ *Daily 9–4; closed Sun., May–Dec.*

■ **NEED A BREAK?**

Café del Teatro Nacional. Duck into the Café del Teatro Nacional, off the theater lobby, to sit at a marble table and sip a hazelnut mocha beneath frescoed ceilings. The frescoes are part of an allegory of seminude figures celebrating the 1897 opening of the theater. Coffee runs from $3 to $5, depending on how much alcohol or ice cream is added. Sandwiches and cakes are $4 to $7. The café keeps the same hours as the theater but is open only until curtain time on performance nights and during intermission. ⊠ *Teatro Nacional, Plaza de la Cultura.*

3

WORTH NOTING

Barrio Chino. We should get one thing straight about the capital's Chinatown: San José is not San Francisco. But the Chinese government has financed the transformation of five blocks of Calle 9 into a pleasant pedestrian mall. A large arch modeled on the architecture of the Tang Dynasty marks the north entrance to the street and several Chinese-Costa Rican businesses line the walkway. ⊠ *C. 9, between Avdas. 2 and 12, Barrio La Soledad.*

Catedral Metropolitana (*Metropolitan Cathedral*). Built in 1871 and completely refurbished in the late 1990s to repair earthquake damage, the neoclassical cathedral, topped by a corrugated tin dome, isn't terribly interesting outside. But inside are patterned floor tiles, stained-glass windows depicting various saints and apostles, and framed polychrome bas-reliefs illustrating the Stations of the Cross. A magnificent 1891 Belgian pipe organ fills the church with music. The renovation did away with one small time-honored tradition: rather than light real candles, the faithful now deposit a 100-colón coin illuminating a bulb in a row of tiny electric candles.

The interior of the small Capilla del Santísimo (Chapel of the Host) on the cathedral's north side evokes ornate old Catholicism, much more so than the main sanctuary itself. A marble statue of Pope John Paul II stands guard over the garden on the building's north side. Masses are held throughout the day on Sunday starting at 7 am, with one in English each Saturday at 4 pm. Although not technically part of the cathedral complex, a small statue of Holocaust victim Anne Frank graces the pedestrian mall on the building's south side. It was donated by the Embassy of the Netherlands. ⊠ *C. Ctl., Avdas. 2–4, Barrio La Merced* ☎ *2221–3820* ⊙ *Mon.–Sat. 6:30–6, Sun. 6:30 am–9 pm.*

Centro Nacional de la Cultura (*National Cultural Center*). Rather than tear it down, the Ministry of Culture converted the sloped-surface, double-block 1853 Fábrica Nacional de Licores (National Liquor Factory) into this 14,000-square-meter cultural center, with government offices, two theaters, and a museum. It might seem strange that the liquor factory was state-run, but the government here also owns the light and water utility, phone company, Internet service provider, bank, insurance, and hospital. The National Liquor Factory was housed here until 1981, when it moved to a modern facility in the Central Valley. The stone-block storage depot next to the water towers at the southeast side of the complex became the Museo de Arte y Diseño Contemporáneo. A stone gate and sundial grace the entrance nearest the museum. The complex sits amid government offices, at the point where downtown's northern reaches fade into the more residential neighborhood of Barrio Otoya. ⊠ *C. 13, Avdas. 3–5, Barrio Otoya* ☎ *2257–5524* ⊕ *www.mjc.go.cr* ⊙ *Weekdays 8–5, Sat. 10–5.*

Teatro FANAL. The metal Teatro FANAL hosts frequent theater and music performances. ☎ *2222–2974* ⊕ *www.mjc.go.cr.*

Teatro 1887. The clay-brick theater dedicates itself to performances by the National Dance Company. What is now the theater's lobby was once a chemical testing lab. ☎ *2222–2974* ⊕ *www.mjc.go.cr.*

Correos de Costa Rica (*Central Post Office*). The handsome, carved exterior of the post office, dating from 1917, is hard to miss among the bland buildings surrounding it. The lobby and the small pedestrian plaza in front are a perpetual beehive of activity. ⊠ *C. 2, Avdas. 1–3, Barrio La Merced* ☎ *2202–2900* ⊕ *www.correos.go.cr* ⊙ *Weekdays 7:30–6, Sat. 8–noon.*

Museo Filatélico (*Philatelic Museum*). Collectors should stop at the second-floor museum for its display of historic stamps. Early-20th-century telegraphs and telephones are also on display. Admission is the purchase (downstairs at one of the post-office windows) of a prepaid postcard sufficient for mailing to North America. ⊠ *Correos de Costa Rica, C. 2, Avdas. 1–3, 2nd fl.* ☎ *2223–9766* ⊙ *Weekdays 7:30–6, Sat. 8–noon.*

Estatua de John Lennon (*Statue of John Lennon*). A whimsical statue of John Lennon sits on a small, slightly out-of-the-way plaza across from La Soledad church. Sculptor José Ramón Villa's work marks the spot where, in 1966, Costa Ricans smashed Beatles records in protest of Lennon's statement that the iconic pop group was "more popular than Jesus." The official name of the statue is *Imagine All the People Living Life in Peace*, evoking the lyrics of Lennon's song *Imagine*. After nearly five decades, bygones are apparently bygones: residents and tourists alike enjoy having their photos taken sitting with the casually seated figure. ⊠ *C. 9, Avda. 4, Barrio La Soledad.*

Mercado Central (*Central Market*). This block-long melting pot is a warren of dark, narrow passages flanked by stalls packed with spices (some purported to have medicinal value), fish, fruit, flowers, pets, and wood and leather crafts. But the 1880 structure is a kinder, gentler introduction to a Central American market; there are no pigs or chickens or their accompanying smells to be found here. A few stands selling tourist souvenirs congregate near the entrances, but this is primarily a place where the average Costa Rican comes to shop. There are dozens of cheap restaurants and snack stalls, including the country's first ice-cream vendor. ⚠ Be warned: the concentration of shoppers makes this a hot spot for pickpockets, purse snatchers, and backpack slitters. Enter and exit at the southeast corner of the building (Avenida Central at Calle 6). The green-and-white "*salida*" signs direct you to other exits, but they spill onto slightly less-safe streets. Use the image of the

Sacred Heart of Jesus, the market's patron and protector, near the center of the building, as your guide; it faces that safer corner by which you should exit. ✉ *Bordered by Avdas. Ctl.–1 and Cs. 6–8, Barrio La Merced* ⊘ *Mon.–Sat. 6–6.*

NEED A BREAK?

Pops. To sample the crème de la crème of locally made ice cream, head to Pops. Mango is a favorite flavor. After a long walk on crowded sidewalks, it may be just what the doctor ordered. You'll find several outlets downtown, as well as around the country and Central America. This longtime institution is now Colombian-owned. ✉ *C. 3, Avda. Ctl., Barrio La Soledad* ☎ *2222–2336* ⊕ *www.pops.co.cr.*

Museo de Arte y Diseño Contemporáneo (*Museum of Contemporary Art and Design*). This wonderfully minimalist space is perfect as the country's premier modern-art venue. The MADC, as it's known around town, hosts changing exhibits by artists and designers from all over Latin America. While the museum holds a permanent collection, space constraints mean that even that must rotate. You will probably not recognize the artists here, but names such as Miguel Hernández and Florencia Urbina tower over the field of contemporary art in Costa Rica. You can arrange for a guided visit with a couple of days' notice. The museum occupies part of a government-office complex in the Centro Nacional de la Cultura. ✉ *Centro Nacional de la Cultura, C. 15, Avdas. 3–5, Barrio Otoya* ☎ *2257–7202* ⊕ *www.madc.ac.cr* ✉ *$3* ⊘ *Mon.–Sat. 9:30–5.*

Museo Nacional (*National Museum*). In the mango-color Bellavista Fortress, which dates from 1870, the museum gives you a quick and insightful lesson in English and Spanish on Costa Rican culture from pre-Columbian times to the present. Cases display pre-Columbian artifacts, period dress, colonial furniture, religious art, and photographs. Some of the country's foremost ethnographers and anthropologists are on the museum's staff. Nearly 1,000 pre-Columbian Costa Rican stone and ceramic objects dating from about AD 1000 are on display here. The artifacts were taken from the country in the late 19th century by businessman Minor Keith during the construction of the Atlantic Railroad and were repatriated from the Brooklyn Museum in 2012. Outside are a veranda and a pleasant, manicured courtyard garden. A former army headquarters, this now-tranquil building saw fierce fighting during a 1931 army mutiny and the 1948 revolution, as the bullet holes pocking its turrets attest. But it was also here that three-time president José "Don Pepe" Figueres abolished the country's military in 1949. ✉ *Bellavista Fortress, Eastern end of Plaza de la Democracia, Barrio La Soledad* ☎ *2257–1433* ⊕ *www.museocostarica.go.cr* ✉ *$8* ⊘ *Tues.–Sat. 8:30–4:30, Sun. 9–4:30.*

Parque Central (*Central Park*). At the city's nucleus, the tree-shaded Central Park is more plaza than park. A life-size bronze statue of a street sweeper (*El Barrendero*) cleans up some bronze litter; look also for *Armonía* (*Harmony*), a sculpture of three street musicians. In the center of the park is a spiderlike gazebo donated by onetime Nicaraguan dictator Anastasio Somoza. ✉ *Bordered by Avdas. 2–4 and Cs. 2– Ctl., Barrio La Merced.*

Parque España. This shady little park is a favorite spot. A bronze statue of Costa Rica's Spanish founder, Juan Vásquez de Coronado, overlooks an elevated fountain on its southwest corner; the opposite corner has a lovely tiled guardhouse. A bust of Queen Isabella of Castile stares at the yellow compound to the east of the park, the Centro Nacional de la Cultura. Just west of the park is a two-story, metal-sided elementary school made in Belgium and shipped to Costa Rica in pieces more than a century ago. Local lore holds that the intended destination for the appropriately named Edificio Metálico (Metal Building) was really Chile, but that Costa Rica decided to keep the mistakenly shipped building components. The bright yellow colonial-style building to the east of the modern INS building is the 1912 Casa Amarilla, home of Costa Rica's Foreign Ministry. The massive ceiba tree in front, planted by John F. Kennedy and the presidents of all the Central American nations in 1963, gives you an idea of how quickly things grow in the tropics. A garden around the corner on Calle 13 contains a 6-foot-wide section of the Berlin Wall donated by Germany's Foreign Ministry after reunification. Ask the guard to let you into the garden if you want a closer look. ✉ *Bordered by Avdas. 7–3 and Cs. 11–17, Barrio El Carmen.*

Parque Morazán. Anchored by the 1920 Templo de Música (Temple of Music), a neoclassic bandstand that has become the symbol of the city, downtown's largest park is somewhat barren, though the pink and gold trumpet trees on its northwest corner brighten things up when they bloom in the dry months. The park is named for Honduran general Francisco Morazán, whose dream for a united Central America failed in the 1830s. Avoid the park late at night, when a rough crowd appears. ✉ *Avda. 3, Cs. 5–9, Barrio El Carmen.*

Parque Nacional (*National Park*). A bronze monument commemorating Central America's battles against North American invader William Walker in 1856 forms the centerpiece of the large, leafy park. Five Amazons, representing the five nations of the isthmus, attack Walker, who shields his face from the onslaught. Costa Rica maintains the lead and shelters a veiled Nicaragua, the country most devastated by the war. Guatemala, Honduras, and El Salvador might dispute this version of events, but this is how Costa Rica chose to commission the work by French sculptor Louis Carrier Belleuse, a student of Rodin, in 1895. Bas-relief murals on the monument's pedestal depict key battles in the war against the Americans. ✉ *Bordered by Avdas. 1–3 and Cs. 15–19, Barrio La Soledad.*

Plaza de la Cultura. The crowds of people, vendors, and street entertainers at the plaza—it's a favored spot for marimba bands, clowns, jugglers, and colorfully dressed South Americans playing Andean music—hide the fact that the expanse is really just a mass of concrete. The ornate Teatro Nacional dominates the plaza's southern half. The Museo del Oro Precolombino, with its highly visited exhibits of gold, lies under the plaza. The plaza's western edge is defined by the Gran Hotel Costa Rica, with its pleasant Café 1930. ✉ *Bordered by Avdas. Ctl.–2 and Cs. 3–5, Barrio La Soledad.*

Plaza de la Democracia. President Oscar Arias built this terraced space west of the Museo Nacional to mark 100 years of democracy and to receive dignitaries during the 1989 hemispheric summit. The view west

The Museo del Oro Precolombino has the largest collection of pre-Columbian gold jewelry in Central America.

toward the dark green Cerros de Escazú is nice in the morning and fabulous at sunset. Jewelry, T-shirts, and crafts from Costa Rica, Guatemala, and South America are sold in a string of stalls along the western edge. The city has been threatening to move the vendors to another location for years, but nothing happens. ✉ *Bordered by Avdas. Ctl.–2 and Cs. 13–15, Barrio La Soledad.*

Plaza del Banco Central. A widening of Avenida Central, this plaza is popular with hawkers, money changers, and retired men, and can be a good place to get a shoe shine and listen to street musicians. Outside the western end of Costa Rica's modern federal-reserve bank building, don't miss *Presentes,* 10 sculpted, smaller-than-life figures of bedraggled *campesinos* (peasants). *La Chola,* a bronze statue of a buxom rural woman, resides at sidewalk level on the small, shady plaza south of the bank. It's public art at its best. △ **Beware: the money changers here are notorious for circulating counterfeit bills and using doctored calculators to shortchange unwitting tourists.** ✉ *Bordered by Avdas. Ctl.–1 and Cs. 2–4, Barrio La Merced.*

Teatro Popular Melico Salazar. Across Avenida 2 on the north side of Parque Central stands San José's second major performance hall (after the Teatro Nacional). The 1928 building is on the site of a 19th-century military barracks felled by an earthquake. The venue was later named for Costa Rican operatic tenor Manuel "Melico" Salazar (1887–1950). It was constructed specifically to provide a less highbrow alternative to the Teatro Nacional. These days it provides the capital with a steady diet of music and dance performances. ✉ *Avda. 2 and C. 2, Barrio La Merced* ☎ *2295–6000* ⊕ *www.teatromelico.go.cr.*

NORTH AND EAST OF DOWNTOWN

Immediately northeast of downtown lie Barrio Amón and Barrio Otoya. Both neighborhoods are repositories of historic houses that have escaped the wrecking ball; many now serve as hotels, restaurants, galleries, and offices. (A few are even private residences.) Where these barrios begin and end depends on who's doing the talking. Locales on the fringes of the city center prefer to be associated with these "good neighborhoods" rather than with downtown. Barrio Escalante, to the east, isn't quite as gentrified but is fast becoming fashionable.

The sprawling suburb of San Pedro begins several blocks east of downtown San José.

It's home to the University of Costa Rica and all the intellect and cheap eats and nightlife that a student or student-wannabe could desire. But away from the heart of the university, San Pedro is awash with malls, fast-food restaurants, and car dealerships—although it manages to mix in such stately districts as Los Yoses for good measure. To get to San Pedro, take a $3 taxi ride from downtown and get off in front of Banco Nacional, just beyond the rotunda with the fountain at its center.

FAMILY **Jardín de Mariposas Spyrogyra** (*Spyrogyra Butterfly Garden*). Spending an hour or two at this magical butterfly garden is entertaining and educational for nature lovers of all ages. Self-guided tours enlighten you on butterfly ecology and let you see the winged creatures close up. After an 18-minute video introduction, you're free to wander screened-in gardens along a numbered trail. Some 30 species of colorful butterflies flutter about, accompanied by six types of hummingbirds. ■ TIP➔ **Try to come when it's sunny, as butterflies are most active then.** A small, moderately priced café borders the garden and serves sandwiches and Tico fare. ⊠ *50 m east and 150 m south of main entrance to El Pueblo shopping center, Barrio Tournón* ☎ *2222–2937* ⊕ *www.butterflygardencr.com* ⊠ *$7* ⊙ *Daily 8–4.*

FAMILY **Museo de los Niños** (*Children's Museum*). Three halls of this museum are filled with eye-catching seasonal exhibits for kids, ranging in subject from local ecology to outer space. The exhibits are in Spanish, but most are interactive, so language shouldn't be much of a problem. The museum's most popular resident is the Egyptian exhibit's sarcophagus; the mummy draws "oohs" and "aahs." Located in a former prison, big kids may want to check it out just to marvel at the castlelike architecture and the old cells that have been preserved in an exhibit about life behind bars. The complex that houses the museum is called the Centro Costarricense de Ciencia y Cultura (Costa Rican Center of Science and Culture), and that will be the sign that greets you on the front of the building. ⚠ **Though just a short distance from downtown, a walk here takes you through a dodgy neighborhood. Always take a taxi to and from.** ⊠ *Centro Costarricense de Ciencia y Cultura, North end of C. 4, Barrio El Carmen* ☎ *2258–4929* ⊕ *www.museocr.org* ⊠ *$2.50* ⊙ *Tues.–Fri. 8–4:30, weekends 9–5.*

■ NEED A BREAK?

Giacomín. We have to admit that Costa Rican baked goods tend toward the dry-as-dust end of the spectrum. But Italian-style bakery Giacomín, near the University of Costa Rica, is an exception—a touch of liqueur added to the batter makes all the difference. Stand European-style at the downstairs espresso bar or take your goodies to the tables and chairs on the upstairs balcony. The place closes from noon to 2. You'll also find branches in Escazú, Santa Ana, and Heredia out in the Central Valley. ⊠ *Next to Automercado supermarket, Los Yoses* ☏ *2224–3463* ⊕ *www.pasteleriagiacomin.com* ⊙ *Weekdays 8–noon and 2–7; Sat. 8–noon and 2–6:30.*

WEST OF DOWNTOWN

3

Paseo Colón, one of San José's major boulevards, heads due west from downtown and leads to vast La Sabana park, the city's largest parcel of green space. La Sabana anchors the even vaster west side of the city. A block or two off its exhaust-ridden avenues are quiet residential streets, and you'll find the U.S., Canadian, and British embassies here.

Museo de Arte Costarricense. Located in La Sabana Park, which was once Costa Rica's international airport, this, the country's foremost art museum, was once its terminal and control tower. A splendid collection of 19th- and 20th-century Costa Rican art, labeled in Spanish and English, is housed in 12 exhibition halls. Be sure to visit the top-floor Salón Dorado to see the stucco, bronze-plate bas-relief mural depicting Costa Rican history, created by French sculptor Louis Feron. Guided tours are offered Tuesday through Friday from 10 to 3. Wander into the sculpture garden in back and take in Jorge Jiménez's 22-foot-tall *Imagen Cósmica,* which depicts pre-Columbian traditions. ⊠ *Parque La Sabana, C. 42 and Paseo Colón, Paseo Colón* ☏ *2256–1281* ⊕ *www. musarco.go.cr* 🖾 *Free* ⊙ *Tues.–Sun. 9–4.*

FAMILY **Parque La Sabana.** Though it isn't centrally located, La Sabana (the Savannah) comes the closest of San José's green spaces to achieving the same function and spirit as New York's Central Park. A statue of 1930s president León Cortes greets you at the principal entrance at the west end of Paseo Colón. Behind the statue, a 16-foot-tall menorah serves as a gathering place for San José's small Jewish community during Hanukkah. La Sabana was once San José's airport, and the white-washed Museo de Arte Costarricense, just south of the Cortes statue, served as terminal and control tower.

The round Gimnasio Nacional (National Gymnasium) sits at the park's southeast corner and hosts sporting events and the occasional concert. A 40,000-seat stadium—a controversial gift from the government of China, which decided to use its own construction workers rather than employ locals—looms over the park's northwest corner. It hosts soccer matches primarily, but Shakira, Pearl Jam, Lady Gaga, and the Red Hot Chili Peppers have all played in the stadium. In between are acres of space for soccer, basketball, tennis, swimming, jogging, picnicking, and kite flying. The park hums with activity on weekend days. You're welcome to join in the early-morning outdoor aerobics classes on Saturday and Sunday. A project is under way to replace many of the park's eucalyptus trees with more bird-friendly species native to Costa Rica. ⊠ *Bordered by Cs. 42 and 68, Avda. de las Américas, and Carretera a Caldera, Paseo Colón.*

WHERE TO EAT

Fed up with all the chicken, rice, and beans you've been eating in your out-country travels? Costa Rica's capital beckons you back with the country's most varied and cosmopolitan restaurant scene. Italian, Spanish, Asian, French, Middle Eastern, Peruvian—they're all here, along with upscale Costa Rican cuisine.

Wherever you eat in San José, be it a small soda or a sophisticated restaurant, dress is casual. Meals tend to be taken earlier than in other Latin American countries; few restaurants serve past 9 or 10 pm. Local cafés usually open for breakfast at 7 am and remain open until 7 or 8 in the evening. Restaurants serving international cuisine are usually open from 11 am to 9 pm. Some cafés that serve mainly San José office workers limit evening hours and close entirely on Sunday. Restaurants that do open on Sunday do a brisk business: it's the traditional family day out (and the maid's day off). ⚠ **Watch your things, no matter where you dine. Even at the best restaurants, thieves target purses slung over chair arms or placed under chairs.**

WHAT IT COSTS IN DOLLARS

	$	$$	$$$	$$$$
Restaurants	under $10	$10–$15	$16–$25	over $25

Prices in the reviews are the average cost of a main course at dinner or, if dinner is not served, at lunch.

DOWNTOWN

$$ ECLECTIC 🍴 **Balcón de Europa.** With walls displaying photographs from a century ago, Balcón de Europa transports you to the year of its inception, 1909. Pasta specialties such as the *plato mixto* (mixed plate with lasagna, tortellini, and ravioli) are so popular that the owners haven't changed much over the years. (Why tamper with success?) French and Mediterranean dishes are on the menu, too—try the blanquette of veal or the couscous. Among the lighter dishes are a scrumptious hearts-of-palm salad and the sautéed corvina. Grab a table away from the door (i.e., from the noise of the nearby bus stop). Old-timers refer to the place as Balcón de Franco; the late, legendary chef Franco Piatti was the restaurant's guiding light for years. [$] *Average main: $14* ✉ *C. 9, Avdas. Ctl.-1, Barrio La Soledad* ☎ *2221–4841* ⏲ *Closed Mon.* ✣ *F3.*

$ CAFÉ 🍴 **Café de la Posada.** The lack of alfresco dining in this tropical city is disappointing, but this café's covered terrace with tables fronting the pedestrian-only Calle 17 is a pleasant exception. The folks here know how to make a great cappuccino. Salads, quiches, and empanadas are specialties. The best bargains are the four rotating *platos del día* (daily specials), with entrée, salad, and dessert for $10. If you opt for dinner, make it an early one: the café closes at 6 on weeknights. [$] *Average main: $9* ✉ *C. 17, Avdas. 2–4, Barrio La Soledad* ☎ *2258–1027* ⏲ *Closed weekends.* ✣ *H4.*

San José's ubiquitous red taxicabs

$$ | **✕ Don Wang.** In a country where "Chinese cuisine" often means rice and
CHINESE | vegetables bearing a suspicious resemblance to *gallo pinto* (the typical
Costa Rican dish of beans and rice), Don Wang's authenticity is a treat.
Cantonese cuisine is the mainstay—the owner comes from that region of
China—but these folks will Szechuan it up a bit if you ask. Don Wang
is known for its immensely popular dim sum, called *desayuno chino*,
literally "Chinese breakfast." You can order it all day. The dining area
is built around a stone garden and small waterfall. $ *Average main:*
$13 ✉ *C. 11, Avdas. 6–8, Barrio La Soledad* ☎ *2233–6484* ⊕ *www.*
donwangrestaurant.com ✛ *G4.*

$ | **✕ La Criollita.** Kick off your day with breakfast here. Mornings are the
COSTA RICAN | perfect time to snag one of the precious tables in the back garden, an
unexpected refuge from noise and traffic. Platters come with eggs on the
side: the *americano* has pancakes and toast; the *tico* comes with bread,
fried bananas, and *natilla* (sour cream); and the huge *criollita* has ham
or pork chops. Government workers from nearby offices start arriving
late in the morning, and the lunchtime decibel level increases appreciably.
(This is the one time of day we recommend avoiding the place.) Everyone
filters out about 2 pm, and once again, you have a quiet place for coffee and dessert. If you come here for dinner, make it an early one; the
place closes at 7. $ *Average main: $9* ✉ *Avda. 7, Cs. 7–9, Barrio Amón*
☎ *2256–6511* ⊗ *Closed Sun. No dinner Sat.* ✛ *G3.*

$ | **✕ Mama's Place.** This is a Costa Rican restaurant with a difference: the
ITALIAN | owners are Italian, so in addition to *corvina al ajillo* (sea bass sau-
téed with garlic) and other standard Tico fare, they serve homemade
seafood chowder, traditional pasta dishes, and meats with delicate
wine sauces. The brightly decorated coffee shop opens onto busy

Avenida 1; the more subdued dining room upstairs accommodates the overflow crowd. (You'll see former Chicago Bears football coach Mike Ditka's autographed picture up there.) At lunchtime it's usually packed with business types drawn to the delicious and inexpensive daily specials—choose from the rotating platos del día with pasta, meat, fish, or poultry—all to the accompaniment of ample focaccia. Mama's closes at 8 pm on weeknights. [$] *Average main: $9* ✉ *Avda. 1, Cs. Ctl.–2, Barrio El Carmen* ☎ *2223–2270* ⏲ *Closed Sun. No dinner Sat.* ✥ *E3.*

$ COSTA RICAN 🍴 **Nuestra Tierra.** Except for the traffic zipping by on one of San José's busiest thoroughfares—opt for a table on the side facing less busy Calle 15—you might think you're out in the rural Central Valley. Bunches of onions and peppers dangle from the ceiling, recalling a provincial ranch. The generous homemade meals are delicious, and the incredibly friendly waitstaff, who epitomize Costa Rican hospitality and dress in folkloric clothing, prepare your coffee filtered through the traditional cloth *chorreador.* The place is open until midnight, just in case those late-night gallo pinto pangs hit. Some disparage the restaurant as "too touristy." Perhaps it is, but it's also fun. [$] *Average main: $7* ✉ *Avda. 2 and C. 15, Barrio La Soledad* ☎ *2258–6500* ✥ *G4.*

$ VEGETARIAN 🍴 **Shakti.** The baskets of fruit and vegetables at the entrance and the wall of herbal teas, health-food books, and fresh herbs for sale by the register signal that you're in a vegetarian-friendly joint. The bright and airy macrobiotic restaurant—much homier than Vishnu, its major vegetarian competition—serves breakfast, lunch, and an early dinner, closing at 7 pm weekdays and 6 pm Saturday. Homemade bread, soy burgers, pita sandwiches (veggie or, for carnivorous dining companions, chicken), fruit shakes, and a hearty plato del día that comes with soup, green salad, and a beverage fill out the menu. The *ensalada mixta* is a meal in itself, packed with root vegetables native to Costa Rica. [$] *Average main: $6* ✉ *Avda. 8 and C. 13, Barrio La Soledad* ☎ *2222–4475* ⏲ *Closed Sun.* ✥ *G5.*

$$$ ASIAN Fodor's Choice ★ 🍴 **Tin Jo.** The colorful dining rooms of this converted house just southeast of downtown evoke Japan, India, China, Indonesia, and Thailand. In the Thai Room, a 39-foot mural depicts a Buddhist temple. You can select from all the above cuisines—there are a few Filipino and Vietnamese dishes, too—with menus to match the various dining areas. Start with a powerful Singapore sling (brandy and fruit juices) before trying such treats as *kaeng* (Thai shrimp and pineapple curry in coconut milk), *mu shu* (a beef, chicken, or vegetable stir-fry with crepes), samosas (stuffed savory Indian pastries), and sushi rolls. The vegetarian menu is extensive. Tin Jo stands out with always-exceptional food, attention to detail, and attentive service that make it, hands down, the country's top Asian restaurant. [$] *Average main: $16* ✉ *C. 11, Avdas. 6–8, Barrio La Soledad* ☎ *2257–3622* 🌐 *www.tinjo.com* ✥ *G4.*

$ VEGETARIAN 🍴 **Vishnu.** "Haciendo un nuevo mundo," proudly proclaims the sign at the door. "Making a new world" might be a bit ambitious for a restaurant goal, but Vishnu takes its vegetarian offerings seriously. The dining area looks institutional—you'll sit at a sterile booth with Formica tables and gaze at posters of fruit on the walls—but the attraction is the inexpensive macrobiotic food. A yummy, good-value bet is usually the plato del día (soup, beverage, and dessert), but the menu also includes soy burgers, salads, fruit juices, and a yogurt smoothie called *morir soñando* (literally, "to die dreaming"). $ *Average main: $5* ⊠ *Avda. 1 west of C. 3, Barrio El Carmen* ☎ *2233–9976* ⊙ *No dinner weekends* ✛ *F3.*

NORTH AND EAST OF DOWNTOWN

$$
CAFÉ
✕ **Café Mundo.** You could easily walk by this corner restaurant without noticing its tiny sign behind the foliage. The upstairs café serves meals on a porch, on a garden patio, or in two dining rooms. The soup of the day and fresh-baked bread start you out; main courses include shrimp in a vegetable cream sauce or *lomito en salsa de vino tinto* (tenderloin in a red-wine sauce). Save room for the best chocolate cake in town, drizzled with homemade blackberry sauce. Café Mundo is a popular, low-key gay hangout that draws a mixed gay-straight clientele. This is one of the few center-city restaurants with its own parking lot. $ *Average main: $11* ⊠ *C. 15 and Avda. 9, Barrio Otoya* ☎ *2222–6190* ⊙ *Closed Sun. No lunch Sat.* ✛ *G2.*

$$$
ECLECTIC
✕ **Jürgen's.** A common haunt for *politicos*, Jürgen's attracts San José's elites. Decorated in gold and terra cotta with leather and wood accents, the contemporary dining room feels more like a lounge than a fine restaurant. In fact, the classy bar, with a large selection of fine wines and good cigars, is a prominent feature. The inventive menu, with such delicacies as medallions of roast duck and tuna fillet encrusted with sesame seeds, sets this place apart from the city's more traditional venues. $ *Average main: $20* ⊠ *Blvd. Barrio Dent, 250 m north of the Subaru dealership, Barrio Dent* ☎ *2283–2239* ⊙ *Closed Sun. No lunch Sat.* ✛ *B5.*

$$$
ECLECTIC
Fodor'sChoice
★
✕ **Kalú.** Camille Ratton, a longtime fixture on San José's restaurant scene, owns and manages one of the capital's hippest dining spots. The panini and pastas are the standouts, but Kalú's menu incorporates Costa Rican, Thai, and American elements, too. For one of those Americanized touches, try the *hambuguesa* Kalú with portobello mushrooms, mozzarella cheese, and hummus. Browse in the adjoining art gallery before or after your meal, or while you wait for your food. The covered back patio offers stupendous views, especially in the evening, although long sleeves are in order if the night is brisk. $ *Average main: $16* ⊠ *C. 7 and Avda. 11, Barrio Amón* ☎ *2221–2081* ⊕ *www.kalu.co.cr* ⊙ *Closed Sun. No dinner Mon. and Tues.* ✛ *F2.*

$$$
FRENCH
✕ **La Terrasse.** This cozy restaurant is the baby of French transplants Patricia and Gérald Richer. (She's your chef; he's your host.) The main-course offerings rotate, but might include a *blanquette de veau* (veal ragout) or a *daube provençale* (a hearty wine-marinated beef stew). Dining here feels as though you are a guest in a private home, and, indeed, the restaurant is located in one of the old Barrio Otoya houses, whose sign is easy to miss. $ *Average main: $25* ⊠ *C. 15, Avdas. 9–9A, 50 m north of Café Mundo, Barrio Otoya* ☎ *8939–8470* ⌚ *Reservations essential* ▭ *No credit cards* ⊙ *Closed Sun. No lunch.* ✛ *G2.*

$ ITALIAN 🍴 **La Trattoria.** The green and gold here might make a Green Bay Packers fan feel right at home, but it's the excellent, reasonably priced homemade pastas that make this popular lunch spot worth the stop. Begin your meal with fresh bread and any number of excellent antipasti, continuing on with your favorite pasta dish. And for dessert, who can resist tiramisu? [$] *Average main: $10* ✉ *Behind Automercado, Barrio Dent, San Pedro* ☎ *2224–7065* ✥ *B5.*

HAVE SOME SAUCE

Any self-respecting Tico home or restaurant keeps a bottle of **Salsa Lizano,** one of the country's signature food products, on hand. Its tang brightens up meat, vegetable, and rice dishes. Bottles of the stuff make great souvenirs, and you can buy them at **Más X Menos** (pronounced Más *por* Menos) supermarkets throughout the country. The main San José branch is at Avenida Central, between Calles 11 and 13.

$$$$ FRENCH 🍴 **Le Chandelier.** San José doesn't get classier than this restaurant, where formal service and traditional sauce-heavy French dishes are part of the experience. The dining room is elegant, with wicker chairs, tile floors, and original paintings. The Swiss chef might start you off with saffron ravioli stuffed with ricotta cheese and walnuts. Main courses include such unique dishes as corvina in a *pejibaye* (peach palm) sauce or hearts of palm and veal chops glazed in a sweet port-wine sauce. The more familiar *pato a la naranja* (duck à l'orange) gets a tropical twist as *pato a la maracuyá* (duck in passion fruit). [$] *Average main: $28* ✉ *C. 49, 50 m west and 100 m south of ICE Bldg., San Pedro* ☎ *2225–3980* 🌐 *www.lechandeliercr.com* ✍ *Reservations essential* ⏲ *Closed Sun. No lunch Sat.* ✥ *C5.*

$ MEDITERRANEAN 🍴 **Olio.** Although this combination pub and restaurant serves the full contingent of Mediterranean cuisine, it's best for drinks and Spanish-style *tapas* (appetizers). The century-old redbrick house with stained-glass windows draws everybody from tie-clad business executives to university students. Groups liven up the large front room—the quieter, smaller back rooms maintain a bit more romance. There are umbrella-covered tables on the sidewalk to enjoy warm evenings. Olio is extremely proud that it offers a copy of its menu in Braille. [$] *Average main: $10* ✉ *C. 33, 200 m north of Bagelmen's, Barrio Escalante* ☎ *2281–0541* ⏲ *Closed Sun. No lunch Sat.* ✥ *H5.*

$ PIZZA 🍴 **Pane e Vino.** Look closely at the extensive menu here: there are 40 varieties of the capital's best thin-crust pizza, and no one will rush you if you spend time pondering what you want. This lively two-level restaurant rounds out its offerings with a complete selection of pastas. You can dine until midnight daily, except on Sunday, when you'll have to finish dinner by 10 pm. The Pizza Allessandre, topped with prosciutto, mozzarella, and olives, is the most popular dish, and for good reason. Pane e Vino has become a small chain—it has even expanded to Nicaragua and Ecuador—but this is the original location. [$] *Average main: $9* ✉ *50 m west and 15 m south of Más X Menos supermarket, San Pedro* ☎ *2280–2869* 🌐 *www.paneevino.co.cr* ✥ *H5.*

WEST OF DOWNTOWN

$$$$ ECLECTIC Fodor's Choice ★

🍴 **Grano de Oro Restaurant.** One of the city's premier lodgings, the Grano de Oro also houses one of its premier dining venues. The hotel's splendid restaurant, open to the public, sits to the left as you enter the lobby and wraps around a lovely indoor patio and bromeliad-filled gardens. That garden area is a perfect spot for lunch on a warm day—choose from among a variety of light sandwiches and salads. Evenings get a tad cooler around here and are time to migrate to the elegant indoor dining area for such dishes as *corvina macadamia* (breaded sea bass with orange sauce and macadamia nuts) or *cerdo en salsa tamarindo* (roasted pork in tamarind sauce). An impressive 100-plus wine selection and decadent dessert menu—the coffee-cream "Pie Grano de Oro" is the must-try option here—round out the offerings. Although elegance is the watchword in this grand coffee-plantation-house-turned-hotel, you'll see everything from diners in business attire to guests in casual garb just back from the hinterlands. [$] *Average main: $25* ✉ *C. 30, Avdas. 2–4, Paseo Colón* ☎ *2255–3322* 🌐 *www.hotelgranodeoro.com* ✥ *A4.*

$$$ ITALIAN

🍴 **L'Olivo.** The same owners who bring you the west-side lodging Suites Cristina also bring you this little bit of Tuscany a few blocks north of La Sabana Park. (The restaurant is most easily entered from around the corner, physically separate from the hotel.) Vaulted ceilings and a vineyard mural on one wall evoke old Italy. Homemade pastas—spinach cannelloni and linguine with clam sauce are popular dishes—make up the fare here, and an extensive wine list rounds out the offerings. Service is attentive—the chef makes the rounds to ensure that you're satisfied. The scant dozen tables mean that reservations are a good idea for dinner. The smallness of the restaurant does create one drawback: it can be difficult to carry on a conversation when things get busy, although that does add to the liveliness of the place. [$] *Average main: $18* ✉ *300 m north, 50 m east of ICE Bldg., Paseo Colón* ☎ *2220–0453* 🌐 *www.cristina.co.cr* ✍ *Reservations essential* ⏲ *Closed Sun.* ✥ *A4.*

$$ MIDDLE EASTERN

🍴 **Lubnan.** Negotiate the quirky wrought-iron-and-burlap revolving door at the entrance and you've made it into one of San José's few Middle Eastern restaurants. The Lebanese owners serve a wide variety of dishes from their native region, so if you can't decide, the *mezza* serves two people and gives you a little bit of everything. For your own individual dish, try the juicy shish kebab *de cordero* (of lamb), or, if you're feeling especially adventurous, the raw ground-meat *kebbe naye* (with wheat meal) and *kafta naye* (without wheat meal). A hip bar in the back serves the same menu. On Wednesday night there is live synthesizer music; on Thursday night check out the immensely popular 9 pm belly-dancing show. [$] *Average main: $11* ✉ *Paseo Colón, Cs. 22–24, Paseo Colón* ☎ *2257–6071* 🌐 *www.lubnancr.com* ⏲ *Closed Mon. No dinner Sun.* ✥ *B3.*

$$ PERUVIAN

🍴 **Machu Picchu.** A few travel posters and a net holding crab and lobster shells are the only props used to evoke Peru, but no matter: the food is anything but plain, and the seafood is excellent. The *pique especial de mariscos* (special seafood platter), big enough for two, presents you with shrimp, conch, and squid cooked four ways. The ceviche is quite different from, and better than, that served in the rest of the country. A blazing Peruvian hot sauce served on the side adds zip to any dish, but be careful—apply it by the drop. One more warning: the pisco sours from the bar go down very easily. $\boxed{\$}$ *Average main: $14 ⊠ C. 32, 130 m north of KFC, Paseo Colón ☎ 2222–7384 ✛ A3.*

$$$
ECLECTIC
✕ **Park Café.** Set within an antiques shop, the all-tapas menu includes such tasty dishes as Thai-style tuna salad or red-snapper couscous. Don't let appearances deceive you: the colonial-style house is only about a decade old, but attention to architectural detail and antique furnishings make you think the building was transplanted from Antigua or Granada. The menu varies from year to year, depending on what the owners have uncovered during their annual two-month European buying trip. Space is limited, so reservations are a must. The January through April dry season takes the pressure off a bit, allowing seating to spill over from the covered veranda to the open courtyard. You dine among the many antiques for sale here, so small children are not allowed. $\boxed{\$}$ *Average main: $25 ⊠ 100 m north of Rosti Pollos, Sabana Norte ☎ 2290–6324 ⊕ parkcafecostarica.blogspot.com ⌲ Reservations essential ⊙ Closed Sun. and Mon. and Sept. and Oct. No lunch ✛ A4.*

$
COSTA RICAN
✕ **Soda Tapia.** One of San José's most popular restaurants fronts the east side of La Sabana Park. Don't expect anything fancy, but food here is cheap and filling. The ubiquitous gallo pinto for breakfast and *casados* (meat, fish, or poultry, accompanied by rice, cabbage salad, and dessert) for lunch are on the menu. The dinner menu has a variety of sandwiches and burgers. You can dine outdoors, but you'll have to contend with the traffic noise and the sight of the guard flagging cars in and out of the tiny parking lot. The place stays open until 2 am and around the clock on weekends. $\boxed{\$}$ *Average main: $5 ⊠ C. 42, Avdas. 2–4, Sabana Este ☎ 2222–6734 ✛ A4.*

WHERE TO STAY

San José may be the big city, but it truly shines in its selection of small to medium-size inns. They're all locally owned, and their friendly, attentive staff will make you feel as if you're staying in an oasis in the middle of Costa Rica's noisy, congested capital.

San José has plenty of chains, including Best Western, Holiday Inn, Radisson, Quality Inn, Meliá, and Barceló (the last two are Spanish chains). But it also has historic houses with traditional architecture that have been converted into small lodgings.

The historic houses are usually without concierge or pool and are found mainly in Barrios Amón and Otoya, and in the eastern suburb of San Pedro. The city also has a lower tier of lodgings with the simplicity (and prices) beloved of backpackers. Most smaller hotels don't have air-conditioning, but it rarely gets warm enough at this altitude to warrant it.

Many lodgings operate at near-full occupancy in high season (December through April), but the capital's status as a business-travel destination means the lodging rates remain constant year-round. Reconfirm all reservations 24 hours in advance. If you're flying out early in the morning and prefer to stay near the airport, consider booking a hotel near Alajuela or San Antonio de Belén in the Central Valley. (⇨ *See Chapter 4)*

Hotel reviews have been shortened. For full information, visit Fodors.com.

3

WHAT IT COSTS IN DOLLARS

	$	$$	$$$	$$$$
Hotels	under $75	$75–$150	$151–$250	over $250

Hotel prices are the lowest cost of a standard double room in high season.

DOWNTOWN

Staying in the downtown area allows you to travel around the city as most Ticos do: on foot. Stroll the parks, museums, and shops, and then retire to one of the many small or historic hotels with plenty of character.

$$ HOTEL 🏨 **Gran Hotel Costa Rica.** You cannot find a more central location than at this grande dame of San José lodgings. **Pros:** central location; good value; great people-watching from ground-floor café. **Cons:** some street noise from the adjoining plaza; some rooms have thin walls; no parking lot of its own. [$] *Rooms from: $64* ✉ *Avda. 2 and C. 3, Barrio La Soledad* ☎ *2221–4000, 800/949–0592 in U.S.* 🌐 *www.granhotelcostarica.com* 🛏 *105 rooms, 5 suites* 🍴 *Breakfast* ✥ *F3.*

$$ HOTEL 🏨 **Holiday Inn San José Downtown – Aurola.** All the amenities a business traveler's heart could desire and the reassuring, familiar name are yours at this conveniently located hotel on the north side of downtown. **Pros:** business facilities; central location. **Cons:** sameness of chain hotel; park across street dicey at night; always take taxi to and from after dark. [$] *Rooms from: $115* ✉ *Avda. 5 and C. 5, Barrio El Carmen* ☎ *2523–1000, 800/315–2521 in North America* 🌐 *www.aurolahotels.com* 🛏 *184 rooms, 12 suites* 🍴 *Breakfast* ✥ *F3.*

$$ HOTEL 🏨 **Hotel Balmoral.** One of the capital's landmark hotels has completed a top-to-toe remodeling at this writing, revealing a much-appreciated modernization of its guest rooms. **Pros:** central location; good restaurant. **Cons:** some street noise. [$] *Rooms from: $105* ✉ *C. 7. Avdas. Ctl.–1, Barrio La Soledad* ☎ *2222–5022, 800/691–4865 in North America* 🌐 *www.balmoral.co.cr* 🛏 *112 rooms, 8 suites* 🍴 *Breakfast* ✥ *F4.*

$$ B&B/INN 🏨 **Hotel Fleur de Lys.** A three-floor Victorian house with a brassy hot-pink-and-lavender exterior offers a quiet elegance that you'd never imagine lies beyond its doors. **Pros:** cozy rooms; close to sights. **Cons:** some noise from downstairs bar. [$] *Rooms from: $88* ✉ *C. 13, Avdas. 2–6, Barrio La Soledad* ☎ *2223–1206* 🌐 *www.hotelfleurdelys.com* 🛏 *24 rooms, 6 suites* 🍴 *Breakfast* ✥ *G4.*

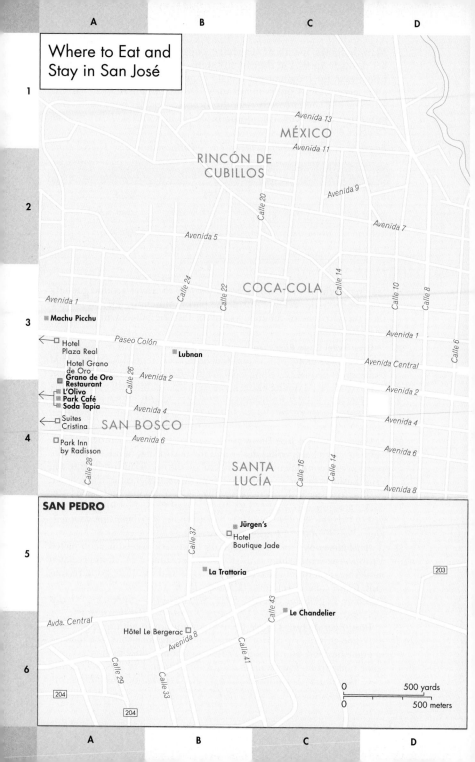

Where to Eat and Stay in San José

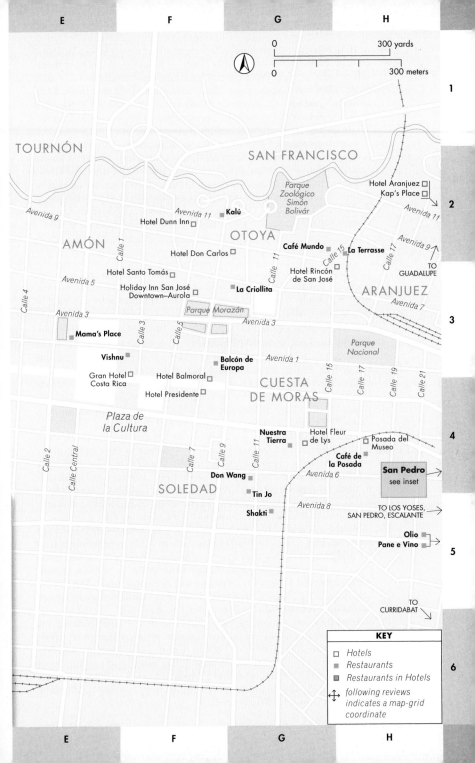

$$
HOTEL
Hotel Presidente. This hotel offers standard, medium-price, business-class accommodations, although plenty of leisure travelers base themselves here as well. **Pros:** central location; eco-friendly hotel. **Cons:** some street noise; some rooms have thin walls. $ *Rooms from: $129 ⊠ Avda. Ctl. and C. 7, Barrio La Soledad* ☎ *2010–0000, 877/540–1790 in North America* ⊕ *www.hotel-presidente.com* ⟲ *80 rooms, 12 suites* ¶⊙¶ *Breakfast* ✛ *F4.*

$
B&B/INN
Posada del Museo. Painted a pretty shade of yellow, this wooden Victorian-style house dating from 1928 is a great place to stay if you're bound for San José's museums (hence the name)—it's diagonally across the street from the Museo Nacional. **Pros:** cozy rooms; near the sights. **Cons:** rush-hour train passes by; fronts busy street. $ *Rooms from: $60 ⊠ Avda. 2 and C. 17, Barrio La Soledad* ☎ *2258–1027* ⊕ *www. hotelposadadelmuseo.com* ⟲ *7 rooms, 3 suites* ¶⊙¶ *Breakfast* ✛ *H4.*

NORTH AND EAST OF DOWNTOWN

Just north of downtown, old homes converted into small lodgings populate Barrios Amón and Otoya, two of the capital's most historic neighborhoods. The small properties just 10 minutes by cab east of downtown, toward the university, offer personalized service and lots of peace and quiet. Plenty of restaurants and bars are within easy reach.

$
HOTEL
Hotel Aranjuez. Several 1940s-era houses with extensive gardens and lively common areas—visitors swap travel advice here—constitute this family-run lodging. **Pros:** good budget value; great place to meet other budget travelers; excellent complimentary breakfast. **Cons:** cumbersome reservations system; far from sights. $ *Rooms from: $56 ⊠ C. 19, Avdas. 11–13, Barrio Aranjuez* ☎ *2256–1825* ⊕ *www.hotelaranjuez. com* ⟲ *35 rooms, 29 with bath* ¶⊙¶ *Breakfast* ✛ *H2.*

$$
HOTEL
Hotel Boutique Jade. The European owners of this small east-side lodging have instilled a standard for attentive service in their staff and the result is a devoted return clientele, mostly from Europe. **Pros:** friendly service; quiet street; close to lots of shopping. **Cons:** can be difficult to find; far from sights. $ *Rooms from: $103 ⊠ Blvd. Dent, 250 m north of the Subaru dealership, Barrio Dent* ☎ *2224–2455* ⊕ *www. hotelboutiquejade.com* ⟲ *29 rooms* ¶⊙¶ *Breakfast* ✛ *B5.*

$$
B&B/INN
Hotel Don Carlos. One of the city's first guesthouses (technically it's three houses), this is the kind of place where you'll meet fellow travelers and swap stories about what you've seen. **Pros:** good value; good place to meet kindred spirits. **Cons:** some noise in interior rooms; some reports of long waits in restaurant. $ *Rooms from: $85 ⊠ C. 9 and Avda. 9* ☎ *2221–6707, 866/675–9259 in North America* ⊕ *www. doncarloshotel.com* ⟲ *30 rooms* ¶⊙¶ *Breakfast* ✛ *G2.*

$
B&B/INN
Hotel Dunn Inn. Adjoining 1926 and 1933 houses fuse to create the cozy Barrio Amón experience at bargain prices. **Pros:** good value; friendly staff; many online specials. **Cons:** difficult to get reservations; interior rooms catch noise from lobby and bar; sits at bottom of steep street. $ *Rooms from: $64 ⊠ Avda. 11 and C. 5, Barrio Amón* ☎ *2222–3232, 888/545–4801 in North America* ⊕ *www.hoteldunninn. com* ⟲ *28 rooms* ¶⊙¶ *Breakfast* ✛ *F2.*

$$ B&B/INN **Fodor's Choice** ★ **Hôtel Le Bergerac.** Quiet elegance doesn't often come at affordable prices, but it's yours here at San José's best small inn. **Pros:** top-notch service; cozy rooms; terrific restaurant. **Cons:** rooms on the small side; not near sights; steep street if walking. [$] *Rooms from: $87* ✉ *C. 35, Avdas. Ctl.–2, 1st entrance to Los Yoses, San Pedro* ☎ *2234–7850* 🌐 *www.bergerachotel.com* 🛏 *25 rooms* 🍴 *Breakfast* ✣ *B6.*

$ B&B/INN **Hotel Rincón de San José.** This elegant little inn has comfortable guest quarters in a charming neighborhood near the Parque España and incorporates environmentally friendly practices into its operations. **Pros:** good value; friendly management; eco-friendly hotel. **Cons:** small rooms; rooms fronting street get some noise; no on-site parking. [$] *Rooms from: $70* ✉ *Avda. 9 and C. 15, Barrio Otoya* ☎ *2221–9702* 🌐 *www.hotelrincondesanjose.com* 🛏 *35 rooms* 🍴 *Breakfast* ✣ *H3.*

$ B&B/INN **Hotel Santo Tomás.** The front of this century-old former coffee-plantation house is along a busy street, but close the front door behind you and you'll find an oasis of quiet in the center of the city. **Pros:** good value; friendly staff; central location; small pool. **Cons:** difficult parking; borders on sketchy neighborhood; small rooms. [$] *Rooms from: $58* ✉ *Avda. 7, Cs. 3–5, Barrio Amón* ☎ *2255–0448, 877/446–0658 in North America* 🌐 *www.hotelsantotomas.com* 🛏 *30 rooms* 🍴 *Breakfast* ✣ *F3.*

$ B&B/INN **Kap's Place.** The owners of this multibuilding lodging are committed to maintaining a family atmosphere, and you'll be guaranteed peace and quiet during your stay here. **Pros:** good budget value; quiet atmosphere. **Cons:** far from sights; small rooms; you can pay with a credit card if you stay in the main building, but not in one of the annexes. [$] *Rooms from: $50* ✉ *C. 19, Avdas. 11–13, 200 m west, 50 m north of Shell station, Barrio Aranjuez* ☎ *2221–1169* 🌐 *www.kapsplace.com* 🛏 *32 rooms, 20 with bath* 🍴 *Breakfast* ✣ *H2.*

WEST OF DOWNTOWN

San José's vast west side contains only a smattering of lodgings, but among them are two of the city's best, Hotel Grano de Oro and the Park Inn by Radisson.

$$$ HOTEL **Fodor's Choice** ★ **Hotel Grano de Oro.** Two wooden houses have been converted into one of the city's most charming inns, decorated throughout with old photos of the capital and paintings by local artists; head up to your room for the old coffee-plantation feel for which the hotel is known. **Pros:** friendly management; top-notch service; superb restaurant. **Cons:** remodeling took away country feel in some areas; far from downtown sights; need taxi to get here. [$] *Rooms from: $180* ✉ *C. 30, Avdas. 2–4* ☎ *2255–3322* 🌐 *www.hotelgranodeoro.com* 🛏 *39 rooms, 3 suites* 🍴 *No meals* ✣ *A4.*

$$ HOTEL **Fodor's Choice** ★ **Park Inn by Radisson.** This chain hotel incorporates local flair—bright, fresh primary colors and a rotating selection of Costa Rican art throughout—while providing business amenities in a clean, modern hotel. **Pros:** impeccable service; friendly staff; quiet neighborhood; local style although a chain hotel. **Cons:** far from sights. [$] *Rooms from: $129* ✉ *Avda. 6, Cs. 28–30, Paseo Colón* ☎ *2257–1011, 800/670–7215 in North America* 🌐 *www.parkinn.com* 🛏 *108 rooms, 9 suites* 🍴 *Breakfast* ✣ *A4.*

$$ HOTEL 🏨 **Suites Cristina.** Our favorite of the capital's many *apartotels*—part apartment house, part hotel—sits on a quiet, out-of-the-way street north of La Sabana Park. **Pros:** friendly staff; quiet street; terrific rates for what is offered. **Cons:** far from sights and center of town. [$] *Rooms from: $87* ✉ *C. Luisa, 300 m north of ICE Bldg., Sabana Norte* ☎ *2220–0453* 🌐 *www.cristina.co.cr* 🛏 *50 suites* 🍴 *Breakfast* ✣ *A4.*

NIGHTLIFE AND THE ARTS

THE ARTS

The best source for theater, dance, film, and arts information is the "Viva" entertainment section of the Spanish-language daily *La Nación*. The paper also publishes the "Tiempo Libre" section each Friday, highlighting what's going on over the weekend. *GAM Cultural* is a free monthly flyer found in many upscale hotels and restaurants, and publishes features about what's going on around town. Listings in both publications are in Spanish but are easy to decipher. The website of the English-language *The Tico Times* (🌐 *www.ticotimes.net*) lists many events of interest to visitors and the expat community.

Unfortunately, arts offerings in the city are nearly nonexistent during the high-season weeks from mid-December through early February. That's school vacation time.

ART GALLERIES

San José's art galleries, public or private, museum or bohemian, keep daytime hours only, but all kick off a new show with an evening opening. They're free and open to the public, and they offer a chance to rub elbows with Costa Rica's art community (and to sip wine and munch on appetizers). Listings appear in *La Nación*'s "Viva" section. Your time in the capital might coincide with one of these by happenstance. (They're rarely announced in the paper more than a day or two in advance.) Look for the term *inauguración* (opening).

FILM

Dubbing of movies is rare; films are screened in their original language, usually English, and subtitled in Spanish. (Children's movies, however, *are* dubbed (*doblada*), although a multiplex cinema may offer some *hablada en inglés*, or screenings in English.) Plan to pay $6 for a ticket. Don't expect anything too avant-garde in most theaters; month-old Hollywood releases are the norm. Following trends seen elsewhere, theaters have fled downtown for the suburban malls.

Sala Garbo. This theater shows arty films, often in languages other than English with Spanish subtitles. ✉ *Avda. 2 and C. 28, Paseo Colón* ☎ *2222–1034* 🌐 *www.salagarbocr.com.*

THEATER AND MUSIC

More than a dozen theater groups (many of which perform slapstick comedies) hold forth in smaller theaters around town. If your Spanish is up to it, call for a reservation. The curtain rises at 8 pm, Friday through Sunday, with some companies staging performances on Thursday night,

"Our first full day in San José was full of wandering through the streets and markets. We happened upon this friendly artist who shared his paintings with us." —Photo by Liz Stuart, Fodors.com member

too. If your Spanish isn't quite theater-ready, there are plenty of dance and musical performances.

Centro Nacional de la Cultura. There are frequent dance performances and concerts in the Teatro FANAL and Teatro 1887, both in the Centro Nacional de la Cultura. ⊠ *C. 13, Avdas. 3–5, Barrio Otoya* ☎ *2257–5524* ⊕ *www.njc.go.cr.*

Eugene O'Neill Theater. This theater has chamber concerts and plays most weekend evenings. The cultural center is a great place to meet North American expatriates. ⊠ *Centro Cultural Costarricense–Norteamericano, Avda. 1 and C. 37, Barrio Dent, San Pedro* ☎ *2207–7554* ⊕ *www.centrocultural.cr.*

Little Theatre Group. Since 1949, the Little Theatre Group has presented English-language community-theater productions several times a year at the near-west-side Teatro Laurence Olivier. ⊠ *Avda. 2 and C. 28, Paseo Colón* ☎ *8858–1446* ⊕ *www.littletheatregroup.org.*

Teatro La Aduana. You'll find frequent dance and stage performances at this theater, and it is home to the Compañía Nacional de Teatro (National Theater Company). ⊠ *C. 25 and Avda. 3, Barrio La California* ☎ *2257–8305* ⊕ *www.mjc.go.cr.*

Teatro Nacional (*National Theater*). This baroque theater is the home of the excellent National Symphony Orchestra, which performs on some Friday evenings and Sunday mornings between March and November. The theater also hosts visiting musical groups and dance companies. Tickets are $5–$50. ⊠ *Plaza de la Cultura, Barrio La Soledad* ☎ *2010–1100* ⊕ *www.teatronacional.go.cr.*

Teatro Popular Melico Salazar. San José's second-most popular theater has a full calendar of music and dance shows, as well as a few offbeat productions. There is always something on several nights a week; tickets are $5–$25. ✉ *Avda. 2, Cs. Ctl.–2, Barrio La Merced* ☎ *2233–5424* ⊕ *www.teatromelico.go.cr.*

NIGHTLIFE

The metro area's hottest nightlife has migrated to the Central Valley suburbs of Escazú and Heredia these days. *(⇨ See Chapter 4.)* Both are about 20- to 30-minute taxi rides from downtown San José. The capital isn't devoid of places to go in the evening, however. There are still plenty of bars, dance clubs, and restaurants and cafés where you can spend the evening. Take taxis to and from when you go; it's the safest option if you're out after dark. Most places will be happy to call you a cab—or, if there's a guard, he can hail you one—when it's time to call it a night. Remember that all venues are nonsmoking.

AREAS

No one could accuse San José of having too few watering holes, but aside from the hotels there aren't many places to have a quiet drink, especially downtown. Barrios Amón and Otoya have little in the way of nightlife outside the occasional hotel bar.

The young and the restless hang out in the student-oriented places around the University of Costa Rica in the eastern suburb of San Pedro. The Calle de la Amargura (Street of Bitterness), named for the route Jesus took to the crucifixion, is much more secular than its name suggests and rocks loudly each night. (Nighttime robberies have occurred on "The Calle," so be wary.)

Don't write off every place around the university as rowdy. There are a few quiet bars and cafés where you can carry on a real conversation. Barrios La California and Escalante, an area anchored by the Santa Teresita church, connect central San José with San Pedro, and house some of the city's trendiest nightspots.

DOWNTOWN

CAFES

Café 1930. The café under the arcades at the entrance to the Grand Hotel Costa Rica pulls duty as a pleasant place for an evening drink or coffee. Listen to live music on the grand piano each night from 6 to 8 pm. ✉ *Grand Hotel Costa Rica, Avda. 2 and C. 3, Barrio La Soledad* ☎ *2221–4011* ⊘ *Daily 10 am–11 pm.*

GAY AND LESBIAN

El Bochinche. This gay bar and dance club gets packed on weekends. It attracts a young crowd and keeps *very* late hours. ✉ *C. 11, Avdas. 10–12, Barrio La Soledad* ☎ *2221–0500* ⊕ *www.bochinchesanjose.com* ⊘ *Wed.–Thurs. 8 pm–5 am, Fri. and Sat. 8 pm–6 am.*

La Avispa. A gay and lesbian crowd frequents La Avispa, which has two dance floors with videos and karaoke, as well as a quieter upstairs bar with pool tables. The last Friday of each month is ladies' night. ✉ *C. 1, Avda. 8, Barrio La Soledad* ☎ *2223–5343* ⊕ *www.laavispa. co.cr* ⊘ *Thurs.–Sun. 8 pm–1 am.*

DID YOU KNOW?

The auditorium floor in the Teatro Nacional was designed to be hoisted up to stage level by a manual winch so that it could also be used as a ballroom.

SAN JOSÉ'S CAFÉS

Costa Ricans are serious about their ritual of *tomando café* (taking a coffee break), but most places they do so in the city feel pretty basic and institutional. The venues we list below capture that café feel and serve export-quality coffee:

Café del Barista. The rain does get a bit loud on the metal roof, but the wide selection of coffee drinks here is worth the occasional racket. ⊠ *C. 19 and Avda. 11, Barrio Aranjuez* 🕾 *No phone* ⊙ *Weekdays 7–7, Sat. 8–6.*

Café Miel Natural. A scant two tables and a small counter are the only seating at this tiny place, which serves up coffee from its own *finca* in Tarrazú in the Los Santos region.

⊠ *Avda. 9 and C. 13, Barrio Otoya* 🕾 *No phone* ⊙ *Mon.–Sat. 9–7.*

Club Unión. The elevated, glassed-in café here lets you survey the ongoing beehive of activity on the small, shaded plaza in front of the post office. ⊠ *C. 2, Avdas. 1–3, Barrio La Merced* 🕾 *2257–1555* ⊙ *Weekdays 8–7, Sat. 10–6.*

Jungle Bean/Jungle Fruit. Peruse a good selection of magazines and newspapers while sipping on a cup of gourmet coffee or a smoothie—that's the "Fruit" part of the place's name. ⊠ *C. 7, Avdas. Ctl.–1, Barrio La Soledad* 🕾 *2256–8251* ⊙ *Weekdays 7–6, Sat. 9–6.*

NORTH AND EAST OF DOWNTOWN

BARS

El Observatorio. El Observatorio strikes an unusual balance between casual and formal: it's the kind of place where folks over 30 go to watch a soccer game but wear ties. Something is on here every night except Sunday, usually a selection of stand-up comedy, live music, or karaoke. ⊠ *C. 23 across from Cine Magaly, Barrio La California* 🕾 *2223–0725* ⊕ *www.elobservatorio.tv* ⊙ *Mon.–Sat. 6 pm–1 am.*

Jazz Café San Pedro. This place draws big crowds for the nightly live music (except Sunday). Although the staple here is jazz, rock and funk acts play here as well—check the website to see what's on. You'll find a branch in the Central Valley suburb of Escazú as well. ⊠ *Avda. Ctl., next to Banco Popular, San Pedro* 🕾 *2253–8933* ⊕ *www.jazzcafecostarica. com* ⊙ *Mon.–Sat. 6 pm–1 am.*

Otoya 1155. This quiet place tucked away in Barrio Otoya—hence the name—has a great selection of wines and is a nice place to go for a drink in the evening. ⊠ *Avda. 9, Cs. 11–13, Barrio Otoya* 🕾 *2222–3636* ⊙ *Wed.–Sun. 6 pm–midnight.*

Vyrus. There is occasionally live music at Vyrus on the weekend, which draws a mixed college student and young professional crowd. Videos from the '60s, '70s, and '80s provide the backdrop other nights. Inside is dark, coupley, and kissy; the outdoor balcony is much more conducive to singing along to that Duran Duran song you haven't heard in ages. ⊠ *100 m west of Spoon restaurant, San Pedro* 🕾 *2280–5890* ⊙ *Mon.–Sat. 4 pm–2 am.*

CAFÉS

Café Mundo. The highly recommended restaurant Café Mundo is a quiet spot for a drink or bite to eat and is frequented by gay and bohemian crowds. ⊠ *C. 15 and Avda. 9, Barrio Otoya* ☎ *2222–6190.*

Olio. Fill up on Spanish-style tapas at the Mediterranean bar and restaurant Olio. It draws a mix of professionals and older college students. ⊠ *C. 33, 200 m north of Bagelmen's, Barrio Escalante* ☎ *2281–0541* ☉ *Mon.– Wed. noon–11, Thurs. and Fri. noon–midnight, Sat. 6 pm midnight.*

Omar Khayyam. Smack-dab in the center of the campus nightlife, Omar Khayyam is a blissfully quiet refuge. Share a jug of wine and falafel or hummus with fried yuca

on the covered patio. ⊠ *C. de la Amargura, San Pedro* ☎ *2253–8455* ☉ *Daily noon–11.*

DANCE CLUBS

Merecumbé. Step into a San José nightclub and you might think Costa Ricans are born dancing. They aren't, but most learn to merengue, rumba, mambo, cha-cha, and swing (called *cumbia* elsewhere) as children. Play catch-up at dance school Merecumbé, which has 16 branches around Costa Rica. With a few days' notice you can arrange a private lesson with an English-speaking instructor. An hour or two is all you need to grasp the fundamentals of merengue and bolero, both of which are easy to master and work with the pop music you're likely to hear back home. ⊠ *100 m south and 25 m west of Banco Popular, San Pedro* ☎ *2224–3531* ⊕ *www.merecumbe.net.*

WEST OF DOWNTOWN

BARS

Mac's American Bar. An older expat crowd hangs out at Mac's, which always has the TV tuned to a sporting event. It gets our nod for serving the city's best burger. ⊠ *South side of La Sabana Park, next to the Costa Rica Tennis Club, Sabana Sur* ☎ *2234–3145* ⊕ *www.macsamericanbar. com* ☉ *Daily 9 am–1 am.*

SOUTH OF DOWNTOWN

FOLKLORIC SHOWS

Ram Luna. In the far, far southern suburbs, Ram Luna is most famous for the views—the lights of the Central Valley sparkle at your feet—and the music. Make reservations if you plan to be here for Wednesday or Thursday evening's folklore show—a bilingual emcee fills you in on the cultural background of what you're enjoying—or Friday evening's dancing to live music. ⊠ *15 km (9 miles) south of San José between Aserrí and Tabarca, Aserrí* ☎ *2230–3022* ⊕ *www.restauranteramluna.com* ☉ *Tues. 4–11, Wed. and Thurs. 7–10, Fri. 4–midnight, Sat. noon–11, Sun. noon–9.*

SHOPPING

Although it might seem more "authentic" to buy your souvenirs at their source, you can find everything in the city, a real bonus if you're pressed for time. If the capital has any real tourist shopping district, it's found loosely in the cluster of streets around Parque Morazán, just north of downtown, an area bounded roughly by Avenidas 1 and 7 and Calles 5 and 9. Stroll and search, because many other businesses congregate in the area as well.

The northeastern suburb of Moravia has a cluster of high-quality crafts and artisan shops—for good reason very popular with tour groups—in the three blocks heading north from the Colegio María Inmaculada. The street is two blocks behind the city's church.

MALLS

Terramall. The mammoth 137-store Terramall is the far eastern suburbs' prime shopping destination. ⊠ *Autopista Florencio del Castillo, Tres Ríos* ☎ *2278–6970* ⊕ *www.terramall.co.cr.*

DOWNTOWN

BOOKS AND MAGAZINES

Casa de las Revistas. With several locations around the metro area, Casa de las Revistas has San José's best selection of magazines in English. ⊠ *C. 5, Avdas. 3–5, Barrio El Carmen* ☎ *2256–5092* ⊕ *www.lacasadelasrevistascr.com.*

CRAFTS

Congo. Congo offers a good selection of wood carvings and ceramic bowls and vases made by local artisans. It's a small chain with four other outlets elsewhere in the country. ⊠ *Arcade in Hotel Balmoral, C. Ctl., Avdas. 7–9, Barrio La Soledad* ☎ *2010–7274* ⊕ *www.congocostarica.com.*

Fodor'sChoice
★ **Galería Namu.** Downtown San José's must-stop shop is Galería Namu, which sells the best indigenous crafts in town. Its inventory brims with colorful creations by the Guaymí, Boruca, Bribri, Chorotega, Huetar, and Maleku peoples—all Costa Rican indigenous groups. Such crafts used to be the exclusive domain of male artisans, but a growing number of works by women are on display here these days. You can also find exquisitely carved ivory-nut Tagua figurines and baskets made by the Wounan people from Panama's Darién region and Tuno textiles and Lenca pottery from Honduras. Take note of carved balsa masks, woven cotton blankets, and hand-painted ceramics.

The store looks expensive—and indeed, the sky's the limit in terms of prices—but if your budget is not so flush, say so: the good folks here can help you find something in the $15–$25 range that will make a cherished souvenir. As a bonus you'll get an information sheet describing your work's creator and art style. ⊠ *Avda. 7, Cs. 5–7, Barrio Amón* ☎ *2256–3412* ⊕ *www.galerianamu.com* ☉ *Mon.–Sat. 9–6:30, Sun. 1–5. Closed Sun., May–Dec.*

SOUVENIRS

Calle Nacional de Artesanía y Pintura (*National Street of Artisanry and Painting*). Some 100 souvenir vendors congregate in a block-long covered walkway on the west side of the Plaza de la Democracia. As you approach, the whole affair looks like a string of metal shacks, but some of the sellers offer bargains in hammocks, wood carvings, and clothing. ⊠ *C. 13, Avdas. Ctl.–2, western side of Plaza de la Democracia* ☉ *Mon.–Sat. 9–5.*

Hotel Don Carlos. The gift shop at the Hotel Don Carlos has a good selection of popular souvenirs and CDs of Costa Rican music. ⊠ *Hotel Don Carlos, C. 9 and Avda. 9, Barrio Amón* ☎ *2221–6707* ☉ *Daily 9–5.*

La Casona. Dozens of souvenir vendors set up shop on the two floors of La Casona, in a rickety, old downtown mansion that dates from 1906. It's much like a flea market, and a fun place to browse. ⊠ *C. 2, Avdas. Ctl.–1, Barrio El Carmen* ☎ *2222–7999* ☉ *Daily 9:30–6.*

La Traviata. The small shop off the lobby of the National Theater has a terrific selection of thespian-themed postcards, tote bags, and glassware. ⊠ *Teatro Nacional, Plaza de la Cultura, Barrio La Soledad* ☎ *2010–1118* ⊕ *www.latraviata.co.cr* ☉ *Mon.–Sat. 9–5 and before evening performances and during intermission.*

Mercado Central. This maze of passageways is where the average Costa Rican comes to stock up on day-to-day necessities, but a few stalls of interest to tourists congregate near the entrances. ⊠ *Bordered by Avdas. Ctl.–1 and Cs. 6–8, Barrio La Merced* ☉ *Mon.–Sat. 6–6.*

Museo del Oro Precolombino. The museum-shop concept barely exists here, but the shop at the entrance of the Museo del Oro Precolombino is the exception. Look for a great selection of pre-Columbian-theme jewelry, art, exclusively designed T-shirts, coin key chains, notebooks, and mouse pads. ⊠ *C. 5, Avdas. Ctl.–2, Barrio La Soledad* ☎ *2243–4202* ☉ *Daily 9:15–5.*

AIRPORT SOUVENIR SHOPS

If you really didn't have time to shop, never fear. Aeropuerto Internacional Juan Santamaría has three noteworthy souvenir shops—**Britt Shop Costa Rica**, **Travel Zone**, and **Green Trails**—for those last-minute purchases. Choose from various blends of coffee ($5 per pound) and such merchandise as hand-carved bowls and jewelry, aromatherapy candles, and banana-paper stationery. There's nary another store in the country carrying such a variety all in one place. The catch is that the airport shops charge U.S. prices.

3

Continued on page 128

LAST-MINUTE SOUVENIR SHOPPING

by Holly K. Sonneland

San José's markets can be crowded, but they're great fun for the savvy shopper. There are plenty of Costa Rican souvenirs for every pocketbook, and the city's bustling downtown is compact enough to make it easy to visit a few markets in a day . . . or even an afternoon. It's a great way to explore the city and take care of last-minute gift shopping.

Some markets have a mishmash of items, whereas others are more specialized. Pick up cigars or peruse antiques in the back of the sleepy La Casona building downtown, or head over to the strip of covered traveler-friendly souvenir stands by Plaza de la Democracia to browse the artsy wares. Festive fake flora in glittery, tropical blue, green, and orange hues can be found at the permanent artisan bazaars.

For a lively experience, head to the gritty and labyrinthine Mercado Central edifice right on Avenida Central where you can jostle among working-class Ticos as you pick up an Imperial beer logo–emblazoned muscle T-shirt or a homemade herbal love potion. Keep a tight hold on your bag, and have fun practicing your Spanish with the vendors.

GREAT GIFT IDEAS

Costa Rica's souvenirs pop with bright color and have that distinct *pura vida* (pure life) flair.

COFFEE: The authentic modern-day Costa Rica souvenir, not to mention most appreciated back home. Load up on whole bean (*grano entero*), or, if you must get ground (*molido*), buy the *puro*, otherwise it might have pre-added sugar. Café Britt is the country's most famous brand (₡2,500/lb).

MAYAN OCARINAS (₡2,500–₡7,000) Calling the ocarina two-faced would be an insult, but only because you wouldn't be giving it nearly enough credit. The Mayan resonant vessel flutes depict over a half-dozen animal faces when flipped around and were often given as gifts to travelers by the Chorotega indigenous group in northwestern Guanacaste.

HAMMOCKS: Swinging in one of these is the official posture of *pura vida*. Structured hammocks with wooden dowels on the ends (₡12,000 and up) are optimal, but dowel-less, cocoon-like hammocks (₡10,000 and up) are infinitely more compactable. Get a chair hammock (₡6,000) if you have limited hanging space back home.

COFFEE BREWERS: The original Costa Rican coffeemaker is called a *chorreador*. It's a simple wooden stand that's fitted with cloth sock-like filters. Finely ground coffee is dumped in the sock, and hot water is filtered into the mug beneath. Unadorned ones to sleek cherry wood cost around ₡5,000. Don't forget to buy extra sock filters (₡250).

OXCARTS: From the Sarchí region, the oxcart has become Costa Rica's most iconic craftsman artifact. Full-size ones can run a few hundred dollars, and many dealers can arrange to have them shipped for you. There's also a coffee table-size version (₡7,000) or, better yet, an oxcart napkin holder (₡1,500).

LOCAL LIBATIONS: If you don't have room for a six-pack, be sure to take home what is probably the world's best beer label, Imperial, on a stein or T-shirt (both ₡2,500). Or, snag a bottle of Costa Rica's signature sugarcane liquor, *guaro*, most commonly sold under the Cacique brand.

JEWELRY: Go for oversized wooden hoop earrings (₡3,000), wire-wrought gold and silver baubles (₡3,500), or plaster-molded earrings adorned with toucans, frogs, and pineapples (₡1,500). Jewelry made from carved-out coco shells are popular, too.

TROPICAL WOODS AND PAPERS: Sleek mango-wood vases (₡8,250), inlaid rosewood cutting boards (₡8,000), and hand-painted rum wood mugs (₡3,850) are among the many elegant woodworks here. There are also scratch-and-sniff writing materials that would make Willy Wonka proud, with banana, mango, lemon, and coffee-scented (sorry, no schnozberry) stationery sets (₡3,700).

BORUCA CEREMONIAL MASKS: The Boruca people, from southern Costa Rica and one of the country's last active indigenous groups, don these masks in their annual end-of-the-year festival, Dansa de los Diablitos (Dance of the Devils). It's an animistic production that depicts the avenging of the people for the decimation wrought by the conquistadors. Cheaper imitations abound, but Galería NAMU has the best—and most authentic—selection (₡65,000 to ₡100,000).

FOLKLORIC DRESSES AND SHIRTS: While they're often only pulled out on national holidays like Independence Day, a flounced dress (₡8,000 and up) or pinafore (₡5,000) might be just the kitschy gift you're looking for. Ranchero-style shirts (₡8,000) and straw hats (₡2,000) are also an option.

MACHETES: Knives and machetes are commonly used in the country's rural jungle areas and happily sold in leather slings to travelers (₡7,000). Also, knives (₡2,000–3,000) and other items, like frogs and butterflies made out of colored resin, might not be considered traditional but represent the Rastafarian side of the country. Be aware, weapons are not welcome in carry-on luggage on planes.

* All prices listed in colones

SAN JOSÉ MARKETS AND SHOPS

San José's navigable city center, and its proximity to the airport, make it the perfect last-minute shopping spot.

MERCADO CENTRAL

This market is geared towards locals and has some of the lowest prices anywhere. Here you can visit flower and medicinal herb (of dubious medicinal properties) shops not found in other markets. ⊠ *Avenidas Central and 1, Calles 6 and 8* ⊗ *Mon.–Sat. 6–6.*

LA CASONA

Souvenirs and tobacco products abound in this rambling, two-story building. At the far eastern end, go up the back stairs to the discount room, where regular items are discounted 25%–30%. Also upstairs is José "Chavo" Navarro's antique shop. ⊠ *Calle Central, between Avenidas Central and 1* ☎ *2222–7999* ⊗ *9:30–6.*

GALERÍA NAMU

Almost inarguably the best—and, importantly, the only free-trade—store selling indigenous artwork and handcrafts. Owner Aisling French and her staff have developed extensive ties with the Costa Rica's few remaining indig-

Shopping for coffee at Mercado Central.

enous peoples, bringing their top-notch artisanship to the city. In particular, NAMU sells the highest quality Bribrí ceremonial masks in the country, and has recently developed ties with the Wounan people in Panama, who produce museum-quality chunga palm baskets. ⊠ *Avenida 7, between Calles 5 and 7 (across from Alliance Française)* ☎ *2256–3412* ⊗ *Mon.–Sat. 9–6:30; closed Sun., May–Nov.*

CALLE NACIONAL DE ARTESANÍA Y PINTURA

This strip of stands across the Plaza de la Democracia from the National Museum is the most traveler-oriented market. Vendors also don't pay taxes here, so while some items (bulk coffee) are more expensive, others (choreadores) are actually cheaper than they are in Mercado Central. Hammocks are at the far north end, and Stand 82 has some of the best woodworks, along with Stands 25 and 66. Custom-made earrings are at Stand 40. ⊠ *Calle 13, between Avenidas Central and 2* ⊗ *Mon.–Sat. 9–5.*

KIOSCO SJO

This stylish shop at the entrance to the hip Kalú restaurant proffers locally made woodwork, fabrics, and ceramics, all crafted with a modern touch. ⊠ *Calle 7 and Avenida 11, Barrio Amón.* ☎ *2221–2018.* ⊗ *Mon.–Tues. noon–7, Wed.–Fri. noon–8, Sat. 10–8.*

SHOPPING KNOW-HOW

Colorful clay piggy banks

MAKING A DEAL

Bargaining isn't the sport it is in other countries, and if Tico vendors do bargain, it's often only with travelers who expect it. Before you try to strike a deal, know that Ticos are not confrontational, and haggling, even if not ill-intended, will come off as rude.

Your best bet for getting a deal is to buy in bulk, or simply suggest you'll come back later and walk away. If the vendors really want to lower the price, they'll call you back. If you're buying a single item, you can ask a vendor to offer you a lower price once, at most twice, but don't push it further.

Costa Ricans are painfully polite and are particularly fond of terms of endearment, and it's worth it to indulge in the gentility when talking with market vendors. If you're comfortable enough with your Tico Spanish, or *pachuco*, use the terms in return. For example, Ticos employ a whole arsenal of royal-themed lingo: *rey* and *reina*, or king and queen, are ubiq-

uitous forms of address, especially with middle-aged Ticos, although *reina* is more common than *rey*. You can easily use a "*Gracias, mi reina,*" to the (female) vendor who's just given you a good price, but "*¿Cómo está mi rey?*" to a 20-something male vendor sounds a little strange. That being said, if you're a 20-something female shopper, be prepared to hear "*¿En cómo puedo servirle mi reina?*" literally, "How can I serve you my queen?" (said endearingly, not lecherously) from every other 50-year-old vendor whose stand you pass. *Regalar*, a verb that literally means "to gift," can be used to ask a vendor to hand you the item that you want to buy (*Puede regalarme esa bolsa verde, porfa?* I'll take that green bag, please?) or to cut you a deal (*Me la regala en tres mil?* Can you sell it to me for three thousand [colones]?)

Of course, if your Spanish is rusty, smiling always helps.

■ TIP→ While most of the shops in these markets take credit cards, vendors will be more likely to cut you a deal if you pay in cash.

PLAYING IT SAFE

Petty crime is on the rise in Costa Rica, but that shouldn't keep you from exploring the markets. It's important to note that what were once recommended precautions are now strongly advised. Keep cash in breast pockets and leave credit cards and important documents in the hotel. Also leave behind jewelry and fancy gear, especially cameras, that will make you stand out. (The lighting in the markets—all of them indoor—is very poor, and photos inevitably don't turn out anyway.) Most of the markets, like the rest of the city, are generally safe during the day but best avoided in the evening.

Ceremonial mask from Namu Gallery

NORTH AND EAST OF DOWNTOWN

BOOKS AND MAGAZINES

Librería Internacional. The city's largest bookstore evokes that Barnes & Noble ambience, though on a much smaller scale. It stocks English translations of Latin American literature, as well as myriad coffee-table books on Costa Rica. ☒ *Plaza Antares, Blvd. Dent and Rotonda La Bandera, Barrio Dent* ☎ *2253–9553* ⊕ *www.libreriainternacional.com.*

CRAFTS

Kiosco SJO. Ensconced inside Barrio Amón's trendy Kalú restaurant, equally trendy Kiosco SJO proffers a good selection of locally made woodwork, fabrics, and ceramics. ☒ *Kalú, C. 7 and Avda. 11, Barrio Amón* ☎ *2221–2081* ⊕ *www.kioscosjo.com* ⊗ *Mon. and Tues. noon–7, Wed.–Fri. noon–8, Sat. 10–8.*

Mi Pueblo Verde. This is a standout among the Moravia shops for its fine carvings made from native *cocobolo* and *guápinol* wood. The salad bowls are especially unusual in their design. ☒ *50 m north of Colegio María Inmaculada, Moravia* ☎ *2235–5742* ⊗ *Mon.–Sat. 9:30–7, Sun. 10–6.*

FARMERS' MARKET

Feria Verde. It's a tad out of the way, but just up the street from the Hotel Aranjuez is one of the city's best Saturday farmers' markets. Stock up on organic fruits and veggies and take in the local scene. For something tropical, try some coconut milk—you'll get a coconut whacked in half by a machete and can sip the water through a straw. ☒ *North end of C. 19, 150 m north of Hotel Aranjuez, then downhill to the left, Barrio Aranjuez* ⊗ *Sat. 7–noon.*

SOUVENIRS

Artesanías Zurquí. You'll find a well-rounded selection of ceramics, wood, and leather at Artesanías Zurquí. ☒ *50 m north of Colegio María Inmaculada, Moravia* ☎ *2240–5342* ⊗ *Mon.–Sat. 8–7, Sun. 9–6.*

Mundo de Recuerdos. If you can't find it at Mundo de Recuerdos, it probably doesn't exist. Here's the largest of the Moravia shops with simply everything—at least of standard souvenir fare—you could ask for under one roof. ☒ *Across from Colegio María Inmaculada, Moravia* ☎ *2240–8990* ⊗ *Mon.–Sat. 9–6, Sun. 9–5.*

WEST OF DOWNTOWN

CRAFTS

Hotel Grano de Oro. The small gift shop at the Hotel Grano de Oro has an impressive selection of carvings and jewelry on hand. ☒ *C. 30, Avdas. 2–4, Paseo Colón* ☎ *2255–3322* ⊗ *Daily 2:30–9:30.*

THE CENTRAL VALLEY

WELCOME TO THE CENTRAL VALLEY

TOP REASONS TO GO

★ **Avian adventures:** Flock to Tapantí National Park to see emerald toucanets, resplendent quetzals (if you're lucky), and nearly every species of Costa Rican hummingbird. Rancho Naturalista is the bird lover's hotel of choice.

★ **Coffee:** Get up close and personal with harvesting and processing on coffee tours at two of the valley's many plantations: Café Britt and Doka Estate.

★ **Poás Volcano:** Peer right down into the witches' cauldron that is the Poás Volcano.

★ **The Orosi Valley:** Spectacular views and quiet, bucolic towns make this area a great day trip or overnight from San José.

★ **Rafting the Pacuare River:** Brave the rapids as you descend through tropical forest on one of the best rivers in Central America.

1 West of San José. The communities immediately west of San José are the capital's booming, upscale suburbs. Things turn more pastoral the farther west you go, and you'll find one of the country's best craft communities, Sarchí, and some luxurious countryside lodges near Grecia and San Ramón. Atenas, a thriving agricultural center known for its coffee plantations and livestock, offers a glimpse into a quintessential Costa Rican town. Heading farther west towards the Central Pacific coast, Carara National Park is home to an impressive collection of plants and animals.

2 North of San José. Coffee farms and small valley towns dominate the area north of San José. Their beautiful hotels attract visitors on their first and last nights in the country. Coffee plantations Café Britt and Doka Estate are both here, as is the international airport, near Alajuela. North of Alajuela, Poás Volcano's

Santa Clara

32

0 ——— 10 mi
0 ——— 15 km

CORDILLERA CENTRAL

Turrialba Volcano
Irazú Volcano
Potrero Cerrado
Turrialba
Juan Viñas
Cartago
Paraíso
Orosi Valley
Río Macho
Tapantí National Park
Tres de Junio
Salsipuedes
CR2
Villa Mills

Guayabo National Monument
Jabillos
Pavones
La Suiza
Tuis
Bajo Pacuare
Moravia
Pacuare River
Río Pacuare

CARTAGO

TALAMANCA

GETTING ORIENTED

The Central Valley is something of a misnomer, and its Spanish name, the *meseta central* (central plateau) isn't entirely accurate either. The two contiguous mountain ranges that run the length of the country—the Cordillera Central range (which includes Poás, Barva, Irazú, and Turrialba volcanoes) to the north and the Cordillera de Talamanca to the south—don't quite line up in the middle, leaving a trough between them. The "valley" floor is 914 to 1,524 meters (3,000 to 5,000 feet) above sea level. In the valley, your view toward the coasts is obstructed by the two mountain ranges. But from a hillside hotel, your view of San José and the valley can be spectacular.

turquoise crater lake and steaming main crater make it many visitors' favorite volcano stop.

3 East of San José. The less visited eastern Central Valley holds Cartago, older than San José, with a couple of historic attractions. Irazú is Costa Rica's tallest volcano. On a clear day you can see both the Atlantic and Pacific oceans from its peak. The nearby Orosi Valley is an

often overlooked beauty. The drive into the valley is simply gorgeous, and a tranquil way to spend a day. Birding destination Tapantí National Park is at the southern edge of the valley. Rafting trips on the Pacuare and Reventazón are based in bustling, growing Turrialba. The nearby Guayabo National Monument, ruins of a city deserted in AD 1400, is Costa Rica's only significant archaeological site.

CARARA NATIONAL PARK

One of the last remnants of an ecological transition zone between Costa Rica's drier northwest and more humid southwest, Carara National Park holds a tremendous collection of plants and animals.

Squeezed into its 47 square km (18 square miles) is a mixed habitat of evergreen and deciduous forest, river, lagoon, and marshland. Much of the park's terrain is blanketed with dramatic primary forest, massive trees laden with vines and epiphytes. This is a birder's and plant lover's haven. The sparse undergrowth makes terrestrial wildlife and ground birds easier to see. The most famous denizens—apart from the crocodiles in the adjoining Río Tárcoles—are the park's colorful and noisy scarlet macaws, which always travel in pairs. An oxbow lake (a U-shaped body of water that was once part of a river) adds an extra wildlife dimension, attracting turtles and waterfowl—and the crocodiles that dine on them. Bring lots of drinking water; this park can get very hot and humid. *(See page 157 for more information.)*

BEST TIME TO GO

Dry season, January to April, is the best time to visit. The trails get very muddy during the rainy season and may even close in the wettest months. This small park can feel crowded at the trailheads, so arrive early and walk far. Bird-watchers can call the day before to arrange early admission.

FUN FACT

The crowning glory of Carara is the successful conservation program that has doubled its scarlet macaw population. You can't miss these long-tailed, noisy parrots—look for streaks of brilliant blue and red in the sky.

BEST WAYS TO EXPLORE

BIRD-WATCHING

With more than 350 species recorded here, Carara is on every bird-watcher's must-visit list. It's an especially good place to see elusive ground birds, such as antpittas (a small ground-dwelling bird that eats ants), early in the morning and late in the afternoon. Around the lake and in the marshy areas, you may also spot roseate spoonbills, northern jacanas, and stately boat-billed herons. The park's most famous fliers are the scarlet macaws. Once almost absent from the area, a decades-long conservation program has revitalized the local population.

HIKING

The best and really only way to explore this park is on foot. Rubber boots or waterproof shoes are essential in the rainy season, and a good idea in the drier months as well. Trails are well marked and maintained but the ground is often muddy—this is rain forest, after all. The shortest—and most popular—loop trail can be done in only 15 minutes. But if you venture farther afield, you'll quickly be on your own, except for the wildlife you're bound to encounter. The longer trail that connects with the Quebrada Bonita loop takes about 90 minutes to hike. There is also a short wheelchair-accessible route that starts at the main entrance. It goes deep enough into the forest to give visitors a sense of its drama and diversity.

WILDLIFE-WATCHING

Carara is famous for an amazing variety of wildlife, given its relatively small area. Keep alert (and quiet) while walking and you'll have a good chance of spotting big and small lizards, coatimundis (a member of the raccoon family), and sloths. You're almost guaranteed to see white-faced monkeys and, with luck, howler and spider monkeys, too. You may even surprise a nine-banded armadillo snuffling along the ground or a northern tamandua (anteater) patrolling low branches.

TOP REASONS TO GO

Birds

With a varied habitat that attracts both forest and water birds, Carara is a treasure trove for birders. Even if you're not a birder, you'll get a thrill hearing the raucous crowing of beautiful scarlet macaws as they soar over the forest canopy.

The Jungle

The forest here is simply magnificent. Even if you don't spot a single bird or animal, you will experience the true meaning of jungle. Carara has one of the most diverse collections of trees in the country. Breathe deeply, be alert to the symphony of forest sounds, and bask in a totally natural world.

Wildlife

For most visitors, wildlife is the park's main attraction. You can count on seeing monkeys and lots of lizards as you walk the trails. Although they are a little harder to spot, look for anteaters, sloths, and armadillos.

POÁS VOLCANO

Towering north of Alajuela, the verdant Poás Volcano is covered with a quilt of farms and topped by a dark green shawl of cloud forest.

That pastoral scene disappears once you get to the summit, and you gaze into the steaming, bubbling crater with smoking fumaroles and a gurgling, gray-turquoise sulfurous lake. You'll swear you're peering over the edge of a giant witches' cauldron. That basin, 2 km (1 mile) in diameter and nearly 305 meters (1,000 feet) deep, is thought to be the largest active volcanic crater in the world.

Poás is one of Costa Rica's five active volcanoes—it has erupted 40 times since the early 1800s—and is one of those rare places that permit you to see volcanic energy this close with minimal risk to your safety. Authorities closely monitor Poás's activity following several eruptions in March 2006, the first significant increase in activity since 1994. The most recent activity took place in October 2012 and involved phreatic eruptions and landslides. Access is normally open, but park officials close the route up here on those occasions of any activity they deem "irregular." *(See page 178 for more information.)*

BEST TIME TO GO

The peak is frequently shrouded in mist, and you might see little beyond the lip of the crater. Be patient and wait awhile, especially if some wind is blowing—the clouds can disappear quickly. Aim to get here before 10 am. The earlier in the day you go, the better the visibility.

FUN FACT

Forgot your umbrella? (It gets wet up here.) Duck under a *sombrilla de pobre* (poor man's umbrella) plant. These giant leaves can grow to diameters of 1 to 1½ meters (4 to 5 feet)— plenty big enough to shelter a few hikers caught out in the rain.

BEST WAYS TO EXPLORE

BIRD-WATCHING

Although birding can be a little frustrating here because of cloud and mist, more than 330 bird species call Poás home. One of the most comical birds you'll see in Costa Rica is usually spotted foraging in plain sight on the ground: the big-footed finch whose oversized feet give it a clownish walk. Its cousin, the yellow-thighed finch, is easy to recognize by its bright yellow, er . . . thighs. Arrive early and bird around the gate before the park opens, and stop along the road to the visitor center wherever you see a likely birding area. In the underbrush you may find spotted wood-quail or the elusive, buffy-crowned wood-partridge. The trees along the road are a favorite haunt of both black-and-yellow and long-tailed silky flycatchers.

HIKING

From the summit, two trails head into the forest. The second trail, on the right just before the crater, winds through a thick mesh of shrubs and dwarf trees to the eerie but beautiful Botos Lake (**Laguna Botos**), which occupies an extinct crater. It takes 30 minutes to walk here and back, but you'll be huffing and puffing if you're not used to this altitude, almost 2,743 meters (9,000 feet) above sea level.

VOLCANIC TIPS

A paved road leads all the way from Alajuela to Poás's 2,708-meter (8,885-foot) summit. No one is allowed to venture into the crater or walk along its edge. ■TIP→ Take periodic breaks from viewing: Step back at least every 10 minutes, so that the sulfur fumes don't overcome you. Be sure to bring a sweater or a jacket—it can be surprisingly chilly and wet up here.

TOP REASONS TO GO

A+ Facilities
You're on your own in many Costa Rican national parks, most lacking in facilities. This wheelchair-accessible park is a pleasant exception, with an attractive visitor center containing exhibits, a cafeteria, gift shop, and restrooms.

Lava and Ash
"Up close and personal with nature" takes on a whole new meaning here. Costa Rica forms part of the Pacific Rim's so-called Ring of Fire, and a visit to the volcano's summit gives you a close-up view of a region of the earth that is still in formation.

Location, Location, Location
Poás's proximity to San José, the western Central Valley, and many destinations in this chapter makes it an easy half-day trip. Mix and match a volcano visit with several other area attractions.

More Than a Volcano
The park is not just about its namesake volcano. A few kilometers of hiking trails wind around the summit and let you take in the cloud forest's lichens, ferns, and bromeliads.

IRAZÚ VOLCANO

The word *Irazú* is likely a corruption of Iztaru, a long-ago indigenous community whose name translated as "hill of thunder." The name is apt.

Volcán Irazú, as it's known in Spanish, is considered active, but the gases and steam that billow from fumaroles on the northwestern slope are rarely visible from the peak above the crater lookouts. The mountain's first recorded eruption took place in 1723; the most recent was a series of eruptions that lasted from 1963 to 1965. Boulders and mud rained down on the countryside, damming rivers and causing serious floods, and the volcano dumped up to 20 inches of ash on sections of the Central Valley.

When conditions are clear, you can see the chartreuse lake inside the Cráter Principal. The stark moonscape of the summit contrasts markedly with the lush vegetation of Irazú's lower slopes, home to porcupines, armadillos, coyotes, and mountain hares. Listen for the low-pitched, throaty song of the *yigüirro*, or clay-color thrush, Costa Rica's national bird. Its call is most pronounced just before the start of the rainy season. *(See page 183 for more information.)*

BEST TIME TO GO

Early morning, especially in the January-through-April dry season, affords the best views, both of the craters and the surrounding countryside. Clouds move in by late morning. Wear warm, waterproof clothing if you get here that early; although rare, temperatures have dropped down close to freezing around dawn.

FUN FACT

Irazú has dumped a lot of ash over the centuries. The most recent eruptive period began on the day that John F. Kennedy arrived in Costa Rica in March 1963. The "ash storm" that ensued lasted on and off for two years.

BEST WAYS TO EXPLORE

BIRD-WATCHING

The road to Irazú provides some of the best roadside birding opportunities in the country, especially on a weekday when there isn't a constant parade of cars and buses heading up to the crater. Some of the most fruitful areas are on either side of the bridges you'll pass over. Reliable bird species that inhabit these roadsides are acorn and hairy woodpeckers; the brilliant flame-throated warbler; and, buzzing around blossoms, the fiery-throated, green violet-ear; and (aptly named) volcano hummingbirds. Once past the main entrance, there are also plenty of opportunities to stop and bird-watch roadside. Look for volcano juncos on the ground and slaty flowerpiercers visiting flowering shrubs.

HIKING

Even before you get to the main entrance, check out the park's Prusia Sector, which has hiking trails that pass through majestic oak and pine forests and picnic areas. They're popular with Tico families on weekends, so if you want the woods to yourself, come on a weekday. Trails in the park are well marked; avoid heading down any paths marked with *"paso restringido"* ("passage restricted") signs.

VOLCANIC TIPS

A paved road leads all the way to the summit, where a small coffee shop sells hot beverages, and a persistent pair of coatis cruise the picnic tables for handouts. (Please resist the urge to feed them!) The road to the top climbs past vegetable fields, pastures, and native oak forests. You pass through the villages of Potrero Cerrado and San Juan de Chicuá before reaching the summit's bleak but beautiful main crater.

TOP REASONS TO GO

Easy to Get to
Irazú's proximity to San José and the entire eastern Central Valley makes it an easy half-day or day trip. Public transportation from the capital, frequently a cumbersome option to most of the country's national parks, is straightforward.

The View
How many places in the world let you peer directly into the crater of an active volcano? Costa Rica offers you two: here at Irazú and at Poás Volcano. Poás's steaming cauldron is spookier, but Irazú's crater lake with colors that change according to the light is nonetheless impressive.

More Views
"On a clear day, you can see forever," goes the old song from the musical of the same name. Irazú is one of the few places in Costa Rica that lets you glimpse both the Pacific and Atlantic (Caribbean) oceans at once. "Clear" is the key term here: clouds frequently obscure the view. Early morning gives you your best shot.

ECO-LODGES IN THE CENTRAL VALLEY

Suburbia oozes out with each passing year, eating up once-idyllic Central Valley land, but it's still surprisingly easy to find vast undeveloped stretches, even in the metro area.

You'd never know it driving the highway west from San José through the valley of shopping malls and car dealerships, but Costa Rica's Central Valley is home to an ample amount of greenery. Three of the country's five active volcanoes (Poás, Irazú, and Turrialba) loom here. Suburbia gives way to farmland above Escazú and Santa Ana, and the rolling hills are perfect for tranquil day hikes. A terrific selection of country lodges populates the hills north of Alajuela and Heredia, and a stay in one of them is certain to give you that "so close (to the international airport) and yet so far" convenience. Tapantí National Park, in the far eastern sector of the valley, contains a real live cloud forest—it's not quite Monteverde, but it is far easier to get to—and Guayabo National Monument nearby is home to Costa Rica's only true archaeological ruins. The medium-size city of Turrialba has fast become the country's white-water center. And the Orosi Valley defines pastoral tranquility.

GOOD PRACTICES

Make a point of getting out and meeting the local people here in the Central Valley. We'd argue that the tidy towns in this region are Costa Rica at its most "authentic," its most "Tico." Folks here still greet you with a hearty "Buenos días" each day. Respond in kind.

Consider taking public transportation in the Central Valley. Communities here are bunched close enough together to be well served by public buses, and taxis can fill in the gaps. Plus, as development increases in the valley, managing your own vehicle here begins to resemble city driving.

TOP ECO-LODGES IN THE CENTRAL VALLEY

FINCA ROSA BLANCA COFFEE PLANTATION RESORT, HEREDIA

The hotel on this 8-acre working coffee plantation just outside Heredia is one of just a handful of properties in the country to have achieved the coveted "Five Leaves" status in the Certification for Sustainable Tourism. In addition to all the amenities you'd expect from one of the Central Valley's most sumptuous accommodations, you can also take Finca Rosa Blanca's unique sustainability tour for a behind-the-scenes look at what a hotel can do to be more eco- and community-friendly. What other tour in Costa Rica lets you take in the workings of the laundry room, the solar panels, and the compost pile? *(Full hotel review on page 176.)*

RANCHO NATURALISTA, TURRIALBA

Some 430 species of birds live on the property—few lodgings can make such a claim, let alone one so close to the metropolitan area. But the fittingly named Rancho Naturalista near Turrialba has fast become the birding center of the Central Valley. From the bird checklist in the welcome packet in your room to the resident professional birding guide to the delightful deck where you can continue to bird-watch even after trekking around the grounds for the day, this is one of Costa Rica's premier locales for bird-watchers of all experience levels. *(Full hotel review on page 194.)*

XANDARI RESORT & SPA, ALAJUELA

Xandari is a favorite of honeymooners who might not be aware of its environmental stewardship. The 40-acre property in the hills above Alajuela maintains an active program of recycling and uses on-site, organically grown fruits and vegetables. The hotel is also turning back a portion of its coffee plantation to tree cover, which has been set aside as a nature reserve. Coffee is still cultivated on the remainder of the plantation and ends up in your morning cup or as part of the coffee-scrub spa treatment. *(Full hotel review on page 165.)*

COMMUNITY OUTREACH

A glance at high schools around the Central Valley reveals a growing number of outdoor eco-theme wall paintings, all part of an ever-expanding annual Environmental Mural Contest. The name says it all: students from area schools compete each year to design and create original murals conveying environmental messages. The works represent combined efforts of schools' art and biology departments, with students devoting an average of four months from the project's start to finish. Many of the murals measure 50 square meters, or around 540 square feet. The competition is designed to foster artistic skills, teamwork, and, of course, environmental awareness among students and faculty who take part. The contest is directed by the nonprofit FUNDECOR foundation, a local nongovernmental organization whose objective is to put the brakes on deforestation and promote environmental consciousness. Local businesses support the effort.

Updated by
Jeffrey Van
Fleet

San José sits in a mile-high mountain valley ringed by volcanoes whose ash has fertilized the soil and turned the region into Costa Rica's historic breadbasket. This will always be the land that coffee built, and the small cities of the Central Valley exhibit a tidiness and prosperity you don't see in the rest of the country. The valley is chock-full of activities and is Costa Rica at its most *típico*, giving you the best sense of what makes the country tick.

You can't find a more ideal climate than out here in the valley. When people refer to Costa Rica's proverbial "eternal spring," they're talking about this part of the country, which lacks the oppressive seasonal heat and rain of other regions. It's no wonder the Central Valley has drawn a burgeoning number of North American and European retirees.

There's no shortage of terrific lodgings out here—everything from family-run boutique hotels to the big international chains are yours for the night. It used to be that everyone stayed in San José and took in the various attractions in the Central Valley on day trips. With the good selection of quality accommodation out here, why not base yourself in the Central Valley, and make San José your day trip instead?

PLANNING

WHEN TO GO
HIGH SEASON: MID-DECEMBER TO APRIL
The Central Valley's elevation keeps temperatures pleasant and spring-like year-round, slightly warmer to the west and slightly cooler to the east. Turrialba and the Orosi Valley represent a transition zone between the valley and the Caribbean slope; expect slightly higher temperatures there. December and January kick off the dry season with sunny days and brisk nights. February, March, and April warm up considerably. Some hotels here keep rates constant throughout the year; others follow high-season/low-season fluctuations.

LOW SEASON: MAY TO MID-NOVEMBER

The rainy season moves in gradually with afternoon showers from May through July. August becomes wetter, and September and October can mean prolonged downpours. The valley's western sector—Alajuela, San Antonio de Belén, Escazú, and Santa Ana—always catches a tad less rain than their eastern counterparts do.

SHOULDER SEASON: MID-NOVEMBER TO MID-DECEMBER

Rains start to wind down by mid-November, and the month before Christmas is a terrific time to enjoy the Central Valley at its most lush and green, and before the big influx of tourists arrives. (As an added bonus, the coffee harvest is under way in earnest in this part of the country, too, always a bustling, fascinating spectacle.)

PLANNING YOUR TIME

You could spend an entire week here without getting bored, but if you have only a week or two in Costa Rica, we recommend a maximum of two days before heading to rain forests and beaches in other parts of the country. Spending a day after you arrive, then another day or two before you fly out gives you a taste of the region, breaks up the travel time, and makes your last day interesting, rather than spent in transit back to San José. The drive between just about any two points in the Central Valley is two hours or usually less, so it's ideal for short trips.

GETTING HERE AND AROUND

AIR TRAVEL

Although Aeropuerto Internacional Juan Santamaría is billed as San José's airport, it sits just outside the city of Alajuela. You can get taxis from the airport to any point in the Central Valley for $8 to $80. Some hotels arrange pickup.

BUS TRAVEL

Many visitors never consider taking a local bus to get around, but doing so puts you in close contact with locals—an experience you miss out on if you travel by taxi or tour bus. It's also cheap. Always opt for a taxi at night or when you're in a hurry.

CAR TRAVEL

All points in the western Central Valley can be reached by car. For San Antonio de Belén, Heredia, Alajuela, and points north of San José, turn right at the west end of Paseo Colón onto the Pan-American Highway (Autopista General Cañas). The eastern Central Valley is accessible from San José by driving east on Avenidas 2, then Central, through San Pedro, then following signs from the intersection to Cartago. To get to the Orosi Valley, head straight through Cartago, turn right at the Basílica de Los Angeles, and follow the signs to Paraíso. The road through Cartago and Paraíso continues east to Turrialba.

The best way to get around the Central Valley is by car. Most of the car-rental agencies in San José have offices at or near the airport in Alajuela. *They will deliver vehicles to many of the hotels listed in this chapter, except those in Turrialba and the Orosi Valley.*

TAXI TRAVEL

All Central Valley towns have taxis, which usually wait for fares along their central parks.

RESTAURANTS

Growing Escazú has become as metropolitan as San José and has the restaurant selection to prove it. Elsewhere, as befits this cradle of the country's tradition, typical Costa Rican cuisine still reigns.

HOTELS

Most international flights fly into Costa Rica in the evening and head out again early the next morning, meaning you likely have to stay your first and last nights in San José or nearby. Think of the Central Valley as "the nearby." For getting away from it all and still being close to the country's main airport, the lodgings around San José make splendid alternatives to staying in the city itself. It may pain you to tear yourself away from that beach villa or rain-forest lodge, but you can still come back to something distinctive here on your last night in Costa Rica. Small mom-and-pop places, sprawling coffee plantations, nature lodges, and hilltop villas with expansive views are some of your options. The large chains are here as well, but the real gems are the boutique hotels, many of which are family-run places and have unique designs that take advantage of exceptional countryside locations. Subtropical gardens are the norm, rather than the exception, and air-conditioning is usually not necessary. *Hotel reviews have been shortened. For full information, visit Fodors.com.*

WHAT IT COSTS IN DOLLARS			
$	**$$**	**$$$**	**$$$$**
Restaurants	under $10	$10–$15	$16–$25	over $25
Hotels	under $75	$75–$150	$151–$250	over $250

Restaurant prices are the average cost of a main course at dinner or, if dinner is not served, at lunch. Hotel prices are the lowest cost of a standard double room in high season.

WEST OF SAN JOSÉ

Believe it or not, as you drive west out of San José, the city's sprawling suburbs and industrial zones do eventually give way to arable land, much of which is occupied by coffee farms. Anchoring the western metro area are snazzy, posh Escazú and getting-snazzier-and-more-posh-all-the-time Santa Ana. Yet, not all has been malled over out here, and both communities remain proud of their histories and traditions. Keep heading west, though, and you'll leave Escazú and Santa Ana's commercialism behind: Grecia, San Ramón, Sarchí, and Atenas are, these days, far more típico Tico communities. Carara National Park, great for birding, is southwest of San José, on the way to the Central Pacific coast.

ESCAZÚ

5 km (3 miles) southwest of San José.

Costa Rica's wealthiest community and the Central Valley's most prestigious address, Escazú nevertheless mixes glamour with tradition, BMWs with oxcarts, trendy malls with farmers' markets, Louis Vuitton with burlap produce sacks. As you exit the highway and crest the first gentle hill, you might think you made a wrong turn and ended up in Southern California, but farther up you return to small-town Central America. Narrow roads wind their way up the steep slopes, past postage-stamp coffee fields and lengths of shoulder-to-shoulder, modest houses with tidy gardens and the occasional oxcart parked in the yard. Unfortunately, the area's stream of new developments and high-rises has steadily chipped away at the rural landscape—each year you have to climb higher to find the kind of scene that captured the attention of many a Costa Rican painter in the early 20th century. In their place are plenty of fancy homes and condos, especially in the San Antonio and San Rafael neighborhoods. Escazú's historic church faces a small plaza, surrounded in part by weathered adobe buildings. The town center is several blocks north of the busy road to Santa Ana, which is lined with a growing selection of restaurants, bars, and shops.

GETTING HERE AND AROUND

To drive to Escazú from San José, turn left at the western end of Paseo Colón, which ends at the Parque La Sabana. Take the first right, and get off the highway at the second exit. The off-ramp curves right, then sharply left; follow it about 1 km (½ mile), sticking to the main road, to El Cruce at the bottom of the hill (marked by a large Scotiabank). Continue through the traffic light for San Rafael addresses; turn right for the old road to Santa Ana. The trip takes about 20 minutes, much longer during rush hour. A steady stream of buses for Escazú runs from several stops around Terminal Coca-Cola in San José (✉ *Avdas. 1–3, Cs. 14–16*), with service from 5 am to 11 pm. ⚠ **Be careful: The Coca-Cola is a dicey part of downtown San José.**

ESSENTIALS

Bank/ATM Banco de Costa Rica ATM ✉ *125 m west of Municipalidad.*
Banco Nacional ✉ *Southwest side of central park* ☎ *2228–0009.*

Internet Bagelmen's ✉ *San Rafael de Escazú, 500 m southwest of Trejos Montealegre shopping center* ☎ *2228–4460* ⊕ *www.bagelmenscr.com.*
Internet CF ✉ *Northwest corner of central park, upstairs in Centro Comercial Escazú mall* ☎ *2289–5706.*

Medical Assistance Farmacia San Miguel ✉ *North side of central park* ☎ *2228–2339.* **Hospital CIMA** ✉ *Next to PriceSmart, just off the highway to Santa Ana, 12 km (7½ miles) west of downtown San José* ☎ *2208–1000* ⊕ *www.hospitalsanjose.net.*

Post Office Correos ✉ *100 m north of church.*

Taxis Coopetico ☎ *2224–7979.*

EXPLORING

FAMILY **Butterfly Kingdom.** Butterflies are the "livestock" at this working farm in the heart of Escazú, where caterpillars are raised and then exported in chrysalis form. A tour of the operation takes you through the stages of a butterfly's life. The highlight is the garden where fluttering butterflies surround you. Sunny days fuel the most activity among them; they are quieter if the day is overcast. Bilingual tours in English and Spanish are included in the admission price. ✉ *Bello Horizonte, 1 km (½ mile) south and 100 m west of Distribuidora Santa Bárbara* ☎ *2288–6667* ⊕ *www.butterflykingdom.net* ✆ *$12* ◷ *Tues.–Sat. 10–3:30.*

Iglesia San Miguel Arcángel (*Church of St. Michael the Archangel*).
According to tradition, ghosts and witches work their spells, good and bad, over Escazú. The founders of this haunted town fittingly chose the archangel Michael, reputed to have driven Satan from heaven, as their patron saint. The original church on this site dates from 1796, but earthquakes took their toll, as they have on so many historic sites throughout Costa Rica. A complete reconstruction was done in 1962, remaining as true as possible to the original design, but up to current earthquake building codes. The results are still impressive more than five decades later. A statue of St. Michael watches from the left side of the main altar. ✉ *central park* ☎ *2228–0635* ◷ *Mon. 8 am–7 pm, Tues.–Fri. 9 am–7 pm, Sat. noon–7 pm, Sun. 6 am–8 pm.*

SPORTS AND THE OUTDOORS

HIKING

High in the hills above Escazú is the tiny community of **San Antonio de Escazú,** famous for its annual oxcart festival held the second Sunday of March. The view from here—of nearby San José and distant volcanoes—is impressive by both day and night. If you head higher than San Antonio de Escazú, brace yourself for seemingly vertical roads that wind up into the mountains toward **Pico Blanco,** the highest point in the Escazú Cordillera, which is a half-day hike to ascend. Our preference is **San Miguel,** one peak east. Although you can hike these hills on your own, it is far safer to go with an outfitter.

Aventuras Pico Tours. The owner of Aventuras Pico Tours was the first Costa Rican to reach the summit of Everest, and can lead you on a variety of less daunting daylong hikes in the hills above town. ✉ *From the Church of San Antonio de Escazú, 300 m east, 1,800 m south, and 50 m east* ☎ *2289–6135* ⊕ *www.picotours.com.*

CITY OF WITCHES

During colonial days, Escazú was dubbed the City of Witches because many native healers lived in the area. Locals say that Escazú is still Costa Rica's most haunted community, home to witches who will tell your fortune or concoct a love potion for a small fee, but you'd be hard-pressed to spot them in the town's busy commercial district. Try a soccer field instead; the city's soccer team is christened Las Brujas ("the Witches"). You'll see a huge number of witch-on-a-broomstick decals affixed to vehicles here, too.

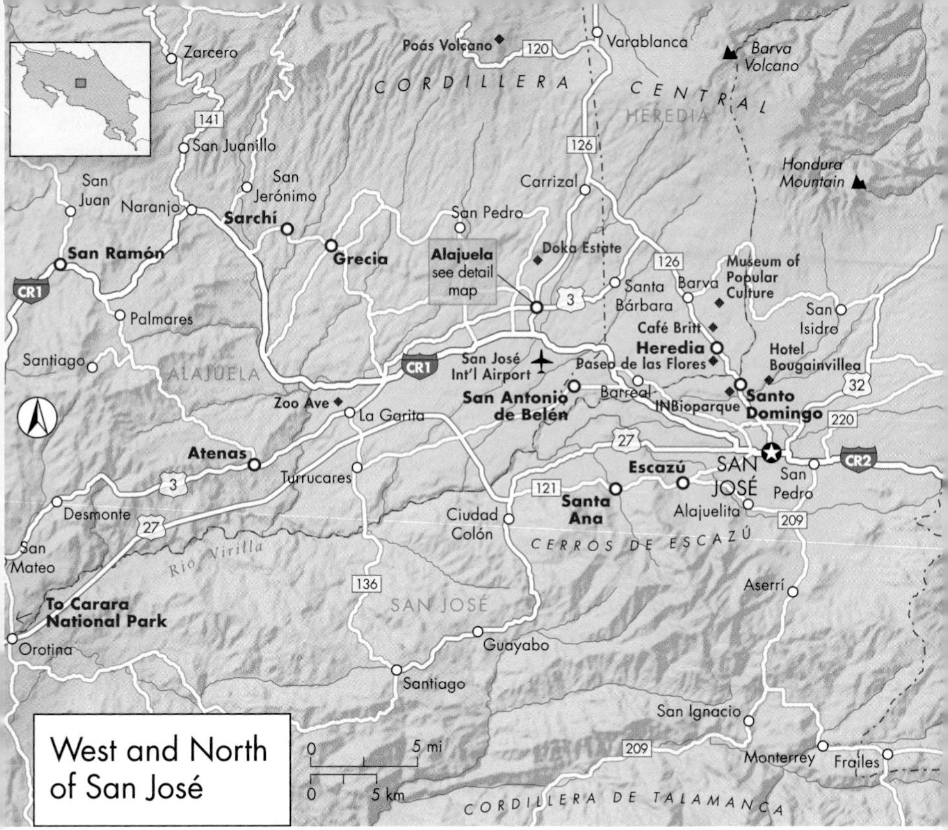

West and North of San José

WHERE TO EAT

$$ BARBECUE
🍴 **Barbecue Los Anonos.** For decades, Costa Ricans have flocked to Los Anonos to enjoy its family-friendly grill fest. The original dining room, a rustic collection of deep booths with wooden benches, has been expanded upon to add a more elegant space decorated with historic photos. The crowd tends toward families on weekend nights, whereas weekdays are busier during lunch, when business executives come for the economical meals. The best bet is the grilled meat, and there is plenty to choose from, including imported U.S. beef and less expensive Tico cuts. Fresh fish, shrimp, and half a dozen salads round out the choices. [$] *Average main: $13* ✉ *400 m west of Los Anonos Bridge* ☎ *2228–0180* ⏲ *Closed Mon.*

$ FRENCH
🍴 **Chez Christophe.** Escazú's very own French-style bistro makes a great place for a breakfast or lunch of sandwiches on baguettes or croissants—the ham or smoked salmon is especially *délicieux*. The pleasant patio has painted murals depicting French food scenes. Even if you don't dine here, stop by for the wonderful selection of French breads and pastries, baked fresh each day. The place closes at 7, so make it an early evening if you're interested in dinner. [$] *Average main: $9* ✉ *75 m south of Centro Comercial Paco* ☎ *2228–2512* ⏲ *Closed Mon.*

$$$$ FRENCH 🍴 **Le Monastère.** This monastery-themed formal restaurant high in the San Rafael hills has a great view of the Central Valley. The dining room is dressed up in antiques, with tables set for a five-course meal; waiters don short friar tunics over their standard black pants and white shirts, which makes the atmosphere too theatrical for some tastes, but the classic French dishes are outstanding. The more casual Cava Grill dining area serves platters of grilled meat. La Cava Bar, beneath the dining room, has tasty appetizers, and live music Thursday to Saturday, and is open into the wee hours. [$] *Average main: $28* ✉ *1½ km (1 mile) southwest of the Paco Shopping Center in San Rafael de Escazú* ✥ *Take old road west to Santa Ana, turn left at Paco and follow signs, always bearing right* ☎ *2228–8515* 🌐 *www.monastere-restaurant.com* ⏲ *Closed Sun. No lunch.*

$$ SPANISH 🍴 **Plaza España.** Generous portions of Spanish tapas and entrées draw diners to this whitewashed adobe house up the hill near San Antonio de Escazú. Wooden-bench tables are distributed along a wraparound porch with views of the Central Valley; inside, tables are arranged in small-to-medium rooms. Presentation isn't the strong suit here: straight-up good food is, as are reasonable prices. Start with a pitcher of sangria and begin sampling; the extensive menu includes dishes such as *tortilla Española* (Spanish omelet). [$] *Average main: $14* ✉ *Del Cruce del Barrio El Carmen, 100 m east and 50 m south, San Antonio de Escazú* ☎ *2228–1850* ⏲ *Closed Mon. No lunch Tues.*

$$$ INDIAN 🍴 **Taj Mahal.** This burst of northern Indian flavor is a real rarity in Central America. Richly swathed in warm fuchsias, red ochers, and golds, the mansion's dining area sprawls through a handful of small, intimate rooms and out to a gazebo in the tree-covered backyard. The price-to-portion ratio is a little high, particularly for North Americans used to good, cheap Indian food, but the sharp tandoori dishes, curries, and *biryanis* (seasoned rice dishes) are a welcome vacation from ubiquitous European and American fare. Vegetarians may swoon at the options. Helpful waiters, in black or maroon traditional Punjabi dress, are frank about recommendations. [$] *Average main: $19* ✉ *1 km (½ mile) west of Paco mall on old road to Santa Ana* ☎ *2228–0980* 🌐 *www.thetajmahalrestaurant.com* ⏲ *Closed Mon.*

WHERE TO STAY

$$ HOTEL 🏨 **Beacon Escazú.** Smack dab in the middle of town, this pleasant respite lets you leave the commotion of central Escazú behind. **Pros:** friendly, service-oriented staff; feels spacious and airy in spite of downtown location; parking beneath the building. **Cons:** so-so restaurant; on congested street in center of town. [$] *Rooms from: $97* ✉ *150 m west of central park* ☎ *2228–3110, 866/978–6168 in North America* 🌐 *www.mybeaconescazu.com* 🛏 *27 rooms* 🍽 *Breakfast.*

$$ HOTEL Fodor's Choice ★ 🏨 **Casa Cristal.** Perched on a hillside in Bello Horizonte, a residential neighborhood of Escazú, this starkly modern lodging offers amazing views of San José and the Central Valley. **Pros:** attentive staff; stupendous views; terrific rates for the offerings. **Cons:** difficult to find; a few rooms face toward the back and lack views. [$] *Rooms from: $99* ✉ *Bello Horizonte, 800 m southeast of Posada El Quijote* ☎ *2289–2530, 786/206–1506 in North America* 🌐 *www.casacristalcr.com* 🛏 *10 rooms* 🍽 *Breakfast.*

Costa Rica's oxcarts are folkloric symbols and a common canvas for local artisans.

$$
B&B/INN **Casa de las Tías.** The gamut of city services is at your doorstep, but you're blissfully apart from them at this tranquil bed-and-breakfast at the quiet end of a short road. **Pros:** tranquility without sacrificing convenience; service that goes the extra mile; excellent breakfast. **Cons:** walls could be a little thicker; slightly dated feel. $ *Rooms from: $100* ⊠ *100 m south and 150 m east of El Cruce* ✚ *Turn east just south of Restaurante Carpe Diem* ☎ *2289–5517* ⊕ *www.casadelastias.com* ⤶ *4 rooms, 1 junior suite* ⊙ *Breakfast.*

$
B&B/INN **Costa Verde Inn.** When they need to make a city run, many beach-living expats head straight for this quiet B&B on the outskirts of Escazú, and you should, too. **Pros:** inviting public areas; excellent value. **Cons:** large student groups in summer; can be difficult to find; pool is for plungers, not swimmers. $ *Rooms from: $70* ⊠ *From southeast corner of second cemetery (the farthest west), 300 m south* ☎ *2289–9509, 800/773–5013* ⊕ *www.costaverdeinn.com* ⤶ *13 rooms, 3 apartments, 3 studios* ⊙ *Breakfast.*

$$
B&B/INN **Posada El Quijote.** Perched on a hill in Escazú's Bello Horizonte neighborhood, with a great view of the city, this bed-and-breakfast strikes the right balance between a small inn and a private residence. **Pros:** peaceful, friendly place to spend first or last night; excellent staff. **Cons:** need a car to get around; can be difficult to find; standard rooms not as nice. $ *Rooms from: $85* ⊠ *Bello Horizonte, 1st street west of Anonos Bridge,1 km (½ mile) up hill* ☎ *2289–8401, 813/287–9996 in North America* ⊕ *www.quijote.cr* ⤶ *8 rooms, 2 apartments* ⊙ *Breakfast.*

NIGHTLIFE

Escazú is the Central Valley's hot spot for nightlife—many Josefinos head here for the restaurants, bars, and dance clubs that cater to a young, smartphone-toting crowd. You can't miss the bright lights as you swing into town off the toll highway.

The high-end **Itskatzú** complex, 1 km (½ mile) east of the Multiplaza mall, has a number of restaurants and bars ranging from the lower-brow (Hooters) to places with sophisticated sushi and live Cuban music.

Cantina La Cava. The cellar tavern beneath Le Monastère restaurant is a great place to stop for a drink before dinner, or stay on and while the evening away. You can dance to live music on Friday and Saturday nights. ✉ *1½ km (1 mile) southwest of Paco Shopping Center in San Rafael de Escazú* ✢ *Take old road west to Santa Ana, turn left at Paco, and follow signs, always bearing right* ☎ *2228–8515* ⊕ *www.monastere-restaurant.com* ⊗ *Mon.–Thurs. 6:30 pm–midnight, Fri. and Sat. 6:30 pm–2 am.*

Henry's Beach Cafe. One of the more popular watering holes with the under-30 set, this spot has televised sports by day, varied music by night, and an island decor of beach paintings and surfboards. Costa Ricans refer to this style of bar as an "American bar," which is fairly accurate. ✉ *200 m north of Centro Comercial Paco, Plaza San Rafael, 2nd fl.* ☎ *2289–6250* ⊕ *www.henrysbeachcafe.com* ⊗ *Weekdays 3 pm–2 am, weekends noon–2 am.*

Jazz Café Escazú. Music fans chill out here. The boxy club hosts an eclectic live-music lineup similar to that of its popular sister venue in San Pedro and has double the capacity. ✉ *Next to Confort Suizo, across the highway from Hospital Cima* ✢ *First exit after the toll booths* ☎ *2288–4740* ⊕ *www.jazzcafecostarica.com* ⊗ *Mon.–Sat. 6 pm–1 am.*

Tintos y Blancos. Although part of the enormous Multiplaza mall, sophisticated wine bar Tintos y Blancos has its own entrance in back. It offers a quality selection of libations, primarily Chilean and Argentine wines, with several French and Italian to round out the choices. ✉ *Multiplaza mall* ☎ *2201–5937* ⊕ *www.tintosyblancos.com* ⊗ *Sun.–Thurs. noon–midnight, Fri. and Sat. noon–1 am.*

SHOPPING

If you get the shopping bug and absolutely must visit a mall while on vacation, Escazú is the place to do it. **Multiplaza,** on the south side of the toll highway, approximately 5 km (3 miles) west of San José, is Costa Rica's most luxurious mall.

Biesanz Woodworks. Expat artist Barry Biesanz creates unique, world-class items from Costa Rican hardwoods, which are turned (a form of woodworking) on-site. Local craftsmen also ply their trade here. It's difficult to find, so take a taxi or call for directions from your hotel. ⊠ *Bello Horizonte, 800 m south of Escuela Bello Horizonte* ☎ *2289–4337* ⊕ *www.biesanz.com* ☉ *Dec.–Apr., weekdays 8–5, Sat. 9–3; May–Nov., weekdays 8–5.*

Multiplaza. Costa Rica's most upscale mall—think Kenneth Cole, Giorgio Armani, Oscar de la Renta, and many of their Costa Rican counterparts—looms over the highway between Escazú and Santa Ana. ⊠ *Caldera Hwy., between Escazú and Santa Ana* ☎ *2201–9097* ⊕ *www. multiplazaonline.com.*

SANTA ANA

17 km (10 miles) southwest of San José.

Santa Ana's tranquil town center, with its rugged stone church, has changed little through the years, even if metro development, with the accompanying condos and shopping malls, spreads out in all directions. The church, which was built between 1870 and 1880, has a Spanish-tile roof, carved wooden doors, and two pre-Columbian stone spheres flanking its entrance. Its rustic interior—bare wooden pillars and beams and black iron lamps—seems appropriate for an area with a tradition of ranching. Because it is warmer and drier than the towns to the east, Santa Ana is one of the few Central Valley towns that doesn't have a good climate for coffee—it is Costa Rica's onion capital, however—and is instead surrounded by pastures and patches of forest; it isn't unusual to see men on horseback here.

GETTING HERE AND AROUND

From San José, turn left at the western end of Paseo Colón, which ends at the Parque La Sabana. Take the first right, and get on the highway. Get off at the sixth exit; bear left at the flashing red lights, winding past roadside ceramics and vegetable stands before hitting the town center, about 2 km (1 mile) from the highway. The trip takes about 25 minutes if there's little traffic. Blue buses to Santa Ana leave from San José's Terminal Coca-Cola every eight minutes. ⚠ **Be careful: the Coca-Cola is a dodgy part of downtown San José.** To get to places along the toll highway or Piedades, take buses marked "Pista" or "Multiplaza." Those marked "Calle Vieja" leave every 15 minutes and pass through Escazú on the old road to Santa Ana. Buses run from 5 am to 11 pm.

ESSENTIALS

Bank/ATM Banco de Costa Rica ⊠ *Northwest corner of central park* ☎ *2203–4281.* **Banco Nacional** ⊠ *100 m south of church* ☎ *2282–2479.*

Internet Internet Café El Sol ⊠ *Southwest corner of church, across from Banco Popular* ☎ *2282–8059.*

Medical Assistance Farmacia Sucre ⊠ *25 m south of church* ☎ *2282–1296* ⊕ *www.farmaciasucre.com.*

Post Office Correos ⊠ *Next to Municipalidad.*

SPORTS AND THE OUTDOORS

GOLF

Valle del Sol. Although it sits inside a residential complex of the same name, Valle del Sol is the Central Valley's preeminent public golf course. Call to reserve tee times at this 7,000-yard, par 72, 18-hole course. Collared shirts and blouses are required; shorts must be "Bermuda" length; denim shorts and jeans are prohibited. ✉ *1,700 m west of Davivienda bank* ☎ *2282–9222* 🌐 *www.vallesol.com* 🎟 *$95 for 18 holes with cart, $81 after 1:30 pm* 🕒 *Mon. 8–6, Tues.–Sun. 6–6.*

WHERE TO EAT AND STAY

$$$ ITALIAN 🍴 **Andiamo Là.** One of the Central Valley's trendiest restaurants stands out with its daily fish and meat specials, including starter carpaccios of salmon, octopus, and beef. The sea bass and jumbo shrimp combination plate comes with a sauce of chopped fresh tomatoes, white wine, and garlic. Surf and turf is pricey, but includes grilled tenderloin and jumbo shrimp with a side of buttery spaghetti and asparagus. Lunch specials are a good value here. Service is as polished as the ample chrome, and there's usually at least one waiter who speaks English. The original restaurant, near San José's east-side Terramall, offers the same menu under more traditional Italian décor. [$] *Average main: $20* ✉ *Next to Más X Menos supermarket* ☎ *2282–7879* 🕒 *No dinner Sun.*

$$$ ECLECTIC 🍴 **Bacchus.** Take a Peruvian chef trained in France and an Italian owner, and you get Bacchus, a welcome addition to the local dining scene. The cuisine is a mix of French and Italian dishes such as duck breast in a port sauce, baked mushroom-and-polenta ragout, and a variety of pizzas. Modern art decorates the simple but elegant interior, and outdoor seating is available. An extensive wine list and reasonable prices make it a great pick for dinner. [$] *Average main: $17* ✉ *200 m east and 100 m north of church* ☎ *2282–5441* 🕒 *Closed Mon.*

$$$ HOTEL 🏨 **AltaHotel.** The view from this hotel perched on a hillside above Santa Ana is impressive, but so is the building itself with its colonial and modern style—think archways, hardwoods, and leather. **Pros:** classy service; panoramic views; excellent value for price. **Cons:** lower-floor rooms lose out on the view; little to do within walking distance. [$] *Rooms from: $180* ✉ *2½ km (1½ miles) west of Paco shopping center, on old road between Santa Ana and Escazú, Alto de las Palomas* ☎ *2282–4160, 888/388–2582 in North America* 🌐 *www.thealtahotel.com* 🛏 *18 rooms, 5 suites* 🍽 *Breakfast.*

$$ B&B/INN 🏨 **Hotel Posada Canal Grande.** This small Italian-owned hotel tucked into the hills to the west of Santa Ana draws an international clientele and is a great value. **Pros:** great value; international feel; second-floor rooms have balconies. **Cons:** spartan bathrooms. [$] *Rooms from: $78* ✉ *On Caldera Hwy. to Ciudad Colón, 500 m south of Piedades de Santa Ana bus terminal* ☎ *2282–4089* 🌐 *www.hotelcanalgrande.com* 🛏 *12 rooms* 🍽 *Breakfast.*

$$ HOTEL 🏨 **Hotel Villa Los Candiles.** You'd never expect to find such a quiet, homey oasis smack-dab in the middle of a suburban business neighborhood, but here it is. **Pros:** attentive staff; suites have kitchenettes; pool; air-conditioning. **Cons:** can be difficult to find. [$] *Rooms from: $100* ✉ *350 m east, 25 m south, 250 m east of Más X Menos supermarket* ☎ *2282–8280, 305/433–4031 in U.S.* 🌐 *www.hotelvillaloscandiles.com* 🛏 *10 rooms* 🍽 *Breakfast.*

CLOSE UP

Speaking Costa Rican

Spanish in Costa Rica tends to be localized. This is a land where eloquent speech and creative verbal expression are highly valued. For example, here the response to a "thank-you" is the gracious "Con *mucho gusto*" ("With much pleasure") instead of *"De nada"* ("It's nothing"), which is used in much of Latin America. In other cases, informality is preferred: the conventional *Señor* and *Señora*, for example, are eschewed in favor of the more egalitarian *Don* and *Doña*, used before a first name. Even President Luis Guillermo Solís is addressed as "Don Luis Guillermo." *Exercise caution when selecting from the list below, however.* Although young Costa Rican men address everyone as *maje* (dude), you'll get a withering look if you, a visitor, follow suit.

agarrar de maje to pull someone's leg

birra beer

brete work

cachos shoes

chunche any thingamajig

clavar el pico to fall asleep

con mucho gusto used in response to "thank you" instead of "de nada"

estar de chicha to be angry

estar de goma to have a hangover

harina money

jupa head

macho, macha a person with blond hair, and nothing to do with "masculine"

mae or maje buddy, dude, mate

mamá de Tarzán know-it-all

maría a woman's name; also a taxi meter

matar la culebra to waste time

montón a lot

muy bien, gracias a Dios very well, thank goodness

muy bien, por dicha very well, luckily

paño towel

pelo de gato cat hair; or fine, misty rain that falls in December

peso colón

pinche a tight-fisted person

ponerse hasta la mecha to get drunk

porfa please

pura vida fantastic, great

rojo red; also a 1,000-colón note

si Dios quiere God willing

soda an inexpensive local restaurant

torta a big mistake or error

tuanis cool

upe anyone home?

SHOPPING

Cerámica Las Palomas. Large glazed pots with ornate decorations that range from traditional patterns to modern motifs are the specialties at Cerámica Las Palomas. Flowerpots and lamps are also common works, and the staff will happily show you the production process, from raw clay to art. ⊠ *Old road to Santa Ana, opposite Alta Hotel* ☎ *2282–7001* ⊕ *www.ceramicalaspalomas.webs.com* ☽ *Mon.–Sat. 7–5.*

GRECIA

26 km (16 miles) (45 mins) northwest of Alajuela, 46 km (29 miles) (1 hr) northwest of San José.

The quiet farming community of Grecia is reputed to be Costa Rica's cleanest town—some enthusiastic civic boosters extend that superlative to all of Latin America—but the reason most people stop here is to admire its unusual church. A growing number of expats now call the town home.

GETTING HERE AND AROUND

From San José continue west on the highway past the airport—the turn-off is on the right—or head into Alajuela and turn left just before the Alajuela cemetery. Buses leave Calle 20 in San José for Grecia every 30 minutes from 5:30 am to 10 pm. From Alajuela, buses to Grecia/Ciudad Quesada pick up on the southern edge of town (Calle 4 and Avenida 10).

ESSENTIALS

Bank/ATM BAC San José ⊠ *100 m north of central park* ☎ *2295–9696.*
Banco Nacional ⊠ *Northwest corner of central park* ☎ *2444–0690.*

EXPLORING

Church of Our Lady of Mercy (*Iglesia de Nuestra Señora de las Mercedes*). The brick-red, Gothic-style church is made of prefabricated iron. It's one of two buildings in the country made from steel frames and iron sheets imported from Belgium in the late-19th century (the other is the metal schoolhouse next to San José's Parque Morazán), when some prominent Costa Ricans decided that metal structures would better withstand the periodic earthquakes that had taken their toll on so much of the country's architecture. The frames were shipped from Antwerp to Limón, then transported by train to Alajuela—from which the metal walls of the church were carried by oxcarts. Locals refer to the building as simply the *Iglesia Metálica* (metal church). The splendid 1886 German pipe organ, regarded as Costa Rica's finest, is worth a look inside. ⊠ *Avda. 1, Cs. 1–3* ☎ *2494–1616* ☉ *Daily 8–4.*

FAMILY **World of Snakes.** On a small farm outside Grecia, this is a good place to see some of the slithering creatures that you are unlikely—and probably don't want—to spot in the wild. Sequestered in the safety of cages here are some 50 varieties of serpents, as well as crocodiles, iguanas, poison dart frogs, and various other cold-blooded creatures. Admission includes a 90-minute tour. ⊠ *Poró, 2 km (1 mile) east of Grecia, on road to Alajuela* ☎ *2494–3700* ⊕ *www.theworldofsnakes.com* 🖅 *$11* ☉ *Daily 8–4.*

SPORTS AND THE OUTDOORS

BUNGEE JUMPING

A 79-meter-tall (265-foot-tall) bridge that spans a forested gorge over the Río Colorado is the perfect place to get a rush of adrenaline in a tranquil, tropical setting. Even if you aren't up for the plunge, it's worth stopping to watch a few mad souls do it.

Tropical Bungee. The first jump is $75 and the second is $45. Transportation is free if you jump; $10 if you don't. Rappelling ($75) and rock-climbing ($95) are among the offerings, too. Reservations are essential. If this is your last hurrah in Costa Rica, a van can take you and your bags straight to the San José airport after your jump. ⊠ *Pan-American*

Hwy., 2 km (1 mile) west of turnoff for Grecia, down a dirt road on the right ☎ *2248–2212 in San José, 8980–5757 cell* 🌐 *www.bungee.co.cr* 🕐 *Daily 8–11:30 and 1–4.*

WHERE TO STAY

$$ B&B/INN Fodor's Choice ★ **Vista del Valle Plantation Inn.** Honeymooners (and many posters to Fodors.com) frequent these handsome cottages on an orange and coffee plantation outside Grecia overlooking the canyon of the Río Grande. **Pros:** attentive staff; secluded cottages; healthful food served. **Cons:** a car is necessary for staying here; jungle bugs and mosquitoes; somewhat difficult to find. [$] *Rooms from: $100* ✉ *On highway 1 km (½ mile) west of Rafael Iglesia Bridge; follow signs* ☎ *2451–1165* 🌐 *www.vistadelvalle.com* 🛏 *16 cottages* 🍴 *Breakfast.*

SARCHÍ

8 km (5 miles) west of Grecia, 53 km (33 miles) (1½ hrs) northwest of San José.

Tranquil Sarchí is Costa Rica's premier center for crafts and carpentry. People drive here from all over the country to shop for furniture, and tour buses regularly descend upon the souvenir shops outside town. The area's most famous products are its brightly painted oxcarts—replicas of those traditionally used to transport coffee.

GETTING HERE AND AROUND

To get to Sarchí from San José, take the highway well past the airport to the turnoff for Naranjo; then veer right just as you enter Naranjo. Direct buses to Sarchí depart from Alajuela (✉ *C. 8 between Avdas. 1 and 3*) every 30 minutes from 6 am to 9 pm; the ride takes 90 minutes.

ESSENTIALS

Bank/ATM Banco Nacional ✉ *South side of soccer field* ☎ *2454–3044* 🌐 *www.bncr.fi.cr.*

Post Office Correos ✉ *South side of soccer field.*

EXPLORING

Eloy Alfaro and Sons Workshop (*Taller Eloy Alfaro e Hijos*). Costa Rica's only real remaining oxcart factory was founded in 1920, and its carpentry methods have changed little since then. The operation still bears the name of founder Eloy Alfaro, but the business and tradition have passed into other hands. The two-story wooden building housing the wood shop is surrounded by trees and flowers—mostly orchids—and all the machinery on the ground floor is powered by a waterwheel at the back of the shop. Carts are painted in the back, and although the factory's main product is a genuine oxcart—which sells for about $2,000—there are also some smaller mementos that can easily be shipped home. ✉ *200 m north of soccer field* ☎ *2454–4131* 🌐 *www.fabricadecarretaseloyalfaro.com* 🕐 *Daily 7–5.*

Else Kientzler Botanical Garden (*Jardìn Botánico Else Kientzler*). Some 2,000 plant species, tropical and subtropical, flourish on 17 acres. The German owner named the facility, affiliated with an ornamental-plant exporter, after his late plant-loving mother. About half of the garden's pathways are wheelchair accessible. The services of a guide cost an extra $25 for groups of up to 15 people. ⊠ *400 m north of soccer field* ☎ *2454-2070* ⊕ *www.elsegarden. com* ⊐ *$12* ⊙ *Daily 8–4.*

Fodor's Choice ★ **La Carreta.** The world's largest oxcart, constructed and brightly painted by longtime local factory Taller Eloy Alfaro e Hijos (Eloy Alfaro and Sons Workshop) and enshrined in the *Guinness Book of World Records,* can be found in Sarchí's central park. The work—locals refer to it as simply *La Carreta* (the oxcart)—logs in at 18 meters (45 feet) and weighs 2 tons. Since no other country is attached to oxcarts quite like Costa Rica, we don't imagine that record will be broken anytime soon. ⊠ *Center of Sarchí, central park.*

> **PAINTED OXCARTS**
>
> Coffee has come to symbolize the prosperity of the Central Valley and the nation. Nineteenth-century coffee farmers needed a way to transport this all-important cash crop to the port of Puntarenas on the Pacific coast. Enter the oxcart. Artisans began painting the carts in the early 1900s. Debate continues as to why: the kaleidoscopic designs may have symbolized the points of the compass, or may have echoed the landscape's tropical colors. In any case, the oxcart has become the national symbol. Give way when you see one out on a country road, and marvel at the sight.

SHOPPING

Sarchí is the best place in Costa Rica to buy miniature oxcarts, the larger of which are designed to serve as patio bars or end tables and can be broken down for easy transport or shipped to your home. Another popular item is a locally produced rocking chair with a leather seat and back.

Fodor's Choice ★ **Chaverrí Oxcart Factory** (*Fábrica de Carretas*). In the nicest of the many stores south of town, you can wander through the workshops and see the artisans in action. Despite the name, offerings extend well beyond oxcarts, and Chaverrí is a good place to buy wooden crafts of all kinds. Chaverrí also runs a restaurant next door, Las Carretas, which serves a variety of local food all day until 6 pm and has a good lunch buffet. ⊠ *Main road, 2 km (1 mile) south of Sarchí* ☎ *2454-4411* ⊕ *www. sarchicostarica.net.*

Plaza de la Artesanía. Sarchí's answer to a shopping mall gathers 35 artisan and souvenir shops under one roof. Expect to find oxcarts, the town's signature symbol, and everything else imaginable. If you can't find it here, it probably doesn't exist in Costa Rica. ⊠ *2 km (1 mile) south of Sarchí, Sarchí Sur.*

SAN RAMÓN

23 km (14 miles) west of Sarchí, 59 km (37 miles) (1½ hrs) northwest of San José.

San Ramón hides its real attractions in the countryside to the north, on the road to La Fortuna, where comfortable lodges offer access to private nature preserves. There's not much to see in the town other than its church, but if you happen to be in San Ramón on Friday or

Saturday, walk through the bustling farmers' market, La Feria del Agricultor. An abundance of locally grown fruits, vegetables, flowers, and even livestock are for sale, and this is a good place to buy fresh tortillas, made by hand.

GETTING HERE AND AROUND

San Ramón is on the Pan-American Highway west of Grecia. Buses leave hourly for San Ramón from San José's Terminal de Puntarenas. From Alajuela, buses to San Ramón/Ciudad Quesada pick up on the southern edge of town (✉ *C. 4 and Avda. 10)*.

ESSENTIALS

Bank/ATM Scotiabank ✉ *Pan-American Hwy., entrance to San Ramón* ☎ *2447–9190.*

EXPLORING

Church of San Ramón. Aside from its poets, San Ramón's claim to fame is this massive church built in a mixture of the Romanesque and Gothic styles. In 1924 an earthquake destroyed the smaller adobe church that once stood here, and the city lost no time in creating a replacement—this great gray concrete structure took a quarter of a century to complete, from 1925 to 1954. To ensure that the second church would be earthquake-proof, workers poured the concrete around a steel frame that was designed and forged in Germany (by Krupp). Step past the formidable facade and you'll discover a bright, elegant interior. ✉ *Across from central park* ☎ *2445–5592* 🕒 *Daily 6–11:30 am and 1:30–7 pm.*

WHERE TO STAY

$$$ HOTEL 🏨 **Villa Blanca.** Lovely casitas, each a replica of a traditional adobe farmhouse, are on a working dairy and coffee farm once owned by former Costa Rican president Rodrigo Carazo and set in the middle of the Los Angeles cloud forest. **Pros:** attentive service; many activities; secluded location; eco-friendly. **Cons:** far from sights; need a car to stay here. [$] *Rooms from: $205* ✉ *20 km (12 miles) north of San Ramón on road to La Fortuna* ☎ *2461–0300, 877/256–8399 in North America* 🌐 *www.villablanca-costarica.com* 🛏 *35 casitas* 🍴 *Breakfast.*

EN ROUTE

Zarcero. The center of this small, tidy town 15 km (9 miles) north of Sarchí on the road to Ciudad Quesada looks as if it was designed by Dr. Seuss. Evangelisto Blanco, a local landscape artist, modeled cypress topiaries in fanciful animal shapes—motorcycle-riding monkeys, a lightbulb-eyed elephant—that enliven the park in front of the town church. Soft lighting illuminates the park in the evening. The church interior is covered with elaborate pastel stencil work and detailed religious paintings by the late Misael Solís, a well-known local artist. Sample some cheese if you're in town, too; Zarcero-made cheese is one of Costa Rica's favorites. The town is frequently included as a short stop on many organized tours heading to the northern region of the country. ✉ *Zarcero.*

ATENAS

42 km (26 miles) west of San José.

By the time you get this far west in the Central Valley, you're likely headed for Costa Rica's famed Central Pacific beaches, but the countryside holds some splendid scenery, from the steep coffee farms around Atenas to the tropical forests of the lowlands. Known for its excellent climate—*National Geographic* once dubbed it the world's best—Atenas ("Athens" in Spanish) is a pleasant, friendly town surrounded by a hilly countryside of coffee and cane fields, cattle ranches, and patches of forest. The small city is off the tourist circuit, which means that here, unlike other highly popular destinations, you'll walk alongside more locals than foreigners and get a more authentic idea of the country. Gazing at the tree-covered peaks and exploring the coffee farms are the main activities in this traditional town. Atenas's center has a concrete church, some well-kept wooden and adobe houses, and a park dominated by royal palms.

GETTING HERE AND AROUND

Atenas lies about one hour west of San José on the route to beaches such as Herradura, Jacó, and Manuel Antonio. Take the Pan-American Highway past the airport and turn right at the overpass with the signs for beach resorts and Zoo Ave. Turn left from the exit and stay on the main road. Alternately, Atenas has its own exit on Highway 27 that connects San José to Caldera. Buses to Atenas leave hourly throughout the day from the Coca-Cola terminal in San José and arrive near the center of town. ⚠ **Be careful: The Coca-Cola is a dicey part of downtown San José.**

ESSENTIALS

Bank/ATM Banco de Costa Rica ✉ *Across from west side of church* ☎ *2446–6034.* **Banco Nacional** ✉ *Across from north side of central park* ☎ *2446–5157.*

Hospital Clínica Pública ✉ *250 m south, 100 m west of the fire station* ☎ *2446–5522.*

Pharmacy Farmacia Don Juan ✉ *West side of Catholic church* ☎ *2446–5055.*

Post Office Correos ✉ *50 m east of southeast corner of market.*

WHERE TO STAY

$ HOTEL 🏨 **Colinas del Sol.** Although it is just a few blocks from the center of Atenas, this pleasant, German-owned lodging manages to capture a country feel with bungalows arranged throughout wooded grounds. **Pros:** friendly owner and staff; huge pool; pleasant Costa Rican restaurant. **Cons:** can be difficult to find; some rooms have yet to be renovated. [$] *Rooms from: $70* ✉ *Calle Boquerón, 600 m east of high school gym* ☎ *2446–4244* 🌐 *www.hotelcolinasdelsol.com* 🛏 *15 bungalows* 🍴 *Breakfast.*

$$ B&B/INN 🏨 **The Orchid Tree.** Like all Atenas lodgings, this countryside inn makes a convenient first or last night on a Costa Rican vacation, but a devoted group of return visitors frequently opts for extended stays here. **Pros:** huge breakfasts; pleasant common area for socializing with other guests. **Cons:** slightly dark rooms; can be difficult to find. [$] *Rooms*

from: $80 ✉ *Calle Oratorio. Río Grande de Atenas* ☎ *2446–0852, 403/755–2530 in North America* ⊕ *www.orchidtreecostarica.com* ⌂ *4 rooms* ¶⊙¶ *Breakfast.*

$

B&B/INN

Fodor'sChoice

★

Vista Atenas. *Vista* means "view" in Spanish, and the name of this comfortable, Belgian-owned lodging perched high on a hillside outside of Atenas fits perfectly. **Pros:** stunning views; attentive service; terrific rates for what's offered. **Cons:** can be difficult to find; steep drive to get here; large, friendly dog on-site, so not a

BASE CAMP

Some visitors to Costa Rica prefer using Atenas as their first- and last-night base camp instead of San José, because Atenas is smaller, friendlier, and more tranquil. The international airport is geographically closer to Atenas, but the hilly roads make the ride slightly longer than the trip on San José's express highway.

4

place to stay if you're not a canine lover. $ *Rooms from: $85* ✉ *Sabana Larga* ☎ *2446–4272, 209/257–4908 in North America* ⊕ *www. vistaatenas.com* ⌂ *6 rooms, 2 cabins, 1 villa* ¶⊙¶ *Multiple meal plans.*

CARARA NATIONAL PARK

43 km (25 miles) southwest of Atenas, 85 km (51 miles) southwest of San José.

In the wilderness of Carara National Park and surroundings, you might encounter white-faced capuchin monkeys in the trees or crocodiles lounging on a riverbank. The region is extremely biologically diverse, making it an excellent destination for bird-watchers and other wildlife enthusiasts.

GETTING HERE AND AROUND

Take Highway 27 west of San José beyond Orotina and follow the signs to Jacó and Quepos. The reserve is on the left after you cross Río Tárcoles. From San José, hop on a bus to Jacó, Quepos, or Manuel Antonio, and ask to be dropped off near the park entrance, about a two-hour drive.

TOURS

Horizontes. The country's premier nature-tour operator can arrange visits to Carara National Park as a day trip from San José or as part of a longer tour. ☎ *2222–2022* ⊕ *www.horizontes.com.*

Jaguar Riders. This Jacó-based tour operator can arrange guided tours through the forests of Carara National Park. ✉ *Avda. Pastor Díaz, next to Pancho Villa restaurant, Jacó* ☎ *2643–0180* ⊕ *www.jaguariders.com.*

EXPLORING

Carara National Park. One of the last remnants of an ecological transition zone between Costa Rica's drier northwest and the more humid southeast holds a tremendous collection of plants and animals. Much of the 47-square-km (18-square-mile) park is covered with primary forest on steep slopes, where the massive trees are laden with vines and epiphytes. The sparse undergrowth makes wildlife easier to see here than in many other parks, but nothing is guaranteed. If you're lucky, you may glimpse armadillos, basilisk lizards, coatis, and any of several monkey species, as well as birds such as blue-crowned motmots, chestnut-mandibled toucans, and trogons.

The first trail on the left shortly after the bridge that spans the Río Tárcoles (a good place to spot crocodiles) leads to a horseshoe-shape *laguna meandrica* (oxbow lake). The small lagoon covered with water hyacinths is home to turtles, crocodiles, and waterfowl such as the northern jacana, roseate spoonbill, and boat-billed heron. It is a two- to four-hour hike from the trailhead to the lagoon and back, depending on how much bird-watching you do. ■TIP➔ **Cars parked at the trailhead have been broken into. If you don't see a ranger on duty at the Sendero Laguna Meandrica trailhead, avoid leaving anything of value in your vehicle. You may be able to leave your belongings at the main ranger station (several miles south of the trailhead), where you can also buy drinks and souvenirs and use the restroom. Otherwise, visit the park as a day trip from a nearby hotel.**

Two trails lead into the forest from the parking lot. The shortest one can be done in 15 minutes, whereas the longer one that connects with the Quebrada Bonita loop takes one to three hours to hike. The latter can be quite muddy during the rainy months, when you may want rubber boots. Carara's proximity to San José and Jacó means that tour buses arrive regularly in high season, scaring some animals deeper into the forest. Come very early or late in the day to avoid crowds. Bird-watchers can call the day before to arrange admission before the park opens. Camping is not permitted. Jacó is the nearest town and the most logical base for trips into the park. Local travel agencies and tour operators arrange transport to and guides through the park *(⇨ Tours, above)*. The park itself has guides, but you must arrange in advance. ⊠ *East of Costanera, just south of bridge over Río Tárcoles* ☎ *2637–1080* ▨ *$10* ☉ *Daily 7–4.*

NORTH OF SAN JOSÉ

As you set out from San José to explore the towns to the north, you first encounter nothing but asphalt, hotels, and malls—not especially scenic. Santo Domingo and San Antonio de Belén blend into the outskirts of San José, and it's only when you get to the heart of these small towns that you feel you've arrived in Central America. Farther north, Alajuela and Heredia are bustling provincial capitals with charismatic central parks. Throughout this area, tucked into the urban scenery and lining volcanic slopes, are fields of that quintessential Costa Rican staple, coffee. North of Alajuela reigns one of the Central Valley's signature sights, the crowd-pleasing Poás Volcano.

SAN ANTONIO DE BELÉN

17 km (10 miles) northwest of San José.

San Antonio de Belén has little to offer visitors but its rural charm and proximity to the international airport. The latter led developers to build several of the San José area's biggest hotels here. The country's sole Mormon temple is also found here, open only to visitors of the faith. The town is a convenient departure point for trips to the western Central Valley, Pacific coast, and northern region. If you stay at the Marriott, you likely won't even see the town, just the busy highway between San José and Alajuela.

GETTING HERE AND AROUND

From San José, turn right at the west end of Paseo Colón onto the Pan-American Highway (Carretera General Cañas). The San Antonio de Belén exit is at an overpass 6 km (4 miles) west of the Heredia exit, by the Real Cariari Mall. Turn left at the first intersection, cross over the highway, and continue 1 km (½ mile) to the forced right turn, driving 1½ km (1 mile) to the center of town. San Antonio is only 10 minutes from the airport.

ESSENTIALS

Bank/ATM Banco de Costa Rica ⊠ *50 m north of rear of church* ☎ *2239–1149.*

Medical Assistance Farmacia Sucre ⊠ *North side of church* ☎ *2239–3485* ⊕ *www.farmaciasucre.com.*

Post Office Correos ⊠ *3 blocks west and 25 m north of church.*

Taxis Asotaxis Belén ☎ *2293–4712.*

WHERE TO STAY

$$$ ⊡ **Costa Rica Marriott San José.** The stately Marriott offers comprehen-
HOTEL sive luxury close to the airport, and, despite being a U.S. chain, offers
FAMILY many distinctively Costa Rican touches. **Pros:** excellent service; lavish grounds; close to airport. **Cons:** tendency to nickel-and-dime guests; tricky car access from highway. $ *Rooms from: $199* ⊠ *¾ km (½ mile) west of Bridgestone/Firestone, off Autopista General Cañas* ☎ *2298–0000, 800/236–2427 in North America* ⊕ *www.marriott. com* ⟿ *290 rooms, 10 suites* ⊠ *No meals.*

$$$ ⊡ **Doubletree by Hilton Cariari San José.** This low-rise hotel was the metro
HOTEL area's original luxury hotel, and it remains popular for its excellent
FAMILY service and out-of-town location. **Pros:** close to both San José and the airport; kid-friendly. **Cons:** tricky car access; close to busy highway. $ *Rooms from: $169* ⊠ *Autopista General Cañas, ½ km (¼ mile) east of intersection for San Antonio de Belén, Cariari* ☎ *2239–0022, 800/222–8733 in North America* ⊕ *www.hilton.com* ⟿ *198 rooms, 24 suites* ⊠ *No meals.*

$$ ⊡ **El Rodeo.** This quiet hotel bills itself as a "country hotel," though
HOTEL this is more in image than fact—El Rodeo's proximity to the airport and major business parks is the real draw. **Pros:** proximity to airport; spacious rooms. **Cons:** generic feel. $ *Rooms from: $125* ⊠ *Road to Santa Ana, 2 km (1 mile) east of central park* ☎ *2293–3909* ⊕ *www. elrodeohotel.com* ⟿ *22 rooms, 7 suites* ⊠ *Breakfast.*

ALAJUELA

20 km (13 miles) northwest of San José.

Because of its proximity to the international airport (5–10 minutes away) many travelers spend their first or last night in or near Ala-juela, but the beauty of the surrounding countryside persuades some to stay longer. Alajuela is Costa Rica's second-most-populated city, and a mere 30-minute bus ride from the capital, but it has a decidedly provincial air compared with San José. Architecturally, it differs little from the bulk of Costa Rican towns: it's a grid of low-rise structures painted in dull pastel colors.

GETTING HERE AND AROUND

To reach Alajuela, head west on the highway past the San Antonio de Belén turnoff and turn right at the airport. Buses travel between San José (⊠ *Avda. 2, Cs. 12–14, opposite north side of Parque La Merced*), the airport, and Alajuela, and run every five minutes from 4:40 am to 10:30 pm. The bus stop in Alajuela is 400 meters west, 25 meters north of the central park (⊠ *C. 3 and Avda. 1*). Buses leave San José for Zoo Ave from La Merced church (⊠ *C. 14 and Avda. 4*) daily at 8, 9, 10, 11 am, and noon, returning on the hour from 10 am to 3 pm.

ESSENTIALS

Bank/ATM Banco de Costa Rica ⊠ *50 m west of southwest corner of central park* ☎ *2440–9039* ⊕ *www.bancobcr.com.* **Banco Nacional** ⊠ *West side of central park* ☎ *2441–0373.*

Hospital Hospital San Rafael ⊠ *1 km (½ mile) northeast of airport, on main road to Alajuela* ☎ *2436–1001.*

Internet Internet Inter@ctivo ⊠ *Across from BAC San José bank, 100 m north of central park* ☎ *2431–1984.*

Medical Assistance Farmacia Chavarría ⊠ *C. 4, Avda. 1–Ctl* ☎ *2441–1231.*

Post Office Correos ⊠ *Avda. 5, C. 1* ⊕ *www.correos.go.cr.*

Taxis Cootaxa ☎ *2442–3030.*

EXPLORING

TOP ATTRACTIONS

Fodor'sChoice ★ **Doka Estate.** Considering the amount of coffee you'll drive past in the Central Valley, you might want to devote an hour or so of your vacation to learning about the crop's production. Doka Estate, a working coffee plantation for more than 70 years, offers a comprehensive tour that takes you through the fields, shows you how the fruit is processed and the beans are dried, and lets you sample the local brew. The best time to take this tour is during the October-to-February picking season. Transportation can be arranged from San José, Alajuela, Heredia, Escazú, or San Antonio de Belén. ⊠ *10 km (6 miles) north of Alajuela's Tribunales de Justicia, San Luis de Sabanilla* ✛ *Turn left at San Isidro and continue 6 km (4 miles), follow signs* ☎ *2449–5152, 800/946–3652 in North America* ⊕ *www.dokaestate.com* ▣ *$22* ☺ *Tours daily at 9, 10, 11, 1:30, 2:30, and 3:30; weekends last tour at 2:30.*

WORTH NOTING

Alajuela Cathedral. The large, neoclassical Alajuela Cathedral has columns topped by interesting capitals decorated with local agricultural motifs, and a striking red metal dome. The interior is spacious but rather plain, except for the ornate cupola above the altar. ⊠ *C. Ctl., Avdas. 1–Ctl.* ☎ *2443–2928* ☺ *Daily 6-6.*

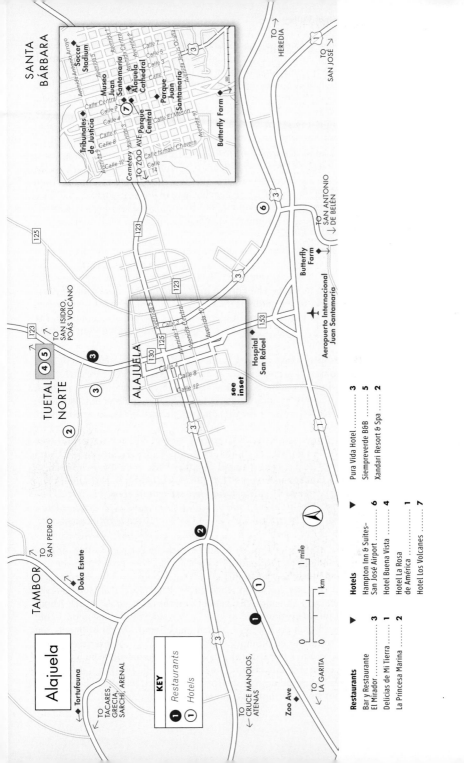

Alajuela

SANTA BÁRBARA

Soccer Stadium
Museo Juan Santamaría
Alajuela Cathedral
Parque Juan Santamaría
Tribunales de Justicia
Parque Central
Butterfly Farm

Avenida Antonio Arroyo
Avenida 5
Avenida 3
Avenida Central
Avenida 1
Calle 7
Calle 5
Calle 3
Calle 1
Calle Central
Calle 2
Calle 4
Calle 6
Calle 8
Calle El Mesón
Calle Ismael Chavern
Calle 14
Avenida 9
Avenida 12
Avenida 10

Cemetery
TO ZOO AVE

TO HEREDIA
TO SAN JOSÉ

TUETAL NORTE

TAMBOR
TO SAN PEDRO
Doka Estate

Tortufauna
TO TACARES, GRECIA, SARCHÍ, ARENAL

TO SAN ISIDRO, POÁS VOLCANO
SAN ISIDRO, POÁS VOLCANO

ALAJUELA
Avenida 3
Avenida 1
Avenida Central
Avenida 7
Calle 1
Calle 2
Calle 4
Calle 6
Calle 8
Calle 12
see inset

Hospital San Rafael

Butterfly Farm
Aeropuerto Internacional Juan Santamaría
TO SAN ANTONIO DE BELÉN

Zoo Ave
TO CRUCE MANOLOS, ATENAS
TO LA GARITA

125
123
130
153
3
1

KEY
1 Restaurants
1 Hotels

1 mile
1 km

Restaurants ▶
Bar y Restaurante El Mirador 3
Delicias de Mi Tierra 1
La Princesa Marina 2

Hotels ▶
Hampton Inn & Suites– San José Airport 6
Hotel Buena Vista 4
Hotel La Rosa de América 1
Hotel Los Volcanes 7
Pura Vida Hotel 3
Siempreverde B&B 5
Xandari Resort & Spa 2

Museo Juan Santamaría. Juan Santamaría's heroic deeds are celebrated in this museum housed in the old jail, one block north of Parque Central. It's worth a quick look if you have the time; Santamaría's story is an interesting one. Following the lead of the Teatro Nacional in San José, the museum holds a series of weekly concerts called *Música al Mediodía* ("Music at Noon") each Thursday from February to early December. Admission is $2. ⊠ *Avda. 3, Cs. Ctl.–2* 🕾 *2441–4775* ⊕ *www. museojuansantamaria.go.cr* 🖾 *Free* ☉ *Tues.–Sun. 10–6.*

Parque Central *(Central park).* Royal palms and massive mango trees fill the Parque Central—residents frequently refer to the park as the Parque de los Mangos—which also has a lovely fountain imported from Glasgow and concrete benches where locals gather to chat. Surrounding the plaza is an odd mix of charming old buildings and sterile concrete boxes, including a somewhat incongruous McDonald's. ⊠ *C. Ctl., Avdas. 1–Ctl.*

Parque Juan Santamaría. Alajuela was the birthplace of Juan Santamaría, the national hero who lost his life in a battle against the mercenary army of U.S. adventurer William Walker when the latter invaded Costa Rica in 1856. The Parque Juan Santamaría, more a small plaza than a park, has a statue of the young hero. After a 2005 restoration, Juan should keep his youthful good looks for years to come. ⚠ **The park gets a little dicey as the sun goes down; confine your visits to daylight hours.** ⊠ *C. Ctl. and Avda. 2.*

FAMILY **Zoo Ave.** Spread over the lush grounds of Zoo Ave is a collection of large cages holding toucans, hawks, and parrots (the macaws range free), not to mention crocodiles, caimans, a boa constrictor, turtles, monkeys, wildcats, and other interesting critters. The zoo, the best in Costa Rica, runs a breeding project for rare and endangered birds, all of which are destined for eventual release. It has 115 bird species, including such rare ones as the quetzal, fiery-billed aracari, several types of eagles, and even ostriches. An impressive mural at the back of the facility shows Costa Rica's 850 bird species painted to scale. Unfortunately, exhibits here are labeled in Spanish only. ⊠ *La Garita de Alajuela* ✦ *Head west from Alajuela center past cemetery, turn left after stone church in Barrio San José, continue on 2 km (1 mile); or head west on Pan-American Hwy. to Atenas exit, then turn right* 🕾 *2433–8989* ⊕ *www.zooavecostarica. org* 🖾 *$21* ☉ *Daily 9–5.*

■ EN ROUTE If you head straight through Alajuela, with the Parque Central on your right, you'll be on the road to Poás Volcano; you should pass the Tribunales de Justicia (the county courthouse) on your right as you leave town. If you turn left upon reaching the Parque Central, and pass the town cemetery on your right, you'll be on the old road to Grecia. About 3 km (2 miles) northwest of town on that road, you'll come upon an old concrete church on the right, which marks your arrival in Barrio San José, a suburban community of Alajuela. A left turn after the church will take you to a lovely rural area called **La Garita**, from which the road continues west to Atenas and the Central Pacific beaches. La Garita is a popular weekend destination for Tico families, who head here for the abundant típico restaurants and *viveros* (greenhouses).

CLOSE UP

A National Hero

When the Costa Ricans drove U.S. invader Walker's army from their country in 1856, they chased his troops to Rivas, Nicaragua. The army of filibusters took refuge in a wooden fort. Juan Santamaría, a poor, 24-year-old drummer with a militia from Alajuela, volunteered to burn it down to drive them out. Legend says that Santamaría ran toward the fort carrying a torch, and that although he was shot repeatedly, he managed to throw it and to burn the fort down. His bravery wasn't recognized at the time, probably because of his modest origins, but in 1891 a statue depicting a strong and handsome soldier carrying a torch was placed in Alajuela, thus immortalizing Santamaría. The entire account may well be apocryphal; some historians doubt there ever *was* such a person. But don't tell that to the average Tico. Juan Santamaría Day is a national holiday in Costa Rica each April 11 and celebrates the victory at the Battle of Rivas.

4

WHERE TO EAT

$$ ECLECTIC 🍴 **Bar y Restaurante El Mirador.** Perched on a ridge several miles north of town, El Mirador has a sweeping view of the Central Valley that is impressive by day but more beautiful at dusk and night when the basin is filled with twinkling lights. Get a window table in the dining room, or one on the adjacent porch if it isn't too cool. The menu, which includes *lomito* (tenderloin) and *corvina* (sea bass) served with various sauces, and several shrimp and chicken dishes, plays second fiddle to the view. Stop in around sunset for drinks and appetizers instead. There are at least two other restaurants nearby with similar names and views—this one is on the main road, close to the Buena Vista Hotel. [$] *Average main: $12* ✉ *Road to Poás, 5 km (3 miles) north of Tribunales de Justicia* ☎ *2441–9347.*

$ COSTA RICAN 🍴 **Delicias de Mi Tierra.** A string of *típico* Costa Rican restaurants lines this road, but the "Delights of My Land" is our favorite. Tasty and traditional Tico favorites are served here: *pozol* (corn-and-pork soup), *casado campesino* (stewed beef with rice, beans, corn, potatoes, and plantains), and *chorreada con natilla* (a corn-bread pancake with sour cream). Long wooden tables and benches are surrounded by cane walls, decorative oxcart wheels, dried gourds, and tropical plants—the kind of decor trying so hard to be traditional that it's anything but. Ordering a few *entraditas* (appetizers) is a good way to sample dishes, as is the *parrillada de campo* (country barbecue), a platter with grilled chicken, beef, pork, rice, beans, fried plantains, and salad, or the larger *fiesta de gallos,* a mixed platter of corn tortillas with various fillings. There are also cheap but hearty breakfasts. Get here early for dinner, as closing time is 7 pm. [$] *Average main: $8* ✉ *1½ km (1 mile) west of the Barrio San José church* ☎ *2433–8536.*

$$ SEAFOOD 🍴 **La Princesa Marina.** This large open-air eatery (part of a chain) at the intersection of the old Alajuela–Grecia road and the road to La Garita is popular with Ticos, who pack it on weekends to feast on inexpensive seafood. The selection is vast, with 10 types of fish, shrimp, or octopus

ceviche; fish fillets served with various sauces; three sizes of shrimp prepared a dozen ways; whole fried fish; lobster tails; and several *mariscadas* (mixed seafood plates). Pastas, rice dishes, beef, and chicken are some other choices, but the seafood is your best bet. The decor is utilitarian—bare tables, ceiling fans, and dividers of potted plants separating the sections—but you avoid that feeling of being in a contrived tourist venue. $ *Average main: $13* ⊠ *Barrio San José, north of church* ☎ *2433–7117* ⊕ *www.princesamarina.com.*

WHERE TO STAY

$$
HOTEL
⊞ **Hampton Inn & Suites – San José Airport.** A longtime favorite for first-night and last-night stays, this U.S. chain outlet lets you ease into and out of Costa Rica in familiar surroundings. **Pros:** airport proximity; U.S. amenities; friendly staff. **Cons:** some noise from planes in the evening; sameness of a chain hotel. $ *Rooms from: $141* ⊠ *Blvd. del Aeropuerto* ☎ *2436–0000, 800/426–7866 in North America* ⊕ *www.hamptoninn. hilton.com* ⇌ *100 rooms* ¶◎¶ *Breakfast.*

$$
HOTEL
⊞ **Hotel Buena Vista.** Perched high above Alajuela, this hotel's superb staff makes up for the somewhat dated, uninspired decor. **Pros:** excellent service; family-friendly. **Cons:** mediocre restaurant; farther from the airport than other options. $ *Rooms from: $139* ⊠ *6 km (4 miles) north of Alajuela's Tribunales de Justicia on road to Poás* ☎ *2442–8595, 800/506–2304 in North America* ⊕ *www.hotelbuenavistacr. com* ⇌ *11 rooms, 6 suites, 5 cabins* ¶◎¶ *Breakfast.*

$$
HOTEL
⊞ **Hotel La Rosa de América.** This small hotel tucked off the road to La Garita is a simple and relaxed place to unwind, with its Canadian owners adding a welcoming energy and a personalized touch to the place. **Pros:** great for families; helpful owners; close to a number of restaurants. **Cons:** lacks flair of other options in this price range; should have car to stay here. $ *Rooms from: $86* ⊠ *1 km (½ mile) east of Zoo Ave* ☎ *2433–2741, 2433–2455* ⊕ *www.larosadeamerica. com* ⇌ *16 rooms* ¶◎¶ *Breakfast.*

$
B&B/INN
⊞ **Hotel Los Volcanes.** Budget travelers looking for airport proximity will find this urban oasis an excellent value. **Pros:** airport proximity; good value; historic ambience. **Cons:** some rooms are noisy; no views. $ *Rooms from: $60* ⊠ *Avda. 3, Cs. 2–Ctl., 100 m north, 25 m east of the northwest corner of central park, across from Juan Santamaría Museum* ☎ *2441–0525* ⊕ *www.hotellosvolcanes.com* ⇌ *15 rooms, 11 with bath* ¶◎¶ *Breakfast.*

$$
B&B/INN
⊞ **Pura Vida Hotel.** Extremely well-informed, helpful owners and proximity to the airport (15 minutes) make this a good place to begin and end a trip. **Pros:** owners active in the local community; stellar breakfast. **Cons:** large dogs may turn off those with less-than-fuzzy feelings for animals; stairs to climb. $ *Rooms from: $95* ⊠ *Tuetal, 2 km (1 mile) north of Tribunales de Justicia; veer left at Y* ☎ *2430–2630* ⊕ *www.puravidahotel.com* ⇌ *2 rooms, 4 bungalows* ¶◎¶ *Breakfast.*

$$
B&B/INN
⊞ **Siempreverde B&B.** A night at this isolated bed-and-breakfast in the heart of coffee plantation Doka Estate might be as close as you'll ever come to feeling like a coffee farmer or to truly getting away from it all. **Pros:** off-the-beaten-path feel; plenty of tranquility most of the day. **Cons:** isolated location; tour groups pass by for breakfast most

The Alajuela Cathedral's painted domed cupola was rebuilt after the 1991 earthquake.

mornings. $ *Rooms from: $80* ✉ *12 km (7½ miles) northwest of Tribunales de Justicia de Alajuela; turn left at high school* ☎ *2449–5562* ⊕ *www.dokaestate.com/siempreverde_eng.html* ⤴ *7 rooms* ¶◯| *Breakfast.*

$$$$
HOTEL
Fodor'sChoice
★
⌂ **Xandari Resort & Spa.** The tranquil and colorful Xandari is a strikingly original inn and spa, tailor-made for honeymooners and romantic getaways. **Pros:** amazing service; ideal setting for romance; guilt-free gourmet delights. **Cons:** some noise from other rooms; should have car to stay here. $ *Rooms from: $265* ✉ *5 km (3 miles) north of Tribunales de Justicia; turn left after small bridge, follow signs* ☎ *2443–2020, 866/363–3212 in North America* ⊕ *www.xandari.com* ⤴ *24 villas* ¶◯| *Breakfast.*

SANTO DOMINGO

18 km (11 miles) northeast of Escazú, 7 km (4½ miles) northwest of San José.

Between Heredia and San José, the pretty town of Santo Domingo de Heredia, established in the early 19th century, has wide streets and fine examples of traditional, tile-roof houses, and a monumental church, the Basílica de Santo Domingo, that stands out as a brilliant white landmark against the surrounding sea of green coffee farms. There's a level of tranquility here that belies its proximity to the capital, a mere 15-minute drive away if the traffic gods smile upon you.

GETTING HERE AND AROUND

For the 30-minute trip from downtown San José, head north on Calle Central 4 km (2½ miles) to the central park in Tibás; continue 100 meters and turn left. Follow this road another 2½ km (1¼ miles) to Santo Domingo. One of the Heredia bus routes leaves from Calle 1, Avenidas 7–9 every three to five minutes and passes through Santo Domingo.

KEEPING COOL

The Central Valley's climate is often a great surprise to first-time visitors—it's not at all the steamy tropics you've imagined. It's usually cool enough at night to go without air-conditioning, so don't be surprised if many hotels don't have it.

ESSENTIALS

Bank/ATM Banco Nacional ⊠ *Across from south side of Iglesia El Rosario* ☎ *2244–0439.*

Post Office Correos ⊠ *Avda. Ctl., Cs. 2 and 4.*

EXPLORING

Basílica de Santo Domingo. The splendid, late-19th-century Basílica de Santo Domingo is one of the country's only two basilicas, with two distinctive towers topped with gold domes. It's often a venue for classical music concerts throughout the year, including the July-to-August International Music Festival. The building keeps limited hours, open only for Masses and confessions. ⊠ *East of the soccer field* ☎ *2244–0168* ⊙ *Mon–Wed. and Fri. 6–7 pm, Thurs. 8–9 am and 6–7 pm, Sat. 4–7 pm Sun. 10–noon and 4–7 pm.*

Iglesia del Rosario. This church is older, built in the 1840s, and simpler than the Basílica de Santo Domingo. It faces the town's palm-shaded Parque Central. The church keeps limited hours depending on masses and confessions. ⊠ *entral park* ☎ *2244–0168* ⊙ *Mon.–Wed., Fri., and Sat. 8–9 am; Thurs. 9–4; Sun. 7–8 am.*

FAMILY **INBioparque.** Santo Domingo's main attraction is INBioparque, which does an excellent job of not only explaining the country's various ecosystems, but also taking you into them. It's a useful, if slightly expensive, primer before heading out to the hinterlands. You'll wander trails through climate-controlled wetlands and out to tropical dry forest. The forests may not look much different, but your English-speaking guide will explain the subtleties. Along the way, stop at the butterfly farm, insect exhibits, and bromeliad garden. For an extra $3 you can visit the 15 species of snakes housed here in the National Serpentarium. The tour is packed with information—perhaps too much—but if you're visiting Costa Rica for its ecology, it's a worthwhile lesson. An open-air, upscale cafeteria serves typical Costa Rican fare, with a playground within view of terrace tables. The gift shop has a great selection of Tagua-nut jewelry and natural history–themed souvenirs and books. Reservations are required for tours. ⊠ *Road between Santo Domingo and Heredia, 400 m north and 250 m west of Shell gas station* ☎ *2507–8107* ⊕ *www.inbioparque.com* ✉ *$25* ⊙ *Fri. 9–5 (last admission at 3), weekends 9–5:30 (last admission at 4). Tours at 9, 11, and 2. Mon.–Thurs. by reservation.*

The verdant Central Valley is Costa Rica's breadbasket.

WHERE TO STAY

$$
HOTEL

Hotel Bougainvillea. True to its name, this modern, very comfortable, three-story hotel is awash in bougainvillea on the outside and decorated with an impressive collection of Costa Rican art on the inside. **Pros:** lush and open spaces; nice bird-watching; balconies in upper rooms; restaurant on-site. **Cons:** slightly institutional feel in the hallways. $ *Rooms from: $108 ⊠ 2 km (1 mile) east of Santo Domingo de Heredia ☎ 2244–1414 ☎ 866/880–5441 in North America ⊕ www.hb.co.cr ➷ 77 rooms, 4 suites ◌ Breakfast.*

HEREDIA

4 km (3 miles) north of Santo Domingo, 11 km (6 miles) northwest of San José.

The lively city of Heredia, capital of the important coffee province of the same name, contains a couple of the country's best-preserved colonial structures, along with a contrasting, youthful buzz provided by a concentration of young people attending the National University (UNA) and century-old *colegios* (high schools) scattered around the town. Heredia is nicknamed the City of Flowers (*La Ciudad de Flores* in Spanish), which refers less to the flowers that decorate the city than to a leading founding family named Flores. Flores also refers to beautiful women, for which Heredia is known. (On the topic of names, remember that "h" is always silent in Spanish. Pronounce the small city's name *air-AY-dee-ah*.) Founded in 1706, the city bears witness to how difficult preservation can be in an earthquake-prone country; most of its colonial structures have been destroyed by the tremors and tropical climate—not to mention modernization. Still, the city and neighboring towns retain a certain historic feel, with old adobe buildings scattered amid the concrete structures. Nearby Barva is also notable for its colonial central square and venerable adobe structures. From Heredia, scenic mountain roads climb northeast, passing through the pleasant, high-altitude coffee towns of San Rafael and San Isidro, each centered by a notable, Tico-style Gothic church and a pleasant central park.

GETTING HERE AND AROUND

The narrow routes from San José to Heredia are notoriously clogged at almost all times; avoid them during rush hours if possible. Turn right at the west end of Paseo Colón. Follow Pan-American Highway 2 km (1 mile); take the second exit, just before the highway heads onto an overpass and just after the Hotel Irazú (on the right). To get to the center of Heredia, follow that road for 5½ km (3½ miles), being careful to note which direction traffic in the alternative middle lane is traveling, then turn left at the Universidad Nacional.

Buses run between San José (300 meters east of Hospital San Juan de Dios) and Heredia every 5 to 10 minutes daily (between 5 am and 10 pm). The steady stream of buses leaving from Calle 1, Avenidas 7–9 every three to five minutes passing through Santo Domingo are sometimes a better bet during rush hour, particularly the *directo* buses that start after 3:30 pm; these buses also run from midnight to 3:30 am on the hour. Better still, hop aboard the new, modern train, departing San José from the vintage Atlantic Station, on the north side of the National Park, and arriving in downtown Heredia 30 minutes later. Trains run every half hour from 5:30 to 8 am, then 3:30 to 7:30 pm—geared more toward the needs of workaday commuters than tourists—and the fare is about 75¢. If you're without a car, a taxi is the best way to get to Café Britt or Barva.

ESSENTIALS

Bank/ATM Banco Nacional ⊠ *25 m south of southwest corner of central park* ☎ *2277–6900.*

Internet La Floresta Internet ⊠ *South side of central park, on 2nd fl* ☎ *2238–4279.*

Pharmacy Farmacia Chavarria ⊠ *South side of central park* ☎ *2263–4668* ⊕ *www.farmaciachavarria.com* ⊙ *Mon.–Sat. 7:30–7:30, Sun. 8–5.*

Post Office Correos ⊠ *Avda. Ctl., C. Ctl.-2, northwest corner of central park.*

Continued on page 174

Picking coffee beans from plant

COFFEE, THE GOLDEN BEAN

Tour a working coffee plantation and learn about the product that catapulted Costa Rica onto the world's economic stage, built the country's infrastructure, and created a middle class unlike any other in Central America.

Costa Rica B.C. (before coffee) was a poor, forgotten little colony with scant infrastructure and no real means of making money. Coffee production changed all of that and transformed the country into one of the wealthier and most stable in Central America. Coffee remains Costa Rica's bread and butter—the industry employs one-fourth of Costa Rica's population full- or part-time—and coffee plantations are sprinkled throughout the Central Valley and Northern Lowlands. All cultivate fine Arabica beans (by government decree, the inferior Robusta variety is not grown here). Visit one and learn what makes the country tick.

By Jeffrey Van Fleet

HISTORY IN A CUP

Coffee plantations near Poás Volcano, Central Valley

The country's first leaders saw this new crop as a tool with which to engineer a better life for their people. After gaining independence, new laws were created to allow average Costa Ricans to become coffee-growing landowners. These farmers formed the foundation of a middle-class majority that has long distinguished the country from the rest of Latin America. Costa Rica's infrastructure, institutional organizations, and means of production quickly blossomed—young entrepreneurs established small import-export houses, growers banded together to promote a better infrastructure, and everyone plowed their profits into improving the country's primitive road system.

SOCIAL TRANSFORMATION

As the coffee business became more profitable, prominent families were sending their children abroad to study, and doctors, lawyers and other skilled professionals in search of jobs began arriving by the

DRINKING THE GOOD STUFF

Here's the kicker for you, dear coffee-loving visitor: it's tough to find a decent cup in Costa Rica. True to the realities of developing-country economics, the good stuff goes for export, leaving a poorer quality bean behind for the local market. Add to that that the typical household here makes coffee with heaps of sugar. Your best bet for a good cup is an upscale hotel or restaurant, which is attuned to foreign tastes and does use export-quality product. The decorative foil bags you see in souvenir shops and supermarkets are also export-quality and make terrific souvenirs.

COFFEE TIMELINE

Local workers harvesting coffee beans in 1800s

1720	Coffee arrives in New World.
1791	Coffee plants introduced to Costa Rica.
1820	First coffee exports go to Panama.
1830	Legislation paves way for coffee profits to finance government projects.
1860	Costa Rican coffee first exported to United States.
1890	Atlantic Railroad opens, allowing for easier port access.

Enjoying a cup of coffee in Montezuma, Nicoya Peninsula

boatload. Returning students and well-educated immigrants brought a new world view that contributed to the formation of Costa Rica's liberal ideology.

MODERN TIMES

Development gobbled up land in the Central Valley by the last half of the 20th century, and coffee production began to spread to other areas of the country. A worldwide slump in coffee prices in the 1990s forced many producers out of the business. Prices have risen since 2002, and the government looks to smooth out any fluctuations with added-value eco-certification standards and innovative marketing.

Today, some 70% of the country's *número uno* agricultural crop comes from small family properties of under 25 acres owned by 250,000 farmers. They seasonally employ over four times that number of people, and kids in rural areas still take class time off to help with the harvest.

CAFÉ CHEAT SHEET

café solo: black

con azúcar: with sugar

con crema: with cream

con leche: with milk

descafeinado: decaffeinated (not easy to find here)

■

grano entero: whole beans

grano molido: ground

tostado claro or *tueste claro:* light roast

tostado oscuro or *tueste oscuro:* dark roast

Oxcarts built in the early 1900s to transport coffee

1897	Coffee barons construct San José's ornate Teatro Nacional.
1992	Costa Rica adopts new environmental laws for coffee industry.
1997	Tourism displaces coffee as Costa Rica's top industry.
Today	Costa Rica turns to eco-certification and fair-trade marketing of coffee.

COSTA RICA'S BEAN COUNTRY

Coffee plantations from Cervantes to Orosi Central Valley

Costa Rica possesses all the factors necessary—moderately high altitude, mineral-rich volcanic soil, adequate rainfall but distinct rainy and dry seasons—to be a major coffee player. Costa Rican growers cultivate only Arabica coffee beans. The industry eliminated the inferior Robusta variety in 1989 and hasn't looked back. The Costa Rican Coffee Institute certifies eight regional coffee varieties.

The coffee-growing cycle begins in April or May, when rains make the dark-green bushes explode in a flurry of white blossoms. By November, the fruit starts to ripen, turning from green to red. The busy harvest begins as farmers race to get picked "cherries" to *beneficios* (processing mills), where beans are removed, washed, machine-dried, and packed in burlap sacks either for export or to be roasted for local consumption.

Coffee plantations, Central Valley

❶ Aficionados wax poetic about the beans that come from **Tarrazú**, the high-altitude Los Santos Region in the Southern Pacific. It has good body, high acidity, and a chocolaty flavor.

❷ Coffee grown in **Tres Ríos**, east of San José, has high acidity, good body, and a nice aroma.

❸ Altitude of the **Valle Central** (around San José, Heredia and Alajuela) affects the size and hardness of the coffee bean and can influence certain components, particularly the acidity. This is an important characteristic of Arabica coffee.

❹ **Valle Occidental,** in the prosperous western Central Valley, gives you hints of apricots and peaches.

Arabica coffee beans

Coffee beans | Coffee bean pickers | Hand picking Coffee beans

Coffee plant

Siquirres
Moín
TURRIALBA
Puerto Viejo de Talamanca
Cahuita
Bribri
Sixaola
CORDILLERA DE TALAMANCA
PANAMA
San Isidro
Buenos Aires
Salitre
BRUNCA
Palmar Norte
Paso Real
Ciudad Cortés
San Vito
Palmar Sur
Pan-American Hwy
Ciudad Neily
Drake
Rincón
Golfito
Río Claro
Osa Peninsula
Puerto Jiménez
Paso Canoas
Carate
Zancudo
Pavones
Matapalo

❺ Tasters describe **Orosi** coffee, from the southeastern Central Valley, as "floral."

❻ The lower altitudes of nearby **Turrialba** give its product a medium body.

❼ The high-altitude **Brunca** region, near San Vito in southern Costa Rica, produces

coffee with excellent aroma, good body, and moderate acidity.

❽ **Guanacaste** is a diverse region that includes Monteverde and the central Nicoya Peninsula. Here they produce a medium-body coffee.

PLANTATIONS WITH TOURS

Wonder where your cup of morning coffee originates? The following purveyors give informative tours of their facilities and acquaint you with the life and times of the country's favorite beverage.

Tours guide you through the plant-to-crop process in English or Spanish, taking you from picking to drying to roasting to packing to brewing.

Reservations are essential. Plan on spending a half-day for any of these outings. The whole package will set you back about $30 per person.

CAFÉ BRITT Barva, Heredia *(see Chapter 4)* Café Britt incorporates a small theater production into its informative tour, presenting the history of Costa Rican coffee in song and dance.

COOPEDOTA SANTA MARIA Santa Maria de Dota *(see Chapter 8)* A tour here acquaints you with the standard bean-to-bag experience, as well as the cooperative's pioneering environmental practices.

DOKA COFFEE ESTATE San Luis de Sabanilla, Alajuela *(see Chapter 4)* Doka Coffee Estate offers a comprehensive tour through the entire growing and drying process and lets you sample the local brew.

DON JUAN COFFEE TOUR Montverde *(see Chapter 5)* A personalized excursion with a small group is the hallmark of this tour to a coffee plantation a few miles outside the town of Santa Elena.

MONTVERDE COFFEE TOUR Montverde *(see Chapter 5)* Montverde Coffee offers you some hands-on experience. Depending on the time of year, you can help with picking, drying, roasting, or packing.

EXPLORING

TOP ATTRACTIONS

Fodor's Choice
★

Café Britt. The producer of Costa Rica's most popular export-quality coffee gives a lively Classic Coffee Tour highlighting Costa Rica's history of coffee cultivation through a theatrical presentation that is admittedly a bit hokey. Your "tour guides" are professional actors, and pretty good ones at that, so if you don't mind the song and dance, it's fun. During the 1½-hour tour, you'll take a short walk through the coffee farm and processing plant, and learn how professional coffee tasters distinguish a fine cup of java. A four-hour Coffee & Nature tour delves into the process at a more expert level. You can also stop in at their Coffee Bar and Factory Store, 8 to 5 daily. Although both coffee tours devote themselves entirely to the production and history of Costa Rica's most famous agricultural product, Britt is also a purveyor of fine chocolates, cocoas, cookies, macadamia nuts, and coffee liqueurs; you'll see its products for sale in souvenir shops around the country and at the airport as you leave. ⊠ *From Heredia, take road to Barva, follow signs* ☎ *2277–1500* ⊕ *www.coffeetour.com* ✉ *$22 Classic Coffee Tour, $39 with transportation; $68 Coffee & Nature Tour, includes transportation* ☉ *Classic Coffee Tours: daily 11 am, 3 pm Dec.– Apr.; Coffee & Nature Tour: Fri.–Sun. 11 am.*

WORTH NOTING

Casa de la Cultura. Next to the Fortín, the tile-roof building with the handsome wood veranda is Heredia's Casa de la Cultura, which almost always has a free exhibition by local artists. Inside is a very small museum of town history, as well as a handsome inner atrium, with wooden galleries, where concerts are often held. The house was originally the stately home of early-20th-century president Alfredo González Flores. ⊠ *Avda. Ctl. and C. Ctl.* ☎ *2261–4485* ⊕ *casadelaculturaalfredogonzalezflores.blogspot.com* ✉ *Free* ☉ *Daily 9–5.*

Feria. On Saturday mornings starting at 5, Heredia's open-air *feria*, a lively famers' market, stretches for almost a kilometer (½ mile) along Avenida 14. ⊠ *Avda. 14.*

Fortín (*Little Fort*). On the north side of the Parque Central in its own little park stands a strange tower. Built as a military post in the 1870s, it never did see action and now serves as the symbol of the province, one of the few military monuments in this army-less country. The tower is closed to the public. The old brick building next to the Fortín is the Palacio Municipal (Town Hall). ⊠ *C. Ctl. and Avda. Ctl.*

Iglesia de la Inmaculada Concepción (*Church of the Immaculate Conception*). On the east side of the park stands this impressive church, built between 1797 and 1804 to replace an adobe temple dating from the early 1700s. It is one of the few structures in Costa Rica remaining from the colonial era. The flat-fronted, whitewashed church has thick stone walls, small windows, and squat buttresses, which have kept it intact through two centuries of earthquakes and tremors. The serene, white interior has two rows of stately, gold-trimmed Ionic columns marching down a long aisle, past lovely stained-glass windows. The church is flanked by tidy side gardens, where you can stroll among sculpted trees along concrete paths incised with a floral pattern. ⊠ *Eastern side of central park* ☎ *2237–0779* ☉ *Daily 6 am–7 pm.*

Mercado Nuevo (*New Market*). Three blocks southeast of the Parque Central is Heredia's covered New Market—that's how everybody refers to it here—officially the Mercado Central, which holds dozens of *sodas* (simple restaurants) along with the usual food stands. ⊠ *C. Ctl. and Avda. 6* ⊗ *Mon.–Sat. 7–6.*

Museo de Cultura Popular (*Museum of Popular Culture*). At the edge of a middle-class neighborhood between Heredia and Barva, this museum is housed in a farmhouse with a large veranda built in 1885 with an adobe-like technique called *bahareque*. Run by the National University, the museum is furnished with antiques and surrounded by a garden and a small coffee farm. Just walking around the museum is instructive, but calling ahead to reserve a hands-on cultural tour (such as one on tortilla making) really makes it worth the trip. An open-air restaurant serves bread baked in a clay oven, and fresh tortillas and tamales. ⊠ *From Musmanni bakery in Santa Lucía de Barva, 100 m north, then turn right 1 km (½ mile) east; follow signs* ☎ *2260–1619* ⊕ *www.museo. una.ac.cr* ⊡ *$2* ⊗ *Sun. 10–5, Mon.–Sat. by appointment.*

Parque Central. Heredia is centered on tree-studded Parque Central, one of the country's loveliest and liveliest central parks, surrounded by some notable buildings spanning more than 250 years of history. The park has a large, round, cast-iron fountain imported from England in 1879 and a Victorian bandstand where the municipal band plays Sunday-morning and Thursday-night concerts. Families, couples, and old-timers sit on park benches, shaded by fig and towering palm trees, often inhabited by noisy and colorful flocks of crimson-fronted parakeets. Drop into Pops, a national ice-cream chain at the south side of the park and pick up an ice-cream cone, then take a seat on a park bench and watch the passing parade. ⊠ *C. Ctl. and Avda. Ctl.*

San Rafael de Heredia. This quiet, tidy, coffee town 2 km (1 mile) northeast of Heredia has a large church notable for its stained-glass windows and bright interior. The road north from the church winds its way up Barva Volcano, ending atop the Monte de la Cruz lookout point. ⊠ *San Rafael de Heredia.*

Sibú Chocolate. Get to know a bean of another kind during a private tasting at the workshop of the country's best artisanal chocolate makers that starts with an informative talk about the historical and cultural significance of the cacao bean, includes a demonstration of tempering chocolate by hand and ends, of course, with a sampling of exquisite chocolates made from 100% organic cacao. Tasters can also stay for an elegant lunch on Sibú's pretty terrace ($17). Reserve 48 hours in advance. ⊠ *Turnoff for San Isidro de Heredia, 2 km (1 mile) off highway to Braulio Carrillo National Park* ☎ *2268–1335* ⊕ *www.sibuchocolate. com* ⊡ *$25, minimum of 4 people* ⊗ *Tues.–Sat. 8:30–4:30.*

WHERE TO EAT

$ ╳ **Barco de los Mariscos.** For an authentic Tico experience, head to this
COSTA RICAN antique hacienda in San Rafael de Heredia for lunch or dinner on the veranda, with a view of the town's imposing, cream-color Gothic church. The 100-year-old wooden house, painted sea blue, was actually moved by oxcart years ago from a nearby coffee *finca* (farmhouse), and now sits

in a rose garden on a busy corner of the town. Ceviche and seafood are the main attractions—marinated sea bass with avocado is the most popular dish—along with daily *casados* (rice, beans, plantains, and salad) and excellent *patacones* (fried, squashed plantain slices) served with *molida*, a smooth, refried bean dip. $ *Average main: $9* ⊠ *Across from Banco de Costa Rica, San Rafael de Heredia* ☎ *2263–3909*.

$ ✕ **L'Antica Roma.** More than 40 ver-

ITALIAN sions of pizza baked in a woodburning oven are the main event at this popular, upscale Italian eatery. Every pizza comes with a trio of condiments to spice it up to your taste: homemade hot chili or a garlicky sauce, and grated cheese. Framed black-and-white photos of famous Italians eating spaghetti may inspire you to try one of the decent homemade pastas. There's also an exhaustive menu of meat and chicken cooked Italian style—juicy beef tenderloin substitutes for veal in all the classic Italian veal dishes. Italian wine can be ordered by the glass, carafe, or bottle. Two large-screen TVs with sports add to the happy buzz indoors on busy nights; the tables out on the wrought-iron-enclosed patio lend themselves better to conversation, once rush-hour traffic has subsided. $ *Average main: $10* ⊠ *C. 7 and Avda. 7, across from Hotel Valladolid* ☎ *2262–9073*.

> ## VOLCANO-VIEWING ON AN EMPTY STOMACH
>
> No question: the earlier you get to Poás, the better the views you'll be afforded. If that means skipping breakfast, a number of roadside stands on the way up the volcano sell strawberry jam, *cajeta* (a pale fudge), and rather bland corn crackers called *biscochos* to tide you over until you can have a hearty típico breakfast in the park visitor center's cafeteria.

WHERE TO STAY

$$$$ ▦ **Finca Rosa Blanca Coffee Plantation Resort.** Set amid fields of green cof-

B&B/INN fee, this exclusive, hilltop bed-and-breakfast hideaway has a much-

Fodor's Choice deserved reputation as one of the country's sumptuous splurges. **Pros:**

★ eco-consciousness; indulgence with style; service par excellence. **Cons:** some units short on closet and drawer space; overpriced restaurant; hard to find if you are driving your own car. $ *Rooms from: $305* ⊠ *800 m north of Café Britt Distribution Center, Santa Bárbara de Heredia* ☎ *2269–9392, 305/395–3042 in North America* ⊕ *www.fincarosablanca.com* ↳ *11 junior suites, 2 master suites* ❘⊚❘ *Breakfast*.

$$ ▦ **Hotel Chalet Tirol.** The replica of a cobbled Tirolean town square, com-

HOTEL plete with fountain and church, may be a bit much, but the cozy, bright, two-story wooden chalets are charming and the Austrian design doesn't seem out of place amid the pines, pastures, and cool air of Volcán Barva's upper slopes. **Pros:** cozy surroundings; most rooms have a fireplace; good restaurant. **Cons:** need a car to stay here; no in-room phones; patchy Wi-Fi. $ *Rooms from: $120* ⊠ *Main road, 10 km (6 miles) north of San Rafael de Heredia, Braulio Carrillo National Park* ☎ *2267–6222, 800/720–1167 in North America* ⊕ *www.hotelchaleteltirol.com* ↳ *15 suites, 20 chalets* ❘⊚❘ *Breakfast*.

$$ ▦ **Hotel Valladolid.** The classiest hotel in downtown Heredia, this four-

HOTEL story narrow building first attracted business travelers and visiting professors at the nearby National University, although guests now are just as likely to be vacationers. **Pros:** central location; friendly staff; extensive buffet breakfast with homemade tortillas. **Cons:** limited parking; a few rooms show their age. [$] *Rooms from: $86* ✉ *C. 7 and Avda. 7* ☎ *2260–2905* 🌐 *www.hotelvalladolid.net* 🛏 *11 rooms, 1 suite* 🍴 *Breakfast.*

SHOPPING

Paseo de Las Flores. This airy, pleasant, and huge shopping mall—with 340 stores, it's Costa Rica's largest—is on the main road south of town. It has a branch of almost every international fashion boutique, as well as a multiplex cinema and a wide choice of cafés and restaurants. ✉ *2 km (1 mile) south of town on highway to San José* ☎ *2261–9898* 🌐 *www.paseodelasflores.com* 🕒 *Mon.–Sat. 10:30–9, Sun. 11–8.*

4

EN ROUTE

Barva de Heredia. About 3 km (2 miles) due north of Heredia, this colonial town is famous for mask making and for its **Parque Central,** still surrounded by the original adobe buildings with Spanish-tile roofs on three sides, and a white-stucco church to the east. The park is filled with whimsical sculptures, including a park bench shaped like an entire seated family, and bizarre masks and clown's heads decorating garbage receptacles. An amphitheater and stage stand ready for the annual mask festival held every August. (A less pleasant part of the August festival is the tradition of smacking one's fellow townspeople with cow or pig bladders.) The stout, handsome church with terra-cotta bas-relief flourishes dates from the late 18th century and has a lovely grotto shrine to the Virgin Mary in the church garden. On a clear day you can see verdant Volcán Barva towering to the north. ✉ *3 km (2 miles) north of Heredia, Barva de Heredia.*

POÁS VOLCANO NATIONAL PARK

37 km (23 miles) (45 mins) north of Alajuela, 57 km (35 miles) (1 hr) north of San José.

Fodor's Choice ★

Arenal may be Costa Rica's most famous volcano, but you can walk right up to the crater here at Poás. That gives it an edge in the "cool volcano visit" department.

GETTING HERE AND AROUND

From the Pan-American Highway north of Alajuela, follow the signs for Poás. The road is in relatively good condition. One public bus departs daily at 8 am from San José (✉ *Avda. 2, Cs. 12–14*) and returns at 2 pm. Taxis from San José are around $100 (and around $50 from Alajuela). A slew of tours from San José take in the volcano and combine the morning excursion with an afternoon at La Paz Waterfall Gardens, or tours of Café Britt near Heredia or the Doka Estate near Alajuela. ✉ *From Alajuela, drive north through town and follow signs* ☎ *2482–2424, 192 national parks hotline in Costa Rica* 🎟 *$10* 🕒 *Daily 8:30–3:30.*

EXPLORING

La Paz Waterfall Gardens. Five magnificent waterfalls are the main attractions at these gardens on the eastern edge of Volcán Poás National Park, but they are complemented by the beauty of the surrounding cloud forest, an abundance of hummingbirds and other avian species, and the country's biggest butterfly garden. A concrete trail leads down from the visitor center to the multilevel, screened butterfly observatory

La Paz Waterfall Gardens attracts 24 different species of hummingbirds and has a huge butterfly garden.

and continues to gardens where hummingbird feeders attract swarms of these multicolor creatures. The trail then enters the cloud forest, where it leads to a series of metal stairways that let you descend into a steep gorge to viewing platforms near each of the waterfalls. A free shuttle will transport you from the trail exit back to the main building if you prefer to avoid the hike uphill. Several alternative paths lead from the main trail through the cloud forest and along the river's quieter upper stretch, providing options for hours of exploration—it takes about two hours to hike the entire complex. (Enter by 3 pm to give yourself adequate time.) The complex's Jungle Cat exhibit serves as a rescue center for felines (jaguars, ocelots, and pumas). The visitor center has a gift shop and open-air cafeteria with a great view. The gardens are a stop on many daylong tours from San José that take in the Poás Volcano or area coffee tours. ✉ *6 km (4 miles) north of Vara Blanca* ☎ *2482–2720, 954/727–3997 in North Ameirca* ⊕ *www.waterfallgardens.com* ✉ *$36, $49 with lunch* ⊙ *Daily 8–5.*

Fodor's Choice **Poás Volcano.** The Northern Lowlands' Arenal Volcano gets all the
★ press, but we nominate Poás, in the far northern Central Valley, as Costa Rica's coolest volcano experience. Arenal requires you to view it from afar, while Poás lets you peer right inside what is thought to be the largest active volcanic crater in the world. The ride up here is disarming: pleasant farms and lush green cloud forest line the volcano's slopes. Friendly fruit and jam vendors along the road beckon you to stop and sample their wares. Only when you get to the bubbling, gurgling, smoking summit do you leave that pastoral scene behind and stare into the crater.

The park is nearly always open, but officials monitor activity closely and close access to Poás's 2,708-meter (8,885-foot) summit at the slightest hint of anything irregular. Volcanic activity has increased, but remained at a steady level here since a series of eruptions in 2006. ⚠ **For your own health and well-being, step away for fresh air at least once every 10 minutes, lest you be overcome by the sulfur fumes.** A good place to take that break is the park's bustling visitor center. With complete park information, a cafeteria, and a gift shop, it is one of the country's best. ⊠ *From Alajuela, drive north through town and follow signs* ☎ *2482–2424, 192 national parks hotline in Costa Rica* ⌧ *$10* ⏰ *Daily 8:30–3:30.*

WHERE TO EAT AND STAY

$
COSTA RICAN

✕ **Jaulares.** All the cooking here is done with wood, which adds to the rustic ambience of terra-cotta floors, bare wooden beams, and sylvan surroundings. The house specialty, *lomito Jaulares* (Jaulares tenderloin), is a strip of grilled meat served with *gallo pinto* (rice and beans) and a mild *salsa criollo* (creole sauce); other grilled meats and several fish dishes are also available. Jaulares stays open until midnight on Saturday for live music. $ *Average main: $9* ⊠ *2 km (1 mile) north of Laguna de Fraijanes* ☎ *2482–2155* ⊕ *www.jaulares.com.*

$
COSTA RICAN
Fodor's Choice
★

✕ **Restaurante Chubascos.** Dine amid tall pines and colorful flowers on the upper slopes of Poás Volcano, enjoying a small menu of traditional Tico dishes that include platters of *gallos* (homemade tortillas with meat, cheese, or potato fillings) as well as delicious daily specials. The *refrescos* (fresh fruit drinks) are top-drawer, especially the ones made from locally grown *fresas* (strawberries) and *moras* (blackberries) blended with milk. $ *Average main: $9* ⊠ *1 km (½ mile) north of Laguna de Fraijanes* ☎ *2482–2280* ⊕ *www.chubascos.co.cr* ⏰ *No dinner Sun.–Fri.*

$$$$
HOTEL

⛺ **Peace Lodge.** These rooms overlooking the misty forests of La Paz Waterfall Gardens seem like something out of the *Lord of the Rings,* with their curved, clay-stucco walls, hardwood floors, stone fireplaces, four-poster beds made of varnished logs, and grottolike bathrooms with private waterfalls. **Pros:** many activities included in rates; whimsical furnishings; excellent river trail; rates include admission to the Waterfall Gardens. **Cons:** pricey; popular with tour groups; sometimes difficult to find space; lukewarm showers; all but the top floors can be noisy because of creaky stairs. $ *Rooms from: $355* ⊠ *6 km (4 miles) north of Vara Blanca* ☎ *2482–2720, 954/727–3997 in North America, 2482–2100 for reservations* ⊕ *www.waterfallgardens.com* ⤶ *16 rooms, 2 villas* ⦵ *No meals.*

$$
B&B/INN
Fodor's Choice
★

⛺ **Poás Volcano Lodge.** Stylish luxury prevails here: king-size beds, outdoor whirlpool tubs, and luxurious fabrics grace the rooms and suites and many have balconies overlooking the volcano. **Pros:** close to volcano; coffeemakers and electric teakettles in rooms; great breakfasts; beautiful surroundings at a good price. **Cons:** hotel is often fully booked. $ *Rooms from: $145* ⊠ *4 km (2½ miles) east of Churrasco restaurant, on road to Vara Blanca* ☎ *2482–2194* ⊕ *www. poasvolcanolodge.com* ⤶ *6 rooms, 5 suites* ⦵ *Breakfast.*

SHOPPING

Neotrópica Foundation. A portion of the profits from the sale of nature-themed T-shirts, cards, and posters in the national park's visitor center goes to conservation projects. ⊠ *Visitor center* ⊕ *www.neotropica.org.*

EAST OF SAN JOSÉ

Cartago, due east of San José, is Costa Rica's oldest city and colonial capital, home to some beautiful old churches, including the country's national shrine, plus other notable historical structures. To the north of Cartago towers massive Irazú Volcano, which is covered with fertile farmland enriched by the volcano's many eruptions and topped by an impressive crater. Southeast of Cartago lies the pastoral Orosi Valley, the cradle of Costa Rican history, and the densely forested Tapantí National Park.

The main attractions near the bustling market town of Turrialba are its namesake volcano, an internationally famous agricultural research center, and the pre-Columbian archaeological ruins of Guayabo. The town lies considerably lower than the rest of the Central Valley, so it enjoys a more moderate climate, a transition between the cooler Central Valley and the sweltering Caribbean coast.

CARTAGO

22 km (14 miles) southeast of San José.

Although earthquakes have destroyed most of its structures from the colonial era, Cartago still has some attractive restored buildings, most of them erected after the devastating 1910 earthquake. The city served as the country's first capital until 1823, when the seat of government was moved to the emerging economic center of San José. Today, Cartago is a bustling market town, shopping center, and vibrant student hub. Most visitors see Cartago on their way to or from the Orosi Valley or Turrialba, and there is little reason (or place) to stay the night. The Orosi Valley, a short drive away, has better choices.

GETTING HERE AND AROUND

For the 25-minute drive from San José, drive east on Avenida 2 through San Pedro and Curridabat to the highway entrance, where you have three road options—take the middle one marked Cartago. Shortly before Cartago, a Y intersection marks the beginning of the route up Irazú, with traffic to Cartago veering right.

Buses between San José and Cartago leave every 10 minutes daily (Avenida 10 and Calle 5, 400 meters south of the Teatro Nacional) from 5 am to 6 pm; after 6 the buses leave from Avenida 2 between Calle 1/3, in front of the National Theater. Cartago buses to San José pick up 300 meters west of the Municipal Museum of Cartago (formerly called the Comandancia), from 4:35 am to 11 pm. Buses to Orosi leave Cartago every 15 minutes from 5:15 to 7:30 am, then every 30 minutes until 7 pm, with a bus at 8 and 9 pm, 100 meters east, 25 meters south of the southeast corner of Las Ruinas.

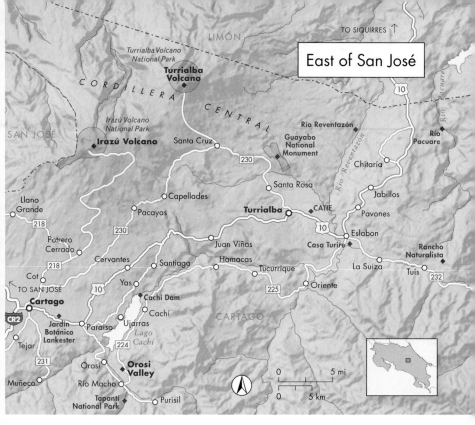

East of San José

ESSENTIALS

Bank/ATM Banco Nacional ⊠ *Southeast corner of Las Ruinas* ☎ *2550–1400.*

Hospital Hospital Dr. Max Peralta ⊠ *200 m south, 150 m east of Las Ruinas* ☎ *2550–1999.*

Pharmacy Farmacia Fischel ⊠ *300 m west of Basílica de Nuestra Señora de los Angeles* ☎ *2552–2430.*

Post Office Correos ⊠ *Avda. 2, Cs. 15–17.*

Taxis Taxis El Carmen ☎ *2551–0836.*

EXPLORING

Basílica de Nuestra Señora de los Angeles (*Our Lady of the Angels Basilica*). This basilica is a hodgepodge of architectural styles from Byzantine to baroque, with a dash of Gothic. The interior is even more striking, with a colorful tile floor, intricately painted, faux-finish wood columns, and lots of stained glass. It is the focus of an annual pilgrimage to celebrate the appearance of La Negrita, or the Black Virgin, Costa Rica's patron saint. To the left as you face the altar is a room decorated with amulets given in dedication to the virgin for her intercession in everything from triumphs over disease to triumphs on the soccer field. ⊠ *C. 16, Avdas. 2–4, 7 blocks east of central square* ☎ *2551–0465* ⊘ *Mon.–Sat. 6 am–7 pm, Sun. 6 am–8 pm.*

Bulls dressed in their finest for an oxcart parade in Cartago

Las Ruinas. Churches in one form or another stood at the site of the present-day central park from 1575 to 1841; they kept being knocked down by earthquakes and reconstructed again and again. After the major earthquake in 1841, the citizens of Cartago began work on a new, Romanesque cathedral. But a devastating earthquake in 1910 ended that project, too. Is there a connection between building churches here and the occurrence of earthquakes? No one knows, but townspeople have decided not to tempt fate any longer. The ruins of this unfinished house of worship now stand in a pleasant park, and the interior has been transformed into a lush garden with fountains, a small pond, and flowers planted in the original stone pillar bases. Among the many legends attributed to the ruins is the gruesome story of the priest who, after falling in love with his sister-in-law, was murdered by his brother. Folks here say his headless ghost still haunts the grounds at night. Although the plaza in front of the ruins is a Wi-Fi hot spot, we recommend not pulling out your laptop or tablet in such a public place—and this has nothing to do with alleged hauntings. Your smartphone should be okay, however. ⊠ *Avda. 2, Cs. 1–2* 🖼 *Free* ⊙ *Weekends 8–4.*

WHERE TO EAT

Although you can find decent pasta and pizza, haute cuisine just doesn't exist here. Cartago does give you a fine opportunity to eat some *comida típica* (typical food). On just about any street downtown you'll find a soda, and the women in the kitchen will serve you the same style of food they cook at home for their own families. One rule of thumb: the busier, the better—the locals know where to eat well.

CLOSE UP

La Negrita: Costa Rica's Patron Saint

On the night of August 1 and well into the early-morning hours of August 2, the road to Cartago from San José clogs with worshippers, some of whom have traveled from as far away as Nicaragua to celebrate the 1635 appearance of Costa Rica's patron saint, *La Negrita* (the Black Virgin). The feast day draws an estimated 1 million pilgrims each year, not bad for a country of just 4 million people. At a spring behind the church, people fill bottles with water believed to have curative properties. Miraculous healing powers are attributed to the saint, and devotees have placed thousands of tiny symbolic crutches, ears, eyes, and legs in a room to the left of the altar. Tour buses and school groups, along with shops selling the saint's likeness, make the scene a bit of a circus.

4

$ COSTA RICAN 🍴 **La Puerta del Sol.** A cut above the usual soda, this large, long-established restaurant across from the basilica has been feeding pilgrims since 1957. Along with hearty portions of seafood, grilled meats, and typical casados, the restaurant has a popular bar and terrace. [$] *Average main: $8* ✉ *North side of basilica plaza* ☎ *2551–0615.*

IRAZÚ VOLCANO

Costa Rica's highest volcano perches on Central America's "continental divide," offering splendid views of the Caribbean and Pacific coasts from the summit, assuming the skies are clear, that is. But look inside the volcano for the real sight here: Irazú's eerie, chartreuse-color crater lake.

GETTING HERE AND AROUND

Follow directions to Cartago (⇨ *above*), but shortly before the city a Y intersection marks the beginning of the road up Irazú; traffic to Cartago veers right, then left immediately past the first lights. From downtown Cartago, a 45-minute trip, take the road to Irazú at the northeast corner of the basilica. Signs from Cartago lead you to the park.

Buses head to Volcán Irazú from San José (✉ *Avda. 2, Cs. 1–3*) daily at 8 and 8:45 am and return at 12:30 pm.

Irazú Volcano (*Volcán Irazú*). Costa Rica's highest volcano, at 3,422 meters (11,260 feet), is one of the most popular with visitors since you can walk right down into the crater. Its presence is a mixed blessing: The ash fertilizes the Central Valley soil, but the volcano has caused considerable destruction through the centuries. ⚠ **Do not leave anything of value in your car while you visit the volcano.** There have been a lot of thefts in the parking lot here, even though it is supposed to be guarded. Most San José and area tour operators include the volcano among its excursions, and this is the easiest way to visit. ⇨ *See the Irazú Volcano feature for more details.* ☎ *2200–5025* 🎟 *$15* 🕒 *Daily 8–4.*

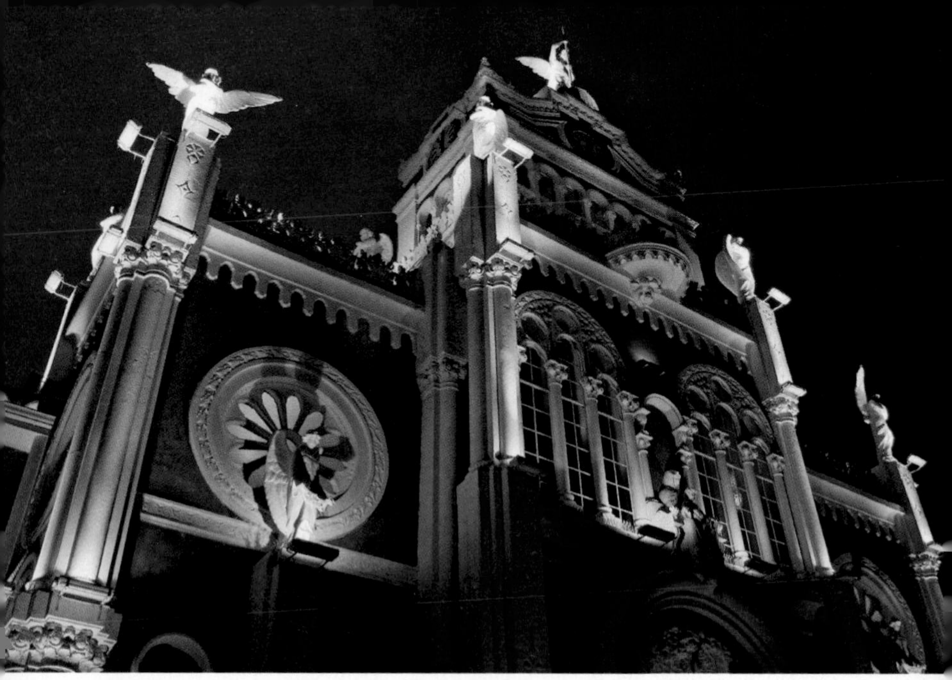

Cartago's Basilica de Nuestra Señora de los Angeles is the focus of the annual pilgrimage to celebrate the appearance of *La Negrita*, the Black Virgin.

WHERE TO EAT

$ COSTA RICAN 🍴 **Restaurant 1910.** Decorated with vintage photos of early-20th-century buildings and landscapes, this upscale restaurant also documents the disastrous 1910 earthquake that rocked this area and all but destroyed the colonial capital of Cartago. The menu is predominantly Costa Rican, with such traditional specialties as *trucha* (trout) and rice with chicken, along with some more-sophisticated dishes, like *corvina* (sea bass) fillet with a coconut liqueur sauce. The Sunday típico buffet is a great introduction to Costa Rican cooking. [$] *Average main: $8* ✉ *Road to Parque Nacional Volcán Irazú, 300 m north of Cot–Pacayas turnoff* ☎ *2536–6063* ⏲ *No dinner Sun.*

THE OROSI VALLEY

If you have a day to spend near San José, this idyllic valley makes a classic day trip, passing through coffee plantations shaded by poró trees—their flame-color flowers make a stunning sight during the dry season—oceans of chayote-squash vines, and small towns backed by verdant landscapes, with countless breathtaking views. It's a popular weekend drive for Costa Ricans, but still relatively off the beaten tourist path. The region is one of the few areas in Costa Rica that has remnants (ruins and churches) of the 17th-century Spanish colonial era. Paraíso, the valley's not-so-interesting metropolis, is your first point of access. Heading counterclockwise around the loop road are the area's real gems: Orosi, Tapantí National Park, Cachí, and Ujarrás.

GETTING HERE AND AROUND

A good road makes a loop around the valley and it's easy to take in all the sights along the loop if you have your own vehicle, or if you go on a guided tour—it's a staple of most San José tour operators' offerings. Buses to the town of Orosi leave Cartago every 15 minutes from 5:15 to 7:30 am, then every 30 minutes until 7 pm, with a bus at 8 and 9 pm, 100 meters east and 25 meters south of the southeast corner of Las Ruinas. Public transportation around the valley is tricky: buses travel clockwise and counterclockwise, but neither route completes the loop.

ESSENTIALS

Bank/ATM Banco Nacional ✉ *200 m south of soccer field* ☎ *2533–1390* ✉ *West side of central park, Paraíso* ☎ *2574–7274.*

Internet PC Orosi ✉ *200 m south of church.*

Pharmacy Farmacia Candelaria ✉ *North side of Retaurante Coto, across from soccer field* ☎ *2533–1919.* **Farmacia Sucre** ✉ *200 m west of central park, Paraíso* ☎ *2574–7286* ⊕ *www.farmaciasucre.com.*

Post Office Correos ✉ *100 m north of Municipalidad, Paraíso.*

EXPLORING

Iglesia de San José de Orosi. The town of Orosi, in the heart of the valley, has but one major attraction: this beautifully restored 1743 church, the country's oldest house of worship still in use, and one of the few structures in Costa Rica remaining from the colonial era. Set in a garden, against a green mountainside, it has a classic Spanish-colonial whitewashed facade and bell tower, with a roof made of cane overlaid with terra-cotta barrel tiles. Inside are an antique wooden altar and ancient paintings of the Stations of the Cross and the Virgin of Guadalupe, all brought to Costa Rica from Guatemala. The religious-art museum next door has a small but exquisite collection of furniture and artifacts from the original Franciscan monastery here. A huge, modern new church is being built beside the historic one, but happily it's just far enough away not to spoil photos of the picturesque church. ✉ *West side of soccer field* ☎ *2533–3051* 🏛 *Museum $1* ⊙ *Church Tues.–Fri. 9–noon and 1–5, weekends 9–noon and 1–7; museum Tues.–Sat. 1–5, Sun. 9–5.*

Iglesia de Ujarrás. Continue past the dam into the small hamlet of Ujarrás, then follow the signs to the site of the romantic ruins of Costa Rica's first church. An unlikely Spanish victory in 1666 over a superior force of invading British pirates was attributed to a stop here to ask for God's protection and blessing. The church was constructed in thanksgiving to honor of the Virgin of Ujarrás. The church, together with the surrounding village, was abandoned in 1833 after a series of earthquakes and floods wreaked havoc here, the lowest point of the Orosi Valley. Today the impressive, often-photographed ruins sit in a beautifully maintained park with lawns, flower gardens, and a pretty picnic area. A final, scenic 6-km (4-mile) winding drive to Paraíso from Ujarrás completes the road that loops the valley. Visitors fill the site on weekends; weekdays, you'll likely have the place to yourself. ✉ *In a small park, 1 km (½ mile) from Restaurante Típico Ujarrás* ☎ *2574–8366* 🏷 *Free* ⊙ *Daily 6–6.*

Iglesia de San José de Orosi is the county's oldest church that is still in use.

Jardín Botánico Lankester. The lush gardens of Lankester Botanical Garden, operated by the University of Costa Rica, house one of the world's foremost orchid collections, with more than 1,100 native and introduced species. Bromeliads, heliconias, and aroids also abound in the 7-acre garden, along with 80 species of trees, including rare palms. A Japanese garden has a graceful bridge and a teahouse. The best time to come is February through April, when the most orchids are in bloom. The garden's gift shop is one of the few places in Costa Rica to buy orchids that you can take home legally. (They come in small bottles and don't flower for four years, so you'll need some serious patience.) The garden is wheelchair-accessible and has excellent restrooms. ✉ *4 km (2 miles) east of Cartago at west entrance to Paraíso, Cartago* ☎ *2552–3247* ⊕ *www.jbl.ucr.ac.cr* 💰 *$7.50* ⊗ *Daily 8:30–5:30, last admission at 4:30.*

Sanchiri Mirador. Just beyond the town of Paraíso on the road to Orosi is the Sanchiri Mirador, a restaurant/bar with excellent food and one of the valley's best *miradores* (lookout points). But our favorite vantage point is at a point on the road just beyond Sanchiri where the earth appears to drop away and the valley comes into view as you make the steep descent to the town of Orosi. Here's a case for letting someone else do the driving. A little farther along, there's free parking at the **Orosi Mirador,** a public park with spectacular views, sheltered picnic tables and grills, and a children's playground. There are some steep steps to climb but the views—and the clean restrooms—at the top are worth it. ✉ *2 km (1 mile) south of Paraíso* ☎ *2574–5454* ⊕ *www.sanchiri.com* ⊗ *Mon.–Thurs. 7 am–9 pm, Fri. and Sat. 7 am–10:30 pm, Sun. 7 am–8 pm.*

Tapantí National Park. Stretching all the way to the Talamanca Mountains, the reserve encompasses 47 square km (18 square miles) of largely pristine, remote cloud forest, refuge for more than 400 bird species, including the emerald toucanet, violaceous trogon, and many of the country's hummingbirds. The rangers' office and visitor center are on the right just after the park entrance. You can leave your vehicle at a parking area 1½ km (1 mile) up the road. From here loop trails head off into the woods on both sides. The Oropéndola trail passes a picnic area and several swimming holes with cold, emerald waters. The entrance to La Pava trail begins up a steep forested hillside, about 1½ km (1 mile) from the parking area and leads down a steep hill to the riverbank. If you continue ½ km (¼ mile) past the trailhead, you arrive at a 91-meter (300-foot) stair trail leading to a lookout. Get an early start—you can enter on foot before 8 am, as long as you pay as you leave. The park clouds over markedly by afternoon and is renowned as the country's wettest national park, so be prepared with a poncho or umbrella.

4

To get to the park, head south of Orosi; the road becomes a rugged track following the Río Grande de Orosi past coffee plantations, elegant *fincas* (farmhouses), and seasonal barracks for coffee pickers before it's hemmed in by the steep slopes of thick jungle. At the bottom of the loop road, follow signs for Tapantí National Park. Though it's worth the trip for just an hour or two of exploring, you could easily fill a day in the park. ✉ *14 km (8 miles) south of Orosi* ☎ *2206–5615* 🎟 *$10* 🕒 *Daily 8–4.*

WHERE TO EAT

$$ COSTA RICAN

🍴 **Bar y Restaurante Coto.** A local institution since 1952, this large rancho restaurant and bar is famous for its huge meat platters—we're talking 1 to 1½ kilos (2.2 to 3.3 pounds) of meat with all the tipíco side dishes. Or you can dine more daintily on sautéed trout. The dining area is actually quite smart, with fresh white tablecloths overlaid with colored cloths, and a view of the lovely Orosi church. [$] *Average main: $12* ✉ *Northeast corner of soccer field* ☎ *2533–3032.*

$$ COSTA RICAN

🍴 **La Casona del Cafetal.** The valley's most scenic and famous lunch stop sits on a coffee plantation overlooking the Cachí Reservoir. It's firmly on the beaten path, which means frequent visits from tour groups. The spacious indoor dining area has a high barrel-tile roof, but the most sought-after tables are out on the tiled, lakeside portico, draped with flowering vines framing gorgeous lake views. The menu has both Costa Rican staples and sophisticated dishes such as *corvina guarumos* (bass stuffed with mushrooms). Expect a wait on weekends, when diners come from miles around for the gargantuan $25 lunch buffet that ends with delicious, coffee-flavored desserts and the casona's own coffee, made cup-by-cup in the old-fashioned Costa Rican way. After lunch, take a stroll down the garden path to the lake or check out the souvenir stalls in the parking lot. [$] *Average main: $12* ✉ *2 km (1 mile) south of Cachí Dam* ☎ *2577–1414* 🌐 *www.lacasonadelcafetal.com* 🕒 *No dinner.*

WHERE TO STAY

$$$ B&B/INN Fodor's Choice ★

🏨 **Hotel Quelitales.** For quiet, get-away-from-it-all seclusion, this eco-friendly lodging can't be beat. **Pros:** quiet seclusion; great views; friendly staff; careful attention to sustainability and environment. **Cons:** rough final road to get here; best to have a car to stay here;

steep walk to a couple of bungalows. $ *Rooms from: $160* ✉ *3 km (2 miles) east of Cachí* ☎ *2577–2222* ⊕ *www.hotelquelitales.com* ⤳ *6 bungalows* ⏐○⏐ *Breakfast.*

$ 📷 **Kiri Mountain Lodge.** Small and very affordable, this family-run hotel

B&B/INN   has easy access to Tapantí park and its own 175-acre private reserve with waterfalls. **Pros:** secluded location; friendly owners; great birding; inexpensive. **Cons:** basic, small rooms; need a car to stay here. $ *Rooms from: $45* ✉ *Turnoff 2 km (1 mile) before Tapantí park entrance* ☎ *2533–2272* ⊕ *www.kirilodge.net* ⤳ *6 rooms* ⏐○⏐ *Breakfast.*

$ 📷 **Orosi Lodge.** Run by a young German couple who have built a warm

B&B/INN   rapport with the community, the little lodge blends in with Orosi's pretty, old-town architecture: whitewashed walls are trimmed in blue, ceilings are high, and natural wood is used throughout. **Pros:** affordable, pleasant; views from second-floor rooms. **Cons:** no restaurant, café only. $ *Rooms from: $58* ✉ *350 m south, 100 m west of soccer field* ☎ *2533–3578* ⊕ *www.orosilodge.com* ⤳ *6 rooms, 1 chalet, 1 house* ⏐○⏐ *No meals.*

$$ 📷 **Río Perlas Spa & Resort.** Thermal springs fill one of the pools at this

B&B/INN   Mediterranean-style spa hotel squeezed into a small, lush valley beside a rushing river, but rooms, while pleasant, are not especially luxurious, with tile floors, wood ceilings, and slightly dated hotel-style furniture. **Pros:** springs nice to bask in after a day of sightseeing; gorgeous river setting; trout fishing. **Cons:** basic rooms; not much peace and quiet during special events. $ *Rooms from: $111* ✉ *6 km (3 miles) south of Paraíso, turn right at bridge, then 2½ km (1½ miles); look for large sign* ☎ *2533–3341, 866/794–6478 in North America* ⊕ *www. rioperlasspaandresort.com* ⤳ *69 rooms* ⏐○⏐ *Multiple meal plans.*

SHOPPING

Casa del Soñador (*House of the Dreamer*). Stop in at this unique artisan shop, a picturesque wood cottage embellished with monumental carvings by local wood sculptor Macedonio Quesada, the creator of the House of the Dreamer. Though Macedonio died years ago, his sons Miguel and Hermes are still here, carving interesting, often comical little statues out of coffee roots, which they sell for only $10. ✉ *2 km (1 mile) south of Cachí Dam* ☎ *2577–1186* ⊙ *Daily 8–6.*

TURRIALBA

58 km (36 miles) east of San José.

The relatively well-to-do agricultural center of Turrialba is a bustling town, with a youthful vibe from the nearby university, a colorful open-air market, and a tree-shaded central park filled with an intriguing collection of large-scale animal sculptures. The region's moist cheese made in nearby Santa Cruz is famous all over Costa Rica. As you begin the descent to Turrialba town, the temperature rises and sugarcane alternates with fields of neat rows of coffee bushes. Turrialba also has a factory you may have heard of: Rawlings makes all the baseballs used in the major leagues. (The Rawlings factory, unfortunately, does not offer tours.) Thanks to some spectacular scenery, patches of rain forest in the surrounding countryside, and a handful of upscale nature lodges,

Costa Rica's first church, Iglesia de Ujarrás, was abandoned in 1833 after a series of earthquakes and floods, along with pirate attacks, wreaked havoc.

ecotourism is increasingly the focus of the town's efforts. Significant numbers of kayakers and rafters also flock here to run the Pacuare and Reventazón rivers. And, of course, looming above the town is Volcán Turrialba. Recent eruptions of ash, along with a heavily damaged road, prevent visitors from going to the top.

GETTING HERE AND AROUND

There are two ways to reach this area from San José, both of which pass spectacular scenery. The more direct route, accessible by heading east through Cartago continues east through Paraíso, where you turn left at the northeast corner of the central park to pick up the road to Turrialba. Marked by signs, this road leads north to Guayabo National Monument. For the second route, turn off the road between Cartago and the summit of Irazú near the town of Cot, heading toward Pacayas. That narrow route twists along the slopes of Irazú and Turrialba volcanoes past some stunning scenery—stately pollarded trees lining the road, riotous patches of tropical flowers, and metal-girder bridges across crashing streams. As you begin the descent to Turrialba town, the temperature rises and sugarcane alternates with fields of neat rows of coffee bushes.

Direct buses between San José and Turrialba leave hourly (8 to 8; slower buses run as early as 5:15 am and as late as 10 pm) from Calle 13, Avenida 6, just west of the downtown court buildings. Direct buses depart from the Turrialba terminal (at the entrance to Turrialba) for San José on the hour from 5 am to 5 pm, on the half hour to Cartago, and every two hours to Siquirres.

White-Water Thrills

You're struggling to hang on and paddle, you can't hear a thing over the roar, and you were just slammed with a mighty wall of water. Sound like fun? Then you're in the right place. The **Río Pacuare** and the **Río Reventazón** draw rafters and kayakers from all over the world to Turrialba. Right next to Turrialba, the Reventazón has Class II, III, and IV rapids. The Pacuare, farther from Turrialba, has a spectacular 29-km (18-mile) run with a series of Class III and IV rapids. The scenery includes lush canyons where waterfalls plummet into the river and expanses of rain forest.

Nearly every outfitter has day trips, many departing from San José, but some also have multiday trips that include jungle hikes. **Ríos Tropicales** even has their own lodges on the river. Age requirements for children vary by outfitter; **Explornatura** in Turrialba runs a family trip on the gentler Pejibaye River that kids as young as five can enjoy. The typical trip starts with a van ride to the put-in; including a breakfast stop, it usually takes about 2½ hours from hotel to river. After the first half of the run, guides flip one of the rafts over to form a crude lunch table. Then you continue up the river to Siquirres, and pile back in the van for the ride home.

Don't choose your company based merely on price: those with bargain rates are probably skimping somewhere. Good outfitters require you to wear life vests and helmets, have CPR-certified river guides with near-fluent English skills, and have kayakers accompany the rafts in case of emergencies. A 5:1 guest-to-guide ratio is good; 10:1 is not. Local Turrialba companies have better prices and allow you to book a trip at the last minute. Hotels and travel agencies book trips with larger outfitters, who can pick you up from nearly anywhere in the Central Valley. Prices range from about $75 to $100.

People fall out of the raft all the time, and it is usually no big deal. The worst-case scenario is getting trapped underwater in an eddy, or under the raft, but surprisingly, most fatalities are heart-attack victims, so don't participate if you're high-risk. You should also be able to swim. Almost every long-standing company has had a death—it is an unfortunate reality of the business. Don't hesitate to ask about safety records. The vast majority of trips, however, are pure, exhilarating fun.

ESSENTIALS

Bank/ATM Banco de Costa Rica ⊠ *Avda. 0 and C. 1* ☎ *2556–0472.* **Banco Nacional** ⊠ *C. 1 and Avda. Ctl.* ☎ *2556–1211.*

Hospital Hospital Dr. William Allen ⊠ *Avda. 2, 100 m west of C. 4* ☎ *2558–1300.*

Pharmacy Farmacia San Buenaventura ⊠ *50 m south of east side of central park* ☎ *2556–0379.*

Post Office Correos ⊠ *Avda. 8 and C. Ctl., 200 m north of central park.*

Taxis Asocut ☎ *2556–7070.*

EXPLORING

Guayabo National Monument. On the slopes of Turrialba Volcano lies Costa Rica's most significant and only true archaeological site. Records mentioning the ruins go back to the mid-1800s, but systematic investigations didn't begin until 1968, when a local landowner out walking her dogs discovered what she thought was a tomb. Archaeologists began excavating the site and unearthed the base wall of a chief's house in what eventually turned out to be the ruins of a large community (around 10,000 inhabitants) covering 49 acres, 10 of which have been excavated. The city was abandoned in AD 1400, probably because of disease or war. Guided tours (about two hours) in Spanish or English make the stones come alive, with knowledgeable guides from the U-Suré Guide Association (the name is the indigenous word for house). Starting from the round, thatch-roof reception center, they'll take you through the rain forest to a *mirador* (lookout) from which you can see the layout of the excavated circular buildings. Only the raised foundations survive, since the conical houses themselves were built of wood. As you descend into the ruins, notice the well-engineered surface and covered aqueducts leading to a trough of drinking water, which still functions today. Next you'll pass the end of an impressive 8-km (5-mile) paved walkway used to transport the massive building stones; the abstract patterns carved on the stones continue to baffle archaeologists, but some clearly depict jaguars, which were revered as deities. Excavations in 2013 have begun to unearth an elaborate system of agricultural terraces. Guayabo has been recognized by the American Society of Civil Engineers as a feat of Latin American civil engineering second only to Machu Picchu. The hillside jungle is captivating, and the trip is further enhanced by bird-watching possibilities: 200 species have been recorded. Facilities at Guayabo are still minimal: there's a souvenir hut opposite the entrance, a pleasant picnic area, and modern restrooms in a replica of a thatched indigenous hut. The access route from the east via the Santa Teresita (Lajas) has some rough spots, but you can make it in any car. The alternative Santa Cruz route is a little rougher, but you can still make it in a regular car, unless the road is wet—in which case you may need a 4WD vehicle to get here. ⊠ *Guayabo National Monument* ✛ *Drive through the center of Turrialba to a girdered bridge; take road signed Guayabo National Monument northeast for a total of 16 km (10 miles) (about 25–30 mins' driving); watch for a signed left turnoff, which will take you the final 3 km (2 miles) to the monument. If you've taken the scenic Irazú foothills route to Turrialba, the Santa Cruz route—11 km (7 miles) (about 35 mins' driving)—is an option. Turn left on rough road from Santa Cruz; climb 5 km (3 miles), past the Escuela de Guayabo; turn right at the sign for the monument; the road descends 6 km (4 miles) to the site.* ☎ *2559–1220, 8534–1063 to reserve a guide* ⊕ *www.accvc.org* ✉ *$5 entrance fee plus $15 guide fee for 1–3 people, $30 for 4–9 people* ☉ *Daily 8–3:30.*

Turrialba Volcano (*Volcán Turrialba*). Although you can't drive up to its summit as you can at Poás and Irazú, Volcán Turrialba is an impressive sight from a distance, albeit with some precautions these days. The volcano has been increasingly active since early 2010, spewing out enough steam and ashes to close off the surrounding area, both to farmers and visitors. A heavy content of sulfur dioxide in fumes emanates from the volcano, a phenomenon that has taken its toll on plant and animal life here. The road to the volcano is closed beyond the Volcán Turrialba Lodge at this writing. ⚠ **If you suffer from a heart or respiratory condition or are pregnant, stay away.** ⊠ *Turrialba Volcano National Park*⊒ *$12.*

Volcán Turrialba Lodge. Ascending to the summit of the Turrialba Volcano is not permitted at this writing, but the Volcán Turrialba Lodge can arrange for guided walks and horseback tours of the area. All are open to day visitors. ✛ *20 km (12 miles) east of Cot, turn right at Pacayas on road to Volcán Turrialba, 4 km (2½ miles) on dirt road; or from the Turrialba side, follow signs in La Pastora for national park, 14 km (7 miles) along a patchily paved road; 4WD advised for last 3 km (2 miles) on rough road* ☎ *2273–4335.*

OFF THE BEATEN PATH

Centro Agronómico Tropical de Investigación y Enseñanza (*Tropical Agricultural Research and Higher Education Center*). A good place for bird-watchers and garden enthusiasts, the center, better known by its Spanish acronym, CATIE, is one of the leading tropical research centers in Latin America, with headquarters here and affiliates in nine other countries. You might catch sight of the yellow-winged northern jacana or the purple gallinule in the lagoon near the main building. The 10-square-km (4-square-mile) property includes landscaped grounds, seed-conservation chambers, greenhouses, orchards, experimental agricultural projects, a large swath of rain forest, labs and offices, and lodging for students and teachers. The most popular attraction is the **Botanical Garden Tour,** a two-hour guided walk to taste, smell, and touch tropical fruits, along with cacao, coffee, and other medicinal and stimulant plants. A favorite stop is the "miracle fruit" tree, whose berries magically make anything sour taste sweet. ⊠ *3 km (2 miles) outside Turrialba, on road to Siquirres* ☎ *2558–2000* ⊕ *www.catie.ac.cr* ⊒ *$25 with guide, $10 on your own; $35 for half-day tour, $50 for full-day tour, including lunch* ☉ *Botanical Garden daily 7–4; reservations recommended for guided tours, especially on weekends.*

SPORTS AND THE OUTDOORS
MULTI-SPORT OUTFITTERS

Ecoaventuras. This adventure company covers all the stops—horseback riding, mountain biking, kayaking, and rafting—with pickup from San José hotels. ⊠ *750 m south of bus terminal* ☎ *2556–7171* ⊕ *www. ecoaventuras.co.cr.*

Explornatura. This downtown company organizes kayaking, horseback riding, mountain biking, and rafting tours, including a family-friendly rafting trip with lots of thrills but fewer chances of spills. ⊠ *40 m west of Hotel Wagelia* ☎ *2556–2070, 866/571–2443 in North America* ⊕ *www.explornatura.com.*

WHITE-WATER OUTFITTERS

Costa Rica Ríos. This outfitter specializes in weeklong rafting, kayaking, and canoeing excursions on the Pacuare and Pejibaye rivers, with rafter to guide ratios of no more than 5:1. ⊠ *50 m north of central park* ☎ *2556–8664, 888/434–0776* ⊕ *www.costaricarios.com.*

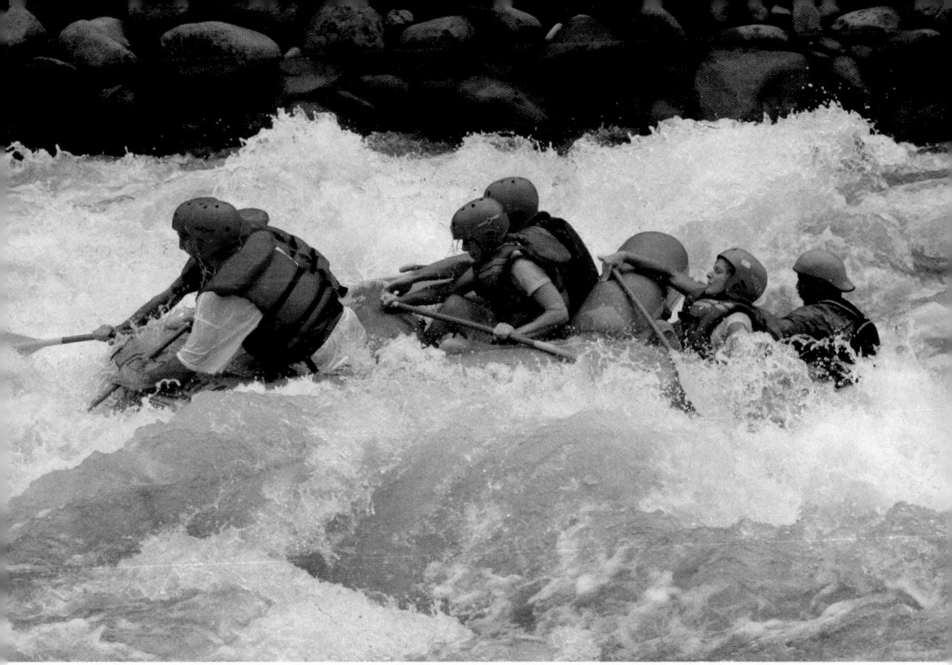

"For a fun ride, try rafting the Pacuare River in October or November when the water is high." —Photo by Linda137, Fodors.com member

Ríos Tropicales. Long-established outfitter Ríos Tropicales begins and ends its Pacuare and Reventazón white-water excursions in San José with the option to overnight on the Pacuare. Rafter-to-guide ratios don't exceed 5:1. ✉ *50 m north of Centro Colón, Paseo Colón, San José* ☎ *2233–6455, 866/722–8273 in North America.*

Tico's River Adventure. Tico's offers all the standard white-water excursions—Pacuare and Reventazón rivers with small groups and a safety kayaker in accompaniment—as well as kayaking classes. ✉ *1 km (½ mile) north of fire station* ☎ *2556–1231* 🌐 *www.ticoriver.com.*

WHERE TO EAT

$ COSTA RICAN 🍴 **La Garza Bar y Restaurante.** With weathered, blond-wood tables and chairs, and big windows with a view out onto the central park, La Garza is a popular meeting spot with a little more atmosphere than most of the eateries in town. The menu runs the gamut from hamburgers to chicken and has a good seafood selection. Open until 11 pm, this is one of the few places in town for a very late bite to eat. There's a pleasant bar here, too, backed by a Latin sound track or karaoke. [$] *Average main: $8* ✉ *Northwest corner of central park* ☎ *2556–1073.*

$$ COSTA RICAN 🍴 **Restaurante La Feria.** A permanent exhibition of local art and the expertise of the owner make this a worthwhile stop. This pleasant, family-style restaurant has the usual mid-scale Costa Rican fare, ranging from fast food to filet mignon; the house specialty is beef tenderloin topped with a Spanish-inspired red-wine-and-mushroom sauce. Casados and gallo pinto compete with more-familiar chicken and seafood dishes. Even paella is on the menu (with three hours' notice), and there's home-baked apple pie for dessert. [$] *Average main:*

$11 ✉ *Across from Enersol gas station at western entrance to town* ☎ *2556–5550* ⏲ *No dinner Tues.*

WHERE TO STAY

$$$ B&B/INN Fodor's Choice ★ 🏨 **Casa Turire.** Lush gardens and manicured lawns surround this gorgeous, hacienda-style, luxury hotel overlooking a scenic lake. **Pros:** excellent value; beautiful grounds; attention to sustainable tourism; luxurious suites. **Cons:** small, one-room spa; standard-room bathrooms could use a little upgrading. [$] *Rooms from: $180* ✉ *8 km (5 miles) south on Carretera a la Suiza from Turrialba* ☎ *2531–1111, 877/750–6855 in North America* 🌐 *www.hotelcasaturire.com* 🛏 *12 standard rooms, 3 suites, 1 master suite* 🍴 *Breakfast.*

$$ B&B/INN 🏨 **Guayabo Lodge.** If fresh mountain air appeals to you, this upscale mountain retreat has comfortable rooms, a first-class restaurant, and spacious, glassed-in sitting areas to enjoy unbeatable volcano and valley views by day and blazing fireplaces by night. **Pros:** cozy and comfortable; high sustainability consciousness; great views. **Cons:** weather can be wet and cool; clouds can obscure the view. [$] *Rooms from: $94* ✉ *2 km (1¼ miles) west of Santa Cruz de Turrialba* ☎ *2538–8400* 🌐 *www.guayabolodge.co.cr* 🛏 *22 rooms, 4 suites* 🍴 *Breakfast.*

$$ HOTEL 🏨 **Hotel Villa Florencia.** This country inn a few miles outside of Turrialba offers peace and quiet, a rural feel, and friendly owners and staff. **Pros:** warm, helpful staff; family-friendly; quiet surroundings. **Cons:** some rooms have dated furnishings; best to have a car to stay here. [$] *Rooms from: $138* ✉ *La Susanita de Turrialba, 800 m west* ☎ *2557–3536* 🌐 *www.villaflorencia.com* 🛏 *10 rooms, 1 suite* 🍴 *Breakfast.*

$$$$ B&B/INN Fodor's Choice ★ 🏨 **Rancho Naturalista.** Unparalleled bird-watching within a 160-acre private nature reserve with more than 400 recorded species, plus first-class food, and comfortable lodging are the reasons nature lovers from all over the world stay here. **Pros:** birder's paradise; hiking trails for guests; warm atmosphere; gourmet meals included. **Cons:** some rooms are a little dated; not a convenient base for day trips; rough final stretch of road to get here. [$] *Rooms from: $301* ✉ *20 km (12 miles) southeast of Turrialba, 1½ km (1 mile) south of Tuís, then up a rough road* ☎ *2554–8100, 888/246–8513 in North America, 2433–8278 for reservations* 🌐 *www.ranchonaturalista.net* 🛏 *12 rooms* 💳 *No credit cards* 🍴 *All meals.*

$ B&B/INN 🏨 **Turrialtico Lodge.** Dramatically positioned on a hill overlooking the valley east of Turrialba, this Costa Rican–owned rustic, wood lodge is a good budget option. **Pros:** rich views at budget prices; coffeemakers in rooms; good opportunity to mingle with Ticos. **Cons:** thin walls in main lodge; less service-oriented than other options. [$] *Rooms from: $75* ✉ *8 km (5 miles) east of Turrialba on road to Siquirres* ☎ *2538–1111* 🌐 *www.turrialtico.com* 🛏 *10 rooms, 8 cabins* 🍴 *Breakfast.*

ARENAL, MONTEVERDE, AND THE NORTHERN LOWLANDS

WELCOME TO ARENAL, MONTEVERDE, AND THE NORTHERN LOWLANDS

TOP REASONS TO GO

★ **Experience a volcano:** When Arenal, one of the world's most active volcanoes, is not dormant, you can hear it rumbling, and, on clear nights, see plumes of gas and rock spouting from its dome.

★ **Walk down to a waterfall:** The reward for a tough hike down to Cataratas de la Fortuna is a magnificent series of waterfalls.

★ **Walk in a cloud:** Explore Monteverde's misty world on treetop walkways up to 41 meters (138 feet) off the ground.

★ **Watch wildlife:** Birds, monkeys, turtles, crocodiles, jaguars, and sloths abound in the 25,000-acre Caño Negro National Wildlife Refuge.

★ **Windsurf:** Lake Arenal is one of the top windsurfing spots on earth; winds can reach 50 to 60 mph mid-November through April.

1 Arenal Volcano Area. Arenal Volcano is one of the most popular tourist destinations in Costa Rica. La Fortuna is the closest town to the volcano; among many nearby diversions are the Tabacón Hot Springs. Tilarán, west of Lake Arenal, is the place to be if you're a windsurfer or kiteboarder.

2 Monteverde Cloud Forest Area. Home to the rainiest of cloud forests, the Monteverde Cloud Forest Area is also the canopy-tour capital of Costa Rica. Hanging bridges, treetop tram tours, and zip lines: it's got it all. As if that's not enough, horseback riding, rappelling, and nature hikes are also available.

Río San Juan

0   10 mi

0   10 km

Acapulco

35

Pangola

Santa
Domingo

Boca
Arenal

Altamira

Puerto
Viejo de
Sarapiquí

4

Angeles

La Fortuna

Platanar

35

Chiles

Braulio Carrillo
National Park

*Puerto Viejo
Loop*

San Isidro

Ciudad
Quesada

San Miguel
Angeles

Poás Volcano
National Park

Naranjo
de Alajuela

CR2

Grecia

Alajuela

SAN JOSÉ

GETTING ORIENTED

The rich, lush terrain of the Zona Norte (Northern Zone), as it is known locally, runs from the base of the Cordillera Central in the south to the Río San Juan, on the border with Nicaragua in the north. Most visitors begin their visit to Costa Rica in San José, and then head north to La Fortuna. This adventure hub is a base for exploring the Arenal Volcano, Cataratas de la Fortuna waterfalls, and Caño Negro Refuge, and participating in activities like sportfishing, windsurfing, and kitesurfing at Lake Arena and rafting on the Sarapiquí River.

5

3 Caño Negro National Wildlife Refuge. In the Far North, this wildlife refuge is great for fishing, bird-watching, and communing with nature.

CAÑO NEGRO

Think a smaller version of Florida's Everglades and you'll have a good picture of the Refugio Nacional de Vida Silvestre Caño Negro.

This lowland rain-forest reserve in the far northern reaches of Costa Rica near the Nicaraguan border covers 98 square km (38 square miles). It looks remote on the map, but is easily visited on an organized day tour, especially from La Fortuna. Caño Negro is the core of a UNESCO biosphere called Agua y Paz (Water and Peace), which encompasses more than 2 million acres of wildlife habitat in Costa Rica and Nicaragua.

Caño Negro has suffered severe deforestation over the years, but most of the length of the Río Frío, its principal river, is still lined with trees. The park's vast lake, which floods according to seasonal rains, is an excellent place to watch waterfowl. On land, pumas, tapirs, ocelots, cougars, and the always-elusive jaguar make up the mammal life found here—consider yourself fortunate if you spot a jaguar. Caimans snap everywhere in the knee-deep marshy waters, too. *(See page 243 for more information.)*

BEST TIME TO GO

It gets *hot* here, with March and April brutally so, but the January-through-March dry season is the best time to spot the reserve's migratory bird population. Opportunities abound the rest of the year, too, though. No matter what the season, bring sunscreen, water, insect repellant, and a brimmed hat.

FUN FACT

In addition to other bird species, the reserve is the best place to spot the Nicaraguan grackle. This New World blackbird is found only in Nicaragua and northern Costa Rica. It is medium size, with a long, graduated tail and fairly long bill and legs.

BEST WAYS TO EXPLORE

BIRD-WATCHING

This is the best place in the country to see water birds. Just sit back in your tour boat and survey the passing parade. You're sure to see anhingas spreading their wings to dry; both glossy and white ibis recognizable by their long curved beaks; roseate spoonbills, often mistaken for flamingos; and the jabiru, king of the storks. Herons and kingfishers lurk on the banks, ready to spear fish, while jacanas, with their huge feet, forage in the water lettuce, looking as though they are actually walking on water. Above the water, watch for gray-color snail kites, which, true to their name, are hunting for snails.

BOAT TOURS

In the dry season you can ride horses, but a visit here chiefly entails a wildlife-spotting boat tour. You could drive up here on your own—roads to the area are in good shape—but once here, you'd need to arrange for boat transportation. Visiting with a tour company out of La Fortuna—it's a 90-minute ride one way—is the easiest way to see the park.

CAIMAN LAND

Famous for its caimans, Caño Negro still boasts a sizable population. They're smaller than crocodiles, though—at most 2½ meters (8 feet) long—and they are relatively unthreatening, because they're too small to eat large mammals (this includes humans). It's a thrill to see them sunning on a bank or see their spectacled eyes floating just above the water line. Unfortunately, the caimans here are under serious threat from hunters who sneak across the Nicaraguan border and slaughter them by the hundreds for their skins. The proof is sadly on display in the souvenir shops in Nicaragua, where you will see purses and belts made from caiman hides.

TOP REASONS TO GO

Bird-Watching
The reserve is one of Costa Rica's lesser-sung bird-watching and wildlife-viewing destinations. Caño Negro is growing in popularity, but, for now, a visit here still gives you that "I'm in on a secret the rest of the world doesn't know about" satisfaction.

Fishing
It's not all about wildlife viewing here: Caño Negro is also one of Costa Rica's prime freshwater fishing destinations, with snook and marlin yours for the catching and the bragging rights during the July through March season. (There's barely enough water in the lake the other months of the year, so fishing is prohibited then.) The two lodges inside the reserve can hook you up.

Great Tours
It's easy to get here from the Arenal area, with top-notch operators and their teams of knowledge-able guides organizing day tours from La Fortuna and so-called evening tours that actually get you here in the very warm mid-afternoon and depart around dusk.

5

ARENAL VOLCANO

The 2-km-high (1-mile-high) Arenal Volcano, Costa Rica's youngest volcano, dominates the region's landscape.

Volcanologists estimate Arenal's age at around 7,000 years, and it was dormant for at least 400 years until 1968. On July 29, 1968, an earthquake shook the area, and 12 hours later Arenal blew.

Until October 2010, Arenal was in a constant state of activity—thunderous, rumbling eruptions sometimes as frequent as one per hour. Now, if you're lucky, you might see a column of ash or hear a faint rumbling in the distance. When the volcano is not in its "resting" state, night is the best time to view the action: on a clear evening you can see rocks spewing skyward. Although everyone refers to it as "lava," a more apt description of what the volcano churns out is "pyroclastic flow," a mix of incandescent rock and gas. *(See page 214 for more information.)*

BEST TIME TO GO

Viewing Arenal can be hit or miss anytime of year. January through April, especially in the early morning, usually means fewer clouds to obscure daytime views. The dry season's clear evenings give the best spectacle of volcanic activity, although Arenal has been quiet since late 2010.

FUN FACT

Researchers at INBio, the National Biological Institute in Santo Domingo, north of San José, have been hard at work around the volcano. They see promise in the lichens growing on Arenal's slopes as a source of new antibiotics.

BEST WAYS TO EXPLORE

BIRD-WATCHING

If you decide to hike the park's Los Tucanes trail, chances are you'll see at least one of the five species of toucan that have been recorded here: chestnut-billed and keel-billed toucans, the yellow-eared and emerald toucanet, and the collared aracari. You'll never look at a box of Froot Loops the same after seeing the real thing. Hummingbirds also abound on the volcano's slope. Look for anything tiny and purple.

HIKING

For intrepid hikers who want to get a little closer to the action, Las Heliconias trail, which starts at the park reception center, wends through secondary forest and passes by the cooled lava flow from the 1968 eruption. Los Tucanes trail also leads to the lava fields, but it's more of an uphill hike, beginning near the entrance to the Arenal Observatory Lodge. There's also a hiking trail up to Cerro Chatto, a lopsided, extinct crater, partially filled with water, creating a pretty lake.

VOLCANIC TIPS

Two words: "from afar." Under no circumstances should you hike even the volcano's lower slopes on your own. Lava rocks and volcanic gas have killed trekkers who got too close. The tour operators we recommend know where the danger lies and take appropriate precautions. Wait until around 2 pm to see if the weather will cooperate, and then book your afternoon volcano hike.

Despite the fact Arenal has entered the "post-eruption era," many visitors still gaze at its majesty from a distance and the safety of several area hotels, restaurants, and hot springs that afford postcard views.

TOP REASONS TO GO

All Budgets Welcome Budget and even moderate travelers are being priced out of the market in certain regions of Costa Rica. Not so here. You'll find everything from backpackers' digs to luxury hotels in the area around Arenal.

A Perfect Volcano Arenal's perfect cone, past images of red-hot lava, plumes of ash, and menacing location close to the tourist town of La Fortuna practically define the term *volcano*. In October 2010, the volcano entered an indeterminate dormant phase, but that status could very well change in a matter of months.

Sports and Adventure No other attraction in Costa Rica has given rise to so extensive a list of accompanying entertainment offerings. Come here to pay your respects to Arenal, and you'll find enough other activities to keep you occupied for days. (You'll also appreciate the backup on those occasions when clouds obscure your view of the volcano.)

5

ECO-LODGES IN THE NORTHERN PLAINS

Cloud forests, rain forests, volcanoes, thermal springs, white-water rivers, waterfalls, coffee and banana plantations, and rolling farmland combine to create the vast landscape that stretches across the northern third of Costa Rica.

That translates into a variety of environmentally themed pursuits unmatched anywhere else in the country. The mists of Monteverde define *cloud forest*, and the original Quaker settlers stamped their environmental consciousness on the area.

The tourist industry up here knows what the region has to offer and is keen to preserve what is green. Hotel owners and tour operators are just as eager to show it off to you with the Certification for Sustainable Tourism Program (CST). Designed to differentiate green businesses of the tourism sector, CST is based on compliance with a sustainable model and is regulated by the Costa Rican National Accreditation Commission on a scale of five levels (or five "leaves") of achievement. Since the program was developed in 1998, more than 220 Costa Rican hotels and 70 tour operators have earned the CST certification.

GOOD PRACTICES

Consider public or semipublic transportation for negotiating the Northern Plains. No question: distances are vast, and your own wheels *do* offer you the greatest convenience. It's surprisingly easy, though, to take shuttle transport, base yourself in Arenal or Monteverde, and use occasional taxis to get around once you arrive. Many tour operators in both places are happy to pick you up at your hotel, too.

Also, ask if your hotel recycles. In Monteverde, the answer will usually be yes, but it'll be less likely in other places. If enough guests keep requesting it, more lodgings just might hop on the eco-bandwagon.

TOP ECO-LODGES IN THE NORTHERN PLAINS

ARCO IRIS LODGE, MONTEVERDE

The German management here eschews the overused word "ecotourism," insisting that many in Costa Rica view the concept as simply e¢otouri$m. But if any lodging were entitled to use the term in its marketing, it would be this one. Comfortable cabins are scattered around the grounds here, and though you're right in the center of town, Arco Iris has managed to create a country feel. That, along with the organic foods, active recycling program, biodegradable materials, and involvement in the community, makes this one of our favorite Costa Rican eco-lodges—even if it doesn't call itself that. *(Hotel review on page 241.)*

LAGUNA DEL LAGARTO LODGE, CIUDAD QUESADA

It doesn't get mentioned in the pantheon of better-known Costa Rican eco-lodges, but this smallish property near the Nicaraguan border offers a variety of nature-themed activities to rival any of the big guys. Accommodation is rustic in this remote locale, but impact on the environment has been minimal. The 1,250-acre rain forest here makes for terrific bird-watching, hiking, and canoeing. Laguna del Lagarto gives back to its community, and has succeeded in bringing employment to a poorer, often forgotten corner of Costa Rica. *(Hotel review on page 209.)*

ARENAL OBSERVATORY LODGE, ARENAL

This working biological station where research biologists make up the primary clientele earned four out of five leaves in sustainability. The lodge promotes recycling, water conservation, and low energy use, in addition to employing locals and protecting flora and fauna through their reforestation program. Their restaurants serve locally grown food and all organic waste is either composted or fed to pigs on their farm. Included in your room rate is a fascinating nature hike. *(Hotel review on page 218.)*

PLANTING TREES

"Costa Rica" equals "forest" in the minds of most visitors. Truth be told, about half the country has been deforested, much of it occurring in this region. The reasons are mostly understandable: coffee, bananas, and dairy cattle make the Northern Plains the country's breadbasket; for decades, trees have been cleared for farmland. Enter the *A Que Sembrás un Árbol* program. Loosely translated, that means "May you plant a tree." It forms part of the United Nations' international Planting for the Planet program, whose goal is to plant 3.5 billion trees worldwide each year. Costa Rica's contribution to the agenda aims for an annual figure of 7 million trees, around one-third of which are targeted for this region.

Like most environmental initiatives here, the program began at the grassroots level, with area students kicking off the tree planting, soliciting support from area businesses, and petitioning the government to become officially involved.

5

Updated
by Marlise
Kast-Myers

The vast expanse that locals call the Zona Norte (Northern Zone) packs in a larger variety of activities than any other part of the country. You'll find almost everything in this region that Costa Rica has to offer, except beaches, of course.

Spend any amount of time here and you can partake of—take a deep breath—volcano viewing, horseback riding, canoeing, kayaking, rafting, rappelling, windsurfing, kitesurfing, wildlife-viewing, bird-watching, bungee jumping, shopping, cloud and rain-forest hiking, swimming, and hot-springs soaking. The zip-line canopy tour deserves special mention. The activity was invented in Costa Rica and has spread to all corners of the planet, while zipping along cables from platform to platform high in the trees has become Costa Rica's signature adventure activity.

We'd argue that those myriad activities make the Northern Plains Costa Rica's most kid-friendly region. Young children especially will "ooh" (and "eeewwww") at various area animal exhibits devoted to bats (Monteverde), frogs (Monteverde), butterflies (Monteverde, La Fortuna), hummingbirds (Monteverde), felines (the Springs Resort in Arenal), and snakes (Monteverde). Guided nature hikes abound; shorter treks can be entertaining and cater to younger ones' shorter attention spans. Most sure-footed and confident teenagers can participate in adult activities. We especially recommend white-water rafting and canopy tours.

A few operators around here will tell you that kids older than eight can participate in canopy tours. We're skeptical of such claims, even if their brochures show children happily zipping from platform to platform. The gondola-like trams (Monteverde) are far safer ways to see the rain-forest canopy.

Most of those activities do go on rain or shine, so don't feel you have to avoid a rainy-season visit here. During the wet months, it's almost a given that you'll get a bit damp on your canopy tour, hike, or horseback ride, and most tour operators provide ponchos. But to avoid a thorough soaking, plan activities for the morning. Rains usually begin around 2 pm, like clockwork, from July through December, although they can be more prolonged in September and October. The clearest time of day is normally before 8 am.

We frequently overhear comments such as "I didn't know it would be so rainy in the rain forest." You heard it here first: that's why they call it the rain forest! During the rainy season it's not unusual for it to rain for several days straight, and even during the dry season, brief showers will come up without notice. Be sure to bring a poncho or rain jacket and waterproof footwear.

PLANNING

WHEN TO GO

HIGH SEASON: MID-DECEMBER TO APRIL

Climate is difficult to pinpoint in this vast region. The Northern Plains link the rainier Caribbean in the east to drier Guanacaste in the west. Precipitation generally decreases from east to west. Monteverde is cool, damp, and breezy much of the time, with high winds in January and February. Elsewhere, rain can occur outside the official wet season since the area's low elevation frequently hosts battles between competing weather fronts. Visibility changes daily (and hourly), so your chances of seeing the Arenal volcano crater is more or less the same year-round, though you may have more luck from February to April, the hottest and driest time of the year.

LOW SEASON: JUNE TO MID-NOVEMBER

Throughout the entire region, the warm and humid rainy season normally lasts from June to December. Many places in Arenal and Monteverde are beginning to impose high-season rates in July and August to correspond with prime North American and European vacation times.

SHOULDER SEASON: MAY TO JUNE

The wet season just starts to kick in by May, but rarely to a degree that will interfere with your travels. A little precipitation provides a welcome clearing and freshness of the air in the countryside.

PLANNING YOUR TIME

Although not centrally located, the Northern Plains can be easily tacked onto stays in other regions of Costa Rica. Fairly decent—decent for Costa Rica, that is—transportation links the region to San José, the Central Valley, and the North Pacific. (Monteverde is the exception, isolated and approached only by rugged roads from all directions.)

If your stay here is limited to two or three days, make La Fortuna your base. Don't miss the volcano, the Tabacón Hot Springs, or a day trip to the Caño Negro Wildlife Refuge.

Most tour operators who have volcano hikes end the day at one of the various thermal springs in the area. ■TIP➔ **There are free public hot springs past the yellow gate next to Tabacón.**

"Half-day" tours to Caño Negro actually take most of a day, from around 7:30 am to 4 pm.

A week in the Northern Plains is more than enough time to experience a great deal of this area—especially if you're longing to get out and get moving. Give yourself four days in La Fortuna/Arenal, a great base for exploring the region. Devote the rest of your week to Monteverde Cloud Forest.

GETTING HERE AND AROUND

AIR TRAVEL

Nature Air has daily flights from its own airport in San José to La Fortuna (FTN). Most travelers to this region fly into San José's Aeropuerto Internacional Juan Santamaría or Liberia's Daniel Oduber Airport. Monteverde and Arenal are equidistant from both. Base your choice of airport on which other areas in Costa Rica you plan to visit in addition to this one.

BUS TRAVEL

Buses in this region are typically large, clean, and fairly comfortable, but often crowded Friday through Sunday. Don't expect air-conditioning. Service tends toward the agonizingly slow: even supposedly express buses marked *directo* (direct) often make numerous stops.

CAR TRAVEL

Road access to the northwest is by way of the paved two-lane Pan-American Highway, which starts from the west end of Paseo Colón in San José and runs northwest to Peñas Blancas at the Nicaraguan border. Turn north at Naranjo for La Fortuna; at Lagarto for Monteverde; and at Cañas for Tilarán. This region manages to mix some of the country's smoothest highways with some of its most horrendous roads. (The various roads to Monteverde are legendary in the latter regard, but the final destination makes it worth the trip.) Four-wheel-drive vehicles are best on the frequently potholed roads. If you don't want to pay for 4WD, at least rent a car with high clearance. (Many rental agencies insist you take a 4WD vehicle if you mention Monteverde as part of your itinerary.) You'll encounter frequent one-lane bridges; if the triangular "CEDA EL PASO" faces you, yield to oncoming traffic. Driving in this region can be slow going if you get behind a large truck transporting sugarcane. As the north is prime sugar country, that's quite likely.

It is possible to rent a car in La Fortuna, but for a far better selection, most visitors pick up their rental vehicles in San José or Liberia. GPS units, programmed with Costa Rica's maps, cost about $12 per day and are available at most car rental agencies. These voice-activated devices are a great way to keep from getting lost.

HEALTH AND SAFETY

This region is Costa Rica's capital of adventure tourism—it gave birth to the canopy tour—so any risks up here are far more likely to be natural than criminal. Before you set out rafting, zip lining, rappelling, or bungee jumping, be brutally frank with yourself about your abilities, your physical condition, and your fear levels. (It's almost impossible to turn back on many excursions once you've started.) Even an activity as innocuous as hiking or horseback riding poses a certain amount of risk, and you should never go alone. Nature here is not an amusement park.

Remember also that there is little government oversight of adventure tourism here. Pay close attention during any safety briefings and orientation. Don't be afraid to ask questions, and don't be afraid to walk away if something seems off to you. Look for canopy tours with built-in brake systems, double cables, and chest harnesses in addition to the normal waist harness. If you have travel insurance, make sure it covers action sports or adrenaline activities—most standard packages do not cover injuries related to kayaking, horseback riding, zip lining, kitesurfing, or other such sports.

MONEY MATTERS

Outside the centers of Monteverde, La Fortuna, and Tilarán, ATMs are still few and far between. Stock up on cash when you get a chance.

RESTAURANTS

You'll never go hungry in this region. The north is the country's bread-basket, and the hotels and restaurants out here make use of the bounty to whip up the best in *típico* Costa Rican cuisine. Don't be afraid to ask for tap water; it is safe to drink in all but the most rural areas. Service is generally slow but well worth the wait at most restaurants. Your final bill will include tax and a 12% service charge, though we suggest you tip a little extra.

HOTELS

A few sumptuous resorts hold court in northern Costa Rica, but this region is largely the province of smaller, nature-themed lodgings that invite you to partake of all their eco-activities, and offer good value for the money. Due to the comfortable inland temperatures, most hotels do not offer air-conditioning. *Hotel reviews have been shortened. For full information, visit Fodors.com.*

WHAT IT COSTS IN DOLLARS			
$	$$	$$$	$$$$
Restaurants Under $10	$10–$15	$16–$25	over $25
Hotels Under $75	$75–$150	$151–$250	over $250

Restaurant prices are the average cost of a main course at dinner or, if dinner is not served, at lunch. Hotel prices are the lowest cost of a standard double room in high season.

ARENAL VOLCANO AREA

Whether you come here from San José or Liberia, prepare yourself for some spectacular scenery—and a bumpy ride. As you bounce along on your way to Arenal, you may discover that "paved" means different things in different places, and that potholes are numerous. Any discomfort you experience is more than made up for by the swaths of misty rain forest and dramatic expanses of the Cordillera Central. Schedule at least 3½ hours for the trip from San José.

CIUDAD QUESADA (SAN CARLOS)

55 km (33 miles) (1 hr) northwest of Zarcero.

Highway signs point you to "Ciudad Quesada," but this friendly hub city is simply "San Carlos" in local parlance. Like so many other places in Costa Rica, the landscape is splendid, but what passes for architecture varies from ordinary to downright hideous. San Carlos is where everyone in the region comes to shop, take in a movie, get medical care, and generally take care of the necessities. There's also an enormous bus terminal (with a shopping center and multiplex movie theater) where you can make connections to almost anywhere in the northern half of the country. If you're traveling from San José to points north, your bus will stop here even if it's a so-called express. This lively mountain market town–provincial capital serves a fertile dairy region and is worth a stop for a soak in the soothing thermal waters in the area.

GETTING HERE AND AROUND

Buses from San José leave Terminal Atlántico Norte on the hour, from 5 am to 7 pm. The trip takes around three hours. The Ciudad Quesada bus terminal is a couple of kilometers from the center of town; taxis wait at the terminal to take you into town. Quesada is just off the Pan American Highway. Driving from San José or other places in the south is straightforward, as long as you don't get stuck behind a slow-moving truck transporting sugarcane to the Central Valley. Try to get an early start if you're driving yourself; the road between Zarcero and Ciudad Quesada begins to fog over by early afternoon.

ESSENTIALS

Bank/ATM BAC San José ⊠ *100 m north and 125 m west of cathedral* ☎ *2295–9797.* **Banco Nacional** ⊠ *Across from north side of cathedral* ☎ *2401–2000.* **Scotiabank** ⊠ *Across from Mercado de Artesanía, east side of the park* ☎ *2461–9660.*

Medical Assistance Hospital de San Carlos ⊠ *2 km (1 mile) north of park* ☎ *2460–1176.*

Post Office Correos ⊠ *Across from Escuela Chávez, 100 m north of park.*

Tourism Information Instituto Costarricense de Turismo ⊠ *75 m north of Universidad Católica* ☎ *2461–9102, 866/2678–27422 in U.S. and Canada* ⊕ *www.visitcostarica.com* ⊙ *Weekdays 8–noon and 1–4.*

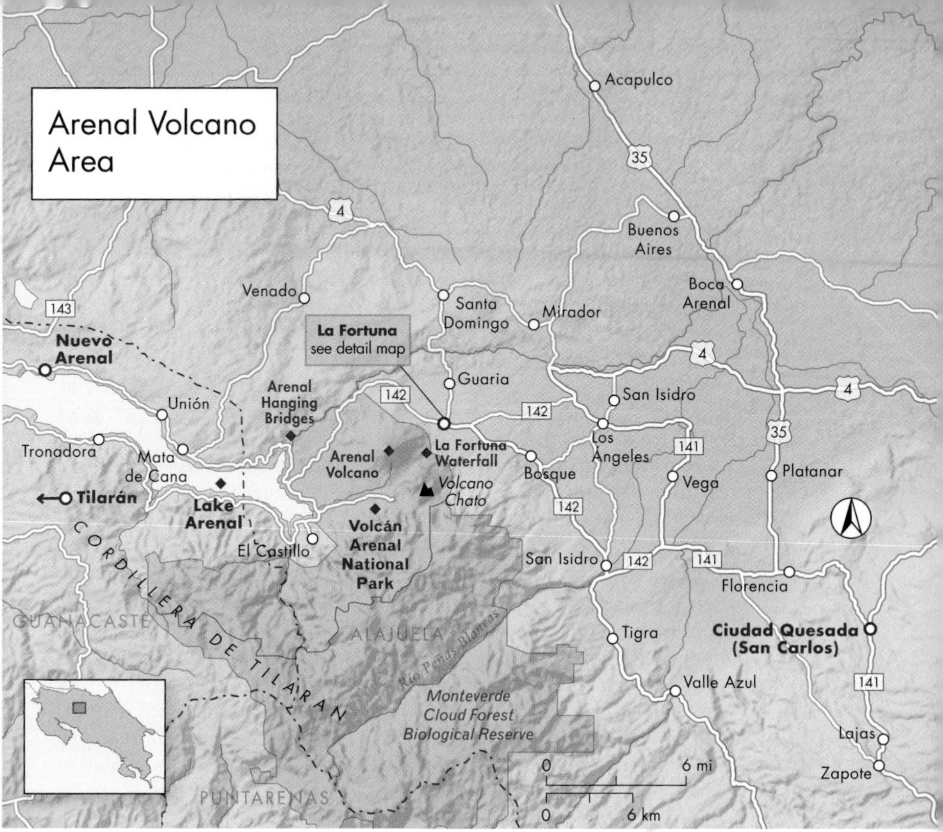
Arenal Volcano Area
Acapulco
35
4
Buenos Aires
Boca Arenal
Venado
Santa Domingo
Mirador
143
La Fortuna
see detail map
Nuevo Arenal
4
Guaria
Arenal Hanging Bridges
Unión
142
San Isidro
142
4
Tronadora
Mata de Cana
Arenal Volcano
La Fortuna Waterfall
Los Ángeles
141
35
Bosque
Vega
Platanar
Tilarán
Volcano Chato
Lake Arenal
142
Volcán Arenal National Park
El Castillo
San Isidro
142
141
Florencia
CORDILLERA DE TILARÁN
GUANACASTE
ALAJUELA
Río Peñas Blancas
Tigra
Ciudad Quesada (San Carlos)
Valle Azul
141
Monteverde Cloud Forest Biological Reserve
Lajas
Zapote
0
6 mi
0
6 km
PUNTARENAS

EXPLORING

Termales del Bosque. Soak those tired muscles as you watch the birds—for less than you'd pay at most of the other hot springs in the region. The day-pass admission price includes breakfast and/or lunch. ✉ *Hwy. 140, 7 km (4 miles) east of Ciudad Quesada* ☎ *2460–1356* 🌐 *www.termalesdelbosque.com* 🎟 *Day pass $21–$33, hot springs only $13* 🕒 *Daily 8 am–10 pm.*

WHERE TO STAY

$ HOTEL 🏨 **Laguna del Lagarto Lodge.** At one of Costa Rica's smaller and more remote eco-lodges, rustic cabins with single beds are surrounded by a 1,250-acre rain forest near the Nicaraguan border that gives shelter to 350 bird species and counting. **Pros:** birders paradise; attentive service; great excursions. **Cons:** last 35 km (20 miles) very rough road; poor lighting in rooms; Wi-Fi in common areas only. [$] *Rooms from: $75* ✉ *7 km (4 miles) north of Boca Tapada, 135 km (78 miles) northeast of Ciudad Quesada* ☎ *2289–8163 in San José* 🌐 *www.lagarto-lodge-costa-rica.com* 🛏 *20 rooms, 18 with bath* 🍴 *No meals.*

ARENAL AND LA FORTUNA

50 km (30 miles) (45 mins) northwest of Ciudad Quesada, 17 km (11 miles) east of Arenal Volcano, 190 km (118 miles) (3½ hrs by car; 25 mins by plane) northwest of San José.

As they say, "Location, location, location." Who would think that a small town sitting at the foot of massive Arenal Volcano would attract visitors from around the world? Nobody comes to La Fortuna—an ever-expanding mass of hotels, tour operators, souvenir shops, and *sodas* (small, family-run restaurants)—to see the town itself. Instead, thousands of tourists flock here each year to use it as a hub for visiting the natural wonders that surround it. The volcano as well as waterfalls, vast nature preserves, great rafting rivers, and an astonishing array of birds are to be found within an hour or less of your hotel. La Fortuna is also the best place to arrange trips to the Caño Negro National Wildlife Refuge.

After the 1968 eruption of Arenal Volcano, La Fortuna was transformed from a tiny, dusty farm town to one of Costa Rica's tourism powerhouses, where visitors converged to see the volcano in action. Don't expect to see any bubbling lava anytime soon. As of 2010, the volcano went into a resting phase, which means it is still "active" below the surface but you'll be lucky if you see anything beyond the occasional puff of steam. Volcano viewing can be hit or miss, especially during the rainy season (May through November). One minute Arenal looms menacingly over the village; the next minute clouds shroud its cone. Early morning, especially in the dry season, is always the best time to catch a longer gaze.

GETTING HERE AND AROUND

Choose from two routes from San José: for a slightly longer but better road, leave the Pan-American Highway at Naranjo, continuing north to Zarcero and Ciudad Quesada. Head northwest at Ciudad Quesada to La Fortuna; or for a curvier but shorter route, continue beyond Naranjo on the Pan-American Highway, turning north at San Ramón, arriving at La Fortuna about 90 minutes after the turnoff. Either route passes through a mountainous section that begins to fog over by afternoon. Get as early a start as possible. Nature Air flies daily to La Fortuna (FTN); flights land at an airstrip at the hamlet of El Tanque, 7 km (4 miles) east of town. Van transport ($6 one way) meets each flight to take you into La Fortuna.

Gray Line has daily shuttle bus service between San José, La Fortuna, and Arenal ($49), and Monteverde ($49). Interbus also connects San José with La Fortuna and Monteverde (each $45) daily, with connections from here to a few of the North Pacific beaches. Public buses depart five times daily from San José's Terminal Atlántico Norte. Travel time is four hours. Although billed as an express route, the bus makes many stops.

Desafío Adventures provides a fast, popular three-hour transfer between Monteverde and La Fortuna via taxi, boat, then another taxi, for $29 each way.

"Our best day in Costa Rica—canyoneering and waterfall rappelling near the active [currently inactive] Arenal Volcano" —Photo by sportster, Fodors.com member

NAVIGATING LA FORTUNA Taxis in and around La Fortuna are relatively cheap and will take you anywhere; a taxi to the Tabacón resort should run about $15. Get a cab at the stand on the east side of Parque Central.

ESSENTIALS

Bank/ATM BAC San José ✉ *75 m north of gas station.* **Banco de Costa Rica** ✉ *50 m east of central park.* **Banco Nacional** ✉ *Central Plaza* ☎ *2479-9355.*

Bus Contacts Interbus ☎ *4100-0888* ⊕ *www.interbusonline.com.*

Internet Expediciones Fortuna ✉ *Across the street from Central Plaza* ☎ *2479-9101.*

Medical Clinic Seguro Social ✉ *300 m east of central park* ☎ *2479-8086.*

Pharmacy Farmacia Fishel ✉ *On the main road, 40 km (25 miles) east of the public park* ☎ *2479-9518.*

Post Office Correos ✉ *Across from north side of church.*

Rental Cars Alamo ✉ *100 m west of church* ☎ *2479-9090* ⊕ *www.alamocostarica.com.* **Mapache** ✉ *800 m west of church* ☎ *2586-6395* ⊕ *www.mapache.com.*

EXPLORING

TOP ATTRACTIONS

Arenal Hanging Bridges. A series of trails and bridges form a loop through the primary rain forest of a 250-acre private reserve, providing great bird-watching and volcano viewing. Fixed and hanging bridges allow you to see the forest at different levels. Trails are open rain or shine, and there are things to do in both types of weather. Shuttle service from La Fortuna and area lodgings can be arranged. ⊠ *4 km (2½ miles) west of Arenal Dam, past Lost Iguana Resort* ☎ *2479–1128 Park Headquarters, 2290–0469 in San José* ⊕ *www.hangingbridges. com* ✉ *$24, natural history tour $36, bird tour $47* ⊘ *Daily 7:30–4; early birding tour at 6 am.*

Eco Termales. Open hours at these family-owned hot springs operate in three 4-hour intervals per day, with only 100 guests entering per segment. This means the six pools and restaurant never get too crowded. Temperatures range from 37° to 41°C (98.6° to 105.8° F), and there is one chilly waterfall to cool you off. This is a great alternative to the overcrowded Baldi Hot Springs across the street. ⊠ *4½ km (2½ miles) west of La Fortuna Park; Across from Baldi, Diagonal from Volcán Look Disco Club* ☎ *2479–8787* ⊕ *www. ecotermalesfortuna.cr* ✉ *$32; lunch or dinner $16.*

Grand Spa at Tabacón. Grab a robe and settle into the jungle Jacuzzi while spa valets serve you smoothies. Treatments like the chocolate body wrap and the couples' two-hour massage utilize locally made products and end with champagne and fresh fruit. For a full day of pampering, request the spa package ($185), which includes access to the thermal baths, lunch or dinner, and $140 in spa services. ⊠ *13 km (8 miles) northwest of La Fortuna on highway toward Nuevo Arenal, across from Tabacón Resort* ☎ *2479–2028* ⊕ *www.tabacon.com* ✉ *Hot springs $60; after 6 pm $45; free for Tabacón guests.*

Fodor'sChoice ★ **La Fortuna Waterfall** (*Cataratas de la Fortuna*). A strenuous walk down ½ km (¼ mile) of precipitous steps (allow 25 to 50 minutes) is worth the effort to swim in the pool under the waterfall. Wear sturdy shoes or water sandals with traction, and bring snacks and water. You can get to the trailhead from La Fortuna by walking, by horseback, or by taking an inexpensive taxi ride. Arranging a tour with an agency in La Fortuna is the easiest option. ⊠ *Yellow entrance sign off main road toward volcano, 7 km (4 miles) south of La Fortuna* ✉ *$10* ⊘ *Daily 8–4.*

Fodor'sChoice ★ **Lake Arenal.** Costa Rica's largest inland body of water, shimmering Lake Arenal, all 125 square km (48 square miles) of it, lies between rolling green hills and a picture-perfect volcano. Many visitors are surprised to learn it's a man-made lake, created in 1973 when a giant dam was built. A natural depression was flooded, and a 32-km-long by 14.4-km-wide (20-mile-long by 9-mile-wide) lake was born. The almost constant winds from the Caribbean make this area a windsurfing and kiteboarding mecca. Outfitters in La Fortuna, Nuevo Arenal, and Tilarán run fishing, windsurfing, and kiteboarding trips on the lake. Desafío, an operator based in La Fortuna and Monteverde, has a half-day horseback trip between the two towns, with great views of the lake. For the best lake views, reserve a hotel in Nuevo Arenal. ⊠ *15 km (9 miles) southwest of La Fortuna.*

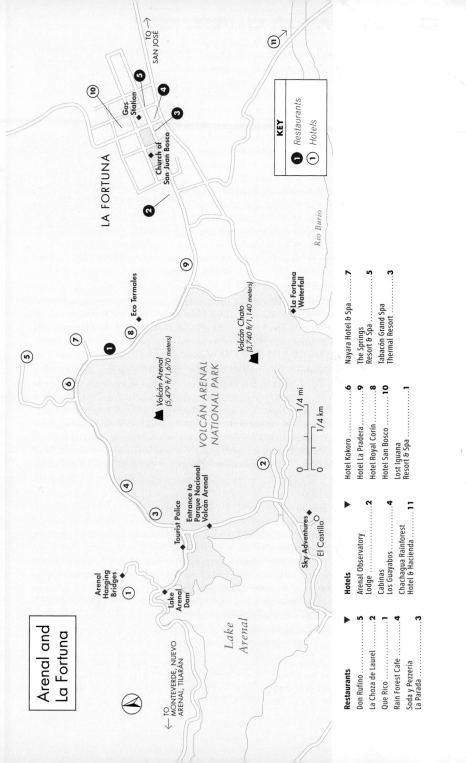

Arenal and La Fortuna

TO MONTEVERDE, NUEVO ARENAL, TILARÁN ←

TO SAN JOSÉ →

LA FORTUNA

Gas Station

Church of San Juan Bosco

Arenal Hanging Bridges

Lake Arenal Dam

Tourist Police

Entrance to Parque Nacional Volcán Arenal

Sky Adventures

El Castillo

Lake Arenal

Eco Termales

Volcán Arenal (5,479 ft/1,670 meters)

VOLCÁN ARENAL NATIONAL PARK

Volcán Chato (3,740 ft/1,140 meters)

La Fortuna Waterfall

Río Burío

0 — 1/4 mi
0 — 1/4 km

KEY

❶ *Restaurants*
① *Hotels*

Restaurants ▶

Don Rufino	**5**
La Choza de Laurel	**2**
Que Rico	**1**
Rain Forest Cafe	**4**
Soda y Pezzeria La Parada	**3**

Hotels ▶

Arenal Observatory Lodge	**2**
Cabinas Los Guayabos	**4**
Chachagua Rainforest Hotel & Hacienda	**11**
Hotel Kokoro	**6**
Hotel La Pradera	**9**
Hotel Royal Corín	**8**
Hotel San Bosco	**10**
Lost Iguana Resort & Spa	**1**
Nayara Hotel & Spa	**7**
The Springs Resort & Spa	**5**
Tabacón Grand Spa Thermal Resort	**3**

Parque Nacional Volcán Arenal (*Arenal Volcano*). Although the volcano is in a resting phase, it is still worth visiting the network of trails leading to old lava flows, rain forest, and a lookout point. The best option is a 4.5-km (2.8-mile) loop that takes you to a memorial and a crater lake formed by the 1968 eruption. You'll see plenty of wildlife and a massive ceiba tree toward the edge of the park. Guides are available for hire at the neighboring tour office, Arenal 1968. Remember, the potential for sudden activity means the park limits how high you can hike.

⊠ *1½- km (1 mile) from police station, on road to Arenal Observatory Lodge* ☎ *2462–1212 guide* ⊠ *$15* ☉ *Daily 8–4.*

> **WORD OF MOUTH**
>
> "Arenal has a lot of great adventure activities. Sky Trek has some of the longest, highest zip lines in the world. You can also raft with Rios Tropicales. We did waterfall rappelling/canyoning with La Roca and loved that too. There are some nice hikes in the Arenal area including the waterfall, the Hanging Bridges, and the volcano."
>
> —volcanogirl

WORTH NOTING

Church of San Juan Bosco. The town's squat, pale, concrete church, unremarkable on its own, wins Costa Rica's most-photographed-house-of-worship award. The view of the church from across the central park, with the volcano in the background, makes a great photo of the sacred and the menacing. ⊠ *West side of central park.*

OFF THE BEATEN PATH

Venado Caverns (*Cavernas de Venado*). In 1945 a farmer in the mountain hamlet of Venado fell into a hole, and thus discovered these eight subterranean, limestone chambers extending about 2½ km (1½ miles). Sunset Tours (⇨ *Tour Operators, below*) runs trips. If you're not claustrophobic, willing to get wet, and don't mind bats—think carefully—this could be the ticket for you. Rubber boots, flashlights, and helmets are provided. ⊠ *45 mins north of La Fortuna and 20 mins southeast of San Rafael* ☎ *2479–9800* ⊠ *$65* ☉ *Daily 7–8; tours at 8:15 and 2:15.*

SPORTS AND THE OUTDOORS

TOUR OPERATORS

FAMILY **Danaus Ecocenter** (*Ecocentro Danaus*). A small ecotourism project outside town exhibits 500 species of tropical plants, abundant animal life—including sloths and caimans—and butterfly and orchid gardens. This is a great place to see Costa Rica's famed red poison dart frogs up close. A two-hour guided evening tour begins at 6 pm and should be reserved in advance. ⊠ *2 km (1 mile) south of La Fortuna, 600 m above the road to community of Agua Azul* ☎ *2479–7019* ⊕ *www.ecocentrodanaus.com* ⊠ *Evening tour $37; day tour with guide $17; self guided $12* ☉ *Daily 8–4.*

Fodor's Choice **Desafío Adventures.** Expert Desafío guides can take you rafting, horse-
★ back riding, hiking, rappelling—you name the adventure.

Desafío pioneered rafting trips in this region, and has day trips on the Toro and Sarapiquí rivers (both Class III–IV) for experienced rafters ($85) and half-day rafting on the Balsa River (Class II–III) for less experienced paddlers ($69). Kayaking outings on Lake Arenal ($49) are ideal for beginners, as is a leisurely safari float on the Peñas Blancas ($55). If you're in the mood for something new, Desafío has half-day stand-up-paddling excursions on the lake ($65), and the popular Mambo Combo tour which combines waterfall rappelling and white-water rafting ($150).

If you're interested in getting up to Monteverde from the Arenal–La Fortuna area without taking the grinding four-hour drive, there's an alternative: Desafío Adventures has a five-hour guided horseback trip ($85). The trip involves taxi or van service from La Fortuna to the southern shore of Lake Arenal, and from that trail's end you ride to Monteverde, circumventing poorly maintained trails. A short boat ride across Lake Arenal is included. You leave La Fortuna at 7:15 am and arrive in Monteverde around 11:30 pm. You can also take the trip in reverse. Desafío will provide a driver to transport your rental vehicle, but you must arrange to include that driver in your rental agreement.

For a break from adventure, a daylong Rainforest Mysteries tour ($90) takes you to an herbal estate to learn about the rain forest and how it relates to what we eat. It includes an interpretive hike and instruction on medicinal plants and sustainable agriculture. Organic lunch is included. ✉ *Behind church* ☎ *2479–0020, 855/818–0020 in North America* ⊕ *www.desafiocostarica.com.*

Jacamar Naturalist Tours. A variety of tours ranges from bird walks and sunset lake cruises to white-water rafting and safari float trips. Sportfishing trips to Lake Arenal and Caño Negro Lagoon operate mornings and afternoons. ✉ *Across from central park* ☎ *2479–9767* ⊕ *www. arenaltours.com.*

Sunset Tours. One of the country's best tour operators pioneered excursions to the Caño Negro Wildlife Refuge and Venado Caverns. ✉ *Across from south side of church* ☎ *2479–9585* ⊕ *www.sunsettourcr.com.*

CANOPY TOURS

Costa Rica Sky Adventures. This canopy tour–bridge walk–tram complex near La Fortuna is operated by the Sky Trek–Sky Walk folks in Monteverde. Alpine-style gondolas transport you to the site, from which you can descend via 3 km (2 miles) of zip lines, hike through the cloud forest along a series of suspended bridges, or go back the way you came, on the tram. Butterfly and orchid gardens round out the offerings. ✉ *26 km (15 miles) west of La Fortuna, El Castillo* ☎ *2479–4100 Sky Adventures* ⊕ *www.skyadventures.travel* ✍ *$89 all offerings, $73 tram and zip lines, $61 tram and walk, $42 tram only, $33 walk only, shuttle $11* ☉ *Daily 7–5.*

Ecoglide Arenal Park. Here's a variation on the standard canopy tour: on the so-called Tarzan swing, you swing between two of the zip-line platforms, but far more securely than Johnny Weismuller ever did on his vine in the old *Tarzan* movies. There are also standard zip lines. As with all zip-line tours in Costa Rica, reservations should be made in advance, with tours starting at 7:40, 10, 12:30, and 3. ✉ *3 km (2 miles) west of La Fortuna* ☎ *2479–7120* ⊕ *www.arenalecoglide.com* ✍ *$55* ☉ *Daily 7–4.*

HORSEBACK RIDING

Many agencies—many nothing more than a guy and a horse—lead riding tours between La Fortuna and Monteverde along treacherous trails. Some riders have returned with stories of terrified horses barely able to navigate the way. It's best to stick with Desafío (⇨ *see Tour Operators above*) or another reputable outfit.

Chaves Tours. One of the most established operators in the area, Chaves Tours offers three-hour horseback excursions from La Fortuna to the Fortuna Waterfall. Tours depart daily at 8 am and 1 pm. The ride is appropriate for both novice and experienced riders. ⊠ *1 km (½ mile) west of town center* ☎ *8354–9159, 2479–0606* ⊕ *www.horsebackridingarenal.com.*

> **CAUTION**
>
> What's the newest craze in Monteverde and Arenal? Four-wheel all-terrain vehicles. Seemingly everybody rents them out these days, but we've heard too many reports of rollover accidents and don't recommend them. They can also disturb vegetation and the ecosystem, not to mention that the noise often frightens wildlife.

RAFTING AND KAYAKING

Desafío (⇨ *see Tour Operators above*) and several other La Fortuna operators offer Class III and IV white-water trips on the Río Toro. The narrow river requires the use of special, streamlined boats that seat just four passengers and go very fast. The easier Balsa, Peñas Blancas, Arenal, and San Carlos rivers have Class II and III rapids and are close enough to town that they can be worked into half-day excursions.

Canoa Aventura. Canoeing trips with ample wildlife viewing on the Río Peñas Blancas are a specialty, as are daylong canoe tours of the Caño Blanco Wildlife Refuge. The three-hour Caño Negro tour takes place on the Rio Frio River near the Nicaraguan border where you're sure to see birds, monkeys, caimans, iguanas, and bats. Tours are appropriate for beginners, with a selection of easy floats if you're not feeling too adventurous, and instruction is provided, but the folks here can tailor excursions if you're more experienced. ⊠ *1 km (½ mile) west of the church* ☎ *2479–8200* ⊕ *www.canoa-aventura.com.*

Flow Trips. Local guides lead rafting excursions on the Sarapiquí River (Classes II, III, and IV), as well as kayaking trips on Lake Arenal and the Peñas Blancas River. ⊠ *1 km (½ mile) west of La Fortuna* ☎ *2479–0075* ⊕ *www.flowtrips.com.*

RAPPELLING

Pure Trek Canyoning. Rappel down four waterfalls and one rock wall ranging in height from 12 to 50 meters (39 to 164 feet). Two guides lead small groups—10 is the maximum size—on a four-hour tour ($98) that departs at 7 am or noon to a private farm near La Fortuna, with plenty of wildlife-watching opportunities along the way. There is a bit of hiking between waterfalls and long periods of waiting for others in your group, so patience and proper shoes are a must. The excursion includes transportation, all rappelling gear, and a light lunch. ⊠ *7 km (4 miles) west of town center* ☎ *2479–1313* ⊕ *www.puretrekcostarica.com.*

EN ROUTE The string of properties on the highway between La Fortuna and the Tabacón resort has led to a noticeable increase in traffic. It is hardly the proverbial urban jungle, and it is one of the country's prettiest stretches of road, but you should drive with caution. Cars dart in and out of driveways. Visitors congregate along the side of the road (likely a sloth-spotting), and drivers gaze up at the volcano that looms over the highway. Keep your eyes on the road.

WHERE TO EAT

$$ ECLECTIC 🍴 **Don Rufino.** Although this is one of the more upscale restaurants in the area, there's no need to dress up here: this is La Fortuna, after all. The L-shape bar fronting the main street has become a popular expat and tourist hangout and lends a relaxed air to the town's most elegant restaurant. The user-friendly menu is marked with symbols of chili peppers for spicy dishes and a check mark for those that are highly recommended. Friendly waitstaff might suggest chicken seasoned with chocolate, coffee, and tarragon or forest lasagna made with wild mushrooms, caramelized onions, and ricotta cheese. The tilapia in bacon-and-tomato sauce is also very good. [$] *Average main: $16* ✉ *Across from gas station* ☎ *2479–9997* 🌐 *www.donrufino.com.*

$ COSTA RICAN 🍴 **La Choza de Laurel.** The smell of rotisserie chicken, porterhouse steak, and fresh fish bathed in garlic attracts passersby to this open-air restaurant a short walk from the center of town. Wooden picnic tables and a cigar shop storefront replicate an old Costa Rican village, adding a cultural touch to your meal. The menu is overwhelmingly large, ranging from pastas and sandwiches to soups and salads. Stick with local favorites like the black bean soup with homemade tortillas or the Choza Plate with chicken, rice, beans, chayote, corn, salad, and plantains. For dessert, banana splits are served in half a pineapple so you can eat the bowl. [$] *Average main: $10* ✉ *800 m northwest of church* ☎ *2479–7063* 🌐 *www.lachozadelaurel.com.*

$$$ ITALIAN 🍴 **Que Rico.** Just below the main road is this lovely Italian-inspired restaurant where wooden tables are draped with orange and lime linens, and soft music and candles add a touch of romance. In typical Costa Rican fashion, the menu is textbook thick, with options ranging from local ceviche and fish carpaccio to Caprese salad and roasted chicken. Stick to the Italian specialties: Brick-oven pizza and ravioli are made with a dough that combines five types of flour from Italy and Costa Rica. The Italian sausage pizza has a kick, and the "Volcán" with ham, mushrooms, bacon, and pepperoni is a local favorite. The chef invites kids to make their own pizzas, or they can order from the children's menu. Wine pairing recommendations are listed next to each item, and there's a "light section" if you're counting calories. Clearly the *boccio perugina* didn't make the cut; these baked pastries are stuffed with Nutella and caramelized almonds and served with vanilla ice cream. [$] *Average main: $20* ✉ *6½ km (4 miles) west of church* ☎ *2479–1020* 🌐 *www.quericoarenal.com.*

$ COSTA RICAN 🍴 **Rain Forest Café.** Reasonable prices, free Wi-Fi, and excellent quality have made this café a traveler's favorite, with meals ranging from *churrasco* and empanadas to salads and sandwiches. Burritos are perfectly toasted (not overly soft) with homemade tortillas, and of course there's always the typical Costa Rican *casado* (chicken, beef, or fish served with rice, beans, plantains, and salad). The tempting dessert display includes options such as carrot cake, flan, and a variety of pastries. For a morning pick-me-up, try the Crazy Monkey made with banana, milk, cinnamon, and coffee. The free Wi-Fi and shelf of books-for-borrow might help you escape from reality, but the ceiling lined with burlap coffee bags will remind you where you are. $ *Average main: $8 ⊠ In front of Hotel Las Colinas, south of the park, La Fortuna* ☎ *2479–7239*.

RICE AND BEANS

"More tico than *gallo pinto*" is an old saying here, but just how Costa Rican is the country's signature dish? Nicaraguans also claim it, and the rivalry has led to five *Guinness Book of World Records* bids for the largest batch. Costa Rica captured the first title in 2003, only to have Nicaragua top it a mere 12 days later. Costa Rica recaptured the prize in 2005. In 2008 Nicaragua snatched the title back with a 22,000-dish batch of rice and beans. Costa Rica more than doubled that amount at a March 2009 event with a whopping 50,000 servings, a record that stands at this writing. Nicaragua, it's your serve.

WHERE TO STAY

$$
HOTEL
Arenal Observatory Lodge. These cozy, comfortable, simply furnished rooms allow you to sleep as close as anyone should to a volcano—it's a mere 2.7 km (1.7 miles) away, and stellar views and outdoor activities are what the place is all about. **Pros:** best volcano views; secluded location; rate includes breakfast, taxes, and guided hike. **Cons:** rough road to get here; isolated location; no in-room phones; patchy Wi-Fi. $ *Rooms from: $128 ⊠ 3 km (2 miles) east of dam on Laguna de Arenal ⚓ from La Fortuna, drive to Tabacón resort and continue 4 km (2½ miles) past resort to turnoff at base of volcano; turn and continue for 9 km (5½ miles)* ☎ *2479–1070 lodge, 2290–7011 in San José* ⊕ *www.arenalobservatorylodge.com* ➟ *46 rooms; 2 suites* ⊚| *Breakfast*.

$
HOTEL
Cabinas Los Guayabos. These orange adobe cabins are basic but clean with big windows and porches facing Arenal. **Pros:** good budget value; friendly owners; great volcano views. **Cons:** rustic rooms; breakfast not included; Wi-Fi at reception only. $ *Rooms from: $65 ⊠ 9 km (5½ miles) west of La Fortuna* ☎ *2479–1444* ⊕ *www.cabinaslosguayabos. com* ➟ *9 cabins* ⊚| *No meals*.

$$$
B&B/INN
Chachagua Rainforest Hotel & Hacienda. At this working ranch, intersected by a brook, you can see *caballeros* (cowboys) at work, take a horseback ride into the rain forest, and look for toucans from your room or the deck of your *cabaña* (cabin). **Pros:** children under 11 stay free; many activities; nice pool area; rate includes breakfast and guided tour; good Web-only promotions. **Cons:** far from sights; thin mattresses; Wi-Fi signal does not reach all rooms. $ *Rooms from: $165 ⊠ 12 km (7 miles) south of La Fortuna* ☎ *2468–1011* ⊕ *www. chachaguarainforesthotel.com* ➟ *9 rooms, 21 bungalows* ⊚| *Breakfast*.

$$
HOTEL
Hotel Kokoro. Rooms at this hot springs hotel are like mini log cabins with hardwood floors and sugarcane ceilings, making the modern flat-screen TVs seem almost out of place. **Pros:** small spa offers massages;

The perfect way to end the day: a nice soak in the hot springs in Arenal Volcano National Park

lovely pool; private hot springs. **Cons:** reception floor slippery after rains; restaurant closed in low season; Wi-Fi in common areas only. $ *Rooms from: $90* ⊠ *500 m west of the Quebrada la Palma, La Fortuna* ☎ *2479–1222* ⊕ *www.arenalkokoro.com* ⤳ *23 rooms; 3 suites* ⦿ *Breakfast.*

$$
HOTEL
🏨 **Hotel La Pradera.** At "The Prairie," simple but comfortable guest rooms have high ceilings, spacious bathrooms, and verandas. **Pros:** good value; excellent views; nice pool. **Cons:** spartan rooms; lackadaisical staff; no Wi-Fi in rooms; no closets. $ *Rooms from: $75* ⊠ *2 km (1 mile) west of La Fortuna* ☎ *2479–9597* ⊕ *www.lapraderadelarenal. com* ⤳ *28 rooms* ⦿ *Breakfast.*

$$$
RESORT
🏨 **Hotel Royal Corín.** Spacious, nicely decorated accommodations come with friendly service, a sense of intimacy, and another big bonus—on-site hot springs and a spa. **Pros:** on-site hot springs; pleasant hotel-style surroundings; excellent showers; friendly service. **Cons:** some street noise; mediocre breakfast buffet; not a lot of local flavor. $ *Rooms from: $342* ⊠ *4.2 km (2.6 miles) west of La Fortuna* ☎ *2479–2200, 877/642–6746 in North America* ⊕ *www.royalcorin.com* ⤳ *42 rooms, 12 suites* ⦿ *Breakfast.*

$
HOTEL
🏨 **Hotel San Bosco.** At the most attractive and comfortable lodgings in the main part of town, clean, bright rooms have polished wood furniture and firm beds and are linked by a long veranda lined with benches and potted plants. **Pros:** gated property; good value; close to center of town. **Cons:** some rooms get street noise; boxy design; no bar or restaurant. $ *Rooms from: $88* ⊠ *220 m north of La Fortuna's gas station* ☎ *2479–9050, 800/393–0902 in North America* ⊕ *www. hotelsanbosco.com* ⤳ *33 rooms* ⦿ *Breakfast.*

$$$ HOTEL 🏨 **Lost Iguana Resort & Spa.** Despite the relative isolation—you're several kilometers beyond Tabacón—this is a favorite among Fodors.com posters, largely because each hillside room has a huge picture window and door opening to an individual balcony with stupendous volcano views. **Pros:** secluded location; great volcano views; many activities; nice spa and gym. **Cons:** removed from sights; ideally, need a car to stay here. [$] *Rooms from: $245* ✉ *20 km (12 miles) west of La Fortuna on highway toward Nuevo Arenal* ☎ *2479–1557, 2267–6148 in San José* 🌐 *www.lostiguanaresort.com* 🛏 *42 rooms* 🍴 *Multiple meal plans.*

WORD OF MOUTH

"Absolutely loved [Lost Iguana]. The rooms are spacious. The view is breathtaking. The hotel truly gives you the feel of being in the jungle. This resort is a bit out of the way and so if you want to go to dinner in town and you do not have a rental car it is recommended you avoid the high taxi fees ($30 one way) by catching the hotel transportation that travels at certain times to drop off employees. We also encountered extra fees when booking excursions as our hotel was considered 'out of the way' and so we paid an extra $20 one way (not per person) to total cost of excursions."

—suzyeq

$$$$ RESORT Fodor's Choice ★ 🏨 **Nayara Hotel, Spa & Gardens.** Expansive grounds are scattered with freestanding casitas, all tastefully decorated with dark-wood furnishings and equipped with luxurious touches like indoor–outdoor showers, four-post canopy beds, plasma TVs, and whirlpool tubs. **Pros:** luxurious rooms; attentive staff; early check-in can be arranged; excellent breakfast; private garden setting. **Cons:** hotel is often full; villas lack volcano views. [$] *Rooms from: $285* ✉ *7 km (4 miles) west of La Fortuna, Arenal* ☎ *2479–1600, 866/311–1197 in North America* 🌐 *www.arenalnayara.com* 🛏 *29 casitas; 21 suites; 16 villas* 🍴 *Multiple meal plans.*

$$$$ RESORT FAMILY 🏨 **The Springs Resort & Spa.** Near-perfect volcano views from individual balconies, a hot-springs complex, and rustically elegant rooms all contribute to a sense of well-being at this luxurious and remote retreat. **Pros:** stupendous volcano views; hot springs rich in minerals; excellent sushi bar. **Cons:** property has a theme-park feel; rooms are pricey. [$] *Rooms from: $515* ✉ *9 km (5½ miles) west of La Fortuna, then 4 km (2½ miles) north* ☎ *2401–3300, 954/727–8939 in North America* 🌐 *www.springscostarica.com* 🛏 *47 rooms, 4 villas* 🍴 *No meals.*

$$$ RESORT Fodor's Choice ★ 🏨 **Tabacón Grand Spa Thermal Resort.** At one of Central America's most famous and compelling resorts, hot springs, a lovely spa, landscaped gardens, and attractive, tile-floored rooms (suites are some of the country's finest lodgings) customarily draw visitors inland from the ocean with no regrets. **Pros:** elegant hotel; luxurious hot springs; great volcano views; good restaurant. **Cons:** crowded with tour groups; breakfast costs $30; two-night minimum stay. [$] *Rooms from: $333* ✉ *13 km (8 miles) northwest of La Fortuna on highway toward Nuevo Arenal* ☎ *2479–2000, 2519–1999 in San José, 877/277–8291 in North America* 🌐 *www.tabacon.com* 🛏 *74 rooms, 28 suites* 🍴 *No meals.*

NIGHTLIFE

People in La Fortuna tend to turn in early, though there's a place or two for night owls.

Lava Lounge. This La Fortuna hot spot has local and imported beers plus plenty of cocktails to get you in the mood for Reggae Nights, every Wednesday and Sunday from 8 to 11. ⊠ *25 m west of Catholic church, La Fortuna* ☎ *2479–7365* ⊕ *www.lavaloungecostarica.com.*

> **IN MEMORIAM**
>
> Those yellow hearts with halos painted on the pavement mark spots where people have died in car accidents or vehicles that have struck and killed pedestrians. An alarming number of them dot streets and roads around the country. Drive (and walk) with utmost caution.

NUEVO ARENAL

40 km (25 miles) (1 hr) west of La Fortuna.

Much of the original town of Arenal, at one of the lowest points near Lake Arenal, was destroyed by the volcano's 1968 eruption, and the rest was destroyed in 1973, when Lake Arenal flooded the region. The *nuevo* (new) town was created about 30 km (19 miles) away from the site of the old. It doesn't have much to interest tourists but is about halfway between La Fortuna and Tilarán, making it a good stop for a break, and an even better base with a couple of truly lovely lodgings nearby.

GETTING HERE AND AROUND

The route from La Fortuna to Nuevo Arenal around the north shore of Lake Arenal is in better shape than it has been in years. Watch out for the raccoonlike coatimundis (*pizotes* in Spanish) that scurry along the road. Longtime human feeding has diminished their ability to search for food on their own, and the cookies and potato chips they frequently get make matters worse. Public buses run twice daily from La Fortuna to Nuevo Arenal and beyond to Tilarán.

ESSENTIALS

Bank/ATM Banco Nacional ⊠ *Across from Restaurante La Muralla.*

Post Office Correos ⊠ *Next to Guardia Rural.*

WHERE TO EAT AND STAY

$$$

ECLECTIC

✕ **Gingerbread.** Ignore the chalkboard menu and let Chef Eyal guide you for what might just be the best meal you'll have in Costa Rica. The Israeli native (who trained in New York) is confident in the kitchen, but his boastfulness is not unwarranted, as you'll discover with fresh dishes like filet mignon, shrimp risotto, organic Greek chicken, and blackened tuna. Portions are large and can be paired with wines from the impressive cellar. Desserts like the macadamia cheesecake are well worth it if you manage to save room. Opt for a table on the patio rather than a booth near the U-shaped bar, unless you like boisterous noise with your meal. Note that the restaurant is open only Tuesday through Saturday from 5 pm to 9 pm and credit cards are not accepted. $ *Average main: $20* ⊠ *Next to Villa Decary* ☎ *2694–0039* ⊕ *www.gingerbreadarenal. com* ⌦ *Reservations essential* ═ *No credit cards* ⊙ *Closed Sun and Mon. No lunch.*

$ **Chalet Nicholas.** John and Cathy
B&B/INN Nicholas (and their three resident
Great Danes) have converted their
hillside home into a charming bed-
and-breakfast with stunning views
of the lake and volcano. **Pros:** attentive owners; great breakfasts; terrific value; birders paradise. **Cons:**
best for dog lovers; need a car to
stay here. *Rooms from: $85*
*3 km (2 miles) west of Nuevo
Arenal* 2694–4041 *www.
chaletnicholas.com 3 rooms*
No credit cards Breakfast.

$$$ **La Mansión Inn Arenal.** Nicely
HOTEL decorated cottages are scattered
Fodor's Choice around 25 acres on Arenal's north-
★ east shore at the point where the
volcano begins to disappear from
sight, but the lake views (and the sunsets) remain as spectacular as
ever. **Pros:** luxurious furnishings; stupendous lake views from private
terraces; great pool area. **Cons:** far from sights; need a car to stay here;
steel bars on windows are an eyesore. *Rooms from: $150 Road
between Nuevo Arenal and La Fortuna 8890–3901, 877/660–3830
in North America www.lamansionarenal.com 12 cottages, 5
suites Breakfast.*

$$ **Villa Decary.** There's much to recommend this hillside lodging, most
B&B/INN of all the large picture windows and balconies overlooking Lake Are-
nal and the attentive service from the owners. **Pros:** attentive owners;
great breakfasts; yoga classes offered. **Cons:** need a car to stay here;
two-night minimum stay in high season; Wi-Fi only reaches lower-level
rooms and common areas. *Rooms from: $119 2 km (1 mile) east of
Nuevo Arenal 800/556–0505 in North America www.villadecary.
com 5 rooms, 3 bungalows Breakfast.*

TILARÁN

*22 km (14 miles) (45 mins) southwest of Nuevo Arenal, 62 km (38
miles) (1½ hrs) west of La Fortuna.*

A windmill farm in the hills high above Tilarán attests to its being the
windiest place in the country, and this lakeside town is used as a base
by bronzed windsurfers. For those days when you get "skunked" (the
wind fails to blow), horseback riding and mountain biking can keep
you busy. A lakeside stroll is a pleasant way to while away a few hours.

GETTING HERE AND AROUND
The road from La Fortuna via Nuevo Arenal is in reasonable shape
these days, with a few short potholed stretches. Give yourself sufficient
time—say, two hours—for the trip, and make the trip during daylight
hours. Public buses travel to and from La Fortuna twice daily, and from
a small terminal at Calle 20 and Avenida 3 in San José five times daily.

If you're coming from Monteverde, keep in mind that the first 40 km (24 miles) are unpaved and slow going.

ESSENTIALS

Bank/ATM **Banco Nacional** ⊠ *Central Plaza* ☎ *2695–5610.*

Hospital **Clínica Tilarán** ⊠ *200 m west of Banco Nacional* ☎ *2695–5093.*

Post Office **Correos** ⊠ *115 m west of municipal stadium.*

SPORTS AND THE OUTDOORS

WINDSURFING AND KITESURFING

Tico Wind. Wind- and kitesurfing equipment is available for rent during the December-to-April season. The company offers three-hour kitesurfing lessons starting at $200, and a multiday course for $530. A one-hour windsurfing lesson costs $50. ⊠ *30 km (18 miles) west of Nuevo Arenal* ☎ *2692–2002* ⊕ *www.ticowind.com.*

Tilawa Windsurf Center. The area's only outfitter open year-round also offers the best selection of wind- and kitesurfing equipment for rent or purchase. Half-day beginner's lessons start at $100. ⊠ *Hotel Tilawa, 8 km (5 miles) north of Tilarán* ☎ *2695–5050* ⊕ *www. windsurfcostarica.com.*

WHERE TO STAY

$$

B&B/INN

🏨 **Mystica Lodge.** It's all about healing, yoga, and relaxation at this Italian-owned lodge, where you can enjoy treetop therapies next to the river or sway in a hammock overlooking Lake Arena. **Pros:** homemade breads at breakfast; hiking trail to stunning Ceiba tree; lovely pool; yoga classes. **Cons:** Wi-Fi in common areas only; no closets; no air-conditioning; limited menu at restaurant. $ *Rooms from: $90* ⊠ *13 km (8 miles) from the center of Tilarán in the direction of Nuevo Arenal, at the turnoff near Plaza del Cafe, Nuevo Arenal* ☎ *2692–1001* ⊕ *www.mysticacostarica. com* ⇆ *6 rooms; 1 villa; 1 house; 1 cabin* ⊠ *Breakfast.*

EN
ROUTE

Viento Fresco Waterfalls. On the road from Monteverde, just south of Tilarán, this private farm boasts five cascading waterfalls and swimming holes. The largest plunges 99 meters (328 feet) into a freshwater pool. The site also offers hiking trails, a dairy farm, several caves, changing facilities, and a restaurant serving Costa Rican fare. Horseback riding is also available. ⊠ *11 km (6 miles) south of Tilarán near San Miguel* ☎ *2695–3434* ⊕ *www.vientofresco.net* ⊠ *$15 waterfalls; $55 horseback riding* ⊙ *Daily 8–5:30.*

MONTEVERDE CLOUD FOREST AREA

Monteverde is a rain forest, but you won't be in the tropics, rather in the cool, gray, misty world of the cloud forest. Almost 900 species of epiphytes, including 450 orchids, are found here; most tree trunks are covered with mosses, bromeliads, ferns, and other plants. Monteverde spans the Continental Divide, extending from about 1,500 meters (4,920 feet) on the Pacific slope and 1,350 meters (4,430 feet) on the Atlantic slope up to the highest peaks of the Tilarán Mountains at around 1,850 meters (6,070 feet). Make Santa Elena your base of operations when visiting this area.

MONTEVERDE CLOUD FOREST BIOLOGICAL RESERVE

GETTING HERE AND AROUND

Buses from San José leave twice daily from the Terminal Atlántico Norte (✉ *C. 12 and Avda. 9*), at 6:30 am and 2:30 pm, stopping in the center of Santa Elena and at various locations on the way up the mountain as far as the Cheese Factory. Buses from Santa Elena leave for San José at 6:30 am and 2:30 pm daily. Taxis from Santa Elena are $7. Buses from Tilarán to Santa Elena leave once a day, at 12:30 pm. The roads to the area are some of the worst in the country.

Monteverde Cloud Forest Biological Reserve. One of Costa Rica's best-kept reserves has well-marked trails, lush vegetation, and a cool, damp climate. The collision of moist winds with the Continental Divide here creates a constant mist whose particles provide nutrients for plants growing at the upper layers of the forest. Giant trees are enshrouded in a cascade of orchids, bromeliads, mosses, and ferns, and in those patches where sunlight penetrates, brilliantly colored flowers flourish. The sheer size of everything, especially the leaves of the trees, is striking. No less astounding is the variety: 2,500 plant species, 400 species of birds, 500 types of butterflies, and more than 100 different mammals have so far been cataloged at Monteverde. A damp and exotic mixture of shades, smells, and sounds, the cloud forest is also famous for its

CLOSE UP

What Is a Cloud Forest?

Cloud forests are a type of rain forest, but are different from the hot, humid lowland forests with which most people are familiar. First of all, they're cooler. Temperatures in Monteverde Cloud Forest, for example, are in the 18°C (65°F) range year-round, and feel colder because of the near-constant cool rain. Cloud forests—also known as montane forests—occur at elevations of around 1,950 to 3,450 meters (6,500 to 11,500 feet). At this altitude, clouds accumulate around mountains and volcanoes, providing regular precipitation as well as shade, which in turn slows evaporation. Moisture is deposited directly onto vegetation, keeping it lush and green. The trees here, on top of high ridges and near the summits of volcanoes, are transformed by strong, steady winds that sometimes topple them and regularly break off branches. The resulting collection of small, twisted trees and bushes is known as an elfin forest. The conditions in cloud forests create unique habitats that shelter an unusually high proportion of rare species, making conservation vital. Monteverde is Costa Rica's most touristed cloud forest, but not its only one. Other cloud forests are in nearby Santa Elena Reserve, Los Angeles Cloud Forest Reserve near San Ramón (⇨ Chapter 4), and around San Gerardo de Dota (⇨ Chapter 8). ⇨ For more information on cloud forests, see Chapter 2: Biodiversity.

population of resplendent quetzals, which can be spotted feeding on the *aguacatillo* (similar to avocado) trees; best viewing times are early mornings from January until September, and especially during the mating season of April and May. Other forest-dwelling inhabitants include hummingbirds and multicolor frogs.

For those who don't have a lucky eye, a short-stay aquarium is in the field station; captive amphibians stay here just a week before being released back into the wild. Although the reserve limits visitors to 250 people at a time, Monteverde is one of the country's most popular destinations. We do hear complaints (and agree with them) that the reserve gets too crowded with visitors at times. Early visitors have the best chance at spotting wildlife.

Allow a generous slice of time for leisurely hiking to see the forest's flora and fauna; longer hikes are made possible by some strategically placed overnight refuges along the way. At the gift shop you can buy self-guide pamphlets and books; a map is provided when you pay the entrance fee. You can navigate the reserve on your own, but a 2½-hour guided tour (7:30 and 11:30 am and 1:30 pm) is invaluable for getting the most out of your visit. You may also take advantage of two-hour guided night tours starting each evening at 6 (reservations required). The reserve provides transport from area hotels for an extra $6. A guided walking bird-watching tour up to the reserve leaves from the park entrance each morning at 6 for groups of two to six people. Advance reservations are required. ✉ *10 km (6 miles) south of Santa Elena* ☎ *2645–5122, 2253–3267 in San José* ⊕ *www.cct.or.cr* ✆ *$17, plus $15 with guide services; $17 night tour; $64 morning bird-watching tour* ☉ *Daily 7–4.*

DID YOU KNOW?

Monteverde's Quakers, or more officially, the Society of Friends, no longer constitute the majority here these days, but their imprint on the community remains strong. (Don't expect to see anyone dressed like the man on the Quaker Oats box.) Their meetinghouse at Escuela de los Amigos, just south of the Cheese Factory on the road to the reserve, welcomes visitors at meetings of worship, 10:30 am Sunday and 9 am Wednesday. Most of the time is spent in quiet reflection.

MONTEVERDE AREA AND SANTA ELENA

Monteverde is 167 km (104 miles) (5 hrs) northwest of San José and 110 km (67 miles) (4 hrs) southwest of La Fortuna; Santa Elena is 6 km (4 miles) (30 mins) north of Monteverde and 35 km (22 miles) (2 hrs) southeast of Tilarán.

The area's first residents were a handful of Costa Rican families fleeing the rough-and-ready life of nearby gold-mining fields during the 1940s. They were joined in the early 1950s by Quakers, conscientious objectors from Alabama fleeing conscription into the Korean War. A number of things drew them to Costa Rica: just a few years earlier it had abolished its military, and the Monteverde area offered good grazing. The cloud forest that lay above the dairy farms soon attracted the attention of ecologists. Educators and artisans followed, giving Monteverde and its "metropolis," the village of Santa Elena, a certain mystique. In any case, Monteverde looks quite a bit different than it did when the first wave of Quakers arrived. New hotels have sprouted up everywhere, traffic grips the center of town, and a small shopping mall has gone up just outside of town on the way to the mountain. A glut of rented all-terrain vehicles contributes to the increasing din that disrupts Monteverde's legendary peace and quiet. Some define this as progress. Others lament the gradual chipping away at what makes one of Costa Rica's most special areas so, well, special. We side with them. Reminiscent of a ski town in summer, Monteverde still lets you get away from it all up here, but you'll have to work harder at it than you used to. In any case, you'll not lack for things to do if seeing nature is a primary reason for your visit.

Note that a casual reference to "Monteverde" generally refers to this entire area, but officially the term applies only to the original Quaker settlement, which is by the dairy-processing plant just down the mountain from the reserve entrance. If you follow road signs exclusively, you'll end up a bit outside the town of Santa Elena.

The only way to see the area's reserves, including the Monteverde Cloud Forest, is to hike them.

GETTING HERE AND AROUND

Getting here means negotiating some of the country's legendarily rough roads, but don't let that deter you from a visit. Years of promises to pave the way up here have collided with politics and scarce funds, but many residents remain just as happy to keep Monteverde out of the reach of tour buses and day-trippers. ("Do we really want this to be a shore excursion for cruise ships?" some residents ask.) Your own vehicle gives you the greatest flexibility, but a burgeoning number of shuttle-van

A leisurely stroll across a suspension bridge in Monteverde

services connect Monteverde with San José and other tourist destinations throughout the country.

If your bones can take it, a very rough track leads from Tilarán via Cabeceras to Santa Elena, near the Monteverde Cloud Forest Biological Reserve, doing away with the need to cut across to the Pan-American Highway. You need a 4WD vehicle, and you should inquire locally about the current condition of the road. The views of Nicoya Peninsula, Lake Arenal, and Arenal Volcano reward those willing to bump around a bit. Note, too, that you don't really save much time—on a good day it takes about 2½ hours as opposed to the 3 required via Cañas and Río Lagarto on the highway.

By car from the La Fortuna area, it's at least four hours by bumpy road around Lake Arenal; some tour companies provide the trip via minibus and boat. Gray Line has daily shuttle bus service between San José, La Fortuna, Arenal ($49), and Monteverde ($49). Interbus also connects San José with La Fortuna and Monteverde (each $45) daily, with connections from here to a few of the North Pacific beaches. There will be times you wish you had your own vehicle, but it's surprisingly easy to get around the Monteverde area without a car. Given the state of the roads, you'll be happy to let someone else do the driving. However, if you do arrive by rental car, the road up the mountain from Santa Elena is paved as far as the gas station near the entrance to the Hotel Belmar. Taxis are plentiful; it's easy to call one from your hotel, and restaurants are happy to summon a cab to take you back to your hotel after dinner. Taxis also congregate in front of the church on the main street in Santa Elena. Many tour companies will pick you up from your hotel and bring you back at the end of the day, either free or for a small fee.

ESSENTIALS

Bank/ATM Banco Nacional ⊠ *50 m north and 50 m west of bus station, Santa Elena* ☎ *2645–5027.*

Medical Clinic Clinica Monteverde ⊠ *150 m south of soccer field, Santa Elena* ☎ *2645–5076.*

Pharmacy Farmacia Vitosi ⊠ *Across from Chamber of Tourism, Santa Elena* ☎ *2645–5004.*

Post Office Correos ⊠ *50 m south of Serpentario, Santa Elena.*

Tourist Information Chamber of Tourism Monteverde ⊠ *Across from Super Compro supermarket, Santa Elena* ☎ *2645–6565* ⊙ *Daily 10–6; closed Sat..*

EXPLORING
TOP ATTRACTIONS

FAMILY **Butterfly Garden** (*Jardín de Mariposas*). Forty species of butterflies flit about in four enclosed botanical gardens. Morning visits are best, since the butterflies are most active early in the day. Your entrance ticket includes an hour-long guided tour under tin roofs meaning you won't get wet on rainy days. Be sure to visit the nonprofit gift shop benefiting the local community. ⊠ *Near Monteverde Inn ⊹ take right-hand turnoff 4 km (2½ miles) past Santa Elena on road to Monteverde, continue for 2 km (1 mile)* ☎ *2645–5512* ⊕ *www.monteverdebutterflygarden.com* 🎟 *$15 adults, $5 kids 4–6, $10 youth 7–18* ⊙ *Daily 8:30–4.*

FAMILY **Monteverde Cloudforest Train.** Riders enjoy a 90-minute excursion in one of three rail cars pulled through the rain forest by an old-fashioned locomotive. After 3 km (2 miles), the train stops for a photo/snack/coffee/hot chocolate break and then returns to the starting station. Tours depart hourly. ⊠ *6 km (4 miles) north of Santa Elena* ☎ *2645–5700* 🎟 *$40* ⊙ *Daily 8–4.*

FAMILY **Monteverde Theme Park** (*Ranario de Monteverde and Frog Pond of Monteverde*). Only in Monteverde would visitors groove to the nightlife at an exhibition of 28 species of frogs, toads, and other amphibians. Bilingual biologist-guides take you through a 45-minute tour of the terrariums in the Frog Pond of Monteverde (Ranario de Monteverde), just outside Santa Elena. For the best show, come around dusk and stay well into the evening, when the critters become more active and much more vocal. (Your ticket entitles you to a second visit the same day, as well as a guided tour.) The complex has a butterfly garden with 40 different species. There's a small cafeteria and a frog-and-toad-and-butterfly theme gift shop. ⊠ *½ km (¼ mile) southeast of Super Compro supermarket, Santa Elena* ☎ *2645–6320* 🎟 *Frog pond and butterfly garden $14 each; combined ticket $24* ⊙ *Frog pond, daily 9–8:30; butterfly garden, daily 9–4.*

Santa Elena Reserve. Several conservation areas near Monteverde are attractive day-trip destinations, especially when the Monteverde Reserve is too busy. The 765-acre Santa Elena Reserve just west of Monteverde is a project of the Santa Elena high school, and has a series of trails of varying lengths and difficulties that can be walked alone or with a guide on tours that depart daily at 7:30, 9, 11:30, and 1 pm.

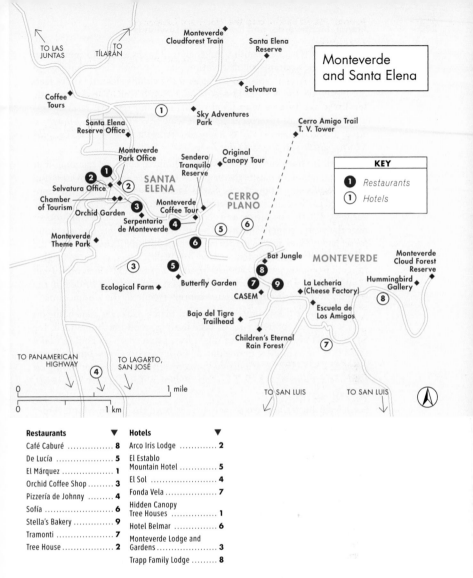

Monteverde and Santa Elena

TO LAS JUNTAS

TO TILARÁN

Monteverde Cloudforest Train

Santa Elena Reserve

Selvatura

Coffee Tours

Sky Adventures Park

Cerro Amigo Trail
T. V. Tower

Santa Elena Reserve Office

Monteverde Park Office

Sendero Tranquilo Reserve

Original Canopy Tour

KEY

1	*Restaurants*
①	*Hotels*

SANTA ELENA

CERRO PLANO

Selvatura Office

Chamber of Tourism

Orchid Garden

Monteverde Coffee Tour

Serpentario de Monteverde

MONTEVERDE

Bat Jungle

Monteverde Cloud Forest Reserve

Monteverde Theme Park

Hummingbird Gallery

Ecological Farm

Butterfly Garden

CASEM

La Lechería (Cheese Factory)

Escuela de Los Amigos

Bajo del Tigre Trailhead

Children's Eternal Rain Forest

TO PANAMERICAN HIGHWAY

TO LAGARTO, SAN JOSÉ

TO SAN LUIS

TO SAN LUIS

0 — 1 mile

0 — 1 km

The 1.4-km (¾-mile) Youth Challenge trail takes about 45 minutes to negotiate and contains an observation platform with views that extend as far as the Arenal Volcano—that is, if the clouds clear. If you're feeling hardy, try the 4.8-km (3-mile) Caño Negro trail. There's a shuttle service to the reserve with fixed departures and returns; reservations are required, and the cost is $3 each way. ⊠ *6 km (4 miles) north of Santa Elena* ☎ *2645–5390* ⊕ *www.reservasantaelena.org* ✉ *$14, plus $15 for guide services* ⊗ *Daily 7–4.*

FAMILY
Fodor'sChoice
★
Selvatura. If your time in Monteverde is limited, consider spending it at Selvatura, a kind of nature theme park—complete with canopy tour and bridge walks—just outside the Santa Elena Reserve. A 100-bird hummingbird garden, an enormous enclosed 50-species *mariposario* (butterfly garden), a *herpetario* (frog and reptile house), and insect exhibition sit near the visitor center. The only zip-line tour built entirely inside a cloud forest has 13 lines and 18 platforms, with an optional Tarzan swing at the end to round out the excursion. Tree Top Walkways takes you to heights ranging from 50 meters (150 feet) up to 170 meters (510 feet) on a 3-km (2-mile) walk. These are some of the longest and strongest bridges in the country and run through the same canopy terrain as the zip-line tour.

You can choose from numerous mix-and-match packages, depending on which activities interest you, or take it all in, with lunch included, for $138. Most visitors get by for much less, given that you couldn't take in all there is to do here in one day. ⊠ *Office across from church, Santa Elena* ☎ *2645–5929* ⊕ *www.selvatura.com* ✉ *Prices vary, depending on package; zip-line tour $45; Tree Tops Walkway $30* ⊗ *Daily 8:30–4:30.*

WORTH NOTING

FAMILY
Bat Jungle. Butterflies, frogs, and snakes have their own Monteverde-area exhibits, and bats get equal time with guided tours that provide insight into the life of one of the planet's most misunderstood mammals. Admission includes a 45-minute guided tour. An adjoining museum documents the history of the region, in particular, its early settlement by the Quakers. ⊠ *Across from El Bosque Lodge* ☎ *2645–7701* ⊕ *www.batjungle.com* ✉ *$12* ⊗ *Daily 9–7:30.*

FAMILY
Children's Eternal Rain Forest (*Bosque Eterno de los Niños*). The 54,000-acre rain forest dwarfs the Monteverde and Santa Elena reserves. It began life as a school project in Sweden among children interested in saving a piece of the rain forest, and blossomed into a fund-raising effort among students from 44 countries. The reserve's **Bajo del Tigre trail** makes for a gentle, self-guided 3.3-km (2-mile) hike through secondary forest. Along the trail are 27 stations at which to stop and learn about the reserve, many with lessons geared toward kids. A separate guided twilight walk ($25) begins at 5:30 pm and lasts two hours, affording the chance to see the nocturnal side of the cloud forest; reservations are required. Much of the rest of the reserve is not open to the public, but the Monteverde Conservation League offers stays at San Gerardo and Poco Sol, two remote field stations within the forest. The $52 packages include dormitory accommodation and meals. ⊠ *100 m south of CASEM* ☎ *2645–5305* ⊕ *www.acmcr.org* ✉ *$28 day tour with guide; $12 self guided; $20 night tour; transportation from area hotels $3* ⊗ *Daily 8–4.*

Continued on page 236

Zip lining is an exhilarating experience.

CANOPY TOURS

Costa Rica invented the concept of the canopy tour, and the idea has spread across the globe. Zip lining through the treetops is a once-in-a-lifetime experience, and exploring the jungle canopy is the best way to see the most eye-catching animals.

A canopy tour is an umbrella term describing excursions that take you to the jungle's ceiling. The experience is distinctly Costa Rican and is one of the country's signature activities for visitors. There are two types of tours: one gives you a chance to see animals (from bridges and platforms), and the other lets you swing through the trees on zip lines. We know of around 80 tours nationwide but recommend only about a third of that number. *You'll find tour information in most chapters of this book.*

By Jeffrey Van Fleet

WHAT EXACTLY IS A CANOPY TOUR?

Canopy cable ride at Monteverde cloud forest

WHAT TO EXPECT

Plan on a half-day for your canopy tour, including transportation to and from your hotel and a safety briefing for zip line excursions. Most zipline tours begin at fixed times and reservations are always required, or at least advised. A tour over hanging-bridges is far more leisurely and can be done at your own pace. The latest craze on zip line tours is an optional Tarzan swing, a freefall drop similar to bungee jumping but with swinging instead of bouncing. Several outfitters also offer rappelling as part of the package. The occasional mega-complex, such as Monteverde's Selvatura, offers both types of tours. For most, it's one or the other.

BRIDGES AND TRAMS

These are canopy tours in a literal sense, where you walk along suspension bridges, ride along in a tram, or are hoisted up to a platform to get a closer look at birds, monkeys, and sloths.

They're also called hanging-bridges tours, sky walks, or platform tours. If seeing nature at a more leisurely pace is your goal, opt for these, especially the bridge excursions. Early mornings are the best time for animal sightings—at 50–250 feet above ground, the views are stupendous.

ZIP LINES

This type of tour is a fast-paced, thrilling experience. You're attached to a zip line with a safety harness, and then you "fly" at about 15–40 miles per hour from one tree platform to the next. (You may be anywhere from 60–300 feet above the forest floor.) Tree-to-tree zip lines date from the 19th century and have been a bona fide activity for visitors to Costa Rica since the mid-1990s when the first tour opened in Monteverde. These tours are tremendous fun, but you won't see any animals. An average fitness level—and above-average level of intrepidness—are all you need.

TOP CANOPY TOURS BY REGION

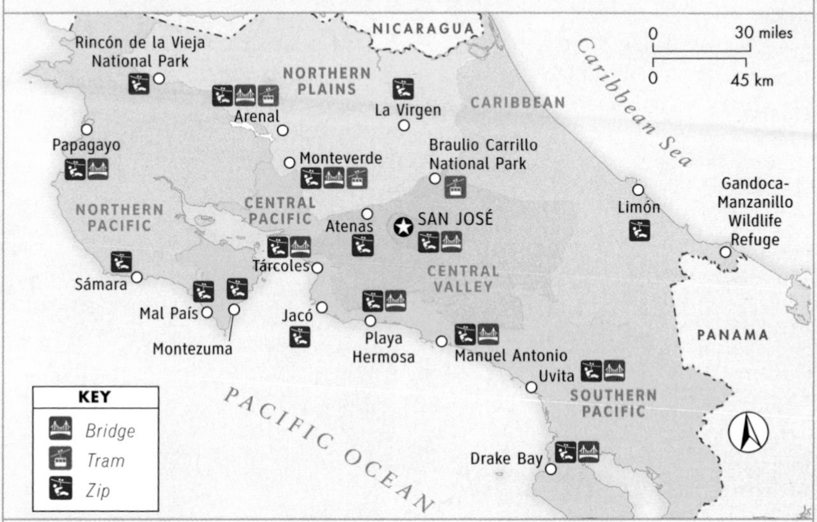

KEY

- Bridge
- Tram
- Zip

TOUR OPERATOR	LOCATION	TYPE		
Arenal Hanging Bridges	Arenal		Bridge	
Sky Adventures	Arenal	Zip	Bridge	Tram
Canopy Safari	Manuel Antonio	Zip	Bridge	
Canopy del Pacífico	Malpaís	Zip		
Cocozuma	Montezuma	Zip		
Ecoglide Arenal Park	Arenal	Zip		
Hotel Villa Lapas	Tárcoles	Zip	Bridge	
Aerial Tram Monteverde	Monteverde			Tram
Original Canopy Tour	Monteverde	Zip		
Original Canopy Tour	Drake Bay	Zip	Bridge	
Original Canopy Tour	Veragua, Limón	Zip		
Rain Forest Adventures	Braulio Carrillo National Park	Zip	Bridge	Tram
Rain Forest Adventures	Jacó	Zip		Tram
Rincón de la Vieja Canopy	Rincón de la Vieja National Park	Zip		
Selvatura	Monteverde	Zip	Bridge	
Tití Canopy Tour	Manuel Antonio	Zip		
Sky Adventures	Monteverde	Zip	Bridge	Tram
Wing Nuts Canopy Tour	Sámara	Zip		
Witch's Rock Canopy Tour	Papagayo	Zip	Bridge	
Osa Canopy Tour	Uvita	Zip	Bridge	
El Santuario Canopy Adventure Tour	Manuel Antonio	Zip	Bridge	

SAFETY FIRST

(top left) Zip lining Aventuras del Sarapiqui. (bottom left) Brown-Throated Three-Toed Sloth. (right) Sky Tram, Rainforest Canopy Tour, Arenal

PLAYING IT SAFE

Flying through the air, while undeniably cool, is also inherently dangerous. Before you strap into a harness, be certain that the safety standards are first rate. There's virtually no government oversight of the activity in Costa Rica. Here is a list of questions you should ask before you book:

1. How long has the company been in business?

2. Are they insured?

3. Are cables, harnesses, and other equipment manufacturer-certified?

4. Is there a second safety line that connects you to the zip line in case the main pulley gives way?

5. What's the price? Plan on paying $50 to $80—a low price could indicate a second-rate operation.

6. Are participants clipped to the zip line while on the platform? (They should be.)

KEEP IN MIND

■ Listen closely to the guides' pre-tour safety briefing and obey their instructions.

■ Never argue with the guide when s/he is making a decision to preserve your safety.

■ Don't attempt to take photos in flight.

■ Gauge your abilities frankly. Remember, once you start, there's no turning back.

■ If anything seems "off" or makes you uncomfortable, walk away.

Don Juan Coffee Tour. Small groups are the hallmark of tours that last about two hours and let you see the coffee process from start to finish at the plantation of Don Juan Cruz, one of the original settlers in the area. Transportation can be arranged from all Monteverde-area lodgings. ⊠ *2 km (1 mile) northwest of soccer field* ☎ *2645–7100* ⊕ *www.donjuancoffeetour.com* ✉ *$30 day tour; $35 evening tour* ☉ *Tours at 8, 10, 1, 3, and 6.*

> ## ANTS ON PARADE
>
> Tread carefully when you see a tiny green parade on the ground before you. It's a troop of leaf-cutter ants carrying compost material to an underground nest.

Ecological Farm. This private, 75-acre wildlife refuge is laced with four trails and houses birds, sloths, agoutis, and coatimundis. You'll also come upon two waterfalls and a coffee plantation. If you can't make it all the way up to the Monteverde Reserve for the day hike, there's a top-notch guided, two-hour twilight walk that begins each evening at 5:30. Reservations are required. ⊠ *Turnoff to Jardín de Mariposas, off main road between Santa Elena and Monteverde* ☎ *2645–5869* ✉ *$12 self-guided; $27 with guide; twilight walk $25* ☉ *Daily 7–5.*

Monteverde Coffee Tour. Bite your tongue before requesting Costa Rica's ubiquitous Café Britt up here. Export-quality Café Monteverde is the locally grown product, and the tour lets you see the process up close from start to finish, from shade growing on the area's Turín plantation, 7 km (4 miles) north of Santa Elena; transport to the *beneficio*, the processing mill where the beans are washed and dried; and finally to the roaster. Reservations are required, and pickup from area hotels is available. ☎ *2645–5901* ✉ *$30* ☉ *Tours at 8 am and 1:30 pm.*

Orchid Garden (*Jardín de Orquídeas*). More than 450 species of orchids, one of which is the world's smallest, are on display. The Monteverde Orchid Investigation Project manages the gardens. Admission includes a 30-minute tour. ⊠ *150 m south of Banco Nacional* ☎ *2645–5308* ⊕ *www.monteverdeorchidgarden.net* ✉ *$10* ☉ *Daily 8–5.*

Sendero Tranquilo Reserve. This 200-acre forest is managed by the Hotel Sapo Dorado and bordered by the Monteverde Cloud Forest Biological Reserve and the Guacimal River. Five kilometers (3 miles) of narrow trails are designed to have as little impact on the forest as possible (only groups of two to six are allowed). A guide leads you through primary and secondary forest and an area that illustrates the effects of deforestation. Because of the emphasis on minimal environmental impact, animals here tend to be more timid than at some other reserves. Your entrance fee includes a guide and transportation. ⊠ *3 km (2 miles) north of Monteverde Reserve entrance, Cerro Plano* ☎ *2645–5010* ⊕ *www.sapodorado.com* ✉ *$35* ☉ *Tours daily at 7:30 and 1; reservations required.*

FAMILY **Serpentarium of Monteverde** (*Serpentario de Monteverde*). Greet 50 species of live Costa Rican reptiles and amphibians with glass safely between you and them. Guided tours in English or Spanish are included in your admission price. ⊠ *Just outside Santa Elena on road to Monteverde, next to Bar Taberna* ☎ *2645–6002* ✉ *$12* ☉ *Daily 9–8.*

NEED A
BREAK?

La Lechería. Long before tourists flocked up here, dairy farming was the foundation of Monteverde's economy. Quakers still deliver dairy to what is locally referred to as the Cheese Factory, or La Lechería. The factory store sells local cheeses and ice cream. Stop in for a cone. It's open Monday through Saturday 7:30 to 5 and Sunday 7:30 to 4. If you have more time, take a two-hour tour of the operation Monday through Saturday at 9 or 2. Tours are $12 and wind up with a cheese-sampling session. Reserve in advance. If you're not heading up the mountain, these folks also operate a stand across from the Tree House restaurant on the main street in Santa Elena. ⊠ *½ km (¼ mile) south of CASEM, halfway between Santa Elena and Monteverde Reserve* ☎ *2645–7090 tours* ⊕ *www.monteverdecheesefactory.com.*

SPORTS AND THE OUTDOORS
HANGING BRIDGES AND TRAMS

FAMILY **Aerial Tram Monteverde.** A two-person carriage on an elevated track takes you an hour-long ride through the rain-forest canopy. You control the speed of your carriage. Alternatively, a 1½-km (1-mile) walk gives you a ground-level perspective. The site opens for night visits with advance reservations. ⊠ *Off main road between Santa Elena and Monteverde, on turnoff to Jardín de Mariposas, 300 m south of the school* ☎ *2645–5960* ⊕ *www.naturalwonderstram.com* ⊞ *$25; $30 night tour* ⊙ *Daily 8–5.*

FAMILY **Sky Adventures.** Here's a tram/zip-line/hanging-bridges entertainment complex all in one. A tram takes you on a mile-long gondola ride through the rain-forest canopy. You can descend via the tram, or along a series of five hanging bridges, at heights of up to 41 meters (138 feet), connected from tree to tree. Your third descent option is 3 km (2 miles) of zip lines through the cloud-forest canopy. Imposing towers, used as support, mar the landscape somewhat. A hummingbird garden rounds out the offerings. ⊠ *Office across from Banco Nacional, Santa Elena* ☎ *2645–5238, 2479–4117* ⊕ *www.skyadventures.travel* ⊞ *$83 all offerings, $66 tram and zip lines, tram and bridges $55, tram only $42, bridges only with guide $33, bridges only without guide $22* ⊙ *Daily 7–4.*

HORSEBACK RIDING

The ride from Monteverde to La Fortuna can be dangerous with outfitters that take inexperienced riders along steep trails. Desafío *(⇨ see Tour Operators under La Fortuna)* should be your only choice for getting from Monteverde to La Fortuna on horseback. ■TIP➜ **During rainy season (July–December), book horseback trips in the morning since rains usually begin around 2 pm.**

Caballeriza El Rodeo. Escorted 1½-hour horseback-riding tours ($30) with Caballeriza El Rodeo are on a private farm. Excursions are for everyone from beginner to experienced rider. A two-hour sunset tour ($35) begins at 3:30 pm. ⊠ *West entrance of town of Santa Elena, at tollbooth, Santa Elena* ☎ *2645–5764* ✎ *elrodeo@ice.co.cr.*

Sabine's Smiling Horses. Owner Sabine—who speaks English, French, German, and Spanish—offers treks starting at $19 per hour. In addition to the regular waterfall and canyon tours, excursions at full moon

are also offered once a month. Pony rides are available for children. ⊠ *1 km (½ mile) west of the cemetery, Santa Elena* ☎ *2645–6894* ⊕ *www.smilinghorses.com.*

ZIP-LINE TOURS

FAMILY **Original Canopy Tour.** The first company to offer zip-line tours in Costa Rica has set up 10 platforms in the canopy. Tours last about 2½ hours and begin at 7:30, 10:30, and 2:30. ⊠ *Cerro Plano* ☎ *2291–4465 in San José for reservations, 305/433–2241 in U.S.* ⊕ *www.canopytour. com* ☜ *$45.*

WHERE TO EAT

$$ ✕ **Café Caburé.** Launched by Argentinean owners who longed for quality
MODERN chocolate made from local cocoa, this remarkable restaurant/bakery/
ARGENTINE chocolateria is one of only four places in Costa Rica to grind its own cocoa beans. Start with a meal in the open-air restaurant serving savory empanadas and chipotle wraps with a creamy secret sauce. The home-made cannelloni with spinach, ricotta, and walnuts is a great vegetarian option, and the mole dishes are about as authentic as you can get, since the owner spent years perfecting her culinary skills in Oaxaca, Mexico. When it comes to the sweet stuff, the ganache with blackberry sauce and the chocolate passion fruit mousse are both decadently delicious, as are the exquisite truffles. Tours of the attached chocolate factory are available daily at 2 and 4 for $12. $ *Average main: $14* ⊠ *Paseo de Stella Tourist Center in Old Monteverde, near the Bat Jungle Tour* ☎ *2645–5020* ⊕ *www.cabure.net* ☽ *Closed Sun.*

$$$ ✕ **De Lucía.** Cordial Chilean owner José Belmar is the walking, talking (in
ECLECTIC five languages) menu here, and he's always on hand to chat with guests. The handsome wooden restaurant with red mahogany tables is given a distinct South American flavor by an array of Andean tapestries and ceramics. Entrées include sea bass with garlic sauce and orange chicken served with grilled vegetables and fried plantains. They also boast the best hamburgers in town. An excellent dessert choice is *tres leches* (three milks), a richer-than-rich cake. $ *Average main: $18* ⊠ *Turnoff to Jardín de Mariposas, off main road between Santa Elena and Monteverde, Cerro Plano* ☎ *2645–5337* ⊕ *www.deluciamonteverde.com.*

$ ✕ **El Márquez.** Seafood is an unexpected treat up here in the mountains,
SEAFOOD and it's fresh: the owner gets shipments from Puntarenas several times a week. The place is nothing fancy—expect wooden tables and chairs, with nautical decor and lots of local flavor—but when area residents want a special meal, this is where they come. Portions are big, but prices aren't. You could have trouble finishing the generous mixed seafood platter with shrimp, crab, and octopus in a white-wine sauce, or the jumbo shrimp with a sauce of mushrooms and hearts of palm. The seafood soup and fish kabobs are smaller portions, allowing you to save room for the coconut flan. $ *Average main: $10* ⊠ *Next to Suárez veterinary clinic, Santa Elena* ☎ *2645–5918* ☽ *Closed daily between 3 and 5:30. No lunch Sun.*

$ ✕ **Orchid Coffee Shop.** It's astonishing the level of culinary perfection that
BAKERY comes out of this A-frame shack. Yes, the menu is enormous, but take
Fodor'sChoice your time and let your appetite guide you. The crepes, pancakes, gra-
★ nola, and French toast are all made from scratch. Tomato soup is comforting on a rainy day, and the veggie panini is stuffed with all kinds of

organic goodness. Choose from more than 25 types of coffee, including the heartwarming "espresso moka" made with hot chocolate, whisky, and mint. The smoothies couldn't be fresher—each one is made with homemade yogurt and local ingredients like pineapple, cucumber, carrot, and basil. With free Wi-Fi, ambient music, and local artwork, the cheerful setting in the center of town is the ideal place to take a break. Save your receipt for a $2 discount on admission to the neighboring Orchid Garden. Ⓢ *Average main: $10* ⊠ *Next to the Orchid Garden, 150 m south of Banco Nacional* ☎ *2645–6850.*

$$
ITALIAN
✕ **Pizzería de Johnny.** Sooner or later everyone makes it to this stylish but informal place with candles and white tablecloths. Paper-thin-crust pizza is cooked in a wood-fire oven; the Monteverde pizza, with the works, is the most popular. Organic lamb and beef are also on the menu, along with homemade mozzarella that is used in salads like the Caprese. Pastas, sandwiches, and a decent wine selection round out the selections. Ⓢ *Average main: $15* ⊠ *Road to Monteverde Reserve, 1½ km (1 mile) southeast of Santa Elena* ☎ *2645–5066* ⊕ *www.pizzeriadejohnny.com.*

$$$
ECLECTIC
✕ **Sofía.** Bilingual waiters in crisp black aprons scurry attentively around the three dining rooms serving a wide variety of dishes. Choose from mouthwatering favorites such as corvina and shrimp in a chipotle cream sauce or chicken served with a guava reduction and a side of diced onions, corn, plantains, and bacon. Other standouts include the sweet-and-sour-fig roasted loin, and the *chile relleno*. There's also an extensive wine and cocktail selection to accompany your meal. Ⓢ *Average main: $18* ⊠ *Turnoff to Jardín de Mariposas, off main road between Santa Elena and Monteverde, Cerro Plano* ☎ *2645–7017.*

$
CAFÉ
✕ **Stella's Bakery.** This local institution is a good place to get an early-morning fix before heading to the Monteverde Reserve. Pastries, rolls, muffins, natural juices, and coffee are standard breakfast fare, and light sandwiches, soups, and quiches are on offer at lunch. There is also a homemade lasagna if you're in the mood for a hearty meal. Ⓢ *Average main: $7* ⊠ *Across from CASEM* ☎ *2645–5560* ☽ *Closes at 5 pm.*

$$
ITALIAN
✕ **Tramonti.** Named for a town in southwestern Italy, this glass-walled restaurant is warm and inviting with dangling fairy lights, hardwood floors, candles dripping onto old wine bottles, and chefs tossing dough high overhead beside a wood-fired oven. The *pulpo* and beef carpaccios are ultrathin, a perfect accompaniment for the homemade rolls dipped in chili-and-garlic olive oil. Pizzas are served on wooden paddles, and come piled high with toppings like asparagus, mushrooms, ricotta, and Gorgonzola. Calzones, eggplant ravioli, and seafood and meat dishes are served in hearty portions. Service is excellent; take-out is available. Ⓢ *Average main: $14* ⊠ *Across from Bat Jungle* ☎ *2645–6120* ⊕ *www.tramonticr.com.*

$$
ECLECTIC
✕ **Tree House.** The name describes the place: this two-story restaurant on Santa Elena's main street is built around a 80-year-old fig tree, and the branches shelter tables from the afternoon mist. The menu mixes pastas and seafood with Costa Rican cuisine; for a taste of everything, try the típico platter. Repeat guests generally order the tilapia with mushroom sauce or the fajitas. The service can be "leisurely" or "slow," depending on your perspective. Ⓢ *Average main: $14* ⊠ *Across from AyA, Santa Elena* ☎ *2645–5751* ⊕ *www.treehouse.cr.*

WHERE TO STAY

Most hotels in Monteverde don't have air-conditioning or heaters in the rooms, so you might have to crack a window or grab an extra blanket depending on your preference. It also helps to pack accordingly.

$ B&B/INN **Arco Iris Lodge.** You're almost right in the center of town, but you'd never know it at this tranquil spot where cozy cabins range from rustic to plush, come with porches, and are set on 4 acres of birding trails. **Pros:** attentive owner and staff; terrific breakfast; ecology-minded place. **Cons:** some obstructed views; steep walk if on foot; not all rooms have Wi-Fi. [$] *Rooms from: $88* ✉ *50 m south of Banco Nacional, Santa Elena* ☎ *2645–5067* 🌐 *www.arcoirislodge.com* 🛏 *20 cabins, 1 suite* 🍴 *No meals.*

$$$ HOTEL **El Establo Mountain Hotel.** The area's largest, grandest hotel gets high marks for its huge suites, plush decor, a long list of amenities, and many activities. **Pros:** luxurious furnishings; spacious rooms; many activities; great views. **Cons:** massive grounds require shuttle van to navigate; Wi-Fi in common areas only; cold pool; rooms lack artwork and patio furniture. [$] *Rooms from: $215* ✉ *3½ km (2 miles) northwest of Monteverde* ☎ *2645–5110* 🌐 *www.hotelelestablo.com* 🛏 *124 rooms; 31 suites* 🍴 *Breakfast.*

$$ B&B/INN **El Sol.** A charming German-Spanish family tends to guests at this quintessential get-away-from-it-all place just 10 minutes down the mountain from—and a noticeable few degrees warmer than—Santa Elena. **Pros:** great views; whimsically decorated cabins. **Cons:** need a car to get here; far removed from sights; Wi-Fi in common areas only; breakfast costs extra. [$] *Rooms from: $100* ✉ *4 km (2½ miles) southwest of Santa Elena* ☎ *2645–5838* 🌐 *www.elsolnuestro.com* 🛏 *3 cabins* 💳 *No credit cards* 🍴 *No meals.*

$$ RESORT **Fonda Vela.** Innovatively designed, steep-roof chalets have large bedrooms with white-stucco walls, wood floors, and huge windows; some have views of the wooded grounds; others, of the far-off Gulf of Nicoya. **Pros:** rustic luxury; secluded location close to reserve; terrific restaurants; large rooms; indoor pool. **Cons:** far from town; rough road to get here; Wi-Fi in common areas only. [$] *Rooms from: $120* ✉ *1½ km (1 mile) northwest of Monteverde Reserve entrance* ☎ *2645–5125* 🌐 *www.fondavela.com* 🛏 *40 rooms* 🍴 *No meals.*

$$$$ B&B/INN Fodor's Choice ★ **Hidden Canopy Tree Houses.** Nestled among 13½ acres of rolling hills nearly 3 km (2 miles) from town, five luxury tree houses have wraparound decks, driftwood headboards, tree stump nightstands, waterfall showers, and skylight ceilings, ultimately fading the line between nature and decor. **Pros:** breathtaking views; unique design; exceptional breakfast; rooms have dehumidifiers. **Cons:** no pool or spa; Wi-Fi in common areas only; no kids under 14; far from town. [$] *Rooms from: $345* ✉ *300 m east of crossroad to Los Nubes, before Sky Adventures Park, Santa Elena* ☎ *2645–5447* 🌐 *www.hiddencanopy.com* 🛏 *7 rooms* 🍴 *Breakfast.*

$$ B&B/INN Fodor's Choice ★ **Hotel Belmar.** Two tall Swiss chalets built into the hillside command extensive views of the Golfo de Nicoya and the hilly peninsula and house elegant, airy, and attractively rustic rooms—all with balconies. **Pros:** good value; friendly staff; beautifully maintained; 5 leaves in sustainability. **Cons:** far from town; steep walk if on foot; no TVs.

5

[$] *Rooms from: $149* ✉ *4 km (2½ miles) north of Monteverde* ☎ *2645–5201* 🌐 *www.hotelbelmar.net* 🛏 *22 rooms* 🍴 *Breakfast.*

$$$ HOTEL Fodor's Choice ★ 🏨 **Monteverde Lodge and Gardens.** The well-established Costa Rica Expeditions operates this longtime favorite, where extremely comfortable rooms have vaulted ceilings and great views and often come as part of a package that includes a long list of nature activities. **Pros:** rustic luxury; attentive service; many activities; great hiking trails. **Cons:** ground-floor rooms can be noisy; rooms have poor lighting; breakfast ends at 8:30. [$] *Rooms from: $198* ✉ *After World of Insects, take right fork, 500 m to lodge entrance on right., Santa Elena* ☎ *2645–5057, 2257–0766 in San José* 🌐 *www.monteverdelodge.com* 🛏 *24 rooms* 🍴 *Breakfast.*

$$ B&B/INN 🏨 **Trapp Family Lodge.** The closest lodge to the Monteverde reserve has enormous rooms, with wood-paneled walls and ceilings, marvelously crafted wood furniture, balconies, and lovely views from most. **Pros:** rustic luxury; good value; closest lodging to reserve entrance. **Cons:** far from town; rough road to get here; no pool or gym. [$] *Rooms from: $100* ✉ *Main road from Monteverde Reserve* ☎ *2645–5858* 🌐 *www.trappfamilylodgecr.com* 🛏 *26 rooms* 🍴 *Breakfast.*

SHOPPING

Librería Chunches. The well-stocked shelves include a good selection of new and used books in English, as well as Spanish-language literature and CDs from Costa Rican artists. ✉ *25 m south of Banco Nacional, Santa Elena* ☎ *2645–5147* ⏲ *Closed Sun.*

ARTS AND CRAFTS

Cooperativa de Artesanía de Santa Elena y Monteverde (*CASEM*). An artisans' cooperative made up of 89 women and three men sells locally made crafts. The prices are higher than they are at most other places, but the high quality and the knowledge that you are contributing to the livelihood of the community justifies paying a bit more. The attached restaurant serves typical Costa Rican dishes. ✉ *Next to El Bosque Lodge* ☎ *2645–5190.*

Coopesanta Elena. This is the distributor for the area's gourmet Monteverde coffee and accoutrements. ✉ *Next to CASEM* ☎ *2645–5901.*

Hummingbird Gallery. Standouts among the books, gifts, T-shirts, Costa Rican coffee, and prints are slides by nature specialists Michael and Patricia Fogden, as well as watercolors by nature artist Sarah Dowell. This is a great place to capture an image of a hummingbird in action as hundreds flutter around the feeders near the coffee shop. ✉ *Outside entrance to Monteverde Reserve* ☎ *2645–5030.*

NIGHTLIFE

"Wild nightlife" takes on its own peculiar meaning here. You can still get up close with nature after the sun has gone down. Several of the reserves have guided evening walks—advance reservations and separate admission are required—and the Frog Pond at Monteverde Theme Park, Serpentario, and Bat Jungle keep evening hours.

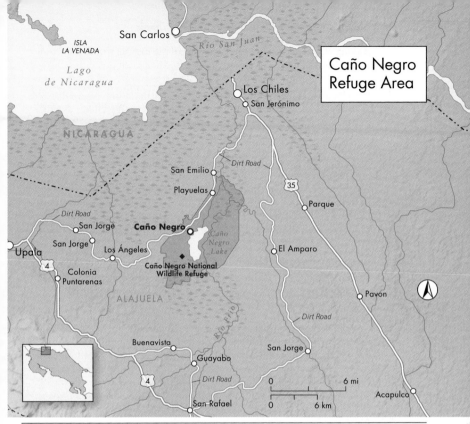

CAÑO NEGRO NATIONAL WILDLIFE REFUGE

Long a favorite among fishing enthusiasts and bird-watchers, this remote area is off the beaten track and may be difficult to get to if your time in Costa Rica is short. You can cross into Nicaragua, via Los Chiles, but there are almost no roads in this part of southern Nicaragua, making access to the rest of the country nearly impossible. The border crossing at Peñas Blancas, near the north Pacific coast, is far more user-friendly (⇨ *Crossing into Nicaragua at Peñas Blancas*, in *Chapter 6*).

CAÑO NEGRO NATIONAL WILDLIFE REFUGE

100 km (60 miles) (2 hrs) north of La Fortuna

GETTING HERE AND AROUND

The highway from La Fortuna to Los Chiles, the gateway to the Caño Negro Refuge, is one of the best maintained in the northern lowlands. You can catch public buses in San José at Terminal Atlántico Norte twice a day for a trip of about five hours to Los Chiles, with many stops. Public buses also operate between La Fortuna and Los Chiles. If they have room, many tour companies (Sunset Tours included) will allow you to ride along on their shuttles for around $10. If you're not staying way up here, an organized tour of the reserve from La Fortuna is the way most visitors get to and from.

EXPLORING

Fodor's Choice ★ **Caño Negro National Wildlife Refuge.** It's a shame that Caño Negro doesn't grab the same amount of attention in wildlife-viewing circles as other destinations in Costa Rica. The reserve is a splendid place to watch waterfowl and resident exotic animals, including cougars, jaguars, and several species of monkeys. If you're not staying at one of the two lodges up here, the refuge is most easily visited as a day trip from La Fortuna. Sunset Tours pioneered the Caño Negro excursions, but most every Arenal-area tour operator can set you up. There are no public facilities in the park, which consists mostly of wetlands fed by the Frio River and can be explored only by boat. Bring a camera, binoculars, and plenty of bug spray. ✉ *180 km (108 miles) north of La Fortuna* 🎟 *$5; fishing license $30* ⏲ *Daily 7–4.*

DID YOU KNOW?

Now you see it, now you don't: Caño Negro's lake forms during the rainy season when the Río Frío floods its banks. By February, dry conditions begin to shrink the lake, and by April, all that's left are a few spotty lagoons.

WHERE TO STAY

$$ HOTEL 🏨 **Hotel de Campo.** Seven white bungalows of high-quality wood each contain two bright, sparkling rooms with terra-cotta tile floors and are arranged around the wooded property. **Pros:** secluded location; close to reserve; tons of wildlife. **Cons:** need a car to get here and road is very rough; food slightly overpriced; cold showers. [$] *Rooms from: $95* ✉ *Caño Negro village; 100 m past supermarket* ☎ *2471–1012* 🌐 *www.hoteldecampo.com* 🛏 *14 rooms* 🍴 *Breakfast.*

$$$ HOTEL 🏨 **Natural Lodge Caño Negro.** It might come as a surprise to find such attractive and comfortable rooms, with nice appointments and high ceilings, in so remote a place, but the lack of pretense and laid-back luxury fits right into the surroundings on the east side of the reserve. **Pros:** secluded location; close to reserve; excellent boat tour; great for bird-watching. **Cons:** need a car to get here; no Wi-Fi in the rooms; rough and bumpy road. [$] *Rooms from: $125* ✉ *Caño Negro village, 250 m west of the school* ☎ *2471–1426, 2265–3302 in San José* 🌐 *www.canonegrolodge.com* 🛏 *42 rooms* 🍴 *Breakfast.*

GUANACASTE AND THE NICOYA PENINSULA

Visit Fodors.com for advice, updates, and bookings

WELCOME TO GUANACASTE AND THE NICOYA PENINSULA

TOP REASONS TO GO

★ **Beaches:** White sand, black sand; palm-fringed strands; beaches for swimming, partying, surfing, and sunbathing—the sheer variety of Guanacaste's beaches can't be beat.

★ **Big wind:** From December to May, the trade winds whip across northern Guanacaste with a velocity and consistency that make the Bahía Salinas a world-class windsurfing and kitesurfing destination.

★ **Endangered nature:** Guanacaste's varied national parks protect some of Central America's last remaining patches of tropical dry forest, a distinctive ecosystem where you might spot magpie jays or howler monkeys in the branches of a gumbo-limbo tree.

★ **Scuba diving:** Forget the pretty tropical fish. Sharks, rays, sea turtles, and moray eels are the large-scale attractions for divers here.

★ **Surfing:** Offshore winds, warm water, and hollow barrels make for epic waves at more than a dozen Guanacaste beaches.

0   10 mi

0   10 km

1 **Far Northern Guanacaste.** Dry, hot Far Northern Guanacaste is traditionally ranching country, but it does include the impressive wildernesses of Santa Rosa and Rincón de la Vieja national parks, the latter of which holds one of Costa Rica's most active volcanoes. Liberia, the capital of Guanacaste province, is the closest town to Costa Rica's second-largest airport. Farther to the north is Bahía Salinas, second only to Lake Arenal for wind- and kitesurfing.

2 **Guanacaste Pacific Coast.** The number and variety of beaches along the northern border of the Nicoya Peninsula, from the Papagayo Peninsula to Tamarindo and down to Playa Junquillal, make it a top tourist destination. Each beach has its specialty, be it surfing, fishing, diving, or just plain relaxing. Hotels and restaurants are in generous supply.

3 **The Nicoya Peninsula.** Lively beach towns dot the coast of the Nicoya Peninsula from Nosara down to Playa Tambor, at the southern tip. In the south, communities are small and quiet, with a funky, European vibe. National parks Palo Verde and Barra Honda are the main attractions in the interior of the peninsula. The former is a prime bird-watching park; the latter has caves and waterfalls to explore.

GETTING ORIENTED

Guanacaste Province—a vast swath of land in northwestern Costa Rica—is bordered by the Pacific Ocean to the west and the looming Cordillera de Guanacaste volcanic mountain range to the east. To the south is the Nicoya Peninsula, with almost continuous beaches along more than 100 km (62 miles) of Pacific coastline, as the crow flies. Many roads are unpaved, especially those to the national parks and those connecting less developed beaches, so the best way to get around is in a 4WD vehicle. Take a plane, bus, or shuttle van to Liberia and pick up your rental car there.

6

PALO VERDE NATIONAL PARK

One of the best wildlife- and bird-watching parks in the country, Palo Verde extends over 198 square km (76 square miles) of dry deciduous forest, bordered on the west by the wide Tempisque River.

With fairly flat terrain and less-dense forest than a rain forest, wildlife is often easier to spot here. Frequent sightings include monkeys, coatis, peccaries, lizards, and snakes. (Keep an eye out for the harlequin snake. It's non-poisonous but mimics the deadly coral snake coloring.)

The park contains seasonal wetlands at the end of the rainy season that provide a temporary home for thousands of migratory and resident aquatic birds, including herons, wood storks, jabirus, and flamingo-like roseate spoonbills. Crocodiles ply the slow waters of the Tempisque River year-round, and storks nest on islands at the mouth of the river where it empties into the Gulf of Nicoya. Trails are well marked, but the weather here can be very hot and windy. Mosquitoes, especially in the marshy areas, are rampant. *(See page 342 for more information.)*

BEST TIME TO GO

The best time of year to visit is at the beginning of the dry season, especially in January and February, when the seasonal wetlands are shrinking and birds and wildlife are concentrated around smaller ponds. Set off early in the morning or after 3 in the afternoon, when the sun is lower and the heat is less intense.

FUN FACT

The park is named after the lacy, light green palo verde bush, also known as the Jerusalem thorn. Even when it loses its leaflets, this tree can still photosynthesize through its trunk, so it can withstand the droughts common to this area.

BEST WAYS TO EXPLORE

BIRD-WATCHING

The greatest number of creatures you're likely to see here are birds, close to 300 recorded species. Many of them are aquatic birds drawn to the park's vast marshes and seasonal wetlands. The most sought-after aquatic bird is the jabiru stork, a huge white bird with a red neck and long black bill. You'll most likely spot it soaring overhead—it's hard to miss. Other birds endemic to the northwest, which you may find in the park's dry-forest habitat, are streaked-back orioles, banded wrens, and black-headed trogons.

PARK STRATEGIES

Unlike many of the other national parks, you can drive 7 km (4½ miles) of fairly rough road from the park entrance to the OTS research station, where most of the trailheads begin. From that point, the best way to see the park is on foot. Plan to spend a couple of nights in the dormitory-style park lodge so that you can get an early-morning start. You'll want to start early because this is a very, very hot area. Hike open areas in the cooler mornings and then choose shaded forest trails for hikes later in the day. Make sure you have a good sun hat, too.

RIVER CRUISE

A river does run through the park, so a delightful and less strenuous wildlife-viewing option is to cruise down the Tempisque River on a chartered boat with a guide who'll do the spotting for you. Without a boat, you are limited to observing the marshy areas and riverbanks from a long distance. Be sure the boat you choose has a bilingual naturalist on board who knows the English names of birds and animals.

TOP REASONS TO GO

Birds, Birds, Birds
Even if you're not used to looking at birds, you'll be impressed by the waves of migratory waterbirds that use this park as a way station on their migratory routes. Think of the 2001 documentary *Winged Migration* and you'll have an idea of the numbers of birds that flock here.

Lots of Wild Animals
Hiking the forest trails is hot work, especially in the dry season. But the wildlife viewing here makes it worthwhile. Watch for monkeys, peccaries, large lizards, and coatis. Take plenty of water with you wherever you walk, and use insect repellent or wear long sleeves and pants.

Outdoor Adventures
The Organization for Tropical Studies has a number of activities that are good for just about any type of group. Choose from guided nature walks, mountain biking, boat tours, and even an occasional nighttime tour. Accommodations can be a little rugged here, but that's half the fun.

6

RINCÓN DE LA VIEJA NATIONAL PARK

Rincón de la Vieja National Park is Costa Rica's mini-Yellowstone, with volcanic hot springs and bubbling mud pools, refreshing waterfalls, and cool forest trails. Often shrouded in clouds, the currently active volcano dominates the landscape northwest of Liberia, rising above the sunbaked plains.

It has two windswept peaks, Santa María, 1,916 meters (6,323 feet) high on the east slope, and Rincón de la Vieja at 1,895 meters (6,254 feet) on the west. The latter slope has an active crater that hardy hikers can climb to when the trail is open (it's occasionally closed when the crater is too active) and easily accessible fumaroles on its lower slope that constantly let off steam. The park protects more than 177 square km (54 square miles) of the volcano's forested slopes. Las Pailas entrance has the most accessible trails, including an easy loop trail that wends past all the interesting volcanic features. When the volcano is very active, the entire park is closed to visitors, so check with lodges or tour operators before you go. *(See page 260 for more information.)*

(See page 260 for more information.)

BEST TIME TO GO

Good times to visit are January through May, during the dry season. January can be very windy, but that means temperatures stay cooler for hiking. May to November—the green season—is when the fumaroles and boiling mud pots are most active, but the crater is often covered in clouds so it's not the best time to hike to the top. Trails can get crowded during school break (mid-December through February). Get here early, well before 9 am, if you plan a long hike or a climb to the crater, since the park officially closes at 3 pm but you can still exit up until 5 pm. The park is closed Monday all year.

BEST WAYS TO EXPLORE

BIRD-WATCHING

Wherever you walk in this park, you are bound to hear the three-note song of the long-tailed manakin. It sounds something like "Toledo," and that's what the locals call this bird. Along with their lavish, long tail feathers, the males are famous for their cooperative courting dance: two pals leap back and forth over each other, but only the senior male gets any girl who falls for this act. The hard-to-spot rock wren lives closer to the top of the volcano. Birding is excellent most of the year here except for January when the weather is dry but often too windy to distinguish between a fluttering leaf or a flittering bird.

HIKING

The only way to explore the park trails is on foot, along well-marked paths that range from easy loops to longer, more demanding climbs. The ranger station at Las Pailas entrance provides maps of the park trails and washrooms before you set off. The easiest hike is Las Pailas loop, which starts just past the ranger station; it takes about two hours to hike. If you want to venture farther afield, follow the signs for La Cangreja trail. After passing through dense, cool forest, you'll emerge through an avenue of giant agave plants into an open, windy, meadow. Your reward is the cool waterfall and swimming hole at the end of the trail. There are also warm springs in the rocks surrounding the pool, so you can alternate between warm and cool water in this natural spa.

ON HORSEBACK

Saddle up to explore the lower slopes of the volcano, just outside the park borders. Local ranches and lodges organize daylong trail rides to waterfalls and sulfur springs. Your nose will tell you when you are approaching the springs—it's not the picnic lunch gone bad, it's the distinctive rotten-egg smell of sulfur.

TOP REASONS TO GO

Wildlife
Here you can find more than 300 species of birds, plus mammals such as white-tailed deer, coyotes, howler and capuchin monkeys, armadillos, and the occasional harlequin snake (not poisonous).

Climbing to the Crater
The hike to the crater summit is the most demanding but also the most dramatic. The trail climbs 8 km (5 miles) through shaded forest, then up a sunbaked, treeless slope to the windswept crater, where temperatures plummet. Be sure to check in at the ranger station before attempting this hike; the trail may be closed when the volcano is dangerously active.

Geological Wonders
Three-kilometer (2-mile) Las Pailas loop trail showcases the park's famous geothermal features. Along the trail you'll see fumaroles with steam hissing out of ground vents, a *volcancito* (baby volcano), and boiling mud fields named after pots (*pailas*) used for boiling down sugarcane.

6

SANTA ROSA NATIONAL PARK

Renowned for its wildlife, Santa Rosa National Park, part of the larger Guanacaste Conservation Area, protects the largest swath of extant lowland dry forest in Central America, about 91,000 acres. *Dry* is the operative word here, with less than 1,500 centimeters (59 inches) of rainfall a year in some parts of the park.

If you station yourself near watering holes in the dry season—January to April—you may spot deer, coyotes, coatis, and armadillos. The park also has the world's only fully protected nesting beach for olive ridley sea turtles. Treetop inhabitants include spider, capuchin, and howler monkeys, as well as hundreds of bird species. The deciduous forest here includes giant kapok, Guanacaste, and mahogany trees, as well as calabash, acacia, and gumbolimbo trees with their distinctive peeling bark. The park is also of historical significance to Costa Rica because it was here, in 1856, that an army of Costa Rican volunteers decisively defeated an invading force of mercenaries led by an American adventurer named William Walker. *(See page 265 for more information.)*

BEST TIME TO GO

Dry season is the best time to visit if you want to see wildlife. The vegetation is sparse, making for easy observation. It's also the best time to drive to the park's beaches. Be aware: it can get very hot and very dry, so take plenty of water if you plan on hiking. In the rainy season, trails can become mud baths.

FUN FACT

Moving from sparse, sunlit secondary forest into the park's shady primary forest areas, you can experience an instant temperature drop of as much as 5C° (9F°). It's a little like walking into a fridge, so wear layers.

BEST WAYS TO EXPLORE

GETTING AROUND

Only the first 12 km (7 miles) of the park's roads are accessible by vehicles. The rest of the park's 20 km (12 miles) of hiking trails have recently been significantly improved. It's easy to drive to La Casona headquarters along a paved road and pick up a short loop hiking trail, but beyond that point you need a four-wheel-drive vehicle. During the rainy season, the roads beyond La Casona are often impassable even to four-wheel-drive vehicles. Get an early start for any hikes to take advantage of cooler temperatures.

A HISTORICAL TOUR

Costa Rica doesn't have many historical sites—relics of its colonial past have mostly been destroyed by earthquakes and volcanic eruptions. So La Casona, the symbolic birthplace of Costa Rica's nationhood, is a particularly revered site. Most Costa Ricans come to Santa Rosa on a historical pilgrimage. Imagine the nation's horror when the place was burned to the ground in a fire purposely set in 2001 by disgruntled poachers who had been fined by park rangers. The government, schoolchildren, and private businesses came to the rescue, raising the money to restore the historic hacienda and replace the exhibits of antique farm tools and historical photos.

TURTLE-WATCHING

Thousands of olive ridley sea turtles emerge from the sea every year, from July to December, to dig nests and deposit eggs on the park's protected beaches at Playa Nancite and Playa Naranjo. Green sea turtles and the huge leatherbacks also clamber ashore, but in much smaller numbers. If you're a hardy outdoors type, you can hike the 12 km (8 miles) to Playa Naranjo and pitch your tent near the beach. Unlike most other turtle-nesting beaches with organized tours, this is a natural spectacle you'll get to witness far from any crowds. Playa Nancite is a totally protected beach and thus off-limits to tourists.

TOP REASONS TO GO

Explore the Forest
The short (about 1-km [½-mile]) La Casona nature-trail loop, which starts from the park headquarters, is a great way to get a sampling of dry tropical forest and to spot wildlife. Look for signs leading to the *Indio Desnudo* (Naked Indian) path, named after the local word for gumbo-limbo trees.

Serious Surfing
Off Playa Naranjo lies the famous Witch's Rock, a towering rock formation famous for its surfing breaks. If you're interested in checking it out but don't feel like walking for miles, take a boat from Playas del Coco, Playa Hermosa, or Playa Tamarindo.

Wildlife-Watching
Wildlife is easy to spot here thanks to the low-density foliage of this tropical dry forest. Scan the treetops and keep an eye out for spider, white-faced capuchin, and howler monkeys. If you're lucky you might even spot an ocelot.

ECO-LODGES IN GUANACASTE AND THE NICOYA PENINSULA

On the mainland, sweeping plains bordered by volcanoes hold remnants of Central America's tropical dry forest. On the Pacific-edged Nicoya Peninsula, conservationists try to protect turtle-nesting beaches from the encroachments of ever-grander resort hotels and vacation houses.

These tropical dry forests change from relatively lush landscapes during the rainy season to desertlike panoramas in the dry months. The national parks of Santa Rosa, Rincón de la Vieja, Palo Verde, and Barra Honda all protect vestiges of dry forest, as do the private reserves of Hacienda Guachipelín and Rincón de la Vieja Mountain Lodge. The Nicoya Peninsula is also the site of Las Baulas National Marine Park, where massive leatherback sea turtles used to lay their eggs on Playa Grande from October to March. Sadly, their numbers have dwindled drastically. For guaranteed sightings of nesting turtles, visit Ostional National Wildlife Refuge, where thousands of olive ridley turtles clamber ashore to nest on moonlit nights, mostly from July to January.

GOOD PRACTICES

After a decade of uncontrolled development in the North Pacific province of Guanacaste, *Guanacastecation* became a pejorative watchword in Costa Rica for unsustainable development.

Playas Junquillal, Negra, Nosara, and Punta Islita are some of the notable exceptions to overdevelopment, managing to maintain a balance between nature and commercial development. Eco-minded tourists who are planning a beach vacation may want to visit these less developed areas and reward lodge owners who have worked hard to keep their pieces of paradise as sustainable as possible.

TOP ECO-LODGES IN THE NORTH PACIFIC

HOTEL PUNTA ISLITA

Proving that sustainability and comfort can go hand in hand, this ultraluxurious resort has won the country's highest five-leaf designation in the national sustainability program. Along with top performances in the technical categories of water management, energy conservation, and waste disposal, this hotel has earned kudos for its outstanding community relations and cultural activities. The Islita Art Museum project transformed an economically disadvantaged community into a living art museum, where colorful murals, art installations, and sculptures decorate every building in the village. The hotel also sponsors a preschool day-care center and after-school programs to foster creative and critical thinking in the community's youngest inhabitants. *(Full hotel review on page 342.)*

THE HARMONY HOTEL

Steps from Playa Guiones in Nosara, this former surfer hotel has been transformed into a luxury resort with a sustainable mind-set. From permaculture-inspired landscaping with native plants and the use of biodegradable cleaning products and toiletries to solar-heated hot water and conscientious recycling and waste-management policies, the hotel owners cover all the eco-stops, garnering the country's five-leaf sustainability certificate. Hotel employees, most of them local hires, also volunteer in the town schools, mentoring and teaching English classes and computer literacy. *(Full hotel review on page 332.)*

HOTEL LAGARTA LODGE

With only 12 guest rooms, the hotel minimizes its environmental impact by keeping a sharp eye on its water and energy consumption, as well as on waste management and recycling. Its eco-friendly hospitality and gardening practices have earned it four leaves in the national sustainability program. By far the most salient eco-aspect of the lodge, though, is its 90-acre private Nosara Biological Reserve. *(Full hotel review on page 332.)*

NESTING LEATHERBACK TURTLES

You simply cannot believe how big a leatherback turtle is. Weighing in at 550 kilos (more than 1,200 pounds), females come ashore under cover of night to lay up to 100 golf ball–size eggs in nests they dig out of the sand with their flippers. People will go to great lengths in the hopes of catching this incredible sight. Your best chance is at Playa Grande in Las Baulas National Marine Park. As night falls, groups of visitors, each shepherded by a local guide, hunker down at the park entrance, waiting for the summons to sprint down the beach to take their turn, standing silently and witnessing the monumental egg laying. A decade ago, it was almost a sure thing to find at least one laying turtle on the beach during the nesting season. But today, some groups will come away disappointed, a sad reminder of how the past 25 years of shore development and commercial fishing have reduced sea turtle populations by 99%.

6

Updated by
Marlise Kast

Reliably sunny, dry weather brings planeloads of sun-starved Northerners to the North Pacific area of Costa Rica every winter, and a windswept coastline makes Guanacaste and the Nicoya Peninsula popular with surfers eager to relive the legendary "Endless Summer" of the sport's early years.

An abundance of marine life and stellar diving spots also lure fishers and underwater aficionados. Add in some stunningly scenic national parks and a range of thrilling outdoor adventures, and you have all the ingredients that make this region an all-around top spot to experience Costa Rica's charms. Although most tourists head here for the dry "high" season, it's even more beautiful—and cheaper, cooler, and less crowded—in the "green" or low season, April to December.

PLANNING

WHEN TO GO

HIGH SEASON: MID-DECEMBER TO APRIL

This is the driest region of the country, with only 165 centimeters (65 inches) of average annual rainfall. It's also the hottest region, with average temperatures around 30°C to 35°C (86°F to 95°F) in high season. It's no wonder that winter-weary Northerners come here for guaranteed sunshine and heat. The beaches and trails can get packed during these drier months, especially mid-December to February, when school is out in Costa Rica. January can be quite breezy, especially along the coast, thanks to the annual Papagayo winds. February through April are the driest months: skies are clear, but the heat is intense and the landscape is brown and parched. Fishing and scuba diving are at their best during this period, though.

LOW SEASON: MAY THROUGH OCTOBER

Major downpours are pretty much guaranteed every afternoon during the rainy season, which brings lower prices, fewer crowds, and a lush green landscape. But mornings are usually fresh and clear. Unpaved beach roads can become quite muddy, though, making travel difficult.

SHOULDER SEASON: NOVEMBER TO MID-DECEMBER

This is the best time to visit, when the rains have abated, the landscape is lush, and the evening air is cool. Hotels and restaurants are prepped for the impending tourist influx, and staff are fresh and eager to please. High-season rates begin mid-December; except for the popular U.S. Thanksgiving week, you can usually make a deal.

PLANNING YOUR TIME

Visiting this region for 10 days to two weeks will introduce you to its wonders and give you a real taste of the North Pacific. Schedule plenty of beach time for lounging, sunbathing, surfing, diving, and snorkeling. Logistically, you also need to take into consideration slow travel over bumpy roads. A beach like Tamarindo with lots of restaurants and nightlife can keep you entertained for a week or more, whereas a more solitary beach might merit only a couple of days. Also plan to visit some protected areas to enjoy canopy tours, wildlife viewing, and hiking. Outdoorsy types should consider spending a few days around Rincón de la Vieja National Park for its amazing hiking, bird-watching, and horseback riding. Other parks to consider are Palo Verde National Park, Santa Rosa National Park, and Barra Honda National Park. Many North Pacific beaches are just a few hours' drive from the Arenal Volcano area *(⇨ Chapter 5),* so the region can be combined with the Northern Plains.

GETTING HERE AND AROUND

AIR TRAVEL

Aeropuerto Internacional Daniel Oduber Quirós (LIR) in Liberia is an international gateway to the coast, with a large, air-conditioned terminal. Tamarindo, Nosara, Playa Sámara, and Punta Islita also have small airstrips. Flying from San José to these airports is the best way to get here if you are already in the country. If your primary destination lies in Guanacaste or Nicoya, make sure you or your travel agent investigates the possibility of flying directly into Liberia instead of San José, which saves some serious hours on the road.

SANSA and Nature Air have scheduled flights between San José and destinations on the Nicoya Peninsula.

BUS TRAVEL

You can ride in a comfortable, air-conditioned minibus with Gray Line Tourist Bus, connecting San José, Liberia, Playa Flamingo, Playa Conchal, Playa Potrero, Playa Brasilito, Playa Hermosa, Playas del Coco, Ocotal, Tamarindo, Rincón de la Vieja, and Playa Langosta. The Gray Line Tourist Bus from San José to Liberia and Tamarindo begins picking up passengers from hotels daily around 8:45 am. The return bus leaves the Tamarindo and Flamingo areas around 8:40 am and 4 pm. Interbus has door-to-door minivan shuttle service from San José to all the major beach hotels (in Papagayo, Flamingo, Tamarindo, Cocos, Ocotal, Nicoya, and Sámara). Fares range from $42 to $57 per person. Reserve 48 hours in advance to guarantee a seat.

Bus Contacts Gray Line Tourist Bus ☎ *2220–2126* ⊕ *www.graylinecostarica. com.* **Interbus** ☎ *4100–0888* ⊕ *www.interbusonline.com.*

CAR TRAVEL

Most unpaved roads here alternate between being extremely muddy and treacherous during the rainy season and being extremely dusty and treacherous during the dry season. That said, it can be a real adventure exploring the coastline if you have a 4WD or a hired driver with a good, sturdy car. The major artery in this region is the Pan-American Highway (CA 1), which heads northwest from San José to Liberia, then due north to the Nicaraguan border. It's fairly well maintained, but the convoys of trucks and buses often create heavy traffic and there are few passing opportunities. Construction to widen the highway south of Liberia began in 2012, creating sporadic delays. To skip the hours of frustrating driving, consider flying into Liberia, whose airport provides easy access to the region. Local hotels and tour companies can help you arrange for ground transportation in many cases. In Guanacaste, it's usually safe to take *pirata* (pirate, or unofficial) taxis, but always negotiate the price before getting into the cab, or ask your hotel to call a reputable driver.

The northwest is accessed via the paved two-lane Pan-American Highway (CA 1), which begins at the top of Paseo Colón in San José. Take the Friendship Bridge (aka Río Tempisque Bridge) across the Tempisque River to get to the Pacific beaches south of Liberia. Once you get off the main highway, dust, mud, potholes, and other factors come into play, depending on which beach you visit. The roads to Playa Flamingo, Playa Conchal, Playa Brasilito, Tamarindo, Playa Grande, Playa Sámara, Playas del Coco, Hermosa, and Ocotal are paved all the way; every other destination may require some dirt-road maneuvering.

FERRY TRAVEL

If you're headed to the southern Nicoya peninsula (Curú, Tambor, Montezuma, Malpaís, or Santa Teresa), the ferry ride from Puntarenas to Paquera across the Gulf of Nicoya is not only the fastest route, it's also the most scenic, with great views of the mountainous coast and islands.

RESTAURANTS

Seafood and fresh fish are tops here, followed by fast food—pizza, tacos, BBQ—to satisfy the hordes of hungry surfers and beachgoers. But there are many sophisticated restaurants, too, offering Asian-fusion, Italian, French, and international cuisine, especially in the tourist-heavy beach towns of Hermosa, Flamingo, Tamarindo, Nosara, and Sámara. ■TIP→ **Many restaurants, especially tourist-oriented ones with dollar-denominated menus, do not include the 13% tax plus mandatory 12% service. By law, menus are required to show the total price including tax, but many owners flout this law. Be sure to ask if taxes are included; otherwise you may be surprised by a bill that's 25% higher than you expected.**

HOTELS

A wide range of lodging options awaits you here, so choose wisely. If your goal is to take leisurely swims and lounge quietly on the beach with a cocktail in hand, then avoid the beaches that are renowned for surfing waves. Super-expensive resorts like the Four Seasons are generally well balanced with budget hotels that charge less than $75 per night. As in all of Costa Rica, the places we recommend most highly are the small owner-operated hotels and bed-and-breakfasts that blend in with unspoiled nature and offer one-on-one attention from the staff and owners. Most hotels will be able to connect you with local tour operators and knowledgeable staff members who can help show you the best aspects of each destination, whether it's a local park with howler monkeys, a great family-run restaurant on the beach, or a thrilling canopy tour. *Hotel reviews have been shortened. For full information, visit Fodors.com.*

WHAT IT COSTS IN DOLLARS			
$	**$$**	**$$$**	**$$$$**
Restaurants	Under $10	$10–$15	$16–$25	over $25
Hotels	Under $75	$75–$150	$151–$250	over $250

Restaurant prices are the average cost of a main course at dinner or, if dinner is not served, at lunch. Hotel prices are the lowest cost of a standard double room in high season.

TOUR OPERATORS

The excellent **Horizontes Nature Tours** (☎ 2222–2022 ⊕ *www.horizontes. com*) has independent, private tours with your own guide/driver and small-group tours.

Swiss Travel Service (☎ 2282–4898 ⊕ *www.swisstravelcr.com*) specializes in Guanacaste and has a new office near the Liberia airport. Despite the name, it's operated by Costa Ricans with lots of local experience. Custom-design a guided private or small-group tour.

FAR NORTHERN GUANACASTE

North from Liberia, all the way to the Nicaraguan border, a towering volcanic mountain range looms over vast plains that end at a windy coastline dotted with pristine beaches. This is Far Northern Guanacaste, one of the lesser-traveled but vastly rewarding parts of Costa Rica. Liberia, the capital of Guanacaste province, is the closest town to Costa Rica's second-largest airport. You'll most likely pass through it on your way to the beaches southwest of the city or to the nearby national parks of Guanacaste, Santa Rosa, or Rincón de la Vieja. This last park is home to Volcán Rincón de la Vieja, an active volcano that spews out fumes on a regular basis.

Northwest of Rincón de la Vieja, on the coast, Parque Nacional Santa Rosa (Santa Rosa National Park) is a former cattle ranch where Costa Ricans defeated the invading mercenary army of American William Walker in 1856. As part of the larger Guanacaste Conservation Area, Santa Rosa protects the country's largest remnant of tropical dry forest, as well as an important nesting beach for olive ridley sea turtles, which lay their eggs in the sand between July and November. Closer still to the Nicaraguan border is the town of La Cruz, overlooking the lovely Golfo de Santa Elena, and the remote, windswept beaches of Bahía Salinas.

RINCÓN DE LA VIEJA NATIONAL PARK

25 km (15 miles) northeast of Liberia.

GETTING HERE AND AROUND

There are two park entrances on the volcano's southern slope: the less traveled one at Hacienda Santa María on the road leading northeast from Liberia (one hour), where there is camping available; and the one at Las Pailas, past Curubandé off the Pan-American Highway. To get to the Las Pailas entrance from Liberia, take the first entrance road 5 km (3 miles) northwest of Liberia off the Pan-American Highway. The turnoff is easy to miss—follow signs for Hacienda Guachipelín or the town of Curubandé. It's a very rough 23-km (14-mile) dirt road, enveloped in white dust, and you have to pay a small toll (about $1.50). The Santa María entrance is 25 km (15 miles) northeast of Liberia along the Colonia Blanca route, which follows the course of the Río Liberia. The turnoff from the Pan-American Highway to the hotels on the western slope of the volcano is 12 km (7 miles) northwest of Liberia, turning right at the road signed for Cañas Dulces. A 4WD vehicle is recommended for all these slow and bone-rattling rides.

EXPLORING

Fodor'sChoice ★ **Rincón de la Vieja National Park.** Rincón de la Vieja National Park is Costa Rica's mini-Yellowstone, with steaming volcanic hot springs and boiling, bubbling mud ponds. The park protects more than 140 square km (54 square miles) of the volcano's upper slopes, which are covered with forest. Often enveloped in clouds, the volcano dominates the scenery to the east of the Pan-American Highway. The park has two peaks: Santa María (1,916 meters [6,323 feet]) and the barren Rincón de la Vieja (1,895 meters [6,254 feet]). The latter has an active crater and fumaroles on its lower slope that constantly let off steam. ■ TIP→ Since 2011, the volcano has been very active, leading park authorities to close some trails and even the entire park on days when the activity is deemed too dangerous. Be sure to check with local lodges and tour operators before you visit.

The wildlife here is diverse: more than 250 species of birds, including long-tailed manakins and blue-crowned motmots; plus mammals such as white-tailed deer, coyotes, howler and capuchin monkeys, and armadillos. There are two main entrances: Santa María and Las Pailas; the latter is the most common place to enter the park because it has the most accessible trails and there are several hotels along the road leading up to it. The park does not have guides; we recommend the guides at Hacienda Guachipelín and Rincón de la Vieja Mountain Lodge. You must sign in and pay at the ranger station. Many of the attractions people visit in Rincón de la Vieja are accessible without actually entering the park, since the ranches that border it also hold significant forest and geothermal sites. Unfortunately that same geothermic energy has now been harnessed by a huge electricity-generating plant, evidence of which you will see on your way to Las Pailas entrance: a huge pipeline now snakes around the scrubby pastureland on the approach to the park. It's unsightly but one of the unavoidable costs of "clean" energy. ☎ 2666–5051 ✉ $15 ⊙ *Tues.–Sun. 7–5; last entry at 3 pm.*

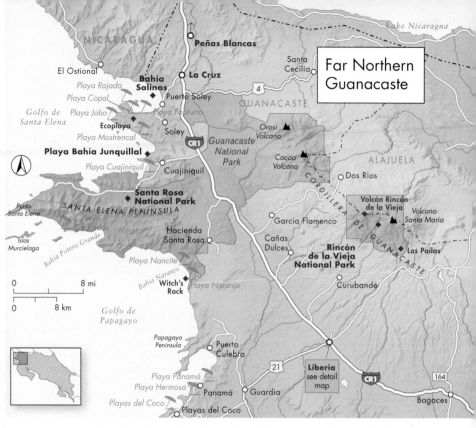

Liberia
see detail
map

La Posada del Tope Tours. There is no bus service to Rincón de la Vieja, but La Posada del Tope Tours arranges shuttle van transportation to the park entrance for $20 round-trip per person, leaving Liberia at 7 am and returning from the park at 4 pm. This agency is also the only place where you can buy tickets for the Tica bus heading north to Nicaragua. ⊠ *C. Real between Avdas. 2 and 4, 150 m south of cathedral entrance, Downtown, Liberia* ☎ 2666–3876 ⊕ *www.laposadadeltope.com.*

SPORTS AND THE OUTDOORS

TOUR OPERATORS

Borinquen Mountain Resort & Spa. A day package here ($80) begins with a horseback ride and a 90-minute canopy tour, followed by lunch and free time to soak in the hotel's hot springs and relax in the natural steam bath. ⊠ *12 km (7½ miles) northwest of Liberia on the Pan-American Hwy., then 23 km (14 miles) north on the dirt road that passes Cañas Dulces* ☎ 2690–1900 ⊕ *www.borinquenresort.com.*

Buena Vista Lodge & Adventure. Located west of the park, this lodge lies on a large ranch where visitors enjoy horseback riding, waterfall hikes, a canopy tour, hanging bridges, a 425-meter (1,394-foot) (long, not steep) waterslide through the forest, and hot springs. Tours are $15 to $45 per person; a combination tour that lasts six to seven hours costs $80, including lunch. ⊠ *Western slope of volcano, 10 km (6 miles) north of Cañas Dulces* ☎ 2690–1414 in Liberia ⊕ *www.buenavistalodgecr.com.*

Fodor's Choice
★ **Hacienda Guachipelín Adventure Tours.** This experienced outfitter has the most exciting tours in the area, including horseback riding, river tubing, hot springs and mud baths, and guided waterfall and hikes on the slopes of the national park volcano (from $25 to $55, special rates for children under 10 and students under 18). The popular canyon tour includes rock climbing, rappelling, zip lines, suspension bridges, and a Tarzan swing. A one-day, all-you-can-do adventure pass, including lunch, is a great deal at $85. ⊠ *Road to Rincón de la Vieja National Park* ☎ *2666–8075* ⊕ *www.guachipelin.com.*

Tours Your Way. Playas del Coco–based Mainor Lara Bustos guides tours to Rincón de la Vieja or Palo Verde for $95 to $115, depending on pickup location, including transportation, entrance fees, lunch, and snacks. ☎ *8820–1829* ⊕ *www.tours-your-way.com.*

CANOPY TOURS

Buena Vista Lodge & Adventure. The zip-line canopy tour ($40) with Buena Vista Lodge & Adventure *(⇨ above)* has cables that are up to 27 meters (90 feet) off the ground and up to 135 meters (450 feet) long. ⊠ *Western slope of volcano, 10 km (6 miles) north of Cañas Dulces* ⊕ *www. buenavistalodgecr.com.*

Rincón de la Vieja Canopy. This combined horseback and canopy tour ($35) at Rincón de la Vieja Lodge includes a 16-platform zip line, a ride to Los Azufrales sulfur springs, or a forest hike to a waterfall with a box lunch. The tours take about 3½ hours. ⊠ *21 km (12 miles) northeast of Pan-American Hwy.; 5 km (3 miles) north of Hacienda Guachipelín; 2 km (1 mile) south of Las Pailas park entrance, at Rincón de la Vieja Mountain Lodge* ☎ *2200–0238* ⊕ *www.hotelrincondelaviejacr.com.*

HIKING

Nearly all the lodges and outfitters in the area offer guided hikes through the park to the fumaroles, hot springs, waterfalls, and (when possible) to the summit or the edge of the active crater.

If you're doing a self-guided hike, stop for trail maps and hiking information at the park stations at both entrance gates. To give yourself enough time to complete the longer hikes, make sure you start out between 7 and 9 am.

Trail to the summit. The 8-km (5-mile) trail to the summit heads up into the forest from Las Pailas park entrance, then emerges onto a windy, exposed shale slope that's slippery and hard going, and has poor visibility owing to clouds and mist. It's a trip for serious hikers, best done in the dry season with preparation for cold weather at the top. ⚠ **The trail is occasionally closed due to volcanic activity. Check with park rangers to make sure the trail is open when you visit.**

Loop through the park. A less-strenuous option is the fascinating 3-km (2-mile) loop through the park, which takes about two hours to complete, starting at Las Pailas entrance. Along the well-marked trail you'll see fumaroles exuding steam, a *volcáncito* (little volcano), and Las Pailas, the boiling mud fields named after pots used for boiling down sugarcane. If you tread softly in the nearby forest, you may spot animals such as howler, capuchin, and spider monkeys, as well as raccoonlike coatis looking for handouts. ■TIP→ **Remember the cardinal rule of wildlife encounters: don't feed the animals.**

La Cangreja Waterfall loop. Another popular hike out of Las Pailas is the four-hour, 10-km (6-mile) La Cangreja Waterfall loop, passing through beautiful primary forests and windswept savannas. The *catarata* (waterfall) has a cool swimming hole below; the surrounding rocks have pockets of hot springs. Check with park rangers to make sure this trail is open.

HORSEBACK RIDING

Buena Vista Lodge & Adventure. This lodge and tour operator *(⇨ above)* has horseback trips to hot springs and to Borinquen Waterfall ($40). If not everyone in your party is a horse lover, tractor transport ($35) is available to the hot springs as well. ⊠ *Western slope of volcano, 10 km (6 miles) north of Cañas Dulces* ⊕ *www.buenavistalodgecr.com.*

Hacienda Guachipelín. This is the premier working ranch in the area, with more than 100 well-bred and well-trained horses, and miles of trails to three waterfalls, tropical dry forest, and hot springs. Horseback tours range from $25 to $35. The Hacienda also offers a cowboy-for-a-day tour ($50, kids $40) that includes harnessing your horse, rounding up cattle, and milking a cow. ⊠ *Hacienda Guachipelín* ⊕ *www.guachipelin.com.*

WHERE TO STAY

$$
RESORT
FAMILY
Fodor'sChoice
★
Blue River Resort. Named for the blue river that flows nearby, this property on the volcano's northern slope is known more for its hot springs and activities than for its rustic cabin accommodations. **Pros:** family-friendly; great activities; nearby waterfalls. **Cons:** room decor needs some help; rough, unpaved road; limited, somewhat pricey menu; Wi-Fi in common areas only. $ *Rooms from: $150* ⊠ *600 m west of Rio Celeste Bridge, Dos Rios* ☎ *2206–5000, 2206–5506, 954/688–3646 in U.S.* ⊕ *www.blueriverresort.com* ↜ *25 rooms* |○| *Multiple meal plans.*

$$$
RESORT
Borinquen Mountain Resort & Spa. The spacious villas on this 4,856-hectare (12,000-acre) ranch are the most upscale—and expensive—accommodations in the area, but the room rate includes access to their hot springs and mud baths. **Pros:** attractive, well-equipped bungalows; peaceful environment; lots of outdoor activities. **Cons:** far from park entrance; 12-km (7-mile) unpaved road; Wi-Fi only in restaurant and reception areas; restaurant a notch below accommodations. $ *Rooms from: $194* ⊠ *13 km (8 miles) northwest of Liberia on Pan-American Hwy., then 19 km (11.8 miles) north on the dirt road toward Cañas Dulces* ☎ *2690–1900* ⊕ *www.borinquenresort.com* ↜ *16 villas, 17 bungalows, 6 junior suites* |○| *Breakfast.*

$$
B&B/INN
FAMILY
Hacienda Guachipelín. One of the best values in the Rincón area for hair-raising adventure and nature tours *(⇨ Sports and the Outdoors, above)*, this hotel also gets top billing for its comfortable rooms, excellent restaurant, and friendly service. **Pros:** near park entrance; lots of activities; excellent value. **Cons:** caters to lots of large groups and day visitors; no air-conditioning in some rooms; vegetarians may have trouble finding meat-free dishes. $ *Rooms from: $110* ⊠ *17 km (10 miles) northeast of the Pan-American Hwy., on road to Las Pailas park entrance* ☎ *2666–8075* ⊕ *www.guachipelin.com* ↜ *52 rooms, 2 suites* |○| *Breakfast.*

6

$

B&B/INN **Rancho Curubandé Lodge.** Convenient to both Rincón de la Vieja and Santa Rosa National Park, these very affordable, equipped bungalows and modern rooms are part of a working farm owned by a Costa Rican family. **Pros:** easy access to highway to Santa Rosa National Park; very affordable, family-friendly bungalows **Cons:** some highway noise; half-hour uphill climb to Rincón de la Vieja National Park (half the route is unpaved). $ *Rooms from: $70 ⊠ Off Pan-American Hwy. on road to Las Pailas ☎ 2665–0375 ⊕ www.rancho-curubande.com ➪ 16 rooms, 2 villas ❍❘ Breakfast.*

SANTA ROSA NATIONAL PARK

35 km (22 miles) northwest of Liberia.

GETTING HERE AND AROUND

The turnoff for Santa Rosa National Park from the Pan-American Highway is well marked, about 30 minutes out from Liberia. From Liberia you can hop on a bus heading north to La Cruz and get off at the park entrance, but you'll have to hitchhike or hike 8 km (5 miles) in the hot sun to La Casona from here. La Posada del Tope *(⇨ above)* arranges shuttle vans from Liberia to the park entrance for $20 per person round-trip.

EXPLORING

Santa Rosa National Park. Renowned for its wildlife, which is easy to spot in the dry season, thanks to sparser foliage, Santa Rosa protects the largest swath of tropical dry forest in Central America. It is officially known now as the Santa Rosa sector of the even larger Guanacaste Conservation Area. Camping expeditions serving bird-watchers, naturalists, and backpackers often venture deep into the interior, but it's possible to experience a good bit of its impressive flora and fauna on a full-day or half-day visit. Treetop inhabitants include spider, capuchin, and howler monkeys, as well as hundreds of bird species. If you station yourself next to water holes during the dry season, you may also spot deer, coyotes, coatis, or armadillos. Typical dry-forest vegetation includes kapok, Guanacaste, mahogany, calabash, acacia thorn, and gumbo-limbo trees.

Santa Rosa's wealth of flora and fauna is due in part to its remoteness, since much of it is still inaccessible to the common tourist. To get anywhere in the park, you must have a vehicle—preferably 4WD. The park headquarters, a historic ranch house and museum called La Casona, and a nearby camping area are 7 km (4½ miles) from the Pan-American Highway via a paved road. Within this dense, shady forest, temperatures drop by as much as 5°C (9°F).

In rainy season the park's rough road to the beach cannot be accessed by even 4WD vehicles, but several short trails head into the forest from its first, flat stretch, and day hikers can easily explore the first stretch of the steep part on foot. Park off the road just before it descends into the forest. From the park headquarters it's 11 km (7 miles) to **Playa Naranjo,** where the famed Witch's Rock surf break is located (surfers often get there by boat). **Playa Nancite**—the site of one of the world's few completely protected olive ridley turtle *arribada,* or mass nesting (accessible primarily to biologists and students; permit required)—is an additional 5 km (3 miles) by footpath north of Playa Naranjo. For more information, visit the park's website. ⊠ *Km 269, Pan-American Hwy. 35 km (22 miles) north of Liberia* ☎ *2666–5051* ⊕ *www.acguanacaste. ac.cr* ⌦ *$15* ⊘ *Daily 8–4.*

SPORTS AND THE OUTDOORS

HIKING

Casona nature-trail loop. The short (about 1-km [½-mile]) Casona nature-trail loop from the park headquarters is worth taking to get a brief sampling of the woods. Look for the "Indio Desnudo," or "Naked Indian," path, named after the local word for gumbo-limbo trees. ■TIP→ **Carry plenty of water and insect repellent.**

Several other short trails lead off the road **to the beaches** before it becomes impassable to vehicles. The hike to Playa Naranjo (11 km [7 miles] west of La Casona) requires good physical condition and lots of water. You can get a map of the trails at the park entrance.

SURFING

Witch's Rock. Witch's Rock towers offshore over a near-perfect beach break off Playa Naranjo in Santa Rosa National Park. If you are interested in surfing Witch's Rock, take a boat tour from Playas del Coco, Playa Hermosa, or Playa Tamarindo, to the south. Tropic Surf offers surf trips to Witch's Rock from their shop at Four Seasons Resort Peninsula Papagayo.

WHERE TO STAY

There are basic, dormitory-style lodgings and a camping area near the park's administrative center; you can also camp within Santa Rosa National Park at the very basic and remote campsites at the beaches of Naranjo and Murcielago. Call the park headquarters (☎ *2666–5051*) for information. Most people visit the park on day trips from Liberia, or nearby Cuajiniquil.

PLAYA BAHÍA JUNQUILLAL

26 km (16 miles) northwest of Santa Rosa National Park entrance.

This 2½-km (1½-mile), tree-fringed, Blue Flag beach is as close as you can get to a white-sand beach in this part of Guanacaste. Not to be confused with the Playa Junquillal on the western coast of the Nicoya Peninsula (that's farther south), this beach is part of the Guanacaste Conservation Area, and is a wildlife refuge to the north of Santa Rosa.

GETTING HERE AND AROUND

From the Pan-American Highway, take the road signed for Cuajiniquil, 43 km (26 miles) northwest of Liberia and 8 km (5 miles) north of Santa Rosa National Park. Follow the paved road 14 km (8 miles) to the beach turnoff, along a dirt road for another 4 km (2½ miles). From the Bahía Salinas area, take the scenic dirt road (4WD recommended); then follow the road near Puerto Soley (signed for Cuajiniquil) 7 km (4½ miles) to the beach entrance. It's about 30 minutes from the Pan-American turnoff and one hour from Bahía Salinas.

BEACHES

Playa Bahía Junquillal (*Junquillal Bay Wildlife Refuge*). The warm, calm water makes this one of the best swimming beaches on the Golfo de Santa Elena. Stay for the day or camp out in the well-kept, shaded camping area with cold-water showers, bathrooms, grills, and picnic tables ($13 onetime park entrance for foreigners, plus $3 per person per night to camp). Compared to other camping areas in Costa Rica, prices are slightly steep since this is part of the Junquillal Bay Wildlife Refuge. You can snorkel if you've got your own gear. **Amenities:** showers; toilets. **Best for:** solitude; swimming. ⊠ *18 km (11 miles) west of Pan-American Hwy., Cuajiniquil turnoff.*

> **WALKER'S LAST STAND**
>
> Santa Rosa Park was the site of the 1856 triumph over American invader William Walker in the famous Battle of Santa Rosa—one of the few historic military sites in this army-less country. The rambling colonial-style ranch house called **La Casona** was the last stand of a ragged force of ill-equipped Costa Ricans who routed the superior mercenary army of the notorious Walker. Disgruntled poachers burned La Casona to the ground in 2001, but it has since been rebuilt.

WHERE TO STAY

$
B&B/INN
Santa Elena Lodge. This simple family-run lodge on the outskirts of Cuajiniquil provides the closest accommodations to both Playa Bahía Junquillal and Santa Rosa National Park, making it a good option for nature lovers and anyone who wants to stray from the vacationing crowds. **Pros:** friendly; near beach and park; lots of outdoor options. **Cons:** little English spoken; basic accommodations. ⓢ *Rooms from: $70* ⊠ *10 km (6 miles) west of Pan-American Hwy., 8 km (5 miles) east of Junquillal, Cuajiniquil* ☎ *2679–1038* ⊕ *www.santaelenalodge. com* ➫ *10 rooms* ⍥ *Breakfast.*

LA CRUZ

40 km (25 miles) northwest of Liberia.

North of Santa Rosa National Park on the west side of the highway is the turnoff to La Cruz, a scruffy, bustling little town, noteworthy only for the stunning views of Bahía Salinas from its bluff and its proximity to the nearby windswept beaches on the south shore of Bahía Salinas, in the hamlet of Jobo, and in the Golfo de Santa Elena. Visit the area sooner rather than later; in 2014, Santa Elena Preserve began the initial development phase of real estate projects near La Cruz.

The Nicaraguan border lies just north of La Cruz at Peñas Blancas. ■TIP➔ **Travelers may be stopped at two checkpoints south of La Cruz for passport and cursory vehicle inspection. Police vigilance is heightened in the region.**

GETTING HERE AND AROUND

La Cruz is a straight shot, one hour's trip north of Liberia on the well-maintained Pan-American Highway. Buses leave Liberia for La Cruz, or you can flag down a bus that says "La Cruz" on its windshield anywhere along the highway north of Liberia.

ESSENTIALS

Bank Banco Nacional ✉ *Pan-American Hwy. across from police station* ☎ *2679–9389.* **Banco Popular** ✉ *75 m east of northeast corner of central park* ☎ *2679–9352.*

Pharmacy Farmacia La Cruz ✉ *1 block north of central park* ☎ *2679–8048* 🕓 *Daily 8–8.*

Post Office Correo ✉ *Behind police station on west side of central park.*

WHERE TO STAY

$ 🏨 **Cabañas y Finca Cañas Castilla.**
B&B/INN Swiss expats Guido and Agi spent their first years in Costa Rica living off the land without running water or electricity, but today their little paradise is a full-fledged farm with cows, horses, chickens, and rustic cabins for overnight guests. **Pros:** friendly owners; nature abounds; all rooms are wheelchair accessible; delicious food. **Cons:** patchy Wi-Fi; no phones; muddy in rainy season; lots of bugs. [$] *Rooms from: $56* ✉ *Approx 5 km (3 miles) from La Cruz, turn off the highway to the right into Sonzapote. Follow the signs to Finca Cañas Castilla.* ☎ *8381–4030 cell* 🌐 *www.canas-castilla.com* 🛏 6 🍴 *Breakfast.*

THIEVES ON THE BEACHES

Guanacaste's idyllic landscapes and friendly people belie an ever-present threat of theft. Sadly, Costa Rica's thieves manage to ruin a lot of vacations by absconding with backpacks, cameras, wallets, and passports, the last of which necessitates a trip to San José. Keep your valuables in your hotel safe—preferably the safe in the hotel office—and don't ever leave anything in an unattended car, even while checking into your hotel. Hotel parking lots are popular spots for local kleptomaniacs, as are beaches.

CROSSING INTO NICARAGUA AT PEÑAS BLANCAS

Costa Rica and Nicaragua share a busy border crossing at Peñas Blancas, 18 km (11 miles) north of La Cruz along a paved highway. **■ TIP→ Rental vehicles may not leave Costa Rica.** Tica Bus and Transnica bus companies *(⇨ Bus Travel in Travel Smart Costa Rica)* travel direct between San José and Managua via this route. You can also take a Tralapa bus to the border from other points in Costa Rica. You'll make your crossing, then catch a Nicaraguan bus or taxi to Rivas, 35 km (22 miles) farther, which is the regional hub for buses departing to other parts of Nicaragua. The fee to cross the border is $7 (paid on the Nicaraguan side), plus a $2 surcharge if you cross from noon to 2 pm or on weekends. Nicaraguan shuttle taxis transport people between the border posts. Returning to Costa Rica is basically the same process in reverse; you are charged a $1 municipal tax and $2 exit tax to leave Nicaragua by land. The crossing is open daily 6 am to 10 pm, but only until 8 pm on Sunday; get there with time to spare or you *will* be stranded. Banks on both sides of the border change their own currency and U.S. dollars. Colones are not accepted or exchanged in Nicaragua; likewise for Nicaraguan córdobas in Costa Rica. Overland border-crossing procedures can be confusing if you don't speak Spanish, but attendants on the cross-border buses can help shepherd you through the formalities. The colonial city of Granada, the twin volcanoes of the island of Ometepe, and the lively beach town of San Juan del Sur—site of two consecutive seasons (2010 and 2011) of the television series *Survivor*—are the draws in southern Nicaragua.

BAHÍA SALINAS

15 km (9 miles) west of La Cruz.

The large windswept bay at the very top of Costa Rica's Pacific coast is the second-windiest area in the country, after Lake Arenal, making it a mecca for windsurfers and kitesurfers, as well as beachgoers looking for breezy, uncrowded, pristine beaches. Strong breezes blow from November to May, when only experienced riders are out on the water and the water grows steadily cooler. The south (bay) side has the strongest winds, and choppy, colder water from January to May.

In July and August the wind is more appropriate for beginners, whereas anytime of year you can enjoy the area's diving and beaches. On the sheltered Golfo de Santa Elena, to the west, are two beaches that rank among the most beautiful in all of Costa Rica: Playa Rajada and Playa Jobo, a far cry from the overdeveloped beaches of Guanacaste's gold coast farther to the south.

6

GETTING HERE AND AROUND

From a high point in La Cruz, the road to Salinas descends both in altitude and condition. It's only 15 km (9 miles) southwest to Hotel Ecoplaya Beach Resort, but after the first 2 km (1 mile) of paved road, the rest of the road varies from bad to worse, so it may take up to 45 minutes or an hour. Signs direct you to Puerto Soley and El Jobo, an end-of-the-road hamlet, about 2 km (1 mile) past the turnoff for Ecoplaya. Playa Copal is about 13 km (8 miles) along the same road from La Cruz.

BEACHES

Playa Copal. Playa Copal is a narrow, dark-beige beach that wouldn't be worth visiting except for the fact that it is one of the main venues for kitesurfing. Winds are often gusty but consistent November to May, which is why several kite schools have set up shop nearby. There are villas and rooms for rent, and the upscale Ecoplaya Hotel is just a mile away. A couple of kilometers to the east, Playa Papaturro also has kitesurfing and simple accommodations. **Amenities:** food and drink. **Best for:** solitude. ⊠ *About 2 km (1 mile) east of the branch road that leads to Ecoplaya.*

Playa Jobo. Playa Jobo is a gem with fine sand and calm water. It's fringed with acacia trees that have sharp thorns, so keep your distance. There's a shady parking area about 150 meters (500 feet) off the beach where you have to leave your car. During rainy season, you'll need a four-wheel-drive vehicle to get here. **Amenities:** parking. **Best for:** solitude; sunset; swimming. ⊠ *3-km (2-mile) walk or drive, west from Ecoplaya Beach Resort.*

Semana Santa

Don't underestimate how completely Costa Rica shuts down for Holy Week, the week preceding Easter. Cities become ghost towns—San José turns beguilingly peaceful—save for religious processions. Many businesses close the entire week; little opens on Thursday or Friday. Tourists, local and international, flock to the beaches. Make reservations months in advance if you plan to be here during that week, and expect greatly inflated room rates. Know that Holy Thursday and Good Friday are, by law, dry days. Bars and liquor stores must close, supermarkets cover up their liquor aisles, and no one, including restaurants or your hotel dining room, is permitted to sell alcohol.

Playa Rajada. Gorgeous, horseshoe-shaped Playa Rajada is a wide sweep of almost-white, fine-grain sand. Shallow, warm waters make it perfect for swimming, and an interesting rock formation at the north end invites snorkelers. It's also a favorite beach for watching sunsets, and for kitesurfing from November to May. **Amenities:** none. **Best for:** snorkeling; sunset; swimming. ⊠ *5 km (3 miles) west of Ecoplaya Beach Resort or 3 km (2 miles) north of the town of El Jobo.*

SPORTS AND THE OUTDOORS

Inshore fishing is quite good in the bay during windy months, when snapper, roosterfish, wahoo, and other fighters abound. Scuba divers also encounter plenty of big fish from December to May, though visibility can be poor then. From May to December the snorkeling is good around the rocky points and Isla Bolaños.

TOUR OPERATOR

Ecoplaya Beach Resort. Local adventure tours organized by this resort hotel include kayaking to Isla Bolaños (a tiny island that is a refuge for such seabirds as the brown pelican), inshore fishing, horseback riding, hiking, and snorkeling and windsurfing, as well as farther-afield adventure tours to Santa Rosa National Park, Palo Verde National Park Hacienda Guachipelín, and the historic city of Granada, in nearby Nicaragua. ⊠ *La Coyotera Beach, 15 km (10 miles) west of La Cruz on a rough dirt road* ☎ *2676–1010* ⊕ *www.ecoplaya.com.*

KITESURFING AND WINDSURFING

Kite Surfing School. Ideally situated on windy Playa Papaturro (11 km [7 miles] west of La Cruz, turn left at sign for Papaturro), this kitesurfing school is run by Nicola Bertoldi, a multilingual instructor with lots of experience; nine hours of beginner's kitesurfing private lessons cost $319, including equipment. But the best deals are all-inclusive packages that include lessons, lodging, and meals at the school's Blue Dream Hotel, on a ridge with ocean views. The hotel also has a wood-oven pizzeria. ⊠ *60 m east Playa Papaturro entrance* ☎ *8826–5221, 2676–1042* ⊕ *www.bluedreamhotel.com.*

WHERE TO STAY

$$ RESORT FAMILY

🏨 **Ecoplaya Beach Resort.** Set between La Coyotera Beach and a mangrove estuary, this Best Western–affiliated small resort has a sprawling collection of equipped villas and two-story concrete buildings (with several types of spacious rooms) that dot ample, landscaped grounds. **Pros:** friendly; lots of activities; large rooms. **Cons:** timeworn; service inconsistent; pool gets packed during holidays; remote. [$] *Rooms from: $125* ✉ *La Coyotera Beach, 15 km (10 miles) west of La Cruz on a rough dirt road* ☎ *2676–1010, 4034–3470 virtual office* 🌐 *www.ecoplaya.com* 🛏 *26 villas, 18 rooms* 🍴 *Breakfast.*

LIBERIA

214 km (133 miles) (4–5 hrs) northwest of San José.

Once a dusty cattle-market town, Liberia has galloped toward modernization, becoming the commercial, as well as the administrative, capital of Guanacaste. There are still a few vestiges of its colonial past on quieter side streets, and the occasional sabanero on horseback still ambles into town. But Liberia has virtually become one big shopping mall, complete with fast-food restaurants—dueling McDonald's and Burger King face off at the entrance to town—and a multiplex theater. Walk a couple of blocks south of the main street along Calle Real, though, and you can still find some whitewashed adobe houses for which Liberia was nicknamed the "White City," as well as some grand town houses that recall the city's glory days. A few have been restored and are now hotels and cafés. Liberia today is essentially a good place to have a meal and make a bank stop at any one of a dozen banks, including Scotiabank, Citibank, and HSBC. Liberia can also serve as a base for day trips to Santa Rosa and Rincón de la Vieja national parks. Keep in mind that Liberia is the hottest city in Costa Rica, getting up to 115° F (46° C) in April. The drive from San José takes between four and five hours, so it makes sense to fly directly into Liberia if you're going only to the North Pacific. It's easy to rent a car near the airport.

NAVIGATING LIBERIA

The *avenidas* (avenues) officially run east–west, whereas the *calles* (streets) run north–south. Liberia is not too big to walk easily, but there are always taxis lined up around the pleasant central park.

GETTING HERE AND AROUND

From San José, follow the Pan-American Highway west past the Puntarenas exit, then north past Cañas to Liberia. The road is paved but is poorly maintained in places. It's a heavily traveled truck and bus route, and there are miles and miles where it is impossible to pass, but many drivers try, making this a dangerous road. South of Liberia, the road is being widened, so expect delays. Hourly direct buses leave San José for Liberia each day, and there are half a dozen daily flights, so it might be worth busing or flying to Liberia and renting a car from here.

ESSENTIALS

Bank/ATM Banco de Costa Rica ✉ *Calle Ctl. at Avda. 1, diagonally across from central park* ☎ *2666–9002.*

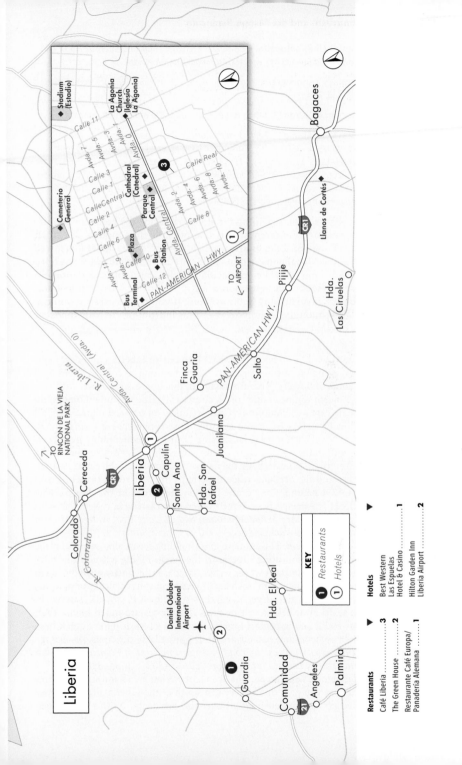

Liberia

KEY
1 *Restaurants*
① *Hotels*

Restaurants ▶
Café Liberia **3**
The Green House **2**
Restaurante Café Europa/
Panadería Alemana **1**

Hotels ▶
Best Western
Las Espuelas
Hotel & Casino **1**
Hilton Garden Inn
Liberia Airport **2**

Hospital Liberia Hospital (*San Rafael Arcangel Medical Center*). ✉ *North end of town* ☎ *2666–1717* 🌐 *www.centromedicosanrafael.com.*

Pharmacy Farmacia Lux ✉ *C. 4 and Avda. Ctl.* ☎ *2666–0061* 🕐 *Mon.–Sat. 8–10, Sun. 8–4 pm.*

Post Office Correo ✉ *300 m west of highway, 200 m north of Avda. Ctl..*

Rental Cars Alamo ✉ *2 km (1 mile) northeast of Liberia airport* ☎ *2668–1111, 800/522–9696 in U.S.* **Budget** ✉ *1 km (½ mile) east of Liberia airport* ☎ *2668–1118.* **Economy** ✉ *5 km (3 miles) east of Liberia airport* ☎ *2666–2816, 2666–7560.* **Hertz** ✉ *Pan-American Hwy., 1 km (½ mile) northeast of the airport; office inside Liberia Airport* ☎ *2668–1048.* **Hola Rentacar** ✉ *6 km (4 miles) southwest of Liberia airport* ☎ *2667–4040.*

EN ROUTE

Yes, that is a life-size dinosaur standing beside the highway 20 minutes north of Puntarenas. It is one of 26 lifelike models of extinct and endangered animals arranged along a 1½-km (1-mile) forest trail at Parque MegaFauna Monteverde (✉ *Pan-American Hwy.* ☎ *2638–8193*). Along with the spectacular models outdoors, an impressive insect museum can be explored for a $5 ($3 for kids) entrance fee. The park is open daily 8 am to 5 pm. If you're just passing, you can still stop and take a photo of your kids in front of the baby dinosaur hatching out of a giant egg.

WHERE TO EAT

$$ FRENCH Fodor's Choice ★

🍴 **Café Liberia.** Step back 150 years into one of Liberia's grandest mansions, complete with an original ceiling painting of cupids, doves, and garlands of flowers. Recently restored, this impressive house, with two magnificent dining rooms and a courtyard garden, is now home to an upscale café and restaurant. Creative takes on tropical ingredients, all with a French twist, make this the most sophisticated restaurant in town. Loyal customers drive over an hour for the incredibly fresh ceviche with mango and cilantro. Don't miss the Wagyu beef burger, the chicken pesto sandwich, or the fish with chimichurri. Herbs are grown on-site and the organic coffee is perhaps the best you'll taste in Costa Rica. Save room for any of the fabulous desserts, like the classic crème brûlée, flambéed crepes, or the molten chocolate lava cake made with Belgian chocolate. [$] *Average main: $12* ✉ *Calle Real Antigua, 125 m south of central park* ☎ *2665–1660* 🕐 *Closed Sun.*

$$ ECLECTIC

🍴 **The Green House.** This modern glass building seems almost out of place on the road connecting Liberia to the coast. Filling a void in healthy cuisine, the restaurant serves wraps, salads, sushi, and sandwiches such as organic chicken with fresh basil. Vegetarians have plenty of options, including a veggie burger, asparagus soup, or a Portobello sandwich. The seafood dishes are hit or miss. The prices are much higher than what you'll find in central Liberia, but it's a good stop for a quick bite. The bruschetta and nachos are both particularly delicious. [$] *Average main: $18* ✉ *Hwy. 21, on road to airport in front of Pájaro Azul, 2 km (1 mile) from Liberia intersection* ☎ *2665–5037, 2665–8901.*

$ GERMAN

🍴 **Restaurante Café Europa.** The aroma of baking bread and strudel is irresistible as you pass this bakery just south of the Liberia airport, whose baked goods are delivered all over the peninsula. Now a full-fledged restaurant, be sure to stop in for strudels, Bundt cakes, and flaky fruit pastries, or for a German breakfast of ham, wurst, cheese, and bread. Heartier meals include salads, bratwurst with sauerkraut, pork schnitzel, and curry wurst—white sausage in a curry tomato sauce. The restaurant recently added a beer garden and playground. It's open daily from 5 am to 7 pm. [$] *Average main: $7* ✉ *2 km (1 mile) west of Liberia airport* ☎ *2668–1081* 🌐 *www.panaleman.com.*

WHERE TO STAY

$$ HOTEL FAMILY 🏨 **Best Western Las Espuelas Hotel.** From the gigantic Guanacaste tree that shades its parking lot to the local paintings, hacienda-style benches, and indigenous stone statues that decorate its lobby and walkways, this motel just south of town has more character than other hotels in town. **Pros:** reasonable rates; big pool; no-smoking rooms; free Wi-Fi. **Cons:** highway noise; few amenities. [$] *Rooms from: $75* ✉ *Pan-American Hwy., 2 km (1 mile) south of Liberia* ☎ *2666–0144* 🌐 *www.hotellasespuelas.com* 🛏 *38 rooms, 7 suites* 🍴 *Breakfast.*

$$ HOTEL 🏨 **Hilton Garden Inn Liberia Airport.** Comfortable and convenient, especially if you're catching an early-morning flight or you need a break from driving before heading south to the beach, this five-story contemporary Hilton has all the mod cons, including Wi-Fi, high-definition TVs, MP3 players, microwaves, and fridges. **Pros:** kids under 12 stay free; very comfortable; free shuttle to and from airport. **Cons:** no shaded parking area; impersonal cookie-cutter rooms; pricey. [$] *Rooms from: $169* ✉ *Across from Liberia International Airport on main highway* ☎ *2690–8888* 🌐 *www.liberiaairport.hgi.com* 🛏 *169 rooms, including 8 handicapped-access rooms, 8 suites* 🍴 *Breakfast.*

6

GUANACASTE PACIFIC COAST

Strung along the southern coast of Guanacaste are sparkling sand beaches lined with hotels and resorts in every price category. As recently as the 1970s, fishing and cattle ranching were the area's mainstays. Development has barreled ahead full speed, though, turning laid-back fishing villages into beach towns with sophisticated restaurants, hotels, shops, and nightlife. Development has also brought congestion, noise, construction chaos, water pollution and shortages, and higher prices. If resort life and the party scene are not your style, there are still some blissfully tranquil beaches just beyond the paved roads.

PAPAGAYO PENINSULA

47 km (29 miles) west of Liberia.

The Papagayo Peninsula, a crooked finger of land cradling the west side of Bahía Culebra (Snake Bay), enjoys guaranteed sun from January to April, making it a prime site for all-inclusive hotels catering to snowbirds escaping northern winters. Five large hotels are already situated around Papagayo Bay, and many others are slated to be built here, all part of a government-sponsored development program modeled after Cancún. Although the hotels are reminiscent of their Caribbean counterparts, the beaches are distinctly Costa Rican, with brown sand and aquamarine water that grows cool from January to April. Isolation is the name of the game here, which means that getting out of man-made "paradise" to explore anything off-property often entails a pricey tour.

High season here coincides with dry season, when the heat is intense and the landscape becomes brown and brittle. In the rainy season (August to December), the landscape is greener and lusher. The sparkling water and spectacular sunsets are beautiful year-round.

GETTING HERE AND AROUND

All hotels here have airport pickup. To get to the Four Seasons from the Liberia airport (the hotel refuses to put up directional signs in order to protect its privacy), drive 10 km (6 miles) south of Guardia, over the Río Tempisque Bridge, then take the turn on the right signed for Papagayo Allegro Resort. Follow this road about 20 km (12 miles) to its end at the entrance to the resort. For Casa Conde Hotel and Hilton Resort, take the road toward Playa Panama.

SPORTS AND THE OUTDOORS

CANOPY TOUR

Witch's Rock Canopy Tour. Taking advantage of one of the few remaining patches of dry tropical forest on the Papagayo Peninsula, Witch's Rock Canopy Tour gives you your money's worth: 23 platforms, with a thrilling 450-meter (1,485-foot) cable zip between two of them; four hanging bridges; a waterfall in rainy season; and hiking trails. The 1½-hour tour is $75 per person; transportation from area hotels is extra. ⊠ *On road to Four Seasons Resort, 17 km (10 miles) west of DYI Center on main highway from Liberia* ☎ *2696–7101, 2696–7103* ⊕ *www.witchsrockcanopy.com.*

SURFING

Tropic Surf. No one mixes surfing and luxury better than this highly professional outfitter, offering excursions to Witch's Rock and Ollies Point aboard their fleet of boats. Their quiver is top notch, ranging from shortboards to stand-up paddleboards. Trained instructors are on hand for all levels, delivering water and sunscreen while you surf. In addition to their location at Four Seasons Resort Peninsula Papagayo, they have more than 20 destinations worldwide. ⊠ *At Four Seasons Peninsula Papagayo* ☎ *61 7/5455–4129* ⊕ *www.tropicsurf.net.*

WHERE TO EAT AND STAY

$$
INTERNATIONAL
Fodor'sChoice
★

✕ **Makoko.** Chefs Sebastian La Roca and Diego Mollenhauer are creating culinary magic at El Mangroove's trendy poolside restaurant, where guests can dine with an ocean view or head indoors to the more formal dining room enclosed in glass. Most ingredients are locally grown and nearly every item on the menu is organic, including the grass-fed beef. Start with red-snapper carpaccio with grapefruit and fennel, or the prosciutto and mozzarella with orange and spiced almonds. Signature entrées include roasted sea bass with shiitake mushrooms, and the remarkably tender Worcestershire-glazed short ribs slow-cooked for 24 hours and served with apple-jalapeño puree (knife optional). Portions are not over the top, which means you'll have room for the chocolate cheesecake that slides off the fork and into your mouth way

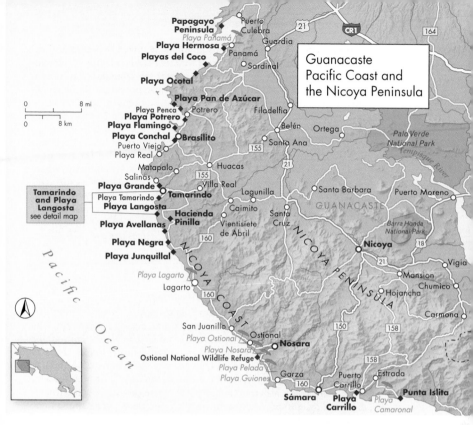

too easily. $ *Average main: $15* ⊠ *At intersection near Hilton Resort, Papagayo Peninsula* ☎ *4701–0000* ⊕ *www.elmangroove.net* ◷ *6–11 pm* ◷ *No lunch.*

$$$$ 🍴 **Andaz Peninsula Papagayo.** Earthy tones and natural details prevail
RESORT in this Hyatt property created by architect Ronald Zürcher, who uti-
lized indigenous woods, sugarcane, and bamboo in the design of the
rooms, each contemporary and bright with ocean views. **Pros:** friendly
staff; free Kids' Club; design reflects culture. **Cons:** pricey breakfast;
rooms have dim lighting; rocky beach; eight-night minimum stay
during holidays. $ *Rooms from: $500* ⊠ *Peninsula Papagayo, next
to Four Seasons Resort, Papagayo Peninsula* ☎ *2690–1234* ⊕ *www.
andazpapagayo.com* ⬅ *132 rooms, 21 suites* ⦿ *No meals.*

$$$ 🍴 **Casa Conde Beachfront Hotel.** Spread over verdant grounds just behind
HOTEL relatively pristine Playa Panama, Casa Conde has an excellent loca-
FAMILY tion with bay views, balmy breezes, and a huge swimming pool. **Pros:**
spacious rooms; immaculate grounds; close to beach. **Cons:** attracts
large tour groups; not all rooms have Wi-Fi; no activities. $ *Rooms
from: $185* ⊠ *Playa Panama, 3 km (2 miles) north of Playa Hermosa*
☎ *2226–0808 San José office, 2672–1008* ⊕ *www.grupocasaconde.
com* ⬅ *26 rooms, including 2 handicapped-accessible rooms, 6 suites*
⦿ *Breakfast.*

$$$
HOTEL

El Mangroove. Barefoot luxury abounds at this chic boutique hotel where an airy courtyard leads to a 45-meter pool lined with beach bungalows and modern rooms. **Pros:** same rates year-round; beautiful spa; attentive service; yoga classes; cool vibe. **Cons:** breakfast not included; only two rooms have ocean views; some mosquitoes in common areas. $ *Rooms from: $320* ✉ *At intersection before Hilton Resort* ☎ *4701–0000* ⊕ *www.elmangroove.net* ⇌ *85 rooms* ⦿ *No meals.*

$$$$
RESORT
Fodor's Choice
★

Four Seasons Resort Costa Rica. By far one of the most luxurious hotels in Costa Rica, the Four Seasons is extremely secluded on a narrow isthmus, meaning you'll have an ocean view from just about anywhere on the property. **Pros:** impeccable service; lovely beach; offers surf trips to Witch's Rock. **Cons:** breakfast not included; 30 minutes from main road; expensive. $ *Rooms from: $725* ✉ *25 km (15 miles) west of Guardia; follow signs to Papagayo Allegro Resort and continue to end of road* ☎ *2696–0000* ⊕ *www.fourseasons.com/costarica* ⇌ *120 rooms, 35 suites, 22 villas* ⦿ *No meals.*

PLAYA HERMOSA

27 km (17 miles) southwest of Liberia airport.

Beautiful Playa Hermosa, once a laid-back, fishing community, has grown like Topsy, with condominiums and villas covering the scrubby hills overlooking the wide, curved beach. Warm, swimmable water, prime dive sites, choice fishing grounds, and sunset views of the Papagayo Peninsula are all reasons why Canadian and American expatriates are buying up those condos. In the early morning, though, Playa Hermosa is still the kind of place where the beach is the town's main thoroughfare, filled with joggers, people walking their dogs, and families out for a stroll. Not to be confused with the mainland surfers' beach of the same name south of Jacó, this Playa Hermosa has long been occupied by small hotels, restaurants, and homes along the length of the beach, so the newer hotel behemoths and other developments are forced to set up shop off the beach or up on the surrounding hillsides.

GETTING HERE AND AROUND

Heading south from Liberia along Highway 21, take the turnoff in Comunidad signed for Playa Hermosa and Playas del Coco. Playa Hermosa is about 15 km (9 miles) northwest. The paved road forks after the small town of Sardinal, the right fork heading into Hermosa and the left leading to Playas del Coco. Local directions usually refer to the first and second entrance roads to the beach, the first entrance being the southern one. There is no through beachfront road, so you have to approach the beach from either of these two roads. Transportes La Pampa buses leave from Liberia for Playa Hermosa daily starting at 4:30, 4:40, 4:50 am (to get workers to their hotel jobs), then at 7:30 and 11:30 am and 1, 3:30, and 5:30 pm. The trip takes about 1½ hours. A taxi from Playa Hermosa to Playas del Coco costs about $15 and takes about 15 minutes.

ESSENTIALS

Playa Hermosa has a large supermarket, Luperón, on the main road, between the first and second beach entrances, open daily 7 am to 8:30 pm—where you can stock up on just about everything you need—food, wine, liquor, toiletries, even fresh-baked French and ciabatta bread.

BEACHES

Playa Hermosa. Not to be confused with the surfers' beach near Jacó by the same name, Playa Hermosa's 2-km-long (1-mile-long) crescent of dark gray volcanic sand attracts heat, making the early morning or late afternoon the best time to visit (with the latter providing spectacular sunsets). The beach fronts a line of shade trees, so there's a welcome respite from the heat of the sun. The crystal clear water—it's a Blue Flag beach—is usually calm, with no strong currents and with comfortable temperatures of 23°C to 27°C (74°F to 80°F). Sea views are as picturesque as they get, with bobbing fishing boats, jagged profiles of coastline, rocky outcroppings, and at night the twinkling lights of the Four Seasons Resort across the bay. At the beach's north end, low tide creates wide, rock-lined tidal pools. **Amenities:** food and drink; water sports. **Best for:** swimming; walking.

SPORTS AND THE OUTDOORS

TOUR OPERATOR

Charlie's Adventure. Operating out of the Hotel Condovac, this tour company organizes ATV tours ($85), and horseback riding ($50), as well as the seven-hour Aqua Combo boat tours of Hermosa Bay, which includes snorkeling, bottom fishing, and a beach barbecue lunch ($90, including drinks). There's also a sunset boat tour ($50). ⊠ *Hotel Condovac, north end of beach* ☎ *2672–0275* ⊕ *www.charliesadventure.com.*

BOATING

Aqua Sport. This outfitter rents every kind of boat and board—kayaks, banana boats, boogie boards—from a storage shed near their seafood restaurant, which bares the same name. ⊠ *Beach road; heading south, take 2nd entrance to Playa Hermosa and follow signs* ☎ *2672–0151.*

Hotel El Velero. This beachfront hotel has a 38-foot sailing yacht for five-hour sunset cruises ($60 per person). Daytime tours include snorkeling and a picnic lunch with soft drinks ($80 per person). ⊠ *100 m north of Aqua Sport* ☎ *2672–1017* ⊕ *www.costaricahotel.net.*

North Pacific Tours. Based in Playa Hermosa, this reliable outfitter has private and customized charters for fishing, surfing, and snorkeling tours aboard a 26-foot center console panga. ☎ *2670–1564* ⊕ *www. northpacifictours.com.*

DIVING AND SNORKELING

Average water temperature of 23°C (75°F), average visibility of 6 meters (20 feet), and frequent sightings of sea turtles, sharks, manta rays, moray eels, and very big fish make Hermosa a great place to dive. There is little coral in the area, but rock reefs attract large schools of fish, and countless critters lurk in their caves and crannies.

Diving Safaris. This is the most experienced dive operation in the area, with a full range of scuba activities, from beginner training to open-water PADI certification and dive master courses. Multitank dives are organized at more than 20 sites. Guides and trainers are very good, and their safety standards have the DAN (Divers Alert Network) seal of approval. This dive shop has also earned the coveted five-star status from PADI. Prices range from $90 for two-tank morning dives to $425 and up for the PADI open-water certification course. ⊠ *2nd entrance road to Playa Hermosa, almost at beach on right side* ☎ *2672–1259* ⊕ *www.costaricadiving.net.*

FISHING

The fishing at Playa Hermosa is mostly close to the shores, and yields edible fish like *dorado* (mahimahi), snapper, amberjack, tuna, and wahoo. Roosterfish, marlin, and sailfish are all catch-and-release. Some local restaurants are happy to cook your catch for you. You can rent a boat with **Aqua Sport** or **North Pacific Tours** *(⇨ above)*. **Charlie's Adventure** *(⇨ above)* runs fishing trips. **Papagayo Gulf Sport Fishing** (☎ *2670–1564* ⊕ *www.papagayofishing.typepad.com)* also runs various fishing tours in the area, as well as snorkeling and surfing tours and water taxis around the bay.

WHERE TO EAT

A few of Playa Hermosa's best restaurants are at hotels *(⇨ Where to Stay, below).*

$$
ECLECTIC
Fodor'sChoice
★

✕ **Ginger Restaurant Bar.** This tapas restaurant, featuring Asian and Mediterranean flavors, is situated in a modernistic glass-and-steel tree house that's cantilevered on the side of a hill and includes a spacious deck. Delectable appetizer-size offerings include seared pepper-crusted tuna atop pickled ginger slaw, or panfried sea bass fillets with a divine ginger–and–mandarin orange butter sauce. Not to be missed are Ginger's crispy shoestring fries, served with roasted garlic mayo. Portions are small, but layers of condiments and garnishes make them surprisingly satisfying. The fun thing to do is order several dishes and share. The varied wine list includes Old and New World wines by the glass, and specialty martinis and tropical cocktails go well with the tapas. For dessert, warm chocolate lava cake is rich enough to share, but only with someone you truly love. Be aware that the menu prices do not include tax and service (another 23%). It's open 5 to 10 pm. $ *Average main: $18* ⊠ *Main highway, south of Hotel Condovac* ☎ *2672–0041* ⊕ *www.gingercostarica.com* ⊘ *Closed Mon.*

WHERE TO STAY

$$
B&B/INN

🛏 **Hotel La Finisterra.** From its perch high above the southern end of Playa Hermosa, this classy, small hotel commands the best view of the beach and bay, along with the best terrace for watching sunsets. **Pros:** good food; very friendly staff; great views. **Cons:** steep climb up from beach; small pool. $ *Rooms from: $185* ⊠ *1st entrance to Playa Hermosa, left before Hotel Playa Hermosa, 250 m up hill* ☎ *2672–0227* ⊕ *www.lafinisterra.com* ⇴ *10 rooms* ❚◎❚ *Breakfast.*

$$$
B&B/INN
Fodor'sChoice
★

🛏 **Hotel Playa Hermosa Bosque del Mar.** This beachfront hotel on the southern end of Playa Hermosa features luxurious rooms and suites on a beautiful, spacious property shaded by century-old, vine-draped trees. **Pros:** superb garden; rare beachfront location; beautiful restaurant; all rooms have terraces. **Cons:** some rooms near the pool are dark; food doesn't match up to restaurant decor; expensive for the area. [$] *Rooms from: $226* ✉ *End of 1st entrance to Playa Hermosa* ☎ *2672–0046* 🌐 *www.hotelplayahermosa.com* 🛏 *20 junior suites, 12 deluxe suites, 1 penthouse suite* 🍴 *No meals.*

$ B&B/INN 🏨 **Villa del Sueño.** Although the handsome garden restaurant ($25) is the main attraction at this elegant hotel, the spacious rooms and well-equipped villas are quite comfortable, too, though the hotel is about a block from the beach. **Pros:** excellent restaurant; good value. **Cons:** not on the beach; can be noisy when there's live music; breakfast not included in high season. [$] *Rooms from: $75* ✉ *1st entrance to Playa Hermosa, 350 m west of main highway* ☎ *2672–0026* 🌐 *www.villadelsueno.com* 🛏 *14 rooms, 27 villas, 3 two-bedroom villas* 🍴 *No meals.*

$ RENTAL FAMILY 🏨 **Villas Huetares.** The best bargain in town, this long-established family hotel offers two-bedroom garden villas as well as a pleasant, two-story annex with 16 spacious rooms. **Pros:** close to beach; good kitchens; beautiful grounds and pool. **Cons:** lots of noise from kids, especially on weekends. [$] *Rooms from: $92* ✉ *2nd entrance road to Playa Hermosa, 100 m (1 block) in from the main highway* ☎ *2672–0052* 🌐 *www.villahuetares.com* 🛏 *16 rooms, 15 villas* 🍴 *Breakfast.*

NIGHTLIFE

Hotel El Velero. This lively beachfront hotel hosts beach barbecues on Wednesday and Saturday nights in high season. The crowd is thirtyish and up. ✉ *2nd entrance to Playa Hermosa, then 100 m north of Aqua Sport on beach road.*

Villa del Sueño. In high season, Villa del Sueño hosts live music (jazz and rock) on Tuesday, Friday, and Sunday nights, as well as occasional concerts featuring top national bands and performers. ✉ *1st entrance to Playa Hermosa, 350 m west of main highway*

SHOPPING

La Gran Nicoya. You can get any souvenir you could possibly want at this lively emporium that also features a restaurant, a coffee tour, and the occasional folklore show. On Monday, Wednesday, and Friday afternoons, from 3:30 to 5, cruise the aisles to the sound of live marimba music. Last-minute shoppers can stop in on their way to nearby Liberia airport. It's open 6 to 6 daily, except Good Friday. ✉ *25 m south of Guardia soccer field, on main highway south of Liberia airport, before turnoff to Hermosa, Hermosa* ☎ *2667–0062* 🌐 *www.lagrannicoya-cr.com.*

Villa del Sueño. The small but upscale gift shop at Villa del Sueño has colorful beach cover-ups, designed and made locally, that will flatter any woman. ✉ *1st entrance to Playa Hermosa, 350 m west of main highway.*

Continued on page 287

Choosing a Beach

From pulverized volcanic rock and steady waves to soft white sand and idyllic settings, all of the beaches along the Nicoya Peninsula's coast have their own distinct merits. Playa Tamarindo has a restaurant so close to the ocean the surf spray salts your food; playas Hermosa and Sámara are family-friendly spots with swimmable waters; and playas Langosta and Pelada are made for contemplative walks.

GUANACASTE PACIFIC COAST

Playa Tamarindo

1 Popular luxury resorts line the beaches of the **Papagayo Peninsula**.

2 **Playa Hermosa** is one of the few Costa Rican beaches with calm, crystal-clear waters.

3 Diving and fishing are the name of the game at **Playas del Coco** and its lively beach town.

4 **Playa Ocotal** is a quiet black-sand beach with great views, diving, and good snorkeling.

5 **Playa Pan de Azúcar** is practically deserted once you get there.

6 **Playa Potrero** is the jumping-off point for diving trips to the Catalina Islands.

7 Busy white-sand **Playa Flamingo** is ideal for swim-ming and sunning.

8 Shells sprinkle the sand at chilled-out **Playa Conchal**, near a small fishing village.

9 Lively **Tamarindo** is a hyped-up surfing and water-sports beach with wild nightlife.

BEACHES KEY

- Diving
- Snorkeling
- Fishing
- Surfing
- Kayaking
- Sailing
- Swimming
- Blue Flag Ecological Award

GUANACASTE AND NORTHERN NICOYA PENINSULA

(top) Playa Avellanas (bottom) Sunset at Sámara

❶ **Playa Langosta** is great for walks up its estuary and watching dramatic sunsets.

❷ **Playa Avellanas** is a perfect spot to relax with a cold drink between surf sessions.

❸ **Playa Negra** has some of Costa Rica's best surfing waves.

❹ Peaceful and difficult to reach, **Playa Junquillal** is all about relaxation.

❺ Hemmed in by rocks, **Playa Pelada** is a calm beach staked out by territorial Tico surfers.

❻ Long, clean **Playa Guiones** is backed by dense jungle.

❼ **Sámara's** gentle waters make it perfect for kayakers, swimmers, and novice surfers.

❽ Perhaps the most beautiful beach in the country, **Playa Carrillo** fronts an idyllic half-moon bay.

❾ Rocky **Punta Islita** has interesting tidal pools to explore.

SOUTHERN NICOYA PENINSULA

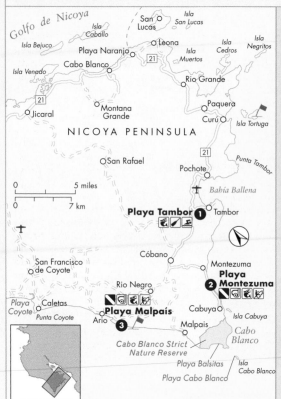

(top) Montezuma (bottom) Surfing at Malpaís

❶ Crescent-shaped, shallow **Playa Tambor** is flanked by an all-inclusive resort and a fishing village.

❷ **Montezuma's** off-beat town is as much a draw as its bayside beach.

❸ Some of the largest surfing waves in Costa Rica are at **Malpaís**.

MAKING THE BEST OF YOUR BEACH VACATION

■ Tamarindo, Nosara, and Sámara are good for beginning surfers. Playas Grande, Avellanas, and Negra are best left to those with experience; other surfing waters are somewhere in between.

■ Tamarindo, Nosara, Sámara, and Tambor are beaches with air service to San José.

■ The beach road connecting most Nicoya Peninsula beaches is hard to stomach any time of year, and virtually impassable during the August through December rains. Take easier inland routes instead.

■ Riptides are seriously dangerous and hardly any Costa Rican beaches have lifeguards; get information from your hotel about where to swim safely.

PLAYAS DEL COCO

25 km (16 miles) southwest of Liberia airport; 10 km (6 miles) south of Playa Hermosa.

Messy, noisy, colorful, and interesting, Playas del Coco has the best souvenir shopping, the most dive shops, and the liveliest nightlife and barhopping on this part of the coast. It's still a working fishing port, with a port captain's office, a fish market, and an ice factory for keeping the catch of the day fresh—not for cooling margaritas, although many are enjoyed here. A beautiful boardwalk built in 2011 made the beach much more attractive, with palm trees, benches, and even cold showers. An explosion of condominium and villa projects has brought new money to the community, along with new commercial development, including the upscale Pacifico Village shopping center at the entrance to town. This center boasts a flagship AutoMercado, the country's top grocery chain, as well as the Arenas Surf Shop, Citron restaurant, fast-food chains, a UPS office, and a few clothing boutiques. Fresh seafood, myriad souvenir shops, and plenty of bars have always drawn tourists here, but Playas del Coco also has a high concentration of tour operators offering diving, fishing, and surfing excursions at remote breaks such as Ollie's Point and Witch's Rock. Because Coco is mere minutes from Playa Hermosa, however, you can just as easily enjoy those sports while staying at that more pleasant beach. If you like to shop and party, and want some local color, Coco's slightly raucous ambience can be appealing.

GETTING HERE AND AROUND

The easy drive from the Liberia airport to Playas del Coco takes about 30 minutes. The paved highway turns into a grand, divided boulevard as you enter town; it ends at the beach. If you don't have a car, the best way to get here from Playa Hermosa is in a taxi, for about $15 each way.

ESSENTIALS

Bank/ATM Banco Nacional ✉ *Main street, at entrance to town.*

Hospital Public Health Clinic ✉ *Next to La Puerta del Sol hotel* ☎ *2670–0987.*

Post Office Correo ✉ *At entrance to town on main road.*

SPORTS AND THE OUTDOORS

DIVING AND SNORKELING

Half a dozen dive shops populate this small town. The standard price for a two-tank dive is $80; Catalina Island dives are $110. This coast doesn't have the coral reefs or the clear visibility of the Caribbean coast, but it does have a lot of plankton (hence the lower visibility) that feeds legions of fish, some of them really, really big. Manta rays and sharks (white-tipped, nurse, and bull varieties) are among the stars of the undersea show. It takes about 20 to 45 minutes to reach most dive sites.

Deep Blue Diving Adventures. This organization has daily scuba diving trips to the top dive spots in the Papagayo Gulf, as well as Catalina and Murciélagos islands. ✉ *50 m before Hotel Coco on main street* ☎ *2670–1004* ⊕ *www.deepblue-diving.com.*

Rich Coast Diving. This longtime operator has enthusiastic guides and is the only PADI five-star CDC facility with the Green Star Award in Costa Rica. They offer daily fun dives, PADI courses, and snorkeling trips. ✉ *Main street, near intersection with road to Playa Ocotal, near medical center* ☎ *2670–0176* 🌐 *www.richcoastdiving.com.*

Summer Salt Dive Center. This longstanding small dive center is great for beginners. They focus on safety and fun in diving and snorkeling, and also offer whale-watching and water tours of the Gulf of Papagayo. ✉ *Main street* ☎ *2670–0308* 🌐 *www.summer-salt.com.*

FISHING

Fishing charter boats go out 24 to 64 km (15 to 40 miles) seeking yellowfin tuna, mahimahi, grouper, and red snapper close in, and sailfish, marlin, and roosterfish offshore (beyond 64 km [40 miles]).

GOLF

Papagayo Golf & Country Club. This 18-hole, par-72 course is very affordable; you can play the whole course for $100, including golf cart and a cooler with ice and water, or play 9 holes for $55. There's a restaurant and bar, and a tournament every Sunday morning. ✉ *10 km (6 miles) southeast of Playas del Coco, Libertad* ☎ *2697–0169 3* 🌐 *www.papagayo-golf.com.*

SURFING

Witch's Rock and Ollie's Point. These legendary surfing spots are a one-hour boat ride away from Playas del Coco off the coast of Santa Rosa National Park. You can surf as long as you pay the $10 park entrance fee.

You can sign up for a surfing trip with any beach-town tour operator, but local authorities allow excursions to Witch's Rock and Ollie's Point to originate only from the main dock at Playas del Coco, in boats owned by local boat owners, in order to curb overcrowding and undue environmental stress. Luxury surf excursions to both breaks are also available through Tropic Surf based at The Four Seasons Resort on Peninsula Papagayo.

WHERE TO EAT AND STAY

$$$ ECLECTIC

🍴 **Citron.** Ignore the strip mall location and step inside this snazzy restaurant with hardwood floors, white brick walls, and a wine bar shaking up divine watermelon martinis. For more ambience, grab a table on the outside deck where dishes like salmon risotto, poached sea bass, and shrimp sautéed in rum are served. For something from the land, try the caramelized pork in a honeyand-lime sauce or the heavily requested Dijon beef tenderloin. Don't be surprised if your taste buds give a standing ovation when you try the Baileys panna cotta with passion fruit coulis. [$] *Average main: $17* ✉ *Pacifico Retail Village, Route 151* ☎ *2670–0942* 🌐 *www.citroncoco.com* 🕒 *Closed Sun. No lunch.*

$$ PERUVIAN

🍴 **Donde Claudio & Gloria.** The coolest dining in Coco is this breezy, pleasant patio restaurant just steps from the beach, specializing in Peruvian seafood dishes. The same family has had a beachfront restaurant here since 1954, but the old place was demolished to make room for the beach boardwalk in 2011. This new incarnation offers seating on a wooden deck, where you can watch fishing boats bobbing in the bay. The updated menu wows with Peruvian *chaufa,* rice and shrimp spiced

THE ECOLOGICAL BLUE FLAG

The tourist industry here estimates that three-quarters of visitors to Costa Rica make a beach excursion. With that in mind, the national water utility, Acueductos y Alcantarillados (AyA), in conjunction with the Instituto Costarricense de Turismo, evaluates and ranks water and environmental quality in coastal communities. Those that achieve at least a 90% score are awarded a Bandera Azul Ecológica (Ecological Blue Flag) to fly as a symbol of excellence. The program, modeled on one begun in Spain in 1986, awards flags as prizes for communities. Participants are required to form a Blue Flag committee, a move that brings together diverse sectors of an area's population, many of which otherwise fiercely compete for tourist dollars. The program has prompted communities to put resources into improving environmental quality of life for themselves and for their guests.

Blue Flag locales receive year-round inspections of water quality—both ocean and drinking water—trash cleanup, waste management, security, signage, and environmental education. (Winners dare not rest on their laurels: a few know the shame of having their flags yanked.) In 2002, the competition was opened to inland communities; 2006 saw schools recognized; eco-friendly businesses and institutions were added in 2008. Even an exceptionally green auto mechanic shop in San José now flies a flag.

Blue flags fly proudly in the following locations covered in this book:

Central Valley: CATIE, Heredia, San Rafael de Heredia.

Arenal, Monteverde, and the Northern Lowlands: La Fortuna, Monteverde Cloud Forest Reserve, Vara Blanca.

Guanacaste and the Nicoya Peninsula: Bahía Junquillal, Bahía Salinas (Playa Copal, Playa Jobo, Playa Rajada), Nosara (Playa Garza, Playa Guiones, Playa Pelada), Ostional, Playa Avellanas, Playa Carrillo, Playa Conchal, Playa Flamingo, Playa Grande, Playa Hermosa, Playa Langosta, Playa Ocotal, Playa Pan de Azúcar, Playa Panamá, Playa Potrero, Playa Sámara, Punta Islita.

Manuel Antonio and the Central Pacific Coast: Curú National Wildlife Refuge, Isla del Coco, Isla Tortuga, Jacó, Malpaís, Manuel Antonio (Playa Manuel Antonio, Playa Espadilla Norte, Playa Espadilla Sur, Playa Gemelas), Playa Bejuco, Playa El Carmen, Playa Hermosa, Puntarenas, Punta Leona (Playa Blanca, Playa Limoncito, Playa Mantas), Santa Teresa.

The Osa Peninsula and the South Pacific: Ballena National Marine Park, Barú, Cabo Matapalo, Carate, Las Cruces Biological Station, Playa Dominical, Playa Nicuesa, Playa Pavones, Puerto Jiménez (Playa Blanca), San Gerardo de Rivas.

Tortuguero and the Caribbean Coast: Cahuita (Puerto Vargas, Playa Blanca, Playa Negra), EARTH, Gandoca-Manzanillo Wildlife Refuge, Puerto Viejo de Talamanca (Playa Chiquita, Playa Cocles, Playa Negra, Punta Uva), Tortuguero.

6

with Japanese flavors, and a Peruvian-style chunky ceviche. Desserts include flans, flambéed Bananas Foster, and key-lime pie. The wine list is notable for a wide range of Spanish and Italian wines, some available by the glass. [$] *Average main: $12* ✉ *75 m east of Lizard Lounge, or just walk east along the beach* ☎ *2670–1514, 2670–0256* 🌐 *www.dondeclaudioygloria.com.*

$$ ITALIAN 🍴 **La Dolce Vita.** This unpretentious restaurant hidden away in a shaded, pleasant courtyard gives diners a taste of life in Italy. Along with well-prepared Italian classics, there are some interesting local specialties like a colorful octopus carpaccio in pesto, and cappellacci pasta studded with lobster meat and zucchini with a sprinkle of peppermint. Seafood lovers should try the tuna tartar or the fettuccine with shrimp. The pizza boasts a thin, crisp crust. For dessert there's an intriguing panna cotta or classic tiramisu. If it's a romantic night, try to get a table outside next to the fountain and be sure to check out the selection of Italian wines. [$] *Average main: $14* ✉ *In El Pueblito shopping center, 350 m north along road running parallel to beach* ☎ *2670–1384* 🌐 *www.ladolcevitacostarica.com.*

$$ SEAFOOD 🍴 **Restaurante Papagayo Seafood.** The food here is straightforward, reliably fresh, and flavorful. Start with fish ceviche, or seafood soup generously packed with shrimp, squid, fish, and crab. Then sink your teeth into the catch of the day (including lobster, most notably), prepared any one of a dozen ways, or Papagayo seafood au gratin, a mix of sautéed seafood in a tarragon cream sauce. Seating is upstairs on a breezy terrace with views of the main street action. The restaurant also sells fresh fish to take home. And for those who like their fish raw, the Papagayo Sushi Boat downstairs wraps up sushi rolls and serves sashimi from a real boat. [$] *Average main: $12* ✉ *Main street, across from Coco Beach* ☎ *2670–0298.*

$$ B&B/INN 🏨 **La Puerta del Sol.** Facing a formal garden with sculpted shrubs and a lovely, small pool just two blocks from the beach, this tranquil enclosure of stylish suites has modern, airy, Mediterranean-style guest rooms shot through with hot, tropical colors. **Pros:** intimate; comfortable. **Cons:** a walk to the beach; hard beds; restaurant open during high season only. [$] *Rooms from: $100* ✉ *180 m to right (north) off main road to town* ☎ *2670–0195* 🌐 *www.lapuertadelsolcostarica.com* 🛏 *8 rooms, 1 suite, 1 apartment* 🍽 *Breakfast.*

NIGHTLIFE

Coconutz. Most local expats meet and greet here at this popular sports bar and grill. It's usually packed around happy hour (3 to 7), with its nightly DJ. They also have pool tables, TVs for *Monday Night Football,* a full range of bar food, and live music on Friday and Saturday. Wednesday night is movie night with all-you-can-eat pizza and pasta, and Tuesday features karaoke at 7:30. There's also free Wi-Fi, but don't expect to be able to hear anything on your laptop over the crowds. ✉ *Main road, across from Hotel Coco Beach* ☎ *2670–1982* 🌐 *www.coconutz–costarica.com.*

Lizard Lounge. At this popular lounge there's Mexican food and dancing every night on a big thatch-roofed dance floor. The reggae, techno, and rap beats appeal to a very young crowd. Happy hour is 11 to 7 and there's free Wi-Fi. ✉ *Main road, west of Hotel Coco Beach* ☎ *2670–0307.*

SHOPPING

Souvenir stalls and shops line the main drag near the entrance to the beach.

Galería & Souvenirs Sussy. If you're looking for something in particular and you can't find it at this cluttered emporium, chances are they don't make it in Costa Rica. Along with a huge selection of interesting notebooks and albums made of botanical materials, the place also sells locally made shell belts. ✉ *Main street, next to Hotel Coco* ☎ *2670–0569.*

PLAYA OCOTAL

3 km (2 miles) south of Playas del Coco.

Just a few minutes south of Coco, this beach couldn't be more different than its rapidly developing neighbor. Quiet and serene, there is little commercial development, aside from a couple of beachfront restaurants. A large resort hotel dominates the beach, and private condominium complexes and luxurious villas pile up on the steep hills overlooking the ocean.

GETTING HERE AND AROUND

The drive is 10 minutes from Playas del Coco on a paved road to the gated entrance of Playa Ocotal. The road winds through a heavily populated Tico residential area, so be on the lookout, especially at night, for bicyclists without lights, children, dogs, cows, and horses on the road. There are no buses from Playas del Coco to Ocotal, but it's about $10 by taxi.

BEACHES

Playa Ocotal. One of the most dramatic beaches in the country, this serene crescent of black sand beach ringed by rocky cliffs contrasts nicely with the sparkling, clean turquoise water. It's only ½ km (¼ mile) long, but the views stretch for miles and include nearby offshore islands and the jagged profile of the Santa Elena Peninsula 34 km (21 miles) away. This is prime fishing, diving, and relaxing territory. Right at the entrance to the Gulf of Papagayo, it's a good place for sportfishing enthusiasts to hole up between excursions. There's good diving at Las Corridas, just 1 km (½ mile) away, and excellent snorkeling in nearby coves and islands, as well as right off the beach around the rocks at the east end of the beach. **Amenities:** food and drink. **Best for:** snorkeling. ✉ *10-min drive south of Playas del Coco.*

SPORTS AND THE OUTDOORS

DIVING AND SNORKELING

The rocky outcrop at the north end of the beach near Los Almendros is good for close-to-shore snorkeling.

Ocotal Beach Resort. The dive shop at this beachfront resort is one of the few PADI Instruction Development Centers in Costa Rica, offering the highest-level diving courses and five diving boats. The shop has excellent equipment, safety standards, and instruction. A regular dive costs $85; equipment rental is $26. Dive trips to the Catalina Islands cost $130. The shop also rents snorkeling equipment for $15 per day. Or you can take a snorkeling boat tour for $50, including gear. ✉ *3 km (2 miles) south of Playas del Coco* ☎ *2670–0321* ⊕ *www.ocotaldiving.com.*

FISHING

Ocotal Beach Resort. This resort has a sportfishing operation with three 32-foot Morgan hulls powered by twin 260-horsepower Cummins engines ($750 half day; $935 full day for up to four fishers, $60 each extra person). Marlins are catch-and-release, but you can keep—and eat—the mahimahi, yellowfin tuna, grouper, and amberjack you catch.

WHERE TO EAT AND STAY

$$$ COSTA RICAN 🍴 **Picante.** It's hot and it's tropical, and, as the name warns (*picante* means "spicy"), some of the dishes here make your taste buds tingle. The menu spices up (literally) local fish and tropical fruits in dishes like grilled mahimahi with an orange chipotle. If you can't face a whole red snapper, try the excellent fish tacos made with fresh snapper. There's also a milder kids' menu. The large terrace restaurant, painted a nautical blue and white, is poolside and faces a gorgeous beach, but it is backed by the cookie-cutter condominium development at Bahía Pez Vela. The long road here is worth it for the delicious coconut cream pie and cheesecake. [$] *Average main: $16* ✉ *At the beach, Bahía Pez Vela, 1½ km (1 mile) south of Ocotal* ☎ *2670–0901* 🌐 *www.bahiapezvela.com.*

$$$ B&B/INN 🏨 **Hotel Villa Casa Blanca.** For romance, you can't beat this Victorian-style bed-and-breakfast on a hillside buried in a bower of tropical plantings. **Pros:** romantic; fabulous breakfasts; use of outdoor kitchen. **Cons:** smallish, dark rooms; noisy parrots; no night staff. [$] *Rooms from: $105* ✉ *Inside gated entrance to El Ocotal Beach Resort* ☎ *2670–0448* 🌐 *www.hotelvillacasablanca.com* 🛏 *10 rooms, 3 suites* 🍽 *Breakfast.*

NIGHTLIFE

Father Rooster. The best place to enjoy a quiet sunset margarita—or make that a rooster-rita—is at this laid-back bar and restaurant right on the beach. You can relax on the wooden deck, or at the tables right on the sand, and enjoy a romantic dinner featuring fresh fish and Tex-Mex favorites. Portions here are huge and there's free Wi-Fi, a pool table, and a big-screen TV to keep you entertained. It's open 11 to 10, though it does close for private parties so you may want to call ahead. ✉ *Next door to El Ocotal Beach Resort, 3 km (2 miles) south of Playas del Coco* ☎ *2670–1246* 🌐 *www.fatherrooster.com.*

PLAYA PAN DE AZÚCAR

8 km (5 miles) north of Flamingo Beach.

Playa Pan de Azúcar literally means "Sugar Bread Beach," though most locals call it simply Sugar Beach. With only two built-up properties, the entire stretch of beach feels practically deserted and very private, qualities that can be hard to find in this area. Sweet, indeed.

GETTING HERE AND AROUND

Getting to the beach area of Playa Pan de Azúcar is a snap now that the road is paved. However, you'll need a 4WD vehicle and an excellent sense of direction, if you want to drive (dry season only) the 16-km (11-mile) Monkey Trail, which cuts through the mountains from Sardinal to Flamingo. The first part of the road is graded, but rapidly deteriorates as it travels over river crossings, through jungle, and down rocky

DID YOU KNOW?

Magnificent beaches and a dramatically sculpted shoreline are southern Guanacaste's trademarks. Here you'll find no shortage of wildlife-watching opportunities. Be sure to check out the tide pools that form on the rocky headlands at each end of Playa Ocotal.

terrain. Even some Ticos get lost on this route, so keep asking for directions along the way. The only buses to Playa Pan de Azúcar are from the Santa Cruz terminal, departing five times daily for $4; a taxi from Playa Flamingo costs about $20.

BEACHES

Playa Pan de Azúcar. A seemingly endless stretch of soft, light-color sand, this Blue Flag beach is the idyllic paradise people picture in their tropical dreams. There is only one property on the entire beach, the upscale Hotel Sugar Beach. The north end of the beach has some good snorkeling when the sea is calm—usually around low tide—and the swimming out from the middle of the beach is relatively safe. But if the swell is big, children and weak swimmers shouldn't go in past their waist. Playa Penca, a short walk south along the beach, can be a good swimming beach as well. A large part of the attraction here is the forest that hems the beach, where you may see howler monkeys, black iguanas, magpie jays, trogons, and dozens of other bird species. **Amenities:** none. **Best for:** solitude; swimming.

SPORTS AND THE OUTDOORS

Most of the operators who work out of Flamingo *(⇨ below)* can pick up guests at the Hotel Sugar Beach for skin diving, sportfishing, sailing, horseback riding, and other excursions.

WHERE TO STAY

$$
RESORT
FAMILY
Fodor'sChoice
★

Hotel Sugar Beach. The theme of this secluded, ultracomfortable hotel with a shimmering infinity pool and thin, curving beach is harmony with nature. **Pros:** friendly; yoga classes; natural setting; practically private beach; kids under 12 stay free. **Cons:** waves and rocks can make the ocean dangerous for kids; small pool. $ *Rooms from: $155 ⊠ 8 km (5 miles) north of Playa Flamingo ☎ 2654–4242 ⊕ www.sugar-beach. com ⇨ 14 rooms, 6 suites, 1 house* ⊙ *Breakfast.*

PLAYA POTRERO

4 km (2½ miles) north of Flamingo.

A typical small town with a school, church, and supermarket arranged around a soccer field, Potrero is not very scenic. The main attraction is the long beach on the curve of Flamingo Bay and the smattering of small hotels and restaurants lining the dusty road to town.

GETTING HERE AND AROUND

Just before crossing the bridge at the entrance to Flamingo, take the right fork signed for Playa Potrero. The road, which is alternately muddy or dusty, is rough and follows the shoreline. Local buses run from Flamingo to Potrero, but it's so close that you're better off taking a taxi.

BEACHES

Playa Potrero. Stretching 4 km (2½ miles), this relatively undeveloped wide, brown-sand beach, across Potrero Bay from built-up Flamingo, catches ocean breezes and spectacular sunsets, which you can watch while bobbing in the warm, swimmable water. The pelican-patrolled beach is anchored at one end by the small Tico community of Potrero and at the other end by the Flamingo skyline. Although large houses and condominium developments have sprung up on any hill with a view, at beach level there is only one unimposing hotel and some low-lying private houses set well back from the beach; beachgoers never feel hemmed in or crowded, thanks to the local folks who keep the beach clean and deserving of Blue Flag status. The best area for swimming is midway between Flamingo and Potrero town, near the hotel Bahía del Sol Hotel. The best beach view and best breeze are from a bar stool at Bar Las Brisas. About 10 km (6 miles) offshore lie the Catalina Islands, a barrier-island paradise for divers and snorkelers; dive boats based in Flamingo can get there in 10 minutes. **Amenities:** food and drink. **Best for:** sunset; swimming; walking.

SPORTS AND THE OUTDOORS

DIVING

Catalina Islands. Marked as Santa Catarina on some maps, the Catalina Islands, as they are known locally, are a major destination for dive operations based all along the coast. These barrier islands are remarkable for their diversity, and appeal to different levels of divers. On one side, the islands have 6- to 9-meter (20- to 30-foot) drops, great for beginners. The other side has deeper drops of 18 to 24 meters (60 to 80 feet), better suited to more-experienced divers. The top dive sites around the Catalina Islands are **Dirty Rock**, **Elephant Rock**, and **Cupcake**. From January to March, when the water is colder, you are almost guaranteed manta-ray sightings at these spots. Cow-nosed and devil rays are also spotted here in large schools, as well as bull and white-tipped sharks, several types of eels, and an array of reef fish. Dive operators from Playa Hermosa south to Tamarindo offer trips to these islands. Reserve through your hotel.

6

Costa Rica Diving. This well-established dive shop has been specializing in Catalina Islands dives for more than 18 years, with two-tank, two-location trips limited to four divers (maximum of five for families) and costing $85 per person. The German owners are also the guides and are noted for their precision and high safety standards. They also offer diving courses and run an animal rescue program inside the dive shop. ✉ *1 km (½ mile) south of Flamingo on the main highway, next door to Banco de Costa Rica* ☎ *2654–4148* 🌐 *www.costarica-diving.com.*

WHERE TO EAT

$$ SEAFOOD 🍴 **Bar Las Brisas.** This quintessential beach bar is a shack with a covered deck and a view of the entire sweep of Playa Potrero. The kitchen went more upscale—and got pricier— in 2012, adding fresh seafood adorned with trendy sauces to the menu. But you can't beat the basic fish tacos, which are outstanding. Wednesday is ladies' night, when the joint really jumps and a DJ plays dance music. The place is decorated with old surfboards, rusty U.S. license plates, and wall murals. It's open noon to 9 or 10 daily. [$] *Average main: $12* ✉ *100 m west of soccer field, across from supermarket* ☎ *2654–4047.*

$$ ITALIAN 🍴 **Ristorante Marco Polo.** They came, they saw, they built a whole Tuscan-style village and imported a chef from Italy to cater to a demanding Italian clientele. Marco Polo, the main restaurant at the Villagio Flor de Pacífico mega-development of red-roof villas east of Potrero, serves properly *al dente* pasta with homemade sauces and a dozen different

wood-oven pizzas. Crusts are thin and crispy and salads are organic and fresh. They also serve more substantial dishes such as grilled tuna, chicken cordon bleu, and tenderloin with a béarnaise sauce. Save room for the panna cotta, of course. $ *Average main: $12* ⊠ *1 km (½ mile) east of Potrero, at Playa Potrero Villagio Flor* ☎ *2654–4905, 8479–6434* ⊘ *Closed Mon. No lunch in low season.*

$$ ✕ **The Shack.** New York expat and owner Harry Baker has somehow
AMERICAN managed to successfully create a menu that blends American favorites with Costa Rican cuisine. Grab a seat under the tin roof and try the fresh fish-and-chips, lobster rolls, seafood soup, hamburgers, or the famous hot dogs (Harry swears they are imported). The breakfast burritos are a good way to start the day. Thursdays draw a crowd with open-mike night. The Shack gimlet with cucumber and basil packs a powerful punch, which can be temptingly dangerous during happy hour from 4 to 6. $ *Average main: $10* ⊠ *200 m west of El Castillo* ☎ *2654–6038* ⊘ *Closed Mon. Closes at 2 pm on Sun.*

WHERE TO STAY

$$$ ⊡ **Bahía del Sol.** Snagging the best spot on the beach, Bahía del Sol has a
RESORT gorgeous, beachfront pool and comfortable rooms built around a mini–
FAMILY rain forest of tropical shrubs and towering trees. **Pros:** on the beach;
Fodor'sChoice lovely grounds; excellent restaurant; friendly, first-rate service. **Cons:**
★ front terraces are not very private. $ *Rooms from: $180* ⊠ *South end of Potrero Beach* ☎ *2654–4671* ⊕ *www.bahiadelsolhotel.com* ⤴ *10 standard rooms, 3 deluxe rooms, 4 one-bedroom suites, 10 two-bedroom suites, 1 beachfront suite* ⦿ *Breakfast.*

$ ⊡ **Hotel Isolina.** This small hotel complex, a little island (*isolina*) of palm
B&B/INN trees shading two pools, is the best and most attractive of the area's affordable lodgings. **Pros:** beautiful garden; affordable; secure parking; clean rooms. **Cons:** beach is a two-minute walk away; breakfast not included for rooms with kitchenettes. $ *Rooms from: $96* ⊠ *100 m north of Restaurant La Perla, on beach road* ☎ *2654–4333* ⊕ *www. isolinabeach.com* ⤴ *9 rooms, 22 equipped rooms, 3 two-bedroom villas* ⦿ *Breakfast.*

PLAYA FLAMINGO

80 km (50 miles) southwest of Liberia.

One of the first northern beaches to experience the wonders of over-development—a fact immortalized in the concrete towers that straggle up the hill above the bay—Flamingo still has some hidden charms. It's perhaps most famous for its large sportfishing fleet, though they've been moored out in the bay for more than eight years now waiting for the government to grant a new concession to update and operate the marina here. Working girls are lured to Flamingo by the boatloads of single-for-the-week fishermen. This adds a faintly salacious whiff to some local nightspots. In recent years, the area has become increasingly popular with the gay and lesbian community, especially at inviting properties like Flamingo Beach Resort.

GETTING HERE AND AROUND

To get to Playa Flamingo from Liberia, drive 45 km (28 miles) south to Belén and then 35 km (22 miles) west on a good, paved road. The trip takes about three hours. If you're coming from the Playas del Coco and Ocotal area, you can take a 16-km (10-mile) shortcut, called the Monkey Trail, starting near Sardinal and emerging at Potrero. It's then 4 km (2½ miles) south to Flamingo. Attempt this only in dry season and in a 4WD. You can also take a bus from Liberia *(⇨ Bus Travel in Travel Smart Costa Rica).*

ESSENTIALS

Bank/ATM Banco de Costa Rica ⊠ *Main road leading to Playa Flamingo, at the intersection of the road to Playa Potrero* ☎ *2654–4984.*

Pharmacy Farmacia Playa Flamingo ⊠ *Plaza beside Marie's Restaurant at entrance to town* ☎ *2654–5524* ⊙ *Mon. –Sat. 9–6:30, Sun. 9–5.*

BEACHES

Playa Flamingo. Hidden away to the southwest of the town, Flamingo Beach is picture-perfect, with almost-white sand sloping into a relatively calm sea, and buttonwood trees separating it from the road. This Blue Flag beach is great for swimming, with a fine-sand bottom and no strong currents, though there are a few submerged rocks in front of the Flamingo Beach Resort, so you should swim a bit farther south. There's sometimes a bit of surf, so if the waves are big, keep your eye on little paddlers. There is little shade along the beach's 1-km-long (½-mile-long) stretch, and no services, though there are restaurants in the beach resort and the adjacent town. To find the beach, go straight as you enter town, and instead of going up the hill, turn left after the Flamingo Beach Resort. **Amenities:** food and drink. **Best for:** swimming; walking. ⊠ *Southwest of town, in front of Flamingo Beach Resort.*

SPORTS AND THE OUTDOORS

BOATING

Lazy Lizard Catamaran Sailing Adventures. Laze away a morning or afternoon sailing or sunbathing on either a 34-foot or 38-foot catamaran. Or jump in the water for a swim or snorkel. The four-hour tours start at 8:30 am (minimum of eight people) and 2 pm and cost $85, with snorkeling equipment, kayaks, drinks, and food included. ⊠ *Flamingo Marina* ☎ *2654–5900* ⊕ *www.lazylizardsailing.com.*

DIVING AND SNORKELING

Aquacenter Diving. Based in the Flamingo Marina Resort, this dive shop runs two-tank dives at the Catalina Islands ($95, including gear rental) and snorkeling trips ($55, including equipment), as well as offering a full range of PADI certification courses. ⊠ *In Flamingo Marina Resort* ☎ *2654–4141* ⊕ *www.aquacenterdiving.com.*

Catalina Islands. Flamingo offers the quickest access to the Catalina Islands, visible from its beach, where big schools of fish, manta rays, and other sea creatures gather. Coastal reefs to the north are visited on day trips that combine snorkeling with time on undeveloped beaches.

Costa Rica Diving *(⇨ See Playa Potrero, above).*

The reclusive zebra moray eel likes to hide its entire body in rock or coral holes.

FISHING

Although the marina is still closed while officials consider bids to rebuild it, there are plenty of sportfishing boats bobbing in Flamingo Bay. Larger boats have moved to moorings in the new Papagayo Marina near the Four Seasons Hotel. In December the wind picks up and many of the smaller, 31-foot-and-under boats head to calmer water farther south. But the wind brings cold water and abundant baitfish, which attract marlin (blue, black, and striped), Pacific sailfish, yellowfin tuna, wahoo, mahimahi, grouper, and red snapper. January to April is consequently prime catch-and-release season for billfish.

WHERE TO EAT

$$
× Angelina's. Named for the owner's grandmother, this Italian restaurant is one of the area's more upscale places to dine, with marble tables, parchment lamps, and driftwood-integrated decor under an open-air patio. Homemade pizzas, like the thin-crust Playa Blanca with wild mushrooms and truffle-scented béchamel, are the draw for most diners. Fresh-from-the-sea dishes include mahimahi with mango salsa or lobster tail served with homemade pasta. A side order of fried brussels sprouts will convert anyone who has avoided this vegetable since childhood. It's worth saving room for the pineapple rum cake and vanilla gelato. $ *Average main: $15* ✉ *2nd floor of Plaza Commercial, Flamingo* ☎ *2654–4839* ⊕ *www.angelinasplayaflamingo.com* ⊗ *Closed Sun.*

ITALIAN

$$
SEAFOOD **× Marie's Restaurant.** A Flamingo institution serving beachgoers and locals for more than three decades, this popular restaurant serves an array of sandwiches and salads, as well as reliably fresh seafood in large portions at reasonable prices. Settle in at one of the wooden tables

beneath the ceiling fans and massive thatched roof for a traditional Costa Rican ceviche, avocado stuffed with shrimp, or heart of palm and *pejivalle* (palm fruit). The main fare includes whole fried red snapper, shrimp and fish kebabs, and a delicious *plato de mariscos* (shrimp, lobster, and fish served with garlic butter, potatoes, and salad). For a lighter meal, you can't beat the scrumptious fish tacos. Save room for Marie's signature banana-chocolate bread pudding. At breakfast, try the unusual papaya pancakes, French toast made with cream cheese and jam, or eggs Benedict. There's free Wi-Fi for customers. [$] *Average main: $15* ✉ *Main road in the new plaza commercial center, near north end of beach* ☎ *2654–4136* 🌐 *www.mariesrestaurantcostarica.com.*

WHERE TO STAY

$$$ RESORT FAMILY 🏨 **Flamingo Beach Resort.** This three-story, modern hotel has a prime location overlooking beautiful Flamingo Beach, along with a huge swimming pool and every water sport that kids of any age could want. **Pros:** beachfront; big pool; excellent value; all-inclusive meal plans available; free Wi-Fi. **Cons:** noisy with kids during vacation times; more than 100 rooms. [$] *Rooms from: $129* ✉ *Hotel entrance on left past Marie's Restaurant* ☎ *2654–4444, 2283–8063 in San José, 877/856–5519 toll-free in U.S.* 🌐 *www.resortflamingobeach.com* 🛏 *112 rooms, 8 suites* 🍴 *Multiple meal plans.*

$ B&B/INN 🏨 **Hotel Guanacaste Lodge.** On the outskirts of Flamingo, a short drive from the beach, this Tico-run lodge offers basic accommodations for a fraction of what the town's big hotels charge. **Pros:** affordable; friendly; nice pool; large rooms. **Cons:** unattractive from the outside; no in-room phones or safes; simple furnishings. [$] *Rooms from: $60* ✉ *200 m south of the Potrero-Flamingo crossroads* ☎ *2654–4494* 🌐 *www.guanacastelodge.com* 🛏 *10 rooms* 💳 *No credit cards* 🍴 *Breakfast.*

NIGHTLIFE

Mariner Inn Bar. This often boisterous bar, thick with testosterone, is the place to be if you enjoy socializing with fishermen trading fish tales. ✉ *Bottom of hill, entering Flamingo* ☎ *2654–4081* 🌐 *www.marinerinn.com.*

BRASILITO AND PLAYA CONCHAL

8 km (5 miles) south of Flamingo.

A small, scruffy fishing village just 1 km (½ mile) north of Playa Conchal, Brasilito has a jumble of houses huddled around its main square, which doubles as the soccer field. It's cluttered, noisy, and totally Tico—a lively contrast to the controlled sophistication of the gated Playa Conchal resort and residential development less than a mile south. Fishing boats moor just off a wide beach, and there's a range of seafood restaurants, from inexpensive *marisquerías* to one notable (but pricey) establishment.

GETTING HERE AND AROUND

The drive south to Brasilito from Flamingo is 10 minutes on a paved highway. Brasilito is just 1 km (½ mile) north of the entrance to the massive Westin Golf Resort & Spa and private Reserva Conchal housing development, which blocks the main road access to Playa Conchal. To reach Playa Conchal without driving through the guard-posted resort, turn left at the end of the town square in Brasilito and follow the dirt road across a stretch of beach and over a steep hill; the beach stretch is impassable at high tide. Buses run from Flamingo to

Brasilito three times daily, at 7:30 and 11:30 am and 2:30 pm. A taxi from Flamingo is about $10.

ESSENTIALS

The closest bank and ATM are in Flamingo.

Hospital Costa de Emergencias. Ambulance and emergency medical services. ⊠ *300 m northwest of crossroads at Huacas* ☎ *2653–6440.*

Pharmacy Farmacia El Cruce ⊠ *Crossroads at Huacas* ☎ *2653–8787* ⊘ *Mon.– Sat. 8–8, Sun. 8–5.*

BEACHES

Playa Brasilito. Fishing boats moor just off this wide beach, about 3 km (2 miles) long and its golden sand flecked with pebbles and a few rocks. The surf is a little stronger here than at Flamingo Beach, but the shallow, sandy bottom keeps it swimmable. There is one hotel almost on the beach, the vintage Hotel Brasilito. The sea is cleaner off nearby Playa Conchal, which is also more attractive. **Amenities:** food and drink. **Best for:** snorkeling; walking.

Playa Conchal. Lovely, secluded Playa Conchal is an idyllic strand of sugary sand sloping steeply into aquamarine water and lined with trees. As its Blue Flag attests, it's clean and invites safe swimming. Although it's dominated by the sprawling Westin Playa Conchal resort, you don't need to stay at that all-inclusive resort to enjoy Conchal, since it's a short beach walk south from Brasilito. Named for the bits of broken shells that cover its base of fine white sand (the Spanish word for shell is *concha*), the southern part of the beach is often deserted. The point that defines Conchal's northern end is hemmed by a lava-rock reef that is a popular snorkeling area—locals rent equipment on the beach. ■ TIP➜ **Despite the availability of shell jewelry, remember that shell-collecting is not officially permitted on Costa Rican beaches. Amenities:** food and drink. **Best for:** snorkeling; swimming; walking.

SPORTS AND THE OUTDOORS
GOLF

Reserva Conchal Golf Course. One of the best golf courses in the country, this 18-hole, par-71 course designed by Robert Trent Jones Jr. is perfectly maintained and reserved for guests of the Westin Golf Resort & Spa, who can try out their swing on 18 holes for $150, cart included; renting clubs costs an extra $40. ⊠ *The Westin Resort & Spa, Playa Conchal, entrance, less than 1 km (½ mile) south of Brasilito* ☎ *2654–3500.*

WHERE TO EAT AND STAY

$ ✕ **Il Forno.** For a break from seafood, try lunch or dinner at this roman-
ITALIAN   tic Italian garden restaurant. There are 17 versions of thin-crust pizzas,
plus fine homemade pastas and risotto. Vegetarians have lots of choices
(if you can get past the thought that veal is on the menu), including
an eggplant lasagna and interesting salads. They also serve some tasty
seafood and meat dishes. At dinner, candles glimmer all through the
garden and on tables grouped under thatched roofs. Spanish and Italian wines are available by the glass or bottle. It's open Tuesday through
Sunday, noon to 9:30 pm. $ *Average main: $10* ⊠ *Main road, 200 m
east of the bridge in Brasilito* ☎ *2654–4125* ▬ *No credit cards* ⊘ *Closed
Mon. and Oct.*

$$ ✕ **Papaya.** Grab a hammock in the tree house lounge and sway away
ECLECTIC   your cares while the kitchen cooks up fresh seafood delivered daily by
local fisherman. If you plan on tasting coconut shrimp on your vaca-
tion, this is where you want to do it. Follow it up with a main dish like
sesame-crusted tuna or Thai curry. Vegetarians will finally get their
chance to gloat thanks to dishes like veggie BLTs with soy bacon and
falafel burritos. There are also delicious salads with shredded papaya
and tangy dressings, as well as local *casados* to remind you that you're
in Costa Rica. The breakfast specials are a bargain. $ *Average main:
$15* ⊠ *At Conchal Hotel, 50 m south of the bridge near the soccer field.,
Brasilito* ☎ *2654–9125* ⊕ *www.conchalcr.com* ⊘ *Closed Wed.*

$ ⌂ **Hotel Brasilito.** Backpackers and travelers who don't need amenities
B&B/INN   will love this vintage, two-story, wooden hotel's affordable price and
seafront location, if not its no-frills but adequate rooms. **Pros:** inexpen-
sive; across the street from beach; knowledgeable manager. **Cons:** boxy
rooms without TVs or phones; can be noisy; Wi-Fi in common areas
only. $ *Rooms from: $44* ⊠ *Between soccer field and beach, Brasilito*
☎ *2654–4237* ⊕ *www.brasilito.com* ⇋ *18 rooms* ⦿⊣ *No meals.*

$$$$ ⌂ **The Westin Golf Resort & Spa, Playa Conchal.** So vast that guests ride
ALL-INCLUSIVE   around in the back of biodiesel trucks and the staff gets around on
FAMILY   golf carts, this all-inclusive resort has been taken over by the Star-
wood hotel group and upgraded, redecorated, and rebranded as an
all-inclusive Westin resort. **Pros:** saltwater pools; Starwood's only all-
inclusive Westin; beach access; abundant activities. **Cons:** massive;
only three rooms have ocean views; easy to get lost; must wear plastic
AI bracelet. $ *Rooms from: $400* ⊠ *Entrance less than 1 km (½ mile)
south of Brasilito* ☎ *2654–3500* ⊕ *www.starwoodhotels.com/westin*
⇋ *282 junior suites, 84 Royal Beach rooms, 38 Royal Beach suites*
⦿⊣ *All-inclusive.*

**EN
ROUTE**   Gas stations are few and far between in these hinterlands. If you're
heading down to Tamarindo from the Flamingo/Conchal area, fill up
first. Your best bet is the 24-hour Oasis Exxon, 3 km (2 miles) east of
Huacas.

6

PLAYA GRANDE

21 km (13 miles) north of Tamarindo.

Down the (long, paved) road from Tamarindo, but only five minutes by boat across a tidal estuary, lies beautiful, pristine Playa Grande, by day one of the best surfing beaches in the country, and by night a nesting beach for the giant leatherback sea turtle. The beach has thus far escaped the overdevelopment of nearby Tamarindo, and is consequently lined with thick vegetation instead of hotels and strip malls. But Playa Grande isn't immune to development; developers have sold hundreds of lots, and there are at least 75 finished houses. The ongoing battle to protect the beach continues. The good thing is that the homes are 200 meters from the beach, thanks to a legislated buffer zone and a decree that no lights can be visible from the beach, to avoid disturbing the turtles. A few hotels and restaurants make this a pleasant, tranquil alternative to Tamarindo. And if you want to go shopping or barhopping, Tamarindo is only a boat ride away. ■ TIP➜ Recent trip reports suggest that crime in the Playa Grande area has increased of late. Take reasonable precautions, choose a hotel with room safes, bring very few valuables, and stay alert.

GETTING HERE AND AROUND

The road from Tamarindo is paved for the duration of the 30-minute drive. The gated community of Palm Beach Estates, where most hotels are, is about 2 km (1 mile) south of the main Playa Grande entrance on a potholed dirt road. Alternatively, you can take a small boat across the Tamarindo Estuary for about $3 per person and walk 30 minutes along the beach to the main surf break. A lesser known break is just a 10-minute walk; boats travel between the guide kiosk at the north end of Tamarindo and either Villa Baulas or Hotel Bula Bula in Playa Grande.

EXPLORING

TURTLE-WATCHING

Nesting giant leatherback turtles. Playa Grande used to host the world's largest visitation of nesting giant leatherback turtles, but the number of turtles has fallen drastically in the past 20 years, from a high of 1,504 in 1989 to less than 50 currently. This loss is due to longline commercial fishing boats that trap turtles in their nets, causing the turtles to drown; along with poaching of turtle eggs and loss of habitat. The beach is still strictly off-limits from 6 pm to 6 am from October 20 to February 15, during the peak nesting season. You can visit only as part of a guided tour, waiting your turn at the park entrance, beside Hotel Las Tortugas, until, if you are extremely lucky, spotters find a nesting turtle. At their signal, you'll walk down the beach as silently as you can, where in the darkness you'll witness the remarkable sight of a 500-pound creature digging a hole in the sand large enough to deposit up to 100 golf ball–size eggs. About 60 days later, the sight of hundreds of hatchlings scrambling toward open water in the early morning is equally impressive. Turtle-watching takes place around high tide, which can be shortly after sunset, or in the early morning. Plan on spending one to four hours at the ranger

Costa Rica's shores are visited by the green turtle, the olive ridley (above), the hawksbill, the loggerhead, and the leatherback turtle.

station waiting for a turtle to come up, during which you can watch a video on the turtles in English (the guides speak mostly Spanish). ⊠ *Playa Grande, 100 m east of main beach entrance* ☎ *2653–0470* ✉ *$25, includes guided tour* ☉ *Oct. 20–Feb. 15 by reservation made between 8 am and 5 pm.*

BEACHES

Playa Grande. In addition to being a paradise for surfers and sunbathers, the narrow woodsy patch that lines this wide, pristine Blue Flag beach holds howler monkeys and an array of birds, and the mangrove estuary on the north end of the beach has crocodiles. Be aware that the surf is a little heavy for safe swimming and there's an abundance of mosquitoes during the rainy months, especially near the estuary, so bring plenty of repellent. The beach's shores and waters are protected within Las Baulas Marine National Park. Admission is free during daylight hours but off-limits at night during the turtle-nesting season (October 20 to February 20), when tourists come on guided turtle tours, hoping to catch the increasingly rare sight of a leatherback turtle building a nest and depositing eggs. The beach's protected status is in part because a surfer who arrived here more than 30 years ago was so upset by the widespread turtle-egg poaching that he adopted a conservationist's agenda. Louis Wilson, owner of Las Tortugas Hotel, spearheaded a campaign to protect the nesting *baulas* (leatherback turtles) that eventually resulted in the creation of Las Baulas Marine National Park. **Amenities:** food and drink. **Best for:** surfing; walking.

SPORTS AND THE OUTDOORS

■TIP→ **Unless you are a strong swimmer attached to a surfboard, don't go in any deeper than your waist here.** There is calmer water for snorkeling about a 30-minute walk north of Las Tortugas, at a black-sand beach called Playa Carbón.

TOUR OPERATORS

All the area hotels can arrange boat tours of the estuary, where you may see crocodiles, monkeys, herons, kingfishers, and an array of other birdlife; go either early in the morning or late in the afternoon, and bring insect repellent.

Hotel Las Tortugas. This turtle-themed hotel right on the turtle-nesting beach has a full menu of nature tours, including guided nature walks, and canoeing with a bilingual nature guide on the estuary; they can also tell you how to get to Playa Carbón, the nearest snorkeling spot. ⊠ *Las Baulas Marine National Park* ☎ *2653–0423* ⊕ *www.lastortugashotel.com.*

Estuary Tours. Two-hour canoe tours of the nearby Tamarindo Estuary ($25) set off at 8 am and 3 pm, with local naturalist guide Jonathan. Kids can join the tour for half price. Hotel Las Tortugas can arrange the tour for you. ☎ *8534–8664.*

SURFING

Playa Grande is renowned for having one of the most consistent surf breaks in the country. Only experienced surfers should attempt riding this beach break, which often features big barrels and offshore winds. The waves are best at high tide, especially around a full moon.

Hotel Bula Bula. You can rent both long- and shortboards for $15 to $25 a day at this surfer-friendly hotel. ⊠ *Palm Beach Estates, 2 km (1 mile) east of Playa Grande* ☎ *2653–0975* ⊕ *www.hotelbulabula.com.*

Hotel Las Tortugas. Hotel Las Tortugas (⇨ *above*) rents boards for $20 to $25 a day and offers surfing lessons at their beachfront Caribbean-style snack bar.

YOGA

Yoga at Rip Jack Inn. Rip Jack Inn has its own yoga shala where classes are held Monday through Friday at 8:30. The cost is $12 and yoga mats are provided. ⊠ *100 m south of Hotel Las Tortugas, at Rip Jack Inn* ☎ *2653–0480* ⊕ *www.ripjackinn.com.*

WHERE TO EAT

$$$ ✕ **Upstairs@the Ripjack.** A block from the beach, this casual place usu-
SEAFOOD   ally has an ocean breeze to complement the ceiling fans, which are best enjoyed from the hammock in the corner. There are rooms for rent and a yoga school downstairs, but most people come to eat, or party at the extensive bar, which occupies about a third of the restaurant. Portions are large so pace yourself, especially if you order the popular flank steak served on homemade pasta. On the seafood side, you can count on ceviche, calamari, and fish fillets spiced, Asian-style, with wasabi and ginger. The quinoa risotto is unbelievably moist thanks to the secret ingredient (shhh . . . it's cream). Prices are on the high side, and service is patchy, especially in low season. The lunch menu tends to be small and overpriced. There's free Wi-Fi and Sunday brunch in

high season. $ *Average main: $18 ⊠ 100 m south of park headquarters* ☎ *2653–0480* ⊕ *www.ripjackinn.com.*

WHERE TO STAY

$$
B&B/INN
🖭 **Hotel Bula Bula.** At the eastern edge of the estuary in the Palm Beach Estates gated community, Bula Bula has its own landing for ferrying guests and restaurant patrons the 1 km (½ mile) to and from Tamarindo. **Pros:** friendly; good food; lots of amenities. **Cons:** rooms small for price; 10-minute walk from beach; restaurant is pricey. $ *Rooms from: $120 ⊠ Palm Beach Estates, 3 km (2 miles) east of Playa Grande* ☎ *2653–0975, 877/658–2880 in U.S.* ⊕ *www.hotelbulabula.com* ⤳ *10 rooms* ⦿ *Breakfast.*

$$
B&B/INN
🖭 **Hotel Las Tortugas.** With a prime location on the beach, steps away from Playa Grande's famous surf break, this place is perfect for surfers, nature lovers, and sun worshippers. **Pros:** on the beach; friendly owners; good value. **Cons:** busy location; spotty service at times. $ *Rooms from: $90 ⊠ Entrance to Las Baulas Marine National Park, 33 km (20 miles) north of Tamarindo* ☎ *2653–0423* ⊕ *www.lastortugashotel.com* ⤳ *11 rooms, 1 suite, 8 dorms, 17 apartments* ⦿ *No meals.*

TAMARINDO

82 km (51 miles) southwest of Liberia.

Once a funky beach town full of spacey surfers and local fishermen, Tamarindo is now a pricey, hyped-up hive of commercial development and real estate speculation, happily accompanied by a dizzying variety of shops, bars, and hotels, and probably the best selection of restaurants of any beach town on the Pacific coast. There's a tiny shopping center at the entrance to town with an upscale AutoMercado supermarket and a Scotiabank branch and ATM. On the downside, still-unpaved roads off the main drag kick up dust and mud alternately, depending on the season. Strip malls and high-rise condominiums clutter the rest of the main street and obscure views of the still-magnificent beach.

Tamarindo serves as a popular base for surfing at the nearby Playas Grande, Langosta, Avellanas, and Negra. There are plenty of outdoor options in addition to surfing, among them diving, sportfishing, wildlife watching, and canopy tours. You can also play 18 rounds at the nearby Hacienda Pinilla golf course, or simply stroll the beach and sunbathe. Some low-life elements are making security an issue, but upscale hotels and inns have their own security and gated parking. Once you're on the beach, almost all the negatives disappear (just keep your eyes on your belongings).

GETTING HERE AND AROUND

Both Nature Air and SANSA fly to Tamarindo from San José. By car from Liberia, travel south on the highway to the turnoff for Belén, then head west and turn left at the Huacas crossroads to Tamarindo. Stretches of the paved road from Belén are sometimes in deplorable states of disrepair. There are no direct bus connections between Playa Grande or Playa Avellanas and Tamarindo. A taxi or a shuttle van is the way to go from nearby towns if you don't have wheels.

6

Tamarindo Shuttle. The Tamarindo Shuttle ferries passengers between the various beaches in a comfortable van and will also pick you up at the Liberia airport, $20 per person, minimum of two; evening flights require a minimum of three passengers. ☎ *2653–4444, 2653–2626* ⊕ *www.tamarindoshuttle.com.*

ESSENTIALS

Bank/ATM Banco Nacional ⊠ *Across from Tamarindo El Diriá Hotel* ☎ *2653–0366.*

Medical Assistance Farmacia Tamarindo. Doctors are on call at this pharmacy. ⊠ *Main road into town, diagonally across from Best Western Tamarindo Villas* ☎ *2653–0210.*

Post Office Correo ⊠ *Across from airport on main road into town.*

Rental Cars Alamo ⊠ *Diagonal to Hotel El Diriá main road* ☎ *2653–0727.* **Budget** ⊠ *Hotel Zullymar, main road* ☎ *2653–0756.* **Economy** ⊠ *Main road entering Tamarindo, across from Witch's Rock Surf Camp* ☎ *2653–0728.* **Hertz** ⊠ *100 m East of Hotel Pasatiempo, Tamarindo* ☎ *2653–1358.*

Taxis A taxi from the airport to the center of Tamarindo costs about $12 for two people with luggage.

BEACHES

Playa Tamarindo. Wide and flat, the sand here is packed hard enough for easy walking and jogging, but swimming and surfing has become questionable since the town lost its Blue Flag clean-beach status (because of overdevelopment and the total absence of water treatment). The water quality is especially poor during the rainy months, when you'll want to do your swimming and surfing at nearby Playa Langosta or Playa Grande. Despite this, surfing is still the main attraction here, and there's a young crowd that parties hard after a day riding the waves. Witch's Rock Surf Shop has showers, toilets, surfboard rental, a swimming pool, and a restaurant where you can watch the surfers over a cold beer. Strong currents at the north end of the beach get a lot of swimmers into trouble, especially when they try to cross the estuary without a surfboard. **Amenities:** food and drink; showers; toilets. **Best for:** partiers; surfing; walking.

SPORTS AND THE OUTDOORS

BOATING

Rocky Isla El Capitán, just offshore, is a close-in kayaking destination, full of sand-dollar shells. Exploring the tidal estuaries north and south of town is best done in a kayak at high tide, when you can travel farther up the temporary rivers. Arrange kayaking trips through your hotel.

Blue Dolphin. Set sail on a 40-foot catamaran for an afternoon of sunning, snorkeling, and kayaking aboard the *Blue Dolphin.* The boat departs at 1 pm from the beach, in front of El Pescador Restaurant, and returns around sunset. It's $85 ($42 for kids under 12) per person, including appetizers and open bar. During high season there's also a morning tour, from 8 am to noon, $70 (half price for kids under 12) including snorkel gear and fishing poles. ☎ *8842–3204* ⊕ *www.bluedolphinsailing.com.*

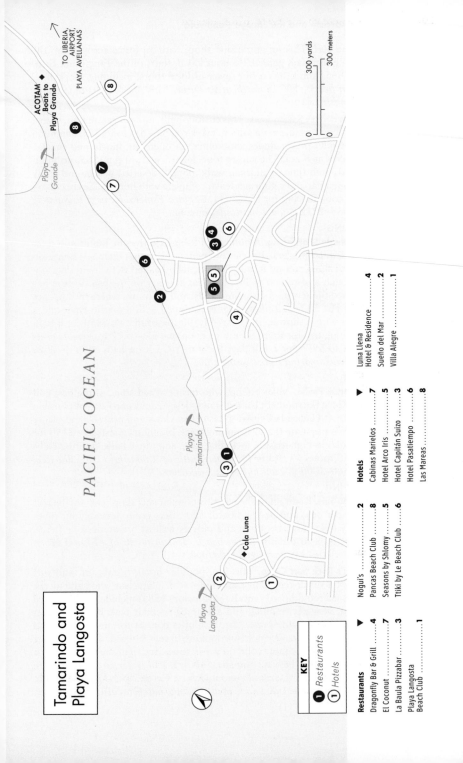

Tamarindo and Playa Langosta

PACIFIC OCEAN

Playa Langosta

Playa Tamarindo

Playa Grande

◆ Cala Luna

TO LIBERIA, AIRPORT, PLAYA AVELLANAS

ACOTAM ◆ Boats to Playa Grande

0 — 300 yards

0 — 300 meters

KEY

▶ Restaurants

① Hotels

Restaurants ▶

Dragonfly Bar & Grill **4**
El Coconut **7**
La Baula Pizzabar **3**
Playa Langosta
Beach Club **1**

Nogui's **2**
Pancas Beach Club **8**
Seasons by Shlomy **5**
Ttiki by Le Beach Club **6**

Hotels ▶

Cabinas Marielos **7**
Hotel Arco Iris **5**
Hotel Capitán Suizo **3**
Hotel Pasatiempo **6**
Las Mareas **8**

Luna Llena
Hotel & Residence **4**
Sueño del Mar **2**
Villa Alegre **1**

Iguana Surf. This longtime surf shop, with an office across from the beach, organizes guided 2½-hour kayak tours of the Tamarindo Estuary ($35) and offers a full roster of local tours, including snorkeling. ✉ *On beach, 100 m north of El Diriá Hotel* ☎ 2653–0148 ⊕ *www. iguanasurf.net.*

Marlin del Rey Sailing Tours. This custom-built, 66-foot catamaran, with a large, comfortable main saloon, takes you on a day tour ($75, minimum 15 people) that includes snorkeling, an open bar, lunch, and snacks. It leaves at 8 am. The sunset tour departs at 1:30 pm ($85, no minimum), with time to snorkel, walk along a deserted beach, and enjoy the open bar and a gourmet feast, complete with homemade chocolate-chip cookies. $60 for kids 5–11. ✉ *Plaza Esmeralda, next to Subway* ☎ 2653–1212 ⊕ *www.marlindelrey.com.*

FISHING

Tamarindo Sportfishing. A number of fishing charters in Tamarindo cater to saltwater anglers. The most experienced among them is Tamarindo Sportfishing, run by Randy Wilson, who has led the way in developing catch-and-release techniques that are easy on the fish. Wilson has roamed these waters since the 1970s, and he knows where the big ones lurk. His 38-foot *Talking Fish* is equipped with a marlin chair and a cabin with a shower, and costs $1,500 for a full day, $850 for a half. A fishing trip for up to four anglers on one of two 27-foot boats costs $825 to $975 for a full day; $550 to $675 for a half. ☎ 2653–0090 ⊕ *www.tamarindosportfishing.com.*

GOLF

Hacienda Pinilla. Mike Young, who has designed some of the best golf courses in the southern United States, designed the par-72 championship course at Hacienda Pinilla. It has ocean views and breezes, and plenty of birds populate the surrounding trees. Nonhotel guests pay $150 for 18 holes in high season, including carts and range balls. Renting clubs is $50 more. ✉ *10 km (6 miles) south of Tamarindo via Villa Real* ☎ 2680–3000 ⊕ *www.haciendapinilla.com.*

SURFING

FAMILY **Iguana Surf.** Right on the beach, this popular surf shop rents surfboards ($20 per day) and boogie boards and offers group lessons four times a day ($45, for ages three and up), as well as private lessons ($80). It's open 8 to 6 daily. ✉ *On beach, 100 m north of El Diriá Hotel* ☎ 2653–0613 ⊕ *www.iguanasurf.net.*

Witch's Rock Surf Camp. This hip, popular hotel, restaurant, and surf school is surfer central in Tamarindo, with a large surf shop and all the latest gear and board rentals. Surf lessons ($85) include all-day board rental, in-water training, and a shaping seminar with Robert August of *Endless Summer* fame. They also offer courses for intermediate and advanced surfers. If you're just looking to rent a board, this is the place as they have the most solid quiver in town. It's right on the beach just steps from the best surf breaks. ✉ *North end of beach, main road in Tamarindo, across from Economy Rent a Car* ☎ 2653–1262, 888/318–7873 *toll-free in U.S. and Canada* ⊕ *www.witchsrocksurfcamp.com.*

WILDLIFE TOURS

ACOTAM. ACOTAM, a local conservation association, conducts turtle-viewing tours in Las Baulas National Marine Park with local guides for $35, including park entrance fee. The group picks you up at your hotel and briefs you at their headquarters on the estuary that separates Tamarindo and Playa Grande. An open boat then takes you across the estuary, where you wait at the park station until a turtle has been spotted. With so few leatherback turtles nesting, you are more likely to see green sea turtles instead. The turtle-nesting season runs from mid-October to mid-February. They also offer covered-boat, mangrove tours along the Tamarindo River year-round for $25 per person (minimum two). ☎ *2653–1687* ✉ *guiaslocalestama@gmail.com.*

WHERE TO EAT

$$ ECLECTIC 🍴 **Dragonfly Bar & Grill.** The minimalist natural ambience here—tree-trunk columns support a tentlike roof—is enlivened by fuchsia and lime table linens, sculptural hanging lamps, and a cool sound track. This trendy restaurant has been a perennial favorite for years. Expect a limited but enticing menu of innovative dishes like mahimahi fish cakes with citrus aioli or chilled avocado cucumber soup. Thick-cut apple pork loin is served over rosemary-infused white beans, and the homemade ravioli is stuffed with ricotta and spinach. Taxes and service are not included on the menu, and credit cards are not accepted. It's open from 6 pm, Monday to Saturday. [$] *Average main: $14* ✉ *100 m past turnoff for Langosta Beach road, then left 50 m* ☎ *2653–1506* 🌐 *www.dragonflybarandgrill.com* 💳 *No credit cards* 🕒 *Closed Sun. and Oct. No lunch.*

$$$ SEAFOOD 🍴 **El Coconut.** The red, black, and dark-wood interior of this high-gloss restaurant with giant pre-Columbian stone sculptures and a coconut tree growing through the roof feels like a lacquered Japanese *bento* box. Seafood is the main event, with the catch of the day—usually mahimahi—served half a dozen ways, but they also serve tenderloin, with a choice of sauces, and the classic surf and turf. The innovative jumbo shrimp or lobster in a pineapple-raisin-and-ginger sauce is delicious, and the list of sauces for the fish includes the traditional Norwegian *sandefjords smor* (a creamy butter sauce with lime)—the owner, Katharina, is from Norway. Service is smooth and more formal than at most beach restaurants, and they have a good wine list. Watch for the occasional $25 lobster special. There's live music some Friday nights. [$] *Average main: $20* ✉ *Main street, 150 m south of Tamarindo Vista Villas* ☎ *2653–0086* 🌐 *www.elcoconut-tamarindo.com* 🕒 *Closed Mon. No lunch.*

$$ PIZZA FAMILY 🍴 **La Baula Pizzabar.** Wildly popular, this casually chic, alfresco pizzeria on a quiet side street has plenty of cars parked outside most nights, particularly Sunday when all the Tamarindo locals seem to meet and greet here. Families are especially fond of La Baula—the Costa Rican name for the leatherback turtle—because of its reasonable prices, noisy buzz, and adjacent playground and picniclike dining area, which keeps expanding to accommodate the crowds. There's also a softly lighted dining area for more-romantic dinners. Everyone enjoys the consistently delicious thin-crust pizzas. The prosciutto, arugula, and Parmesan pizza is perfect. If you're not a fan of pizza, there's little other choice on the menu. They also serve Italian wine by the glass and a tasty little

tiramisu, followed by a glass of Limoncello or Sambuca. $ *Average main: $15 ⊠ Next door to Dragonfly Bar & Grill, behind Banco Nacional* ☎ *2653–1450* ⊙ *No lunch.*

$$$
SEAFOOD

✕ **Nogui's.** Pleasing a loyal legion of local fans since 1974, Nogui's offers a hearty Costa Rican menu and an ocean view. It is one of Tamarindo's best options for lunch, with a good selection of sandwiches, huge salads, and excellent fish tacos at reasonable prices. At dinner they offer a full seafood menu and various meat dishes. The recipes and presentation are nothing fancy, but the seafood is fresh and instead of the ubiquitous rice and beans on the side, Nogui's has a puree of *tiquisque,* a potatolike tuber. The homemade pies are legendary, notably the coconut cream and apple pie à la mode, and they open at 6 am for breakfast. Their signature margarita is made with tamarind fruit. On the downside, the waitresses here often seem sullen and put out. $ *Average main: $16 ⊠ South side of Tamarindo Circle, on beach* ☎ *2653–0029* ⊙ *Closed Wed. and first 2 wks in Oct.*

$$$
FRENCH

✕ **Pangas Beach Club.** You can't get any closer to the water than at this outdoor beach garden, where rustic tables are shaded by enormous ficus trees dangling with wicker lamps. Dig your toes into the raked sand or grab a table in the two-story restaurant where chef Jean Luc Paul blends classic French cuisine with Costa Rican flavors. The menu highlights fresh seafood with fruit reductions and organic meats seared on hot lava stones. For something light, try the tropical goat cheese salad with mango chutney or the fajitas with yellowfin tuna. There's a Sunday brunch from 9 to 3 and daily happy hour from 5 to 7. For a dash of entertainment with your meal, come on Wednesday, Friday, or Sunday evening when they have live music. Better yet, start early with the coconut French toast and stay all day nursing a tamarind margarita or star fruit colada. $ *Average main: $25 ⊠ 500 m southwest of Automercado* ☎ *2653–0024* ⊕ *www.lasmareas.com.*

$$$
MEDITERRANEAN
Fodor's Choice
★

✕ **Seasons by Shlomy.** At his intimate, poolside restaurant in the casually chic Hotel Arco Iris, innovative chef Shlomy Koren, Israeli-born and Cordon Bleu–trained, transforms fresh local ingredients into sophisticated Mediterranean-fusion dishes you would pay a small fortune for on the Riviera. Even the bread basket here is enticing: fresh-baked rolls topped with cumin seeds, salty soft focaccia, and a tasty eggy bread with raisins. The snapper cooked in rice paper is so moist, it's almost fluffy; add the savory sun-dried tomato and mushroom sauce, and you are in fish heaven. Sashimi comes doused in ginger-flavored, sizzling sesame oil, and masala chicken is cooked with almonds and sage. Chocolate lovers will long remember Seasons' version of Toblerone— dense chocolate with almond nougat combined with a rich chocolate ganache. Service is swift and attentive and the occasional live jazz adds to the pleasant atmosphere. $ *Average main: $18 ⊠ Hotel Arco Iris, uphill from turnoff to Langosta beach road* ☎ *8368–6983* ⊕ *www. seasonstamarindo.com* ▭ *No credit cards* ⊙ *Closed Sun. and mid-Sept.–mid-Oct. No lunch.*

$$
FRENCH FUSION

✕ **Ttiki by Le Beach Club.** The proper French chef at this beachfront restaurant beckons diners with his perfectly executed cuisine, like a whole snapper grilled in salt, crunchy on the outside, moist and tender inside, and served with a finely sliced potato gratin, plump herb-roasted tomatoes, and a vegetable skewer. Add a glass of French rosé and *voilà*—you're in France. The dessert specialty is profiteroles, dark chocolate-bathed, choux pastries filled with ice cream. The chef also produces not-to-be-missed crème brûlée. Presentation is artistic and service is polished and friendly. With a world-music sound track, white tablecloths, and candles, dinner here is serene and sophisticated but never stuffy. ⓢ *Average main: $15* ✉ *100 m south of Diria Hotel* ☎ *2653–0178.*

WHERE TO STAY

$

B&B/INN

🛏 **Cabinas Marielos.** The rooms at this centrally situated, locally owned hotel are among the best of the budget category in Tamarindo. **Pros:** cheap; near beach; pretty garden; relatively quiet. **Cons:** basic rooms; no air-conditioning or hot showers in some rooms; no pool; cash only. ⓢ *Rooms from: $55* ✉ *Across main dirt road from beach, on left after Best Western* ☎ *2653–0141* ⊕ *www.cabinasmarieloscr.com* ⤢ *24 rooms, 2 apartments* ⊟ *No credit cards* �𝌆 *No meals.*

$$

B&B/INN

🛏 **Hotel Arco Iris.** Beautiful bungalows dot the grounds of this chic compound, half a block off one of Tamarindo's main drags. **Pros:** transportation service; boutique feel; great restaurant. **Cons:** not a lot of privacy in bungalows; dusty walk to beach; very small pool. ⓢ *Rooms from: $125* ✉ *Follow signs past turnoff to Playa Langosta and go up hill to right* ☎ *2653–0330* ⊕ *www.hotelarcoiris.com* ⤢ *5 bungalows, 8 rooms* �𝌆 *Breakfast.*

$$$$

B&B/INN

Fodor'sChoice

★

🛏 **Hotel Capitán Suizo.** For folks who value nature, tranquility, and an unbeatably beautiful beach setting, along with luxurious rooms and an idyllic swimming pool, this is the classiest choice in town. **Pros:** beachfront; secluded; friendly; lovely gardens and pool; high sustainability rating. **Cons:** not a lot of privacy in garden bungalows; pricey; Wi-Fi in common areas only. ⓢ *Rooms from: $280* ✉ *Right side of Playa Langosta road, halfway between Tamarindo and Langosta* ☎ *2653–0075* ⊕ *www.hotelcapitansuizo.com* ⤢ *22 rooms, 8 bungalows, 1 beachfront suite, 2 beachfront garden rooms* �𝌆 *Breakfast.*

$$

B&B/INN

FAMILY

🛏 **Hotel Pasatiempo.** A longtime local hangout, this pretty collection of bungalows is clean, comfortable, and well priced, making it a good option for moderate budgets and families. **Pros:** affordable; gorgeous pool and garden; great restaurant. **Cons:** 10-minute walk to beach along dusty road; rooms close to pool can be noisy; bland breakfast. ⓢ *Rooms from: $89* ✉ *100 m southeast of high-rise Pacific Park condo at turnoff for Playa Langosta Rd.* ☎ *2653–0096* ⊕ *www.hotelpasatiempo.com* ⤢ *17 rooms, 4 family rooms, 1 family suite* �𝌆 *Breakfast.*

$$$$

RENTAL

🛏 **Las Mareas.** If space, privacy, luxury, and location are your priorities, then these 2,800-square-foot villas are your best option, with Balinese decor and all the comforts of home. **Pros:** ideal for large groups; five-minute walk to central Tamarindo; high-end amenities; built in 2013. **Cons:** no meals; one-week minimum stay during holidays; maid service every other day. ⓢ *Rooms from: $400* ✉ *Across from Las Pangas Beach Club, at entrance to Tamarindo* ☎ *2653–1561, 8832–5773* ⊕ *www. lasmareas.com* ⤢ *6 villas* �𝌆 *No meals.*

A group of local musicians rocking out in Tamarindo

$$ B&B/INN 🏨 **Luna Llena Hotel & Residence.** Looking a little like a cheerful Fellini film set of a fantasy tropical village, this collection of bright yellow, conical huts is fun and affordable. **Pros:** secluded; lush grounds; cheerful decor. **Cons:** several blocks away from beach; small pool; lots of kids. [$] *Rooms from: $90* ✉ *From road to Playa Langosta, 1st left (uphill)* ☎ *2653–0082* 🌐 *www.hotellunallena.com* 🛏 *7 rooms, 7 bungalows* 🍴 *Breakfast.*

NIGHTLIFE

Tamarindo is one of the few places outside San José where the nightlife really jumps. Although party-hearty hot spots come and go with the tides, Tamarindo does have some perennially popular nightspots, along with a couple of low-key options.

Aqua Discoteque. With a waterfall in the middle of the dance floor and an oceanfront patio, this trendy disco is open Monday, Wednesday, Friday, and Saturday nights, from about 10 pm, with changing DJs and live bands. There's a $4 cover charge. ✉ *75 m north of Hotel El Diriá* ☎ *8702–2925.*

Crazy Monkey Bar. Popular with the older surfing crowd, Crazy Monkey Bar features live salsa music that attracts locals who really know how to move—and a crowd of appreciative onlookers. Friday night is ladies' night. ✉ *Tamarindo Vista Villas, main road entering Tamarindo* ☎ *2653–0114.*

Hotel Capitán Suizo. For a pleasant Wednesday or Friday evening, try barbecue on the beach at the Hotel Capitán Suizo, starting at 6:30 with a cocktail, then on to a lavish barbecue buffet and live folk music and dancing ($36 with reduced rates for kids; reserve in advance). ✉ *Right side of road toward Playa Langosta; veer left before circle.*

Jazz at Playa Langosta Beach Club. Sink into a comfortable chair at this chic poolside lounge on Playa Langosta to watch the sunset over the Pacific and listen to jazz under the stars, Friday 7 to 9 pm. ✉ *200 m north of Hotel Capitán Suizo, road between Tamarindo and Playa Langosta.*

Sharky's. This is the biggest, most popular sports bar in town, with huge TV screens showing up to six games at once. After the game, both floors play extremely loud music for dancing. Karaoke is on Tuesday and beer pong is on Sunday, which you may or may not want to avoid. If sports aren't your thing, the bar food is amazingly good. The action starts at 5 pm and goes to 2:30 am. ✉ *On road to Hotel Pasatiempo, across from Plaza Conchal shopping center* ☎ *2653–4705.*

SHOPPING

Most stores in the strip malls lining the main road sell the same souvenirs. It's hard to leave town without at least one sarong or T-shirt in your suitcase. There are a few upscale clothing and jewelry shops worth a visit.

Amo La Vida. One of the most beautiful and intriguing shops in town, this eclectic emporium has exquisite local jewelry, plus exotic home-decorating items from Morocco and Egypt, including atmospheric wall sconces and accent lamps. ✉ *Main street, beside El Diriá Hotel* ☎ *2653–1507.*

Calypso. Owner Celine Price Annecy has raised the bar on beach fashion with fabulous Indonesian- and Mexican-style cover-ups and elegant, summery dresses, all available in real women's sizes. She also sells exotic jewelry. ✉ *Main street, at Tamarindo El Diriá Hotel* ☎ *2653–1436.*

PLAYA LANGOSTA

2 km (1 mile) south of Tamarindo.

A chic bedroom community of Tamarindo, just five minutes away by car, Playa Langosta is tranquil and elegant. It has not totally escaped development, but most of the low-rise buildings on the northern half are tucked behind the mangrove trees, so you can enjoy an unsullied dramatic beachscape, with surf crashing against rocky outcroppings. A few high-rise condominiums have invaded the area, but they are mostly set back.

GETTING HERE AND AROUND

The dirt road from Tamarindo is alternately dusty or muddy, but reliably rough. To keep down the dust, the road is periodically spread with an industrial mixture of molasses, which accounts for the stickiness and the lovely sweet smell. You can walk along the beach, at low tide, all the way from Tamarindo Beach, but be careful not to get caught on the headland rocks as the tide comes in. Most hotels offer pickup in Tamarindo for car-free visitors. Or you can take a taxi.

BEACHES

Playa Langosta. This Blue Flag beach is actually two beaches: To the north is an upscale, residential area where every foot of beachfront has been built up; the beach here is rather narrow, since the coast is lined with rocks, and the light gray sand is coarse. To the south, the beach is a pristine, protected annex of Las Baulas National Marine Park, where the occasional leatherback turtle nests at night and beachcombers and surfers roam by day. The dividing point is the San Francisco Estuary, the mouth of which is a knee-high wade at low tide, and a deep river with dangerous currents around high tide. The beach here is wider and less rocky, and it's where surfers find the best surf breaks. If you walk up the river at low tide, you may see snowy egrets, baby blue herons, tail-bobbing spotted sandpipers, and, if your eyes are sharp, tiny white-lored gnatcatchers, endemic to these parts. The rockier parts of the beach are excellent for spotting seabirds, including American oystercatchers. **Amenities:** none. **Best for:** surfing; sunset; walking. ⊠ *Playa Langosta.*

SPORTS AND THE OUTDOORS

Tour operators in Tamarindo, just a few miles north, offer activities in the Playa Langosta area.

WHERE TO EAT

$$$ ✕ **Playa Langosta Beach Club.** Looking for romance with spectacular
FRENCH food that matches the ambience? This beach club/restaurant/lounge/ jazz club is the most romantic and the most sophisticated dining spot on the beach. At dinner, tables set with white linens and candles are arranged under swaying palms around two glowing pools, while the sound of waves breaking on the beach blends with the very cool soft-jazz sound track. Start with a lobster-and-mango salad or a flaky pastry nest filled with goat cheese and spinach. Move on to a divine fillet of sole bathed in a velvety, peppery champagne cream sauce. There's a good wine list and light, refreshing Spanish wines by the glass. For dessert, try the caramelized apple crepes with honey and ice cream. Live sunset jazz starts at 7 on Sunday. At lunch, the menu features panini, fresh tuna salad, lobster, and mussels with french fries. You can work off your meal at the attached fitness center for $10 per day. $ *Average main: $25* ⊠ *Langosta Beach road, 200 m north of Capitán Suizo* ☎ *2653–1127.*

WHERE TO STAY

$$$ 🛏 **Sueño del Mar.** The name of this beachfront bed-and-breakfast means
B&B/INN "Dream of the Sea," and the front gate opens into a dreamy world of intimate gardens, patios, and hand-painted tiles. **Pros:** intimate; well appointed; friendly service; great beachfront. **Cons:** tiny pool; lack of privacy in small rooms; pricey. $ *Rooms from: $205* ⊠ *130 m south of Capitán Suizo, veer right for 45 m, then right again for about 90 m to entrance gate, across from back of Cala Luna Hotel, Playa Langosta* ☎ *2653–0284* ⊕ *www.sueno-del-mar.com* ⇱ *3 rooms, 1 suite, 2 casitas* ¡○¡ *Breakfast.*

$$$ ⌂ **Villa Alegre.** A visit here is like coming to stay with dear friends who
B&B/INN   just happen to have a really terrific house on one of the most scenic
beaches in Costa Rica. **Pros:** lovely grounds; friendly; good value.
Cons: some dark rooms; beach is a bit rocky. $ *Rooms from: $170*
⊠ *300 m south of Hotel Capitán Suizo, Playa Langosta* ☎ *2653–
0270* ⊕ *www.villaalegrecostarica.com* ⇆ *4 rooms, 2 villas, 1 casita*
⋈ *Breakfast.*

PLAYA AVELLANAS

17 km (11 miles) south of Tamarindo.

Traditionally a far cry from its northern neighbor's boom of real estate
development, Avellanas has seen Tamarindo escapees slowly encroach-
ing on it for years, building private houses and a smattering of small
hotels. The 2008 opening of the massive gated community of Hacienda
Pinilla—complete with a JW Marriott and golf course—marked the
beginning of major development. As you bump along the dusty, rough
beach road, most of the cars you pass have surfboards on top. But
nonsurfers are welcome, as Avellanas (pronounced ah-vey-ya-nas) is a
lovely spot for anyone who just likes sea and sand.

GETTING HERE AND AROUND

You have to drive inland from Tamarindo to Villa Real, where you turn
right for the 13-km (8-mile) trip down a bumpy road to reach Playa
Avellanas. It takes about 20 minutes. There are rivers to cross in rainy
season, when you may want to drive via Paraíso and Playa Negra. All
of the roads in the gated community of Hacienda Pinilla are paved.

Tamarindo Shuttle. If you're without a car, take the Tamarindo Shut-
tle van; call for current rates. ☎ *2653–2626, 2653–1326* ⊕ *www.
tamarindoshuttle.com.*

BEACHES

Playa Avellanas. This beach's main claims to fame are surfing and hang-
ing around at Lola's (⇨ *see below*), a very cool beach restaurant/bar.
Wide and sandy at the main access point, the beach itself is beautiful,
with a line of palms and beach almonds for shade. Rocky outcrop-
pings and a small river mouth mark its southern end, and a mangrove
swamp lies behind its northern half. Its Blue Flag designation means
the water is clean, but you shouldn't go in deeper than your waist when
the waves are big, because of rip currents. That's when the surfers take
over. Jellyfish can be a problem so you might want to wear a rash-
guard. Unfortunately, security is an issue here, as at most Costa Rican
beaches; posted signs warn visitors not to leave anything of value in
parked cars or unattended on the beach. There is guarded parking at
the beach entrance near Lola's but be sure to have small bills to tip the
attendant when you leave. If you are staying in the gated resort com-
munity of Hacienda Pinilla, it is better to park in the private lot and
enter from their beach club. **Amenities:** food and drink; parking. **Best
for:** surfing; walking.

SPORTS AND THE OUTDOORS

SURFING

Locals claim there are eight breaks here when the swell is big, which means Avellanas doesn't suffer the kind of overcrowding the breaks at Playas Negra and Langosta often do. Tamarindo-based surf schools can arrange day trips here.

Cabinas Las Olas. You can rent boards at Cabinas Las Olas for $15 a day. ✉ *Main road, on right* ☎ *2652–9315.*

WHERE TO EAT AND STAY

$$ VEGETARIAN 🍴 **Lola's.** In deference to Lolita, the owners' pet pig (the original Lola used to freely roam the beach and enjoy the surf), the menu at this hip beach café is heavily vegetarian. It has exactly the kind of ambience one comes to Costa Rica for, with tables scattered along the beach amid palm and almond trees, hammocks swinging in the wind, palm fronds rustling, and surfers riding the glistening waves in front. Seating, or more precisely, lolling, is on reclining, African-style hardwood chairs, or at shaded tables. Along with fresh-fruit smoothies, ultrathin vegetarian pizzas, and veggie soy burgers, the menu includes organic chicken and "responsible fish" (fish caught in nets that don't also trap turtles). Seared ahi tuna with sun-dried tomatoes and olive tapenade served on ciabatta bread is a winner, as are the ceviche, fish-and-chips, and assorted salads. You can arrange in advance for private beach dinners (minimum 10 people) by candlelight. Operating hours are 10 to 5, but you can order fruit smoothies between 8 and 10 am. [$] *Average main: $11* ✉ *At main entrance to Playa Avellanas* ☎ *2652–9097* ⏲ *Closed Mon. No dinner.*

$$ B&B/INN 🏨 **Cabinas Las Olas.** Frequented mainly by surfers, this is a good option for anyone seeking easy beach access, relative solitude, and comfortable, if not fancy, lodging. **Pros:** near beach; great surf shop with board rental; secluded. **Cons:** mosquitoes a problem in rainy season; simple rooms. [$] *Rooms from: $90* ✉ *1 km (½ mile) before Avellanas, on right* ☎ *2652–9315* 🌐 *www.cabinaslasolas.co.cr* 🛏 *10 rooms* ⏲ *Closed Oct.* 🍽 *Breakfast.*

$$$$ RESORT 🏨 **JW Marriott Guanacaste Resort & Spa.** In the gated community of Hacienda Pinilla, this luxury resort is centered around a 25,000-square-foot infinity pool that merges with a short stretch of beach in the west, making every sunset a major event. **Pros:** height of luxury; largest infinity pool in Central America; equestrian center. **Cons:** very pricey; remote location keeps you captive if you don't have a car; beach is small. [$] *Rooms from: $500* ✉ *In Hacienda Pinilla Beach resort and residential community* 🌐 *www.marriott.com/sjojw* 🛏 *289 rooms, 21 suites* 🍽 *No meals.*

$$$$ B&B/INN Fodor's Choice ★ 🏨 **Los Altos de Eros Luxury Inn & Spa.** This intimate adults-only inn is the place to be for honeymooning couples with enough money left over after the wedding to pamper themselves, or for stressed-out high achievers in need of some serious relaxation therapy. **Pros:** secluded location; excellent service; peaceful; romantic spa. **Cons:** scheduled mealtimes; not a lot of privacy in rooms; no kids under 18; difficult to find. [$] *Rooms from: $450* ✉ *Cañafistula, 14 km (8½ miles) southeast of Tamarindo, Avellanas* ☎ *8850–4203* 🌐 *www.losaltosdeeros.com* 🛏 *5 rooms, 1 suite* 🍽 *Some meals.*

Continued on page 322

BIRD-WATCHING

by Dorothy MacKinnon

Even if you've never seen yourself as a bird-watcher, Costa Rica will get you hooked. Waking you before dawn, calling to you throughout the day, and serenading you through tropical nights, birds here are impossible to ignore here.

Luckily, Costa Rica has a wealth of world-class ornithologists and local bird guides who can answer all your questions. Every licensed naturalist guide also has some birding expertise, so virtually every tour you take in the country will include some bird-watching.

The sheer variety and abundance of birds here make bird-watching a daily pastime—with less than 0.03% of the planet's surface, Costa Rica counts some 900 bird species, more than the United States and Canada combined. You don't have to stray far from your hotel or even need binoculars to spot, for instance, a kaleidoscopic-colored Keel-billed Toucan, the bird of Fruit Loops cereal fame. But armed with a pair of binoculars and a birding guide, the sky is literally the limit for the numbers of birds you can see.

Part of the thrill of walking along a jungle trail is the element of surprise: what is waiting around the path's next curve? Catching sight of a brilliantly colored bird is exciting, but being able to identify it after a couple of encounters is even more thrilling. For kids, spotting birds makes a great game. With their sharp, young eyes, they're usually very good at it—plus it's wildly educational.

About 10% of Costa Rica's birds are endemic, so this is a mecca for bird-watchers intent on compiling an impressive life list.

BEST BIRDING DESTINATIONS

The most sought-after bird is the aptly named Resplendent Quetzal, sporting brilliant blue, green, and red plumage and long tail feathers. The best places to spot it are the new **Los Quetzales National Park** in the Cerro de la Muerte highlands, the **San Gerardo de Dota valley,** and the **Monteverde Cloud Forest Reserve.**

Another bird high on many bird-watchers' lists is the Scarlet Macaw, the largest of the parrot family here. You'll see pairs performing aerial ballets and munching in beach almond trees in **Corcovado National Park,** along the **Osa Peninsula's coastline,** and around **Carara National Park** in the Central Pacific region.

The **Tempisque River delta's** salty waters, at the north end of the Gulf of Nicoya, are famous for a wealth of water birds, notably Wood Storks, Glossy Ibis, and Roseate Spoonbills. A little farther north, in **Palo Verde and Caño Negro National Parks,** look for the rarest and largest of wading birds, the Jabiru.

The network of jungle-edged natural canals in **Tortuguero National Park,** in the northern Caribbean, is home to a host of herons, including the spectacular Rufescent Tiger-Heron and the multi-hued Agami Heron.

More than 50 species of hummingbirds hover around every part of the country. Look for them around feeders at lodges in the **Cerro de la Muerte area, Monteverde,** and the **Turrialba region.**

WHEN TO GO: The best time to bird is November to May, when local species are joined by winter migrants. Breeding season, which varies by species throughout the year, is the easiest time to spot birds, as males put on displays for females, followed by frequent flights to gather nesting material and then food for the chicks. Also keep your eye on fruit-bearing trees that attract hungry birds.

6

IN FOCUS BIRD-WATCHING

IDENTIFYING BIRDS

Quetzal in Río Savegre Valley; Krasinsky, Fodors.com member

Binoculars are the most important piece of equipment. They don't have to be a very expensive pair, but they should have good light-gathering lenses and be waterproof. A magnification of 7 to 8 is ideal; any higher and your range of vision becomes very limited.

A good guidebook is essential. The standard "bible" has been a comprehensive tome written by Dr. Alexander Skutch, but beginners (and experienced birders) will probably find the new field guide, written by Richard Garrigues and illustrated by Robert Dean, much more useful—and lighter to carry. It has range maps for every bird and lists the most obvious field marks to help you identify each species. Gift shops and hotels also sell plastic-laminated, one-page guides with local birds that can get you started.

The most important advice for new birders is to find the bird with your naked eye and then bring your binoculars to your eyes, without losing your focus on the bird. Look for beak shape; characteristic rings around the eye; bars, stripes, spots, and mottling on plumage; and, of course, colors on feathers, eyes, beaks, legs, and feet.

10 EASY-TO-IDENTIFY BIRDS FOR BEGINNERS

❶ Blue-Crowned Motmot

Unmistakable with those long tail feathers that look like tennis racquets, this gorgeous turquoise-and-green bird perches low in trees often close to a stream. They're usually silent but their call is easy to identify: a repeated, low "whoop."

❷ Keel-Billed Toucan

Half a dozen of these rainbow-colored, huge-billed birds often travel together, hunting for berries and fruits. Look for them in Cecropia trees, and listen for the loud, rapid beat of their wings.

❸ Great Kiskadee

You can tell the kiskadee from the similar-looking flycatchers by its *pecho amarillo* (yellow breast), black-and-white-striped head, rufous tinted wings, and its call—it really does say *Kiss-kah-deeee*!

❹ Orange-fronted Parakeet

Found in forest canopy on the Pacific side of the country, these highly social and noisy little birds feed in flocks of up to 100. The adults are mainly green, and have shorter tails than their crimson-fronted cousins. The head is distinctive, with a blue crown and orange forehead. Sadly, the population has been decreasing for a number of years thanks to the pet trade.

❺ Rufous-tailed Hummingbird

Stake out hibiscus hedges or any flowering shrub for the country's most common hummingbird. An iridescent green color, with a long red beak and reddish-brown tail, it makes a loud "tse, tse" chipping sound as it goes about its business.

❻ Scarlet Macaw

Look for this huge scarlet, yellow, and blue parrot in the beach almond trees that edge South Pacific beaches. They usually travel in pairs and you'll probably hear their raucous squawks before you see them.

❼ Blue-Gray Tanager

Abundant everywhere—cities, towns, gardens, and countryside—this bluish-gray bird, always seen in pairs, loves fruit. You'll often find them at feeding platforms and in fruiting fig trees.

❽ Black Vulture

Almost every large black bird you see circling high in the sky will be a vulture; some have white-tipped wings. You'll also see them hopping along the roadside feasting on roadkill.

❾ Roadside Hawk

This raptor sits quietly on low perches in trees alongside fields and roads, waiting to pounce on lizards, large insects, and small mammals. It has a gray head, a yellow beak and legs, and a brown and white striped chest.

❿ Cherrie's Tanager (on Pacific slope), aka Passerini's Tanager (on Carribean slope)

The unmistakable scarlet-rumped, velvety-black male travels with a harem of olive-and orange-colored females, making a lot of scratchy noises as they hunt insects in dense shrubbery.

PLAYA NEGRA

3 km (2 miles) south of Playa Avellanas.

Surfer culture is apparent here in the wave of beach-shack surfer camps along the road that leads to the rocky strand of beach. But Playa Negra is growing up fast, with some interesting cafés and restaurants popping up to cater to beachgoers and residents of an upscale residential development called Rancho Playa Negra.

GETTING HERE AND AROUND

From Playa Avellanas, continue south 10 minutes on the rough beach road to Playa Negra. If it's rainy season and the road is too rough, you can approach along a slightly more civilized route from Santa Cruz. Drive 27 km (16½ miles) west, via Veintisiete de Abril, to Paraíso, then follow signs for Playa Negra for 4 km (2½ miles). Taxis are the easiest way to get around if you don't have a car; they cost about $30 from Tamarindo.

BEACHES

Playa Negra. Contrary to the name, the beach is not black, but rather beige with dark streaks. This is primarily a surfer's beach, so it's not great for swimming because it tends to have fast hollow waves and is lined with rocks. There is one calm, short stretch of clear sand to the south of the Playa Negra Hotel, and at low tide a large tidal pool forms there. The spindly buttonwood trees that edge the beach provide sparse shade. The dirt road to Playa Negra is bumpy and muddy during rainy season so drive with caution. **Amenities:** parking. **Best for:** surfing; walking.

SPORTS AND THE OUTDOORS

SURFING

Surfing cognoscenti dig the waves here, which are almost all rights, with beautifully shaped barrels. It's a spectacular, but treacherous, rock-reef break for experienced surfers only. There's also a small beach break to the south of the rocks where neophytes can cut their teeth. Both breaks can be ridden from mid- to high tide.

Hotel Playa Negra. The point break is right in front of the only beachfront hotel, which can arrange surfing classes ($35 per hour for a private lesson), and rents boards ($20 per day). ⊠ *4 km (2½ miles) northwest of Paraíso on dirt road, then follow signs carefully at forks in road; or 10 minutes south of Playa Avellanas on rough beach road* ☎ *2652–9298* ⊕ *www.playanegra.com.*

WHERE TO EAT

$ ✕ **Kon Tiki.** A favorite local hangout, this rustic pizzeria is run by viva-
ITALIAN   cious Peruvian owners Martin and Giovanna. Martin mans the outdoor clay oven, while inside the restaurant Giovanna kneads dough and mixes up fresh sangrias in the open kitchen. Among the 14 types of pizza, we like the house special with goat cheese, pesto, and caramelized onions. They also serve gluten-free pizzas and homemade ravioli and barbecued meats from the pizza oven (with 24 hours' notice). If you can't find a pizza that sounds good, you can build your own from a list of endless toppings. As the area's top local hangout, the place

gets packed, so plan to wait awhile for your food and bill. $ *Average main: $10* ✉ *700 m after the soccer field at Los Pargos* ☎ *2652–9117* ⊕ *www.kontikiplayanegra.com* ☾ *No lunch.*

A SURF CLASSIC

Americans—surfer Americans, at least—got their first look at Playa Negra in 1994's *The Endless Summer II,* a film by legendary surf documentarian Bruce Brown.

$$$
FRENCH FUSION
Fodor's Choice
★

✕**Restaurant Deevena.** An unexpected outpost of divine French cuisine, this oasis of elegance is run by chef Patrick Jamon, formerly executive chef of the Regency Club in California, who brought his culinary skills, extensive wine cellar, and family to the wilds of Guanacaste. The alfresco restaurant overlooks a sparkling blue pool edged by lush palms, while lounge chairs shaded by orange umbrellas beckon diners to stay overnight (six stylish rooms are available). Lunch and dinner feature lots of local seafood, produce, and goat cheese from the chef's nearby farm. Try the fresh grouper fillet bathed in lemon herb butter sauce, or the seared ahi tuna with ginger-carrot puree. Vegetarians can feast on ravioli stuffed with wild mushrooms, sage, and sun-dried tomatoes. Desserts include classic French options—fruit crepes, crème brûlée—as well as chocolate lava cake with raspberry compote. The service here is exemplary. You can order wonderful wines by the glass or bottle—a rare opportunity in these remote parts. While waiting for your meal to arrive, ask to view the photo album of the chef's famous clients. $ *Average main: $17* ✉ *25 m off main road that runs through Playa Negra; watch for Villa Deevena sign* ☎ *2653–2328* ⊕ *www.villadeevena.com* ☾ *Closed Mon.*

6

WHERE TO STAY

$$
RESORT

Hotel Playa Negra. Pastel-color, round cabinas are sprinkled across sunny lawns strewn with tropical plants at this gorgeous oceanfront place with a huge round pool. **Pros:** in front of reef break; friendly; comfortable accommodation; family suites available. **Cons:** not a great swimming beach; rocky road to hotel. $ *Rooms from: $100* ✉ *4 km (2½ miles) northwest of Paraíso on dirt road (watch signs for Playa Negra), then follow signs carefully at forks in road; or 10 mins south of Playa Avellanas on beach road* ☎ *2652–9134* ⊕ *www.playanegra. com* ⊅ *10 bungalows, 7 bungalow suites* ☾ *Restaurant closed Sept. 1–Nov. 1* ⊙ *No meals.*

PLAYA JUNQUILLAL

4 km (2½ miles) south of Paraíso, 34 km (22 miles) southwest of Santa Cruz.

Seekers of oceanfront tranquility need look no further than Junquillal (pronounced hoon-key-*yall*), a beach town as far away from the crowd as you can get on a decent road. A surprisingly cosmopolitan mélange of expats has settled in this out-of-the-way area, and there's a supermarket at the entrance to an upscale housing development. But Junquillal is still barely on the tourist map; consequently its few hotels offer some of the best deals on the North Pacific coast.

GETTING HERE AND AROUND

In rainy season, the 4-km-long (2½-mile-long) beach road from Playa Negra to Playa Junquillal is sometimes not passable. The alternative is driving down from Santa Cruz one hour on a road that's paved most of the way. The Castillos bus company runs a bus to Junquillal from the central market in Santa Cruz four times a day (at 5 and 10 am, and 2:30 and 5:30 pm); the trip takes about 40 minutes. A taxi from Santa Cruz or Tamarindo costs about $40; from the Liberia airport, $90 to $100.

> **DID YOU KNOW?**
>
> Guanacaste was a political monkey-in-the-middle for centuries, bouncing between Spain, Nicaragua, and independence. In 1858, Guanacastecans finally voted to annex themselves to Costa Rica, an event celebrated every July 25 with a national holiday.

ESSENTIALS

The closest town for most services is Santa Cruz, 34 km (22 miles) northeast.

Hospital Clínica ⊠ *16 km (10 miles) northeast of Playa Junquillal, Veintisiete de Abril.*

BEACHES

FAMILY **Playa Junquillal.** This wide swath of light-brown sand stretches over 3 km (2 miles), with coconut palms lining much of it and hardly a building in sight. Two species of sea turtle nest here, and a group of young people collect and protect their eggs, releasing the baby turtles after sunset. The surf is a little strong, so watch children carefully. There's a kids' playground right at the beach, and a funky little restaurant with concrete tables amid the palms. It's also a perfect beach for taking long, romantic strolls. Surfers head here to ride the beach break near Junquillal's northern end, since it rarely gets crowded. **Amenities:** food and drink. **Best for:** surfing; walking.

WHERE TO STAY

$ **Guacamaya Lodge.** Spread across a breezy hill with expansive views
B&B/INN above the treetops of the surrounding forest and the sea, the Guaca-
FAMILY maya is a real find, with affordable, spacious cabinas surrounding a
Fodor's Choice generous-size pool, lawn, and tropical plants. **Pros:** excellent value;
★ clean; friendly. **Cons:** hilly 10-minute walk to the beach. $ *Rooms from: $65* ⊠ *275 m east of Playa Junquillal* ☎ *2658–8431* ⊕ *www.guacamayalodge.com* ↩ *6 bungalows, 4 studios, 2 two-bedroom villas* ⊗ *Closed Sept. and Oct.* ⏴*No meals.*

$$ **Mundo Milo Eco Lodge.** This hidden eco-lodge with a kidney-shaped
B&B/INN pool is made up of five bungalows themed after Africa, Persia, and Mexico. **Pros:** 300 meters from the beach; great value; delicious food at restaurant. **Cons:** rooms might be too themed for some; closed in October; bumpy road. $ *Rooms from: $77* ⊠ *Calle Mundo Milo, 300 m from the beach* ☎ *2658–7010* ⊕ *www.mundomilo.com* ↩ *5 rooms* ⏴*Breakfast.*

THE NICOYA PENINSULA

South of Tamarindo, you'll find the interesting anomaly of a trendy restaurant or upscale hotel plunked at the end of a tortuous dirt road. The key to enjoying the Nicoya Peninsula is to pick your spot—happening beach town or off-the-beaten-path seclusion.

The parks and wildlife refuges in and around the Río Tempisque are prime places to hike, explore caves, and spot birds and other wildlife. And there's a smattering of culture, too, in the town of Nicoya, with its colonial-era church, and in Guaitil, with pottery made in the pre-Columbian Chorotega tradition. The town of Nicoya is the commercial and political hub of the northern Nicoya Peninsula. By road, Nicoya provides the best access to Sámara, Nosara, and points south and north, and is linked by a smooth, well-paved road to the artisan community of Guaitil and the northern Nicoya beach towns.

The southern tip of the Nicoya Peninsula is one of Costa Rica's less developed regions, where some of the country's most gorgeous beaches, rain forests, waterfalls, and tidal pools lie at the end of some of its worst roads. Within the region are quiet, well-preserved parks where you can explore pristine forests or travel by boat or sea kayak to idyllic islands for bird-watching or snorkeling. Other outdoor options include horseback riding, gliding through the treetops on a canopy tour, or surfing on some of the country's most consistent waves. In the laid-back beach towns of Montezuma, Santa Teresa, and Malpaís, an international cast of surfers, nature lovers, yoga enthusiasts, and expatriate massage therapists live out their dreams in paradise.

NOSARA

28 km (17 miles) southwest of Nicoya.

One of the last beach communities for people who want to get away from it all, Nosara's attractions are the wild stretches of side-by-side beaches called Pelada and Guiones, with surfing waves and miles of sand on which to stroll, and the tropical dry forest that covers much of the hinterland. Regulations here limit development to low-rise buildings 180 meters (600 feet) from the beach, where they are, thankfully, screened by trees. Americans and Europeans, with a large Swiss contingent, are building at a fairly rapid pace, but there appears to be an aesthetic sense here that is totally lacking in Tamarindo. The town of Nosara itself is inland and not very interesting, but the surrounding flora and fauna keep nature lovers entertained.

For years, most travelers headed here for the surf. The wide range of surf schools and waves varying from beginner to expert levels makes Nosara one of the best places to learn to surf. Along with surfing, the Nosara Yoga Institute, which offers instructor training and daily classes for all levels, is increasingly a draw for health-conscious visitors. Healthy-food options, spas, and exercise classes abound. You'll see lots of yoga practitioners on the beaches around sunrise and sunset.

Bird-watchers and other nature enthusiasts can explore the tropical dry forest on hiking trails, on horseback, or by floating up the tree-lined

Nosara River in a kayak, guide boat, or paddleboard. The last leg of the access road to Nosara is abysmal, and the labyrinth of woodsy roads around the beaches and hard-to-read signs make it easy to get lost, which is why most hotels here provide local maps for their guests. Don't get in your car without one—especially at night. For local news and tourist information, pick up a free copy of the excellent monthly newspaper *Voice of Nosara*.

CAUTION

To approach Nosara along the coast from Junquillal used to involve fording many rivers, some of them impassable during the wet season. The good news is that new bridges now span the Rosario, Juanillo, and Montaña, the widest and deepest rivers. But there are still a couple of small creeks to cross, so 4WD is a good idea. If you have a compact car and it has been raining a lot, you are better off driving via Nicoya on the paved road.

GETTING HERE AND AROUND

From Nicoya, drive south, almost to Sámara, but take the very first road sign for Nosara, 1 km (½ mile) south of the big gas station before Sámara. This high road is rough for about 8 km (5 miles), but there are bridges over all the river crossings. When you join up with the beach road near Garza, you still have a very bumpy 10 km (6 miles) to go. The roads into Nosara are in really bad shape, so a 4WD vehicle is definitely recommended. Budget about one hour for the trip. You can also fly directly to the town of Nosara on daily scheduled SANSA and Nature Air flights, or take an air-conditioned shuttle van from San José. A couple of major rent-a-car companies have offices in Playa Guiones.

ESSENTIALS

Bank/ATM Banco Popular ⊠ *Next door to Café de Paris, Main St., Playa Guiones.* **Banco de Costa Rica** ⊠ *Next to Servicentro Nosara gas station, main road* ⊙ *Weekdays 9–4.*

Hospital Centro Médico Nosara. Medical and dental specialists, including pediatric dentists and a periodontist, opens daily at 8 am. ⊠ *100 m west of Café de Paris, on road to Playa Guiones* ☏ *2682–1212.*

Internet Café de Paris ⊠ *At entrance to Playa Guiones* ☏ *2682–0087.*

Pharmacy Farmacia Nosara ⊠ *In town, on right side of air strip* ☏ *2682–5149* ⊙ *Mon.–Sat. 8–noon and 1 to 7.*

Post Office Correo ⊠ *Next to soccer field in town.*

Rental Cars Alamo/National ⊠ *Café de Paris shopping center, Playa Guiones road* ☏ *2682–0052.* **Economy** ⊠ *Below Marlin Bill's Restaurant, Playa Guiones main road* ☏ *2682–1146.*

Taxis Abel's Taxi. Independent drivers provide taxi service. Abel's Taxi is reliable. A taxi ride from Nosara to Sámara will set you back $50, a measure of how punishing the road is. ☏ *8812–8470.*

Beginning surfers love Sámara's almost placid water and its undeveloped palm-fringed beach.

EXPLORING

Nosara Biological Reserve. This 90-acre private reserve is a natural treasure, with trails through a huge mangrove wetland and old-growth forest along the Nosara River. A concrete walkway passes over an eerily beautiful mangrove swamp, with fantastical stilt roots and snap-crackling sound effects from respiring mollusks. More than 270 bird species have been spotted here, including long-tailed manakins. There are always crabs, lizards, snakes, and other creatures rustling in the grass and howler monkeys and iguanas in the trees. Pick up a self-guided trail map from the Hotel Lagarta Lodge when you pay your admission fee, or better yet, hire Gabriele, the resident nature guide, for a two-hour tour; call ahead if you want to hire a guide. The best times to do the hike, which takes about two hours, are early in the morning or late in the afternoon, which means you can follow your trek with breakfast, or sunset cocktails at the Hotel Lagarta Lodge. ⊠ *Trailhead 168 steps down from Hotel Lagarta Lodge, top of hill at the north end of Nosara* ☎ *2682–0035* ⤬ *$6 self-guided tour; $15 with guide (reserve 1 day in advance).*

Ostional National Wildlife Refuge (*Refugio Nacional de Fauna Silvestre Ostional*). This wildlife refuge protects one of Costa Rica's major nesting beaches for olive ridley turtles. Locals have formed an association to run the reserve on a cooperative basis, and during the first 36 hours of the *arribadas* (mass nesting) they are allowed to harvest the eggs, on the premise that eggs laid during this time would likely be destroyed by subsequent waves of mother turtles. Though turtles nest here year-round, the largest arribadas, with thousands of turtles nesting over the courses of several nights, occur from July to December, though smaller arribadas take place between January and May. They usually occur around high tide, the week of a new moon. People in Nosara usually know when an arribada has begun. The mandatory guide-led tours of the nesting and hatching areas cost $10 per person. Stop at the kiosk at the entrance to the beach to arrange a tour, or at the Association of Guides office, 25 meters south of the beach entrance on the main road, next to Cabinas

Ostional. A new bridge over the Río Montaña has made access easier from Nosara. ⊠ *7 km (4½ miles) north of Nosara* ☎ *2682–0428* 🎫 *$12.*

BEACHES

Playa Guiones. With some of the most consistent surf on the Pacific coast, Playa Guiones attracts a lot of surfboard-toting visitors, but the breezy beach, with vegetation rising up from the high-tide mark for its length, is also a haven for sun lovers, beachcombers, and anyone who wants to connect with nature. The only building in sight is the bizarre Hotel Nosara, which was originally the only choice for lodging in town but is now a rambling private residence complete with an eccentric observation tower. Otherwise, this glorious Blue Flag beach has 7 km (4½ miles) of hard-packed sand, great for jogging, riding bikes, and saluting the sun. Because there's a 3-meter (9-foot) tide, the beach is expansive at low tide but rather narrow at high tide, when waves usually create strong currents that can make the sea deadly for nonsurfers. Most hotels post tide charts. Guiones is at the south end of the Nosara agglomeration, with three public accesses. The easiest one to find is about 300 meters (1,000 feet) past the Harmony Hotel, heading straight at the intersection. **Amenities:** none. **Best for:** surfing; walking.

Playa Pelada. North along the shore, Playa Guiones segues seamlessly into crescent-shape Playa Pelada, where the water is a little calmer and just as clean, also designated a Blue Flag beach. There are tide pools to explore and a blowhole that sends water shooting up when the surf is big. Lots of trees provide shade. This is the locals' favorite vantage point for watching sunsets—great photo ops, with beached fishing boats adding color and interest to the foreground. Olga's Bar, a recently renovated Tico beach bar, is an atmospheric place for a cool beer. More upscale and romantic are the Balinese settees in front of La Luna Bar & Grill. **Amenities:** food and drink. **Best for:** sunset; surfing; swimming.

SPORTS AND THE OUTDOORS

TOUR OPERATORS

Experience Nosara. For in-depth insights into the natural world, join bilingual naturalist/ecologist Felipe Lopez on a three-hour kayak tour along the Río Nosara ($60 per person), or on a leisurely hike to a hidden waterfall with swimming holes ($50). Out on the ocean, the company offers surfing and stand-up paddleboat lessons and tours. ☎ *8705–2010* ⊕ *www.experience-nosara.com.*

Harbor Reef Surf Resort. This long-established hotel has an excellent tour desk that can arrange fishing, surfing, nature tours, and river expeditions. They can also arrange educational visits to the Refuge for Wildlife, which specializes in rescued howler monkeys. ⊠ *Follow signs from Café de Paris turnoff, Playa Guiones* ☎ *2682–0059, 2682–1000* ⊕ *www.harborreef.com.*

BIRD-WATCHING

Experience Nosara. Experience Nosara *(⇨ above)* bilingual naturalist Felipe Lopez leads serious bird-watchers on bird-watching tours, with an early-morning expedition on foot in the Nosara Biological Reserve or a kayak paddle up river to catch sight of some of the 270 species recorded here ($60 each tour).

FAMILY **River Safari.** Glide up the Nosara and Montaña rivers in a flat-bottom catamaran with an almost noiseless electric motor. Wading herons, egrets, roseate spoonbills, ospreys, and kingfishers are common sights. The German-born naturalist guide also knows where crocodiles hunker down in mud caves along the riverbank. Trips are $38 per person. ⊠ *Boat moored at bottom of hill leading to Hotel Lagarta Lodge, follow signs to the boca [mouth] of Nosara River* ☎ *2682–0610* ⊕ *www.riversafari.de.*

FISHING

Fishing Nosara. This outfit can hook you up with local English-speaking captains who can take you fishing for 2½ hours, a half day, or full day, on boats ranging from 6 to 10 meters (20 to 32 feet). Rates start at $200 for 2½ hours and top out at $850 for a full day on the largest, best-equipped boat. ⊠ *In Paradise Rentals office on main road to Playa Guiones, Playa Guiones* ☎ *2682–0606* ⊕ *www.fishingnosara.com.*

HORSEBACK RIDING

FAMILY **Boca Nosara Tours.** German equestrienne Beate Klossek and husband Hans Werner take small groups of up to six people on 2½-hour horseback nature tours through the jungle and along the beach ($50 to $70 per person, according to group size). They can also take a group of up to 12, with one guide for every four riders. Horses are well mannered and well treated. There are smaller saddles for kids, from six years old and up. ATV tours, starting from $50, are also offered. ⊠ *150 m below Hotel Lagarta Lodge, at mouth of Nosara River* ☎ *2682–0280* ⊕ *www.bocanosaratours.com.*

SURFING

In 2012, the *New York Times* listed Nosara as the best place in the world to learn how to surf, so if you've always wanted to try it, this is the place. Guiones is the perfect beginners' beach, with no rocks to worry about. Local surf instructors say that the waves here are so consistent that there's no week throughout the year when you won't be able to surf. In March and April, the Costa Rican National Surf Circuit comes here for surf trials.

Coconut Harry's Surf Shop. This Nosara surfing institution on the main road has boards ($15 to $20 per day), gear, and lessons ($45 for 1½ hours, board included, for a group of three; a private lesson is $70). The shop also has a beach location 100 meters (328 feet) from the main

Playa Guiones beach entrance, where surfers can also store their boards. ✉ *Main road, across from Café de Paris* ☎ *2682–0574* 🌐 *www.coconutharrys.com.*

Corky Carroll's Surf School. Named after a renowned, veteran American surfer, this school has its own hotel for surfing students, with prebooked lodging and lessons packages. They also offer one-on-one hourly lessons ($60) including board rental for the day. ✉ *Rocky Ricker Rd., near Casa Romántica, off Playa Guiones road* ☎ *2682–0384, 888/454–7873 toll-free in U.S.* 🌐 *www.surfschool.net.*

> **CAUTION**
>
> Many restaurants do not include the legally required 13% tax and 10% service charge in their menu prices, but tack them onto the bill at the end. It might be indicated somewhere on the menu that tax and tip are not included, but that's not always the case. If you're not sure, ask.

Nosara Surf Shop. This large surf shop offers group lessons ($40 per hour), rents boards by the day ($10 to $15), and has lots of gear for sale, too. Have a credit card handy to pay a deposit on the rental board. They also rent bicycles and ATVs. ✉ *500 m west of Café de Paris, on road to Playa Guiones* ☎ *2682–0186* 🌐 *www.nosarasurfshop.com.*

Safari Surf School. Run by Tim and Tyler Marsh, surfing brothers from Hawaii, this popular school with its own beachfront location called Olas Verdes, is certified by the International Surfing Association. There are special packages for women, as well as a kids' surf camp. Most students come on package deals that include transportation and a choice of lodging. You can also pay as you learn, $45 per hour for a group lesson, surfboard included. ✉ *Olas Verdes, beach road past Harbor Reef Hotel, Playa Guiones* ☎ *2682–0113* 🌐 *www.safarisurfschool.com.*

YOGA

Harmony Hotel Healing Center. Closer to Playa Guiones, the Harmony Hotel *(⇨ below)* holds yoga classes daily for $12 a session. They also have a wide selection of new age therapeutic massages and a full range of herbal spa services.

The Nosara Yoga Institute. This reputable, internationally known institute focuses on teacher certification, but also offers several daily 90-minute yoga classes to the public ($10), as well as weeklong workshops and retreats throughout the year. ✉ *Southeast end of town, on main road to Sámara* ☎ *2682–0071, 866/439–4704 in U.S.* 🌐 *www.nosarayoga.com.*

WHERE TO EAT

$$ ECLECTIC 🍴 **Café de Paris.** Swiss-French owners have turned this corner bakery into a chic, alfresco eatery. In addition to hearty sandwiches, they have such Continental treats as fish and vegetables baked in papillote, plus tagliatelle with shrimp, and hamburgers spiced with chipotle peppers. The pastry shop is great for take-out beach picnics, with classic French baguettes, savory croissants and quiches, chocolate bread, and a mouth-watering array of pastries, tarts, and rum-flavored truffles. The rich chocolate mousse is ready to go in a plastic cup. Open 7 to 5, for breakfast and lunch only. [$] *Average main: $12* ✉ *Main road, at Playa Guiones entrance* ☎ *2682–1036.*

$$ ITALIAN 🍴 **Giardino Tropicale.** Formerly famous for its wood-oven pizzas, the original pizza maker has moved on and opened his own place (⇨ *see Pepperoni's below),* but this restaurant still makes decent, if not spectacular, pizza, and bowls of homemade chili-pepper sauce still grace every table. Beyond pizza, this thatch-roof, multilevel restaurant casts a wide net to include daily fresh seafood and fish specials, such as ravioli stuffed with snook or tuna carpaccio. Sit on one of the upper decks and you'll dine amid the treetops. The downstairs part of the restaurant is quite sophisticated and romantic, with elegant white tablecloths. The owners are also working to make the restaurant ecologically sustainable. Service is always fast and very friendly. Dinner only from 5 pm. [$] *Average main: $15* ✉ *Giardino Tropicale Hotel, main street, north of entrance to Playa Guiones* ☎ *2682–0258* ⏲ *Closed Mon. No lunch.*

$$ AMERICAN 🍴 **Marlin Bill's.** Sink your teeth into a classic New York strip steak or pork chops in American-size portions at this open-air restaurant with a great sunset view. Lighter choices include eggplant parmigiana, homemade spinach-and-ricotta ravioli in marinara sauce, and delicious "dorado fingers"—battered fish fillet strips served with tartar sauce. Rum-based drinks and margaritas flow, and beer drinkers can try Libertas, a Costa Rican craft beer, on draft. Homemade desserts are delicious, including key lime pie. The decor is decidedly fishy, with fish-themed art on the walls. Fishing and real estate talk over beer and chicken wings keeps the U-shape bar abuzz. The kitchen is open from 11 to 3; then 6 to 9, and on Sunday for lunch only. Sporting events, like play-off NFL football games, are aired on the big-screen TV. There's also free Wi-Fi and the friendly waitresses speak English. [$] *Average main: $14* ✉ *Hilltop above main road, near Coconut Harry's Surf Shop* ☎ *2682–0458* ⏲ *No dinner Sun.*

$$ ITALIAN 🍴 **Pepperoni's.** Head to this spot for the best pizza in town. The owners (nicknamed Kike and Fofo) became known for their irresistible pies at Giardino Tropicale before opening this restaurant and pizzeria in a beautiful garden setting near Playa Pelada. You can sit at tables in the shaded garden and watch your pizza being made in a wood-fired, freestanding brick oven, or sit under the roof of the terrace restaurant and choose from a full menu of salads, pasta, fish, seafood, meat, and chicken dishes, all Italian style. On Sunday, there's live music at dinner. [$] *Average main: $15* ✉ *Across from Condominios Las Flores, road to Playa Pelada* ☎ *2682–0545.*

$ VEGETARIAN 🍴 **Robin's Wholesome Foods Cafe.** Famous for homemade ice creams and tropical-fruit sorbets, this casual patio café also serves full meals with a focus on wholesome foods, including vegetarian and raw-food dishes. Over-stuffed veggie quesadillas will appeal to all tastes, along with pad thai rolls and yummy vegan veggie burgers. Locals line up to buy the dense, fudgy brownies when they come out of the oven. [$] *Average main: $8* ✉ *Road to Playa Guiones, 25 m west of Banco Popular* ☎ *2682–0617* 💳 *No credit cards* ⏲ *No dinner.*

6

WHERE TO STAY

$$ B&B/INN **Casa Romántica Hotel.** The name ("Romantic House") says it all: the Spanish colonial–style house has a balustraded veranda upstairs and below, a graceful arcade with views of a crystal-blue kidney-shape pool surrounded by a glorious tropical garden. **Pros:** very close to beach; good restaurant; good value. **Cons:** rooms not spectacular; can be noisy. [$] *Rooms from: $105* ✉ *200 m west of Giardino Tropicale, on left* ☎ *2682–0272* 🌐 *www.casa-romantica.net* 🛏 *12 rooms, 1 house* 🍴 *Breakfast.*

$$ B&B/INN **Giardino Tropicale Hotel.** In the lush gardens downhill from the popular restaurant *(⇨ above)*, shaded by large trees, you'll find comfortable suites and cabinas, and a sparkling 17-meter (56-foot), salt-filtered swimming pool—the only good lap pool in town. **Pros:** good value; environmentally friendly; laptop-size safety boxes. **Cons:** road noise; extra charge for air-conditioning; short walk to beach. [$] *Rooms from: $85* ✉ *Main street, past entrance to Playa Guiones* ☎ *2682–4000* 🌐 *www.giardinotropicale.com* 🛏 *3 standard rooms with kitchen, 2 standard without kitchen, 4 deluxe suites, 1 apartment* 🍴 *No meals.*

$ B&B/INN **The Gilded Iguana.** This lively hotel/bar/restaurant has been a Nosara fixture for more than 25 years. **Pros:** very economical rooms; laid-back; lively bar. **Cons:** spotty service; can be noisy; cheaper rooms don't have air-conditioning. [$] *Rooms from: $50* ✉ *Playa Guiones* ☎ *2682–0259* 🌐 *www.thegildediguana.com* 🛏 *10 rooms, 2 suites* 🍴 *No meals.*

$$ B&B/INN **Harbor Reef Lodge.** It's easy to lose yourself in the junglelike gardens of this comfortable surfer hotel, where rooms and suites cater to surfers of every age, with plenty of space for boards and gear inside. **Pros:** attractive grounds; near beach and surf breaks; good restaurant. **Cons:** bland rooms; very small pools. [$] *Rooms from: $110* ✉ *Follow signs from Café de Paris turnoff toward Playa Guiones* ☎ *2682–1000* 🌐 *www.harborreef.com* 🛏 *9 standard rooms, 4 deluxe rooms, 12 suites, 5 houses* 🍴 *Breakfast.*

$$$$ B&B/INN Fodor's Choice ★ **The Harmony Hotel.** Surf's up, *upscale*, that is; this ultracool, holistic retreat gets top marks for both comfort and sustainability, thanks to American owners who are surfers of an age where comfort, quiet, and thinking ecologically are more appealing than partying. **Pros:** near beach; excellent food; loaner laptops and laptop-size safe boxes; one free yoga class per guest. **Cons:** pricey; not overly kid-friendly but babies welcome; standard rooms are smallish. [$] *Rooms from: $300* ✉ *From Café de Paris, take road almost all the way to Playa Guiones, look for sign leading to tree-shaded parking lot on right* ☎ *2682–4114, 2682–1073* 🌐 *www.harmonynosara.com* 🛏 *10 rooms, 13 one-bedroom bungalows, 1 two-bedroom suite* 🍴 *Breakfast.*

$$ B&B/INN Fodor's Choice ★ **Hotel Lagarta Lodge.** A birders' and nature lovers' Valhalla, this magnificent property on a promontory has amazing views of the forest, river, and coast north of Nosara from both its comfortable rooms and terrace restaurant. **Pros:** amazing views and grounds; close to nature; sustainable; very good value. **Cons:** not on the beach; some steps to rooms; steep, rough road to get here. [$] *Rooms from: $80* ✉ *Top of hill at north end of Nosara* ☎ *2682–0035* 🌐 *www.lagarta.com* 🛏 *12 rooms* 🍴 *No meals.*

$$$ B&B/INN 🏨 **Luna Azul.** Sequestered in the green hills above Playa Ostional, several miles north of Nosara, tranquil, tasteful Luna Azul is full of clever design and healthful attributes; birds and wildlife abound in the surrounding private nature reserve. **Pros:** isolated in a picturesque environment; good restaurant; luxurious rooms; excellent breakfast. **Cons:** off the beaten path; restaurant prices do not include tax and service. [$] *Rooms from: $160* ✉ *1 km (½ mile) north of Ostional, 5 km (3 miles) north of Nosara* ☎ *8821–0075, 2682–1400* 🌐 *www.hotellunaazul.com* 🛏 *3 bungalows, 2 duplex bungalows with 2 rooms each* 🍴 *Breakfast.*

NIGHTLIFE

The Gilded Iguana. Live acoustic music on Tuesday and Friday nights draws a big crowd. ✉ *Playa Guiones* ☎ *2682–0259.*

Olga's Bar. Sunset is the main event in the evening, and both locals and tourists gather to watch it here at this unpretentious beach shack with the best view. ✉ *End of the road to Playa Pelada.*

Restaurante La Luna. Sip an exotic tropical cocktail or munch on hummus and pita bread while watching the sun set at this lovely Mediterranean restaurant, which has exotic Indonesian daybeds and rattan chairs set out on the sand, as well as seats in the chic new indoor lounge. ✉ *Beachfront, Playa Pelada* ☎ *2682–0122.*

Tropicana Discobar. The popular Tropicana is where the action is on Friday and Saturday nights, from 9:30 pm to 2:30 am, for locals who love to dance and visitors who want to join in. ✉ *Downtown Nosara, beside the soccer field* ☎ *2682–0140.*

SHOPPING

Arte Guay. This is the place to find the largest selection of local crafts and every imaginable souvenir, plus beachwear and sun hats. Open 9 to 4:30, Monday to Saturday. ✉ *Just past Café de Paris on road to Playa Guiones, right-hand side.*

Arteinti Glass. This Italian-owned shop sells lovely, handmade glass-bead jewelry and enchanting wind chimes, plus unique hangings, lamp shades, and mobiles made from handmade paper. ✉ *Road to Playa Guiones, across from Centro Medico* ☎ *2682–1406.*

Coconut Harry's Surf Shop. Along with surfing wear and gear, this funky, jam-packed shop has an interesting selection of jewelry and bottled hot sauces that will spice up the local *comida tica* (typical fare). ✉ *Main road, across from Café de Paris.*

The Silver Tree. This elegant jewelry store is a cut above the usual souvenir shop, with beautiful, handmade pieces from local artists as well as items from around the world. There are also unusual, high-quality handcrafted gifts and art. ✉ *2nd floor in minimall beside Café de Paris, on Playa Guiones road.*

SPAS

Tica Massage and Nosara Pilates Studio. Relaxing massages, facials, and salt glows in a jungle setting ($60 per hour) are available by appointment at Tica Massage. Under the same management and in the same location, Nosara Pilates offers Pilates and yoga classes, as well as surfers' stretch sessions. A range of dance and movement classes in this studio includes a kids-in-motion class; check the website for exercise and dance class schedules. ✉ *Heart of Guiones Wellness Center, across from Casa Tucan and Harmony Hotel, Playa Guiones* ☎ *2682–0096* ⊕ *www.ticamassage.com; www.studioguiones.com.*

SÁMARA

36 km (23 miles) southwest of Nicoya, 26 km (16 miles) south of Nosara.

Sámara has miles of palm-shaded beach, safe swimming water, and an abundance of budget accommodations and seafront restaurants, making it especially popular with budget travelers, both Tico and foreign. This can be a lively place on weekends, with beach bars and handicraft vendors setting up on the main drag. A sandy roadway with the occasional car runs alongside the coconut palms and Indian almond trees that line the beach, so be sure to look both ways when you move between the surf and the town. Like nearby Nosara, Sámara is becoming more nature-and-health-conscious, with a weekly farmers' market, Friday from 3 to 6, selling goat and cow cheeses, *kombucha* (a probiotic brewed tea), artisan breads, local honey, salsas, jellies, and handicrafts.

GETTING HERE AND AROUND

The drive from Nicoya to Sámara is one of the most scenic in Costa Rica, passing through rolling hills and green vistas before descending to the wide, south-facing bay hemmed by palm-lined sand. The road is paved all the way and takes about an hour. ■TIP➜ **Potholes are spreading, so drivers need to keep their eyes on the road instead of the beautiful views.** A rough beach road from Nosara is passable in dry season (it's more direct, but takes just as long); do not attempt this road when it rains. To get from Nosara to Sámara via the paved road, drive south, 5 km (3 miles) past Garza. At the T in the road, ignore the road toward Sámara (the beach road) and take the road to the left, toward Nicoya. This will take you uphill to merge with the main Nicoya–Sámara highway. Sámara-bound buses leave Nicoya from a stop 300 meters (1,000 feet) east of the central park. They depart almost hourly from 5 am to 3 pm (there's no bus at 7 am) and then at 4:30, 6:30, 8, and 9:45 pm. For the latest bus schedule, look online at ⊕ *www.samarabeach.com.* There's also a direct Tracopa-Alfaro bus from San José daily at noon (☎ *2221–4214*); the trip takes about 4½ hours and costs $8.

ESSENTIALS

Bank/ATM Banco de Costa Rica ✉ *North side of soccer field, downtown* ☎ *2656–2112.* **Banco Nacional** ✉ *50 m west of Catholic church* ☎ *2656–0089.*

Hospital Clinica ✉ *1 km (½ mile) west of Sámara in Cangreja* ☎ *2656–0166.*

Pharmacy Farmacia Sámara ✉ *Mini plaza Patio Colonial, main road at entrance to Sámara* ☎ *2656–3400.*

Post Office Correo ✉ *Beside church, across from soccer field.*

Rental Cars Alamo ✉ *Main road into town, beside Hotel Giada* ☎ *2656–0958.*

BEACHES

Playa Sámara. This is the perfect hang-out beach, with plenty of shade, bars, and seafront restaurants to take refuge in from the sun. Its wide sweep of light gray sand is framed by two forest-covered hills jutting out on either side. The waves break out on a reef that lines the entrance of the cove several hundred yards offshore, which keeps the water calm enough for safe swimming without rip currents and leaves enough surf to have fun in. The reef holds plenty of marine attractions for diving and snorkeling excursions. Isla Chora, at the south end of the bay, provides a sheltered area that is especially popular for kayakers and snorkel- ers—it even has a tiny beach at lower tides. After years of hard work to clean up the beach, Sámara Beach now sports a Blue Flag. Those seeking solitude should head to the beach's western or eastern ends. **Amenities:** food and drink; water sports. **Best for:** snorkeling; surfing; swimming.

SPORTS AND THE OUTDOORS

TOUR OPERATORS

Sámara is known more for gentle water sports such as snorkeling, kaya- king, and paddleboarding than for surfing, although the calmer waters provide a good place for learning, so surf schools have multiplied fast. There are also two high-flying adventures here: a zip-line tour and ultralight flights and flying lessons. ATV tours, tearing along dirt roads, are popular with travelers who are particularly fond of dust, or mud, according to the season. For information on area activities, visit the town's official website at ⊕ *www.samarabeach.com* or try the informa- tive ⊕ *www.samarainfocenter.com.*

Carrillo Adventures. Horseback riding, river and sea-kayaking, dolphin- watching, fishing, snorkeling, and trips to Palo Verde, Arenal, and Mon- teverde national parks can all be booked here. This long-established, local tour company also provides daily shuttle service to the Liberia airport at 8:30 am ($50 per person, minimum two people) and to Tama- rindo for the same price. ✉ *Miniplaza next door to Palí supermarket in downtown Sámara* ☎ *2656–0606* ⊕ *www.carrilloadventures.com.*

Samara Adventure Company. This tour operator offers an array of local tours and arranges transportation by air and private shuttle to other parts of the country; they also rent bicycles, motorcycles, scooters, and ATVs. ✉ *Main street, beside Hotel Giada* ☎ *2656–0920* ⊕ *www. samara-tours.com.*

CANOPY TOURS

Wing Nuts Canopy Tour. Named after a famous surfer, this three-hour, 10-platform zip-line tour ($60) flies through a patch of tropical forest just south of town, with ocean views from some of the platforms. It's small but just right for younger or timid kids, and they have special kid-size harnesses for kids as young as 2 years old ($40 for kids 12 and under). ✉ *In hills above Sámara, office 1 km (½ mile) east of down- town Sámara, near Hotel Las Brisas del Pacifico* ☎ *2656–0153* ⊕ *www. wingnutscanopy.com.*

DIVING AND SNORKELING

The reef offshore is the best place to snorkel. Kayakers also paddle out to Isla Chora to snorkel on the leeward side of the island.

KAYAKING

Plastic sit-on-top kayaks can be rented at Villas Playa Sámara (⇨ *below*), which is quite close to Isla Chora and the reef.

C&C Surf School. This established surf school runs three-hour, guided kayak snorkeling tours to Isla Chora and the nearby reef ($40, including gear and a fruit snack). You can also rent single kayaks for $10 per hour. Samara Adventure Company and Carrillo Adventures (⇨ *see above*) also organize kayaking tours, on both ocean and river. ☒ *On beach next to Tree House Inn* ☎ *5006–0369* ⊕ *www. cncsurfsamara.webs.com.*

SURFING

The surf is relatively gentle at Sámara, so it's a good place for beginners. The challenging waves for more experienced surfers are farther south, at Playa Camaronal, which has both left and right breaks.

C&C Surf School. This beachfront surf school offers lessons from beginner up ($40 per 90-minute private lesson, including seven-day board rental) with certified instructors, and a huge selection of boards for rent ($4 for the first hour, $2 per hour after). ☒ *On beach in center of town* ☎ *5006–0369* ⊕ *www.cncsurfsamara.webs.com.*

ULTRALIGHT FLIGHTS

Flying Crocodile Lodge. Take off for a thrilling ride over Sámara from the beach near this beach lodge, which gives ultralight flights ($110 cash for 20-minute tour, $150 for 30 minutes) and flying lessons. ☒ *Playa Buena Vista, 6 km (4 miles) northwest of Sámara* ☎ *2656–8048* ⊕ *www. autogyroamerica.com.*

WHERE TO EAT

$$
ITALIAN

✕ **Al Manglar.** Hidden on a rutted side street near a mangrove, this authentically Italian eatery beneath a large thatch roof may not look like much at first, but it's been a local favorite for more than 15 years. Two ladies of Verona are in the kitchen from 6 pm on, preparing fresh pasta, fish, and meat dishes to order, or sliding superthin, crispy pizzas out of the oven. They make the best pizza in town, with more than two dozen varieties to choose from. The ricotta-and-spinach ravioli with a sauce of porcini mushrooms have made many a mouth water, as have the homemade gnocchi—but ask for the salmon ravioli, which isn't on the menu but is often available, smothered in creamy shrimp sauce. Nearly everything is fresh, which means you have to wait a little longer. Wines are available by the carafe, and don't miss the homemade tiramisu. You can order a pizza for takeout. $ *Average main: $15* ☒ *200 m west and 150 m south of Banco Nacional* ☎ *2656–0096* ⊗ *No lunch.*

$$$
BARBECUE

✕ **El Lagarto.** Close enough to the sea to hear the surf above the mix of Latin music on the stereo, El Lagarto serves up real surf and turf, and Sámara's best buzz by far. Varnished wooden tables are scattered across the sand amid ficus and Indian almond trees. The food—fresh, local seafood and high-quality meat from lean Brahman cattle, is grilled to perfection on a massive, open-air barbecue. Sink your teeth into juicy tenderloin, lamb chops, mahimahi, prawns, tuna, mussels, chicken breast stuffed with mushrooms and cheese, portobello mushrooms, or a whole grilled lobster. You won't find any barbecue sauce here; everything is simply brushed with extra-virgin olive oil and seasoned with a bit of garlic, salt, and pepper to complement the flavor of the wood. Dinners include grilled vegetables and potatoes; a salad is à la carte. There's also a kids' menu, an ample wine list, and an extensive cocktail selection, not to mention banana splits. The restaurant is open for dinner only, though they open at 3 pm for cocktails. Tax and service are not included on the menu prices, so expect to pay 23% more than advertised. $ *Average main: $20 ⊠ 200 m west and 200 m south of Banco Nacional or just walk west along the beach past Las Olas ☎ 2656–0750 ⊕ www.ellagartobbq.com ۞ Closed last 2 wks of Sept. and Oct. No lunch.*

$$
ITALIAN
✕ **Pizza & Pasta a Go-Go.** An ample selection of good Italian food, including 14 versions of crispy pizzas, 19 pastas, generous salads, and a lengthy Italian wine list (available by the glass, too), is just one reason to drop in at this sidewalk trattoria. Tuna carpaccio is a lighter option or try their insalata caprese with fresh basil. Unlike the checkered tablecloths you'd find elsewhere, here you have glass tabletops showcasing shells, or plain wooden tables by the pool. Save room for a delicious Tico-Italian version of tiramisu or a mint-chocolate panna cotta. $ *Average main: $14 ⊠ Hotel Giada lobby, main strip, 150 m north of beach ☎ 2656–0132.*

$
VEGETARIAN
✕ **Sámara Organics Market Café.** Proving that healthy food can also be delicious food, this café serves up outrageously good salads and sandwiches featuring locally grown vegetables, fresh local cheeses, and cured meats along with vegetable dips and spreads, and homemade cakes, brownies, and other desserts. Gluten-free and vegan dishes are also on the menu. You can shop here for imported olive oils and other gastronomic rarities in these parts. To drink, there's an array of vegetable and fruit juices in interesting combinations. Chow down at sidewalk tables or under cover in the new lounge. Everything can be packed to go, and the place hosts a weekly farmers' market on Friday, 3 to 5:30, to catch incoming weekenders. $ *Average main: $7 ⊠ In front of Natural Center Gym, on road that runs parallel to beach, across from Sporting Club Gusto Beach ☎ 2656–3046 ⊕ www.samaraorganics.com.*

$$
COSTA RICAN
✕ **Tabanuco Beachfront Restaurante & Bar.** Right on the beach, this lively nightspot also has an elegant terrace restaurant that's romantically torch-lighted at night. Come for fresh ceviche and grilled fish and seafood, Tico-style, as well as chicken and meat dishes. It's open from 11 am to 10 pm, with lots of shade under massive trees and cool breezes off the ocean. $ *Average main: $14 ⊠ On the beach, 30 m west of main beach entrance ☎ 2656–1056 ۞ Closed Sun.*

WHERE TO STAY

$
B&B/INN
⛫ **Hotel Belvedere.** After a day on the beach, it's refreshing to retreat to this small hotel buried in a dense, cool garden on a breezy hill overlooking Sámara. **Pros:** affordable; clean; quiet. **Cons:** 15-minute walk to beach and a bit of a climb back up the hill. $ *Rooms from: $75 ⊠ Entering Sámara, go 100 m left at the 1st cross street ☎ 2656–0213 ⊕ www.belvederesamara.net ⮌ 20 rooms, 2 apartments ⵜ Breakfast.*

$ ⊞ **Hotel Casa del Mar.** Less than a block from the beach, this pleasant, well-
B&B/INN   tended hotel is one of Sámara's best values. **Pros:** helpful staff; easy on
the wallet; free Wi-Fi. **Cons:** close, but not right on the beach; no swimming pool; some noise from road. Ⓢ *Rooms from: $45* ⊠ *Main beach
strip, 45 m east of school* ☎ *2656–0264* ⊕ *www.casadelmarsamara.net*
⤳ *17 rooms, 6 with shared bathroom* ⓄⅠ *No meals.*

$$ ⊞ **Hotel Giada.** Giada means "jade" in Italian, and this small hotel in the
B&B/INN   heart of town, with two small swimming pools surrounded by green-
ery and brilliant bougainvillea, has been decorated with the artistic
Italian owners' precious, polished creations. **Pros:** affordable; friendly;
hair dryers in rooms. **Cons:** not right on the beach; smallish rooms.
Ⓢ *Rooms from: $82* ⊠ *Main strip, 250 m from beach* ☎ *2656–0132*
⊕ *www.hotelgiada.net* ⤳ *24 rooms* ⓄⅠ *Breakfast.*

$$ ⊞ **Sámara Tree House Inn.** One of the few hotels right on the beach, this
B&B/INN   small inn has lofty, breezy bungalows up at palm-tree level, perfect for
folks who love the open air and looking down on the beach action. **Pros:**
right on the beach; small and cozy. **Cons:** neighboring bars and restaurants can be noisy; very small pool. Ⓢ *Rooms from: $135* ⊠ *Beach road,
across from supermarket* ☎ *2656–0733* ⊕ *www.samaratreehouse.com*
⤳ *4 tree houses, 2 rooms* ⓄⅠ *Breakfast.*

$$$ ⊞ **Villas Kalimba.** You may never want to leave this tranquil oasis of
RENTAL   luxury villas hidden behind scrolled white-and-orange walls, where the
architecture is Mexican but the style is all Italian. **Pros:** spacious villas;
all the comforts of home; lovely garden. **Cons:** not right on beach; some
noise from beach road. Ⓢ *Rooms from: $153* ⊠ *200 m east of Sámara
Police Station, along beach road* ☎ *2656–0929* ⊕ *www.villaskalimba.
com* ⤳ *6 villas, 4 casas* ⓄⅠ *No meals.*

$$ ⊞ **Villas Playa Sámara.** Families come back to this property year after
RESORT   year for good reason: there's lots to do, the villas are spacious and prac-
FAMILY   tical, and the beach setting is fabulous. **Pros:** great location; spacious
villas; ample grounds; excellent sportfishing. **Cons:** no phones in rooms;
15-minute walk along the beach to Samara center. Ⓢ *Rooms from: $129*
⊠ *Off main road, 2 km (1¼ miles) south of town* ☎ *2656–1111* ⊕ *www.
villasplayasamara.com* ⤳ *59 villas, 16 deluxe rooms* ⓄⅠ *No meals.*

NIGHTLIFE

La Vela Latina Beach Bar. This is the best spot around for grown-up soft
music and cocktails on the beach at sunset. It's also your best late-night
option for nightcaps, since it's open until midnight. ⊠ *Across from Villas Kalimba, on beach* ☎ *2656–2286.*

Las Olas. The noisiest beach bar is at Cabinas Las Olas, where bright
lights and a pulsing Latin sound track attract a mix of locals and young
backpackers. There's also live music some nights. ⊠ *On beach, 200 m
west and 200 m south of Banco Nacional.*

Mister Lelluz. This local dance club, formerly called Tutti Frutti, is right
on the beach, packed with young Ticos and energetic young visitors. It
swings on Friday and Saturday nights into the early hours of the morning with DJs and live music. ⊠ *50 m west of police station.*

Sporting Club Gusto Beach. This is Sámara's latest incarnation of a hopping beach hangout, with tables and chairs spread out across the

Idyllic Playa Carrillo is perfect for swimming, snorkeling, or just sunning.

sand. Fruit shakes, drinks, excellent espresso, and a creative Italian-flavored menu feed the mostly 25-and-unders who come here for the music, music, music all day and much of the night. The excellent food tends to draw an older crowd at lunch. There's also beach volleyball and great people-watching all day long. ⊠ *On beach, center of town* ☎ *2656–0252.*

Tabanuco. This beachfront restaurant and bar (⇨ *see above*) is a little more upscale and attracts a slightly older, better-heeled crowd than the backpackers at Las Olas. The action heats up on the dance floor after 10 pm, with a high-tech sound-and-light system; live music includes a reggae night. ⊠ *On beach* ☽ *Closed Sun.*

SHOPPING

Souvenir stands are set up along the main street and the entrance to the beach, along with the inevitable handmade-jewelry stalls. Most shops here have pretty much the same beachwear and souvenirs for sale.

CoCo Tales. Delicate coconut carvings and sophisticated, one-of-a-kind jewelry made with polished amber, turquoise, and orange-toned spondylus shells are the specialty of Carloa, a skilled local artisan. You'll find him in his workshop, 9 to 7 daily, on Sámara's main street into town. ⊠ *In front of Cabinas Arenas, main street into town* ☎ *8807–7056.*

Dragonfly Galería. Weird and wonderful, this arts-and-crafts gallery sells local art and carvings, plus shell, feather, and bead jewelry. The owner also paints temporary henna tattoos. Just follow the trail off the main road through the trees decorated with fantastical glowing lamps. ⊠ *Across the street from Century 21 office, main road leading to beach.*

PLAYA CARRILLO

7 km (4½ miles) southeast of Sámara.

With its long, reef-protected, crescent beach backed by an elegant line of swaying coconut palms and sheltering cliffs, Playa Carrillo (interchangeably called Puerto Carrillo) is a candidate for the most picturesque beach in Costa Rica. A smooth, paved boulevard runs along the beach, with sparkling turquoise waters on the seaside and a hedge of scarlet bougainvillea on the land side. The main landmark here is the Hotel Guanamar, high above the south end of the beach. Unfortunately, the former private fishing club and previously grand hotel has been bought and sold so often that its charm has faded. But its bar still has the best view.

GETTING HERE AND AROUND

It's an easy 15-minute drive south on the smooth, paved road from Sámara. If you're not staying at a hotel in Carrillo, you'll have to park your car either in a sunbaked concrete lot halfway along the beach or on the grassy median at the south end of the beach. You can also take a taxi from Sámara or hop on the local bus.

ESSENTIALS

Sámara is the closest town for banks and other services.

EXPLORING

FAMILY **La Selva Wildlife Refuge & Zoo.** Most nature lovers are no fans of zoos, but this modest collection of mostly rescued small animals offers a great chance to see them up close in chest-high corrals under the shade of trees. The Italian owners are a little eccentric, and the place is not terribly well kept. There are plenty of usually hard-to-see nocturnal animals, so the best time to visit is just before sunset, when the roly-poly armadillos and big-eyed kinkajous are starting to stir. There are also skunks, spotted pacas, raccoons, bats, and scarier species like boas, poison dart frogs, caimans, and crocodiles. A bromeliad and orchid collection is artistically arranged around the zoo. If you come early in the day, the best time to see the day animals in action, your ticket is also good for a return early-evening visit. It's pricey, but the ticket price helps to buy food for the animals. Kids under 12, $10; under 6 years, free. ⊠ *Look for signed road on left, just after crossing bridge at south end of beach* ☎ *2656–2236* ⊠ *$15* ☉ *Daily 8–7; last admission 6:30 pm.*

BEACHES

Fodor'sChoice **Playa Carrillo.** Unmarred by a single building, this picture-perfect, Blue
★ Flag beach is ideal for swimming, snorkeling, strolling, and lounging—just remember not to sit under a loaded coconut palm. Signs posted by the municipality cleverly announce that the only entry "fee" is: make no fires, and take your garbage away with you. There are some concrete tables and benches, but they get snapped up quickly. This is a popular beach with locals, and it gets quite busy on weekends. The only commercial activity is a hand-wheeled cart selling fruit ices. **Amenities:** none. **Best for:** snorkeling; swimming; walking.

SPORTS AND THE OUTDOORS
FISHING

Kingfisher. From January to April, the boats moored off the beach take anglers on fishing expeditions for catch-and-release marlin and sail fishing, as well as good-eating dorado, yellowfin tuna, and wahoo.

Captain Rick Ruhlow, a U.S. Coast Guard–licensed skipper with 21 years' experience fishing Costa Rican waters, takes up to five anglers out on *Kingfisher,* a fully equipped 31-foot Palm Beach fishing boat; it's the only boat that stays full-time in Carrillo from November to September. A full day's fishing offshore costs $1,250; inshore $800. ☎ *8834–7125, 2656–0091 ⊕ www.costaricabillfishing.com.*

WHERE TO EAT

$$

ARGENTINE

✕ **El Colibrí Steakhouse.** Tired of fish? Sink your chops into steak—rib eye, New York, or T-bone—grilled on an open fire and served Argentine-style with garlicky chimichurri sauce at this family-run, pleasant rancho restaurant. Other specialties include grilled chorizo sausages or Milanesa, the classic Argentine breaded steak, served with French fries. Wash it down with a glass or bottle of South American *vino tinto.* There's salad, chicken, and, yes, fish when available on the menu, but people come here mainly because of the meat. Six air-conditioned cabinas, some with kitchens, face a small pool next to the restaurant. There's free transportation from Sámara for a party of four or more. $ *Average main: $15 ✉ From main beach road, turn left at soccer field, then left again ☎ 2656–0656 ⊕ www.cabinaselcolibri.com ⊙ Closed Mon. during low season.*

PUNTA ISLITA

16 km (11 miles) south of Playa Carrillo in dry season, 30 km (21 miles) south of Carrillo by alternative mountain route in rainy season.

Punta Islita is named for a tiny tuft of land that becomes an island at high tide. It's synonymous in Costa Rica with Hotel Punta Islita, one of the country's most exclusive, luxurious, and gorgeous resorts, popular with honeymooners and romantics of any age. Just about everything in Punta Islita—from outdoor activities to food—revolves around, and is available through, this resort. Just up the beach, the small village is an artistic work in progress, thanks to a community art project led by a few renowned Costa Rican artists who have turned almost all the buildings into galleries, workshops, or works of art in themselves.

GETTING HERE AND AROUND

During the dry season, January to May, it's a quick trip south of Playa Carrillo in a 4WD vehicle with high-enough clearance to get across the soft-bottom river; but in the rainy season, it's often impossible to cross the Río Ora, so you have to make a longer detour along a winding, mostly paved road, via Santa Marta, with spectacular mountain views. Most well-heeled guests consequently fly into the hotel's private airstrip.

BEACHES

Punta Islita. The curved beach here is rocky but good for walking, especially at low tide when tidal pools form in the volcanic rock. Sunsets are gorgeous, but despite its Blue Flag designation, this is not a great swimming beach. Be sure to take a stroll through the small village up from the beach, which has become an artistic work in progress ⇨ *see above*. Outdoor activites, food, and drinks are all available through the beachside resort. **Amenities:** food and drink. **Best for:** sunset; walking.

WHERE TO STAY

$$$$ RESORT Fodor's Choice ★ 🏨 **Hotel Punta Islita.** Overlooking the ocean from a forested ridge, this secluded and sublime hotel is luxury incarnate, with villas, casitas, suites, and spacious rooms sprinkled around the bougainvillea-bedecked hillside. **Pros:** gorgeous views; ultraluxurious rooms; top-notch service. **Cons:** isolated; distant beach; very pricey; steep paths to and from restaurant and beach club but there is a shuttle van. [$] *Rooms from: $330* ✉ *16 km (11 miles) south of Playa Carrillo* ☎ *2231–6122 in San José, 2656–2020 hotel, 866/446–4053 toll-free U.S.* 🌐 *www.hotelpuntaislita.com* 🛏 *14 rooms, 8 suites, 8 casitas, 25 villas* 🍴 *Breakfast.*

PALO VERDE NATIONAL PARK

52 km (32 miles) south of Liberia.

GETTING HERE AND AROUND

To get to Palo Verde from Liberia, drive south along the Pan-American Highway to Bagaces, then turn right at the small, easy-to-miss sign for Palo Verde, along a rough dirt road for 28 km (17 miles). Count on an hour to drive the distance from the main highway to the park entrance; it's a very bumpy road. You'll have to pay the $10 park entrance fee to get to the Organization for Tropical Studies station. The OTS station is about 7 km (4½ miles) beyond the park entrance; the park headquarters is less than 1 km (½ mile) farther. The gatekeeper takes lunch from noon to 1 pm. The drive from Liberia should take a total of about 1½ hours.

EXPLORING

Palo Verde National Park. One of the best wildlife- and bird-watching parks in Costa Rica, Palo Verde protects a significant amount of deciduous dry forest and its denizens, along with seasonal wetlands that provide a temporary home for thousands of migratory birds toward the end of the rainy season. The park is bordered on the west by the Río Tempisque and encompasses more than 198 square km (76 square miles). The terrain is fairly flat—the maximum elevation in the park is 268 meters (879 feet)—and the forest is less dense than a rain forest, which makes it easier to spot the fauna. While crocodiles ply the Tempisque's waters year-round, from September through March you can see dozens of species of migratory and resident aquatic birds, including herons, wood storks, jabirus, and elegant, flamingo-like roseate spoonbills. White-tailed deer, coatis, collared peccaries, and monkeys are easy to spot, too. It's almost always hot and humid in these lowlands—March is the hottest month—so be prepared with water, hat, and insect repellent.

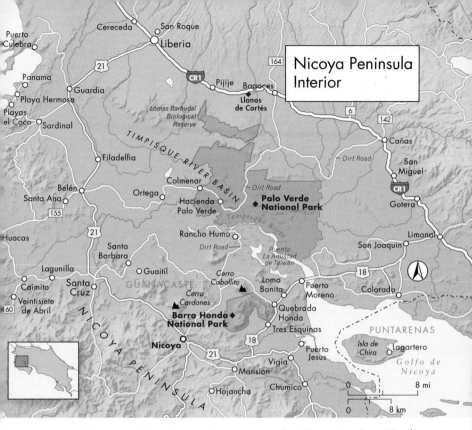

TIP→ A rickety observation tower near the OTS station, about 8 km (5 miles) past the park entrance, gives you a vantage point over a marsh filled with ducks and jacanas. But be prepared to climb a narrow metal ladder. For a good look at hundreds of waterfowl, there's also a long boardwalk jutting out over the wetlands. Hostel-type lodging in rustic dormitory facilities with bunk beds and shared bathrooms ($13), and family-style meals for overnight guests only ($7 breakfast; $9 for lunch or dinner) can be arranged through the park headquarters. ⊠ *29 km (18 miles) southwest of Bagaces* ☎ *2206–5965* ⊠ *$12* ⊙ *Daily 8–dusk; entrance gates open 8–noon and 1–4.*

Llanos de Cortés. Just 3 km (2 miles) north of the Palo Verde road at Bagaces, take the dirt road signed for Llanos de Cortés to get to this hidden waterfall less than 2 km (1 mile) off the highway. About ½ km (¼ mile) along the dirt road you'll see on your right a large rock with "Cataratas" scrawled on it. Follow this bumpy road about 1.3 km (0.8 mile) to its end and then clamber down a steep path to the pool at the bottom of a spectacular, wide, 15- meter (50-foot) waterfall. This is a great place for a picnic; avoid weekends if you can when it's often crowded and noisy. **TIP→** Don't leave anything of value in your car. ⊠ *Off Pan–American Hwy., Bagaces.*

Las Pumas Rescue Shelter. Sad but sobering, one of the few places left in the country where you are guaranteed to see large wild cats, including a jaguar, is this animal rescue center (Centro de Rescate Las Pumas). The small enclosures also hold jaguarundis, pumas, margays, ocelots, and oncillas. Some small animals and birds are rehabilitated and released into the wild. The larger cats are probably here for life, as it's dangerous for them to be released. There's also a nature trail guests can hike, along the Corobici River. Donations to the nonprofit foundation are welcomed. ⊠ *4½ km (3 miles) north of Cañas on main highway* ☎ *2669–6044, 2669–6019 for reservations* ⊕ *www.laspumas.net* ⊠ *$10; children $5* ⊙ *Daily 8–4.*

SPORTS AND THE OUTDOORS

TOUR OPERATOR

Organization for Tropical Studies. This nonprofit, scientific consortium of universities offers overnight packages with a guided walk, excellent family-style meals, and lodging in very basic, no-frills rooms with bunk beds, overhead fans, and private bathrooms ($93 per person). The biological research station overlooks the Palo Verde wetlands, and expert naturalist guides can arrange a boat tour along wetlands lining both sides of the Tempisque River, as well as long hikes on the trails. ■TIP➜ **Bring binoculars and cameras. Guides can direct you to a perennial nest where jabirus (giant storks) are in residence with their chicks, January through February.** Guests still have to pay the $12 entrance fee to the national park. ⊠ *7 km (4½ miles) past park entrance* ☎ *2524–0607* ⊕ *www.ots.ac.cr.*

BIRD-WATCHING

The best bird-watching in Palo Verde is on the wetlands in front of the Organization for Tropical Studies' (OTS) biological station. The OTS has expert guides who can help you see and identify the varied birds in the area, but if you have good binoculars and a bird book, you can identify plenty of species on your own. A boat excursion to Isla Pájaros south of the Río Tempisque is particularly interesting for birders. Toward the end of rainy season this 6-acre island near Puerto Moreno is an exciting place to see hundreds of nesting wood storks, cormorants, and anhingas. You can get close enough to see chicks being fed in nests. ■TIP➜ **The best time to go is very early in the morning, to avoid heat and to guarantee the most bird sightings.**

Aventuras Arenal. This adventure tour company specializes in ecological tours and has guides with good eyes who usually know the English names for birds. Their boat tours up the Río Tempisque ($45, including juice and lunch) depart from the dock at Bebedero or Puerto Humo. ☎ *2479–9133* ⊕ *www.arenaladventures.com.*

Rios Tropicales. Paddle down the easy Class I and II rafting route on the Río Corobicí with this experienced, national rafting company. The two-hour trips ($55 including lunch and excluding ground transportation) are great for bird- and monkey-watching and are safe enough for kids ages seven and older. ⊠ *Km 193, Pan-American Hwy., Cañas* ☎ *2233–6455* ⊕ *www.riostropicales.com.*

FAMILY **Safaris Corobici.** This small, local company specializes in two-hour Class I and II floats down the Río Corobicí ($40) that put in (and end at) their office location, near Km 192 on the Pan-American Highway. They also offer an early-morning bird-watching float tour ($48 including a snack) and a half-day float, with lunch in their Cocobolo restaurant afterward ($65). Boats are launched from 7 am to 3:30 daily. There are also trips on the Tenorio River, including a gentle float trip or a wilder Class IV white-water tour on the upper reaches of the river ($90 including lunch). Their office is right at the entrance to Las Pumas Rescue Shelter. ✉ *Main highway to Liberia, 4½ km (3 miles) north of Cañas, Cañas* ☎ *2669–6191* 🌐 *www.safaricorobici.com.*

WHERE TO STAY

$ B&B/INN 🏨 **La Ensenada Lodge.** Part of a national wildlife refuge, this is the most comfortable and affordable base for bird-watching, crocodile spotting, and nature appreciation on this side of the Río Tempisque. **Pros:** wildlife; interesting setting; good value. **Cons:** very simple rooms; large tour groups at times; no air-conditioning. [$] *Rooms from: $66* ✉ *Take the signed turnoff at Km 155 of the Pan-America Hwy. and drive along a gravel road, about 13 km (8 miles) southwest to the lodge* ☎ *2289–6655* 🌐 *www.laensenada.net* 🛏 *25 cabin rooms* 💳 *No credit cards* 🍴 *No meals.*

BARRA HONDA NATIONAL PARK

100 km (62 miles) south of Liberia, 13 km (8 miles) west of Río Tempisque Bridge.

GETTING HERE AND AROUND

From the Río Tempisque Bridge, drive west along a paved highway. Then follow a dirt road (signed off the highway) for 10 km (6 miles) to the park entrance. If you don't have a car, there is a bus that departs from the town of Nicoya at 7:30 am, Monday through Saturday. You can also take a taxi from Nicoya to the park entrance or go with one of many tour companies in beach towns on the Nicoya Peninsula.

EXPLORING

FAMILY **Barra Honda National Park.** Once thought to be a volcano, 390-meter (1,184-foot) **Barra Honda Peak** actually contains an intricate network of caves created millions of years ago by erosion after the ridge emerged from the sea. You can explore the resulting calcium carbonate formations on a guided tour, and perhaps catch sight of some of the abundant underground animal life, including bats, birds, blindfish, salamanders, and snails. The caves are spread around almost 23 square km (14 square miles), but many of them remain unexplored.

Every day from 8 am to 1 pm, local guides take groups rappelling 18 meters (58 feet) down into **Terciopelo Cave,** which shelters unusual formations shaped (they say) like fried eggs, popcorn, and shark's teeth. You must wear a harness with a rope attached for safety. The tour costs $29 per person (minimum of two) including equipment rental, guide, and entrance fee. Kids under 10 are not allowed into this cave, but they can visit the kid-size La Cuevita cavern ($6), which also has interesting stalagmites. Both cave visits include interpretive nature hikes. ■TIP→ The caves are not open during the wet season, for fear of flooding.

If you suffer a fear of heights, or claustrophobia, the cave tour is not for you, but Barra Honda still has plenty to offer, thanks to its extensive forests and abundant wildlife. You can climb the 3-km (2-mile) Los Laureles trail (the same trail that leads to Terciopelo Cave) to Barra Honda's summit, where you'll have sweeping views over the surrounding countryside and islet-filled Gulf of Nicoya. Wildlife you may spot on Barra Honda's trails includes howler monkeys, white-faced monkeys, skunks, coatis, deer, parakeets, hawks, dozens of other bird species, and iguanas. It's a good idea to hire a local guide from the **Asociación de Guias Ecologistas**. The park has camping facilities, and the ranger station, open 8 am to dusk, has potable water and restrooms. ⊠ *13 km (8 miles) west of Río Tempisque Bridge* ☎ *2659–1551* 🖃 *$12* ⊘ *Daily 8 am–dusk.*

NICOYA

27 km (15 miles) west of the Río Tempisque Bridge.

Once a quaint provincial town, Guanacaste's former colonial capital is now a bustling shopping center, thanks to the bridge over the Río Tempisque that brings tourists headed for the nearby coast. But there are still a few historical remnants around the central park. A noticeable Chinese population, descendants of 19th-century railroad workers, has given Nicoya numerous Chinese restaurants. The town has supermarkets, 24-hour service stations, and ATMs that take international cards.

GETTING HERE AND AROUND

The town of Nicoya is 40 minutes west of the Río Tempisque Bridge on a paved road. If you're running out of gas, oil, or tire pressure, the Servicentro Nicoyano on the north side of Nicoya, on the main road, is open 24 hours.

ESSENTIALS

Bank/ATM Banco de Costa Rica ⊠ *West side of central park* ☎ *2685–5110.* **Coopmani ATH** ⊠ *Main street, beside Fuji Film store.*

Hospital Hospital de L'Anexion ⊠ *Main road into town from highway* ☎ *2685–8400.*

Pharmacy Farmacia y Clinica Medica Nicoyana ⊠ *Main street, near Restaurante Nicoya* ☎ *2685–5138* ⊘ *Weekdays and Sat. 8 am–10 pm, Sun. 9–5.*

Post Office Correo ⊠ *Southwest corner of park.*

EXPLORING

Church of San Blas. Nicoya's last remaining colonial landmark is the impressive, whitewashed, mission-style Church of San Blas. Originally built in 1644, the church was reconstructed after the first church was leveled by an 1831 earthquake. The spare interior is made grand by seven pairs of soaring carved-wood columns. Inside are folk-art wood carvings of the Stations of the Cross arrayed around the stark white walls, a small collection of 18th-century bronze mission bells, and some antique wooden saints. Arched doorways frame verdant views of park greenery and distant mountains. ✉ *North side of central park* 🎟 *By donation* 🕒 *Erratic hrs.*

WHERE TO EAT AND STAY

$ CHINESE 🍴 **Restaurante Nicoya.** Nicoya has a few Chinese restaurants, but this one is the most central and atmospheric, with hanging lanterns, a colorful collection of international flags, and an enormous menu with 85 Asian dishes. The sea bass sautéed with fresh pineapple, chayote, and red peppers is excellent. It's open from 10:30 am to 3 pm; then from 5 to 10:30 for dinner. [$] *Average main: $9* ✉ *Main road, 70 m south of Coopeallianza Bldg.* ☎ *2685–5113.*

$ HOTEL 🏨 **Hotel Río Tempisque.** There aren't many reasons to stay overnight in Nicoya, but if you get stuck here, this lush garden hotel is the best option. **Pros:** quiet; convenient; affordable. **Cons:** simple; not memorable; very busy in January. [$] *Rooms from: $66* ✉ *Hwy. north to Santa Cruz, outside Nicoya* ☎ *2686–6650* 🌐 *www.hotelriotempisque.com* 🛏 *106 rooms* 🍽 *No meals.*

> **CHOROTEGAN POTTERY**
>
> In the country village of Guaitil, 24 km (15 miles) north of Nicoya, artists—most of them women—have revived a vanishing tradition by producing clay pottery handmade in the manner of pre-Columbian Chorotegans. The town square is a soccer field, and almost every house facing it has a pottery shop out front and a round, wood-fired kiln in back. Pottery designs range from imitation Mexican to inspired Cubist abstractions. Prices range from $12 to $300, depending on size; most are around $30. Pieces do crack easily, so pack them carefully.

6

PUNTARENAS

82 km (50 miles) west of San José.

Most commonly used as a cruise ship port and launching pad for ferries heading southeast to the coast of the Nicoya Peninsula and for cruises sailing out on the Gulf of Nicoya, Puntarenas is also a major fishing port with a lively fish market. The town's reputation suffers from the unimpressive parts you see from your car as you roll through town on the way to the ferry dock. But the town has a lot of character off the main drag, thanks to its illustrious past as an affluent port town and principal vacation spot for San José's wealthy, who arrived by train in the last century. Once the port was moved and roads opened to other beaches, Puntarena's economy crashed, but it's starting to make a comeback. Sitting on a narrow spit of sand—*punta de arenas* literally means "point of sand"— that protrudes into the Gulf of Nicoya, the town boasts a beautifully groomed, wide Blue Flag beach with views of the Nicoya Peninsula and spectacular sunsets, along with a new public swimming pool, the San Lucas Beach Club, and a marine-life museum. Ticos arrive by bus and car to enjoy the beach and stroll the Paseo de los Turistas, a beachfront promenade lined with tree-shaded concrete benches and seafood restaurants. Crowds of locals, called porteños, cruise by on bicycles, the town's most popular form of transport.

GETTING HERE AND AROUND

The drive from San José to Puntarenas takes just over one hour. From San José, take the new toll Highway 27 to the port of Caldera, then swing north toward Puntarenas. From here it's another 15 minutes to the ferry dock. Buses run every 40 minutes between San José (Avenida 12, Calle 16) and Puntarenas. If you travel to Puntarenas by public bus, take a taxi to the ferry dock.

Ferries shuttle passengers between Puntarenas and Paquera on the Nicoya Peninsula, where they board buses bound for Cóbano, Montezuma, and Malpaís/Santa Teresa.

Coonatramar. The ferries of Coonatramar ply the route four times daily between Puntarenas and Playa Naranjo, farther north than the Tambor port on the peninsula side of the Gulf of Nicoya. Boats depart Puntarenas at 6:30 and 10 am and 2:20 and 7:30 pm; departures are at 8 am and 12:30, 5:30, and 9 pm from Playa Naranjo. Passengers pay $2 for the crossing. Standard vehicles are charged $18. Bicycles cost about $3. There are no reservations; if you are driving, get there early, especially on weekends. ■TIP➡ If you are heading south on the Peninsula, be aware that the road from Naranjo is in very bad shape. ☏ 2661–1069 ⊕ www.coontramar.com.

Naviera Tambor. The passenger and car ferries run by Naviera Tambor depart both Puntarenas and Paquera at 9 and 11 am, and 2 and 5 pm. Additional departures take place from Puntarenas at 5 am and 8:30 pm, and from Paquera at 6 am and 8 pm. The trip takes about 60 minutes. Passengers pay about $1 for the crossing; vehicles are charged $22–$32 depending on size. This is the more popular route and the ferries are jammed with people in December and January. Music blasts through loudspeakers and the atmosphere is "muy fiesta." Off-season, the atmosphere is much calmer and you may be able to get a seat on deck. ☏ 2661–2084 ⊕ www.navieratambor.com.

ESSENTIALS

Bank/ATM Banco de Costa Rica (BCR). ✉ 100 m west of municipal market. **Banco Nacional** ✉ 200 m west of municipal market ☏ 2661–0233.

Hospital Hospital Monseñor Sanabria ✉ 8 km (5 miles) east of Puntarenas ☏ 2663–0033.

Pharmacy Don Gerardo Farmacia. ✉ 2 blocks north of bus station ☏ 2661–4963.

Post Office Correos ✉ Avda. 3 near Parque Victoria, across from Banco Nacional.

Tourist Information Cámara de Turismo ✉ Plaza El Pacífico, in front of Muelle de Cruceros, Paseo de Los Turistas ☏ 2661–2980 ☉ Weekdays 8–5, weekends when cruise ships are in port.

WHERE TO EAT AND STAY

$$$

ECLECTIC

✕ **Gugas.** In a quiet rancho, surrounded by huge *tabacón* plants and cooled by ceiling fans, Gugas receives high praise from locals for its alfresco fine dining. "Chicken of the Sea" (fish stuffed with shrimp and spices), pasta dishes, vegetarian options, seafood, and meat plates are all on the menu of

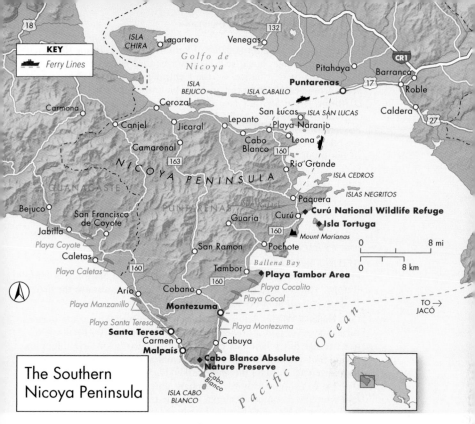

The Southern
Nicoya Peninsula

KEY
Ferry Lines

this German-owned restaurant. There's a long bar to perch at and tables sport red and white napery. It's just one block north of the bustle of the Paseo de los Turistas. ⑤ *Average main: $18* ✉ *From the cruise-ship dock on Paseo de Los Turistas, 100 m due north* ☎ 2661–0707.

$$$
SEAFOOD
✕ **Steakhouse La Yunta.** In a 1928 wooden building painted peach, originally a vacation home for San José's upper class, this old-fashioned steak house is presided over by mounted ox heads (*yunta* means "a yoked pair of oxen"). Seating is on a large veranda with views of the ocean and passersby strolling down the Paseo de los Turistas. The specialty is *churrasco* (tenderloin), but the diverse menu includes seafood dishes such as lobster and sea bass cooked 10 different ways. The liquor list is impressively long. ▪**TIP**➔ **If you order lobster, ask for it to be cooked lightly; the kitchen has a tendency to overcook crustaceans.** ⑤ *Average main: $16* ✉ *West end of Paseo de los Turistas, east of Hotel Tioga* ☎ 2661–3216.

$$
HOTEL
⬚ **Hotel Las Brisas.** Right on the beach, this white, three-story building with Greek columns is centered around a pool deck that features stunning sunset views over the Nicoya Peninsula. **Pros:** unbeatable ocean views; good restaurant; very close to ferry dock. **Cons:** can be noisy when families gather around the pool. ⑤ *Rooms from: $139* ✉ *West end of Paseo de los Turistas* ☎ 2661–4040 ⊕ *www.lasbrisashotelcr.com* ⬏ *25 rooms* ⑩ *Breakfast.*

$$ HOTEL **Hotel Tioga.** This grande dame of Puntarenas hotels facing the beach is showing its age, but it still evokes a bygone era when Puntarenas was the major destination on the Central Pacific coast. **Pros:** across street from beach. **Cons:** timeworn; a bit cramped; busy on weekends. [$] *Rooms from: $90* ✉ *Paseo de los Turistas, 8 blocks west of cruise ship dock* ☎ *2661–0271* 🛏 *52 rooms* 🍴 *Breakfast.*

EN ROUTE **Paquera.** If you take the ferry from Puntarenas to the southern tip of the Nicoya Peninsula, you'll arrive at a ferry dock 5 km (3 miles) north of the small community of Paquera. You can pick up supplies at the supermarkets, fill up your tank on the way to the beach, and grab a quick bite to eat at a pizza joint en route.

CURÚ NATIONAL WILDLIFE REFUGE

7 km (4½ miles) south of Paquera, 1½ to 2 hrs southwest of Puntarenas by ferry.

GETTING HERE AND AROUND

From the town of Paquera it's a short drive to Curú National Wildlife Refuge. You can also take a bus bound for Cóbano, just ask the driver to drop you off at the entrance to the refugio.

FAMILY **Curú National Wildlife Refuge.** Established by former farmer and logger-turned-conservationist Frederico Schutt in 1933, this 106-hectare (262-acre) refuge has a fabulous beach and bay, perfect for kayaking; plus hiking trails leading through forest and mangrove swamps. Named after the indigenous word for the spiky-barked *pochote* trees that flourish here, the reserve is home to hordes of phantom crabs on the beach, howler and white-faced capuchin monkeys in the trees, red brocket deer grazing in open fields, and plenty of hummingbirds, kingfishers, woodpeckers, trogons, and manakins (including the coveted long-tailed manakin). The refuge, classified as a Blue Flag project, is working on building an artificial reef. Visitors can stay in very basic beachfront cabins with solar power ($30 per person, including entrance fee); meals are $10 each. Call ahead to arrange for lodging, guides, horseback riding, kayaking tours, and early-morning bird-watching walks. The entrance fee is $10. ✉ *7 km (4½ miles) south of Paquera on road to Cóbano, left side of road* ☎ *2641–0100* 🌐 *www.curuwildliferefuge.com* 🎟 *$12* 🕒 *Daily 7–4.*

SPORTS AND THE OUTDOORS

TOUR OPERATOR

Seascape Kayak Tours. From November to May, experienced Canadian guide Bruce Smith leads half- and full-day kayak excursions in Ballena Bay, leaving from Curú and Playa Tambor ($85 to $165, minimum two people). ✉ *Curú National Wildlife Refuge* ☎ *8314–8605.*

Turismo Curú. Horseback tours of the Curú National Wildlife Refuge ($10 per hour, plus $10 admission to refuge) are a specialty of this tour operator, along with 90-minute guided nature walks ($15). The company also offers inexpensive kayaking trips to nearby Isla Tortuga, including snorkeling; half-day tour is $65, full day is $125, including lunch. Or you can rent kayaks by the hour ($10 single, $15 double). There's an office in Paquera and a dive shop on-site at the refuge, with tanks, tours, and diving lessons. ⊠ *Main road, across from Esso station* ☎ *2641–0004* ⊕ *www.curutourism.com.*

EN
ROUTE

Cóbano. Paquera is the closest city to Tambor, but if you're headed to Montezuma or Malpaís, you'll pass through Cóbano, 12 km (7½ miles) southwest of Tambor. The town has a supermarket, two gas stations, and a large Banco Nacional with the area's only consistently reliable ATM. (Montezuma and Malpaís/Santa Teresa now have cash machines, but they frequently run out of money.) ⊠ *Cóbano.*

PLAYA TAMBOR AREA

27 km (17 miles) south of Paquera.

Much of the huge Bahía Ballena shoreline is taken up by a massive all-inclusive hotel and an adjoining private residential development and golf course. But to the south, near the actual village of Tambor, visitors can explore the barely developed Playa Tambor, a beautiful flat beach with nothing more than a volleyball net, a few concrete tables set under shade trees, and one beach shack serving pizza. This beach was never developed as much as Montezuma or Malpaís, making it a better destination for those who want to get away from the crowds. It can serve as a convenient base for fishing excursions, bird-watching, horseback-riding trips, and day trips to Curú National Wildlife Refuge and Isla Tortuga.

GETTING HERE AND AROUND

You can fly directly to Tambor (TMU) from San José on SANSA and Nature Air. Taxis meet every flight and can take you to a nearby hotel ($10 to $15), to Montezuma ($40), or to Malpaís ($40–$50).

SPORTS AND THE OUTDOORS

Unlike other beach towns, tiny Tambor doesn't have tour operators on every corner or rental shops of any kind—not even for a basic bike. The receptionist at your hotel can set up tours of the area's diverse natural attractions.

FISHING

In the open sea off the Gulf of Nicoya, sailfish, marlin, tuna, mahimahi, and wahoo are in abundance from November to March. Local fishermen in small boats are your best guides to finding fish in the gulf, including snapper, sea bass, and jacks, almost year-round. Prices for fishing range from $375 for half-day trips to $900 for full-day excursions.

Dive Academy Ballena Blanca. This PADI-certified dive outfit operates fishing tours aboard 27-foot Apex boats. Inshore half-day is $450; offshore whole day is $900. Their dive excursions include trips to three wrecks nearby and a cave dive that offers a chance to see a white-nosed shark. A two-tank dive, including equipment, is $110. ⊠ *Los Delfines center, next door to Tambor airport* ☎ *2683–0015* ⊕ *www. diving-costa-rica.com.*

HIKING

An easy and quick excursion from Tambor is the 1-km (½-mile) hike south of town to the secluded beach of Palo de Jesús. From the town's dock, follow the road south until it becomes a shady trail that winds its way over rocks and sand around Punta Piedra Amarilla. The trees along

Isla Tortuga, just off the coast near Curú National Wildlife Refuge

the way resound with squawks of parakeets and the throaty utterings of male howler monkeys.

HORSEBACK RIDING

The Tango Mar Resort has its own stables and offers horseback tours that can take you down trails through the rain forest or down to the beach to see an array of wildlife. Set off early in the morning or late in the afternoon, when it is cooler and you are more likely to see birds and animals. Tours range from $40 to $60, depending on the duration.

WHERE TO STAY

$$$ RESORT **Tambor Tropical.** Centered on the scenic sweep of placid Bahía Tambor with its warm, shallow water, intimate Tambor Tropical offers "beds with a view" in spacious suites, along with sportfishing, horseback riding, bird-watching, and just lolling in a hammock by the pretty, blue-tile pool. **Pros:** spacious suites; tranquil, beautiful setting; easy access. **Cons:** no air-conditioning in two suites; no kids; Continental, not full breakfast, included. [$] *Rooms from: $175* ✉ *From Tambor main street, turn left at beach* ☎ *2683–0011, 866/890–2537 in U.S.* 🌐 *www.tambortropical.com* 🛏 *12 suites* 🍴 *Breakfast.*

$$$ RESORT FAMILY Fodor's Choice ★ **Tango Mar Resort.** Set on stunning, palm-fringed Playa Quizales (a Blue Flag beach) and backed by 5 acres of exuberant gardens and a 9-hole executive golf course, this comfortable, contemporary resort has a wide range of luxurious lodging options that appeal to families, couples of every age, and honeymooners. **Pros:** gorgeous setting; friendly service and attention to details; lots of activity options. **Cons:** quiet evenings; large groups on occasion; stairs to climb to villas and some rooms. [$] *Rooms from: $210* ✉ *Playa Quizales, 3 km (2 miles) south of Tambor*

☎ *2683–0001, 800/297–4420 in North America* 🌐 *www.tangomar.com* ⇨ *18 rooms, 17 suites, 5 villas* 🍽 *Breakfast.*

ISLA TORTUGA

90 mins by boat from Puntarenas.

Soft white sand and casually leaning palms fringe this island of tropical dry forest off the southern coast of the Nicoya Peninsula. Sounds heavenly? It would be if there weren't quite so many people. Tours from Jacó, Herradura, San José, Puntarenas, and Montezuma take boatfuls of visitors to drink from coconuts and snorkel around a large rock. On the boat ride from Playa Tambor or Montezuma you might spot passing dolphins. Though state owned, the island is leased and inhabited by a Costa Rican family. It makes for an easy day trip out to sea, costing $20 to $109, depending on the duration and departure point.

GETTING HERE AND AROUND

Every tour operator in Playa Tambor and Montezuma *(⇨ below)* offers trips to Isla Tortuga, one of the area's biggest attractions, or you can kayak from the nearby Curú National Wildlife Refuge. Admission to the island is $7 (included in tour prices).

6

BEACHES

FAMILY **Isla Tortuga.** This idyllic, unpopulated island has clear turquoise water, where you'll see a good number of colorful fish, though in the company of many tourists. A 40-minute hiking trail (small fee) wanders past monkey ladders, strangler figs, bromeliads, orchids, and the fruit-bearing *guanábana* (soursop) and *marañón* (cashew) trees up to a lookout point with amazing vistas. **Amenities:** water sports. **Best for:** snorkeling; swimming.

SPORTS AND THE OUTDOORS

KAYAKING

Calypso Cruises Island Tours. This company pioneered excursions in the Gulf of Nicoya with tours aboard a luxury catamaran yacht to Isla Tortuga. Depart from San José, Manuel Antonio, or anywhere in between. A typical itinerary includes a Tico breakfast en route to the port, snorkeling, banana boat rides, and five hours on the island, with a first-class lunch served with chilled white wine—all for about $139. ■ **TIP→ If you're in Puntarenas, the Calypso Cruises dock has an air-conditioned, elegant restaurant, the Shrimp Shack, serving excellent lunches.** ☎ *2256–2727, 800/887–1969 in North America* 🌐 *www.calypsocruises.com.*

Turismo Curú. Turismo Curú arranges year-round kayak excursions to Isla Tortuga for $25 (minimum two), including entrance fee to the island. Snorkeling equipment is available for an additional $5 fee. ✉ *Main road, across from Esso station, Paquera* ☎ *2641–0004* 🌐 *www.curutourism.com.*

MONTEZUMA

7 km (4½ miles) southeast of Cóbano, 45 km (28 miles) south of Paquera, 18 km (11 miles) south of Tambor.

Beautifully positioned on a sandy bay, Montezuma is hemmed in by a precipitous wooded shoreline that has prevented the overdevelopment that has affected so many other beach towns. Its small, funky town center is a pastel cluster of New Age health-food cafés, trendy beachwear shops, jaunty tour kiosks, lively open-air bars and restaurants and, at last count, three ice cream shops, one advertising organic Italian gelato. Most hotels are clustered in or around the town's center, but the best ones are on the coast to the north and south, where the loudest revelers are the howler monkeys in the nearby forest. The beaches north of town, especially Playa Grande, are lovely.

Montezuma has been on the international vagabond circuit for years, attracting backpackers and alternative-lifestyle types. Yoga is a main attraction with a wide range of classes, and the town is becoming more of a cultural draw, with a low-key film festival of shorts and documentaries, and an occasional poetry festival. At night, the center of town often fills up with tattooed travelers and artisans who entertain each other and passersby. When college students are on break, the place can be a zoo. Wags used to refer to the town as Monte*fuma,* with *fuma* meaning "smoke" in Spanish—get it?—but, for better or for worse, Montezuma is being tamed and becoming more civilized and attractive with plenty of grown-up lodging and dining options to choose from.

North and south of the town center have always been quiet, and the attractions here include swaths of tropical dry forest, waterfalls, and beautiful virgin beaches that stretch across one national park and two nature preserves. One especially good walk (about 2 hours) or horseback ride leads to a small waterfall called El Chorro that pours into the sea, where there is a small tidal pool at lower tides.

GETTING HERE AND AROUND

Most people get here via the ferry from Puntarenas to Paquera, which is an hour's drive from Montezuma, with a bumpy dirt-road stretch, from Cóbano to Montezuma. The quickest way to get here, however, is to fly to nearby Tambor. One of the taxis waiting at the airstrip will take you to Montezuma for $45–$50, about a 1½-hour drive. There are also one-hour water taxis ($40) that travel every morning between Jacó and Montezuma, departing from Montezuma at 9:30 am and Jacó at 10:45 am.

ESSENTIALS

ATM Banco Nacional ⊠ *Main road, Cóbano* ☎ *2642–0210.*

SPORTS AND THE OUTDOORS

In Montezuma it seems that every other storefront is occupied by a tour operator. In spite of the multitude of signs advertising "Tourist Information," none are officially sanctioned by the Costa Rican tourist office.

Cocozuma Traveller. Montezuma's oldest and most experienced tour company offers horseback riding to a beachfront waterfall ($40), a full-day snorkeling trip to Isla Tortuga with lunch ($55), and various

Jumping through one of the two waterfalls in Montezuma

sportfishing options ($250–$800). ⊠ *Main road, next to El Sano Banano* ☎ *2642–0911* ⊕ *www.cocozumacr.com.*

Zuma Tours. This reliable agency organizes local tours, transport by shuttle van, and taxi boats between Jacó and Montezuma. ⊠ *Main street, south of El Sano Banano Hotel* ☎ *2642–0024* ⊕ *www.zumatours.net.*

HIKING

Hiking is one of the best ways to explore Montezuma's natural treasures, including beaches, lush coastline, jungles, and waterfalls. There are plenty of options around town or in nearby parks and reserves. Just over a bridge, 10 minutes south of town, a slippery path patrolled by howler monkeys leads upstream to two waterfalls and a fun swimming hole. If you value your life, don't jump or dive from the waterfalls. Guides from any tour operator in town can escort you, but save your money. This one you can do on your own. The path is very crowded on weekends, especially in January and around Easter.

El Chorro. To reach the beachfront waterfall called El Chorro, head left from the main beach access and hike about two hours to the north of town along the sand and through the woods behind the rocky points. The trip takes you across seven adjacent beaches, on one of which there is a small store where you can buy soft drinks. Bring water and good sunblock. El Chorro can also be reached on a horseback tour with a local tour operator.

WHERE TO EAT

$$$ × **Cocolores.** Follow the glow of multicolor lanterns to this dinner-only,
ECLECTIC open-air eatery within sight and sound of the ocean. The simple wooden tables are on a patio bordered with gardens or, during the drier months,

practically on the beach. The Italian and Argentine owners serve an eclectic menu ranging from shrimp curry to squid in spicy puttanesca sauce to tenderloin with porcini mushrooms. The restaurant usually opens just in time for sunset. [$] *Average main: $16* ✉ *Behind Hotel Pargo Feliz* ☎ *2642–0348* ▭ *No credit cards* ⏲ *Closed Mon. and Oct.*

$$ ECLECTIC 🍴 **El Sano Banano Restaurant.** Freshly caught seafood, organic chicken, sushi, Thai dishes, pizza, and a half dozen pasta dishes are included on the menu at Montezuma's first natural-food restaurant. Named after the chewy, dried bananas made by the owners, who also own the upscale Ylang Ylang Beach Resort nearby, the popular eatery serves the best vegetarian fare in town, including Thai tofu curry and some excellent wraps and salads. On the terrace, which is the best people-watching spot in town, you can enjoy a delicious Mocha Chiller, made with frozen yogurt, or a fruit smoothie made with local coconut milk. The homemade cakes and pies are scrumptious. A battalion of ceiling fans keeps the air moving in the spacious dining room decorated with murals of tropical beach scenes. A free movie is shown nightly at 7:30-ish in the dining room ($6 minimum consumption)—don't expect a romantic dinner during this time. [$] *Average main: $14* ✉ *Main road* ☎ *2642–0944* 🌐 *www.ylangylangbeachresort.com.*

$$$ ITALIAN Fodor's Choice ★ 🍴 **Playa de los Artistas.** Low driftwood tables scattered along the rocky beach and an inventive Mediterranean menu have made this one of the most scenic, as well as one of the best, restaurants in the country for more than 20 years. The decor is funky with "found" art and hanging lamps, and every guest gets a warm welcome from the chef's gracious wife, Daniela, and a bevy of notably gorgeous, multilingual waitresses. The restaurant is most spectacular at night, when flickering lanterns combine with crashing surf to create a dramatic and romantic dinner experience. The eclectic menu changes daily and features local seafood, lamb, beef, and even duck. Portions are plentiful and artistically presented on huge platters. On weekends, Italian owner/chef Nicola fires up the barbecue and wood-fired pizza oven. Don't pass up the velvety, dark-chocolate tart if it's on the dessert menu. [$] *Average main: $18* ✉ *275 m south of town, near Los Mangos Hotel* ☎ *2642–0920* ▭ *No credit cards* ⏲ *Closed Sun. No lunch Sun.–Fri.*

$$$ ECLECTIC 🍴 **Ylang Ylang Restaurant.** One of Montezuma's most scenic restaurants, Ylang Ylang is nestled between the beach and the jungle offering views of waves crashing against the rocks. The lunch menu—a selection of sushi, salads, wraps, and sandwiches—is similar to the owners' restaurant in town at El Sano Banano, but the ocean view and elegant terrace setting make it worth the 10-minute walk down the beach. The inventive dinner menu ranges from a Thai-style teriyaki tuna steak to penne in a seafood sauce. There are also various vegan and raw live dishes. Whatever you choose, you'll want to save room for one of the scrumptious desserts, such as the tiramisu espresso crepe. At night, they can provide transportation from town if you make a reservation earlier in the day at the Sano Banano. [$] *Average main: $18* ✉ *On beach, ½ km (¼ mile) north of town, at Ylang Ylang Beach Resort* ☎ *2642–0636* 🌐 *www.ylangylangbeachresort.com.*

WHERE TO STAY

$ B&B/INN **El Sano Banano Village Café Suites.** If quiet and cool is what you are seeking, these comfortable, tastefully decorated rooms above the popular restaurant of the same name are air-conditioned and soundproofed—and they are a bargain. **Pros:** budget-friendly; beach resort privileges; excellent restaurant. **Cons:** most guest rooms lack windows; can feel a little claustrophobic. [$] *Rooms from: $75* ✉ *Main road* ☎ *2642–0636* 🌐 *www.ylangylangbeachresort.com* 🛏 *12* 🍴 *Breakfast.*

$ B&B/INN **Horizontes de Montezuma.** Montezuma's only Spanish-language center is perched on a hill 2 km (1 mile) from town, and rents its rooms to students and travelers. **Pros:** friendly; terrific value; nice respite from the heat of town. **Cons:** outside town; need car to stay here. [$] *Rooms from: $60* ✉ *2 km (1 mile) north of Playa Montezuma* ☎ *2642–0534* 🌐 *www.horizontes-montezuma.com* 🛏 *7 rooms* 🍴 *No meals.*

$$ HOTEL **Hotel Amor de Mar.** About ½ km (¼ mile) south of town, this charming, small hotel with a spectacular sea view sits on a grassy lawn between the rocky shoreline and the entrance to Montezuma's famous waterfall hike. **Pros:** beautiful property; friendly. **Cons:** most of the rooms are small; some noise and commotion from nearby parking lot for waterfall. [$] *Rooms from: $90* ✉ *South of town, past bridge* ☎ *2642–0262* 🌐 *www.amordemar.com* 🛏 *9 rooms, 2 houses* 🍴 *No meals.*

$$ HOTEL **Hotel El Jardín.** Spread across a hill a few blocks from the beach, this hotel has rooms and villas with ocean, pool, and garden views. **Pros:** central location; good value. **Cons:** a few rooms catch a bit of noise from bars in town; steep paths to climb. [$] *Rooms from: $85* ✉ *West end of main road* ☎ *2642–0074* 🌐 *www.hoteleljardin.com* 🛏 *14 rooms, 2 villas* 🍴 *No meals.*

$ HOTEL **Hotel Los Mangos.** The rhythmic sounds of the nearby ocean make these affordable octagonal wood bungalows spread across a shady, green mango grove the perfect place to practice yoga or just relax. **Pros:** great pool; lots of wildlife; yoga central. **Cons:** road noise; could use updating; slightly uphill concrete paths to cabins. [$] *Rooms from: $60* ✉ *Near entrance to waterfall trail, ½ km (¼ mile) south of town* ☎ *2642–0384* 🌐 *www.hotellosmangos.com* 🛏 *10 rooms, 6 with bath; 9 bungalows* 🍴 *No meals.*

$$ HOTEL FAMILY **Luz de Mono.** About 50 meters from the beach, downtown Montezuma's most upscale hotel has comfortable, tastefully decorated rooms amidst a lush, almost jungle-like garden. **Pros:** secluded feel although in center of town; lots of shade in huge garden; conveniently located. **Cons:** some steeper inclines to reach villas. [$] *Rooms from: $85* ✉ *End of the main road, across from beach entrance* ☎ *2642–0090* 🌐 *www.luzdemono.com* 🛏 *12 rooms, 6 casitas* 🍴 *Breakfast.*

$$$ RESORT Fodor's Choice ★ **Ylang-Ylang Beach Resort.** Secluded and serene, this gorgeous tropical resort with a holistic slant sits in an exuberant garden, nestled between the sea and a lush forest. **Pros:** gorgeous, natural setting; great restaurant; eco-friendly. **Cons:** ocean-view tent cabins offer limited privacy; the standard, ground-level rooms are dark. [$] *Rooms from: $203* ✉ *700 m north of school in Montezuma* ☎ *2642–0636, 888/795–8494 in North America* 🌐 *www.ylangylangbeachresort.com* 🛏 *8 bungalows, 1 treetop tent cabin, 3 suites, 3 standard rooms, 6 ocean-view tents* 🍴 *Some meals.*

NIGHTLIFE

Montezuma's nightlife is focused on a handful of bars where locals and foreigners mix, a refreshing change from larger beach towns where the clientele tends to be more segregated. A few venues boasting live music have recently appeared on the scene, including El Sano Banano, where along with the nightly movie showing, guest musicians and bands appear. Street-side artisans selling their creations often animate the area with drumming and dancing that draws passersby to stop and shake their hips, too.

Cafe Restaurant Organico. Every Monday is open mike at this Italian-owned hot spot. The fun gets started around 4:30 and goes late into the night if enough performers show up. ⊠ *Across from Cocolores, beach road* ☎ *2642–1322.*

Chico's Bar. Chico's Bar blasts music from its dark, uninviting entrance, but farther back is a brighter, spacious deck with pool tables and dancing. Directly behind is an open-air beach bar with a more laid-back atmosphere. ⊠ *Next to Hotel Moctezuma.*

SHOPPING

Beachwear, banana paper, wooden crafts, and indigenous pottery are some of what you find in colorful shops in the town's center. During the dry season, traveling artisans from around the world unfold their street-side tables just before the sun begins to set; candles light up the handmade leather-and-seed jewelry, dream catchers, and knit tops.

Deep Forest Aquamarine. Among the many craft and souvenir stands and shops in town, this artisans' cooperative stands out for fabulous mosaic-tiled mirrors, original jewelry, carved-wood bird mobiles, pottery, and charming, painted wooden porcupines with colored toothpicks for spines. It's open 9 to 9 daily in high season. ⊠ *Beside El Sano Banano Restaurant, main street* ☎ *8848–0146.*

Librería Topsy. For some intellectual stimulation at the beach, head to Librería Topsy, where you can buy or exchange books. There are also local newspapers for sale along with a wide selection of the best nature and local guidebooks, kids' books (mostly in Spanish), and school and office stationery supplies. The owner also provides a postal service, where you can drop off postcards and letters to be mailed (since there is no post office at the southern tip of the peninsula). ⊠ *Next door to school* ☎ *2642–0576* ⊘ *Closed Sun. and Sept.–Nov.*

CABO BLANCO ABSOLUTE NATURE PRESERVE

10 km (6 miles) southwest of Montezuma, about 11 km (7 miles) south of Malpaís.

Cabo Blanco Absolute Nature Preserve. Conquistadores named this area Cabo Blanco on account of its white earth and cliffs, but it was a more benevolent pair of foreigners—Swede Nicolas Wessberg and his Danish wife, Karen Mogensen, arriving here in the 1950s—who made it a preserve (Reserva Natural Absoluta Cabo Blanco, in Spanish). Appalled by the first clear-cut in the Cabo Blanco area in 1960, the pioneering couple launched an international appeal to save the forest. In time their efforts led not only to the creation of the 12-square-km (4½-square-mile) reserve but also to the founding of Costa Rica's national park service, the National Conservation Areas System (SINAC). Wessberg was murdered on the Osa Peninsula in 1975 while researching the area's potential as a national park. A reserve just outside Montezuma was named in his honor. A reserve has also been created to honor his wife, who dedicated her life to conservation after her husband's death.

Informative natural-history captions dot the trails in the humid evergreen forest of Cabo Blanco. Look for the sapodilla trees, which produce a white latex used to make gum; you can often see V-shape scars where the trees have been cut to allow the latex to run into containers placed at the base. Wessberg cataloged a full array of animals here: porcupine, hog-nosed skunk, spotted skunk, gray fox, anteater, cougar, and jaguar. Resident birds include brown pelicans, white-throated magpies, toucans, cattle egrets, green herons, parrots, and blue-crowned motmots. A fairly strenuous 10-km (6¼-mile) round-trip hike, which takes about two hours in each direction, follows a trail from the reserve entrance to **Playa Cabo Blanco.** The beach is magnificent, with hundreds of pelicans flying in formation and paddling in the calm waters offshore—you can wade right in and join them. Off the tip of the cape is the 698-square-meter (7,511-square-foot) **Isla Cabo Blanco,** with pelicans, frigate birds, brown boobies, and an abandoned lighthouse. As a strict reserve, Cabo Blanco is open only five days a week. It has brand new restrooms (in honor of the park's 50th anniversary in 2013), picnic tables at the entrance, and a visitor center with infomation panels on park history and biological diversity, but no other tourist facilities, and overnight camping is not permitted. Most visitors come with their own guide. ■ TIP→ **This is one of the hottest parks in the country, so be sure to bring lots of water with you. An official sign at the entrance warns people with cardiovascular problems NOT to walk the strenuous trail to Cabo Blanco beach.** ✉ *10 km (6 miles) southwest of Montezuma via Cabuya, Montezuma* ☎ *2642–0093* 🖂 *$12* ☉ *Wed.–Sun. 8–4.*

GETTING HERE AND AROUND

The road to the reserve from Montezuma is usually passable and well-graded in the dry season. It's also scenic, with rows of huge, spiky pochote trees and one massive ficus tree with its own historical plaque. The road from Malpaís is much rougher and a 4WD is recommended, especially in the rainy season. From Montezuma or Malpaís, take the road signed to Cabuya. Taxis can take you to or from Montezuma for $15 one way—that's always the easiest option—but buses to Cabuya also leave from Montezuma daily at 8:30 am, 10:30 am, 12:30 pm, 2:30 pm, and 4:30 pm.

MALPAÍS AND SANTA TERESA

12 km (7½ miles) southwest of Cóbano, 52 km (33 miles) south of Paquera.

Once frequented mostly by die-hard surfers in search of some of the country's largest waves and by naturalists en route to the nearby Cabo Blanco Absolute Nature Preserve, this area is now a 10-km (6-mile) stretch of hotels, restaurants, and shopping centers strung along a mostly dirt road that is choking with dust in the dry season and awash in mud the rest of the year. The lovely beaches and consistent surf are still the main draw here, along with new health-oriented spas, organic restaurants, and yoga classes that are attracting a very international, young crowd, from Europe, Australia, and North America.

Coming from Cóbano, the bumpy dirt road hits an intersection, known locally as El Cruce, marked by a cluster of shopping centers, banks, restaurants, and hotel signs. To the left is the partially paved route to relatively tranquil Malpaís, and to the right is the road to Santa Teresa, which has a few paved sections but is mostly a rutted, narrow, busy dirt road. Playa Carmen, straight ahead, is the area's best place for surfing, though swimmers will want to be careful of rip currents. Malpaís and Santa Teresa are so close that locals disagree on where one begins and the other ends. You could travel up the road parallel to the ocean that connects them and not realize you've moved from one town to the other.

GETTING HERE AND AROUND

From Paquera it's a 90-minute drive to Malpaís via Cóbano. After Cóbano, the road quickly deteriorates. It can become quite muddy in the rainy season, so you'll want a 4WD vehicle. There is now a direct bus from San José, leaving at 6 am and 2 pm to Santa Teresa, crossing with the ferry from Puntarenas (Transportes Hermanos Rodríguez, ☏ 2642–0219). The trip takes about six hours and costs about $15, including ferry fare. Taxis waiting at Tambor's airstrip will take up to four people to Malpaís for $45–$50.

Tropical Tour Shuttles. The trip between Jacó and Malpaís takes about two hours, thanks to a fast daily boat service between Jacó and Montezuma, followed by an hour's drive ($50 total). Tropical Tours can also set you up with a shuttle to San José ($50), about 5½ hours, using vans and the Puntarenas to Paquera ferry. ⊠ *50 m north of El Cruce* ☏ *2640–1900* ⊕ *www.tropicaltourshuttles.com.*

ESSENTIALS

ATM Banco Nacional ⊠ *Centro Comercial Playa Carmen, at the crossroads* ☏ *2640–0640.*

Medical Center Lifeguard Urgent Medical Centre. This medical center at the crossroads in Malpaís stands on guard 24 hours a day and will make hotel visits if you're injured or too sick to move. ⊠ *At the crossroads, around the corner from BCR bank* ☏ *2220–0911.*

Pharmacy Farmacia Amiga ⊠ *Centro Comercial Playa Carmen, at the crossroads* ☏ *2640–0463* ⊘ *Mon.–Sat. 8–8.*

Taxi Taxi. For a reliable taxi driver, ask for Richard. ☏ *8360–8166.*

SPORTS AND THE OUTDOORS
TOUR OPERATOR
Olingo Ecotours. You'll see and learn more at Cabo Blanco or Curú nature reserves in the company of a private naturalist guide from this outfit. Half-day wildlife tours, 7 am to 1 pm, are $100 per person, minimum two people; $75 for three or more, transportation included. Bird-watching tours, 6 to 10 am or 3 to 6 pm, are $105 per person (minimum two) or $80 (three or more), transportation included. Out on the water, surf lessons are $50 per person for two hours. ☎8707–1782 ⊕ www.olingosurfandnaturetours.com.

Tropical Tours. Tropical Tours can set you up with a horseback-riding jaunt ($35), or a day trip to Isla Tortuga ($55). ✉ 50 m north of El Cruce ☎2640–1900 ⊕ www.tropicaltourshuttles.com.

CANOPY TOUR
Canopy del Pacífico. Here you'll find the only canopy tour in the area, an 11-platform adventure that takes about an hour and a half ($45). You can walk, glide, or rappel through 60 acres of forest. This operator also rents ATVs by the hour, day, or week. ✉ In front of fishermen's village ☎2640–0360, 8875–8452 to reserve ATVs ⊕ www.canopymalpais.com.

SURFING
From November to May, the Malpaís area has some of Costa Rica's most consistent surf, as well as clear skies and winds that create idyllic conditions. **Playa Carmen** is the area's best surf spot for all levels, and has dozens of beach breaks scattered along its shores. The sea grows rough and dirty during the May-to-December rainy season, with frequent swells that sometimes make it impossible to get out. **Playa Santa Teresa** is a better option when the waves at Playa Carmen are too gnarly. In Malpaís, at **Mar Azul,** more advanced surfers can try the break over a rock platform.

Kina Surf Shop. This shop stands out among the dozens of surf shops scattered along the beach road for its surfing expertise and wide range of boards and accessories. If you're a first-time surfer, they can fit you with the correct board from their stock of 60 different shapes and sizes. Surf lessons for all levels are available as well. ✉ Next door to Pizza Tomate, Santa Teresa ☎2640–0627 ⊕ www.kinasurfcostarica.com.

WHERE TO EAT
$$$ ✕ **Koji's Restaurant.** North of Santa Teresa, this trendy sushi place off a SUSHI dusty dirt road is currently the most popular restaurant in the area. About 20 wood tables are scattered around a poor man's Zen-like, sand-and-gravel garden with palm trees and a stand of bamboo. The "decor" is mainly votive candles, flaming torches, and tin-can hanging lamps. So why the stampede to eat here? Fabulous sushi, sashimi, and tempura carefully crafted by a charismatic Japanese chef named, of course, Koji. All the usual hand rolls and wraps are on offer, expertly made and artistically presented. One of the most popular dishes on the blackboard menu is the Koji wrap: a double dose of shrimp and shrimp tempura, with avocado, cucumber, spicy tuna, and a "special" sauce. There's also tempura shrimp, beef tenderloin, and ginger pork main dishes. Vegetarians can order veggie curry *korroke*—a

Santa Teresa beach, southern tip of the Nicoya Peninsula

Japanese deep-fried patty. To wash it down, there are coconut-milk fruit shakes, sake, Costa Rican craft beer, and wine. It's not cheap but the crowd, both young and older, seems happy to bring along wads of cash to spend. Dinner only, starting around 5:30. $ *Average main: $16 ⊠ 200 m north of Pranamar, near Playa Hermosa, Santa Teresa ☎ 2640–0815 ⌂ Reservations essential ▭ No credit cards ⊙ Closed Mon. No lunch.*

$$$ ✕ **Nectar.** Savor the experience of the Florblanca Resort's fabulous gar-
SEAFOOD den setting at this poolside alfresco restaurant. Fresh seafood is the specialty here, with inventive daily specials that focus on the day's catch prepared with Asian and Mediterranean flavors, say a fresh tomato-and-olive-tapenade sauce with citrus mash. The dedicated sushi chef produces such treats as Panko-crusted prawn roll with ahi tuna, mango, and avocado. Come for lunch and enjoy the calming sea view peeking through the tropical foliage, or come for a special-occasion, candlelit dinner backed by the sound of the surf. It's pricey but worth the splurge if you crave a sophisticated scene. $ *Average main: $23 ⊠ Resort Flor-blanca, 2 km (1 mile) north of soccer field ☎ 2640–0232 ⌂ Reserva-tions essential.*

$$ ✕ **Restaurante Al Chile Viola.** Sit yourself down amidst a sea of chili-
MODERN ITALIAN pepper red—tabletops, chandeliers, hangings, and funky *objets d'art* all tinted red—for an Italian meal like you have never tasted before. Chef Emilio from Florence will challenge your taste buds with imaginative dishes using authentic Italian ingredients, while his lovely wife, Luz, works her Tica charm in the dining room. The exciting menu includes traditional homemade pastas, osso buco à la Romana, and seafood such as sea bass rolled around grilled vegetables. A standout dish is

Bulls Balls Ravioli—yes, tasty testes finely minced with spices, stuffed into pasta purses, and served with a creamy prosciutto sauce. For dessert, Emilio makes a killer dark-chocolate mousse sprinkled with sea salt crystals. Lunch is from noon to 3; dinner 6 to 9:30. $ *Average main: $14* ⊠ *200 m north of Super La Hacienda, Santa Teresa* ☎ *2640–0433* ⊟ *No credit cards* ☺ *Closed Sun.*

WHERE TO STAY

$ 🏨 **Blue Jay Eco-Lodge.** Perched along
B&B/INN a forested mountainside, these wooden cabins feel like tree houses; you'll hear howler monkeys and an array of birdsong from your bed. **Pros:** natural setting; good value; nice respite from lowland heat and dust, since road in front is paved. **Cons:** steep terrain; most bungalows don't have air-conditioning. $ *Rooms from: $73* ⊠ *From El Cruce, 800 m south toward Malpaís, Sant Teresa* ☎ *2640–0089* ⊕ *www.bluejaylodgecostarica.com* ↩ *14 cabins* ⦿ *Breakfast.*

$$$$ 🏨 **Florblanca.** Named for the white flowers of the frangipani trees grow-
RESORT ing between the restaurant and the beach, this ultraluxurious resort
Fodor's Choice is dedicated to relaxation and rejuvenation. **Pros:** gorgeous villas and
★ grounds; friendly; great yoga classes. **Cons:** very expensive; on rocky stretch of beach; insects sometimes a problem. $ *Rooms from: $550* ⊠ *2 km (1 mile) north of soccer field, Santa Teresa* ☎ *2640–0232* ⊕ *www.florblanca.com* ↩ *11 villas* ⦿ *Breakfast.*

$$ 🏨 **Hotel Tropico Latino.** This beachfront hotel has everything—a spectacu-
HOTEL lar beach with major surf break; a trendy restaurant with ocean views; a round, palm-fringed pool; bungalows and rooms sprinkled throughout a mature garden; twice-daily yoga sessions on the beach; and a full-service spa. **Pros:** location; beach; pool; garden. **Cons:** cheaper rooms are close to dusty; noisy road. $ *Rooms from: $129* ⊠ *700 m north of the crossroads, Santa Teresa* ☎ *2640–0062* ⊕ *www.hoteltropicolatino. com* ↩ *8 bungalows, 1 two-bedroom house, 1 equipped studio, 11 rooms* ⦿ *No meals.*

$$$$ 🏨 **Latitude 10°.** Totally removed from the crowd, this exclusive and
B&B/INN exquisite beach resort is for well-heeled couples who want to enjoy the action of the Santa Teresa beach scene without actually staying in it. **Pros:** serene and private; outstanding service; direct beach access. **Cons:** very quiet; for people who can amuse themselves. $ *Rooms from: $310* ⊠ *Just north of Florblanca, Santa Teresa* ☎ *2640–0396* ⊕ *www. latitude10resort.com* ↩ *5 villas* ⦿ *Breakfast.*

BATTLE OF THE BAKERIES

The morning lineup for pastry and coffee at **The Bakery** in Playa Carmen, just 30 meters from the Cruce, attests to its popularity. This self-advertised "artisan bakery" delivers sweet buns along with an all-day "Ultimate breakfast" of eggs, chopped salad, focaccia with olive tapenade, mini-brownie, fresh OJ, and coffee or tea. But if you hanker after an authentic, flaky French croissant, head for **Marianne's Panadería/Pastelería Francesca** in Plaza Kahuna in Santa Teresa, where you can enjoy a true Continental breakfast on a quiet terrace.

6

$ HOTEL FAMILY [Fodor's Choice] **Ritmo Tropical.** Tranquil, comfortable, and nicely priced, this small hotel a short walk from the beach is consistently the best deal in Malpaís. **Pros:** very clean rooms; economical; lively restaurant. **Cons:** a bit of a walk to town, but on a paved road. [$] *Rooms from: $75* ✉ *100 m south of El Cruce on road toward Malpaís* ☎ *2640–0174* 🌐 *www.hotelritmotropical.net* 🛏 *7 bungalows* 🍴 *No meals.*

SHOPPING

Boutique Jungle Avenue. In the Centro Commercial Playa Carmen, this small store sells funky beachwear, as well as versatile skirts and tops, made by local designers. Open Monday to Saturday, 9 to 7. ✉ *Centro Comercial, at the Cruce, Playa Carmen* ☎ *2640–0817.*

Pranamar. At the far end north end of Santa Teresa, the gift shop in this yoga-centered retreat sells exquisite jewelry from Bali, France, and local artisans. Delicate filigree silver armlets, headbands, and bracelets made with freshwater pearls, abalone, amethyst, and other semiprecious stones add soulful bling to yoga princesses. Open daily. ✉ *Pranamar Oceanfront Villas & Yoga Retreat, north end of Playa Santa Teresa* ☎ *2640–0852* 🌐 *www.pranamarvillas.com.*

NIGHTLIFE

CocoLoco. The musical action is hopping here every night, with Latin, reggae, and electro dance music enjoyed by a mixed crowd. Each month there's also a full-moon party. ✉ *Santa Teresa.*

La Lora Amarilla. In the middle of Santa Teresa, this venue features live and DJ music daily, from noon to 2:30 am. Monday is reggae night; Wednesday and Sunday it's karaoke; Friday features Latin beats; and on Saturday, live performers take to the stage as the international tourist crowd dances to disco beats. ✉ *On main road, across from Chiropractic Clinic, Playa Santa Teresa* ☎ *2640–0132.*

Ranchos Itauna. This beachfront restaurant/lounge in Santa Teresa is a fixture on the nightlife scene, with "Sunset Sessions," Tuesday to Sunday, featuring international live and DJ music, from 3 to 10 pm. Bonfires and fireworks add to the excitement. The crowd is a mix of locals and tourists. ✉ *150 m north of Super Costa, Santa Teresa* ☎ *2640–0095* 🌐 *www.ranchos-itauna.com.*

7

MANUEL ANTONIO AND THE CENTRAL PACIFIC COAST

WELCOME TO MANUEL ANTONIO AND THE CENTRAL PACIFIC COAST

TOP REASONS TO GO

★ **Adventure sports:** Snorkel among colorful fish, get muddy on mountain adventures, and zip through treetops near Jacó and Manuel Antonio.

★ **Fishing:** Deep-sea fishing at Quepos, Jacó, or Herradura gives a chance to hook a sailfish, marlin, wahoo, or yellowfin tuna.

★ **Nature and wildlife:** Explore the seaside forest and see sloths, iguanas, agoutis, monkeys, and 350 species of birds at Manuel Antonio National Park.

★ **Sunsets:** Whether you view it from the beach or while sipping hilltop cocktails in Manuel Antonio, this region has some of the country's best venues for watching the sunset.

★ **Surfing:** This is Costa Rica's surf central. Jacó and Playa Hermosa swarm with surfers, from beginners to pros.

1 Central Pacific Coast.
From Tárcoles, the highway along the coast connects the lively surf towns of Jacó and Playa Hermosa to several quiet beach communities dotting the South Pacific. This is the place to surf, do a multitude of activities, party, and laze on the beach.

2 Manuel Antonio.
Boutique hotels and sustainable resorts cradle the steep cliffs of this coastal town, where white sand coves border the wildlife-rich Manuel Antonio National Park.

GETTING ORIENTED

Most of the Central Pacific is mountainous, and beach towns are backed by forested peaks. Humid evergreen forests, oil-palm plantations, and cattle pastures blanket the land. The coastal highway connects all towns from Tárcoles to the southern Pacific. The hub town of Jacó makes a good base for visiting surrounding beaches and wildlife areas. Farther south are neighboring Quepos and Manuel Antonio, Costa Rica's most popular destination, followed by smaller towns barely touched by tourism.

7

Atenas

Carara National Park

SAN JOSÉ

Pavona

Esterillos Este

PUNTARENAS

Parrita

Esterillos Oeste **Playa Bejuco**

Playa Hermosa

Paquita

Quepos

Manuel Antonio

Manuel Antonio National Park

Rey

34

0   10 mi

0   10 km

MANUEL ANTONIO NATIONAL PARK

At only 7 square km (3 square miles), Manuel Antonio National Park—Costa Rica's smallest park—has an impressive collection of natural attractions: wildlife, rain forest, white-sand beaches, and rocky coves with abundant marine life.

The forest is dominated by massive gumbo-limbo trees, recognizable by their peeling bark. It's home to both two- and three-toed sloths, green and black iguanas, agoutis (similar to the guinea pig, but with longer legs), three species of monkeys, and more than 350 species of birds.

Trails are short, well maintained—and heavily traveled. Make no mistake about it: this is no undiscovered wilderness. In fact, Manuel Antonio is Costa Rica's most visited attraction. There are 5 km (3 miles) of coastline, and it's one of the few parks where you can combine nature walks with swimming off idyllic beaches. There's absolutely no commercial beach development, so the beaches are picture-perfect. *(See page 405 for more information.)*

BEST TIME TO GO

Visit any day but Monday, when the park is closed, and any month but September or October, when it's very wet. Come early, ideally between 7 and 8 am, because park rangers allow only 800 people at a time inside.

FUN FACT

The park's territory is too small to support all of its monkeys, so forested corridors and suspended bridges have been built to allow the monkeys to come and go.

BEST WAYS TO EXPLORE

HIKING

Don your hiking shoes and set off on the main trail from the ranger station. You'll immediately find yourself in rain forest and then emerge onto sparkling Playa Espadilla Sur. Another trail leads to Playa Manuel Antonio, which has a good coral reef for snorkeling. These two beaches lie on either side of a *tombolo*, a sandy strip that connects the mainland to rocky Punta Catedral, which used to be an island. Farther east, where fewer visitors venture, Playa Escondido is rocky and secluded. Trails from the entrance to Punta Catedral and Playa Escondido are in good shape. Trails farther east are progressively rougher going. Sturdy walking sandals are good enough for most of the trails, but light hiking boots or closed shoes will help you avoid nasty encounters with biting ants.

WILDLIFE-WATCHING

Manuel Antonio is famous for its monkeys, especially the noisy white-faced monkeys that pester tourists at the beach. A troop of rarer squirrel monkeys also lives here, one of the few places in the country where you can still find them. These tiny monkeys—*mono titi* in Spanish—are an endangered species. Catching sight of them is a real wildlife coup. The smallest of Costa Rica's four monkey species, these little guys have squirrel-like bushy tails, but they only use them for balance—they can't swing from them.

Watch, too, for less active creatures, such as the more-or-less stationary sloth, especially along the park's Sloth Trail. They sleep much of the day, curled up high in the trees. Look for clumps of green and brown and watch carefully to see if they move.

You'll see many more animals and birds with a guide than without one. You can hire an official guide at the park entrance. If you're interested in seeing birds, be sure to hire a guide that is certified and carrying a scope, so you can get close-up views.

TOP REASONS TO GO

Beaches
Gorgeous beaches without any commercial clutter or noise are one of the best reasons to visit Manuel Antonio. Bring your own snorkeling gear, snacks, and drinks because there's nowhere to buy them. There are basic toilet facilities and cold-water, open-air showers.

Monkeys
Along with the ubiquitous white-faced monkeys performing for visitors on the beaches, you'll also find howler monkeys (*congos*) draped over tree branches in the forest, and more rarely, the endangered, diminutive squirrel monkey.

Pelicans
Just off Playa Espadilla, you can swim out to some rocks and tread water while pelicans dive for fish, oblivious to visitors who bob quietly in the water.

Views
For a fabulous coastal view, take the steep path that leads up to Punta Catedral's rocky hill, draped with thick jungle. You'll pass a lookout point from which you can gaze out at the Pacific and the park's islets.

7

ECO-LODGES IN THE CENTRAL PACIFIC

The Central Pacific is more renowned for its hedonistic Pacific beaches and resort nightlife than for wildlife or ecotourism. But there are some small pockets of original forest and habitat, and a couple of greener lodging choices.

An ecological transition zone between the dry forests of the North Pacific and the rain forests of the South Pacific, the Central Pacific is home to animals and plants of both regions. It is one of the easiest places to get a good look at the American crocodile, many of which gather near the bridge over the Tárcoles River. At Manuel Antonio National Park, you can see wildlife and enjoy an ocean swim at the same time. Just outside the park are a handful of luxury resorts that have earned four and five leaves in sustainability, a remarkable achievement considering the stringent guidelines of the CST Certification System.

GOOD PRACTICES

No matter how many warning signs are posted, visitors still feel compelled to feed the animals. At Manuel Antonio National Park, the white-faced monkeys have become a nuisance at the beach and at nearby hotels, begging for food and even stealing backpacks and ripping food packages open. They are very cute, but they can also be quite mean and deliver nasty bites to the hands that feed them.

It's not only animal behavior, but also animal health that has been compromised. The white-faced monkeys in Manuel Antonio show elevated levels of cholesterol from all the fried chips they have been fed over recent decades.

TOP ECO-LODGES IN THE CENTRAL PACIFIC

ARENAS DEL MAR BEACHFRONT AND NATURE RESORT

One of the newest hotels in the Central Pacific, this luxury hotel has an impressive eco-pedigree. It is the brainchild of Teri and Glenn Jampol, owners of Finca Rosa Blanca in the Central Valley, one of the first lodges in the country to achieve five-leaf sustainability status. The first most obvious eco-aspect guests encounter is the reception center in a forest clearing, where you leave your car behind and ride an electric golf cart to the main open-air lobby. For 20 years, the Jampols reforested and allowed these formerly farmed slopes to regenerate before they began building, often wrapping terraces around established trees. The result is a totally natural landscape, home to lots of wildlife. Other green practices include ionization systems for the swimming pools, biodegradable cleaning products, solar-heated water, a recycling program, and a black water treatment system. A behind-the-scenes sustainability tour is free to hotel guests. *(Full hotel review on page 413.)*

HOTEL SÍ COMO NO

From its meticulous recycling policy and energetic reduction of waste and energy consumption to its innovative conservation programs, Sí Como No has led the way in sustainable tourism. Perched on a hillside in the center of developed Manuel Antonio, this luxury hotel is not a classic eco-lodge. But owner Jim Damalas has worked hard to minimize the hotel's environmental impact. By creating a harmonious workplace, the hotel has retained a well-trained, happy staff, who in turn do their best to make guests happy, too.

The hotel's most notable contribution to local ecotourism is the nearby Butterfly Garden and a 30-acre wildlife refuge. Sí Como No also promotes local culture in Quepos and its surrounding farm villages. The hotel is a member of the Green Hotels of Costa Rica and has attained the five leaves for sustainability. *(Full hotel review on page 414.)*

FROM OUR WRITER

"Conserving natural habitat is not only a good idea, ecologically speaking, but also makes for potentially unpredictable and memorable wildlife sightings. On a visit to Arenas del Mar Beach and Nature Resort, in Manuel Antonio, I was relaxing by one of the hotel's two swimming pools, watching white-faced monkeys scrambling among branches over the nearby restaurant roof, throwing down half-eaten fruits and the occasional partially vivisected grasshopper (headless but still squirming).

Suddenly, my peripheral vision caught sight of a coatimundi emerging from the forest at the far side of the pool. He dove into the pool, dog-paddled diagonally across, climbed out, and made a beeline into the forest. It was a surprise to me to learn that coatis could even swim. This one was obviously so at home here that he thought nothing of using the hotel pool as a cool shortcut."

—Dorothy MacKinnon

7

Updated
by Marlise
Kast-Myers

The Central Pacific region of Costa Rica is a long swath of gorgeous land, encompassing sublime coastline dotted with national parks and palm-lined beaches and inland stretches of ranches, coffee plantations, small villages, and forested mountains. There's a reason this is a popular place to visit: the region has a lot of *pura vida* to offer.

If you're a first-timer to Costa Rica, this region is all about Manuel Antonio and the acclaimed national park of the same name. (Manuel Antonio and the Arenal Volcano in the Northern Plains make the classic "get your feet wet" visit to Costa Rica.) For Costa Ricans, the Central Pacific means Jacó, the closest beach town to San José, and an odd mix of burgeoning condo developments and surf shacks. But you need not limit yourself to these two anchors: Playas Hermosa, Herradura, and Bejuco along this stretch of coast offer a little more solitude, although development is slowly creeping up here, too.

The region has become more accessible than ever, thanks to the opening of the spiffy San José–Caldera Highway, more than 30 years on the drawing board but finally completed in 2010.

PLANNING

WHEN TO GO
HIGH SEASON: DECEMBER TO APRIL
Dry season means high season here. Your payback for braving the crowds is nearly ideal weather. Expect warm, sunny days and pleasant evenings. If however, you're not big on heat, March and April may feel stiflingly hot. Lots of visitors push hotel prices up and crowd the beaches, especially on dry-season weekends. Weekdays offer a slight respite from the crowds. During Holy Week and the last week of December, rooms are even harder to come by. If you're in the area during the high season and want to visit one of the parks, especially Manuel Antonio, get an early start and arrive by 7 am.

LOW SEASON: SEPTEMBER TO NOVEMBER

This is the wettest of the rainy season, when showers become frequent and prolonged. The landmass and wind patterns that cause hurricane activity off the Caribbean coast create significant rain in the Central Pacific. Nature-themed activities usually go on rain or shine, but beach-lazing plans may well go awry.

SHOULDER SEASON: MAY TO AUGUST

The rains begin in mid-May, but the first half of the wet season sees warm, mostly sunny days with lighter afternoon showers. It's easy to plan around them, and the precipitation keeps everything lush and green. Mid-year school vacations fall in early July, with Costa Rican families flocking to the beach, especially Jacó and Manuel Antonio.

PLANNING YOUR TIME

A week gives you enough time to visit several beaches on the central coast, and still explore the wildlife of Manuel Antonio National Park. Adventure seekers might want to set aside a day for a surf lesson, forest hike, or canopy tour. The perfect balance is three days in scenic Manuel Antonio, two days at a secluded beach near Tárcoles or Playa Bejuco, and a couple of days for surfing and action close to bustling Jacó.

GETTING HERE AND AROUND

AIR TRAVEL

The 20-minute flight between San José and Quepos, on Nature Air or SANSA, can save you the three-hour drive and cost just under $80 one way. From San José, both airlines have four daily flights to Quepos departing between 8 and 3. Flights from San José to Tambor, on Nature Air or SANSA, take 30 minutes—a fraction of the time it takes to drive to Puntarenas and ferry over.

BUS TRAVEL

Public buses to and within this entire region are timely and economical, and local shuttles from San José can drop you off at your hotel's doorstep. Public buses leave San José almost hourly between 6 am and 7:30 pm and take four hours to reach Quepos. From here you have to take local transportation to your hotel in Manuel Antonio. Gray Line and Interbus are more direct, with hotel pickup in San José and Quepos or Manuel Antonio. Both companies offer a morning and afternoon trip for around $40 one way.

Bus Contacts Gray Line ☎ 2220–2126 ⊕ *www.graylinecostarica.com.* **Interbus** ☎ 4100–0888 ⊕ *www.interbusonline.com.*

CAR TRAVEL

Highway 27 connects San José to the Pacific port of Caldera, near Puntarenas. The 77-km (46-mile) toll road eliminates a winding drive through the mountains and puts the coast just one hour from the capital. Costa Ricans call the modern road the *Carretera a Caldera* (Caldera Highway). Before the coast, an exit to the two-lane paved coastal highway, or *Costanera*, leads southeast to Tárcoles, Herradura, Jacó, Hermosa, Bejuco, and Quepos. An asphalt road winds its way over the hill between Quepos and Manuel Antonio National Park—plan on about 1½ hours to drive to Jacó and 2½ hours to Quepos.

TOUR OPERATORS

King Tours. A roster of tours includes trips to renowned attractions like Manuel Antonio National Park, as well as crocodile boat adventures, deep-sea and coastal fishing trips, horseback rides, and canopy tours. The company can also book tours to destinations elsewhere in the country, such as Poás and Arenal volcanoes, Monteverde Cloud Forest, and Isla Tortuga. ⊠ *Main road into Playa Herradura, in front of Los Sueños, Playa Herradura* ☏ *2643–2441, 800/213–7091 in North America* ⊕ *www.kingtours.com.*

Rios Tropicales. High-quality adventure tours include white-water rafting trips on rivers near Manuel Antonio; excursions cost $68 to $99. ⊠ *Central Colon Bldg., San José* ☏ *2233–6455, 866/722–8273 in North America* ⊕ *www.riostropicales.com.*

Team CRT. The many services include a variety of Central Pacific tours, plus car rentals, private drivers, shuttle vans, and a 4WD off-the-beaten-path "adventure" transfer between San José and Manuel Antonio. ☏ *2508–5000, 888/236–4447 in North America* ⊕ *www.costarica4u.com.*

BIRD-WATCHING GUIDES

Costa Rica Gateway. Since 1993, expert birders (and brothers) Kevin and Steven Easley have been organizing comprehensive and customized bird-watching tours. They know where the birding hot spots are, as well as all the best birding places to stay and how to capture the birds on film. ⊠ *Alajuela* ☏ *2433–8278, 888/246–8513 in U.S.* ⊕ *www.costaricagateway.com.*

Costa Rica Living and Birding. Guide Patrick O'Donnell is not only knowledgeable but also particularly good at helping new birders see the birds. He offers custom birding tours, mostly day trips from the San Jose area. For up-to-date birding news, check out his informative blog. ⊠ *Santa Barbara de Heredia* ☏ *8318–3329, 716/778–2091* ⊕ *birdingcraft.com/wordpress.*

RESTAURANTS

You'll find the liveliest dining mix in the country outside San José here, especially in Manuel Antonio. The crowd of international visitors has brought about a crowd of international cuisines, but, as you'd expect in a coastal region, seafood still reigns here.

HOTELS

The Central Pacific has a good mix of high-quality hotels, nature lodges, and *cabinas* (low-cost Tico-run hotels, often laid out like motels), including some of the country's priciest lodgings. As a rule, prices drop 20% to 30% during the rainy season. Reserve as far in advance as possible during the busy dry season, especially on weekends. Near Manuel Antonio National Park, Manuel Antonio is the more activity-rich, attractive, and expensive place to stay (though we've culled the best budget options). *Hotel reviews have been shortened. For full information, visit Fodors.com.*

WHAT IT COSTS IN DOLLARS				
	$	$$	$$$	$$$$
Restaurants	under $10	$10–$15	$16–$25	over $25
Hotels	under $75	$75–$150	$151–$250	over $250

Restaurant prices are the average cost of a main course at dinner or, if dinner is not served, at lunch. Hotel prices are the lowest cost of a standard double room in high season.

THE CENTRAL PACIFIC COAST

From Tárcoles to Quepos along Costa Rica's Pacific coast, you'll find patches of undeveloped jungle, small surf towns, and some of the country's most accessible beaches. The proximity of these strands to San José leads Costa Ricans and foreigners alike to pop down for quick weekend beach vacations. Surfers have good reason to head for the consistent waves of Playas Jacó and Hermosa, and anglers and golfers should consider Playa Herradura for its golf courses and ocean access. You might find Herradura and Jacó overrated and overdeveloped, but the latter is a good option if you're looking for shopping and nightlife.

TÁRCOLES

90 km (54 miles) southwest of San José.

Crocodile boat tours on the Río Tárcoles are this small town's claim to fame. You don't actually have to drive to Tárcoles to do the tour, operators can pick you up in Herradura or Jacó. Budget (or time-conscious) travelers may want to simply stop near Río Tárcoles bridge where dozens of crocodiles gather on the banks. It's easy to snap a few photos from the top of the bridge, but be sure to lock your car and watch for oncoming traffic and Tourist Police, who make this a regular ticketing location for speedy drivers. The muddy river has gained a reputation as the country's dirtiest, thanks to San José's inadequate sewage system, but it amazingly remains an impressive refuge for wildlife. A huge diversity of birds results from a combination of transitional forest and the river, which houses crocodiles, herons, storks, spoonbills, and other waterbirds. This is also one of the few areas in the country where you can see scarlet macaws, which you may spot on a boat tour or while hiking in a private reserve nearby.

GETTING HERE AND AROUND

By car, head west from San José on the new Highway 27 to Orotina and follow the signs to Herradura, Jacó, and Quepos. After crossing the bridge over the Rio Tárcoles, look for the entrance to the town of Tárcoles on the right. On the left is the dirt road that leads to the Hotel Villa Lapas and the waterfall reserve. Any bus traveling to Jacó can drop you off at the entrance to Tárcoles. Let the driver know in advance.

SPORTS AND THE OUTDOORS

BOAT TOURS

FAMILY On the two-hour riverboat tours through the mangrove forest and Tárcoles River, you might see massive crocodiles, Jesus lizards, iguanas, and some of roughly 50 colorful bird species, including the roseate spoonbill and boat-billed heron. Tours reach the river's mouth, providing nice sea views, especially at sunset. **■TIP→ Around noon is the best time to spot crocs sunbathing; bird enthusiasts prefer afternoon rides to catch scarlet macaws. During the rainy season (May to November), the river may grow too rough for boats in the afternoon.**

Crocodile Man Tour. Small scars on the hands of the two brothers who run the company are the result of the tour's most original (and optional) attraction: feeding fish to the crocs. The boats are small enough to slide up alongside the mangroves for a closer look. Transportation is provided from nearby beaches, but not from San José. Daily tours take place every two hours from 8 to 4. ✉ *Main road into Tárcoles* ☎ *2637–0771* 🌐 *www.crocodilemantour.com* 🎟 *$30* 🕒 *Daily 7–4.*

CANOPY TOUR

Hotel Villa Lapas. The hotel manages a suspension-bridge nature walk and a zip-line tour. **Sky Way** consists of five suspension bridges spread out over a 2½-km (1½-mile) old-growth-forest nature trail. You can do the trail with a guide ($20). A shuttle picks you up at the hotel. **Villa Lapas Canopy** has zip lines through primary forest ($30). ✉ *Off Costanera, after bridge over Río Tárcoles* ☎ *2637–0232* 🌐 *www.villalapas.com.*

WHERE TO STAY

$$ RESORT FAMILY 🏨 **Hotel Villa Lapas.** These stucco rooms within a tranquil rain-forest preserve are nothing special, but they have white tile floors, hardwood ceilings, and large baths and are a great escape for nature lovers. **Pros:** surrounded by forest; lots of activities; birds; kid-friendly. **Cons:** rooms sometimes musty; property is a bit tired looking; often busy with tour groups. [$] *Rooms from: $104* ✉ *Off Costanera, 3 km (2 miles) after bridge over Rio Tárcoles, turn left on dirt road, up 600 m* ☎ *2637–0232* 🌐 *www.villalapas.com* 🛏 *56 rooms* 🍴 *Multiple meal plans.*

EN ROUTE

Even if you choose to bypass Tárcoles and its crocodile tours, you can still get a peek at the huge reptiles as they lounge on the riverbanks: on the Costanera, pull over just after crossing the Río Tárcoles bridge and walk back onto it. Bring binoculars if you have them. **■TIP→ Be sure to watch for traffic and lock your car—vehicles have been broken into here.**

PUNTA LEONA

Past Tárcoles, the first sizable beach town of the Central Pacific coast is Playa Herradura *(see below)*. In between, the road passes tiny Playa La Pita, then heads inland where it crosses the entrance to Punta Leona, a vast hotel and residential complex. The road then winds its way up a steep hill, atop which is the entrance to the luxury hotel Villa Caletas. On the other side of that ridge is the bay and beach of Herradura.

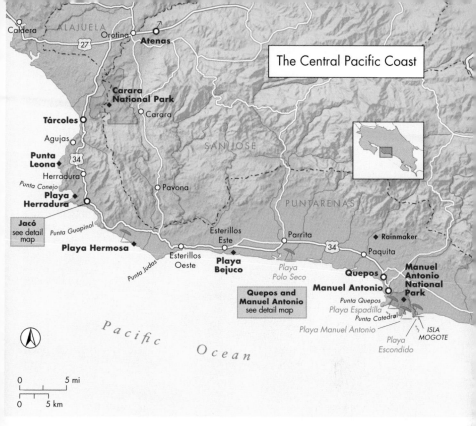

The Central Pacific Coast

BEACHES

Playa La Pita. About a kilometer (½ mile) south after the entrance to Tárcoles, the Costanera passes this small beach that provides your first glimpse of the Pacific if you're coming down from San José or the Central Valley. The beach is rocky, and its proximity to the crocodile-infested Río Tárcoles makes the water murky and dangerous for swimming, but it's a nice spot to stop and admire the ocean and birds. **Amenities:** food and drink at hotels. **Best for:** sunset; walking.

WHERE TO EAT AND STAY

$$$ ✕ **El Mirador Restaurant.** White tablecloths, glass walls, and yellow-and-
ECLECTIC blue-checkered curtains contribute to the sophisticated but not overly stuffy atmosphere of this hotel dining room. Expensive prix-fixe meals include your choice of appetizer, main dish, and dessert. Appetizers range from the traditional escargots to a shrimp and lobster bisque. The entrées include beef tenderloin with chimichurri, jumbo shrimp sautéed with white wine and passion fruit, and roasted duck with truffle oil. A covered terrace below the restaurant is popular for sunset viewing over a cocktail, and offers a tapas menu that is much less expensive than choices in the main restaurant. The extensive wine list includes several blends from the region. $ *Average main: $50* ⊠ *Villa Caletas hotel, off coastal highway, 3 km (1½ miles) south of Punta Leona* ☎ *2637–0505* ⊕ *www.hotelvillacaletas.com/mirador* ��� *No breakfast or lunch.*

¿HABLA INGLÉS?

Although some Central Pacific areas like Jacó and Manuel Antonio are very touristy, don't assume everyone speaks English. Taxi and bus drivers often won't understand your directions in English. To make traveling smoother, write down the name of the place you're headed to or ask someone at your hotel's reception desk to write out directions in Spanish, which you can pass on with a smile to your driver. This is good advice for any destination in Costa Rica.

$$ RESORT FAMILY 🏨 **Punta Leona Hotel & Club.** This 740-acre private reserve and resort community with hotel-style rooms, apartments, and chalets is an odd and sometimes overwhelming mix of residential development, vacation spot, and natural attractions—including two beaches and a tropical forest. **Pros:** ample beachfront; lots of variety in activities; range of accommodation options. **Cons:** far from town; spotty service; compound feel; caters more toward condominium owners than hotel guests. [$] *Rooms from: $220* ✉ *15 km (9 miles) south of Tárcoles on west side of road to Jacó* ☎ *2630–1000, 2231–3131 in San José, 888/301–9473 in North America* 🌐 *www.hotelpuntaleona.com* 🛏 *108 rooms, 13 suites, 27 apartments* 🍴 *Breakfast.*

$$$$ RESORT 🏨 **Villa Caletas.** Perched 1,200 feet above the sea on a promontory south of Punta Leona, these elegant rooms sequestered in the jungle have jaw-dropping views of the surrounding foliage and sea below. **Pros:** gorgeous views; secluded setting; on-site spa; good food. **Cons:** abundant insects and spiders; lots of stairs; 20 minutes to nearest beach; pricey food and drinks. [$] *Rooms from: $350* ✉ *Off coastal highway, 3 km (1½ miles) south of Punta Leona, on right* ☎ *2637–0505, 2257–3653 in San José* 🌐 *www.hotelvillacaletas.com* 🛏 *33 rooms, 13 villas, 8 suites* 🍴 *No meals.*

PLAYA HERRADURA

20 km (12 miles) south of Tárcoles.

Just north of bustling Jacó, this small beach town, named for its horseshoe-shaped bay, is made up of hotels, a golf course, and a marina. Once a sleepy fishing village, it has recently transformed into one of the country's fastest-developing areas. The entrance to town is marked by a shopping complex complete with fast-food chains and a surf shop. A paved road connecting the coastal highway to the beach dead-ends at the sand where three seafood shacks line the shores; the best is the more upscale El Pelicano. Golfers and sportfishing fans alike are drawn to the pristine beauty of Playa Herradura, and the placid waters tend to keep surfers farther down the coast, where waves are abundant.

GETTING HERE AND AROUND

By car, head 20 minutes straight down the Pacific Highway. The town's entrance is on the right-hand side, where a long paved road leads to the beach. Follow the signs to the Marriott.

CLOSE UP

Diving the Deep at Cocos Island

Rated one of the top diving destinations in the world, Isla del Coco is uninhabited and remote, and its waters are teeming with marine life. It's no place for beginners, but serious divers enjoy 30-meter (100-foot) visibility and the underwater equivalent of a big-game park: scalloped hammerheads, white-tipped reef sharks, Galápagos sharks, bottlenose dolphins, billfish, and manta rays mix with huge schools of brilliantly colored fish.

Encompassing about 22½ square km (14 square miles), Isla del Coco is one of the largest uninhabited islands on Earth. Its isolation has led to the evolution of dozens of endemic plant and animal species. The rocky topography is draped in rain forest and cloud forest and includes more than 200 waterfalls. Because of Isla del Coco's distance from shore (484 km [300 miles[) and its craggy topography, few visitors to Costa Rica—and even fewer Costa Ricans—have set foot on the island.

Costa Rica annexed Coco in 1869, and it became a national park in 1978.

Today only extremely high-priced specialty-cruise ships, park rangers, volunteers, and scientists visit this place. The dry season (November to May) brings calmer seas and is the best time to see silky sharks. During the rainy season large schools of hammerheads can be seen, but the ocean is rougher.

Two companies offer regular 10- to 12-day dive cruises to Isla del Coco that include 3 days of travel time on the open ocean and cost roughly $4,595 to $6,610, depending on the boat and dates.

Okeanos Aggressor. Ten-day dive safaris to Cocos Island operate year-round. The cost is around $5,000 per person. ☎ 2289–2261, 800/348–2628 in U.S. ⊕ www.aggressor.com.

Undersea Hunter. The boat operates 10- and 12-day dive trips to Cocos Island year-round and is part of a fleet that also includes *Argo* and *Sea Hunter.* ☎ 2228–6613 in San José, 800/203–2120 in North America ⊕ www.underseahunter.com.

7

BEACHES

Playa Herradura. If sportfishing and golf are your priorities, this is a good option. If you're looking for nature, seclusion, a beautiful beach, or a bargain, keep driving. Rocky Playa Herradura, a poor representative of Costa Rica's breathtaking beaches (although its tranquil waters make it considerably safer for swimming and stand-up paddleboarding than most central and southern Pacific beaches), gets its name from the Spanish word for "horseshoe," referring to the shape of the deep bay in which it lies. Playa Herradura's safety factor coupled with its proximity to the city (it is the closest beach to San José), has turned it into a popular weekend getaway for *Josefinos*, who compete for shade beneath the sparse palms and Indian almond trees that line the beach. On the north end of the beach is Los Sueños development, which includes a large marina, shopping center, hundreds of condos, a golf course, and a massive Marriott hotel. This is also the sportfishing capital of Costa Rica, though the black sand makes the water look somewhat dark at times. **Amenities:** food and drink at hotels; toilets at marina. **Best for:** swimming.

SPORTS AND THE OUTDOORS

Few activities are available directly in Playa Herradura, but that doesn't mean you have to settle for less. Most of the area's diverse outfitters can pick you up at your hotel for activities near Jacó and Playa Hermosa. Your hotel's reception desk is often a good source of information.

Costa Rica Dreams. One of the area's oldest and most reputable sportfishing outfitters offers trips to fishing grounds just an hour offshore in calm waters. ✉ *Los Sueños Marina* ☎ *2637–8942, 337/205–0665 in North America* 🌐 *www.costaricadreams.com.*

RIPTIDES

Riptides (or rip currents), common in Jacó and Manuel Antonio's Playa Espadilla, are dangerous and have led to many deaths over the years. If you get caught in one, don't panic and don't try to swim against it as paddling to shore will simply exert your energy. Riptides are generally less than 100 feet wide, so simply swim parallel to shore until you feel the power dissipate. Once you are out of the current, swim back to the beach. The best policy is not to go in deeper than your waist when the waves loom large, and never swim alone.

WHERE TO EAT AND STAY

$$$ LATIN AMERICAN 🍴 **Nuevo Latino.** The most formal restaurant at the Los Sueños Resort (though dress is still Costa Rican casual) has large arched windows facing cascading water on one wall and large still-lifes of fruits on the other. As the name implies, the menu uses basic Latin American ingredients, like yucca, sweet potato, corn, and beans, in creative ways, fusing them with flavors from other parts of the world. The "Simply Fish" concept allows you to select your fish, choose the style of preparation, and an accompaniment. The main menu includes pork chops with mint pesto, and sea bass with curry and coconut. [$] *Average main: $32* ✉ *Marriott Los Sueos Resort* ☎ *2630–9000.*

$$ SEAFOOD 🍴 **Restaurante El Pelícano.** It may not look like much at first glance, but this open-air restaurant across the street from the beach serves some dishes you'd be hard-pressed to find in other casual beach-town places. The decor is limited to green-tile floors, thin wooden columns, turquoise tablecloths, and soft candlelight. Starters include fish croquettes in a lemon sauce, green peppers stuffed with shrimp and mushrooms, and clams *au gratin*. Grilled tuna in a mango sauce, sea bass in a heart-of-palm sauce, lobster, and tenderloin are a few of the main dishes. The most "formal" option on the beachfront, this lovely restaurant has been in operation since 1983. [$] *Average main: $30* ✉ *Turn left at end of main road into Playa Herradura* ☎ *2637–8910.*

$$$$ RESORT FAMILY Fodor's Choice ★ 🏨 **Los Sueños Marriott Ocean and Golf Resort.** This mammoth multimillion-dollar resort in a palatial colonial-style building has a gorgeous view of Herradura Bay and combines modern amenities with traditional Central American decorative motifs, such as barrel-tile roofing and hand-painted tiles. **Pros:** impeccable grounds; kids' club; swimming pool the size of a soccer field. **Cons:** expensive; so-so rooms and service; beach can be dirty. [$] *Rooms from: $319* ✉ *800 m west of road to Jacó from San José, follow signs at entrance of road to Playa Herradura* ☎ *2630–9000, 888/236–2427 in North America, 2298–0000 in San José* 🌐 *www.marriott.com* 🛏 *191 rooms, 10 suites* 🍽 *Breakfast.*

JACÓ

7 km (4 miles) south of Playa Herradura, 114 km (70 miles) southwest of San José.

Its proximity to San José has made Jacó the most developed beach town in Costa Rica. Nature lovers and solitude seekers should skip this place, which is known mostly for its nightlife, surf scene, and prostitution. More than 80 hotels and cabinas back its long, gray-sand beach, and the mix of restaurants, shops, and bars lining Avenida Pastor Díaz (the town's main drag) give it a cluttered appearance devoid of any greenery. Any real Costa Rican–ness evaporated years ago; U.S. chain hotels and restaurants have invaded, and you can pretty much find anything you need, from law offices and dental clinics to tattoo parlors and appliance stores. The town does provide everything in terms of tours and outdoor activities, and makes a convenient hub for exploring neighboring beaches and attractions. Theft can be a problem here; watch your things like a hawk.

GETTING HERE AND AROUND

The drive from San José takes less than two hours; take the new Highway 27 west of San José beyond Orotina, and then take the exit to Jacó and Quepos. The exit, on the right after Herradura, is well marked. There's a gas station at the second entrance to town close to Club del Mar. Buses leave from San José's Coca-Cola station seven times daily, with an extra run on weekends.

ESSENTIALS

Bank/ATM BAC San José ⊠ *Centro Comericial Il Galeone* ☎ *2295–9797.*
Banco Nacional ⊠ *Avda. Pastor Díaz* ☎ *2643–3621.*

Hospital Clínica Pública ⊠ *In front of Plaza de Deportes* ☎ *2643–1767.*

Pharmacy Farmacia Jacó ⊠ *Diagonally across from Más X Menos supermarket* ☎ *2643–3205.*

Post Office Correos ⊠ *Avda. Pastor Díaz, next to the soccer field, across from the municipality.*

Rental Cars Alamo ⊠ *Avda. Pastor Díaz* ☎ *2643–1752* ⊕ *www.alamocostarica. com.* **Budget** ⊠ *Avda. Pastor Díaz* ☎ *2643–2665* ⊕ *www.budget.co.cr.* **Economy** ⊠ *Avda. Pastor Díaz* ☎ *2643–1098* ⊕ *www.economyrentacar.com.* **Hertz** ⊠ *Beside Hotel Tangerí, in front of Kentucky Fried Chicken* ☎ *2221–1818.*

Taxis Taxi services ☎ *2643–2020, 2643–2121, 2643–3030.*

BEACHES

Playa Jacó. This long, palm-lined beach west of town is a pleasant enough spot in the morning but can burn the soles of your feet on a sunny afternoon. Though the gray sand and beachside construction make this spot less attractive than most other Costa Rican beaches, it's a good place to soak up the sun or enjoy a sunset. The beach is popular with surfers for the consistency of its waves, but when the surf is up, swimmers should beware of dangerous rip currents. During the rainy months the ocean here is not very clean. Smaller waves make this beach ideal for surf lessons or longboarders. Bigger waves are found 5 km (3 miles) south at Playa Hermosa. **Amenities:** food and drinks; toilets at local restaurants and hotels. **Best for:** sunset; surfing.

SPORTS AND THE OUTDOORS

TOUR OPERATORS

You don't have to physically step into any tour office, because everyone from a reception desk attendant to a boutique salesperson can book you a local adventure. Almost every tour can pick you up at your hotel's doorstep. ■**TIP**→ Keep in mind that part of your price tag includes the salesperson's commission, so if you hear higher or lower prices from two different people, it's likely a reflection of a shift in the commission. You can try negotiating a better deal directly from the outfitter.

Gray Line Costa Rica. Dealing primarily with large groups, this tour company arranges day trips from Jacó to Arenal and Poás volcanoes, Manuel Antonio National Park, Sarchí, Isla Tortuga, and raft trips on the Savegre River. ✉ *Best Western Jacó Beach Resort* ☏ *2220–2126 in San José, 800/719–3905 in US* ⊕ *www.graylinecostarica.com.*

ATV TOURS

Because ATV tours have only been popular in Costa Rica for about a decade, the vehicles are in relatively good condition. But they're not exactly the most eco-friendly way to see the area's rain forest and wildlife, and rollovers always pose a risk to you. Some operators will ask you to put up a credit card voucher of roughly $500.

Adventure Tours. Locals will tell you this company provides the best ATV tours with the longest routes. Options include a two-hour tour ($69), a three-hour waterfall tour ($89), and full-day trips ($175). Their automatic ATVs are inspected by a licensed mechanic after each use. ✉ *In the center of Playa Jacó, behind Subway* ☏ *2643–5720, 877/561–7263 in North America* ⊕ *www.adventurtourscostarica.com.*

CANOPY TOURS

Fodor'sChoice ★ **Rainforest Adventures.** A modified ski lift offers easy access to the rainforest canopy, with eight-seat gondolas that float through the treetops within a 222-acre private reserve. The company offers guided tours that explain a bit of the local ecology ($60), as well as early-morning bird-watching tours ($100). There is also a small serpentarium and medicinal plant garden ($10). A $75 "Tranopy" tour combines the tram with a 10-cable zip-line tour. The latest attraction is a 164-foot waterfall climbing tour that includes a zip line and rappelling section ($39). The International Ecotourism Society named Rainforest Adventures one of the most sustainable theme parks in the world. It is also considered to be one of the safest due to their double cables, chest harnesses, certified guides, and high-tech equipment inspected annually. ✉ *3 km (2 miles) west of Jacó* ☏ *2257–5961, 866/759–8726 in North America* ⊕ *www.rainforestadventure.com.*

HORSEBACK RIDING

Discovery Horseback Tours. A British couple runs 2½-hour trail rides on healthy horses. You'll spend some time in the rain forest and also stop at a small waterfall where you can take a dip. Another tour takes you on a sunset ride on the beach. Either runs $75. An alternate tour ($85) runs three hours and takes in a small village and butterfly farm. Tours start at 8:30 and 2:30, Monday to Saturday (8:30 only on Saturday). ☏ *2643–7151* ⊕ *www.horseridecostarica.com.*

KAYAKING AND CANOEING

Kayak Jacó. Looking for waters calmer than those at Jacó Beach? Kayak Jacó takes you to Playa Agujas for sea-kayaking tours and Hawaiian-style outrigger canoe trips ($60). The half-day tours include snorkeling (conditions permitting) at secluded beaches. Transportation to/from your hotel costs an additional $20. ⊠ *Playa Agujas* ☏ *2643–1233* ⊕ *www.kayakjaco.com.*

SURFING

Jacó has several beach breaks, all of which are best around high tide. Surfboard-toting tourists abound in Jacó, but you don't need to be an expert to enjoy the waves—the swell is often small enough for beginners, especially around low tide. Abundant surf shops rent boards and give lessons. Prices range from $40 to $60 for two hours and usually include a board and transportation. If you plan to spend more than a week surfing, it might be cheaper to buy a used board and sell it back at the standard half price before you leave *(⇨ Shopping, below)*. Otherwise, you'll be paying airline transportation fees around $150 (one way), and most likely your board will arrive damaged despite your bubble-wrapping efforts. For rental, Jacó has plenty of surf shops with solid quivers, with cheaper boards starting at $10 an hour. If you don't have much experience, don't go out when the waves are really big—Jacó sometimes gets very powerful swells, which result in dangerous rip currents. During the rainy season, waves are more consistent than in the dry months, when Jacó sometimes lacks surf.

School of the World. This unique language school offers one-day workshops in everything from photography and salsa dancing to yoga and stand-up paddleboarding. They specialize in Spanish and surf lessons. ⊠ *Off Avda. Pastor Díaz, 300 m east of POPS; turn left after Condominiums Nasua, 50 m on the left* ☏ *2643–2462, 305/517–7689 in U.S.* ⊕ *www.schooloftheworld.org.*

SWIMMING

The big waves and dangerous rip currents that make surfing so popular here can make swimming dangerous. Lifeguards are on duty only at specific spots, and only sporadically. If the ocean is rough, stay on the beach—dozens of swimmers have drowned here over the years.

When the ocean is calm, especially around low tide, you can swim just about anywhere along Jacó Beach. The sea is always calmer near the beach's northern and southern ends, but the ocean bottom is littered with rocks there, as it is in front of the small rivers that flow into the sea near the middle of this beach.

WHERE TO EAT

$$ ✕**Graffiti Restro Cafe and Wine Bar.** The ghetto gourmet concept of this
ECLECTIC Jacó hot spot plays with the senses, starting with the decor that blends
Fodor'sChoice graffiti with soft candlelight and jazz. Chef Danny Clark's menu relies
★ on only fresh, locally grown ingredients and has dishes ranging from sushi to vegetarian, with creations like cacao and coffee-rubbed beef

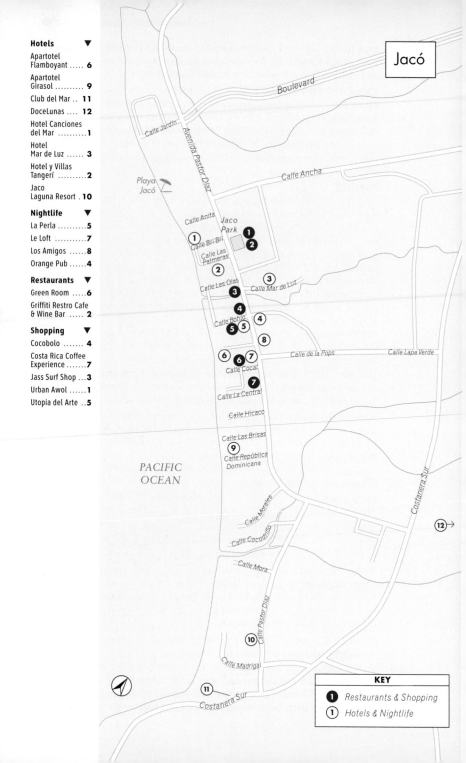

Jacó

Boulevard

Calle Jardín

Avenida Pastor Díaz

Calle Ancha

Playa
Jacó

Calle Anita

Jaco
Park

Calle Bri Bri

Calle Las
Palmeras

Calle Las Olas

Calle Mar de Luz

Calle Bohío

Calle de la Pops

Calle Lapa Verde

Calle Cocal

Calle La Central

Calle Hicaco

Calle Las Brisas

Calle República
Dominicana

PACIFIC
OCEAN

Calle Morales

Costanera Sur

Calle Cocodrilo

Calle Mora

Calle Pastor Díaz

Calle Madrigal

Costanera Sur

KEY

1 *Restaurants & Shopping*

(1) *Hotels & Nightlife*

tenderloin, and a tuna-tartar tower that melts in your mouth. For something with a kick, try the snook seasoned with five Caribbean spices and topped with caramel soy. If you've dined elsewhere, drop by this understated spot to listen to live music on Friday and Saturday. Sample a signature martini with lemongrass and ginger or cucumber and basil, and indulge in one of the extraordinary desserts like chocolate cheesecake or peanut-butter banana flambé. Take home Graffiti's flavors with their homemade spices and recipes, sold at the attached gallery, Urban Awol. $ *Average main: $15* ⊠ *Avda. Pastor Díaz; Pacific Center #23, across from Hotel Tangeri, behind Pacific Center Plaza* ☎ *2643–1708* ⊕ *www.graffiticr.com* ⊙ *Closed Sun. No lunch.*

$ ✕ **Green Room.** Bordered by a white picket fence, this charming café
CAFÉ serves meals prepared with organic ingredients delivered daily by local farmers. A tin roof draped in silk, concrete floors, wooden tables, and local art offer a cheerful escape from the grime of Avenida Pastor Díaz. The ever-changing chalkboard menu usually features home-ground burgers with fresh baked buns or seared ahi on buckwheat noodles with roasted vegetables. Breakfasts are hearty, ranging from banana pancakes to eggs Florentine. Salads are topped with fresh strawberries, and cocktails are made with natural fruit juice—try the lemon basil margarita. You're likely to hear Jack Johnson on the stereo by day and live acoustic by night. $ *Average main: $10* ⊠ *Corner of Avda. Pastor Díaz and C. Cocal* ☎ *2643–4425* ⊙ *Closed Mon.*

WHERE TO STAY

$$ ⛳ **Apartotel Flamboyant.** Though nothing special, these small beachfront
HOTEL rooms and apartments, many with kitchenettes, are a good deal. **Pros:**
FAMILY beachfront; good value; quiet; centrally located. **Cons:** very simple rooms; no meals; not all rooms have air-conditioning. $ *Rooms from: $95* ⊠ *100 m west of Centro Comercial Il Galeone* ☎ *2643–3146, 2643–1732* ⊕ *www.apartotelflamboyant.com* ⇄ *18 rooms, 4 apartments* ⚭ *No meals.*

$$$ ⛳ **Apartotel Girasol.** These cozy apartments face a small pool and grill
HOTEL area and are just across a manicured lawn from the beach. **Pros:** beach-
FAMILY front; quiet grounds; big apartments great for families. **Cons:** far from town center; often full. $ *Rooms from: $162* ⊠ *100 m west of Moto-shop, end of C. República Dominicana* ☎ *2643–1591, 800/923–2779 in North America* ⊕ *www.girasol.com* ⇄ *16 apartments* ⚭ *No meals.*

$$$ ⛳ **Club del Mar.** Secluded far from the crowds at the beach's south-
RESORT ern end, Jacó's nicest lodgings include green-and-cream-hue rooms with private teak balconies and extremely comfortable condos. **Pros:** beachfront; tranquil; friendly; lush grounds; tasteful decor. **Cons:** some highway noise reaches back to condos; some insects; no bathtubs in standard rooms. $ *Rooms from: $179* ⊠ *Costanera, 300 m south of El Arroyo gas station* ☎ *2643–3194, 866/978–5669 in North America* ⊕ *www.clubdelmarcostarica.com* ⇄ *10 rooms, 22 condos, 1 suite* ⚭ *No meals.*

$$$ ⛳ **DoceLunas.** The spacious teak furniture–filled rooms at "Twelve
HOTEL Moons" are a couple of miles from the sea and sand, set amid 5 acres
Fodor'sChoice of lawns shaded by tropical trees and luxuriant gardens with a moun-
★ tainous green backdrop. **Pros:** more secluded than other Jacó lodgings;

terrific restaurant; two handicap rooms; beautiful grounds. **Cons:** 10-minute walk to beach; some rooms are rather dark. [$] *Rooms from: $180* ✉ *On coastal highway from San José, pass the 1st entrance to Jacó; take dirt road on left with signs for Docelunas at main entrance to Quebrada Seca* ☎ *2643–2211* 🌐 *www.docelunas.com* 🛏 *12 rooms, 8 suites* 🍴 *Breakfast.*

$$ RESORT 🏨 **Hotel Canciones del Mar.** The poetically named "Songs of the Sea" is tranquil, intimate, and charming, with tastefully and individually decorated rooms and suites that overlook the sea or lush gardens. **Pros:** close to ocean; rooms have kitchens; some units with nice porches; handicap room available. **Cons:** too close to Jacó; rooms feel worn; pool could be cleaner. [$] *Rooms from: $140* ✉ *End of C. Bri Bri* ☎ *2643–3273, 888/260–1523 in U.S.* 🌐 *www.cancionesdelmar.com* 🛏 *16 suites* 🍴 *Breakfast.*

$$ B&B/INN FAMILY 🏨 **Hotel Mar de Luz.** It may be a few blocks from the beach, and it doesn't look like much from the street, but this surprisingly pleasant place full of flowering plants and bird-attracting trees offers nice, comfortable rooms of varying size and decor. **Pros:** attentive owner; plenty to do; close to the beach. **Cons:** rooms a bit dark and dated; service can be spotty; website photos not true representation. [$] *Rooms from: $130* ✉ *East of Avda. Pastor Díaz, on C. Mar de Luz behind Subway* ☎ *2643–3000, 2643–1682* 🌐 *www.mardeluz.com* 🛏 *27 rooms, 2 suites* 🍴 *Breakfast.*

$$ RESORT FAMILY 🏨 **Hotel y Villas Tangerí.** A mix of accommodations, ranging from spacious rooms by the sea to villas big enough for a large family, are scattered across ample grounds shaded by coconut palms. **Pros:** beachfront; spacious rooms; centrally located. **Cons:** rooms a bit timeworn; musty; staff does not speak English. [$] *Rooms from: $167* ✉ *Avda. Pastor Díaz, north of river* ☎ *2643–3001, 2222–2924 in San José* 🌐 *www.hoteltangeri.com* 🛏 *14 rooms, 11 villas* 🍴 *Multiple meal plans.*

$$$ HOTEL 🏨 **Jacó Laguna Resort.** Despite its name, this new addition to Jacó is more of a basic hotel than a resort, but it's clean and comfortable, steps from the beach, and just far enough from town to offer a peaceful night of sleep. **Pros:** kids under six stay free; good food; ideal location. **Cons:** hallway noise; poor lighting in rooms; weak Wi-Fi signal in some rooms; mattresses lack support. [$] *Rooms from: $175* ✉ *Corner of C. Madrigal and Avda. Pastor Díaz* ☎ *2643–3362, 215/942–5135 in U.S.* 🌐 *www.jacolagunaresort.com* 🛏 *26 rooms* 🍴 *Breakfast.*

NIGHTLIFE

Whereas other beach towns may have a bar or two, Jacó has an avenue full of them, with enough variety for many different tastes. After-dinner spots range from restaurants perfect for a quiet drink to loud bars with pool tables to dance clubs.

BARS

La Perla. The large corner bar and wooden chairs and tables are great for a laid-back cocktail, people-watching, and tropical feel. Occasionally you'll hear live music. ✉ *Avda. Pastor Díaz, across from Orange Pub* ☎ *2643–3326, 2643–3332.*

"I caught this beautiful heron just outside our beachfront hotel at Jacó." —Photo by Leethal33, Fodors.com member

Le Loft. This chic club is popular with locals and surfers who stop by for a few drinks before heading to other after-hour spots. Plan to stand in line behind a velvet rope for a while, unless you have an "in" with the bouncer. Above all, dress to impress. ⊠ *Red building across from Los Amigos and Pops; 2nd floor* ☎ *2643–5846* ☉ *Thurs.–Sat 9 pm–2:30 am.*

Los Amigos. Sports fans can get their fix at this lively restaurant and bar with nine plasma TVs, two projectors, and six satellite feeds hosting every sporting event imaginable. Local DJ's, cheap eats, and draft beers make this one of the most popular spots in town. ⊠ *Corner of Avda. Pastor Díaz and C. Pops* ☎ *2643–2961* ⊕ *www.losamigosjaco.com.*

Orange Pub. This is a good choice for a cocktail, after-dinner drinks, or a late-night meal. It has a big bar in back, pool tables, and DJs and dancing on weekends. ⊠ *Avda. Pastor Díaz, north of Il Galeone mall across from El Bohio St.* ☎ *2643–3387* ☉ *Closed Tues and Sun.*

SHOPPING

Souvenir shops with mostly the same mass-produced merchandise are crowded one after the other along the main street in the center of town. Most of the goods, like wooden crafts and seed jewelry, are run-of-the-mill souvenir fare, but a few shops have more unusual items.

Cartón. Cartón sells new and used boards and shapes for some of Costa Rica's top surfers. Their two-hour surf lessons are held just past the surf-shop at Madrigal Beach. ⊠ *C. Madrigal, near the gas station* ☎ *2643–3762* ⊕ *www.cartonsurfboards.com.*

Cocobolo. Named for the tropical hardwood of the Cocobolo tree, this large shop is jam-packed with wooden handicrafts hanging from the ceiling, walls, and shelves. It's much of what you find in other stores, but with more tasteful items and a richer variety. In addition to wood carvings, they sell clothing, hammocks, jewelry, and locally made crafts. ⊠ *Avda. Pastor Díaz, 300 m north of Banco Nactional, next to Jass Surf Shop* ☎ *2643–3486.*

Costa Rica Coffee Experience (*Fruity Monkey Poop*). For locally grown coffee and reasonably priced artisan crafts, this place offers the best shopping in Jacó. They serve marvelous iced coffees, natural iced teas, and fresh roasted coffee. Be sure to try a sample of their chocolate, cashews, and "Fruity Monkey Poop" (actually just candied nuts). ⊠ *Across from Banco Nacional and Más X Menos market* ☎ *2643– 6197* ⊕ *www.discovercoffee.net.*

Jass Surf Shop. As Jacó's first surf shop, this well-stocked store has a good variety of surf gear at decent prices. They sell new and used surfboards and stand-up paddleboards, and will buy back your board at the end of your trip for half the purchase price. Two-hour surf lessons cost $45. ⊠ *Avda. Pastor Díaz, next to La Perla, 200 m north of Banco Nacional* ☎ *2643–3850* ⊕ *www.jasssurfshop.com.*

Urban Awol. Appropriately located next to Graffiti Restro, this surf boutique and art gallery sells everything from clothing and jewelry to crafts and surfboards. They also sell a variety of spices, rubs, and salsas—all of which are used at Graffiti Restro. ⊠ *Pacific Center #25* ☎ *2643–1709* ⊗ *Opens Mon.–Sat. at 5 pm.*

Utopia Del Arte. Every item here is handmade, including jewelry, clothing, dreamcatchers, and paintings on driftwood. ⊠ *C. Bohio, across from Hotel Poseidon* ☎ *2543–4140, 8575–3136* ⊗ *Daily 1–6.*

PLAYA HERMOSA

5 km (3 miles) south of Jacó, 113 km (70 miles) southwest of San José.

On the other side of the rocky ridge that forms the southern edge of Jacó Beach is Playa Hermosa, a swath of dark gray sand and driftwood stretching southeast as far as the eye can see with consistent waves for surfers. For nonsurfers, outdoor options include horseback and canopy tours in the nearby forested hills. But all of these can be done from other beaches. As for the town itself, there's really not much, which is part of the attraction for travelers who want to escape Jacó's crowds and concrete towers. Most of the restaurants, bars, and hotels have cropped up one after the other on a thin stretch separating the highway and the beach. From June to December, olive ridley turtles nest on the beach at night, especially when there's not much moonlight. ■ TIP→ **Note: there is a second Playa Hermosa on the Guanacaste Pacific coast.**

GETTING HERE AND AROUND
If you have a car, take the coastal highway 5 km (3 miles) past Jacó. You'll see the cluster of businesses on the right. If you don't have your own transportation, take a taxi from Jacó or a local bus toward Quepos.

BEACHES

Playa Hermosa. Despite its name, "Beautiful Beach" is hardly spectacular. The southern half of the wide beach lacks palm trees or other shade-providing greenery; its sand is scorching hot in the afternoon; and frequent rip currents make it unsafe to swim when there are waves. But board riders find beauty in its consistent, hollow surf breaks. Beginner surfers might want to stick to Jacó since waves here are powerful and punchy. The beach's northern end is popular because it often has waves when other spots are flat, and the ocean is cleaner than at Jacó, except after heavy rains when there is floating debris. There is also plenty of forest covering the hills, and scarlet macaws sometimes gather in the Indian almond trees near the end of the beach. **Amenities:** food and drink; showers and toilets at Backyard Bar. **Best for:** sunset; surfing. .

NOT THAT PLAYA HERMOSA

"¡Ojo!" as they say. Watch out: Costa Rica has two Playa Hermosas. Don't confuse this one with the larger, more developed beach of the same name on the Guanacaste Pacific coast. Each has its fans, but the Central Pacific's Playa Hermosa is better known to Costa Ricans and to surfers.

SPORTS AND THE OUTDOORS

You can arrange activities throughout the Central Pacific from Playa Hermosa. Most tour operators and outfitters include transportation in their prices. *For more options, see Sports and the Outdoors in Jacó, above, or consult your hotel's reception.*

CANOPY TOUR

Chiclets Canopy Tour. Guided daily tours (7 and 9 am; 1 and 3:30 pm) take you through the rain-forest canopy ($60) to 15 platforms and a suspension bridge. Cables strung between platforms perched high in a dozen trees have views of tropical foliage, wildlife, and the nearby coast. ⊠ *West of Costanera, ½ km (¼ miles) north of Hermosa* ☎ *2643–1880* ⊕ *www.jacowave.com.*

TURTLE TOURS

Playa Hermosa Turtle Tours. Raúl Fernández takes small groups to look for nesting sea turtles on Playa Hermosa between July and December ($45) as part of a project to collect the eggs and raise them in a hatchery. Tour times vary depending on the tide; he can provide transportation from hotels in Jacó. ☎ *8817–0385.*

SURFING

Most people who bed down at Playa Hermosa are here for the same reason—the waves that break just a shell's toss away. There are half a dozen breaks scattered along the beach's northern end, and the surf is always best around high tide. Because it is a beach break, though, the waves here often close out, especially when the surf is big. If you don't have much experience, don't go out when the waves are really big—Hermosa sometimes gets very powerful swells, which result in dangerous rip currents. If you're a beginner, don't go out at all. Surf instructors in Hermosa take their students to Jacó, an easier place to learn the sport.

Continued on page 398

SURFING
COSTA RICA

Costa Rica's big surfing community, consistent waves, and not-too-crowded beaches make surfing accessible to anyone who is curious enough to give it a whirl; surf schools, board rentals, and beachside lessons are plentiful. At the most popular beaches, surf tourism is a regular part of the scene. Many instructors are able to bridge generational divides, giving lessons tailored for anyone from tots to retirees. First-timers would be wise to start at a beginner beach and take some lessons.

by Leland Baxter-Neal

Costa Ricans are known for their laid-back attitude, and this usually translates into a welcoming vibe in the water. Of course, as the waves get more intense, and the surfers more serious, the unspoken rules get stricter, so beginners are advised to stay close to the shore. A good instructor should help keep you out of the way anywhere you go, and if you're on your own, just steer clear of the hot shots until you know the

COSTA RICA'S SURF FINDER

THE PACIFIC COAST

For those new to surfing, destinations on the Pacific coast are more welcoming in a number of ways. There are more beaches, hotels, bars, and surf schools than in the Caribbean, and the waves are friendlier. Access to the Northern and Central Pacific coast is also made easy by (sometimes) paved and well-marked roads. As you head southward down the coast, the route becomes untamed. The remoteness of the Osa Peninsula has guarded a couple of world-class breaks surrounded by some of the country's most untouched jungle.

WHEN TO GO: Waves are most consistent from December through April. As you move southward down the coast, the breaks are best from May to November.

THE CARIBBEAN

Costa Rica's truncated Caribbean has comparatively few beaches and they draw only the most dedicated surf seekers. The laid-back culture of that coast seems a perfect match for the surfer vibe. Among the Caribbean waves is perhaps Costa Rica's most famous: Puerto Viejo's Salsa Brava.

WHEN TO GO: Best conditions January through April.

TYPES OF BREAKS

BEACH BREAK: The best type for beginners. Waves break over sandbars and the seafloor. Jacó, Hermosa, and Sámara are all beach breaks.

POINT BREAK: Created as waves hit a point jutting into the ocean. With the right conditions, this can create very consistent waves. Pavones is a point break.

REEF BREAK: Waves break as they hit a reef. It can create great (but dangerous) surf. There's a good chance of getting smashed and scraped over extremely sharp coral or rocks. Salsa Brava, in Puerto Viejo, is a reef break.

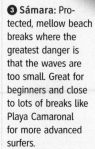

PACIFIC

❶ Tamarindo: Very popular with all levels of surfers. It is most famous for its reef breaks like Ollie's Point, Playa Negra (south), and Witch's Rock (north), made famous by the film *Endless Summer*. Nice waves are formed at a point break called Pico Pequeño and at the river mouth called El Estero at the beach's north end.

❷ Playa Guiones: If not the best surf in the vicinity of Nosara, it's the best beach break for beginners and longboarders, second only to Sámara. Lots of long, fun rights and lefts.

❸ Sámara: Protected, mellow beach breaks where the greatest danger is that the waves are too small. Great for beginners and close to lots of breaks like Playa Camaronal for more advanced surfers.

❹ Malpaís: A variety of beach breaks plus a point break that's good when waves get big. Good for beginners and advanced surfers, but hard to reach.

❺ Jacó: Unless the surf gets too big, the consistent beach breaks produce forgiving waves that are good to begin and advance on. The

Tamarindo

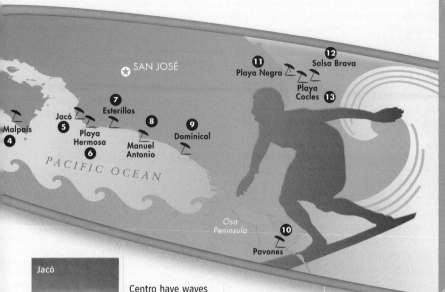

SAN JOSÉ

11 Playa Negra **12** Salsa Brava

Playa Cocles **13**

7 Esteríllos

Jacó **5**

Playa Hermosa **6**

Manuel Antonio

8

9 Dominical

Malpaís **4**

PACIFIC OCEAN

Osa Peninsula

10 Pavones

7

IN FOCUS SURFING COSTA RICA

Jacó

Centro have waves much like Hermosa. Oeste has a variety of beach breaks with softer, friendlier waves.

south end is best for beginners.

6 Playa Hermosa: A steep beach break just south of Jacó with some of the country's best waves and surfers. Waves can get big, mean, and thunderously heavy.

7 Esteríllos: Divided into three beaches, going north to south: Oeste, Centro, and Este. A beautiful stretch of coast, uncrowded to the point of desolation. The surf and currents can be tough for beginners, and Este and

8 Manuel Antonio: Just outside the national park you'll find a variety of beach breaks. Playitas, at the park's north end, is perhaps the most consistent. This spot only gets good at hightide, about three hours per day. September through December it's usually flat.

9 Dominical: At the foot of beautiful, forested coastal mountains. A long set of beach breaks that are fun and great for advanced levels. When waves get too

Manuel Antonio

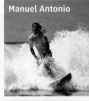

big, head south to Dominicalito. This wave is fast, hollow, and powerful.

10 Pavones: Legendary, remote, and surrounded by rain forest, Pavones is said to be one of the world's longest, left-breaking waves, with a perfect ride lasting nearly three minutes. But with fickle conditions and a tough drive to get here, it's best for the very experienced.

CARIBBEAN

11 Playa Negra: A largely undiscovered but quality reef break for all skill levels. Be careful at low tide when rocks are exposed.

12 Salsa Brava: When the conditions are right, this is arguably Costa Rica's best and most powerful wave; it's placed right over a shallow coral reef. For advanced surfers only.

13 Playa Cocles: Plenty of beach breaks to pick from, good for all levels. But beware the currents or you'll drift out to sea.

SURF SCHOOL TIPS

Surf lesson

Surfing is for the young and the young at heart. At many of Costa Rica's top surf beaches, a wide range of ages and skill sets can be found bobbing together in the water. With the right board and some good instructions, just about anybody can stand up and have some fun in the waves. We strongly recommend taking a lesson or two, but be sure to take them from an actual surf school (there's one on just about every beach) rather than from the eager kid who approaches you with a board. Trained instructors will be much better at adapting their lesson plans to different skill levels, ages, and body types.

If you're a first-timer, there are a few things you need to know before getting in the water.

■ **Pick your beach carefully.** Sámara is a good choice, as is Jacó or Tamarindo. You want beach breaks and small, gentle waves. Make sure to ask about rip tides.

■ **Expect introductory lessons to cover the basics.** You'll learn how to lie on the board, paddle out, duck the incoming waves, and how to pop up on your board. If you're a natural, you'll be able to hop up and stay standing in the white wash of the wave after it breaks.

■ **Have realistic expectations.** Even if you have experience in other board sports, like snowboarding or skateboarding, don't expect to be surfing on the face of the wave or tucking into barrels on your first day. It literally takes years before you can reach that level.

■ **Choose the right gear.** If you're a beginner, start on a longboard, preferably made of foam (aka, "soft top surfboard"). Be sure to wear a rashguard or a wet suit to help protect your chest and stomach from getting scraped or stung by jellyfish. Hydrate, and apply sunscreen.

SURF SLANG (or, how not to sound like a kook)

Barrel: The area created when a wave breaks onto itself in a curl, creating a surfable tube that's the surfer's nirvana. Also called the "green room."

Drop in: To stand up and drop down the face of a wave. Also used when one surfer cuts another off: "Hey, don't drop in on that guy!"

Duck dive: A maneuver where the surfer first pushes his or her board underwater and then dives with it, ducking under waves that have already broken or are about to break. It's difficult with a longboard (⇨see Turtle roll).

Goofy foot: Having a right-foot-forward stance on the surf-board. The opposite is known as "regular."

Close out: When a wave or a section of a wave breaks all at once, rather than breaking steadily in one direction. A frustrating situation for surfers, giving them nowhere to go as the wave comes crashing down.

Ding: A hole, dent, crack, or other damage to a board.

Grom: A young surfer, usually under 15, who "RIPs" (is amazing).

Kook: Someone (usually a beginner) trying to pass as a surfer.

Outside: The area farther out from where waves are most regularly breaking. Surfers line up here to catch waves.

Stick: A surfboard.

Turtle roll: A maneuver where the surfer rolls over on the surfboard, going underwater and holding the board upside down. Used by longboarders and beginners to keep from being swept back toward shore by breaking waves.

BOARD SHAPES

Longboard: Lengthier (about 2.5–3 m/ 9–10.5 feet), wider, thicker, and more buoyant than the often-miniscule shortboards. Offers more flotation and speedier paddling, which makes it easier to get into waves. Great for beginners and those with relaxed surf styles. Skill level: Beginner to Intermediate.

Funboard: A little shorter than the longboard with a slightly more acute nose and blunt tail, the Funboard combines the best attributes of the longboards with some similar characteristics of the shorter boards. Good for beginners or surfers looking for a board more maneuverable and faster than a longboard. Skill level: Beginner to Intermediate.

Fishboard: A stumpy, blunt-nosed, twin-finned board that features a "V" tail (giving it a "fish" like look, hence the name) and is fast and maneuverable. Good for catching small, steep slow waves and pulling tricks. At one point this was the world's best-selling surfboard. Skill level: Intermediate to Expert.

Shortboard: Shortboards came on the scene in 1967–70 when the average board length dropped from 9'6" to 6'6" (2.9 m to 2 m) and changed the wave riding styles in the surf world forever. This board is a short, light, high-performance stick that is designed for carving the wave with a high amount of maneuverability. These boards need a fast steep wave, completely different than a longboard break, which tends to be slower with shallower wave faces. Skill level: Expert.

7

IN FOCUS SURFING COSTA RICA

Beginner			Expert
		Fish	
	Funboards		
	Longboards	Shortboards	
Shallow wave faces, easiest surfing			Steeper wave faces, difficult surfing

WHERE TO EAT AND STAY

$
ECLECTIC
✕ **The Backyard Bar.** Playa Hermosa's original nightlife spot has two seating areas, each with its own bar. Television sets on the wraparound bar in the front room show sports matches and surf videos. A wooden deck in back overlooking the beach is great for lunch and sunset, mostly because of the pleasant sea breezes and view of the surfers. The usual bar food—Tex-Mex standards and burgers—is complemented by fresh seafood, including ceviche, grilled tuna, lobster, and jumbo shrimp. It's popular especially on Saturday, when there's a surf contest at 4 pm and live music at 6 pm. $ *Average main: $11* ✉ *Costanera, southern end of town next to The Backyard hotel* ☎ *2643–7011* ⊕ *www.backyardhotel.com.*

$$
HOTEL
🛏 **The Backyard Hotel.** Surfers are the main clientele in these nice rooms with high ceilings, clay-tile floors, and sliding-glass doors that open onto semiprivate balconies and terraces, most of which have good views of Playa Hermosa. **Pros:** steps from the surf; nice views from second floor; friendly staff; good Web-only packages. **Cons:** bar next door noisy on weekends; low water pressure; thin sheets and towels. $ *Rooms from: $133* ✉ *Costanera, southern end of town* ☎ *2643–7011, 2643–7133* ⊕ *www.backyardhotel.com* ⤴ *6 rooms, 2 suites* ⦿| *Breakfast.*

$$
HOTEL
Fodor's Choice
★
🛏 **Casa Mia.** Hidden from public view behind high walls and a large fortress-style wooden door, intimate Casa Mia (formerly Casa Pura Vida) underwent major renovations in 2011, transforming it into the best property in Playa Hermosa. **Pros:** well maintained; communal kitchen; beachfront. **Cons:** not all rooms have ocean views; no meals. $ *Rooms from: $85* ✉ *Costanera, 200 m south of soccer field* ☎ *2643–3490, 800/575–9568 in US.* ⊕ *www.casamiacostarica.com* ⤴ *7 rooms, 1 apartment* ⦿| *No meals.*

$$
B&B/INN
🛏 **Surf Inn.** Right in front of Hermosa's beach break, a mural of tall palms and peeling waves marks the entrance to this well-priced inn which offers small apartments and studios. **Pros:** surfers' paradise; decent rates; kitchens in rooms; almost half price in low season. **Cons:** noise from neighboring bar; studios are dark; no meals. $ *Rooms from: $120* ✉ *Next to Backyard Hotel* ☎ *8899–1520* ⊕ *www.surfinnhermosa.com* ⤴ *4 studios, 2 apartments* ⦿| *No meals.*

PLAYA BEJUCO

27 km (16 miles) south of Playa Hermosa, 32 km (19 miles) south of Jacó.

Serious surfers wanting to escape the crowds at Jacó and Playa Hermosa, or anyone simply seeking to stray from the beaten path, need drive only 20 minutes south to Playa Bejuco's relatively deserted, palm-lined beach. One could stroll for an hour along the light gray swath of sand and hardly encounter a soul. Several vacation homes and two small hotels sit behind the first part of the beach, and behind them is a large mangrove forest where you might see macaws or white-faced monkeys. Just 3 km (2 miles) north of Playa Bejuco is Playa Esterillos Este where head-high waves break year-round. Here you'll find several boutique hotels capitalizing on the seclusion and beachfront location. Most locals survive on farming and fishing, meaning this area is relatively undeveloped other than the occasional *soda* (casual eatery) serving up rice and beans.

GETTING HERE AND AROUND

If you have a car, take the coastal highway 27 km (16 miles) south past Playa Hermosa to the turnoff for Playa Bejuco, which is 1 km (½ mile) west of the highway. If you don't have a car, take a taxi from Jacó, or local bus toward Quepos.

BEACHES

Playa Bejuco. The surf here is as big and consistent as at Playa Hermosa, but with a fraction of the surfers. As at Hermosa, dangerous rip currents develop, so swimmers should go in no deeper than their waist when the waves are big. Aside from surfing and beachcombing, there is little to do here, which makes it a good place for people wanting to do nothing at all. Like most surrounding beaches, the sand is dark brown with the occasional palm tree offering shade on the shore. Delfín Beach Resort has foam and plastic surfboards for $20 per day. The mosquitoes can be quite fearsome during the rainy months. **Amenities:** food, drink, and toilets at neighboring Delfín Beach Resort and Hotel Playa Bejuco. **Best for:** surfing; beachcombing; isolation. ⊠ *35 km (21 miles) north of Manuel Antonio and 30 km (18 miles) south of Jacó.*

SPORTS AND THE OUTDOORS

SURFING

There are various high-tide beach breaks scattered along Playa Bejuco. Waves tend to close out here when the swell is big, but then you can try the mouth of the estuary, 1 km (½ mile) south of the hotels. Bejuco is a do-it-yourself beach, without surf schools or decent board rentals nearby, and because the waves break so close to shore, it's not a good spot for beginners. Delfín Beachfront Resort has a few plastic surfboards for desperate surfers traveling without their own gear.

WHERE TO STAY

$$$$ ⛩ **Alma Del Pacifico Beach Hotel & Spa.** Combining Costa Rica's vibrant
HOTEL architecture with modern design, this tranquil property offers spacious rooms and colorful beach bungalows with indoor/outdoor rain showers and private gardens. **Pros:** promotions on website; plenty of activities; creative design; very private. **Cons:** wild beach; hard mattresses; simple breakfast; far from town. ⑤ *Rooms from: $295* ⊠ *3 km (2 miles) north of Playa Bejuco, Playa Esterillos Este* ☎ *303/459–7939, 1–888/960–ALMA* ⊕ *www.almadelpacifico.com* ➥ *20 rooms, 3 condos* ⑩ *Breakfast.*

$$ ⛩ **Delfín Beachfront Resort.** Expect swan towels and plastic flowers at
HOTEL this comfortable but slightly dated hotel, best known for its proximity to good surf and fresh fish. **Pros:** beachfront; clean rooms; great views. **Cons:** cramped bathrooms; beach has rip currents; so-so management; pool is often dirty. ⑤ *Rooms from: $124* ⊠ *On beach, Playa Bejuco* ☎ *2779–4245* ⊕ *www.delfinbeachfront.com* ➥ *14 rooms* ⑩ *Breakfast.*

$$ ⛩ **Hotel Playa Bejuco.** In exchange for being 150 feet away from the
HOTEL beach, you get spacious, well equipped, ocher-walled rooms with views
FAMILY of the pool and gardens rather than surf and sand. **Pros:** big pool; decent restaurant; spacious rooms. **Cons:** lacks ocean view; beach has rip currents; slightly dated rooms. ⑤ *Rooms from: $124* ⊠ *Road to Playa Bejuco, on left* ☎ *2779–2000* ⊕ *www.hotelplayabejuco.com* ➥ *20 rooms* ⑩ *Breakfast.*

7

MANUEL ANTONIO

South of the beach communities and surf stops along the Central Pacific coast are the towns of Quepos and Manuel Antonio, as well as the popular Manuel Antonio National Park. Unless you're stocking up on supplies or making a bank run, it's better to bypass Quepos, a former banana port and now a somewhat run-down fishing town, and head to Manuel Antonio, where boutique hotels and luxury resorts are perched on beachside cliffs. Between surf lessons, canopy tours, exploring the national park, and relaxing on the beach, it's easy to fall in love with this quaint town where the jungle meets the shore. Equally impressive is the town's reputation for sustainability practices, from green hotels to organic cuisine. Although some consider Manuel Antonio overdeveloped, nobody can deny its spectacular natural beauty.

QUEPOS

23 km (14 miles) south of Parrita, 174 km (108 miles) southwest of San José.

This hot and dusty town is the gateway to Manuel Antonio, and also serves as the area's hub for banks, supermarkets, and other services. Because nearby Manuel Antonio is so much more attractive, there is little reason to stay here, but many people stop for dinner, for a night on the town, or to go sportfishing. Quepos's name stems from the indigenous tribe that inhabited the area until the Spanish conquest wiped them out. For centuries the town of Quepos barely existed, until the 1930s, when the United Fruit Company built a banana port and populated the area with workers from other parts of Central America. The town thrived for nearly two decades, until Panama Disease decimated the banana plantations in the late 1940s. The fruit company then switched to less lucrative African oil palms, and the area declined. Only since the 1980s have tourism revenues lifted the town out of its slump, a renaissance owed to the beauty of the nearby beaches and nature reserves. Forests around Quepos were destroyed nearly a century ago, but the massive Talamanca Mountain Range, some 10 km (6 miles) to the east, holds one of the largest expanses of wilderness in Central America.

GETTING HERE AND AROUND

The drive from San José to Quepos is under three hours. Follow the directions for Jacó and continue south another 40 minutes. Buses from San José's Tracopa bus station (Avenida 5 and Calle 14/16) drop you off in downtown Quepos. SANSA and Nature Air run multiple flights per day, 20 minutes one way, between San José and Quepos (XQP), as well as direct flights between Quepos and Palmar Sur in the Southern Pacific and La Fortuna in the Northern Plains.

ESSENTIALS

Bank/ATM BAC San José ⊠ *Avda. Ctl.* ☎ *2777-0781.*
Banco Nacional ⊠ *50 m west and 100 m north of bus station* ☎ *2777-0113.*

Hospital Ambulance ☎ *911.* **Hospital de Quepos** ⊠ *4 km (2½ miles) on road to Dominical* ☎ *2774-9510.*

Post Office Correos ✉ *C. Ctl., next to soccer field in central Quepos.*

Rental Cars Alamo ✉ *Downtown, 50 m south of Korean school* ☎ *2242–7733, 800/462–5266 in U.S.* **Hertz** ✉ *75 m south of the Catholic church* ☎ *2777–3365, 1–888/HERTZCR.*

Taxis Taxi services ☎ *2777–3080, 2777–1207.*

Tourist Information Instituto Costarricense de Turismo ✉ *25 m east of docks* ☎ *2777–4217, 866/26782–7422 from U.S or Canada* ⊕ *www.visitcostarica.com* ⊙ *Weekdays 8–noon and 1–4.*

EXPLORING

Rainmaker Conservation Project. This private nature reserve is spread over Fila Chota, a lower ridge of the Talamanca Range 22 km (13 miles) northeast of Quepos, and protects more than 1,500 acres of lush and precipitous forest. The lower part of the reserve can be visited on guided tours from Manuel Antonio, or as a stop on your way to or from Quepos. If you get here on your own, the guided river-walk and canopy-bridge tour runs $25 ($15 for self-guided tour). The park also offers an early-morning bird-watching tour ($25) and a night reptiles and amphibians hike ($35). The restaurant serves lunch for $8 and there's a new on-site microbrewery that utilizes Rainmaker's mountain waters. The reserve is home to many of Costa Rica's endangered species, and you may spot birds here that you won't find in Manuel Antonio. It isn't as good a place to see animals as the national park, but Rainmaker's forest is different from the park's—lusher and more precipitous—and the view from its bridges is impressive. It's best to visit Rainmaker in the morning, since—true to its name—it often pours in the afternoon. ✉ *22 km (13 miles) northeast of Quepos* ☎ *2777–3565, 540/349–9848 in North America, 8960–3836 park cell* ⊕ *www.rainmakercostarica.org* ⌾ *$25–$35 for guided tours* ⊙ *Daily 7:30–4:30.*

SPORTS AND THE OUTDOORS

There's a tour operator or travel agency on every block in Quepos that can sell you any of about a dozen tours, but some outfitters give discounts if you book directly through them. The dry season is the best time to explore the area's rain forests. If you're here during the rains, do tours first thing in the morning.

CANOPY TOUR

Canopy Safari. There are many zip-line tours in the area that take you flying through the treetops, but Canopy Safari has earned a reputation for long and fast-paced rides. The company's privately owned forest is about a 45-minute car ride from Quepos, and the tour ($75) includes gliding down 10 zip lines, a Tarzan swing, two rappel lines, and a visit to the on-site butterfly garden and serpentarium. Tours take place at 7:30 am and 10:30 am and include either breakfast or lunch. ✉ *Office downtown, next to the Poder Judicial* ☎ *2777–0100, 888/765–8475 in North America* ⊕ *www.canopysafari.com.*

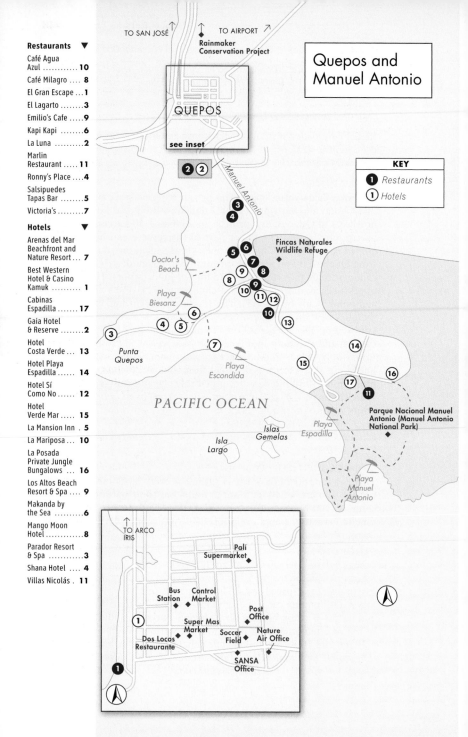

Quepos and Manuel Antonio

TO SAN JOSÉ   TO AIRPORT

Rainmaker Conservation Project

QUEPOS

see inset

Manuel Antonio

KEY

❶ *Restaurants*
① *Hotels*

Fincas Naturales Wildlife Refuge

Doctor's Beach

Playa Biesanz

Punta Quepos

Playa Escondida

PACIFIC OCEAN

Islas Gemelas

Isla Largo

Playa Espadilla

Parque Nacional Manuel Antonio (Manuel Antonio National Park)

Playa Manuel Antonio

TO ARCO IRIS

Palí Supermarket

Bus Station   Control Market

Post Office

Super Mas Market

Soccer Field   Nature Air Office

Dos Locas Restaurante

SANSA Office

FISHING

Quepos is one of the best points of departure for deep-sea fishing in southwestern Costa Rica. The best months for hooking a marlin are from October to February and in May and June, whereas sailfish are abundant from November to May, and are caught year-round. From May to October you're more likely to catch yellowfin tuna, roosterfish, mahimahi, and snapper.

Bluefin Tours. A fleet of 26-, 28-, and 33-foot boats is used for catch-and-release sportfishing, conventional fishing, and fly-fishing. Full-day charters run $845 to $1,350. ⊠ *Downtown, across from the soccer field* ☎ *2777–0000* ⊕ *www.bluefinsportfishing.com.*

Costa Mar Fishing. The largest fleet in Quepos has six boats ranging from 25 to 60 feet, and consequently has a wide range of rates. Full-day charters start at $750. ⊠ *Entrance to Quepos, next to Café Milagro* ☎ *2777–0593* ⊕ *www.costamarsportfishing.net.*

Luna Tours Sport Fishing. Half-, three-quarter-, and full-day catch-and-release fly and conventional trips ($850–$1,250 for a full day) with Luna Tours Sport Fishing are available on 28-, 32-, and 33-foot boats. ⊠ *Downtown, in lobby of Best Western Hotel Kamuk* ☎ *2777–0725, 727/242–5982 in U.S.* ⊕ *www.lunatours.net.*

KAYAKING AND RAFTING

Iguana Tours. Guides show off the area's natural beauty on white-water rafting trips on the Naranjo (Class III–IV) and Savegre (Class II–III) rivers and kayak adventures at sea or in a mangrove estuary. They also offer bird-watching, horseback riding, and canopy tours. ⊠ *Downtown Quepos, across from soccer field* ☎ *2777–2052* ⊕ *www. iguanatours.com.*

WHERE TO EAT AND STAY

$$
SEAFOOD
✕ **El Gran Escape.** A favorite with sportfishermen ("You hook 'em, we cook 'em"), this is the town's best place for seafood, serving everything from shrimp scampi to fresh tuna with mushrooms to bouillabaisse and paella. You can also get hearty burgers or a handful of Mexican dishes, and there's a kids' menu. You won't find any billfish (like marlin or swordfish) on the menu, owing to the restaurant's conservation policy, but the back wall is covered with pictures of them—and their proud reelers. Weathered fishing caps hang from the bar's ceiling. $ *Average main: $20* ⊠ *Marina Pez Vela* ☎ *2777–0395* ⊕ *www.elgranescape.net* ☉ *Closed Tues.*

$
HOTEL
Best Western Hotel & Casino Kamuk. The town's best and priciest accommodations (though they pale in comparison to Manuel Antonio properties) have all the perks and ho-hum blandness of a chain hotel, and only two rooms have sea views (blocked by electric lines). **Pros:** reassurance of chain name; decent value given cleanliness; good service. **Cons:** sameness of chain hotel; far from beach; some street noise. $ *Rooms from: $70* ⊠ *Downtown, 100 m after last bridge into Quepos* ☎ *2777–0811, 800/780–7234 in North America* ⊕ *www.bestwestern.com* ⋑ *44 rooms* ⦿| *Breakfast.*

Dos Locos Restaurante. Older American expats often congregate day and night to people-watch or, on Wednesday at 7 pm and Saturday at noon, to listen to live music. ⊠ *Avda. Ctl. at C. Ctl., near bus station* ☎ *2777– 1526* ⊗ *Closes Sun. at 7 pm.*

MANUEL ANTONIO

3 km (2 miles) south of Quepos, 179 km (111 miles) southwest of San José.

Fodor's Choice
★

You need merely reach the top of the forested ridge on which many of Manuel Antonio's hotels are perched to understand why it is one of Costa Rica's most popular destinations. That sweeping view of beaches, jungle, and shimmering Pacific dotted with rocky islets confirms its reputation. And unlike the tropical forests in other parts of the country, Manuel Antonio's humid tropical forest remains green year-round. The town itself is spread out across a hilly and curving 5-km (3-mile) road that originates in Quepos and dead-ends at the entrance to Manuel Antonio National Park. Along this main road, near the top of the hill, or on Punta Quepos are the area's most luxurious hotels and fine-dining restaurants, surrounded by rain forest with amazing views of the beaches and offshore islands. The only problem with staying in one of those hotels is that you'll need to drive or take public transportation to and from the main beach and national park, about 10 minutes away. More hotel and restaurant options are available at the bottom of the hill, within walking distance of the beach, but they lack the sweeping view.

Manuel Antonio is a gay-friendly town. Many hotels and bars cater to gay travelers, and all of them offer a warm welcome to anyone walking in the door. The area doesn't especially cater to budget travelers, but there are a few cheap places and various midrange lodging options closer to the park.

GETTING HERE AND AROUND

Manuel Antonio is a 15-minute drive over the hill from Quepos and 25 minutes from the Quepos airport. Between SANSA and NatureAir, there are eight flights per day linking San José and Quepos (XQP)—flying time is 20 minutes—as well as direct flights between Quepos and La Fortuna in the Northern Plains and Palmar Sur in the Southern Pacific. Buses depart from San José's Tracopa bus station (Avenida 5, Calle 14/16) for Manuel Antonio four times a day, at 6 am, noon, and 6 and 7:30 pm, traveling the opposite direction at 6 and 9:30 am, noon, and 5 pm. They pick up and drop off passengers in front of hotels on the main Quepos–Manuel Antonio road. Shuttle services Gray Line and Interbus offer hotel-to-hotel service to and from San José, Jacó, Monteverde, Arenal, and major North Pacific beaches. The trip from San José takes about 2½ hours by car or 3½ hours by bus. A local public bus makes the 20-minute trip from Quepos to Manuel Antonio every half hour from 7 to 7, then hourly until 10 pm.

"I was in complete awe as my fantastic local Quepos guide led me along a delightful path up in the hills outside of Quepos." —Photo by Colleen George, Fodors.com member

ESSENTIALS

Bank/ATM Banco Promérica ⊠ *Main road, next to Economy Rent a Car* ☎ *2777–5101.*

Pharmacy Farmacia La Económica ⊠ *Main road, across from soccer field, in front of the market* ☎ *2777–2130.*

Rental Cars Economy ⊠ *Next to Banca de Costa Rica, across from Salsi Puedes* ☎ *2777–5353.*

Taxis Taxi services ☎ *2777–3080, 2777–1207.*

EXPLORING

FAMILY **Fincas Naturales Wildlife Refuge.** A former teak plantation has been reforested to allow native trees to spring back among the not-so-native ones. A footpath winds through part of the 30-acre tropical forest, and naturalist guides do a good job of explaining the local ecology and identifying birds. The reserve is home to three kinds of monkeys, as well as iguanas, motmots, toucans, tanagers, and seed-chomping rodents called agoutis. Guided walks are given throughout the day, plus a nighttime jungle trek that departs at 5:30 pm. The quickest and least expensive tour is an hourly walk through displays on butterflies, reptiles, and amphibians. Unfortunately, you can't explore the reserve at your own pace. ⊠ *Entrance across from Sí Como No Hotel* ☎ *2777–0850* ⊕ *www. wildliferefugecr.com* ⊒ *$15–$39, depending on tour* ☉ *Daily 8–4.*

FAMILY
Fodor's Choice
★
Parque Nacional Manuel Antonio (Manuel Antonio National Park). Costa Rica's smallest park packs in an impressive collection of natural attractions: lots of wildlife, rain forest, white-sand beaches, and rocky coves

with abundant marine life. Trails are short, well maintained, and easy to walk. The forest is dominated by massive ficus and gumbo-limbo trees, and is home to two- and three-toed sloths, green and black iguanas, agoutis, four species of monkeys, and more than 350 species of birds. This is one of two places in Costa Rica to see adorable squirrel monkeys. It's also one of the best places to see white-faced capuchin monkeys. The great diversity of wildlife is easily spotted from the well-marked trails, and because the animals are so used to humans, this is one of the best places to see them up close.

From the ranger station a trail leads through the rain forest behind Playa Espadilla Sur, the park's longest beach. It's also the least crowded because the water can be rough. The coral reefs and submerged volcanic rocks of white-sand Playa Manuel Antonio make for good snorkeling. The 1-km-long (½-mile-long) beach, tucked into a deep cove, is safe for swimming. At low tide you can see the remains of a Quepos Indian turtle trap on the right—the Quepos stuck poles in the semicircular rock formation, which trapped turtles as the tide receded. Olive ridley and green turtles come ashore on this beach May through November. Espadilla and Manuel Antonio beaches lie on opposite sides of a *tombolo*, or a sandy strip that connects the mainland to Punta Catedral (Cathedral Point), which used to be an island. The steep path that leads up Punta Catedral's rocky hill draped with thick jungle passes a lookout point from which you can gaze over the Pacific at the park's islands.

Farther east, Playa Escondido (Hidden Beach) is rocky and secluded, but it's also more difficult to access. Before you head out to Escondido, find out when the tides come in so you're not stranded. Kayaking trips might take you down to Punta Serrucho near the southern border of the park, whose jagged peaks explain its name. (*Serrucho* means "saw.")

Despite being Costa Rica's smallest national park, Manuel Antonio is its second most visited, after Volcán Poás, so it is no undiscovered wilderness. A few tips to make the most of a visit:

Hire a private guide with certification from the Costa Rica Tourism Board—you'll walk away with a better understanding of the flora and fauna and see things you probably would have missed otherwise.

Get here as early as possible—between 7 and 8 am is ideal. Rangers permit only 800 people inside at a time, and during peak season visitors line up to enter. Early morning is also the best time to see animals (and it's cooler, too.)

■ TIP→ Beware of manzanillo trees (indicated by warning signs)—their leaves, bark, and applelike fruit secrete a gooey substance that irritates the skin. ⊠ *Manuel Antonio* ☎ *2777–5185* ⌨ *$16* ⊙ *Tues.–Sun. 7–4.*

BEACHES

When the surf is up, riptides are a dangerous problem on Playa Espadilla, Manuel Antonio's main beach, which runs parallel to the road near the park's entrance. ■ TIP→ Never leave your valuables unattended while you're swimming.

Playa Biesanz. For a less-turbulent swim and smaller crowds, head to this beach within a sheltered cove. There are a few tide pools near a cluster of rocks, and during low tide, you can see fragments of turtle traps dating back to AD 900, when the area was inhabited by Quepoa Indians. Today the beach is best known for snorkeling and isolation. You're likely to see monkeys and butterflies on the trail connecting the road to the sand. **Amenities:** none. **Best for:** solitude; snorkeling. ⊠ *Near Hotel Parador.*

Playa Espadilla. As the road approaches Manuel Antonio National Park, it skirts the lovely, forest-lined beach of Playa Espadilla, which stretches for more than 2 km (1 mile) north from the rocky crag that marks the park's border to the base of the ridge that holds most of the hotels. One of the most popular beaches in Costa Rica, it fills up with sunbathers, surfers, volleyball players, strand strollers, and sand-castle architects on dry-season weekends and holidays, but for most of the year it is surprisingly quiet. Even on the busiest days it is long enough to provide an escape from the crowd, which tends to gather around the restaurants and lounge chairs near its southern end. Though it is often safe for swimming, beware of rough seas, which create deadly rip currents. **Amenities:** food and drink. **Best for:** surfing.

Playa Manuel Antonio. Manuel Antonio's safest swimming area is sheltered Playa Manuel Antonio, the second beach in the national park. Its white sand makes it attractive for lounging around, and it's also a good place for snorkeling. There are plenty of palm trees where you can find shade on this wide stretch of sand, and just outside the park are vendors selling fresh coconut water and lychees. Huge mounds of lava rock shelter this cove on both sides. Several shacks rent beach chairs for about $10 a day. **Amenities:** food and drink. **Best for:** swimming. ⊠ *6 km (4 miles) south of Quepos; near park entrance.*

SPORTS AND THE OUTDOORS

TOUR OPERATORS

Manuel Antonio's list of outdoor activities is almost endless. Tours generally range from $40 to $100 per person and can be booked through your hotel's reception desk or directly through the outfitter. During the rainy season, some outdoor options might lose their appeal, but clouds usually let loose in the afternoon, so take advantage of sunny mornings. Most nature-themed activities go on rain or shine.

Manuel Antonio Tours. A small company run by friendly young locals with a good grasp of the area can arrange any kind of activity, from white-water rafting and parasailing to horseback riding and canyoning. They can also arrange a private guide to Manuel Antonio Park ($30 for 2½ hours). ⊠ *Next to Musmanni bakery* ☎ *2777–5334* ⊕ *www. manuelantoniotourscr.com.*

CANOPY TOURS

El Santuario Canopy Adventure Tour. Just 20 minutes from Manuel Antonio National Park, this canopy tour boasts the longest single zip line in Costa Rica, extending nearly 2 km (1 mile) over the treetops. Tours include 14 platforms, 3 towers, 6 bridges, 3 nature walks, and 1 double belay rappel. The company has double anchored zip lines

You can hike to white-sand beaches in Manuel Antonio National Park—just one of the reasons it is so popular.

with built-in braking systems. Transportation and lunch are included in the $75 tour fee. ☎ *2777–6908, 877–914–0002 in U.S.* ⊕ *www. elsantuariocanopyadventure.com.*

Tití Canopy Tour. You'll find a relatively slow-paced zip-line tour ($60) here, a rarity in Costa Rica, through a forest reserve that is contiguous with the national park. A night canopy tour runs $75. Guides go above and beyond to make you feel comfortable and safe and will help you spot animals. ✉ *150 m past Quepos Hospital* ☎ *2777–3130* ⊕ *www. titicanopytour.com.*

HIKING

Highly visited Manuel Antonio National Park is the obvious place to go, but in private reserves like Fincas Naturales (⇨ *above*) and Rainmaker (⇨ *Quepos, above*) you can also gain a rich appreciation of the local forests' greenery and wildlife. ■ TIP→ Bring binoculars!

HORSEBACK RIDING

Brisas del Nara. This outfitter takes riders of all ages and levels through the protected Cerro Nara mountain zone, 32 km (20 miles) from Manuel Antonio, and ends with a swim in a natural pool at the foot of a 107-meter (350-foot) waterfall. Full-day tours ($75) include three hours on horseback, with breakfast and lunch included; the ride on the half-day tour ($65) lasts two hours. ☎ *2779–1235* ⊕ *www.horsebacktour.com.*

Finca Valmy Tours. Five-hour horseback tours take you through the forested mountains above Villa Nueva, east of Manuel Antonio ($70). Lunch and swimming in a pool below a small waterfall on their property are included. Tours take place from 8:30–1:30 and in dry season (December to May) from 1:30 to 6:30. ✉ *Villanueva* ☎ *2779–1118.*

Rancho Savegre. Beach riding is the specialty here. Trips set out from a cattle ranch 40 minutes north of Manuel Antonio and include a stop at a waterfall for swimming or trail walking. The morning tour (7:30) ends with lunch; the afternoon tour (2:30) finishes up with dinner. The meeting point for beach tours is next to Monterey Hotel. ⊠ *Monterey Hotel, Esterillos Este, Puntarenas* ☎ *8834–8687* ⊕ *www.ranchosavegre.com* ⊙ *Closed Thurs.–Sun.*

KAYAKING

Iguana Tours. Half-day sea-kayaking trips ($65) to the islands of Manuel Antonio National Park require some experience when the seas are high. On a mellower paddle through the mangrove estuary of Isla Damas ($65) you might see monkeys, crocodiles, and various birds. ⊠ *Downtown Quepos, across from Catholic church, Quepos* ☎ *2777–2052* ⊕ *www.iguanatours.com.*

SNORKELING AND DIVING

The islands that dot the sea in front of Manuel Antonio are surrounded by volcanic rock reefs with small coral formations. They attract schools of snapper, jacks, barracudas, rays, sea turtles, moray eels, and other marine life.

Oceans Unlimited. This is one of the few diving companies in the area that has an on-site training pool. They offer all-day diving excursions to Caño Island ($165), local dives (from $98), PADI-certification courses, and snorkeling tours; rental equipment is included. ⊠ *At Hostel Plinio* ☎ *2777–3171, 407/385–6598 in U.S.* ⊕ *www.scubadivingcostarica.com.*

SURFING

Local Surf School. Located at the isolated section of Playa Espadilla near Arenas Del Mar Resort, this surf school has bilingual instructors and a decent quiver of long and short boards. Several of the surf instructors are certified lifeguards. Showers, drinking water, beach security, and one-on-one training make this a good option. Two-hour group lessons cost around $50. Surfboard rental is $15 per hour or $30 per day. Boogie boards are available for $10 per day. ⊠ *Playa Espadilla near Arenas Del Mar Resort* ☎ *848–66401, 606–13019.*

Manuel Antonio Surf School. Beginner surfers are in good hands with this reputable surf school. Three-hour group lessons start at $65 and include transportation, gear, snacks, and certified instruction. Half-day tours to Damas Island include lunch ($75). ☎ *2777–4842* ⊕ *www.masurfschool.com.*

WHITE-WATER RAFTING

The three white-water rivers in this area have limited seasons. The rains from August to October raise the rivers to their perfect peak.

Adventure Manuel Antonio. Manuel Antonio's original rafting outfitter leads half-day trips down the Naranjo River ($69) and full-day tours down the Savegre River ($98). Naranjo tours can be combined with kayaking in the nearby estuary. ☎ *2777–1084* ⊕ *www.adventuremanuelantonio.com.*

H2O Adventures. The Manuel Antonio franchise for Ríos Tropicales, the biggest rafting outfitter in the country, runs kayaking excursions and rafting trips on the Naranjo River ($65). ✉ *75 m from Catholic church, Quepos* ☎ *2777–4092, 888/532–3298 in U.S.* 🌐 *www.h2ocr.com.*

Río Naranjo. A short but exciting run on this Class III to IV river requires some experience and can be done only from April to November.

Río Parrita. In the dry season this relatively mellow white-water route (Class II to III) can be navigated only in two-person, inflatable duckies.

Río Savegre. Two navigable stretches include the lower section (Class II to III), which is a mellow trip perfect for neophytes, and the more rambunctious upper section (Class III to IV). The river flows past patches of rain forests usually navigable all year long.

WHERE TO EAT

$$ SEAFOOD 🍴 **Cafe Agua Azul.** Follow your nose to this simple second-floor room offering breathtaking views by day and a deliciously inventive selection of seafood by night. The lunch menu is strong on salads and sandwiches, but the dinner options include some of the best entrées in town. In addition to nightly fish and pasta specials, they offer such inventive delicacies as seared tuna over a tequila-and-lime cucumber salad, calamari sautéed with capers and olives, and coconut-crusted mahimahi. [$] *Average main: $18* ✉ *Main road, above the Villas del Parque office* ☎ *2777–5280* 🌐 *www.cafeaguaazul.com* 🕒 *Closed Wed. and Oct.*

$$ CAFÉ 🍴 **Café Milagro** (*El Patio de Café Milagro*). Colorado native Adrienne Pellizzari first came to Manuel Antonio in 1993 on a summer vacation, but it was her quest for good coffee and cuisine that made her stay. In the end, she created her own *milagro* (miracle) blend, making this cozy café the only place in town that serves its own fresh-roasted coffee. The eclectic menu is heavy on vegetarian and organic dishes, like chilled avocado soup, mango chayote salad, and grilled vegetables with quinoa. They also serve pulled pork on corn cakes and dorado with a Caribbean salsa. The breakfast burritos, baked goods, and inventive selection of sandwiches make this a top breakfast and lunch spot. Tables on the front porch overlook the road, but there's also seating in the back garden. At the time of writing, the owners were looking to open a second location at the marina in Quepos. [$] *Average main: $12* ✉ *Main road to park, across from Los Altos* ☎ *2777–0794* 🌐 *www.cafemilagro.com.*

$$$$ STEAKHOUSE 🍴 **El Lagarto.** Carnivores can get their fix at this local grill, where sizzling cuts are seared on a wood-fire grill and served on chopping blocks. Anyone with a fondness for woodwork will appreciate the floors inlaid with tree stumps and the tabletops made from driftwood. A palapa bar serves powerful margaritas and daiquiris, but it's the grass-fed beef from neighboring La Fortuna that you'll want to try. Other specialties include whole red snapper, pork ribs, or lamb (with 24-hour notice). All mains include a baked potato, tomato, and grilled zucchini. Vegetarians can opt for the portobello mushrooms smothered in garlic and cheese, served in a cast-iron skillet. There's a second location in Samara. [$] *Average main: $35* ✉ *200 m north of the soccer field* ☎ *2777–6932* 🌐 *www.ellagartobbq.com* 🕒 *No lunch.*

Espadilla Beach, not far from Quepos, is one of the few beaches in Costa Rica with lifeguards.

$ 🍴 **Emilio's Café.** Sweeping views, organic cuisine, and a Bohemian vibe
MEDITERRANEAN are what you'll get at this popular café where soft jazz sets the stage for all kinds of good eats. Start early with eggs Benedict, waffles, or delectable French toast—fluffy on the inside and crunchy on the outside. At lunch or dinner, try the chicken lemongrass soup, falafel pita, or one of the vegetable sandwiches served with homemade pesto or salsa picante. If you're looking for a sweet treat, try the passion fruit pie or peanut butter cake with fresh fruit juice, frozen mint lemonade, or a frothy cappuccino. Vegetarians and gluten-free eaters have plenty to choose from, as does anyone obsessed with chocolate. They often host live music events. [$] *Average main: $8* ✉ *40 m before Hotel Mariposa* ☎ *2777–6807* 💳 *No credit cards* 🕒 *Closed Tues.*

$$$ 🍴 **Kapi Kapi.** Low lighting, ocher walls, dark hardwood, and potted
ASIAN FUSION palms provide Manuel Antonio's best ambience for dinner, despite the lack of an ocean view. The name is a greeting in the indigenous Maleku language, but the menu is a cosmopolitan invention and includes such un–Costa Rican starters as lemongrass coconut soup, and "seafood cigars"—a mix of fresh tuna, shrimp, and mahimahi deep-fried in an egg-roll wrapper and served on a cabbage salad. The main courses include such Asian-inspired dishes as prawns with a tamarind-coconut-rum glaze and macadamia-encrusted mahimahi with a plum chili sauce. Be sure to order the chocolate soufflé in advance, otherwise you'll be stuck listening to the table next to you rave about its perfection. [$] *Average main: $24* ✉ *East side of main road, across from Pacífico Colonial condos* ☎ *2777–5049* 🌐 *www.restaurantekapikapi.com* 🕒 *Closed Oct. No lunch.*

$$$
INTERNATIONAL
Fodor'sChoice
★

✕**La Luna.** It's hard to know what's more impressive—the view or the cuisine at this restaurant without walls, where the sun melts into the Pacific and La Luna (the moon) takes center stage. Innovative starters range from Gorgonzola and tomato tarts to roasted squash-papaya soup. For something tender and moist, try the tequila lime chicken or the ginger and Panko-crusted tuna. The service is outstanding and there's often live jazz. Happy hour, from 3 to 6, includes half-price tapas and cocktails. If you want to learn the secrets of the young prodigy chef, reserve a spot in the cooking class. Ⓢ *Average main: $22* ⊠ *Km 2.7 Carretera Quepos, at Gaia Hotel* ☎ *2777–9797* ⊕ *www.gaiahr.com.*

$$$
COSTA RICAN

✕**Marlin Restaurant.** The outdoor tables are pretty much always full, owing to a location on Manuel Antonio's busiest corner, across the street from the beach. This is a convenient place to grab breakfast after an early-morning hike through the park—maybe banana pancakes or a *típico*, with eggs and *gallo pinto* (black beans and rice). The lunch and dinner menu ranges from the ubiquitous *arroz con pollo* (rice with chicken) to tenderloin with french fries, and jumbo shrimp in garlic-and-lemon butter. The fresh mahimahi and tuna are always a good bet. Ⓢ *Average main: $25* ⊠ *Main road, south of the hill, on corner across from bus stop and beach* ☎ *2777–1134.*

$$
COSTA RICAN

✕**Ronny's Place.** A spectacular sunset view comes with friendly, attentive service and a small but tempting menu that includes such typical Tico dishes as *sopa negra* (black-bean soup), ceviche, shrimp and fish on a skewer, and filet mignon wrapped with bacon and topped with a mushroom sauce. This is the best place in town to soak in the view—especially when accompanied by a glass of their famous white wine–and–vodka sangria. Ronny's is somewhat secluded down a long dirt road that crosses a green valley on a narrow ridge in front of the sea. Ⓢ *Average main: $15* ⊠ *1 km (½ mile) west of main road, down dirt road across from Amigos del Río* ☎ *2777–5120* ⊕ *www.ronnysplace. com* ⊙ *Closed Sept.*

$
ECLECTIC

✕**Salsipuedes Tapas Bar.** A spot nestled behind a rock formation at the edge of the forest has one of the best sunset views in town, making this a great choice for cocktails and appetizers. The tapas range from sashimi and grilled tuna and mahimahi to fajitas. Such Costa Rican favorites as *frijolitos blancos* (white beans stewed with chicken) and *chicharrones con yuca* (fried pork and cassava root) are also available. The kitchen offers half a dozen full dinners, including larger cuts of fish, and some rice and pasta dishes, and is willing to turn any of the tapas dishes into a full meal. At the other end of the day, this is one of the few restaurants around that serves breakfast, and you can expect hearty offerings to get you through the morning. Live Latin music kicks off at sunset from December through March. Ⓢ *Average main: $15* ⊠ *Main road, across from Banco Proamérica* ☎ *2777–5019* ⊙ *Closed Tues.*

$$$
ITALIAN

✕**Victoria's.** If the sound of live music by Rafa Mora (Costa Rica's leading classical guitarist) isn't enough to lure your senses, then the smell of brick oven pizza surely will be. Thin and crispy, top picks include shrimp pizza or pesto chicken with toasted walnuts and caramelized onions. Staying true to Italian cuisine are the homemade meatballs, advertised as "to die for, but not recommended on first dates." The tuna chipotle and filet mignon are hearty dishes and come with a side of roasted potatoes and vegetables. There's a children's menu and a banana flambé worth saving room for. Live music is performed Sunday through Thursday from 6 to closing. $ *Average main: $24* ✉ *Across from Pacifico Colonial Condominiums* ☎ *2777–5143* ⊕ *www.victoriasgourmet.com* ☾ *No lunch.*

WHERE TO STAY

$$$$
RESORT
Fodor's Choice
★

🏨 Arenas del Mar Beachfront and Nature Resort. On hillsides sloping down to two pristine, almost-deserted beaches, chic and elegant rooms are decorated with gorgeous natural fabrics and flamboyant local art and have huge private terraces with comfortable outdoor seating. **Pros:** best of both worlds: luxury and eco-consciousness; best beach access in Manuel Antonio; wonderful bird-watching and wildlife viewing; beach with surf lessons and lifeguard. **Cons:** very steep paths and stairs; humidity can leave bathrooms somewhat musty; pricey. $ *Rooms from: $350* ✉ *Far west end of Playa Espadilla, down El Parador road, in Manuel Antonio* ☎ *2777–2777* ☎ *888/240–0280 in U.S.* ⊕ *www.arenasdelmar. com* ⬎ *38 rooms, 10 suites* ⊚ *Breakfast.*

$$
HOTEL
FAMILY

🏨 Cabinas Espadilla. These quiet cabinas open onto porches overlooking a tropical garden and a wide lawn, shaded by hammock-strung palm trees, and a large pool. **Pros:** good value; short walk from beach and national park; nice grounds. **Cons:** mediocre rooms; street noise in some units; Wi-Fi does not reach all rooms. $ *Rooms from: $120* ✉ *On road beside Marlin Restaurant* ☎ *2777–2113* ⊕ *www.espadilla. com* ⬎ *16 cabinas* ⊚ *Breakfast.*

$$$$
HOTEL

🏨 Gaia Hotel & Reserve. On 14 acres of private reserve, this adults-only boutique hotel is the essence of contemporary chic, with rooms rendered in slate, hardwood, and rattan with Italian fittings. **Pros:** outstanding service; free shuttle to beach and town; best spa in Manuel Antonio; personal concierge; 24-hour room service. **Cons:** no kids under 12; rooftop pools are shallow and impractical; 3 km (2 miles) from the beach. $ *Rooms from: $290* ✉ *Km 2.7 Carretera Quepos, near Plaza Yara, in Manuel Antonio* ☎ *2777–9797, 1–800/226–2515 in U.S.* ⊕ *www. gaiahr.com* ⬎ *20 rooms* ⊚ *Breakfast.*

$$
RESORT

🏨 Hotel Costa Verde. You're likely to see monkeys, iguanas, and all kinds of birds on the forest trails surrounding these varied accommodations. Some are scattered with screened walls that let the breeze through, some with kitchens and ocean views, one converted from a Boeing 727 fuselage. **Pros:** great ocean views; wildlife; daily yoga; studios and Building D efficiencies a good value. **Cons:** most efficiencies suffer road noise; no beach access; service inconsistent; some rooms are dated. $ *Rooms from: $172* ✉ *Road to park, south side of hill, on left* ☎ *2777–0584, 866/854–7958 in North America* ⊕ *www.costaverde.com* ⬎ *75 rooms* ⊚ *No meals.*

$$$
HOTEL
FAMILY

🏨 Hotel Playa Espadilla. Simple but spacious mint-green rooms with big windows are a short walk from the beach and surrounded by green lawns bordered on two sides by the tall trees of Manuel Antonio National Park. **Pros:** surrounded by forest; close to beach and park; guests can use amenities at sister property Cabinas Espadilla. **Cons:** service inconsistent; very small pool; basic rooms. $ *Rooms from: $188* ✉ *150 m up side road from Marlin Restaurant, 1st left* ☎ *2777–0903* ⊕ *www.espadilla.com* ⬎ *16 rooms* ⊚ *Breakfast.*

7

The Pacific coast is backed by mangrove, rain, transitional, and tropical dry forests.

$$$
RESORT
FAMILY

Hotel Sí Como No. Scattered through the rain forest in nine buildings, rooms are decorated in earth tones to complement the surrounding nature; spacious deluxe rooms have sea views and private balconies, smaller "superior" rooms have less impressive ocean views, and standard rooms face the jungle. **Pros:** free butterfly garden; spa; nice views; environmentally sustainable; good restaurants. **Cons:** 3 km (2 miles) from beach; standards overpriced; a few suites too close to road. $ *Rooms from: $250 ⊠ Road to park, just after Villas Nicolás, right-hand side* ☎ *2777–0777, 888/742–6667 in North America* ⊕ *www.sicomono.com* ↘ *39 rooms, 19 suites* ⦿ *Breakfast.*

$$
HOTEL

Hotel Verde Mar. The turquoise buildings at this friendly though basic hotel house small rooms with queen beds, pineapple print interiors, kitchenettes, and large windows with views of the ubiquitous tropical foliage. **Pros:** good value; mere steps from beach; in the rain forest; friendly. **Cons:** no meals; rooms smallish and basic; no in-room safes. $ *Rooms from: $115 ⊠ ½ km (¼ mile) north of park* ☎ *2777–2122* ⊕ *www.verdemar.com* ↘ *29 rooms* ⦿ *No meals.*

$$$$
B&B/INN

La Mansion Inn. White silk curtains, black onyx flooring, and classical music welcome you to the reception area of this five-star boutique hotel, where all rooms boast ocean views, white tile floors, leather chairs, and balconies. **Pros:** excellent views; unique bar; free shuttle to Manuel Antonio National Park. **Cons:** steep driveway with limited parking; deluxe rooms not as impressive as common areas. $ *Rooms from: $350 ⊠ Next to Hotel Makanda, in Manuel Antonio* ☎ *2777–3489, 1–800/360–2071 in U.S.* ⊕ *www.lamansioninn.com* ↘ *24 rooms* ⦿ *Breakfast.*

$$$
RESORT

[icon] **La Mariposa.** The best view in town—a sweeping panorama of verdant hills, the aquamarine ocean, and offshore islands—is the claim to fame for this array of spacious rooms and suites tucked between the jungle and gardens ablaze with colorful flowers. **Pros:** gorgeous views; central location; website often has last-minute specials; large bathrooms. **Cons:** 2 km (1 mile) from beach; some ocean-view balconies lack privacy; lots of stairs to reach some rooms; slightly dated. [$] *Rooms from: $215* ✉ *West of main road, right after Barba Roja* ☎ *2777–0355, 800/572–6440 in U.S.* ⊕ *www.lamariposa.com* ☞ *62 rooms* ❙○❙ *Breakfast.*

$$
RESORT
Fodor'sChoice
★

[icon] **La Posada Private Jungle Bungalows.** This cluster of distinctive A-frame bungalows, nestled on the edge of the national park and also just a short walk from the beach, is as close as you'll get to sleeping in the park. **Pros:** good value; near beach and park; wildlife; friendly. **Cons:** a bit isolated; small pool. [$] *Rooms from: $135* ✉ *250 m up side road from Marlin Restaurant* ☎ *2777–1446* ⊕ *www.laposadajungle.com* ☞ *4 bungalows, 2 apartments, 1 villa, 1 house* ❙○❙ *Breakfast.*

$$$$
RESORT

[icon] **Los Altos Beach Resort & Spa.** These three- and four-bedroom Balinese-inspired luxury condo suites boast 2,500 square feet with industrial kitchens, slate floors, granite counters, rich hardwoods, and rattan furnishings. **Pros:** great views; kids under six stay free; ideal for families; enormous rooms. **Cons:** higher level suites cost more; $75 charge per person over two guests; only high-rise in Manuel Antonio; a bit of an eyesore. [$] *Rooms from: $450* ✉ *Km 4 on road to Manuel Antonio National Park, across from Café Milagro, in Manuel Antonio* ☎ *2777–8888, 888/803–1332 in U.S.* ⊕ *www.thepreserveatlosaltos.com* ☞ *28 condos* ❙○❙ *Breakfast.*

$$$$
RESORT

[icon] **Makanda by the Sea.** These bright, spacious, white-and-cream villas are among the area's most tasteful (and expensive) accommodations, and the hypnotic views of the jungle-framed Pacific Ocean make this secluded rain-forest retreat worth it. **Pros:** tranquil; surrounded by nature; ocean views; stocked kitchens. **Cons:** far from beach; a few studios need updating; no children under 12. [$] *Rooms from: $315* ✉ *1 km (½ mile) west of La Mariposa* ☎ *2777–0442, 888/625–2632 in North America* ⊕ *www.makanda.com* ☞ *6 villas, 5 studios* ❙○❙ *Breakfast.*

$$
B&B/INN

[icon] **Mango Moon Hotel.** The cream-color rooms vary in size and amenities, but the intimate atmosphere and hospitable staff make you feel as if you're staying with a friend rather than at a hotel. **Pros:** nice view; tranquil area; friendly. **Cons:** far from main beaches; not much privacy; some rooms dark and dated; relatively expensive. [$] *Rooms from: $150* ✉ *Between La Mariposa and Makanda* ☎ *2777–5323* ⊕ *www.mangomoonhotel.com* ☞ *10 rooms* ❙○❙ *Breakfast.*

$$$$
RESORT

[icon] **Parador Resort & Spa.** Terra-cotta floors, steamer trunks, marble statues, bronzed knights, and elaborate antiques create a high-end Spanish colonial style at this beachfront resort perched on the end of a secluded peninsula. **Pros:** outstanding service; tranquil location. **Cons:** it's a hike to some rooms; 15-minute drive to Manuel Antonio National Park; not ideal setting for kids. [$] *Rooms from: $325* ✉ *End of Peninsula at Biesanz Beach, in Manuel Antonio* ☎ *2777–1414* ⊕ *www.hotelparador.com* ☞ *92 rooms, 30 suites.*

7

$$$$
RESORT

⊡ **Shana Hotel.** Everything—walls, furniture, decor, pools, staff uniforms—is blindingly white, a striking contrast to the lush greens of the hillside grounds, and the service might seem over the top if you just want a quiet beach vacation. **Pros:** sumptuous luxury; attentive service; relaxing spa; sleek design. **Cons:** not oceanfront; weak Wi-Fi signal in some rooms; steep driveway. Ⓢ *Rooms from: $280* ⊠ *Road to Quepos, 300 m downhill from La Mansión Inn* ☎ *2774–6747, 2272–7036* ⊕ *www.shanahotel.com* ⤶ *28 rooms* ⍾⋌ *Breakfast.*

$$
RESORT
Fodor's Choice
★

⊡ **Villas Nicolás.** On a hillside about 3 km (2 miles) from the beach, terraced Mediterranean-style, privately owned (and rented) villas have impressive views and offer one and two bedrooms, kitchens, and (in most) large balconies with hammocks. **Pros:** great location; most rooms have great views; grounds are well maintained. **Cons:** some units need updating; lukewarm Jacuzzi; a bit of hike to the beach. Ⓢ *Rooms from: $180* ⊠ *Road to park, across from Hotel Byblos* ☎ *2777–0481* ⊕ *www. villasnicolas.com* ⤶ *19 rooms* ⍾⋌ *Breakfast.*

NIGHTLIFE

BARS

Billfish Bar. With large-screen TVs and pool tables, Manuel Antonio's consummate sports bar fills up on game nights. Ladies' Night is on Monday and Friday. ⊠ *Main road, across from Barba Roja* ☎ *2777–0411.*

Salsipuedes Tapas Bar. This colorful tapas bar hidden behind tropical foliage is a great sunset venue. It's one of the few places you can enjoy a quiet drink. ⊠ *Main road, north of Barba Roja, in front of Banco Promérica* ☎ *2777–5019* ⊗ *Closed Tues.*

DANCE CLUB

Barba Roja. A dance club on Saturday night, this bar also has a popular sunset cocktail hour daily. ⊠ *Main road, across from Hotel Divisamar* ☎ *2777–0331* ⊕ *www.barbarojarestaurant.com* ⊗ *Closed Mon.*

Victoria's. This upscale Italian restaurant is also a popular nightspot, with classical guitarist Rafa Mora performing most evenings. ⊠ *Main road, across from Pacifico Colonial Condominiums* ☎ *2777–5143* ⊕ *www.victoriasgourmet.com.*

SHOPPING

There's no shortage of shopping in this town. The beach near the entrance to the park is lined with a sea of vendors who sell T-shirts, hats, and colorful beach wraps. More-authentic handicrafts are sold at night by artisans positioned along the sidewalk in central Manuel Antonio.

Regalame. This appealing art gallery is a showplace for paintings, drawings, pottery, and jewelry by area artists. ⊠ *Next to Sí Como No Hotel* ☎ *2777–0777.*

THE OSA
PENINSULA AND
THE SOUTH PACIFIC

WELCOME TO THE OSA PENINSULA AND THE SOUTH PACIFIC

TOP REASONS TO GO

★ **Bird-watching:** Spot beauties such as the scarlet macaw and resplendent quetzal.

★ **Enormous Corcovado National Park:** The last refuge of endangered jaguars and tapirs.

★ **Kayaking:** Head to the Golfo Dulce or along the jungly channels of the Sierpe or Colorado rivers.

★ **Mountain hikes:** Hiking paths here range from easy daytime treks around luxurious lodges to Costa Rica's toughest: 3,820-meter (12,532-foot) Cerro Chirripó.

★ **Wild places to stay:** Relax in the country's top eco-lodges, rustic thatch-roof beach bungalows, and cozy mountain cabins.

1 The Central Highlands. The main road climbs more than 2,134 meters (7,000 feet) over mountains and above the clouds of the Central Highlands before descending into the huge Valle de El General agricultural region. Highlights are fabulous mountain lodges, world-class bird-watching, and high-altitude hikes.

2 Valle de el General Region. This prosperous region, centered around the bustling market town of San Isidro de El General, is the gateway to Chirripó National Park, home of the country's highest peak.

3 Dominical and Ballena Marine Park. The coast has miles of beaches peppered with small beach communities, including Dominical, a scruffy but lively surfer haven, and Ojochal, a French-accented enclave. Parque Nacional Marino Ballena offers 10 km (6 miles) of pristine beaches and a chance to watch dolphins and migrating whales, for which the park is named.

4 The Golfo Dulce. The eastern Golfo Dulce draws anglers and kayakers to Golfito, beachcombers to slow-paced Zancudo, and serious surfers to Pavones.

5 The Osa Peninsula. The wild Osa Peninsula consists almost entirely of Corcovado National Park, 1,156 square km (445 square miles) of primary and secondary rain forest straight out of a David Attenborough nature documentary.

División — San Gerardo de Rivas — **2** Cerro Chirripó National Park

CR2

San Isidro

1

SAN JOSÉ — 18 — 22 — Juntas — Mercedes

CR2

Dominical

VALLE DE EL GENERAL

3 Pejibaye

Uvita — 244

Ballena Marine National Park — Punta Mala

Palmar Norte — 18

Sierpe

Sierpe R.

Drake — Rincón

OSA PENINSULA

San Pedrillo

Corcovado National Park

Sirena

GETTING ORIENTED

The most remote part of Costa Rica, the South Pacific encompasses the southern half of Puntarenas Province and La Amistad International Biosphere. The region descends from mountainous forests just an hour south of San José to the humid Golfo Dulce and the richly forested Osa Peninsula, seven to nine hours from the capital by car.

0   10 mi

0   10 km

CORDILLERA DE TALAMANCA

LIMÓN

La Amistad National Park

Cabagra

Buenos Aires

Brujo
Terraba

Helechales

Paso Real

Alturas

Jabillo

237

PUNTARENAS

Union

San Vito

Chacarita

16   PANAMA

245

Piedras Blancas National Park

CR2   Río Claro

Ciudad Neily

4   Golfito

14

245

Golfo Dulce

Zancudo

Paso Canoas

Puerto Jiménez

Laurel

5

Conte

Madrígal

El Higo

Pavones

Carate

Banco

Cabo Matapolo

Punto Banco

Pacific Ocean

8

CHIRRIPÓ NATIONAL PARK

Chirripó National Park is all about hiking. The ascent up Mt. Chirripó, the highest mountain in Costa Rica, is the most popular and challenging hike in the country. It's also the most exclusive, limited to 40 hikers per day.

From the trailhead to the peak, you gain more than 2,438 meters (8,000 feet) of elevation, climbing through shaded highland forest, then out into the wide-open, windswept wilds of the *páramo*, scrubby moorland similar to the high Andes. It's a 48-km (30-mile) round-trip, and you need at least three days to climb to the base, explore the summits, and descend. The modern but chilly stone hostel is the only available accommodation, with small rooms of four bunks each, shared bathrooms, and a cooking area. A generator and solar panels provide some electricity, but the hostel is still bare-bones rustic. Trails from the hostel lead to the top of Chirripó—the highest point in Costa Rica—and the nearby peak of Terbi, as well as half a dozen other peaks and glacier lakes. *(See page 442 for more information.)* ■ TIP➔ **Pack plenty of warm clothes.**

BEST TIME TO GO

Between sometimes freezing temperatures and more than 381 centimeters (150 inches) of rain a year, timing is of the essence here. The best months are in the dry season, January to May. The park is closed the last two weeks in May, all of October and often in November and December as well if the trails are too wet and slippery for safety.

FUN FACT

A climb up Chirripó is a rite of passage for many young Costa Ricans, who celebrate their graduation from high school or college with a group expedition.

BEST WAYS TO EXPLORE

HIKING

There's no getting around it: the only way to explore this park is on foot. And the only way is up. It's a tough climb to Mt. Chirripó's base camp—6 to 10 hours from the official park entrance, depending on your physical condition—so most hikers head out of San Gerardo de Rivas before the first light of day. You can hire porters to lug your gear up and down for you, so at least you can travel relatively light.

People who live in Costa Rica train seriously for this hike, so be sure you are in good enough shape to make the climb. Smart hikers also factor in a couple of days in the San Gerardo de Rivas area to acclimate to the high altitude before setting out. The hike down is no picnic, either: your knees and ankles will be stretched to their limits. But it's an adventure every step of the way—and the bragging rights are worth it.

MOUNTAIN HIGHS

The base-camp hostel at Los Crestones is at 11,152 feet above sea level, so you still have some hiking ahead of you if you want to summit the surrounding peaks. Take your pick: Chirripó at 12,532 feet; Ventisqueros at 12,467 feet; Cerro Terbi at 12,336; and, for the fainter of heart, Mt. Uran at a measly 11,811 feet. Mountain hikers who collect "peaks" can add all four mountaintops to their list.

BIRD-WATCHING

Although your eyes will mostly be on the scenery, there are some highland species of birds that thrive in this chilly mountain air. Watch for the volcano junco, a sparrowlike bird with a pink beak and a yellow eye ring. Only two hummingbirds venture up this high—the fiery-throated hummingbird, which lives up to its name; and the volcano hummingbird, which is the country's smallest bird. If you see a raptor soaring above, chances are it's a red-tailed hawk.

TOP REASONS TO GO

Did It!
The sheer sense of accomplishing this tough hike is the number one reason hikers take on this challenge. You don't have to be a mountain climber, but you do need to be in very good shape.

Ocean Views
On rare, perfectly clear days, the top of Chirripó is one of the few places in the country where you can see both the Pacific and Atlantic oceans.

Top of the World
The exhilaration of sitting on top of the world, with only sky, mountain peaks, and heath as far as the eye can see, motivates most visitors to withstand the physical challenges and the spartan conditions in the hostel.

Unique Environment
A climb up Chirripó gives visitors a unique chance to experience extreme changes in habitat, from pastureland through rain forest and oak forest to bleak, scrubby *páramo* (a high-elevation ecosystem). As the habitat changes, so does the endemic wildlife, which thins out near the top, along with the air.

8

CORCOVADO NATIONAL PARK

For those who crave untamed wilderness, Corcovado National Park is the experience of a lifetime. Covering one-third of the Osa Peninsula, the park is blanketed primarily by virgin rain forest and holds Central America's largest remaining tract of lowland Pacific rain forest.

The remoteness of Corcovado and the difficult access to its interior make it one of the country's most pristine parks—barely disturbed by human presence—where massive, vine-tangled primary-forest trees tower over the trails and birds and wildlife abound. Your chances of spotting endangered species are better here than anywhere else in the country, although it still takes a combination of luck and determination. The rarest and most sought-after sightings are the jaguar and Baird's tapir. Corcovado also has the largest population of scarlet macaws in the country. Bordering the park are some of Costa Rica's most luxurious jungle lodges and retreats, all of which are contributing to the effort to save Corcovado's wildlife. *(See page 488 for more information.)*

BEST TIME TO GO

Dry season, January to May, is the best time to visit, but it's also the most popular. With so few accommodations available, it's crucial to reserve well in advance. June through August will be wetter, but may also be a little cooler. The long-distance trails are virtually impassable from September to December, when most visitors arrive in boats.

STAY ON TRAILS

Warning signs to stay on the trails should be heeded: in 2007, the Minister of Tourism got lost and wandered around in a daze for three days after following a baby tapir off the trail and being attacked by its mother.

BEST WAYS TO EXPLORE

BIRD-WATCHING AND WILDLIFE

The holy grail of wildlife spotting here is a jaguar or a Baird's tapir. You may be one of the lucky few to see one of these rare, elusive animals. In the meantime, you can content yourself with coatis, peccaries, and agoutis on the ground and, in the trees, some endemic species of birds you will see only in this part of the country: Baird's trogon, riverside wren, and black-cheeked ant-tanager, to name a few.

GETTING HERE AND AROUND

The easiest way to visit the park is on a day trip by boat, organized by a lodge or tour company in Drake Bay, Sierpe, or Uvita. The well-heeled can fly in on an expensive charter plane to the Sirena airfield. But no matter how you arrive, the only way to explore is on foot. There are no roads, only hiking trails. If you have a backpack, strong legs, and a reservation for a tent site or a ranger station bunk, you can enter the park on foot at three staffed ranger stations and spend up to five days deep in the wilds.

HIKING

There are two main hiking routes to Corcovado. When you're planning your itinerary, keep in mind that the hike between any two ranger stations takes at least a day. The hike from La Leona to Sirena is about 16 km (10 miles) and requires crossing a wide river mouth and a stretch of beach best negotiated at low tide. Some people plan this hike before dawn to avoid the blistering sun. The 17.4-km (10.8-mile) route from Los Patos to Sirena is the coolest trail, through forest all the way.

TOP REASONS TO GO

Flora and Fauna
The sheer diversity of flora and fauna and the chance to see wildlife completely in the wild are the main draws here. The number of cataloged species, to date, includes 500 trees (49 of them in peril of extinction), 150 orchids, 375 birds, 124 mammals (11 on the endangered list), 123 butterflies, 71 reptiles, 46 amphibians, and more than 8,000 insects.

Off the Beaten Track
Day visitors get to taste the thrill of being completely off the beaten track, in an untamed natural world. But for campers and guests at the park's main lodge, La Sirena, the chance to spend days roaming miles of trails without hearing a single man-made sound is a rare treat.

Test Your Limits
The physical challenges of hiking in high humidity and living very basically, along with the psychological challenge of being completely out of touch with "the real world" can be rewarding.

8

WHALE MARINE NATIONAL PARK

Great snorkeling, whale-watching, and beach-combing draw visitors and locals to Parque Nacional Marino Ballena (Whale Marine National Park), which protects four relatively tranquil beaches stretching for about 10 km (6 miles), as well as a mangrove estuary, a recovering coral reef, and a vast swath of ocean.

Playa Uvita, fronting the small town of Bahía Ballena, is the longest, widest, and most visited beach, and the embarkation point for snorkeling, fishing, and whale-watching tours. Restaurants line the nearby main street of the town. Playa Colonia, the most easily accessible beach, has a safe swimming beach with a view of rocky islands. Playa Ballena, south of Playa Colonia, is a lovely strand backed by lush vegetation. Finally, tiny Playa Piñuela is the prettiest of the park beaches, in a deep cove that serves as the local port. It's also the narrowest beach, with a pebbled slope down to the sand. Along with the tropical fish you'll see while snorkeling, you may be lucky enough to see humpback whales and dolphins. (*See page 456 for more information.*)

BEST TIME TO GO

December to April is the best time for guaranteed sunny beach weather, as well as for sightings of humpback whales with their young. The whales also roam these waters in late July through late October. Bottlenose dolphins abound in March and April. Avoid Easter Week and weekends in December to February, when locals camp in the park by the hundreds.

FUN FACT

Playa Uvita features a *tombolo*, a long swath of sand connecting a former island to the coast. At low tide, the exposed brown sandbar resembles a whale's tail.

(See page 456 for more information.)

BEST WAYS TO EXPLORE

BEACHCOMBING

The park's beaches are ideal to explore on foot, especially Playa Uvita, which has the longest and widest stretch of sand. Visitors and locals flock here in the late afternoon to catch spectacular sunsets. Don't forget your camera! At low tide, you can walk out onto the Whale's Tail sandbar. During the day, you'll see moving shells everywhere—hermit crabs of every size are constantly scuttling around. Although it all looks idyllic—and it mostly is—don't leave valuables unattended on the beach.

CAMPING

If you brought a tent, pitch it here. Camping on the beach is allowed at Playas Ballena, Colonia, and Piñuela. You can't beat the price, as camping is included in the park admission. Every beach has *sanitarios* (basic toilets) and cold-water showers. But bring your own drinking water. Costa Ricans are avid—and often noisy—campers, so try to avoid busy weekends and school holidays.

IN, ON, AND OVER THE WATER

Swimming here is relatively safe, but check with the park ranger or your hotel about the best swimming spots. Watch for the *banda amarilla* (yellow ribbon) signs, which indicate dangerous currents. Or just watch where the locals are frolicking in the water. Get a little farther out in the water on a fishing charter and try your hand at reeling in mahimahi, tuna, and mackerel. Whale- and dolphin-watching excursions are also a fun option—bottlenose dolphins are most often spotted, but humpback whales, especially mothers with babes, are the stars of the show. If you want to be the captain of your boat, sea kayaks are a popular way to explore the park's mangroves and river estuaries. Playa Ventanas, just south of the park's official border, has tidal rock caves you can kayak through. You can also paddle out to close-in islets and look for brown boobies, the tropical seabirds that nest here. For the ultimate bird's-eye view, take an ultralight flight over the park.

TOP REASONS TO GO

Alone Time
If solitude is what you're after, the park's beaches are relatively uncrowded, except on weekends and school holidays when locals come to camp and relax. Neither Playa Colonia nor Playa Piñuela sees a lot of traffic, so you can have them virtually to yourself almost anytime. There have been some nighttime drug-trafficking problems on these beaches, so don't hang out after dark.

Beaches
Miles of wide, sandy beach backed by palm trees and distant green mountain ridges make this one of the most scenic and accessible coastlines in the country. Playa Uvita and Playa Ballena, with their warm, swimmable waters and soft sand, attract the most beachgoers.

Whales and Dolphins
Catching sight of a humpback whale with her youngster swimming alongside is a thrill you won't forget. And watching dolphins cavorting around your excursion boat is the best entertainment on water.

ECO-LODGES IN THE SOUTH PACIFIC

The South Pacific Zone is Costa Rica's last frontier, with a wealth of protected biodiversity. It's also the cradle of the country's ecotourism, including some of the world's best eco-lodges.

Costa Rica's wildest corner has vast expanses of wilderness ranging from the majestic cloud forests and high-altitude *páramo* (scrubby alpine terrain) of the Talamanca highlands to the steamy, lowland rain forest of Corcovado National Park. Quetzals and other high-elevation birds abound in the oak forests of the San Gerardo de Dota Valley, and scarlet macaws congregate in beach almond trees lining the shores of the Osa Peninsula. The Southern Zone has some of the country's most impressive, though least accessible, national parks—towering Chirripó and mountain-studded La Amistad; and Corcovado, where peccaries, tapirs, and, more rarely, jaguars still roam. Stunning marine wonders can be found in the Golfo Dulce, the dive and snorkeling spots around Caño Island Biological Reserve, and Ballena Marine National Park, famous for seasonal whale migrations.

GOOD PRACTICES

The signage you'll often see in natural areas sums up ecotourism's principal tenets: leave nothing but footprints; take away nothing but memories.

A few more tips:

Walk softly on forest trails and keep as quiet as you can. You'll spot more wildlife and maintain the natural atmosphere of the forest for other visitors, too.

Stay on marked trails and never approach animals; use your zoom lens to capture close-ups.

Ecotourism is also about getting to know the locals and their culture. Visit a local farm, an artisan's co-op, or a village school.

TOP ECO-LODGES IN THE SOUTH PACIFIC

CASA CORCOVADO JUNGLE LODGE

This jungle lodge, bordering Corcovado National Park, gets top eco-marks for its energy-saving solar and microhydroelectric systems, and its recycling and waste-management leadership in the area. The lodge financed the building of a recycling center in Sierpe, and all the area's glass and aluminum is now recycled. Guests receive a refillable bottle to use throughout their stay. Owner Steve Lill is cofounder and president of the Corcovado Foundation, a major supporter of local initiatives to preserve wildlife on the Osa Peninsula. *(Full hotel review on page 497.)*

LAPA RÍOS

Lapa Ríos is the premier eco-lodge in Costa Rica. The lodge's mission is to protect the 1,000 acres of forest in its private preserve edging Corcovado National Park. Its main weapon is education, through local school programs and community involvement. The lodge owners spearheaded the building of the local school and provide direct employment to more than 45 area families. Lapa Ríos was the first area lodge to offer a free sustainability tour, highlighting innovative eco-friendly practices. *(Full hotel review on page 492.)*

PLAYA NICUESA RAINFOREST LODGE

From its initial construction to its daily operations, this Golfo Dulce lodge, accessible only by boat, has been committed to sustainability. The main lodge and guest cabins were built with fallen wood and recycled materials. Solar power, an organic septic system, composting, and a chemical-free garden also attest to the owners' eco-credentials. The kitchen uses local produce and cooks up fish caught in the gulf. Lodge owners Donna and Michael Butler match guests' donations to the Osa Campaign, a cooperative conservation program. They also help guests purchase carbon credits to help offset the carbon footprint of their flights to Costa Rica. *(Full hotel review on page 468.)*

AFTER DARK

The first night in a remote Southern Zone eco-lodge can be unnerving. You may have looked forward to falling asleep to the sounds of nature, but you may not be prepared for the onslaught of night noises: the chirping of geckos as they hunt for insects in the thatch roof, the thwack of flying insects colliding against window screens, and the spine-tingling calls of owls and nightjars. Add in the chorus of croaking frogs and you may have trouble falling asleep. Once you realize that you're safe under your mosquito net, you can start to enjoy the nocturnal symphony. And after the first day of waking up at dawn to the roars of howler monkeys and the chatter of songbirds, you'll be more than ready to crash early the next night. Most guests are asleep by 8 pm and rise at 5 am, the best time to spot birds and wildlife as they start their day, too. For nighttime visits to the bathroom, be sure to keep a flashlight and shoes handy.

8

By Dorothy
MacKinnon

Visitors go south to heed the call of the wild. The jewels in the South Pacific crown are the idyllic Golfo Dulce and the wild Osa Peninsula, brimming with wildlife and natural adventures. There is no place like it, especially when you travel off the grid, far from the sounds of modern civilization. With miles of undulating Pacific coastline, there is rarely a crowded beach. Up in the highlands, the hiking and birdwatching are unsurpassed.

The South Pacific encompasses everything south of San José, down to the border with Panama, and all the territory west of the Talamanca Mountains, sloping down to the Pacific coast. Adventures abound in this rugged region. On land, hiking, bird-watching, horseback riding, and wildlife viewing are the main activities, along with some thrilling tree-climbing, zip-lining, and waterfall-rappelling opportunities. On the water, there's surfing, snorkeling, diving, fishing, sea-kayaking, and whale- and dolphin-watching, as well as swimming and beachcombing. There's even a sky option, flying in a two-seater ultralight plane.

What makes many of these activities special is that, given the wildness of the locations, the focus is more on nature than on entertainment. No matter what you're doing, you'll come across interesting flora and fauna and natural phenomena. Another key to what sets the Southern Zone apart is the large number of trained naturalist guides. Most eco-lodges have resident guides who know not only where to find the birds and wildlife, but also how to interpret the hidden workings of the natural world around you.

PLANNING

WHEN TO GO
PEAK SEASON: JANUARY TO APRIL
The dry season has the most reliably sunny weather. But be aware that the climate swings wildly in the south, from bracing mountain air to steamy coastal humidity. In the mountains it's normally around 24°C (75°F) during the day and 10°C (50°F) at night. Temperatures can fall close to freezing on the upper slopes of Cerro de la Muerte and elsewhere, so be sure to pack a sweater. Temperatures in coastal areas are usually 24°C–32°C (76°F–90°F), but it's the humidity that does you in.

OFF-SEASON: SEPTEMBER TO DECEMBER
The rainy season can be very wet indeed, especially September through November. The rainy season is longest in the Osa Peninsula, where showers usually last through January. Roads sometimes flood and many lodges close in the rainiest months (October and November). Elsewhere during the long rainy season, mornings tend to be brilliant and sunny, with refreshing rain starting in mid-afternoon. Many lodges offer discounted "green season" rates. Often, there is a two-or three-week period of dry weather with brilliant sunshine in late June into July, a mini-summer called *el veranillo*.

SHOULDER SEASON: EARLY DECEMBER AND APRIL TO MAY
Early December, when the landscape is lush and green after months of rain and crowds of tourists have yet to arrive, can be delightful in most of the Southern Zone. April into May is another good time to visit, when crowds have thinned out and the rains are just starting to freshen up the landscape

PLANNING YOUR TIME
You need at least a week to truly experience any part of the Osa Peninsula. Even if you fly, ground transportation to your lodge may be painfully slow, so plan two days for travel alone. It's best to choose one base and take day trips from there. In three weeks, you can experience the entire region, including mountains, beaches, and the Osa Peninsula.

If you are driving south, keep in mind that Cerro de la Muerte is often covered with fog in the afternoon, so plan to cross the mountains in the morning. This mountain road has been much improved, but it's safer—not to mention more scenic—to drive it in dry, clear weather. More and more visitors take the coastal highway these days, but they miss out on the dramatic mountain vistas.

Don't try to cover too much ground on a set schedule. It is simply impossible to estimate how long it takes to drive a certain route or make transportation connections in this part of the country, especially during rainy season when flooding and landslides can close roads and bad weather can delay flights. But remember, getting there is part of the adventure.

GETTING HERE AND AROUND

AIR TRAVEL

SANSA and Nature Air have direct flights to Drake Bay, Palmar Sur, and Puerto Jiménez. SANSA flies Cessna planes and has the most flights to Golfito. Nature Air flies DeHavilland planes with larger windows that are great for sightseeing. The company prides itself on its sustainability, claiming to be the world's first carbon-neutral airline. *For more information about air travel to the South Pacific from San José, see Air Travel in Travel Smart Costa Rica.*

Alfa Romeo Aero Taxi, at the Puerto Jiménez airport (really more of an airstrip), flies small charter planes to Carate, Tiskita, and Corcovado National Park's airstrip at La Sirena. The one-way price to Corcovado is $390 for up to five people.

Airline Contacts Alfa Romeo Aero Taxi ⊠ *Puerto Jiménez Airport* ☎ *2735–5178.*

BUS TRAVEL

Bus fares from San José average about $10, depending on distance and number of stops. The best way to get around the region's roads is by bus—let someone else do the driving. Bus fares are cheap, and you'll meet the locals. But the going is generally slow, departures are often very early in the morning, and schedules change so frequently that you'll want to confirm the day before you travel.

Based in Dominical, Monkey Ride has shuttle-van services in each direction between San José and the Dominical/Uvita/Ojochal area starting at $44 per person.

Bus Contacts Monkey Ride. Shared rides in large, air-conditioned vans, from San Jose to Dominical and points south, start at $44 per person. ⊠ *Pueblo del Río, main street, Dominical* ☎ *2787–0454, 8651–9090* ⊕ *www.monkeyridecr.com.*

CAR TRAVEL

Owing to the often dismal state of the roads (deteriorated bridges and potholes galore) and hazardous driving conditions (flooded rivers), we don't recommend driving in the southern reaches of the South Pacific, especially in rainy season. If you decide to drive, make sure your vehicle has 4WD, high clearance, and a spare tire. Give yourself lots of daylight time to get to where you are going (the sun sets around 5:30). You can also fly to Golfito or the Osa Peninsula and rent a 4WD vehicle.

HEALTH AND SAFETY

You are more likely to suffer from dehydration than any other health issue. Carry plenty of water wherever you go, wear a hat, and use sturdy hiking boots and long pants when hiking trails where biting insects may strike or the occasional snake might be sleeping in the sun. Do not leave any valuables in your car or your room—always put them in the safe provided by your hotel or lodge.

MONEY MATTERS

ATMs are sprouting up everywhere in the Southern Zone. The places you won't find a bank are remote communities, for example the beaches south of Golfito on the mainland, or in Drake Bay and lodges south of Puerto Jiménez.

RESTAURANTS

Count on finding lots of fresh fish and tropical fruits on the menu, whether at a roadside *soda* (casual eatery) serving *comida tipica* (typical food) or a sophisticated restaurant in Dominical or Ojochal. Up in the mountains, don't miss out on eating fresh, farmed trout. The food at most remote eco-lodges is excellent.

HOTELS

Expect reasonable comfort in unbelievably wild settings. Most accommodations are in small hotels, lodges, and cabins run by hands-on owners, many of them foreigners who fell in love with the country during a vacation here and stayed. Generally speaking, the farther south and more remote the lodge, the more expensive it is. Bad roads (causing supply problems) and lack of electricity and communications make hotel-keeping costly, especially in the Osa Peninsula and Golfo Dulce, where a fresh egg can cost up to a dollar. When comparing per-person prices, take into account that most of these places include meals, transport, guides, and unique locations.

The country's premier eco-lodges are almost all in the Southern Zone, ranging from simple tents to sophisticated lodges. But keep in mind that if you yearn to be close to nature, you have to be prepared for encounters of the natural kind in your shower or bedroom. Keep a flashlight handy for nighttime trips to the bathroom and always wear sandals. *Hotel reviews have been shortened. For full information, visit Fodors.com.*

WHAT IT COSTS IN DOLLARS				
	$	$$	$$$	$$$$
Restaurants	under $10	$10–$15	$16–$25	over $25
Hotels	under $75	$75–$150	$151–$250	over $250

Restaurant prices are the average cost of a main course at dinner or, if dinner is not served, at lunch. Hotel prices are the lowest cost of a standard double room in high season.

TOURS

Costa Rica Expeditions. This is the original ecotourist outfit in Costa Rica, specializing in customizing countrywide nature tours and led by expert, bilingual, local naturalist guides. ☎2521–6099 ⊕ *www.costaricaexpeditions.com.*

Horizontes Nature Tours. This expert ecotourist company arranges small-group and custom tours with naturalist guides and ornithologists, including nature-photography tours. ☎2222–2022, 888/7868–748 toll-free ⊕ *www.horizontes.com.*

TRAVELING WITH KIDS

The Southern Zone is like Outward Bound for families, where kids and parents can face challenges—such as no TVs or video games!—and have fun together. Plunge the family into real-life adventures with added educational value. You might inspire a future herpetologist or marine biologist among your progeny.

Go horseback riding to waterfalls and swimming holes. Steal into the night with infrared flashlights to scout out frogs and other fascinating, nocturnal creepy-crawlies. Enjoy kayaking in a calm gulf where dolphins play. Rappel down a waterfall, climb inside a hollow tree, or zip-line through the trees.

The more remote areas of the south are ideal for kids ages seven and up. Babies and all their paraphernalia are hard to handle here, and toddlers are tough to keep off the ground where biting insects and snakes live.

VISITOR INFORMATION

There aren't many official tourist offices in the south. The excellent Uvita Information Center provides up-do-date information and books tours and hotels in Uvita and points south. The Dominical Information Center is also a great source for everything from bus schedules to maps to tour arrangements. There is also a hard-to-find, official government tourist office in Río Claro, en route to Golfito. Always ask for recommendations from your hosts. Lodge and hotel owners know their turf and they want happy guests, so they are unlikely to steer you astray.

THE CENTRAL HIGHLANDS

Famous for spectacular mountain vistas, high-altitude coffee farms, cloud-forest eco-lodges, and challenging mountain hikes, the Central Highlands of Cerro de la Muerte are less than an hour south of San José, climbing up the Pan-American Highway.

ZONA DE LOS SANTOS

Santa María de Dota is 65 km (40 miles) south of San José.

Empalme, at Km 51 of the Pan-American Highway, marks the turnoff for Santa María de Dota, the first of the picturesque coffee-growing towns named after saints that dot this mountainous area known as the Zona de Los Santos (Zone of the Saints). The route itself is about 24 km (15 miles) long.

GETTING HERE AND AROUND

From San José, drive southeast on the paved Pan-American Highway, heading toward Cartago, then follow the signs south for San Isidro de El General. The two-lane road climbs steeply, and there are almost no safe places to pass heavy trucks and slow vehicles. Make an early start, because the road is often enveloped in mist and rain in the afternoon. It typically takes about 90 minutes to reach Km 51, where you turn right at Empalme to reach Santa María de Dota, 14 km (8½ miles) along a wide, curving, paved road.

EXPLORING

Ruta de Los Santos (*Route of the Saints*). The scenic road that winds through the high-altitude valleys from Empalme to San Pablo de León is appropriately called the Ruta de Los Santos. It's nicely paved to facilitate shipping the coffee produced in the region. On the 30-minute drive from Empalme to San Pablo de León Cortés, you travel through misty valleys ringed by precipitous mountain slopes terraced with lush,

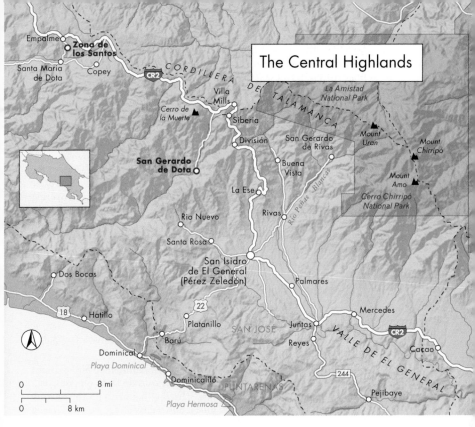

The Central Highlands

green coffee plants. The 24-km (15-mile) route also captures the essence of a fast-disappearing traditional Tico way of life built around agriculture. Stately churches anchor bustling towns full of prosperous, neat houses with pretty gardens and vintage 1970s Toyota Land Cruisers in a rainbow of colors.

WHERE TO EAT AND STAY

$ ✕ **Café de Los Santos.** This pretty café, within sight of the town's majestic
CAFÉ church in San Marcos de Tarrazú, showcases the area's high-altitude *arabica* Tarrazú coffee, the "celestial drink" for which this zone is famous. There are more than 30 specialty coffee drinks, plus homemade sweet and savory pastries, and light lunches available here. The café is open weekdays 8 to 6:30 and Saturday 2 to 7:30. $ *Average main: $5* ✉ *6 km (4 miles) west of Santa María de Dota, San Marcos de Tarrazú* ☎ *2546–7881* ☺ *Closed Sun.*

$ 🛏 **El Toucanet Lodge.** For serenity and mountain greenery, you can't beat
B&B/INN this family-run lodge with plenty of pastoral scenery and close-up views of hummingbirds from the glassed-in dining room. **Pros:** fresh mountain air; tranquility; affordable; good birding. **Cons:** simple furnishings; limited menu. $ *Rooms from: $58* ✉ *Rt. 315, 7 km (4½ miles) east of Santa María de Dota, Copey* ☎ *2541–3045* ⊕ *www.eltoucanet.com* ⇆ *6 rooms, 2 junior suites* ☺ *Closed Sept. and Oct.* 🍴 *Breakfast.*

SHOPPING

Coopedota Santa Maria. The best place to buy local coffee is where 800 farmers bring their raw coffee beans to be roasted and packed into jute bags. This is the first carbon-neutral coffee producer in the world. You can buy three dozen different coffee beverages and export-quality coffee at the shop for about $16 per kilo (2.2 pounds). Choose between light or dark roast and *en grano* (whole bean) or *molido* (ground). A variety of tours are offered ($19 to $32), covering everything from processing to tasting to the cooperative's innovative recycling. The classic two-hour Coffee Experience tour ($22), which reveals the process from bean to bag, is offered weekdays 7–5, and weekends by appointments. Check out the website for details of tours or e-mail experience@coopedota.com to make reservations. ⊠ *C. Ctl., Santa María de Dota* ☎ *2541–2828 for coffee tour, 2541–0102 café* ⊕ *www.coopedota.com* ⊙ *Mon.–Sat. 8:30–6, Sun. 1–6.*

> **THE FINAL FRONTIER**
>
> The Southern Zone was the very last part of Costa Rica to be settled. The first road, from San José to San Isidro, wasn't begun until the 1950s.

SAN GERARDO DE DOTA

89 km (55 miles) southeast of San José, 52 km (32 miles) south of Santa María de Dota.

Cloud forests, invigorating mountain air, well-maintained hiking trails, and excellent bird-watching make San Gerardo de Dota one of Costa Rica's premier nature destinations. The tiny hamlet is in the narrow Savegre River valley, 9 km (5½ miles) down a twisting, partially paved track that descends abruptly to the west from the Pan-American Highway. The peaceful surroundings look more like the Rocky Mountains than Central America, but hike down the waterfall trail and the vegetation quickly turns tropical again. Beyond hiking and bird-watching, activities include horseback riding and trout fly-fishing.

GETTING HERE AND AROUND

The drive from San José takes about three hours, and from Santa María de Dota about an hour. At Km 80 on the Pan-American Highway, turn down the dirt road signed "San Gerardo de Dota." It's a harrowing, twisting road with signs warning drivers to gear down and go slow. Some newly paved sections help ease the steepest curves. Tourist vans often stop along the road when the guides spot birds; grab your binoculars and discreetly join them!

SPORTS AND THE OUTDOORS

BIRD-WATCHING

Although you can see many birds from your cabin porch, most bird-watching requires hiking, some of it along steep paths made extra challenging by the high altitude (from 7,000 to 10,000 feet above sea level). Come fit and armed with binoculars and layers of warm clothing. The early mornings are brisk up here, but you'll warm up quickly with the sun and the exertion of walking.

Fodor's Choice ★ **Savegre Hotel, Natural Reserve & Spa.** With the best bird guides in the area, including veteran birder Marino Chacon ($75 for a half day), this hotel organizes the best highland birding and hiking tours in the oak forests and surrounding mountains. ✉ *Savegre Hotel, Natural Reserve & Spa, off the Pan-American Hwy.* ☎ *2740–1028* 🌐 *www.savegre.co.cr.*

THE RESPLENDENT QUETZAL

The damp, epiphyte-laden oak-tree forest around San Gerardo de Dota is renowned for resplendent quetzals, considered by many to be the most beautiful bird in the Western world. Male quetzals in full breeding plumage are more spectacular than females, with metallic green feathers, crimson stomachs, helmetlike crests, and extravagantly long tail feathers. Ask guides or hotel staff about common quetzal hangouts; early morning during the March-to-May nesting season is the best time to spot them.

HIKING

Some of the best hiking in the country is in this valley.

Savegre Hotel, Natural Reserve & Spa. This hotel runs a daylong, guided, natural-history hike (about $155 for up to eight people, including transportation) that starts with a drive up to the *páramo* (high-altitude ecosystem) of Cerro de la Muerte. The trail begins at the cluster of communication towers and descends through the forest into the valley. Miles of prime bird-watching and hiking trails wind through the private forest reserve. ■ TIP→ **Night temperatures on the slopes of Cerro de la Muerte can approach freezing. Pack accordingly for cold mornings.** ✉ *Savegre Hotel, Natural Reserve & Spa, off the Pan-American Hwy.* ☎ *2740–1028* 🌐 *www.savegre.co.cr.*

Río Savegre. The most scenic and interesting trail in the area is the one that begins at the Savegre Hotel, Natural Reserve & Spa and follows the Río Savegre to a spectacular waterfall. To get to the trailhead, follow the main road past the hotel to a fork, where you veer left, cross a bridge, and head over the hill to a pasture that narrows to a footpath. Although it is only 2 km (1¼ miles) each way and there are some steps to help you negotiate the steepest parts, the hike can be slippery, especially near the bottom, and takes about two hours. ⚠ **Do not attempt to swim in the pool below the waterfall. The current is very swift and dangerous.**

8

WHERE TO STAY

$ B&B/INN 🏨 **Cabañas y Senderos Las Cataratas.** One of the best deals—and fresh-trout meals—in the valley is at this family-run restaurant and bed-and-breakfast, set beside a scenic trout pond. **Pros:** excellent fresh trout; authentic Tico culture. **Cons:** very simple accommodations; call ahead on weekdays to make sure someone is there. [$] *Rooms from: $50* ✉ *3 km (2 miles) from main highway, along road to San Gerardo de Dota* ☎ *2740–1064, 2740–1065* 🛏 *4 cabins* 🍴 *Multiple meal plans.*

$$$ B&B/INN FAMILY Fodor's Choice ★ 🏨 **Dantica Lodge and Gallery.** High style at high altitude, this avant-garde lodge clinging to the side of a mountain has unbeatable valley views, great bird-watching, luxury accommodations, and the top ecological sustainability rating. **Pros:** stylish casitas; gorgeous natural setting with miles of trails; excellent restaurant. **Cons:** steep access along narrow

A male white-throated mountain-gem hummingbird in a defense posture. Río Savegre, San Gerardo de Dota.

trails to forest casitas; some casitas close to road. $ *Rooms from: $167* ✉ *Road to San Gerardo de Dota, 4 km (2 miles) west of Pan-American Hwy.* ☎ *2740–1067* ⊕ *www.dantica.com* ⤵ *6 casitas, 1 deluxe suite, 2 two-bedroom bungalows* ⦿ *Breakfast.*

$$
B&B/INN
🔲 **Paraíso Quetzal Lodge.** Nestled in a cloud forest just minutes off the main highway, this recently upgraded lodge is, indeed, a paradise for resplendent quetzals and for those who want to spot this sought-after bird. **Pros:** scenic views; pristine cloud forest; amazing hikes and bird watching. **Cons:** very simple food; steep paths to some cabins; very cold nights. $ *Rooms from: $144* ✉ *Km 70 Pan-American Hwy., Cerro de la Muerte* ☎ *2200–0241, 8810–0234* ⊕ *www.quetzalsparadise.com* ⤵ *8 cabins, 4 junior suites* ⦿ *Some meals.*

$$
B&B/INN
Fodor's Choice
★
🔲 **Savegre Hotel, Natural Reserve & Spa.** Famous for its miles of bird-watching trails and its expert guides, this once-rustic lodge has been upgraded to include cabin suites with handsome wood furnishings, crackling fireplaces, and deep bathtubs, plus a full-service, riverside spa. **Pros:** great trails; amazing birdlife; excellent guides. **Cons:** unexciting buffet-style meals when hotel has lots of groups; older cabins are very simple and lack privacy; be prepared for very cold nights. $ *Rooms from: $106* ✉ *At Km 80 on Pan-American Hwy., take road to San Gerardo de Dota, 9 km (5½ miles) down very steep gravel road* ☎ *2740–1028* ⊕ *www.savegre.com* ⤵ *21 rooms, 29 cabin suites* ⦿ *Multiple meal plans.*

$$
B&B/INN
🔲 **Trogón Lodge.** Set in a garden filled with fuchsias, hydrangeas, and hummingbirds, the Trogón Lodge is more a relaxing hideaway than a hiking-heavy destination. **Pros:** lush garden; convivial public area; small but excellent gift shop. **Cons:** steep, short trails that end at road;

limited privacy except in honeymoon suite. $ *Rooms from: $94 ⊠ Road to San Gerardo de Dota, 7½ km (4½ miles) down a dirt road from the Pan-American Hwy. ☎2740–1051, 2293–8181 in San José ⊕ www. grupomawamba.com ⤴22 rooms, 1 suite ⦿ Breakfast.*

VALLE DE EL GENERAL REGION

The Valle de El General (The General's Valley) area encompasses vast expanses of highland wilderness on the upper slopes of the Cordillera de Talamanca and the high-altitude *páramo* of Chirripó National Park, as well as prosperous agricultural communities amid vast, sunbaked fields of pineapple and sugarcane. It is bounded to the north and west by the central highlands of the massive Cordillera de Talamanca and to the south by La Amistad International Park. The valley is named for the Río de El General, one of the many rivers that rise in the Talamancas and run down through the valley, making it ideal for farming.

SAN ISIDRO DE EL GENERAL

54 km (34 miles) south of San Gerardo de Dota.

Although San Isidro de El General has no major attractions, the bustling market town is a good place to have lunch, get cash at one of the many ATMs (most accept Visa/Plus cards), or fill your tank—the main highway into town is lined with service stations, some operating 24 hours. Advice to map readers: there are other San Isidros in Costa Rica, but this is the only San Isidro de El General. Just to confuse matters more, this town also goes by the name Peréz Zeledón. The town is the jumping-off point for hiking the scenic highlands around San Gerardo de Rivas, and climbing the country's highest peak, Chirripó. There's also excellent bird-watching in nearby nature reserves, including the original homestead, now a museum, of famed ornithologist Alexander Skutch.

GETTING HERE AND AROUND

The Pan-American Highway takes you straight into San Isidro de El General. It's 129 km (80 miles) south of San José and about 1½ hours' drive south of the San Gerardo de Dota highway exit. Truck traffic can be heavy and painfully slow. Buses to Dominical leave from the San Isidro de El General bus terminal, southeast of the cathedral, near the Pan-American Highway. Buses bound for San Gerardo de Rivas, the starting point of the trail into Chirripó National Park, depart from San Isidro de El General at 5:30 am from the central park and at 2 pm from a stop at the central market.

ESSENTIALS

Banks/ATM **ATH Coopealianza** ⊠ *South side of central park beside Hotel Chirripó, San Isidro de el General.* **Banco Nacional** ⊠ *North side of central park, San Isidro de el General* ☎ *2771–3287.*

Hospital **Hospital Escalante Pradilla** ⊠ *Off main street, east of municipal stadium, San Isidro de el General* ☎ *2771–3122.*

Pharmacy **Farmacia Santa Marta** ⊠ *Northwest of central park, across from cultural center, San Isidro de el General* ☎ *2771–4506.*

Post Office Correo ⊠ *South side of park, San Isidro de el General.*

Visitor Information Camara de Turismo de la Region Brunca (*Chamber of Commerce, Tourism, Industry and Agriculture of Perez Zeledón*). ⊠ *On main highway, behind the MUSOC bus station, San Isidro* 🕾 *2771–2003* ⊕ *www.camaradecomerciopz.com.*

EXPLORING

FAMILY **Centro Biológico Las Quebradas** (*Las Quebradas Biological Center*). In a lush valley 7 km (4½ miles) northeast of San Isidro de El General, this community-managed nature reserve protects 1,853 acres of dense forest in which elegant tree ferns grow in the shadows of massive trees, and colorful tanagers and euphonias flit about the foliage. A 3-km (2-mile) trail winds uphill through the forest and along the Río Quebradas, which supplies water to San Isidro de El General and surrounding communities. There's also an easily accessible sensory garden, with plants to smell and taste, and a butterfly garden. To get here from the Pan-American Highway, head 7 km (4½ miles) northeast at the sign for Las Quebradas. The reserve is 2 km (1 mile) north of town on an unpaved road. ⊠ *Off Pan-American Hwy., 7 km (4½ miles) northeast of San Isidro de El General, Las Quebradas* 🕾 *2771–4131* 🖃 *$5* 🕒 *Tues.–Sun. 8–4.*

> ### HITTING THE TRAILS
>
> The hiking in the south is simply spectacular, so don't leave home without your hiking boots. The most challenging hike in the country is Chirripó Mountain, a 6- to 10-hour haul up to the national-park hostel, a base camp for exploring surrounding peaks. Dramatic but less challenging hikes include the well-maintained, wide trails in the cool high-altitude forests of the Savegre Valley; the narrow Coastal Path south of Drake; and forest trails to waterfalls and swimming holes in the Golfo Dulce, Osa Peninsula, and around Dominical.

Los Cusingos Bird Sanctuary. Here you'll find birding trails and a museum dedicated to the late Dr. Alexander Skutch, the region's preeminent ornithologist and coauthor of *A Guide to the Birds of Costa Rica*, the birders' bible. His 190-acre estate, an island of forest amid a sea of new farms and housing developments, is now run by the nonprofit Centro Cientifico Tropical (Tropical Science Center), which has improved 2 km (1 mile) of trails and restored the simple house where Dr. Skutch lived—without electricity—from 1941 until his death in 2004, just a week shy of his 100th birthday. Bird species you might see include fiery-billed araçaris—colorful, small members of the toucan family—and mixed tanager flocks. The sanctuary is 12 km (7½ miles) southeast of San Isidro de El General in the town of Quizarrá. Just show up, or call ahead if you want a guided tour. ⊠ *12 km (7½ miles) southeast of San Isidro de El General, Quizarrá* 🕾 *2738–2070* ⊕ *www.cct.or.cr/reservas/reserva_cusingos.xhtml* 🖃 *$13* 🕒 *Mon.–Sat. 7–4, Sun. 7–1.*

SPORTS AND THE OUTDOORS

TOUR OPERATORS

Selva Mar. The most experienced Southern Zone tour operator, Selva Mar organizes nature, horseback, waterfall, and birding tours, as well as boat transportation to remote Osa lodges. The company also runs

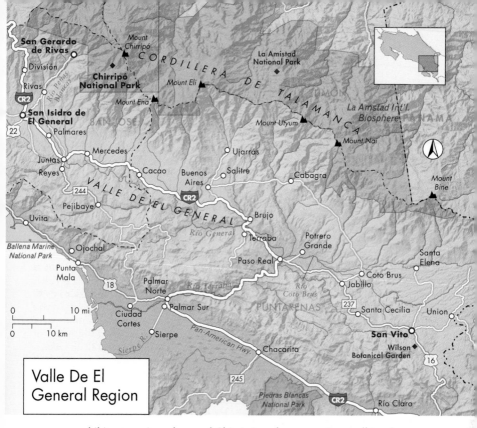

Valle De El
General Region

hiking tours in and around Chirripó; make reservations well in advance. ✉ *South of southeast corner of central park, San Isidro* ☎ *2771–4582* ⊕ *www.selvamar.com.*

BIRD-WATCHING

Tropical Feathers. Run by expert birder Noel Ureña, with over 15 years of experience, Sunny Travel/Tropical Feathers offers multiday bird-watching packages and arranges customized tours in the San Isidro de El General and Dominical area and points south. Check the website for excellent photos and bird lore. ✉ *San Isidro de el General* ☎ *2771–9686* ⊕ *www.costaricabirdingtours.com.*

HIKING

The major tourist draw is climbing Mt. Chirripó (the highest peak is 3,820 meters or about 12,532 feet) in Chirripó National Park.

Because of national park limitations on the number of climbers, even tour operators have trouble reserving space. Your best bet is to show up at the national park office in San Gerardo de Rivas in hopes of setting off the next day. Alternatively, opt for a different hike in the area.

Costa Rica Trekking Adventures. Run by Selva Mar, Costa Rica Trekking Adventures can arrange everything you need to climb the mountain, including transportation, guide, porters to carry your gear, meals, snacks, and beverages—as long as you give them at least three months' notice.

You still have to make the tough climb yourself, about eight hours uphill to the park lodge, and five hours to come down. The two-night, three-day packages are approaching $600 per person. The company also offers a four-day, three-night ($600 per person) hike that gives you the same vistas and challenges, without the complications of national park reservations. ✉ *San Isidro* ☎ *2771–4582* 🌐 *www.chirripo.com.*

WHERE TO EAT AND STAY

$ COSTA RICAN FAMILY 🍴 **El Trapiche de Nayo.** The panoramic valley view is worth a stop at this rustic roadside restaurant that serves the kind of food Ticos eat at *turnos* (village fund-raising festivals), including hard-to-find *sopa de mondongo* (tripe soup). Easier to stomach are the *gallos,* thick tortillas cooked on a woodstove, which you stuff with cooked hearts of palm, root vegetables, or chicken in salsa. Some Saturdays, raw sugarcane is pressed in an antique mill and boiled in huge iron cauldrons to make smooth *sobado,* a molasses-flavored fudge. Service is leisurely, to say the least, but the restrooms have been upgraded, so it's a decent pit stop. It's open 7 am to 7 pm daily. [$] *Average main: $8* ✉ *Pan-American Hwy., 6 km (4 miles) north of San Isidro de El General, San Isidro de el General* ☎ *2771–7267.*

$ COSTA RICAN 🍴 **Kafe de la Casa.** This is as hip as it gets in downtown San Isidro de El General. Along with excellent cappuccino and homemade muffins, you can enjoy breakfast here all day long, in a funky, retro rustic atmosphere combining '50s diner and Tico country. There's also a full menu of meat and chicken dishes. Sample them all in the Bandeja de la Casa, a monster plate of cheese fingers, chicken or beef fajitas, platano, refried beans, and tortillas. Healthier options include yogurt smoothies and omelets. This is the place to find out what's happening culturally around town and perhaps chance upon an art exhibit, an acoustic concert, or a poetry reading in the café. It's open weekdays 7–8 and Sunday 8–2. [$] *Average main: $8* ✉ *C. 4 at Avda. 3, just behind the Musoc bus station, San Isidro de el General* ☎ *506/2770–4816* 🕒 *Closed Sat.*

$ DINER 🍴 **Restaurante Bazooka's.** The slogan here is "American as apple pie," and there is indeed apple pie, as well as all-day breakfast and a selection of hearty burgers, triple-decker sandwiches, and meal-size salads at this popular roadside diner. Pancakes, waffles, and ice-cream sundaes will satisfy your sweet tooth. Hungrier eaters can chow down on hearty servings of barbecue ribs or steak. There are Tico touches, too, with local fish and shrimp with rice and *tres leches* cake, the classic Tico dessert. The $5 lunch specials are an excellent value. Tables are spread through different rooms of the cheerfully updated wooden hacienda, all of them pleasant with lots of natural light. If you're in a hurry, everything is available "to go." An added attraction: the eatery is on the main highway, so you don't have to negotiate San Isidro de El General's sometimes confusing one-way streets. Just look for the big pink Bazooka's sign at the northern entrance to town. [$] *Average main: $8* ✉ *Pan-American Hwy., next door to Beto Solis gas station, San Isidro de el General* ☎ *2771–2050.*

$ COSTA RICAN 🍴 **Restaurant La Georgina.** Since 1947, this large cafeteria in a white clapboard building has been the traditional roadside stop for busloads of travelers crossing the highlands of Cerro de la Muerte. Along with comfortable restrooms, the eating area has recently been brightened up with new blond-wood tables and chairs. Grab a tray and choose from a steam table of Costa Rican specialties—beef in salsa, cheesy tortillas, grilled sweet platanos stuffed with cheese, and homemade muffins and sweet rolls. Or just order a hot chocolate and take a seat at the counter along the back wall and enjoy the main attraction: a row of hummingbird feeders abuzz with birds, notably fiery-throated hummingbirds. Make sure you wear a jacket or sweater—the altitude here is over 10,000 feet and it gets chilly. It's open 7–6 daily. $ *Average main: $6* ⊠ *Km 95 on the Pan-American Hwy., San Isidro* ☎ *506/2200–4313* ▭ *No credit cards.*

$ ⊤ **Hotel Los Crestones.** Flowering hedges give this pleasant and affordable
HOTEL motel a homey feel, even though it's near the sometimes-noisy stadium (the quietest rooms are numbers 18 to 21). **Pros:** affordable prices; pleasant rooms; secure parking and easy wheelchair access. **Cons:** avoid noisy rooms at the front; a few cheaper rooms lack air-conditioning. $ *Rooms from: $65* ⊠ *Road to Dominical, southwest side of stadium, San Isidro de el General* ☎ *2770–1200* ⊕ *www.hotelloscrestones.com* ⟿ *27 rooms* ⊤⊙⊤ *No meals.*

$ ⊤ **Hotel Zima.** Especially popular with backpackers heading up to Chirripó, this upgraded hotel is within walking distance of the main bus station.
HOTEL **Pros:** handy to bus station and restaurants; bargain price. **Cons:** not a scenic location, just off main highway; smallish rooms; not all rooms have air-conditioning. $ *Rooms from: $47* ⊠ *Half a block east of Pan-American Hwy., across from MUSOC bus terminal, San Isidro de el General* ☎ *2770–1114* ⊕ *www.hotelzima.net* ⟿ *28 rooms* ⊤⊙⊤ *No meals.*

SAN GERARDO DE RIVAS

20 km (12½ miles) northeast of San Isidro.

Chirripó National Park is the main reason to venture to San Gerardo de Rivas, but if you aren't up for the physically challenging adventure of hiking up to Chirripó it's still a wildly scenic place, reminiscent of the Himalayas, to spend a day or two. Spread over steep terrain at the end of the narrow valley of the boulder-strewn Río Chirripó, San Gerardo de Rivas has cool mountain air, excellent bird-watching, spectacular views, and an outdoor menu that includes waterfall hikes and hot springs.

GETTING HERE AND AROUND
From San Isidro de El General, more than half the one-hour drive to San Gerardo de Rivas is along a very rocky, very hilly, dirt road, so a 4WD is strongly recommended. Buses run three times a day from San Isidro, but it's a slow, dusty ride up the mountain.

EXPLORING
FAMILY **Cloudbridge Private Nature Reserve.** This private nature reserve staffed by volunteers and a senior biologist has an easy trail to a waterfall, plus almost 20 km (12 miles) of river and ridge trails bordering Chirripó National Park. It's a pleasant alternative for hikers who aren't up to the challenge of Chirripó. There's also an art gallery featuring nature paintings, and basic accommodations in a few simple cabins, including one en route to Chirripó. Volunteers often occupy the simple rental cabins, so check the website for availability. ⊠ *2.6 km (1½ mile) northeast of San Gerardo de Rivas* ⊕ *www.cloudbridge.org* ▱ *By donation* ⊙ *Daily sunrise–sunset.*

8

FAMILY **Gevi Hot Springs.** On a farm above the road to Herradura, Gevi Hot Springs is a favorite stop. To get here, you must cross a raging river on a high bridge, then manage a steep climb on foot or by 4WD vehicle to a combination of natural rock and concrete pools in a forested area. It's nothing fancy, and can be crowded with locals and kids on weekends, so aim for a weekday soak. ⊠ *1½ km (1 mile) past the ranger station, north of Herradura, Herradura* 🕾 *2742–5210* 🖃 *$6* ⊘ *Daily 7–5:30.*

WHERE TO STAY

$ 📺 **Hotel de Montaña El Pelícano.** On a precipitous ridge south of town, B&B/INN this budget lodge is named for a chunk of wood that resembles a pelican—one of dozens of idiosyncratic sculptures carved out of tree roots by owner Rafael Elizondo. **Pros:** close to Chirripó; free ride to the trailhead; very cheap. **Cons:** smallish rooms; very steep drive to hotel. 🟈 *Rooms from: $50* ⊠ *Main road, south of national park office* 🕾 *2742–5050* ⊕ *www.hotelpelicano.net* ⤳ *8 rooms, 4 cabins, 1 apartment* 🍽 *Breakfast.*

$$$$ 📺 **Monte Azul.** Set in a private nature reserve bordering the rushing Chir-
B&B/INN ripó River, this sleek and chic boutique hotel is an artistic triumph, both
Fodor'sChoice inside and out, with luxurious accommodations unmatched in the area.
★ **Pros:** gorgeous natural setting; stunning design aesthetic; excellent food. **Cons:** pricey ($199 per person) but worth it—price includes all meals. 🟈 *Rooms from: $398* ⊠ *Off main road, 5 km (3 miles) south of San Gerardo de Rivas, Chimirol* 🕾 *2742–5222* ⊕ *www.monteazulcr.com* ⤳ *4 bungalows* ⊘ *Closed Oct.* 🍽 *Multiple meal plans.*

CHIRRIPÓ NATIONAL PARK

Park entrance is a 4-km (2-mile) hike uphill from San Gerardo de Rivas.

Chirripó National Park is the ultimate challenge for serious local and visiting hikers. But the rewards are worth it—from the visitors' hut you can summit even higher surrounding peaks and on a clear day, see both the Atlantic and Pacific oceans. It does, however, require top fitness and advance planning, since the number of hikers is limited each day, in order to preserve the sensitive ecosystems hikers traverse.

EXPLORING

Chirripó National Park. The main attraction of this national park is Mt. Chirripó, the highest mountain in Costa Rica and a mecca for both hikers and serious summiteers. It's a 48-km (30-mile) round-trip hike, with an elevation gain of 2,100 meters (6,890 feet) to reach the hostel, and another 340 meters (1,000 feet) to reach the summit. You need to plan gear and food carefully, be very fit, and acclimatize before setting out. The round-trip usually takes three days—one day to climb to the hostel, one day to explore the surrounding summits, and one day to descend.

With the number of hikers limited to 40 per day, it's becoming ever more difficult to hike here, since most advance reservations are quickly snapped up by local schools and organizations. Phone reservations are accepted, but only on the first Monday of May and November. Outside of national holiday weeks, there is always the possibility that spaces will be available to hikers who show up without reservations, because not all the spots are reserved. So your best bet is to try your luck and check in between 6:30 am and 4 pm at the San Gerardo de Rivas National Parks Service office the day before you want to hike. Entrance is on a first-come, first-served basis. The maximum stay at the hostel is three days, two nights. Admission to the park is $15 per day, plus $10 per day for lodging. Ask for trail maps at the office. ⚠ **Don't try to sneak in: a park ranger will stop you at a checkpoint on the trail and ask to see your reservation voucher.** ✉ *San Gerardo de Rivas National Parks Service, main street, San Gerardo de Rivas* ☎ *2742–5083* ⊕ *www. parquenacionalchirripo.com* ✉ *$18 per day* ☉ *Closed 2 wks in Nov.*

DID YOU KNOW?	Although it takes the fittest hikers at least four hours to get to the base camp of Chirripó, hundreds of competitors from around the world converge on tiny San Gerardo de Rivas every February to run a 34-km (22-mile) race up and down Chirripó. A local family of hardy brothers shares the record time: three hours and 15 minutes!

SPORTS AND THE OUTDOORS

Hikes and other activities in the park are arranged by the **Guides and Porters Association of San Gerardo** (☎ *2742–5225* ✉ *arrierosdechirripo@ gmail.com*), which provide guides, porters, and provisions for Chirripó hikes, as well as an alternative hike up the Ruta Urán.

SAN VITO

110 km (68 miles) southeast of San Isidro, 61 km (38 miles) northeast of Golfito.

Except for the tropical greenery, the rolling hills around the bustling hilltop town of San Vito could be mistaken for a Tuscan landscape. The town actually owes its 1952 founding to 200 Italian families who converted forest into coffee, fruit, and cattle farms. A remnant of the Italian flavor lingers on in the statue dedicated to the *pioneros* standing proudly in the middle of town. San Vito today is a bustling agricultural market town, the center of the Coto Brus coffee region. Many coffee pickers are from the Guaymí indigenous group, who live in a large reserve nearby and also over the border in Panama. They're easy to recognize by the women's colorfully embroidered, long cotton dresses.

GETTING HERE AND AROUND

If you are driving south from San Isidro, your best route is along the wide, smooth Pan-American Highway via Buenos Aires to Paso Real, about 70 km (43 miles). Then take the scenic high road to San Vito, 40 km (25 miles) farther along. This road has recently been repaved and it's the most direct and prettiest route. Another route, which many buses take, is via Ciudad Neily, about 35 km (22 miles) northeast of Golfito, and then 24 km (15 miles) of winding steep road up to San Vito, at almost 1,000 meters (3,280 feet) above sea level. At this writing, the road is potholed and in *mal estato* (bad shape). There are direct buses from San José four times a day, and buses from San Isidro twice a day.

8

A ginger flower at the Wilson Botanical Garden in San Vito

ESSENTIALS

Most of the banks in town have cash machines that accept foreign cards.

Banks/ATM ATH Coopealianza ✉ *Center of town, north of hospital.*
Banco Nacional ✉ *Across from south side of central park* ☎ *2773–3601.*

Hospital Hospital San Vito ✉ *South of town, on road to Wilson Botanical Garden* ☎ *2773–3103.*

Pharmacy Farmacia Assisi ✉ *Center of town, across from La Flor pastry shop* ☎ *2773–3281.*

Post Office Correo ✉ *Far north end of town, beside police station.*

EXPLORING

La Amistad National Park. At more than 1,980 square km (765 square miles), La Amistad is by far the largest park in Costa Rica. However, it's a mere portion of the vast La Amistad Biosphere Reserve that stretches into western Panama. Altitudes range from 1,000 meters (3,280 feet) to 3,500 meters (11,480 feet). There are miles of rugged, densely forested trails and plenty of wildlife (two-thirds of the country's vertebrate species live here), but because access is extremely difficult, it's not worth visiting the park unless you plan to spend several days, making this a trip only for experienced hikers. To get to the official park entrance at Altamira (4WD essential), drive 31 km (20 miles) west from San Vito along the road to Paso Real. Turn right at the park sign at Guacimo (also known as Las Tablas), near two small roadside restaurants. Then drive about 20 km (13 miles) uphill on a rough road, very muddy in rainy season. The last couple of kilometers are on foot.

Hire a local guide for $40 a day from ASOPROLA (☎ *2743–1184* ⊕ *www.actuarcostarica.com*), a local guide association that also organizes strenuous three-day guided trips ($170 per person). ASOPROLA operates a rustic lodge near the Altamira park entrance, with both private and dormitory rooms with hot-water showers ($12), as well as an organic restaurant run by a local women's cooperative. You can also arrange a home stay with a local family. The alternative is rustic campsites for $6 per person. Reserve space about a week in advance. ■TIP→ Call or write for exact directions, since very few maps show these roads or Altamira de Biolley. ⊠ *Altamira de Biolley, 31 km (20 miles) west of San Vito, then 20 km (13 miles) uphill* ☎ *2200–5355 National Park* 🖅 *$10 per day* ☉ *Daily sunrise–sunset.*

Fodor'sChoice   **Wilson Botanical Garden.** A must-see for gardeners and bird-watchers,
★   the world-renowned Wilson Botanical Garden is enchanting even for those who are neither. Paths through the extensive grounds are lined with exotic plants and shaded by avenues of palm trees and 50-foot-high bamboo stalks. In 1961, U.S. landscapers Robert and Catherine Wilson bought 30 acres of coffee plantation and started planting tropical species, including palms, orchids, bromeliads, and heliconias. Today the property extends over 635 acres, and the gardens hold around 2,000 native and more than 3,000 exotic species. The palm collection—more than 700 species—is the second largest in the world. Fantastically shaped and colored bromeliads, which usually live in the tops of trees, have been brought down to the ground in impressive mass plantings, providing one of many photo opportunities.

The garden was transferred to the Organization for Tropical Studies in 1973, and in 1983 it became part of Amistad Biosphere Reserve. Under the name Las Cruces Biological Station, Wilson functions mainly as a research and educational center, so there is a constant supply of expert botanists and biologists to take visitors on natural-history tours in the garden and the adjoining forest trails. Birders can hike to the new canopy tower in the forest, funded by the local San Vito Birding Club, to get up to eye level with birds in the treetops. ■TIP→ Twice a month, members of the San Vito Bird Club lead free birding tours of the garden, complete with binoculars and field guides to share. Check ⊕ *www.sanvitobirdclub.org* for the bird walk schedule. If you spend a night at the garden lodge, you have the garden all to yourself in the late afternoon and early morning, when wildlife is most active. Guests also have access to the Río Java trail, where monkeys abound. ⊠ *Road to Ciudad Neily, 6 km (4 miles) south of San Vito* ☎ *2773–4004* ⊕ *www. esintro.co.cr/lascruces_general_info.shtml* 🖅 *$8 garden; $15 canopy tower trail* ☉ *Weekdays 7–5, weekends 8– 5.*

WHERE TO EAT AND STAY

$ ✕ **Pizzería Liliana.** Treat yourself to authentic pizza made from all-natural
ITALIAN   ingredients at the classiest restaurant in town, or dig into the macaroni *sanviteña*-style: with white sauce, ham, and mushrooms. The classics are here as well, and they're all homemade—lasagna, cannelloni, and ravioli—as well as hearty chicken and meat dishes. If you can't decide between pasta or meat, try the *plato mixto*: a half portion of lasagna

along with a quarter chicken and fries or salad. The authentic vinaigrette is a welcome change from more acidic Tico salad dressings. In true Italian fashion, the friendly, family-run restaurant can be noisy, but it's a happy buzz. For a more romantic dinner, ask for a table on the pretty garden terrace. It's open until 10 every evening, making it one of the few places in town where you can eat late. [$] *Average main: $10* ✉ *West of central square* ☎ *2773–3080.*

$ B&B/INN 🏨 **Casa Botania B&B.** Book a comfortable room with a sweeping view of forest and mountains at this delightful hilltop bed-and-breakfast, owned by a charming young Belgian–Costa Rican couple. **Pros:** affordable rates; great views; amiable hosts; great food. **Cons:** close to road but not much traffic noise at night; friendly dog. [$] *Rooms from: $65* ✉ *Road to Wilson Botanical Garden, 5 km (3 miles) south of San Vito, Linda Vista* ☎ *2773–4217, 8711–3008* 🌐 *www.casabotania.com* 🛏 *2 bungalows* 🍴 *Breakfast.*

$ B&B/INN 🏨 **Cascata del Bosco.** Just 200 meters from the entrance to Wilson Botanical Garden, this attractive new hotel has four totally private, round cabins, in a garden and forest setting, far back from the road. **Pros:** close to Wilson Botanical Garden; attractive cabins; affordable. **Cons:** no phones in rooms. [$] *Rooms from: $60* ✉ *200 m from entrance to Wilson Botanical Garden, Las Cruces* ☎ *2773–3208* 🌐 *www.cascatadelbosco.com* 🛏 *4 cabins* 🍴 *Breakfast.*

$ HOTEL 🏨 **Hotel El Ceibo.** The best deal in town, this arcaded, two-story hotel with decorative balustrades overlooking potted palms is tucked in a cul-de-sac behind the main street. **Pros:** central location; good price; relative quiet. **Cons:** rooms are quite small; furnishings are nothing special. [$] *Rooms from: $50* ✉ *East of central park, behind Municipalidad* ☎ *2773–3025* 🛏 *40 rooms* 🍴 *No meals.*

$$ B&B/INN Fodor's Choice ★ 🏨 **Wilson Botanical Garden.** The best features of the dozen comfortable rooms here, in three modern buildings built of glass, steel, and wood, are the private balconies cantilevered over a forested ravine, perfect for bird-watching. **Pros:** unparalleled setting with 24-hour access to botanical garden and nature trails; excellent birding and wildlife viewing. **Cons:** not all rooms have been renovated yet; family-style meals are served strictly on schedule so be ready to sit at the table when the dinner bell rings. [$] *Rooms from: $180* ✉ *Las Cruces Biological Station, Road to Ciudad Neily, 6 km (4 miles) south of San Vito* ☎ *2524–0628 in San José, 2773–4004* 🌐 *www.esintro.co.cr* 🛏 *12 rooms* 🍴 *All meals.*

SHOPPING

Finca Cántaros. In a vintage farmhouse between San Vito and Wilson Botanical Garden, Finca Cántaros sells crafts by indigenous artisans from near and far, including charming calabash gourds painted by Maleku artists, and colorful *molas* (appliqué work) made by Kuna women from the San Blas Islands in Panama. The owner's own mixed-media prints celebrate tropical nature with watercolor, colored pencil, and hand-carved rubber blocks used as printing stamps. You can also find a great selection of colorful, high-glaze ceramics from San José artists, as well as Sibú artisanal chocolates. Profits help support the adjacent free lending library, where English classes are also held.

■TIP→ **Walk bird-filled nature trails around a lake behind the shop and explore an indigenous archaeological site.** ✉ *Linda Vista, road to Ciudad Neily, 3 km (2 miles) south of San Vito* ☎ *2773–3760.*

EN
ROUTE

San Vito to Ciudad Neily. The 33-km (21-mile), recently paved road from San Vito to Ciudad Neily is twisting and spectacular, with views over the Coto Colorado plain to the Golfo Dulce and Osa Peninsula beyond. You can stop halfway to admire the view at Mirador La Torre to enjoy excellent fruit *naturales* and views from their counter stools. ⚠ **Watch out for some tricky curves where there are no guardrails.**

San Vito to Paso Real. The scenic road from San Vito to Paso Real, recently repaved, travels along a high ridge with sweeping valley views on either side. Halfway between Boca Limon and Las Vueltas, stop to enjoy a *refresco* and the views at open-air **Restaurante La Carreta.** As the road descends, the wide valley of El General River opens up before you, planted with miles of spiky pineapples and tall sugarcane. ⚠ **Few passing opportunities require a lot of patience, especially in the valley if you find yourself caught in a slow-moving convoy of trucks hauling pineapple and sugar cane.**

DOMINICAL AND BALLENA MARINE PARK

On the other side of a mountain ridge, just a scenic hour-long drive west of San Isidro de El General, you reach the sunny southern Pacific coast, with its miles of beaches for surfing, strolling, kayaking, and snorkeling. Ballena National Marine Park alone encompasses almost 10 km (6 miles) of protected beaches. Scattered along the coast are small communities with increasing numbers of international residents and interesting restaurants and lodging options.

8

DOMINICAL

34 km (21 miles) southwest of San Isidro, 40 km (25 miles) south of Quepos.

Sleepy fishing village–turned–surfer town, Dominical is changing again as luxury villas pop up all over the hillsides above the beaches, bringing new wealth that is boosting the economy. It's still a major surfing destination, attracting surfers of all ages, with a lively restaurant and nightlife scene. Favorite local hangouts come and go, so don't hesitate to try something new.

Dominical's real magic lies beyond the somewhat scruffy town, in the surrounding terrestrial and marine wonders: the rain forest grows right up to the beach in some places, and the ocean offers world-class surfing.

Much of the lush forest that covers the steep hillsides above the beaches is protected within private nature reserves. Several of these reserves, such as Hacienda Barú, protect significant tracts of the rain forest.

GETTING HERE AND AROUND

The road west over the mountains and down to Dominical is scenic at its best and fog-shrouded and potholed at its worst. There are lots of curves and dicey landslide areas, and potholes pop up unexpectedly, so take your time and enjoy the scenery along the hour-long drive from San Isidro de El General. From Quepos, the paved Costanera Highway makes for an easy half-hour drive to Dominical, although you do have to contend with huge trucks barreling along. Buses from San Isidro de El General leave six times a day, three times a day from Quepos. If you want to avoid driving altogether, Monkey Ride has air-conditioned vans with room for six to eight passengers that make trips to and from San José (starting at $44).

ESSENTIALS
Bank/ATM Banco de Costa Rica ⊠ *Plaza Pacífica* ☎ *2787–0381.*

Rental Cars Solid Car Rental ⊠ *Hotel Villas Río Mar, on bumpy river road, 1 km (½ mile) west of Dominical* ☎ *2787–0052* ⊕ *www.solidcarrental.com.*

Tour Companies Costa Rica Dive and Surf ⊠ *Main street, across from Sundancer Hotel* ☎ *8319–5392, 2787–0362* ⊕ *www.costaricadiveandsurf.com.* **Dominical Surf Adventures** ⊠ *Main street, across from church* ☎ *8897–9540, 2787–0431* ⊕ *www.dominicalsurfadventures.com.*

Visitor Information Dominical Information. Along with providing free bus schedules and town maps, this all-in-one information center also arranges adventure tours on, over, and under the water, along with horse tours, zip lines, and rappelling down waterfalls. ⊠ *Pueblo del Río, main street* ☎ *2787–0454* ⊕ *www.dominicalinformation.com.*

EXPLORING

FAMILY
Fodor'sChoice
★

Hacienda Barú. A leader in ecotourism and conservation, this wildlife refuge offers spectacular bird-watching and excellent naturalist-led hikes, as well as a turtle-protection project and nature-education program in the local school. You can stay at the cabins and poolside rooms or on platform tents in the jungle, or just come for the day to walk the forest and mangrove trails, zip through the canopy on cables, climb trees, or stake out birds on an observation platform. ⊠ *Costanera Hwy., 3 km (2 miles) north of Dominical* ☎ *2787–0003* ⊕ *www.haciendabaru.com* ⊠ *$7, tours $25–$125* ☉ *Daily 7 am–dusk.*

FAMILY
Fodor'sChoice
★

Nauyaca Waterfalls. This massive double cascade, the longer tumbling down 45 meters (150 feet), is one of the most spectacular sights in Costa Rica. The falls—also known as Barú River Falls—are on private property, so the only way to reach them is to take a horseback tour. ⇨ *See Sports and the Outdoors for tours.* ⊠ *Highway to San Isidro de El General, 10 km (7 miles) northeast of Dominical.*

FAMILY

Parque Reptilandia. With more than 300 specimens, this impressive collection includes snakes, lizards, frogs, turtles, and other reptilian creatures, housed in visitor-friendly terrariums and large enclosures. Stars of the exhibit are a Komodo dragon, Gila monsters, and a 150-pound African spur-thighed tortoise that likes to be petted. Kids love the maternity ward showcasing newborn snakes. More mature snakes live under a retractable roof that lets in sun and rain. Although snakes are generally more active in sunlight, this is still a great rainy-day activity. Guided night tours can also be arranged to watch nocturnal animals. ■TIP➔ If you're not squeamish, feeding day is Friday. ⊠ *Road to San Isidro, 11 km (7 miles) east of Dominical* ☎ *2787–0343* ⊕ *www.crreptiles.com* ⊠ *$12* ☉ *Daily 9–4:30.*

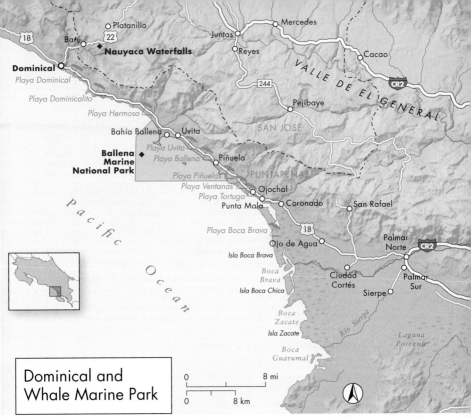

Dominical and Whale Marine Park

0   8 mi

0   8 km

FAMILY **Pozo Azul.** Hidden in a forest about 5 km (3 miles) south of town, this waterfall is considerably smaller than Nauyaca Waterfalls. Off the main highway, head up the road toward Bella Vista lodge and take the first road to the right, past the new school and through a stream; follow the road straight uphill for about 300 meters (1,000 feet) to where the road widens. If the stream is too high to cross, go back to the highway and drive south to the next left turn, where there's a bus stop, and go through a small village, over the new bridge, then turn right up the mountain for 300 meters (1,000 feet). You can park here and climb down the steps to the river on the right, where there is a lovely swimming hole and waterfall, often populated by local kids when school is out. ⚠ **Pay strict attention to the posted sign that warns not to leave anything of value in your parked car.**

BEACHES

Playa Dominical. Long, flat, and rarely crowded, Playa Dominical is good for beachcombing among all the flotsam and jetsam that the surf washes up onto the brown sand. There's shade and parking under palm trees along the dirt road that parallels the beach. Although it lost its Blue Flag status, the water is relatively clean and local businesses make sure things look tidy. Photo opportunities abound here, with buff surfers riding the waves and vendors' clotheslines of colorful sarongs flapping in the sea breeze. Tortilla Flats restaurant is practically on the beach. ■TIP→ **Huge waves and dangerous rip currents make it primarily a surfing beach.** In high season, flags mark off a relatively safe area for swimming, under the watchful gaze of a professional lifeguard. **Amenities:** food and drink; lifeguards; parking. **Best for:** surfing; walking.

Playa Dominicalito. About 1 km (½ mile) south of Playa Dominical, this wide beach is usually calmer and more suited to boogie boarding. There are hidden rocks near the shore, so the best time to swim is at low tide. This is one of the best walking beaches, with lots of shade under tall palms and beach almond trees. The sun sets behind a huge rocky outcropping topped with tiny palm trees, an ideal shot for photographers. There is a campground running parallel to the beach, which is popular with locals, especially during Easter, Christmas, and school holidays. **Amenities:** parking. **Best for:** sunset; walking.

> ## PACK YOUR BOARD
>
> The surfing is great in Dominical, thanks to the runoff from the Barú River mouth, which constantly changes the ocean bottom and creates well-shaped waves big enough to keep intermediate and advanced surfers challenged. The best surfing is near the river mouth, and the best time is two hours before or after high tide, to avoid the notorious riptides.

SPORTS AND THE OUTDOORS

FISHING

Angling options range from expensive sportfishing charters to a trip in a small boat to catch red snapper and snook for supper. The five most common fish species here, in the order in which you are likely to catch them, are sailfish, dorado, yellowfin tuna, wahoo, and marlin.

Captain Isidro. Go fishing for wahoo and roosterfish the Tico way in a *panga*, a locally made, roofed-over boat, with a bilingual captain. Casual fishers can try their luck inshore for $60 an hour; more serious fishers can try for tuna and dorado around Caño Island, for $570 for the day or $360 for half a day. ☎ 2787–0341.

Las Rocas Marea Alta Sportfishing. Cast off with Captain George or Captain Allan on a 24-foot, center-console sportfishing boat equipped with outriggers. Inshore fishing costs $90 per hour, with a minimum of three hours, while a whole day offshore is $850 for up to four anglers, with lunch, drinks, and snacks. If you want to try your luck close in, you can dip a rod from a 15-foot *panga*, a traditional fishing boat, for $200 for a half day. The boats are also available for snorkeling tours and for whale- and dolphin- watching. ⊠ *Km 146 on Pan-American Hwy., south of Hotel Roca Verde* ☎ 2787–0480, 8606–5118.

HORSEBACK RIDING

Don Lulo. Horseback riding tours to Nauyaca Waterfalls depart Monday to Saturday at 8 am from Don Lulo's stables. The tour ($60) includes a light breakfast and lunch at the family homestead near the falls. You can swim in the cool pool beneath the falls, so bring a bathing suit and sunscreen. There is a river to cross, but otherwise the 12-km (7-mile)

"Nauyaca waterfall is a three-tiered waterfall. Well worth the visit." —Photo by Richard Bueno, Fodors.com member

ride is easy. Be sure to reserve a day in advance. ⊠ *Road to San Isidro, 10 km (6 miles) northeast of Dominical* ☎ *2787–0541, 2787–0542* ⊕ *www.cataratasnauyaca.com.*

SURFING

Dominical Surf Adventures. Offering more than surfing lessons, this outfitter can arrange white-water rafting trips on nearby rivers, as well as kayaking tours in the Terraba River mangroves and in the ocean in Ballena Marine National Park. ⊠ *Main street, across from church* ☎ *2787–0431, 8897–9540* ⊕ *www.dominicalsurfadventures.com.*

Green Iguana Surf Camp. Learn to surf with two-hour private lessons for $50, or small-group lessons for $40 per person. The company also offers weeklong packages that include lodging, board rental, lessons, and transportation to whichever nearby beach has the best waves each day (from $680 per person). Packages include transportation to and from San José and other locations. ☎ *8825–1381* ⊕ *www. greeniguanasurfcamp.com.*

WHERE TO EAT

$$
COSTA RICAN

✕ **La Parcela.** Picture a dream location: a high headland jutting out into the sea with vistas up·and down the coast. Throw in a breeze-swept terrace, polished service, and some fine seaside cuisine. This restaurant has had its ups and downs, often relying on its unmatched location, but the newest incarnation, painted in nautical blue and white, is worth a stop. Shrimp and lobster dishes, if pricey, are excellent. Less expensive is the grilled fish fillet, cooked perfectly and served with a medley of fresh, local vegetables and rice. Desserts here are rich— mud pie and a delectable chocolate cake—and substantial enough to share. If you're just passing through Dominical, this is a good place for a cold beer or a *naturale,* a tall glass of freshly whipped fruit juice. Sunsets here are spectacular. There is some controversy about this restaurant's eco-sensitive location, so call ahead to make sure it's still up and running. [$] *Average main: $12* ✉ *4 km (2½ miles) south of Dominical* ☎ *2787–0016.*

$ VEGETARIAN 🍴 **Maracatù.** Who says vegetarian food has to be boring? From spicy pad Thai with tofu to crunchy falafel served with brown rice and organic salad, this sophisticated restaurant can make vegetarians ecstatic and even the most committed carnivore happy. The fish tacos are delicious and priced right for budget-conscious beachgoers. The eclectic decor reflects the global reach of the kitchen: Moroccan stained-glass lamps, bamboo furniture, and cushions covered in East Indian fabrics. The colorful linens and cloth napkins here are a rarity at the beach. It's definitely the most romantic restaurant in Dominical. For the less romantically inclined, there's free Wi-Fi and an interesting world music sound track. [$] *Average main: $10* ✉ *Main street, across from soccer field* ☎ *2787–0091.*

$$ ECLECTIC 🍴 **Restaurante Charter.** Is that a plane that just crash-landed in the jungle? It's hard to miss Charter Restaurant's Boeing 727 as you approach Dominical from San Isidro de El General. Kids of all ages will delight in stopping here if only to get close to a real plane (minus the engine), transported here, piece by piece, by the aircraft-enthusiast owner. The gimmick is irresistible and the food in the rancho restaurant next to the plane beats any airplane food. There are succulent grilled pork ribs and a sirloin steak special loaded with shrimp in a garlic-and-wine sauce. For lunch there's the Plane Burger, which is anything but plain, with bacon, chili peppers, lettuce, and tomato. Fish and seafood are fresh and the excellent pastas include a standout penne a la vodka. If the kids tire of checking out the plane, there's also a swimming pool to keep them amused while grown-ups enjoy lunch. Dinners are candlelit and romantic—a little like dining on the set of the TV show *Lost.* [$] *Average main: $11* ✉ *1½ km (1 mile) northeast of Dominical, on road from San Isidro de El General* ☎ *506/2787–0172* ✉ *info@restaurantecharter.com.*

$ SOUTHWESTERN 🍴 **San Clemente Bar & Grill.** Signs you're in the local surfer hangout: a real Volkswagen van, balanced atop a pole at the entrance, with life-size, loony caricatures (including Elvis) spilling out of the windows, and broken surfboards affixed to the restaurant's ceiling. Fresh seafood, sandwiches, and such Tex-Mex standards as burritos and nachos make up the menu, which you can enjoy at inside tables or picnic tables on a terrace. Owner Mike McGinnis is famous for making a blistering hot sauce, which you can buy by the bottle. [$] *Average main: $8* ✉ *Main St.* ☎ *2787–0055.*

$ SOUTHWESTERN 🍴 **Tortilla Flats.** A perennially popular surfer hangout, this casual, breezy place has the advantage of being right across from Dominical Beach, which you can spy through a fringe of palm trees. Surf videos play on big screens, and there's free Wi-Fi. The most popular items on the menu are the fresh-baked baguette sandwiches stuffed with interesting combinations. Try the grilled chicken, avocado, tomato, and mozzarella sandwich. Light eaters can opt for half a sandwich. Fresh-fish specials, notably the fish tacos, and typical Mexican fare round out the casual menu. Desserts are decadent, along with excellent margaritas and flavored daiquiris, downed at the huge U-shape bar. There's a stage for live bands and a DJ, usually Wednesday, Friday, or Saturday nights. $ *Average main: $9* ⊠ *Across from Dominical Beach* ☎ *2787–0033.*

WHERE TO STAY

Lodgings in the lowlands of Dominical and the area a little to the north tend to be hot and muggy and not as comfortable as the more luxurious, private, and breezy places up in the hills above Dominicalito, to the south.

$
RENTAL
Coconut Grove Oceanfront Cottages. Right on the beach, this well-maintained cluster of cabins and beach houses, set in a gorgeous garden with magnificent trees, is ideal for couples or families who want to fend for themselves. **Pros:** best location in town: right on beach; close to cool ocean breezes; friendly owners. **Cons:** furnishings are simple and a little tired; guests must love animals; cabin 4 doesn't have the best air circulation. $ *Rooms from: $75* ⊠ *Domincalito Beach, Costanera Hwy. at Km 147, 3 km (2 miles) south of Dominical* ☎ *2787–0130* ⊕ *www.coconutgrovecr.com* ⇆ *3 cabins, 2 beach houses* ⊟ *No credit cards* ⊚ *No meals.*

$$
B&B/INN
Cuna del Angel Hotel and Spa. Decorative angels abound at this hotel, a perfect spot for those who like to indulge themselves, with a small spa offering a selection of soothing massages. **Pros:** delightful decor; excellent restaurant; friendly service in hotel and spa. **Cons:** rooms that face the pool can be noisy; water pressure is sometimes low; steep steps to Jungle Rooms. $ *Rooms from: $108* ⊠ *Puertocito, 9 km (5 miles) south of Dominical* ☎ *2787–8012* ⊕ *www.cunadelangel.com* ⇆ *23 rooms* ⊚ *Breakfast.*

$
B&B/INN
FAMILY
Fodor'sChoice
★
Hacienda Barú National Wildlife Refuge and Ecolodge. Base yourself in this wildly family-friendly, comfortable eco-lodge and you can explore vast tracts of surrounding forest, both primary and secondary, plus mangroves, and a Blue Flag beach with nesting turtles. **Pros:** prime wildlife viewing; excellent guides; trails and outdoor activities; great value. **Cons:** older cabins are not fancy; no air-conditioning but cabins are well ventilated with ceiling and wall fans. $ *Rooms from: $75* ⊠ *Off Costanera Hwy., 3 km (2 miles) north Dominical* ☎ *2787–0003* ⊕ *www.haciendabaru.com* ⇆ *6 cabins, 6 guest rooms* ⊚ *Breakfast.*

$
B&B/INN
Pacific Edge. Private, spacious wood cabins—one sleeps six, others sleep four—have kitchenettes, tiled bathrooms, hammocks strung on wide porches, and comfortable mattresses covered with colorful Guatemalan bedspreads. **Pros:** fabulous views; bargain prices; serene setting. **Cons:** very steep road that requires 4WD; must love dogs. $ *Rooms from: $60* ⊠ *At Km 148 of Costanera Hwy., head up a rough road for 1.2 km (1 mile), 4 km (2½ miles) south of Dominical* ☎ *8935–7905* ⊕ *www.pacificedge.info* ⇆ *4 cabins* ⊚ *No meals.*

$$$
B&B/INN
Río Magnolia Nature Lodge. Hidden away in a spectacular mountain valley, this luxury eco-lodge has the best of everything: a huge stone fireplace inside and an infinity pool outside with distant ocean views

LIVING OFF THE GRID

Many hotels in the more remote areas of the South Pacific generate their own electricity, so don't count on air-conditioning, using a hair dryer, calling home, checking your email, or paying with a credit card (unless it's arranged in advance). Some lodges do have radio contact with the outside world and satellite phone systems you can use in emergencies, but bad weather can often block the satellite signal. On the positive side, you really can get away from it all in the Southern Zone. Pack as though you are a castaway from modern civilization. Be sure to bring the following:

- Flashlight with extra batteries, or better still, one of the new kinetic flashlights that don't need batteries
- Insect repellent (lots of it)
- Sunscreen (ditto)
- After-sun lotion
- All toiletries and medications you could conceivably need, in small travel containers
- Sturdy, breathable hiking shoes and lots of socks (your feet will get wet)
- Waterproof walking sandals
- Binoculars
- Sun hat
- Refillable water bottle
- Portable, battery-operated reading light or a head lamp
- Zip-style baggies of all sizes to keep cameras, snacks, etc., dry and bug-free

from wrap-around decks. **Pros:** seclusion; magnificent views; excellent food; lots of books and field guides. **Cons:** very difficult access over rough roads; must love dogs; be prepared for cool mountain nights. $ *Rooms from: $145* ✉ *14 km (8½ miles) northeast of Dominical, off the main highway between San Isidro and Dominical, turn at sign for La Alfombra, Tinamaste* ☎ *8307–1036* 🌐 *www.riomagnolia.com* 🛏 *4 suites, 1 cabin* 🍴 *Breakfast.*

$$ B&B/INN 🏨 **Roca Verde.** Small and friendly, this is the only hotel with direct beach access in the area, so it's no surprise it's popular with surfers, anglers, and beach-lovers. **Pros:** right on the beach; friendly bar; reasonably priced. **Cons:** can be noisy Friday night if you don't join the party. $ *Rooms from: $85* ✉ *Dominical Beach, 1 km (½ mile) south of Dominical* ☎ *2787–0036* 🌐 *www.rocaverde.net* 🛏 *9 rooms* 🍴 *No meals.*

$$ B&B/INN 🏨 **Villas Alturas.** One of the best lodging deals on this coast, these seven, no-frills villas are in a lovely setting, with a large swimming pool and a huge terrace with a million-dollar view of the Pacific. **Pros:** excellent value, especially weekly rates; fabulous views; personal service. **Cons:** long steep drive requiring all-wheel or 4WD; long way down to beach and activities. $ *Rooms from: $164* ✉ *7 km (4½ miles) south of Dominical, 800 m up steep hill* ☎ *2200–5440* 🌐 *www.villasalturas.com* 🛏 *7 villas* 🍴 *Some meals.*

$$ HOTEL FAMILY 🏨 **Villas Río Mar.** Upriver from the beach on exquisitely landscaped grounds, this upscale yet very affordable hotel is awash in clouds of terrestrial orchids and aflame with bright bougainvillea and hibiscus. **Pros:** huge pool; lovely grounds; excellent restaurant. **Cons:** some rooms lack

air-conditioning and TV; 15-minute walk to the main beach. $ *Rooms from: $102* ⌧ *Off main highway into town, 1 km (½ mile) west of Dominical* ☎ *2787–0052* ⊕ *www.villasriomar.com* ⇆ *40 rooms, 12 suites* ⏏ *Breakfast.*

NIGHTLIFE

During the high season, Dominical hops at night, and when the surfers have fled to find bigger waves, there are enough locals around to keep some fun events afloat.

Maracatù World Music Bar. The crowd is young and edgy here, with live music Saturday night. Check the restaurant window for posters advertising special DJ nights and visiting bands. Wednesday is Ladies' Night, with free shots from 10 to midnight. ⌧ *Main street, across from San Clemente* ☎ *2787–0091.*

Roca Verde. Friday nights feature local bluesy rock band Ben Jammin' and the Howlers, with electric jazz fiddler Nancy Buchan electrifying the happy, upbeat crowd, which consists of a mix of families, ex-pats, and tourists. ⌧ *Roca Verde, 1 km (½ mile) south of Dominical* ☎ *2787–0036.*

Tortilla Flats. This lively restaurant also has a stage for live bands and DJ music, usually Wednesday, Friday, or Saturday nights, so check out their program when you are in town. ☎ *2787–0033.*

SHOPPING

Mama Kiya Art Gallery. This is the showplace for local artists and artisans, with canvasses spilling out onto the sidewalk in front of the colorful shop, brimming with oil paintings, sculptures, stained glass, textiles, and indigenous crafts. Owner Pedro Monzón always has a smile for passersby. If he can't help you find a one-of-a-kind artistic souvenir here, you won't find it anywhere. ⌧ *Centro Comercial Pueblo del Rio, main road* ☎ *2787–0215.*

Tucan Souvenir & Gifts. The most upscale souvenir shop in town has the usual assortment of local handmade crafts made of exotic woods, hammocks and T-shirts, candles and incense, and field guides. But they are good quality and artistically presented in a pleasant, fan-cooled shop. ⌧ *Plaza Pacifica, Costanera Hwy.* ☎ *2787–0020.*

PARQUE NACIONAL MARINO BALLENA

20 km (12 miles) southeast of Dominical.

GETTING HERE AND AROUND

The park area includes the communities of Uvita, Bahía Ballena, and Ojochal, all easily accessible off the Costanera, a wide, paved highway. As soon as you get off the highway, however, the roads are mostly bumpy and dusty. Alternatively, take a taxi or bus from Dominical. Buses leave Dominical at 10:30 am and 5:30 pm daily, and there are longer-haul buses that pass along the Costanera and can drop you off in Uvita. Each of the park's four sectors has a small ranger station where you pay your $6 admission.

The best place in the area to get information on tours and hotels is the Uvita Information Center. A bonus: it's air-conditioned inside.

8

ESSENTIALS

Hospital Dome Plaza Medical Services. A dentist, an on-call doctor for general services, minor surgeries, and dermatology, lab tests and a full-service pharmacy with an English-speaking pharmacist combine to give the most comprehensive medical services in one convenient location on the Costanera Highway. ⊠ *Dome Plaza, 50 m south of the bridge, Uvita* ☎ *2743–8595 doctor, 2743–8418 dentist, 2743–8558 pharmacy.*

Visitor Information Uvita Information Center ⊠ *Beside the Costanera Hwy., across from BM Supermarket, Uvita* ☎ *8843–7142, 2743–8889* ⊕ *www.uvita.info.*

EXPLORING

Oro Verde Private Nature Reserve. You'll find excellent bird-watching and hiking in this nature preserve, uphill from the Costanera. Family run, this property has well groomed trails through a majestic, primary forest reserve. Early-morning, three-hour birding tours ($30) end with a hearty home-cooked breakfast. There are also three- to four-hour morning horseback tours to a waterfall, including lunch ($35). ⊠ *Off the Costanera Hwy. at Km 159, 3 km (2 miles) uphill from Rancho La Merced, Uvita* ☎ *2743–8889, 8843–8833* ⊗ *By reservation only.*

FAMILY

Fodor's Choice

★

Parque Nacional Marino Ballena (*Whale Marine National Park*). Named for the whales who use this area as a nursery, Ballena Marine National Park has four separate beaches, stretching for about 10 km (6 miles), and encompasses a mangrove estuary, a remnant coral reef, and more than 12,350 acres of ocean, home to tropical fish, dolphins, and humpback whales. Playa Uvita is the most popular sector of the park. It has the longest stretch of beach and shallow waters calm enough for kids. Fishing boats, kayaks, snorkeling tours, and dolphin- and whale-watching cruises all leave from the Playa Uvita sector of the park. Restaurants line the road to the Playa Uvita park entrance, but there are no food concessions within the park. Access to each of the four beaches—from north to south, Uvita, Colonia, Ballena and Piñuela—is off the Pan-American Highway. ⊠ *Entrance at Playa Uvita, about 20 km (12 miles) south of Dominical, Uvita* ☎ *2743–8236* 🎫 *$12* ⊗ *Daily 6–5.*

FAMILY

Rancho La Merced National Wildlife Refuge. Ride the range on a 1,250-acre property combining forest and pasture ($45) or gallop along the beach at sunset on horseback ($50). Explore the forest on a nature hike ($35) or go bird-watching ($45) with an excellent guide. Riding tours also include a guide and helmets and kid-size saddles. All tours begin at the pleasant reception center, where you can freshen up in clean, modern restrooms. The full-day, Cowboy for a Day tour ($45) includes roping and riding and herding cattle. For $6 you can explore the 10 km (6 miles) of hiking trails on your own with a trail map that includes a wildlife picture guide. There's also a night tour with a naturalist guide ($35). ⊠ *Km 159 of Costanera Hwy., north of Uvita, Uvita* ☎ *2743–8032* ⊕ *www.rancholamerced.com* 🎫 *$35–$50* ⊗ *By reservation only.*

Uvita Market. From 8 am to noon on Saturday, the place to be is this combination farmers' market and weekly gathering place for locals. About 20 vendors show up to sell organic produce, homemade cheeses, fresh fish, baked goods, jams and pickles, and frozen gourmet dinners

CLOSE UP

Wildlife-Watching Tips

If you're accustomed to nature programs on TV, with visions of wildebeest and zebra swarming across African savanna, your first visit to a tropical forest can be a bewildering experience. If these forests are so diverse, where are all the animals? Websites, brochures, and books are plastered with lovely descriptions and close-up images of wildlife that give travelers high hopes. Reality is much different but no less fascinating. Here are some tips to make your experience more enjoyable.

■ Don't expect to see rarely sighted animals. It might happen; it might not. Cats (especially jaguars), harpy eagles, and tapirs are very rare sightings.

■ Monkeys can be the easiest animals to spot, but although they are as reliable as the tides in some locations, in others they are rare indeed.

■ Remember that nearly all animals spend most of their time avoiding detection.

■ Be quiet! Nothing is more unsettling to a wary animal than 20 *Homo sapiens* conversing as they hike. It's best to treat the forest like a house of worship—quiet reverence is in order.

■ Listen closely. Many visitors are surprised when a flock of parrots overhead is pointed out to them, despite the incredible volume of noise they produce. That low-pitched growl you hear is a howler monkey call, which is obvious if nearby, but easily missed over the din of conversation. Try stopping for a moment and closing your eyes.

■ Slowly observe different levels of the forest. An enormous caterpillar or an exquisitely camouflaged moth may be only a few inches from your face, and the silhouettes in the tree 100 meters (330 feet) away may be howler monkeys. Scan trunks and branches where a sleeping sloth or anteater might curl up. A quick glance farther down the trail may reveal an agouti or peccary crossing your path.

■ In any open area such as a clearing or river, use your binoculars and scan in the distance; scarlet macaws and toucans may be cruising above the treetops.

■ Cultivate some level of interest in the less charismatic denizens of the forest—the plants, insects, and spiders. On a good day in the forest you may see a resplendent quetzal or spider monkey, but should they fail to appear, focus on an intricate spider web, a column of marching army ants, mammal footprints in the mud, or colorful seeds and flowers fallen from high in the canopy.

8

and soups to take home. You can also feast on ready-to-eat breakfast burritos, tamales, cakes, and cookies. Artists sell painted masks, colorful textiles, and beautiful photographs. Every third Saturday there's a garage-sale table, too. This is a great place to meet English-speaking locals as they meet and greet. Some weeks, there's live music by local bands. You'll find the market just off the Costanera Highway, across from the Banco de Costa Rica and down a short side road. Just look for the parked cars. ⊠ *Off Costanera Hwy., across from Banco de Costa Rica, Uvita.*

BEACHES

Playa Ballena. Playa Ballena, 4 km (2½ miles) from Playa Colonia, is a lovely strand backed by lush vegetation and easy to get to from the main highway. **Amenities:** showers; toilets. **Best for:** swimming; walking. ⊠ *Parque Nacional Marino Ballena, Ojochal.*

Playa Colonia. Playa Colonia, 2 km (1¼ miles) south of Playa Uvita, has a safe swimming beach with a view of rocky islands, which you can visit by kayak. It's the only beach where cars can park practically on the beach. **Amenities:** food and drink; showers; toilets. **Best for:** swimming. ⊠ *Parque Nacional Marino Ballena, Colonia.*

Playa Piñuela. Tiny Playa Piñuela is the prettiest of the Parque Nacional Marino Ballena beaches, nestled in a deep cove. It's not the best beach for swimming, however, since the shore is pebbled and the waves can be a little rough. **Amenities:** showers; toilets. **Best for:** walking. ⊠ *Parque Nacional Marino Ballena, 3 km (2 miles) south of Colonia, Ojochal.*

Playa Uvita. At the northern end of Parque Nacional Marino Ballena, wide, palm-fringed Playa Uvita stretches out along a *tombolo* (a long swath of sand) connecting a former island to the coast. This is the most popular beach, especially on weekends, with shallow waters for swimming. On weekdays you may have it almost to yourself. It's also the launching spot for boat tours and the favorite vantage point for spectacular sunsets. **Amenities:** food and drink; showers; toilets. **Best for:** sunset; swimming; walking. ⊠ *Parque Nacional Marino Ballena, Uvita.*

Playa Ventanas. Just 1½ km (1 mile) south of Ballena Marine Park, off the Costanera Highway, you'll find a scenic beach with interesting tidal caves, popular for sea-kayaking. Coconut palms edge the beach, which is sometimes pebbly, with quite a dramatic surf, especially at high tide when the waves break against huge offshore rock formations. The ocean views are rivaled by the vistas of green, forested mountains rising up behind the beach. Sometimes there is guarded, private parking here for about 75¢ an hour. ■TIP→ Do not leave anything of value in your car. **Amenities:** some parking. **Best for:** walking. ⊠ *1½ km (1 mile) south of Ballena National Park, Ojochal.*

SPORTS AND THE OUTDOORS

DIVING AND SNORKELING

The best spot for snorkeling in the park is at the north end of Playa Ballena, near the whale's tail.

Bahía Aventuras. Bilingual guides lead half-day tours in covered boats that combine whale- and dolphin-watching with snorkeling for $85. A boat tour of the Terraba Sierpe Mangrove costs $85. If you want to try your luck, you can fish from a 23-foot locally designed and built boat; a half day costs $750 or full day around Caño Island costs $950. ⊠ *Bahía Ballena* ☎ *2743–8362, 8846–6576* ⊕ *www.bahiaaventuras.com.*

Dolphin Tours of Bahía Ballena. This tried-and-true tour company takes a minimum of two people on four-hour boat tours that combine dolphin- and whale-watching with snorkeling, a visit to ocean caverns, and a rocky island bird sanctuary for $70 per person. All-day fishing trips for snook and red snapper cost $600 for up to four anglers. ☎ *2743–8013, 8825–4031* ⊕ *www.dolphintourcostarica.com.*

"Strolling across Playa Uvita, I saw this iguana; I think it was as interested in me as I was in him." —Photo by Justin Hubbell, Fodors.com member

Mystic Dive Center. Specializing in dive and snorkel trips to Caño Island, about 50 km (31 miles) offshore, this long-standing dive operation takes a minimum of four divers or eight snorkelers ($115 full-day snorkeling; $158 full-day diving). The tour leaves at 6:30 am and returns around 2 pm. Or you can dive or snorkel closer in, only a 15-minute boat ride from Playa Ventanas, morning or afternoon, with a minimum of four people ($85 for snorkelers, $100 for divers). You can also rent surf- and boogie boards or take PADI dive lessons. ⊠ *West side of Costanera Hwy., near entrance to Ojochal, Ojochal* ☎ *2786–5217* ⊕ *www. mysticdivecenter.com* ⊗ *Open only during dry season, Dec.–Apr.*

ULTRALIGHT FLIGHTS

Ultralight Tour. For a thrilling bird's-eye view of the Whale's Tail in Bahía Ballena, take off in a two-seater ultralight flying machine with aeronautical engineer Georg Kiechle. The fee is about $140 for 30-minute trips. You can also fly south to Corcovado National Park or north to Manuel Antonio National Park. Be sure to bring your camera. ⊠ *PapaKilo Airstrip, north of Costanera Hwy., at entrance to Colonia Beach* ☎ *2743–8037, 8816–6901* ⊕ *www.flyadventurescr.com.*

ZIP LINING

Osa Canopy Tour. Zip lines are a dime a dozen in Costa Rica but this relatively new one is getting rave reviews. With 14 platforms and more than 3 kilometers (2 miles) of cable, you will certainly get your money's worth. For the really adventurous, there are also two rappelling stations and a Tarzan swing. Count on flying through the forest, 100 feet high at times, for two to three hours, all for $55 per person. ⊠ *Ticket office at Km 196, Costanera Hwy., south of Uvita, Bahía Ballena* ☎ *2788–7555* ⊕ *www.osacanopytour.com.*

WHERE TO EAT

$$$ MEDITERRANEAN

🍴 **Azul Restaurante y Bar.** Ojochal's gourmet scene has been enhanced by this *intime* restaurant with an *au courant* Mediterranean menu, as well as an unbeatable view overlooking the sky, the sea, and a picturesque barrier island on the horizon. Sunsets here are spectacular, sometimes accompanied by pairs of scarlet macaws winging past at eye level. The well-priced menu suits the scene, with hummus and pita bread, delicately fried calamari, and goat cheese ravioli. The seafood soup is chock-full of shrimp and shellfish, and the pan-seared fish of the day can't be beat. For dessert, the standout item is the passion fruit pie, creamy and not too tart, balanced by a buttery cookie crust. The innovative pricing here is affordable: a main course is $15, two courses are $20, and three are $25 (plus tax and service). Thursday nights feature designer pizzas and salad. Service is a little uneven, but who cares when you have that view? [$] *Average main: $15* ✉ *El Castillo Hotel, off the Costanera Hwy., Ojochal* ☎ *2786–5543* 🕒 *Closed Mon.*

$ SEAFOOD

🍴 **Boca Coronado Bar y Restaurante.** Along the Costanera Highway from Dominical to Punta Mala you'll see signs shouting "Ceviche," sold from carts with cooler chests or in rickety roadside ranchos. If you're interested in trying this local specialty—raw fish and seafood marinated in lime juice and spiced up with onions and red peppers—try the ceviche at this breezy, open-air restaurant that's just steps from the sea. The ceviche is the freshest you'll find: among the various versions, the shrimp and sea bass marinated in coconut milk is a specialty. But don't stop at the ceviche: the fish and seafood are fresh and well prepared, along with a few more exotic dishes, including an excellent chicken curry. **TIP→ This airy space is sometimes the venue for food festivals organized by El Sabor de Ojochal, an association of local restaurants.** [$] *Average main: $9* ✉ *West side of Costanera Hwy., just south of entrance to Ojochal, Ojochal* ☎ *2786–5082* 🕒 *Closed Tues.*

$$$ ECLECTIC
Fodor's Choice ★

🍴 **Citrus Restaurant.** This sophisticated, Moroccan-inspired restaurant lives up to its name: it's tangy, tart, and refreshing. The intriguing menu offers sophisticated world cuisine, ranging from a Moroccan-style hamburger served with spicy harissa mayonnaise to Indian chicken curry in coconut milk, sweetened with dried plums, to a tuna tartare served with a peppery Thai *sriracha* sauce and a seaweed salad. There's a *soupçon* of French flavor, too, with garlicky escargots, *moules marinières* (mussels) with a touch of curry, and *steak frites* (steak with french fries). New on the menu is a dish of scallops in a creamy orange and sun-dried-tomato sauce scented with sage. Desserts are among the best in the country; if you like chocolate, don't pass up the divine Choco-Choco flourless chocolate cake with vanilla ice cream. Choose from tables in the elegant dining room, on the torch-lighted terrace, or in the riverside garden. In the high season great-value, three-course lunch specials are available until 5 pm. [$] *Average main: $18* ✉ *Off Costanera Hwy., first left turn at entrance of Ojochal, Ojochal* ☎ *2786–5175* 🕒 *Closed Sun. No lunch May–Dec.*

$$$ FRENCH
Fodor's Choice ★

🍴 **Exotica Restaurant.** In the tiny French-Canadian enclave of Ojochal, this intimate thatch-roofed restaurant, where 10 tables are encased in greenery, has been serving superb French-inspired fare with exotic flavors culled from France's colonial past, for more than a decade.

You'll be warmly welcomed by Lucy, the restaurant's chic and charming owner. Subtitled *Cuisine du Monde*, the menu starts off with a tangy and refreshing avocado, pineapple, lime, and cilantro appetizer, or an intriguing Tahitian fish carpaccio with bananas. Don't miss out on a hearty serving of fish or shrimp in a banana-curry sauce, or a spicy Vietnamese chicken soup. French favorites include cognac liver pâté and a pricey but excellent duck breast with orange sauce. Presentation is artistic, with garnishes of flowers and sprigs of exotic greenery. Desserts are all homemade, luscious, and reasonably priced. Chocoholics won't want to miss the chocolate chiffon cake with chocolate sauce and an accompanying shot glass of cocoa liqueur. [$] *Average main: $18* ✉ *Main road into Ojochal, off Costanera Hwy., Ojochal* ☎ *2786–5050* ✍ *Reservations essential* ⏲ *Closed Sun. and Sept. and Oct. No lunch.*

$ FRENCH 🍴 **Pancito Café.** Besides crusty baguettes, buttery croissants, and divine pastries to go, this French-owned bakery near the entrance to Ojochal serves hearty breakfast omelets and does a booming lunch business with crepes, quiches, meal-size salads, soups, pizzas, and sandwiches. You can also order roasted, free-range chickens to eat here or take to go. Customers perch on high stools at tables and counters in this casual, thatch-roofed café. Many have their laptops open, taking advantage of the free Wi-Fi. Get here early on Tuesday for the popular weekly *plat du jour.* [$] *Average main: $8* ✉ *Plaza de Los Delfines, off Costanera Hwy., Ojochal* ☎ *506/8729–4155* 💳 *No credit cards* ⏲ *Closed Sun. No dinner.*

$$ PIZZA 🍴 **Pizzeria El Jardín Tortuga.** Pizza is the claim to fame here, and it's served in a casual garden patio and a cool upstairs rancho. The German pizza baker can make only six individual pizzas at a time in his wood-fired clay oven, but it's worth the wait for thin-crust pies heaped with toppings. For something a little different, try the roast pork in beer sauce. While you wait for your meal, you can enjoy the birds flitting in the garden by day, or in the evening have a drink in the bar, which is popular with locals. [$] *Average main: $12* ✉ *Ojochal, past supermarket, left on bridge and 1st right* ☎ *2786–5059* 🌐 *www.theturtlesgarden.com* 💳 *No credit cards* ⏲ *Closed Tues. Closed Mon. and Tues. Sept.–Dec.*

$$ SPANISH 🍴 **Sabor Español.** Authentic paella, made with nutty, saffron-infused Spanish rice and the freshest seafood, is the main reason to wend your way along a rutted dirt road behind Playa Ballena to this jungle outpost of Catalan cuisine. The smallish, open-air rancho is nothing fancy, with wooden chairs and tables and a few potted palms, but the warm welcome along with the extensive menu quickly dispel any qualms about the seriousness of this restaurant. There's a classic, spicy, Andalusian gazpacho for starters or tapas to share. The long list of seafood specialties includes whisky-flambéed shrimp. Meat lovers can sink their teeth into sirloin slathered with a wine and fresh grape sauce. Chicken takes on tropical flavors with sauces featuring mango, rum, and curry. The pace is a little leisurely, but a pitcher of excellent sangria, studded with tropical fruit chunks, helps to pass the time enjoyably. There are only five tables, so reservations are advised, especially in the evenings. [$] *Average main: $12* ✉ *1 km (½ mile) south of Uvita BM Supermercado along Costanera, Bahía Ballena* ✥ *turn right at Cabinas Gato and look for left-turn sign onto dirt road parallel to Playa Ballena* 💳 *No credit cards* ⏲ *Closed Mon.*

$ ✕ **Tilapias El Pavón.** To enjoy an authentically Tico day in the country,
COSTA RICAN follow a winding river road up to this family-run tilapia fish farm in
the tiny hamlet of Vergel. You can work up an appetite on a short
hike to a spectacular, nearby waterfall with a swimming hole (bring
your swimsuit and binoculars for bird-watching), then catch your own
tilapia. The cooks at the open-air wooden restaurant overlooking the
tidily kept fishponds will fry up your fish in 10 minutes, presenting it
whole or filleted, with rice, salad, yuca, and excellent *patacones* (fried,
mashed plantains), plus a pitcher of refreshing fruit *naturale*, a feast
for only $9. There's also chicken for non-fish fans, plus wine and beer.
It's open 9–6 weekdays, 9–8 weekends, so it's a good spot for lunch
or an early dinner. $ *Average main: $9* ✉ *2 km (1 mile) south of Ojochal, then just before bridge in Punta Mala, follow a dirt road 4 km
(2½ miles) uphill to tiny hamlet of Vergel, Vergel* ☎ *8311–8213* ▭ *No
credit cards* ⊘ *Closed Mon.*

$$ ✕ **Villa Leonor.** Can't decide between lunch or the beach? You can get
BARBECUE both at this cheerful, casual restaurant-cum-beach-club, complete with
FAMILY swimming pool and showers, just steps from Playa Ballena. Famous
for barbecue pork ribs, the menu also offers skewers of barbecued
chicken, calamari, or shrimp. The mixed chicken and fish fajitas are
popular, too, served with a salad. Chill out with ice-cold beer, excellent
fruit smoothies, and tropical cocktails while the kids play in the pool.
Or stroll down to the beach between courses. Sunday, the all-inclusive
brunch menu includes soup, salad, sautéed rosemary potatoes, and a
barbecued main of your choice. Dinner is also served daily in high sea-
son, except Tuesday, until 8 pm. Service is sprightly, and the friendly
American owner is usually on hand to greet customers. $ *Average
main: $11* ✉ *Between Km 170 and 171 on Costanera, Bahía Ballena*
⊕ *1 km (½ mile) south of road to Hotel Cristal Ballena, turn right on
road to Playa Ballena* ☎ *506/2786–5380* ▭ *No credit cards* ⊘ *Closed
Tues. No dinner Sept.–Dec.*

WHERE TO STAY

$$$ ⬚ **Cristal Ballena Hotel Resort.** High on a hillside with spectacular ocean
B&B/INN views framed by giant travelers palm trees, this Austrian-owned hotel
FAMILY is the most luxurious base for exploring the area, with a 400-square-
meter (4,400-square-foot) swimming pool that commands both
mountain and sea views. **Pros:** wonderful swimming pool for serious swimmers and loungers; great ocean, mountain, and sky views;
luxurious rooms. **Cons:** restaurant service can be slow; steep walk to
beach. $ *Rooms from: $189* ✉ *Costanera Hwy., 7 km (4 miles) south
of Uvita, Uvita* ☎ *2786–5354* ⊕ *www.cristal-ballena.com* ⇱ *19 suites*
⦿| *Breakfast.*

$$ ⬚ **Diquis del Sur Hotel Resort & Garden.** At this ideal—and affordable—
RENTAL tropical retreat for the winter-weary, five bungalows are sprinkled
around lush grounds with views of both mountains and ocean. **Pros:**
reasonable daily rates and weekly bargains; great breakfasts; well-
spaced bungalows. **Cons:** some bungalows lack air-conditioning; spare
but adequate furnishings; rough road from main highway. $ *Rooms
from: $85* ✉ *Off Costanera Hwy., 1 km (½ mile) up dirt road signed*

"Calle Papagayo," Ojochal ☎ *2786–5013* 🌐 *www.diquiscostarica.com* 🛏 *10 bungalow rooms, 1 cabin* 🍴 *Breakfast.*

$$$$ B&B/INN Fodor's Choice ★ 🏨 **Kurá Design Villas.** Stunning contemporary design, high-tech comforts, and a lofty location overlooking the Pacific combine to set a whole new standard of luxury on this coast. **Pros:** the ultimate in contemporary design and comfort; saltwater infinity pool; excellent restaurant. **Cons:** the ultimate in price (but worth the splurge); a long, steep drive down to the beach. [$] *Rooms from: $590* ✉ *1 km (½ mile) above Uvita, to parking lot; hotel transport up to Kurá, Bahía Ballena* 🌐 *www.kuracostarica.com* 🛏 *4 villas, 2 junior suites* 🍴 *Breakfast.*

$$ B&B/INN FAMILY 🏨 **La Cusinga.** Along with one of the best sunset views along the coast, this comfortable eco-lodge on a high cliff bordering Ballena Marine National Park has spacious, airy cabins and a forest trail to a pristine beach. **Pros:** comfortable cabins; forest and beach access. **Cons:** steep path between cabins and lodge; uncomfortable concrete benches on private terraces. [$] *Rooms from: $140* ✉ *Between Km 166 and 167 on the Costanera Hwy., south of Dominical, Bahía Ballena* ☎ *2770–2549* 🌐 *www.lacusingalodge.com* 🍴 *Breakfast.*

$ B&B/INN FAMILY 🏨 **Rio Tico Safari Lodge.** You'll feel as though you're on a luxury safari when you step inside one of these spacious South African–made tents. **Pros:** gorgeous natural setting; dry and airy tents; helpful hosts. **Cons:** some steps to climb up and down from main lodge to tents. [$] *Rooms from: $55* ✉ *4 km (2½ miles) up dirt road between Ojachal and Vergel de Punta Mala, turnoff just before bridge in Punta Mala, Vergel de Punta Mala* ☎ *8996–7935* 🌐 *www.riotico.com* 🛏 *9 tents, 3 rooms* 🍴 *No meals.*

$$ B&B/INN 🏨 **Villas Gaia.** Conveniently just off the highway, these spacious, tasteful villas owned by a Dutch couple are hidden behind a ridge overlooking forest ravines leading to Playa Tortuga. **Pros:** easy access off the highway; serene setting; good restaurant. **Cons:** you must climb some stairs to get to the villas; pool is small; beach is down a steep path. [$] *Rooms from: $85* ✉ *Off the Costanera Hwy., 15 km (9 miles) south of Uvita, Playa Tortuga* ☎ *2786–5044, 2241–3393 in San José* 🌐 *www.villasgaia.com* 🛏 *14 cabinas, 1 house* 🍴 *Breakfast.*

SHOPPING

Green Leaf Arts & Artesania. Along with a great selection of high-quality local art, indigenous crafts, and souvenirs, this well-stocked shop has eclectic home accessories, plus field guides and interesting jewelry. Next door at the **Super Feliz** you can pick up snacks, cheeses, and treats for a beach picnic, as well as imported beer and wine. Both stores are open daily from 9 to 6. Need some beach reading? Check out the store's used-book exchange, the **Rainforest Book Trader**, open daily 7 to 6. ✉ *West side of Costanera Hwy., next to Mystic Dive Center, Ojochal* ☎ *2786–5313.*

THE GOLFO DULCE

One of only three tropical fjords in the world, the Golfo Dulce has 180-meter-deep (600-foot-deep) waters in the center of a usually placid gulf where you can watch dolphins swim and humpback whales feed. At Chacarita, 33 km (20 miles) south of Palmar Sur, the southern coast assumes a split personality. Heading west, you reach the Osa Peninsula and, eventually, the Pacific Ocean and the wildest region of Costa Rica. Continuing due south brings you to the Golfo Dulce, which means "Sweet Gulf," reflecting the usually tranquil waters. This gulf creates two shorelines: an eastern shore that is accessible only by boat above Golfito, and a western shore, which is the eastern side of the Osa Peninsula. South of Golfito the coast fronts the Pacific Ocean once again (rather than the calm gulf), with wilder beaches that beckon surfers and nature lovers.

GOLFITO

130 km (81 miles) south of Uvita, 339 km (212 miles) southeast of San José.

Overlooking a small gulf (hence its name) and hemmed in by a steep bank of forest, Golfito has a great location. Lodges supply kayaks for paddling the gulf's warm, salty, and crystal-clear waters. When the sun sets behind the rolling silhouette of the Osa Peninsula, you can sometimes spot phosphorescent fish jumping. Fishing, both commercial and for sport, is the main activity here, with two large marinas providing slips to visiting yachts and charter fishing boats.

Golfito was once a thriving banana port—United Fruit arrived in 1938—with elegant housing and lush landscaping for its plantation managers. After United Fruit pulled out in 1985, Golfito slipped into a state of poverty and neglect. The town itself consists of a pleasant, lushly landscaped older residential section and a long strip of scruffy commercial buildings. Visiting U.S. Coast Guard ships dock here, and small cruise ships moor in the harbor. The Costa Rica Coast Guard Academy is also here.

GETTING HERE AND AROUND

From San José the trip used to take eight hours, along paved roads crossing over often-foggy mountains. But with the new toll road from San José, connecting to the paved Costanera Highway, travel time has been cut to five hours. Your best bet, especially if you are visiting a lodge on the gulf, is to fly to Golfito, which takes only about an hour. Direct buses from San José leave twice daily, at 7 am and 3 pm.

Taxis and boats take you wherever you need to go in and around Golfito. You can hire taxi boats at the city dock in Golfito (about $90 round-trip, often negotiable, to go to area lodges or across to Puerto Jiménez). The only way to reach the remote Golfo Dulce lodges above Golfito is by boat. Early morning is the best time, when the water in the gulf is at its calmest. Most lodges include the boat transport in their rates.

For tour, lodging, and general tourist information, check out ⊕ *www.golfitocostarica.com*, a website managed by longtime Golfito residents.

The Golfo Dulce

0   8 mi

0   8 km

Pacific Ocean

ESSENTIALS

Banks/ATM ATH Coopealianza ✉ *North end of town, across from hospital.* **Banco Nacional** ✉ *South of hospital* ☎ *2775–1101.*

Hospital Regional Hospital. This is the main hospital for the Southern Zone, including Puerto Jiménez and the Osa Peninsula. This is where you go—by boat, ambulance, or charter plane—if you need anti-venom for a serious snake bite. ✉ *American Zone, near Deposito* ☎ *2775–7800.*

Pharmacy Farmacia Golfito ✉ *Main street, across from city park* ☎ *2775–2442* ⊙ *Daily 8 am–7 pm.*

Post Office Correo ✉ *Off the main road, south of central park.*

Taxi Taxi service. Most taxis here are *colectivos,* meaning you will probably share your ride with passengers picked up along the way. ✉ *Taxi stand beside park at center of town, San Vito* ☎ *2773–3939.*

Visitor Information Land Sea Services. Check their website for accommodation in rental villas, boat charters, restaurant info, and what to do in Golfito. ✉ *Next to Banana Bay Marina* ☎ *2775–1614* ⊕ *www.golfitocostarica.com.*

EXPLORING

American Zone. The northwestern end of town is the so-called American Zone, full of handsome wooden houses where the expatriate managers of United Fruit lived amid flowering trees imported from all over the world. Many of these vintage houses, built of durable Honduran hardwoods, are now being spruced up. Eccentric garden features, such as a restored railway car, make the neighborhood worth a stroll. If you're on foot, there's also excellent birding in and around the gardens.

Fodor'sChoice **Casa Orquideas.** A Garden of Eden with mass plantings of ornamental
★ palms, bromeliads, heliconias, cycads, orchids, flowering gingers, and spice trees, Casa Orquideas has been tended with care for more than 25 years by American owners Ron and Trudy MacAllister. The 2½-hour tour, available Sunday and Thursday at 8:30 am, includes touching, tasting, and smelling, plus spotting toucans and hummingbirds. Trudy is also a font of information on local lore and medicinal plants. Guided tours, given for a minimum of three people, are $10 per person. Self-guided visits, any day but Friday, cost $8. The garden is accessible only by boat; a water taxi to the garden (about $90 round-trip for four or more people) is a tour in itself. ⊠ *On the Golfo Dulce, north of Golfito* ☎ 8829–1247 🖃 *$8–$10* ☉ *Guided tours Thurs. and Sun. at 8:30 am. Closed Fri.*

Piedras Blancas National Park. There is some good birding in the dense forest here, which is also an important wildlife corridor connecting to Corcovado National Park. Follow the main road northwest through the American Zone and past the airstrip and a housing project. The place where a dirt road heads into the rain forest is great for bird-watching. There are no marked trails actually in the park; the best birding is along the road. ⊠ *Adjacent to Golfito National Wildlife Refuge* 🖃 *$10* ☉ *Daily dawn–dusk.*

BEACHES

Playa Cacao. Golfito doesn't have a beach of its own, but Playa Cacao is a mere five-minute boat ride across the bay. It's not the prettiest beach, but it has a picturesque view of boats bobbing in Golfito Bay. The fastest way to get here is to hire a boat at the city dock or from a mooring opposite the cruise-ship dock. Playa Cacao has two casual restaurants and one collection of basic cabinas, but it makes a cooler, quieter option when the heat and noise in Golfito get unbearable, and it's a good putting-in spot for kayaks. **Amenities:** food and drink. **Best for:** walking.

SPORTS AND THE OUTDOORS
FISHING

The open ocean holds plenty of sailfish, marlin, and roosterfish during the dry months, as well as mahimahi, tuna, and wahoo during the rainy season; there's excellent bottom fishing any time of year. Captains are in constant radio contact with one another and tend to share fish finds.

Banana Bay Marina. This marina houses a fleet of five charter fishing boats, fitted with tournament-quality tackle and skippered by English-speaking, world-record-holding captains. A day's fishing for up to four averages $1,450. You can also charter a boat for overnight trips to Drake Bay. ☎ *2775–0255, 2775–0003* ⊕ *www.bananabaymarinagolfito.com.*

WHERE TO EAT

$$ AMERICAN 🍴 **Banana Bay.** For consistently good American-style food, you can't beat this breezy marina restaurant with a view of expensive yachts and sport-fishing boats. Locals complain that the prices are high, but portions are hefty, and include generous salads, sizzling hamburgers, excellent chicken fajitas, and a delicious grilled dorado sandwich with a mountain of fries. Shrimp and fish plates are pricier—$15 to $22—but they couldn't be fresher, straight off the local boats. It's open for breakfast, too. Try the Eggs in Hell, consisting of two poached eggs smothered in hot sauce. While you're waiting for your order, take advantage of the free Wi-Fi. [$] *Average main: $12* ✉ *Main street, south of town dock* ☎ *2775–0383.*

$$ SEAFOOD 🍴 **Restaurante Mar y Luna.** This casual terrace restaurant jutting out into the harbor has the best harbor view in Golfito, along with jaunty nautical decor and cool breezes. The seafood-heavy lineup includes grilled whole fish served in a variety of ways, including Caribbean-style with coconut milk and a side of *patacones* (fried green plantain). Mixed chicken and beef fajitas are also on the menu, along with a few vegetarian dishes. The quality varies, depending on who's at the stove. The bar is a great place to hang out, with two large flat-screen TVs. Inexpensive, motel-style rooms and larger suites with the same view are available for rent. [$] *Average main: $12* ✉ *South end of main street, north of Hotel Las Gaviotas* ☎ *2775–0192* 🌐 *www.marylunagolfito.com.*

WHERE TO STAY

The atmosphere of the in-town hotels differs dramatically from that of the lodges in the delightfully remote east coast of the Golfo Dulce. The latter is a world of jungle and blue water, birds and fish, and desert-island beaches, with lodges accessible only by boat from either Golfito or Puerto Jiménez.

$$ HOTEL 🏨 **Casa Roland Marina Resort.** Everything at this luxury resort, designed like an art-deco ocean liner incongruously dry-docked in Golfito's American Zone, is first class. **Pros:** style and luxury; excellent service; resort facilities for bargain price. **Cons:** dark hallways and low ceilings on lower floor; often deserted and too quiet with few guests. [$] *Rooms from: $135* ✉ *American Zone* ☎ *2775–3405* 🌐 *www.casaroland.com* 🛏 *41 rooms, 6 suites* 🍽 *Breakfast.*

$$$$ RESORT 🏨 **Esquinas Rainforest Lodge.** This well-managed eco-lodge in a 35-acre nature preserve is run by Austrians who have tried to instill a sense of Teutonic order (which might be why more than 80% of the guests are from Germany and Austria). **Pros:** top-notch trails and wildlife-viewing opportunities in unique natural setting; excellent meals. **Cons:** no air-conditioning and it can get hot here; some trails are challenging, and you need to be steady on your feet; lodge is geared to nature lovers who aren't looking for luxury. [$] *Rooms from: $256* ✉ *Near the village of La Gamba, 5 km (3 miles) west of Villa Briceño turnoff* ☎ *2741–8001* 🌐 *www.esquinaslodge.com* 🛏 *14 rooms, 1 two-bedroom villa* 🍽 *All meals.*

$$ B&B/INN FAMILY 🏨 **Hotel Samoa del Sur.** Nautical kitsch at its corniest, this dockside hotel has a ship-shape bar complete with mast, a billowy sail, a mermaid figurehead, and a collection of U.S. Coast Guard caps donated by visiting personnel at the nearby Costa Rican Coast Guard Academy. **Pros:** affordable and fun; lively restaurant. **Cons:** can be lots of rambunctious

kids; noisy bar in evenings; guard dogs at night may frighten some guests. [$] *Rooms from: $85* ✉ *Main street, 1 block north of town dock* ☎ *2775–0233* 🌐 *www.samoadelsur.com* 🛏 *14 rooms* 🍴 *Breakfast.*

$$$$ ALL-INCLUSIVE Fodor's Choice ★ **Playa Nicuesa Rainforest Lodge.** Hands down, this is the best eco-lodge on the gulf, combining comfortable, upscale accommodations and great food with an emphasis on adventure on both land and sea. **Pros:** everything you need to have an active vacation; excellent food and service; idyllic setting. **Cons:** no air-conditioning; cabins are fairly open to nature, so there will be some insects outside the mosquito netting at night. [$] *Rooms from: $410* ✉ *Golfo Dulce, accessible only by boat from Golfito or Puerto Jiménez* ☎ *2258–8250 in San José, 2222–0704 in San José, 866/504–8116 in U.S.* 🌐 *www.nicuesalodge.com* 🛏 *5 cabins, 4 rooms, 1 house* 🕑 *Closed Oct. 1.–Nov. 15* 🍴 *All-inclusive.*

SHOPPING

Depósito Libre. Ticos are drawn to Golfito's duty-free bargains on such imported items as TV sets, stereos, and tires, but it's also a good place to stock up on wine and liquor. To shop at the Depósito Libre you have to register in the afternoon with your passport to shop the next morning; this means spending the night in Golfito. Shopping is sheer madness in December. The place is closed on Monday, but you can stop in and pick up your *boleta* for the next day. ✉ *North end of town* 🕑 *Tues. 8–3:30, Wed.–Sat. 8–4:30, Sun. 7–3.*

Tierra Mar. This shop has a small but excellent selection of painted wood masks made by the Boruca indigenous group. It also has one-of-a-kind local crafts, such as woven straw hats, cloth dolls, cotton purses, painted gourds, and local paintings. ✉ *Main street, next to Banana Bay Marina* ☎ *2775–1614.*

NIGHTLIFE

Happy hour is popular in Golfito, and locals and ex-pats alike need to wet their whistles. The bar at Banana Bay Marina is hopping every day from 5 to 7, when drinks are half price. The lively bar at Samoa del Sur has a mix of Ticos and foreigners, mostly of the hard-drinking, fishermen type. Friday nights there's karaoke and dance music at the huge, high-tech disco/bar by the pool at the Casa Roland Marine Resort.

Fish Hook Marina & Lodge. The curved, polished-wood bar at this marina is cooled by breezes off Golfito Bay. It's a pleasant place to meet locals, tell fish tales, and sit and watch the sunset over the bay. ✉ *Main street, south of Banana Bay* 🌐 *www.fish-hook-marina.com.*

PLAYA ZANCUDO

51 km (32 miles) south of Golfito.

Life here is laid-back and casual, centering on walking the beach, fishing, kayaking, paddle-boarding, swimming, and hanging out at the local bars and restaurants. Zancudo has a good surf break at the south end of the beach, but it pales in comparison with Playa Pavones a little to the south. Swimming is especially good two hours before or after high tide, especially at the calmer north end of the beach. The water is always warm.

"Taken on the road to Puerto Jiménez. It was such a beautiful view of Gulfo Dulce." —Photo by jamie722, Fodors.com member

If you get tired of playing in the surf and sand, you can arrange a boat trip to the nearby mangrove estuary to see birds and crocodiles. Zancudo is also home to one of the area's best sportfishing operations, headquartered at The Zancudo Lodge.

GETTING HERE AND AROUND

The road from Golfito is fully paved for the first 11 km (7 miles), but after the turnoff at El Rodeo, you'll encounter some rough patches. A bridge has finally replaced the ancient cable ferry, making the trip a little shorter, but count on 1½ hours to get here. Instead of driving, you can hire a boat at the municipal dock in Golfito for the 25-minute ride ($40 for two) or take a cheaper *collectivo* (communal) boat that leaves from Golfito's Samoa del Sur Hotel twice a week; check the schedule at the hotel because it varies throughout the year. A taxi ride from Golfito to Zancudo costs about $70, so the boat is a bargain.

Getting around Playa Zancudo doesn't take much, since there's really only one long, dusty road parallel to the beach. You can rent a bike at Cabinas Sol y Mar or Tres Amigos Supermercado, both on the main road in Zancudo, for about $10 per day.

Cabinas Los Cocos. There is water-taxi service to Golfito ($60 for up to three passengers; $20 each extra) and Puerto Jiménez ($80, up to three people) here. ⊠ *Beach road* ☎ 2776–0012.

BEACHES

Playa Zancudo. For laid-back beaching involving hammocks strung between palms and nothing more demanding than watching the sunset, you can't beat breezy Playa Zancudo, with its miles of wide, flat beach and romantic views of the Osa Peninsula across the Golfo

Dulce. The water is amazingly warm for swimming and except for local holiday times, this beach is pretty much deserted. It isn't picture-perfect: the 10 km (6 miles) of dark, volcanic sand is sometimes strewn with flotsam and jetsam. But there's a constant breeze and a thick cushion of palm and almond trees between the beach and the dirt road running parallel. Away from the beach breezes, be prepared for biting *zancudos* (no-see-ums). **Amenities:** food and drink. **Best for:** sunset; swimming; walking.

SPORTS AND THE OUTDOORS

FISHING

If you've got your own gear, you can do some good shore fishing from the beach or the mouth of the mangrove estuary, or hire a local boat to take you out into the gulf. The main edible catches are yellowfin tuna, snapper, and snook; catch-and-release fish include marlin, roosterfish, and swordfish.

Captain Ronny. Born and raised in Golfito, Captain Ronny has experience working at all the area fishing lodges. His new 27-foot boat has a big enough engine to go farther offshore fast, embarking from either Zancudo or Golfito. The daily rate is an all-inclusive $1,200 for a maximum of four fishers. ☎ *2776–0201, 8826–5439 cell phone* ✉ *golfitocr@yahoo.com.*

The Zancudo Lodge. This luxury lodge runs the biggest charter operation in the area, with 15 boats ranging in length from 28 to 36 feet, including TwinVee catamarans and a state-of-the-art Contender 32ST. A day's fishing includes gear, food, and drinks ($900–$1,500 for two), and you can arrange to be picked up in Golfito or Puerto Jiménez. ✉ *Main road, north end of town* ☎ *2776–0008* ⊕ *www.zancudolodge.com.*

KAYAKING

The kayaking is great at the beach and along the nearby Río Coto Colorado, lined with mangroves. You can also test your balance on a paddleboard over ocean waves or on the river.

Cabinas Los Cocos. Their popular tour ($50 per person, minimum three passengers) takes you for a 1½-hour motorboat ride up the Coto Colorado River, then a magical 2-hour kayak tour along a jungly mangrove channel and a relaxing paddle, moving downstream with the current, back to the river mouth. Captain Susan can identify the birds you'll see along the way. Or you can paddle a loop through the mangrove, balanced on a paddleboard. The company also rents user-friendly sit-on-top kayaks with backrests for $5 per hour, and paddleboards (with instruction) at $25 for two hours. ✉ *Beach road, north of Cabinas Sol y Mar* ☎ *2776–0012.*

WHERE TO EAT

$ ✕ **Coloso del Mar Restaurant.** Fabulous fish cakes, tasty fish burritos, and
SEAFOOD a savory fillet of sea bass with a smoky jalapeño cream sauce are a few of the delights at this screened-in porch restaurant in a bright-yellow clapboard cottage on the beach. Chicken or fish curry is popular with the locals. Attention is paid to sides, too, including creamy mashed potatoes, cheese-topped toasted garlic bread, and perfectly cooked vegetables. Beer and wine by the glass or bottle are available. Service here

is with a smile, and everything is cooked to order, so relax—you're at the beach. If you want to try the banana pancakes at breakfast, consider staying at one of the four beachfront cabins. $ *Average main: $9* ✉ *Main road, 100 m north of Soda Tranquilo* ☎ *2776–0050* ⊕ *www. colosodelmar.com* ☾ *No lunch.*

$$$
CONTEMPORARY
Fodor'sChoice
★

✕**The Gamefisher Restaurant.** Famous for its sportfishing, the Zancudo Lodge's new terrace restaurant excels in cooking fish—all caught by guest fishers that day. Mahimahi sautéed to crusty perfection on the outside and moist on the inside, might be served with a carrot-ginger broth, or over a salad of mixed greens and white beans, with a tangy citrus dressing. Carpaccio-thin slices of smoked tuna, sprinkled with finely minced garlic, capers, onions, and parsley, burst with flavor. Meat lovers can indulge in aged New York–style steaks and tender ribs. Nightly four-course dinners ($35–$45, plus tax) have a meat or fish option. There's also a regular menu with salad, shrimp, pasta, burgers (tuna or beef) and taco options for diners not hungry enough for the mulit-course dinner. Crusty, flavorful breads are baked daily. Desserts are delicious and inventive: try the caramelized *maduro* (sweet banana) à la mode with house-made *dulce de leche* (caramel) ice cream. The setting is ultra-luxe: large lanterns and candles illuminating teak tables and chairs, and throwing shadows on the impressive marlin replica suspended over the chic bar. Service is very attentive and polished. This is simply the best restaurant this remote area has ever seen, and well worth the journey and the price. It's open to the public for lunch and dinner; reservations are a must for dinner. $ *Average main: $16* ✉ *The Zancudo Lodge, north end of town* ☎ *2776–8791* ⊕ *www.zancudolodge. com* ⚐ *Reservations essential.*

$
ECLECTIC

✕**Oceano Bar & Restaurant.** This beachfront restaurant has a wide-ranging menu that's popular with locals. Choose from tropical seafood fresh from the gulf, tangy ceviche, crispy fish-and-chips, Mexican-style burritos, and made-from-scratch pizzas. For beachgoers with a sweet tooth there are homemade brownies and the only ice cream parlor in town. Watch for special theme nights when the joint is jumping. Bring your laptop and surf on their Wi-Fi connection. There are also two rooms to rent here. $ *Average main: $8* ✉ *Beach road, south of Supermercado Bellavista* ☎ *2776–0921* ⊕ *www.cabinas-costa-rica.com* ☾ *Closed Sept.–Nov.*

$
ECLECTIC

✕**Restaurant Sol y Mar.** On a breezy porch with a palm-fringed beach view, this thatch-roofed restaurant has an eclectic menu ranging from spicy quesadillas and burritos to fresh fish with an array of exotic sauces. There's a touch of Thai here, too; one of the most popular dishes is mahimahi in a coconut-curry sauce. For a change from fish, try their thick-cut pork chops slathered in a teriyaki or creamy mushroom sauce. The hearty bar food includes chicken wings, and there are barbecue specials on Monday and Friday night. Homemade desserts are decadent and delicious, including a standout carrot cake, and a key lime pie with a cinnamon cookie crust below and meringue on top. Breakfasts are huge and hearty, from healthy granola to giant burritos. Credit cards are accepted but incur an extra 5% fee. $ *Average main: $9* ✉ *Cabinas Sol y Mar, main road, south of Cabinas Los Cocos* ☎ *2776–0014.*

8

WHERE TO STAY

$$
RENTAL

🏠 **Cabinas Los Cocos.** This secluded cluster of self-catering cabins right on the beach, under palm trees swaying in the breeze, is designed for people who want to kick back and enjoy the beach. **Pros:** like having your own beach house on an idyllic beach; friendly, amusing hosts help you get the most out of your stay. **Cons:** no air-conditioning, but there are ceiling fans and ocean breezes; no phone in cabins. $ *Rooms from: $75* ✉ *Beach road, north of Cabinas Sol y Mar* ☎ *2776–0012* ⊕ *www. loscocos.com* 🛏 *4 cabins* ▭ *No credit cards* 🍽 *No meals.*

$
B&B/INN

🏠 **Cabinas Sol y Mar.** Just as the name implies, Cabinas Sol y Mar have plenty of sun and sea, as well as a beach fringed by coconut palms and apricot-color wooden cabinas with porches where you can take in the spectacular views of the Osa Peninsula. **Pros:** beach location; bargain price; lively restaurant and bar. **Cons:** no air-conditioning; bare-bones furniture; no-frills bathrooms. $ *Rooms from: $50* ✉ *Main road, south of Cabinas Los Cocos* ☎ *2776–0014* ⊕ *www.zancudo.com* 🛏 *5 cabinas, 1 house* 🍽 *No meals.*

$$$$
ALL-INCLUSIVE
Fodor'sChoice
★

🏠 **The Zancudo Lodge.** Most guests here are well-heeled, avid anglers on all-inclusive sportfishing packages, but the young owners have completely transformed this beachfront property into a top-notch luxury resort that can be enjoyed by those who have never dropped a line. **Pros:** luxurious hotel; excellent fishing boats and captains; air-conditioned, rare in these parts; Wi-Fi. **Cons:** pricey for the area; very quiet evenings since fishers go to bed early in order to rise at 5 am. $ *Rooms from: $450* ✉ *Main road, northern end of town* ☎ *2776–0008, 800/ 854–8791 in U.S.* ⊕ *www.zancudolodge.com* 🛏 *12 rooms, 4 suites* 🍽 *All-inclusive.*

PLAYA PAVONES

53 km (33 miles) south of Golfito.

Surfing is the main draw here, especially from April to September when the waves are most reliable. But the dramatic scenery, looking across the Golfo Dulce to the Osa Peninsula, along with a very laid-back vibe make it a popular destination year-round. The area is not heavily developed but there are some excellent restaurants in town, and nearby Tiskita Jungle Lodge is a birder's paradise.

GETTING HERE AND AROUND

There's no avoiding the bumpy road from Golfito to Conte, where the road forks north to Zancudo and south to Pavones. But the dirt road to Pavones is usually well graded. A public bus leaves from Golfito twice a day, and the trip takes about two hours. A taxi from the airstrip in Golfito costs upward of $90.

BEACHES

Playa Pavones. Driving along remote Playa Pavones, one of the most scenic beaches in Costa Rica, you catch glimpses through the palms of brilliant blue water, white surf crashing against black rocks, and the soft silhouette of the Osa Peninsula. This area at the southern edge of the mouth of Golfo Dulce attracts serious surfers, but also has pristine black-sand beaches and virgin rain forest. The coast is very rocky, so it's important to ask locals before surfing or swimming. One of the best places to swim is in the Río Claro, under the bridge or at the river mouth (dry season only). The town of Pavones itself is a helter-skelter collection of guest houses and sodas a few blocks from the beach. **Amenities:** food and drink. **Best for:** surfing; swimming; walking.

> **CAUTION**
>
> In the unlikely event that you are bitten by a snake, stay calm, move slowly, and try to remember what the snake looked like, to tell the clinic staff. Allow antivenom to be administered only by trained medical personnel, in case of side effects. Five hours is the window before any tissue loss. To avoid snakebites, stay on trails and wear long, loose pants; in some areas high rubber boots are recommended.

SPORTS AND THE OUTDOORS

SURFING

Pavones is famous for one of the longest waves in the world, thanks to the mouth of the Río Claro. The most consistent waves are from April to September, and that's when the surfing crowd heads down here from the Central Pacific beaches. But even at the crest of its surfing season, Pavones is tranquility central compared with the surfing hot spots farther north.

Clear River Sports & Adventures. Down by the beach, this outfit rents surfboards for $10 a day and sea kayaks for $15 a day, with a weekly rate of $75. Bicycles go for $10 the first day, $5 each following day. There are a couple of computers, plus Wi-Fi access, a library, and rooms for surfers for $25 a night. They can also arrange local tours. ✉ *Main street, north of soccer field* ☎ *2776–2016.*

8

Sea Kings Surf Shop. You can buy top-of-the-line surfboards and other gear here, along with heavy-duty sunscreen, board wax, and the latest in surfer wear. You can also rent surfboards for $15 a day and boogie boards for $10. ✉ *Main street, near Cafe de la Suerte* ☎ *2776–2015* 🌐 *www.seakingssurf.com.*

WHERE TO EAT

$ VEGETARIAN 🍴 **Café de la Suerte.** Fortunately for food lovers, the "Good Luck Café" serves truly astonishing vegetarian food, along with intriguing exotic juices and thick fruit smoothies. The homemade yogurt is a revelation: light, almost fluffy, and full of flavor, served over a cornucopia of fruits, sprinkled with the café's own granola, and mixed into refreshing fruit-flavor *lassis* (a yogurt-base drink from India). Healthful sandwiches include excellent hummus, and hot daily specials might include curried hearts of palm or authentically Italian cannelloni. Don't leave without buying a fudgy brownie or a brown-sugar oatmeal square for the road. Bring your laptop and use the Wi-Fi—the fee of $1 an hour is donated to local community projects. It's open 7 to 5. [$] *Average main: $8* ✉ *Main street, next to soccer field* ☎ *2776–2388* 🌐 *www.cafedelasuerte.com* 💳 *No credit cards* 🕓 *Closed Sun. and Oct. and Nov. No dinner.*

$$$ ITALIAN 🍴 **Ristorante Italiano La Bruschetta.** This casually chic spot within earshot of the surf serves savory bruschetta and 16 varieties of crispy, thin-crusted pizza, all made with flair by Rosella, a glamorous native of Naples who

everyone calls Lella. Her four-seasons pizza is a triumph, with thin, spicy pepperoni, flavorful ham, olives, eggplant, peppers, onion, and zucchini. Save room for the knockout gnocchi, pillow-soft dumplings made with potatoes and cheese and bathed in olive oil and rosemary. Other choices include tortelloni in cream sauce and filet mignon. Tiramisú and key-lime pie do dessert duty. Japanese lanterns add a romantic touch to the wooden tables and chairs, which are painted in sherbet colors and placed in intimate nooks. To find the place, look for the La Piña sign. [$] *Average main: $12* ✉ *Main road between Pavones and Punto Banco, north of La Ponderosa Beach and Jungle Resort* ☎ *2776–2174.*

WHERE TO STAY

$$ B&B/INN 🏨 **La Ponderosa Beach and Jungle Resort.** The world-famous Playa Pavones surf break is a 10-minute walk from La Ponderosa, the area's only beach resort and a cut above the usual surfer hangout. **Pros:** affordable rates; close to beach and town; pleasant pool and garden. **Cons:** tends to attract a younger crowd; mosquitoes love the garden when there's no breeze. [$] *Rooms from: $70* ✉ *Road betweeen Pavones and Punta Banco, on the beach* ☎ *2776–2076, 954/771–9166 in U.S.* 🌐 *www.laponderosapavones.com* 🛏 *6 rooms, 1 two-bedroom house* 💳 *No credit cards* 🍴 *Multiple meal plans.*

$$$$ ALL-INCLUSIVE Fodor's Choice ★ 🏨 **Tiskita Jungle Lodge.** This last-outpost lodge is one of the premier eco-lodges in the Southern Zone, attracting nature lovers, bird-watchers, yoga enthusiasts, and people who want to get away from it all in comfort. **Pros:** unrivaled wildlife viewing and birding; splendid natural isolation; friendly, knowledgeable owners. **Cons:** some steep walks to cabins in forest; no air-conditioning; not a lot of privacy in joined double and triple cabins, which share verandas. [$] *Rooms from: $320* ✉ *On road between Pavones and Punta Banco, 6 km (4 miles) south of Playa Pavones* ☎ *2296–8125* 🌐 *www.tiskita.com* 🛏 *17 rooms arranged in 4 single cabins, 3 doubles, 1 triple, 1 quadruple* 🕒 *Closed June–Nov.* 🍴 *All-inclusive.*

NIGHTLIFE

La Manta. This is where the action is at night during high surfing season, March to September. Surfers can watch their own filmed surf sessions projected onto a huge screen while refueling with burgers, burritos, and lots of beer and tropical cocktails. ✉ *Near the beach, Playa Pavones* ☎ *No phone* 🌐 *www.la-manta.com* 🕒 *Closed Oct.–Mar.*

THE OSA PENINSULA

If you came to Costa Rica seeking wilderness and adventure, this is it. You'll find the country's most breathtaking scenery and most abundant wildlife on the Osa Peninsula, a third of which is protected by Corcovado National Park. You can hike into the park, take a boat, or fly in on a charter plane. Corcovado also works for day trips from nearby luxury nature lodges, most of which lie within private preserves. And complementing the peninsula's lush forests and pristine beaches is the surrounding sea, with great fishing and some surfing.

There are two sides to the Osa: the gentler Golfo Dulce side, much of it accessible by car, albeit along rocky roads; and the much wilder and dramatic Pacific side, which is accessible only by boat, by plane, or by hiking a sublimely beautiful coastal trail.

PUERTO JIMÉNEZ

130 km (86 miles) west of Golfito, 364 km (226 miles) from San José.

You might not guess it from the rickety bicycles and ancient pickup trucks parked on the main street, but Puerto Jiménez is the largest town on the Osa Peninsula and the main gateway to the Osa Peninsula and Corcovado National Park. This one-iguana town has a certain frontier charm, with an interesting, funky edge provided by eco-lodge owners and backpacking nature lovers. A bayside promenade has added a touch of class, with benches where you can admire the gulf views. At night, elegant street lamps light your way to the restaurants along the waterfront.

This is the last civilized outpost on the peninsula. Heading south, you fall off the grid. That means no public electricity or telephones. So make your phone calls, send your email, get cash, and stock up on supplies here. Be prepared for the humidity and mosquitoes—Puerto Jiménez has plenty of both.

If you need a refreshing dip, head southeast of the airport to Playa Platanares, where there is a long stretch of beach with swimmable, warm water. At low tide, you can also walk out onto a narrow, pebbly beach beside the town dock.

The main reason to come to Puerto Jiménez is to spend a night before or after visiting Corcovado National Park, since the town has the best access to the park's two main trailheads and an airport with flights from San José. It's also the base for the *colectivo* (public transport via pickup truck) to Carate.

GETTING HERE AND AROUND

Since the drive is grueling and long, most visitors fly to Puerto Jiménez from San José. Driving from Golfito is a little easier these days thanks to the newly paved road all the way from Rincón to Puerto Jiménez, though the road between Chacarita and Rincón still has the occasional, jarring pothole. A better option from Golfito is the motorboat launch. A rickety old passenger launch ($3 each way) leaves Golfito at 11:30 am every day and takes 90 minutes. Faster motorboat launches ($6) make the trip in 45 minutes, leaving Golfito at 7, 10:15, 1:15, 2:30, and 3:15. Going in the opposite direction, the fast launches to Golfito leave Puerto Jiménez at 6, 8:45, 11:30, and 2, and 4:15. The schedule changes frequently, so check before you head to the dock. Be sure to arrive 15 minutes early, because the boats often depart as soon as they are full. You can also hire private taxis at the city dock in Golfito for about $90, and they can drop you off in Puerto Jiménez or at your lodges.

A colectivo taxi—actually an open truck with bench seats—leaves Puerto Jiménez daily at 6 am and 1:30 pm for Cabo Matapalo and Carate. At $8 it's the cheapest way to travel, but the trip is along a bumpy road and is not recommended in rainy season (May through December). It leaves from a stop 200 meters west of the Super 96.

Once you arrive in Puerto Jiménez, you can get around on foot or bicycle.

ESSENTIALS

Bank/ATM Banco Nacional ⊠ *Main street, south of Super 96* ☎ *2735–5020.*

Hospital Public Clinic and First Aid Station ⊠ *Main street, west of post office* ☎ *2735–5063.*

Internet CaféNet El Sol ⊠ *Main street, south of soccer field* ☎ *2735–5719* ☾ *Daily 7 am–10 pm.*

Pharmacy Farmacia Hidalgo ⊠ *Main street, north of Cabinas Marcellina* ☎ *2735–5564* ☾ *Mon.–Sat. 8–7:30.*

Post Office Correo ⊠ *Main street, west side of soccer field.*

Rental Cars Solid Car Rental ⊠ *Road running parallel to airstrip* ☎ *2735– 5777* ⊕ *www.solidcarrental.com.*

Visitor Information National Parks Service Headquarters. The National Parks Service office has information about hiking trails in Corcovado National Park. The office is open weekdays 8 to 4. ⊠ *Road running parallel to airport* ☎ *2735–5036.*

EXPLORING

Finca Köbö. Go right to the source to see how cacao grows and becomes chocolate at this organic cacao plantation. The two-hour tour includes a naturalist-guided walk around the roughly 50-acre property, which includes gardens, orchards, and both primary and secondary forest. The highlight of the tour is the tasting—dipping an array of tropical fruits grown on-site into a pot of homemade chocolate fondue. ⊠ *Off main road, 18 km (11 miles) west of Puerto Jiménez, La Palma* ☎ *8398–7604* ⊕ *www.fincakobo.com* ✉ *$32* ☾ *Dec.–Sept., tours at 9 and 2.*

SPORTS AND THE OUTDOORS

TOUR OPERATORS

Osa Tropical. Isabel Esquivel runs the best general tour operation on the peninsula. Whatever travel question you ask the locals, they will usually reply, "Ask Isabel." Along with arranging flights, ground transportation, hotel rooms, guided tours, and car rentals, Osa Tropical is the radio communications center for some of the off-the-grid Osa lodges and tour operators. ⊠ *Main street, across from Banco Nacional* ☎ *2735–5062* ⊕ *www.osa-tropical.com.*

BIKING

Main Street Rent-a-Bike. If you want to cruise around town like the locals do, you can rent a bike here for $10 a day. ⊠ *150 m north of Banco Nacional, main street* ☎ *No phone.*

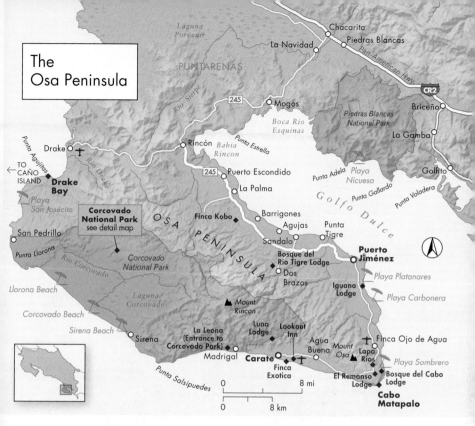

The Osa Peninsula

BIRD-WATCHING

The birding around the Osa Peninsula is world renowned, with more than 400 species. Endemic species include Baird's trogon, yellow-billed cotinga, whistling wren, black-cheeked ant tanager, and the glorious turquoise cotinga. There have even been sightings of the very rare harpy eagle in the last couple of years.

Fodor's Choice ★ **Bosque del Río Tigre Lodge.** The best English-speaking birding guides are Liz Jones and Abraham Gallo, who run Bosque del Río Tigre Lodge, just west of Puerto Jiménez. They lead birding trips all around the peninsula, including visits to Corcovado National Park. ⊠ *12 km (7½ miles) northwest of Puerto Jiménez, Dos Brazos del Tigre* ⊕ *www. osaadventures.com.*

Rincón. One of the best spots on the peninsula to find a rare yellow-billed cotinga is beside the bridge over the river at Rincón. Make sure to get there before 7 am. ⊠ *Main road, 40 km (25 miles) north of Puerto Jiménez, Rincón.*

Continued on page 484

Scuba Diving
and *Snorkeling*

by Gillian Gillers

For snorkelers and scuba divers, Costa Rica is synonymous with swarms of fish and stretches of coral that hug the country's 910 miles of coastline. Submerge yourself in crystalline waters and enter another world, with bull sharks, brain coral, and toothy green eels. The variety and abundance of marine life are awe-inspiring.

WHEN AND WHERE TO GO

Swimming with the turtles on Cocos Island

The Pacific tends to be clearer than the Caribbean, and the fish are bigger and more abundant. Northern waters are generally best May through July, after winds die down and the water turns bluer and warmer. The southern Osa Peninsula is popular during the dry season, from January to April.

The Caribbean, known for its diverse coral and small fish, is good for beginners because it has less surge. The best months are September and October, when the ocean is as calm and flat as a swimming pool. April and May also offer decent conditions, but steer clear during the rest of the year, when rain and strong waves cloud the water.

CAHUITA Mounds of coral and a barrier reef (dubbed Long Shoal) run from Cahuita to Punta Mona, along 25 kilometers of Caribbean coastline. Arches, tunnels, and canyons in the reef form a playground for small fish, crabs, and lobsters. Even though sediment and waste water have damaged much of the coral, the healthy sections are dense, colorful, and delightfully shaped. Gentle pools right off the beach allow for some of the country's best snorkeling.

ISLA DEL COCO (Cocos Island) Some 295 nautical miles and a 36-hour sail from Puntarenas, Cocos Island is one of the world's premier sites for advanced divers. Visibility is good all year, and hammerhead and white-tipped reef sharks are the main attractions.

ISLA DEL CAÑO (Caño Island) With visibility of 20 to 80 feet, strong currents and very changeable conditions, Caño is best suited for advanced divers. The huge schools of large fish and potential shark sightings are the attractions here. Novice snorkelers can frolic in the Coral Garden, a shallow area on the north side of this biological reserve.

ISLA SANTA CATALINA (Santa Catalina Island) Known for sightings of golden cownose rays and giant mantas, these big rocks near Playa Flamingo have spots for beginner and advanced divers. Snorkelers should head to shallow waters near the beach.

GOLFO DE PAPAGAYO (Papagayo Gulf) This northern gulf has Costa Rica's highest concentration of snorkel and dive shops. Calm, protected waters make it the best place for beginner divers on the Pacific.

ISLA MURCIÉLAGO (Bat Island) Located inside Santa Rosa National Park, this cluster of rocks is good for advanced divers and famous for its fearsome bull sharks.

DIVING SCHOOLS

The beach towns on both coasts are riddled with diving schools and equipment rentals shops. If you're a first-timer and plan to go diving just once, taking a basic half-day class isn't difficult, and it will allow you to dive up to 40 feet with an instructor. A three- or four-day certification course gets you a lifetime license and allows you to dive up to 130 feet and without a guide. Outfitters can point snorkelers towards pristine spots. *We list only the most reputable schools under the Sports and Outdoors section throughout every chapter.* Look for outfitters that are PADI (Professional Association of Diving Instructors) trained or give PADI certifications.

IN CASE OF AN EMERGENCY

DAN (Divers Alert Network) is an organization that provides emergency medical advice and assistance for underwater diving injuries. Doctors, emergency medical technicians, and nurses are available 24 hours a day to answer questions. If you would like to discuss a potential diving-related health problem, contact the non-emergency DAN switchboard (☎ *800/446–2671*) or check out their website (⊕ *www. diversalertnetwork.org*). Their emergency telephone line is ☎ *919/684– 9111* for international calls.

SNORKELING TIPS

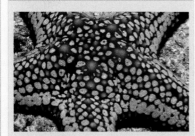

Sea Star in Santa Catalina Island

■ Never turn your back on the ocean, especially if the waves are big.

■ Ask about rip tides before you go in.

■ Enter and exit from a sandy beach area.

■ Avoid snorkeling at dusk and never go in the water after dark.

■ Wear lots of sunscreen, especially on your back and butt cheeks.

■ Don't snorkel too close to the reef. You could get scratched if a wave pushes you.

■ Be mindful of boats.

DIVING TIPS

■ Make sure your instructor is certified by a known diving agency, such as PADI.

■ Stick to the instructor's guidelines on depth and timing.

■ Never hold your breath.

■ Never dive or snorkel (or swim or surf) alone. Also, never touch the coral or the fish—this is for your own good and the good of the marine life.

■ Don't drink alcohol before diving.

■ Never dive while taking medicine unless your doctor tells you it's safe.

■ Diving can be dangerous if you have certain medical problems. Ask your doctor how diving may affect your health.

■ If you don't feel good or if you are in pain after diving, go to the nearest emergency room immediately.

■ Don't fly for 12 hours after a no-decompression dive, even in a pressurized airplane.

CREATURES OF THE SEA

Underwater exploration is as close to visiting another world as you can come. Here you'll encounter some of the most bizarre creatures on this planet.

Pillar Coral

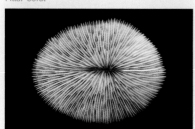

Calcareous skeleton of the coral

CORAL

Coral tends to cluster in colonies of identical individuals. The most diverse coral (at least 31 types) in Costa Rica can be found on the Caribbean coast, near Puerto Viejo. Like other plant-looking sea animals, many types of coral reproduce by spawning.

SEAHORSE

These magical little creatures are hard to spot because they are often camouflaged within black coral trees, with their tails curled around the branches. They are bottom feeders and usually found in 10-meter deep water.

FIREWORM

Look but don't touch! These stunning, slow-moving worms have poisonous bristles that flare out when disturbed. Getting stung is no fun; it will burn and itch for hours afterwards. Try taking the bristles out with adhesive tape and dabbing the infected area with alcohol.

GREEN EEL

Eels have a reputation for being vicious and ill-tempered, but they're really shy and secretive. Eels will only attack humans in self-defense. Though they may accidentally bite the hand that feeds them, it's just because they can't see or hear very well.

SPONGES

Common in the Caribbean, these strange animals don't have nervous, digestive, or circulatory systems. Instead, they rely on a constant water flow for food and oxygen, and to remove wastes. To reproduce, some sponges release both sperm and eggs into the water and hope the two collide.

Orange sponge

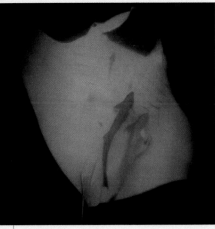

BOTTLENOSE DOLPHIN
Everybody loves dolphins. In some parts of the world they work with local fishermen, driving schools of fish into the nets and then eating the fish that escape. They've also been known to help injured divers to the surface.

GIANT MANTA RAY
Commonly spotted near Isla Santa Catalina, mantas often hang out at reef-side "cleaning stations" where small fish (like wrasses and angelfish) congregate. These cleaner fish feed in the manta's gills and over its skin, simultaneously scrubbing it free of parasites and dead skin.

BARRACUDA
Barracudas are not aggressive towards humans, but are vicious predators. Their diet consists of all sorts of fish. Large barracudas, when gorged, will even try to herd a school of fish into shallow water so that they can guard over them and eat them off when they're hungry again.

PARROTFISH
Parrotfish are named for their external set of tightly packed teeth that look just like a parrot's beak. These strange looking teeth are used to rasp the algae off of coral and rock, thus feeding themselves and keeping the coral clean and healthy.

HAMMERHEAD SHARK
These sharks are distinctive not only for their strangely shaped, mallet-like head but also because they're one of the few creatures in the animal kingdom (besides humans and pigs) that can tan. If they spend too much time in shallow waters, they'll become noticeably darker. In 2007, scientists also discovered that hammerheads can reproduce asexually through a rare process called parthenogenesis: female hammerheads can actually develop an embryo without ever having been fertilized.

FISHING

Puerto Jiménez is a major fishing destination, with plenty of billfish and tuna, snapper and snook, almost all year, with the exception of June and July, when things slow down. The best offshore fishing is between December and April. Charter captains follow the fish up and down the Pacific coast, so ask at your hotel for their recommendation of the best fishing boats currently in town.

Tropic Fins Adventures. Head out onto the Golfo Dulce or the open ocean on a sportfishing adventure aboard a custom-built 27-foot Ocean Runner, equipped with all the latest fishing equipment. Captain Cory, a transplanted Canadian, has been fishing these waters for more than a decade. The boat comfortably accommodates four anglers. Half-day excursions are $650; full-day trips, which can last up to nine hours, depending on how the fish are biting, are $950. Package tours include flight from San José, plus lodging, meals, and fishing. ⊠ *Playa Platanares* ☎ *8834–6079* ⊕ *www.tropicfins.com.*

HIKING

Osa Aventura. This company specializes in multiday hiking adventures led by Mike Boston, an ebullient tropical biologist who sounds like Sean Connery and looks like Crocodile Dundee. Hikers stay in way-off-the-beaten-track rustic lodges or in basic cabins in Corcovado National Park. Boston also employs bilingual biologists to lead hikes and conduct scientific research projects in which visitors can sometimes participate. ☎ *2735–5670, 8372–6135* ⊕ *www.osaaventura.com.*

Osa Wild. The focus here is on sustainable tourism, including horseback-riding treks, nighttime insect tours, and low-impact, low-cost biologist-guided tours into Corcovado National Park. ⊠ *Main street, north of Banco Nacional* ☎ *2735–5848* ⊕ *www.osawildtravel.com.*

Tigre Sector. If you have a sturdy vehicle, it's just a 30-minute drive west to the village of Dos Brazos and the Tigre Sector of Corcovado Park. There is a park office along the way where you can check with rangers on trail conditions. Few hikers come to this pristine part of the park because it's difficult to access, which means you'll likely have it to yourself. ⊠ *road to Dos Brazos del Tigre, off main highway between Rincón and Puerto Jiménez.*

HORSEBACK RIDING

FAMILY **Río Nuevo Horse Tour.** The wildest horse trails in the area are at this remote lodge west of Puerto Jiménez. Rides along the river and up onto scenic forested ridges last from three to seven hours and include transportation there and back and snacks and drinks for $65 per person. Most hotels and tour agencies can reserve a spot for you, including Osa Tropical and Osa Wild. ⊠ *12 km (7½ miles) west of Puerto Jiménez* ☎ *2735–5062.*

Beach views at Drake Bay on the Osa Peninsula

KAYAKING

FAMILY Puerto Jiménez is a good base for sea-kayaking trips on the calm Golfo Dulce and for exploring the nearby mangrove rivers and estuaries.

Aventuras Tropicales Golfo Dulce. Alberto Robleto has amassed an impressive fleet of kayaks with excellent safety equipment at Aventuras Tropicales Golfo Dulce. There are snorkeling, dolphin-watching, and bird-watching tours, but the most popular is the three-hour mangrove tour ($45). A three- to five-day tour (four-person minimum) teaches survival skills in the tropical forest, including fishing, camping, and cooking with coconuts and wild herbs. Outrigger canoe trips ($20 for three hours, minimum six paddlers) are offered at sunset when dolphins are often jumping. All tours longer than three hours include a picnic lunch. ✉ *Road to Playa Platanares, southeast of airport* ☎ *2735–5195* ⊕ *www.aventurastropicales.com.*

La Sirena Adventure Boat Tour. If you just want to get out onto the water, this company offers 5½-hour tours on a covered boat. You can explore the gulf, look for dolphins, do some snorkeling, or try plane boarding. Lunch and snacks are included ($60 per person, minimum six people). For $25 extra, you can visit the Osa Wildlife Sanctuary, a refuge for orphaned and injured wildlife. The boat sails at 7:30 am. ✉ *Cabinas Jiménez, on the waterfront* ☎ *2735–5090* ⊕ *www.cabinasjimenez.com.*

WHERE TO EAT

$ ╳ **Corcovado Marisquería, Restaurante y Bar.** If you're hungry for a bargain
SEAFOOD and want to enjoy a little local atmosphere, join the anglers, families, and backpackers at this tiny restaurant that has spilled over into a large waterfront garden. Wooden tables are nattily covered with blue and white tablecloths and are shaded by palm trees. The menu is truly vast, with more

than 40 *bocas* (small bites) and dozens of *platos fuertes* (main courses) that run the gamut from seafood rice to whole lobsters to sirloin steaks. You can make a meal of one or two bocas—say, clams in garlic butter and a cup of tangy ceviche or a shrimp omelet with salad—and walk away for less than $5. Or spend $20 on lobster. Wash it down with the only draft beer served in town, and gaze out at Golfo Dulce. An added bonus: there's free Wi-Fi and it is open 11 to 11 daily. $ *Average main: $8* ⊠ *On the waterfront, east of city dock* ☎ 2735–5659, 8898–2656.

$$ ✕ **Il Giardino a la Playa.** Northern
ITALIAN   Italian cooking, in the form of tasty pastas and excellent salads, is alive and well at this popular garden restaurant. It sits on the waterfront, taking advantage of the views and fresh breezes off the gulf. Fresh fish and sushi round out the menu, as well as barbecued meats. Sadly, wood-oven pizzas are not the restaurant's forte, and service can be painfully slow. But sitting under a lime-green umbrella, enjoying the breeze and the view, isn't a hardship. $ *Average main: $12* ⊠ *Waterfront promenade, near the public dock* ☎ 2735–5129.

$ ✕ **Mail It Pizza.** This cheerful, family-run café comes with an authentic
ITALIAN   pedigree: the Colovattis are from the Italian city of Trieste, and the pizza is simply the best in the area. The crust is toasty crisp on the outside and chewy inside, topped with high-quality fixings and sauce made fresh every day. Calzones and homemade pastas are also on the menu, but pizza reigns supreme. Eat in the dining room—the fresh blue-and-white decor is reminiscent of the owners' hometown on the Adriatic Sea—or order takeout and bring your meal back to your hotel. The restaurant's rather odd name refers to the fact that this building used to be the post office. It's open 4 pm to 10 pm in high season and closed Tuesday in low season. $ *Average main: $9* ⊠ *Main street, across from soccer field* ☎ 2735–5483 ▭ *No credit cards* ⊘ *No lunch.*

$ ✕ **Restaurante Carolina.** This simple alfresco restaurant in the heart of
COSTA RICAN   Puerto Jiménez is a meeting place for locals and every foreigner in town, making it a good place to pick up information. It serves decent *comida típica*, salads, pasta, reliably fresh seafood, and excellent fruit smoothies. It's open 7 am to 10 pm daily. $ *Average main: $8* ⊠ *Main street* ☎ 2735–5185.

NEED A BREAK?

The best way to beat the heat in Puerto Jiménez is to make a stop at the Jade Luna Ice Cream cart on Main Street, in front of the farmacia (Monday–Saturday 10–6). The luscious array of refreshingly different dairy-free sorbets, made with coconut milk and coconut water, includes creamy ginger and tropical fruit. The signature flavor of the decadently delicious ice creams, packed into personal-size little tubs complete with spoon, is Aztec chocolate, made with local cacao spiced with chili pepper and cinnamon.

WHERE TO STAY

Playa Platanares is only about 6 km (4 miles) outside of Puerto Jiménez, but lodgings there have a different feeling from those in town because they are on a lovely and quiet beach. Bosque del Río Tigre is also outside of town, but inland, in a forested area beside a river, on the northeastern edge of Corcovado Park.

$$$$ RESORT Fodor's Choice ★ **Bosque del Río Tigre Lodge.** You can't get any closer to nature than this off-the-grid lodge, famous for its excellent birding and hiking trails, wedged between forest and the banks of the Río Tigre. **Pros:** a birder's paradise; great hiking trails; fabulous food. **Cons:** shared bathroom and outdoor showers; limited electricity; must love living very close to nature. [$] *Rooms from: $324* ✉ *12 km (7½ miles) northwest of Puerto Jiménez, Dos Brazos del Tigre* ☎ *8705–3729 leave messages only* 🌐 *www.bosquedelriotigre.com* 🛏 *4 rooms with shared baths, 1 ensuite cabin* 🕒 *Closed Sept. and Oct.* 🍴 *All meals.*

$ B&B/INN **Cabinas Jiménez.** Overlooking the harbor, these air-conditioned rooms set in a lush garden are the most comfortable in town, and have the best water views. **Pros:** water views; air-conditioning; some rooms with pleasant, private terraces. **Cons:** rooms are on the small side; no food service; some rooms have no view. [$] *Rooms from: $50* ✉ *On the waterfront, west of town dock* ☎ *2735–5090* 🌐 *www.cabinasjimenez.com* 🛏 *14 rooms* 🍴 *No meals.*

$ B&B/INN **Cabinas Marcelina.** Two Italian sisters run the best bargain hotel in Puerto Jiménez. **Pros:** very affordable; pleasant oasis in middle of town; safe parking. **Cons:** rooms are quite small; fan-only rooms are cheap but can be hot and sticky. [$] *Rooms from: $45* ✉ *Main street, north side of church* ☎ *2735–5007, 2735–5286* 🛏 *8 rooms* 💳 *No credit cards* 🍴 *No meals.*

$$ B&B/INN FAMILY **Danta Corcovado Lodge.** Follow the giant tapir footprint signs to this rustic lodge, reminiscent of an Adirondacks camp, within hiking distance of the western edge of Corcovado National Park. **Pros:** proximity to Corcovado National Park; comfortable rusticity; affordable rates. **Cons:** no air-conditioning; close encounters of the insect kind in cabins. [$] *Rooms from: $108* ✉ *Road from La Palma to Guadalupe, 3 km (2 miles) northwest of La Palma, La Palma* ☎ *2735–1111* 🌐 *www.dantalodge.com* 🛏 *3 rooms, 1 suite, 5 cabins sleeping 3–8 people* 🍴 *Breakfast.*

$$$$ B&B/INN Fodor's Choice ★ **Iguana Lodge.** If a long stretch of deserted beach is your idea of heaven, check out this idyllic lodge with two-story cabins set in an exquisite botanical garden. **Pros:** top-of-the-line accommodation and food in tranquil tropical setting; complimentary kayaks; breakfast and dinner included in casita rooms. **Cons:** no air-conditioning; club rooms are small and can be noisy; be prepared to get friendly with an insect or two. [$] *Rooms from: $370* ✉ *Playa Platanares, 5 km (3 miles) south of airport* ☎ *8848–0752* 🌐 *www.iguanalodge.com* 🛏 *8 rooms, 4 cabins, 1 house* 🍴 *Some meals.*

NIGHTLIFE

Pearl of the Osa. With pulsing salsa music and a pasta buffet, this beachfront bar attracts a big crowd on Friday nights, starting at 7. There's a mix of ages, and the music is loud and a lot of fun. Tuesday nights there's a beach barbecue with tiki torches and tables right on the beach. Come at 5:30 to watch the sun set; it's a good idea to reserve ahead. ✉ *Playa Platanares, next to Iguana Lodge* ☎ *8848–0752.*

SHOPPING

Fodor'sChoice **Jagua Arts & Crafts.** The area's fin-
★ est arts and crafts are displayed
in this impressive shop, including exquisitely detailed bird carvings made by a family in nearby
Rincón;   stained-glass   mosaic
boxes, mirrors, and trivets made
by a San José artist; and serious art
ceramics. A gallery features mixed-
media nature paintings. The shop
is famous for local artisan Karen
Herrera's exquisite glass-bead jewelry. There's an excellent selection
of natural-history field guides and
books, and you can also stock up
on locally made organic chocolate.
✉ *Road beside airport.*

CORCOVADO NATIONAL PARK

The crown jewel of the country's national park system, Corcovado is
the ultimate in off-the-grid adventure. The only way to see it is on foot,
with a naturalist guide to interpret the incredible biodiversity that has
made this park the most rewarding and challenging natural experience
in the country.

GETTING HERE AND AROUND

The easiest way to visit remote Corcovado National Park is by boat
from Drake Bay or on foot from Carate. A 20-minute boat trip from
Drake Bay gets you to the San Pedrillo entrance. The boat trip from
Drake Bay to Sirena takes 45 minutes to one hour. From Carate airfield, where the collective taxi from Puerto Jiménez stops, it's about a
45-minute walk along the beach to La Leona park entrance.

For getting to Corcovado from elsewhere in the country, the most
expensive option—but also the easiest way to get into the heart of the
park—is flying in on a small charter plane through **Alfa Romeo Aero Taxi**
(✉ *Puerto Jiménez Airport* ☎ *2735–5178*).

Less expensive is hiring a taxi in Puerto Jiménez ($90) to take you to
the Los Patos trailhead or the first crossing of the Río Rincón (where
you can hike a few miles upriver to the trailhead). The cheapest, and
least convenient, option is to take an 8 am bus from Puerto Jiménez
to La Palma (less than $1). You can also take a taxi ($70) to the Los
Patos entrance.

EXPLORING

Fodor'sChoice **Corcovado National Park.** This is the last and largest outpost of virgin
★ lowland rain forest in Central America, and it's teeming with wildlife.
Visitors who tread softly along the park's trails may glimpse howler,
spider, and squirrel monkeys, peccaries (wild pigs), poison-dart frogs,
scarlet macaws, and, very rarely, jaguars and tapirs.

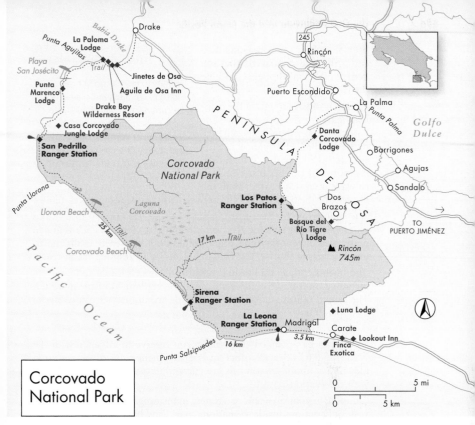

Corcovado
National Park

Most first-time visitors to Corcovado come on a daylong boat tour from Drake Bay or hike in from Carate. But to get to the most pristine, wildlife-rich areas, you need to walk, and that means a minimum of three days: one day to walk in, one day to walk out, and one day inside.

Ranger stations are officially open from 8 am to 4 pm daily, but you can walk in almost any time as long as you pay in advance. ⚠ **At this writing, a new park policy requires every visitor entering the park to be accompanied by a certified guide. If this policy stands, count on paying around $50 per person per day for a guide.** ✉ *Corcovado National Park* 🔅 *$15.*

SPORTS AND THE OUTDOORS

If your reason for coming to the Osa Peninsula is Corcovado National Park, choose a lodge that has resident naturalist guides. On the Drake Bay and gulf sides of the park, all the lodges arrange guided trips into Corcovado, most with their own guides. Tour operators in Puerto Jiménez and Drake Bay also run guided trips in the park.

HIKING

There are two main hiking routes to Corcovado. One begins near La Palma, at the Los Patos entrance. There is one beach trail to the park, an easy 45-minute beach walk from Carate to the La Leona entrance. The former beach trail from San Pedrillo to La Sirena has been closed for safety reasons. You can still take a boat to the San Pedrillo station, though, and hike the trails there.

Hiking is always tough in the tropical heat, but the forest route (Los Patos) is cooler than the beach hike to La Leona. Although it is possible to hike La Leona at high tide, it's more difficult because you have to walk on a slope rather than the

> **WARNING**
>
> Swimming on the beach near Sirena is not advised because of rip currents and bull sharks. Also steer clear of the brackish Río Sirena, home to crocs, bull sharks, and snakes. The only advisable swimming area is the Río Claro.

flat part of the beach. The hike between any two stations takes all day.

The hike from La Leona to Sirena is about 16 km (10 miles) and requires crossing one big river mouth and a stretch of beach that can be crossed only at low tide. Some guides do it very early in the morning, just before sunrise, to avoid the blistering heat along the beach.

The 14-km (9-mile) trail from Los Patos to Sirena is lovely and forested, including an 8-km (5-mile) walk along the verdant Río Rincón Valley. The Sirena ranger station has great trails around it that can easily fill a couple of days.

WHERE TO EAT AND STAY

Meals can be arranged at Sirena if you reserve in advance with the National Parks Service office in Puerto Jiménez. It's always a good idea to ask about what meals are currently available when you make your reservation.

Camping in your own tent or sleeping in the ranger station in Sirena are your only options inside the national park, and both take planning and preparation. You must reserve in advance, especially during the peak season. Reservations for the entire year can be made starting January 1 each year. The 26 very basic bunks at the ranger station cost $8 per night. Meals, decent but relatively expensive, are $20 for breakfast, $25 for lunch or dinner. Prices are slated to rise in 2015. Camping costs $4 per person per night. Bring your own sheets, a pillow, and a good mosquito net. Bring your own tent, gear, and food. The maximum stay is four nights and five days.

To make reservations you must fill out a request via email or in person at the park office in Puerto Jiménez, make a deposit in the park's bank account, then email, fax, or present the receipt in person to the park office. Park rules are constantly changing, so your best bet is to book a tour with a local outfitter who can make reservations for you.

DID YOU KNOW?

Corcovado has 13 ecosystems within its boundaries, ranging from mangroves and swamps to lowland rain forest. The park also has more forest giants—trees that stand 50 to 80 meters (165 to 264 feet) high—than anywhere in Central America.

CABO MATAPALO

21 km (14 miles) south of Puerto Jiménez.

The southern tip of the Osa Peninsula, where virgin rain forest meets the sea at a rocky point, retains the kind of natural beauty that people travel halfway across the world to experience. From its ridges you can look out on the blue Golfo Dulce and the Pacific Ocean, sometimes spotting whales in the distance. The forest is tall and dense, with the highest and most diverse tree species in the country, usually draped with thick lianas.

The name Matapalo refers to the strangler fig, which germinates in the branches of other trees and extends its roots downward, eventually smothering the supporting tree by blocking the sunlight. Flocks of brilliant scarlet macaws and troops of monkeys are the other draws here.

GETTING HERE AND AROUND

If you drive one hour south from Puerto Jiménez, be prepared for a bumpy ride and a lot of river crossings. In rainy season cars are sometimes washed out along rivers to the ocean. Most hotels arrange transportation in 4WD taxis or their own trucks. The cheapest—and the roughest—way to travel is by colectivo ($8), which leaves Puerto Jiménez at 6 am and 1:30 pm. Buses do not serve Cabo Matapalo.

SPORTS AND THE OUTDOORS

TOUR OPERATORS

Everyday Adventures. Andy Pruter is an engaging, experienced outfitter who will take you on anything-but-everyday, adrenaline-pumping adventures: rappelling down waterfalls ($85), climbing up a 185-meter (70-foot) strangler fig vine ($55), and rain-forest hiking ($45). Or you can go all out with a combination rappelling and climbing tour for $120. ✉ *Cabo Matapalo* ☎ *8353–8619* 🌐 *www.psychotours.com.*

8

SURFING

On the eastern side of Cabo Matapalo, waves break over a platform that creates a perfect right, drawing surfers from far and wide, especially beginners.

Pollo Surf School. Local surf expert Oldemar (aka Pollo) Fernandez offers daily lessons at Pan Dulce Beach at his Pollo Surf School. Expect to pay $55 per person for a group lesson, or $110 for private lessons. ✉ *Cabo Matapalo* ☎ *8366–6559* 🌐 *www.pollosurfschool.com.*

WHERE TO STAY

$$$ RESORT Fodor's Choice ★

🏨 **Bosque del Cabo.** Atop a cliff at the tip of Cabo Matapalo, this lodge has unparalleled views of the Golfo Dulce merging with the endless blue of the Pacific, as well as hundreds of acres of primary forest, home to plenty of monkeys and peccaries, as well as the occasional puma and ocelot. **Pros:** luxurious bungalows; fabulous trails and guides; congenial atmosphere among guests at cocktail hour and dinner. **Cons:** steep trail to beach and back; very small pool; limited electricity supply; rates do not include $30 round-trip transfer fee per person. [$] *Rooms from: $270* ✉ *Road to Carate, 22 km (14 miles) south of Puerto Jiménez, Cabo Matapalo* ☎ *2735–5206, 8389–2846 at lodge* 🌐 *www.bosquedelcabo.com* 🛏 *12 cabins, 4 houses* 🍴 *All meals.*

$$$
B&B/INN
Fodor's Choice
★

El Remanso. This quiet, sophisticated retreat sits in a forest brimming with birds and wildlife, 122 meters (400 feet) above a beach studded with tide pools. **Pros:** gorgeous natural setting; jungle views; easy access to beach. **Cons:** no air-conditioning; no hair dryers; steep drive down to lodge. $ *Rooms from: $320* ✉ *Main road to Carate, 22 km (14 miles) south of Puerto Jiménez, Cabo Matapalo* ☎ *2735–5569 office, 8814–5775* ⊕ *www.elremanso.com* ⤳ *4 rooms, 2 suites, 6 cabinas* ❖❘ *All meals.*

$$$$
ALL-INCLUSIVE
Fodor's Choice
★

Lapa Ríos. Hands down the first and still the most spectacular eco-resort in Costa Rica, Lapa Ríos has won numerous awards for its mix of conservation and comfort in a huge private nature reserve that brims with wildlife. **Pros:** excellent, professional service; Tico-flavor atmosphere with well-trained, local employees; delicious typical and international dishes. **Cons:** many steps to climb to farther cabins; steep trail to beach, but there is a shuttle service; no phone or Internet. $ *Rooms from: $660* ✉ *Road to Carate, 20 km (12 miles) south of Puerto Jiménez, Cabo Matapalo* ☎ *2735–5130* ⊕ *www.laparios.com* ⤳ *16 cabinas* ❖❘ *All-inclusive.*

CARATE

60 km (37 miles) west of Puerto Jiménez.

Carate is literally the end of the road. The black volcanic-sand beach stretches for more than 3 km (2 miles), with surf that's perfect for boogie boarding and body surfing but not for serious surfing or safe swimming. The main entertainment at the beach is watching the noisy but magnificent scarlet macaws feasting on almonds in the beach almond trees that edge the shore. Carate has no phone service; a couple of lodges have satellite phones and iffy Wi-Fi and cell-phone connections.

GETTING HERE AND AROUND

The road from Matapalo to Carate covers 40 suspension-testing km (25 miles); there is a bridge over the Agua Buena River and the road is periodically graded and relatively smooth, but that can all change with one drenching wet season. You're better off taking the colectivo from Puerto Jiménez (➪ *Getting Here and Around in Puerto Jiménez, above*). Or give yourself a break and fly via charter plane to Carate's small airport, which has been upgraded recently; arrange flights through your lodge. From here it's 3 km (2 miles), roughly a 40-minute walk along the beach to La Leona ranger station entrance to Corcovado National Park. In rainy season (May to December) it is sometimes impossible to cross the raging Río Carate that separates the landing strip from the beach path to the park, and you may end up stranded on either side. Parking at the store in Carate is $5 per day.

SPORTS AND THE OUTDOORS

Activities here revolve around Corcovado National Park and its environs. Hiking, horseback riding, canopy tours, and other adventures must be organized through your hotel.

"This is the view from the deck of the Toucan cabina at Bosque del Cabo." —Photo by Monica Richards, Fodors.com member

WHERE TO STAY

$$ B&B/INN **Finca Exotica.** A garden paradise that lives up to its name, this combination organic farm, botanical garden, and sophisticated eco-lodge is an otherworldly experience. **Pros:** gorgeous gardens; exotically delicious food; charming hosts. **Cons:** no air-conditioning; must enjoy being in a totally natural setting. [$] *Rooms from: $150* ✉ *Main road, east of Carate Airstrip* ☎ *506/8828–0817 in Puerto Jiménez* 🌐 *www.fincaexotica.com* 🛏 *5 cabins, 7 tents, 1 house* 🕒 *Closed Oct.* 🍴 *All meals.*

8

$$$ B&B/INN **Lookout Inn.** This lively, barefoot inn—shoes come off at the bottom step—is set on a precipitous hillside with a spectacular panorama that includes a colorful garden and scarlet macaws foraging in the almond trees that line the beach. **Pros:** proximity to beach and access on foot to Corcovado Park; excellent food; party atmosphere. **Cons:** very steep trip to lodge and down to beach; limited communication with outside world; cabins have more privacy than lodge rooms. [$] *Rooms from: $250* ✉ *Main road to Carate, east of Carate landing strip* ☎ *2735–5431, 757/644–5967 in U.S.* 🌐 *www.lookout-inn.com* 🛏 *3 rooms, 4 cabins, 2 cabins with shared bath* 🍴 *All meals.*

$$$$ B&B/INN Fodor's Choice ★ **Luna Lodge.** Perched on a sublime mountaintop overlooking rain forest and ocean, Luna Lodge is the ultimate in yoga retreats, but its ultimate charm is its end-of-the-road remoteness and wild setting. **Pros:** scenic setting for peace, yoga, and therapeutic massage; comfortable lodging and healthful food; excellent birding; free Wi-Fi. **Cons:** extremely steep road up to lodge; beach is quite a hike. [$] *Rooms from: $350* ✉ *2 km (1 mile) up a steep, partially paved road from Carate* ☎ *2206–5859, 2206–5860, 888/760–0760 in U.S/Canada* 🌐 *www.lunalodge.com* 🛏 *8 bungalows, 3 rooms, 5 tents* 🍴 *All meals.*

Snorkelers' Paradise

Most of uninhabited 2½-square-km (1-square-mile) **Caño Island Biological Reserve** is covered in evergreen forest that includes fig, locust, and rubber trees. Coastal Indians once used it as a burial ground, and the numerous bits and pieces unearthed here have prompted archaeologists to speculate about pre-Columbian long-distance maritime trade. But virtually nothing remains of indigenous interest. The main attraction is the ocean around the island, offering advanced scuba diving and snorkeling. The snorkeling is best around the rocky points flanking the island's main beach; if you're a certified diver, you'll want to explore Bajo del Diablo and Paraíso, where you're guaranteed to encounter thousands of good-size fish, and if you're lucky, white-tip, nurse, and trigger sharks. As of this writing, visitors are once again allowed to land on the island, to hike a trail that climbs to the island's summit. But no picnicking is allowed on the beach and there are no toilet facilities owing to runoff that was damaging the surrounding coral.

The only way to get to the island, 19 km (12 miles) due west of the Osa Peninsula, is by boat arranged by your lodge or a tour company. Ocean Safaris and Jinetes de Osa tour companies in Drake Bay run half-day trips here, as do tour companies in Dominical, Uvita, and Sierpe.

DRAKE BAY

18 km (11 miles) north of Corcovado, 40 km (25 miles) southwest of Palmar Sur, 310 km (193 miles) south of San José.

This is castaway country, a real tropical adventure, with plenty of hiking and some rough but thrilling boat rides to get here. The rugged coast that stretches south from the mouth of the Río Sierpe to Corcovado probably doesn't look much different from what it did in Sir Francis Drake's day (1540–96), when, as legend has it, the British explorer anchored here. Small, picture-perfect beaches with surf crashing against dark volcanic rocks are backed by steaming, thick jungle. Nature lodges scattered along the coast are hemmed in by the rain forest, which is home to troops of monkeys, sloths, scarlet macaws, and hundreds of other bird species.

The cheapest accommodations in the area can be found in the town of Drake, which is spread out along the bay. A trio of upscale nature lodges—Drake Bay Wilderness Resort, Aguila de Osa Inn, and La Paloma Lodge—are clumped near the Río Agujitas on the bay's southern end. They all offer comprehensive packages, including trips to Corcovado and Caño Island. Lodges farther south, such as Punta Marenco Lodge and Casa Corcovado, run excursions from even wilder settings.

GETTING HERE AND AROUND

The fastest way to get to Drake Bay is to fly directly to the airstrip. You can also fly to Palmar Sur and take a taxi to Sierpe and then a thrilling, if bumpy, boat ride to Drake Bay. From the airport, it's a 25-minute taxi ride to Sierpe; small, open boats leave at low tide, usually 11 to 11:30 am for the one-hour trip to Drake. There is also a late-afternoon

Boat trips are a must to explore the wild Osa Peninsula.

boat service. Captains will often stop along the way to view wildlife in the river mangroves. Many lodges arrange boat transportation from Drake Bay or Sierpe. From Rincón you can drive to Drake on a 30-km (19-mile) (sometimes) graded dirt road, but only in dry season when the rivers are low enough to cross. Buses leave Puerto Jiménez for La Palma about every two hours from 6 am to 8 pm, connecting in La Palma with buses to Drake Bay at 11:30 am and 4:30 pm. Buses leave Drake at 4 am and 1 pm for La Palma, to connect with buses to either Puerto Jiménez or San José. These bus schedules often change, so be sure to check with a local source. The drive from San José to Drake is scenic, but an exhausting seven hours long.

SPORTS AND THE OUTDOORS

TOUR OPERATORS

Jinetes de Osa. Experienced guides run popular diving tours ($110 for a two-tank dive, plus $20 for gear), plus snorkeling ($75), and dolphin-watching tours ($105), as well as a canopy tour ($45) with some interesting bridge, ladder, and rope transitions between platforms. ⊠ *West side of bay* ☎ *2231–5806* ⊕ *www.costaricadiving.com.*

FAMILY

Fodor's Choice

★

Night Tour. When you're on the Osa Peninsula, the wildest nightlife is outdoors. Join entomologist Tracie Stice (also known as the Bug Lady) and herpetologist Gianfranco Gomez on their night tour of insects, bats, reptiles, and anything else creeping or crawling around at night. Tracie is a wealth of bug lore, with riveting insect stories from around the world. Top-of-the-line Petzl headlamps help you see in the dark. Tours are $35 per person. Book ahead because these nightly tours, at 5:30 and 7:30 pm, are popular. ☎ *8701–7356* ⊕ *www.thenighttour.com.*

Understanding Costa Rica's Climate

Although you may associate the tropics with rain, precipitation in Costa Rica varies considerably, depending on where you are and when you're here. This is a result of the mountainous terrain and regional weather patterns. A phenomenon called rain shadow—when one side of a mountain range receives much more than the other—plays an important ecological role in Costa Rica. Four mountain ranges combine to create a continental divide that separates the country into Atlantic and Pacific slopes; because of the trade winds, the Atlantic slope receives much more rain than the Pacific. The trade winds steadily pump moisture-laden clouds southwest over the isthmus, where they encounter warm air or mountains, which make them rise. As the clouds rise, they cool, lose their ability to hold moisture, and eventually dump most of their liquid luggage on the Caribbean side.

During the rainy season—mid-May to December—the role of the trade winds is diminished, as regular storms roll off the Pacific Ocean and soak the western side of the isthmus. Though it rains all over Costa Rica during these months, it often rains more on the Pacific side of the mountains than on the Atlantic. Come December, the trade winds take over again, and while the Caribbean prepares for its wettest time of the year, hardly a drop falls on the western side until May.

Climate variation within the country results in a mosaic of forests. The combination of humidity and temperature helps determine what grows where; but whereas some species have restricted ranges, others seem to thrive just about anywhere. Plants such as strangler figs and bromeliads grow all over Costa Rica, and animals such as the collared peccary and coati—a long-nose cousin of the raccoon—can pretty much live wherever human beings let them. Other species have extremely limited ranges, such as the mangrove hummingbird, restricted to the mangrove forests of the Pacific coast, and the volcano junco, a gray sparrow that lives only around the highest peaks of the Cordillera de Talamanca.

Ocean Safaris. Local marine conservationist and dive master Shawn Larkin offers eco-sensitive tours doing just about anything you can think of in or above the water, including his signature Super Ocean Safari ($150 per person, four-person minimum), which can include underwater photography, snorkeling, free-diving, scuba-diving, sea-kayaking, or just staying on the boat as he locates dolphin mega-pods. Private tours, for up to eight people, cost $750. Larkin can also arrange an aerial photo tour for up to four passengers ($800 for one hour), flying in a Cessna with the door open, over the ocean in search of dolphins and other bird's-eye photo opportunities. ⊠ *Drake Bay* ☎ *8702–1248 text messages* ⊕ *www.costacetacea.com.*

WHERE TO STAY

$$$$

B&B/INN

⌂ **Aguila de Osa Inn.** No longer only a sportfisher's dream lodge, Aguila de Osa has newly renovated, luxurious, high-ceilinged rooms with handsome, hardwood interiors, king-size beds, and all-new, glass-brick and granite bathrooms that will please the fussiest traveler. **Pros:** great for fishing enthusiasts; elegant lodge and rooms. **Cons:** steep climb to rooms; no air-conditioning but rooms have good air circulation, ceiling fans, and screens; some verandas are shared, not private. [$] *Rooms from: $500* ✉ *South end of town, at mouth of Río Agujitas* ☎ *2296–2190 in San José, 8840–2929 lodge, 866/924–8452 U.S. toll-free* 🌐 *www.aguiladeosa.com* 🛏 *11 rooms, 2 suites* 🍴 *All meals.*

> **WORD OF MOUTH**
>
> "We enjoyed our stay very much at La Paloma Lodge in Drake Bay. They make everything so easy. The food was good. Our guide to Corcovado was fantastic—we learned so much from him! We saw as many animals on their property as we saw in the park. We did the Caño Island snorkeling trip. We knew the snorkeling would not be comparable to some of the Caribbean Islands, but we did see quite a few fish and sharks."
>
> —wego

$$$$ ALL-INCLUSIVE Fodor'sChoice ★ 🏨 **Casa Corcovado Jungle Lodge.** This hilltop jungle lodge has it all: exquisite bungalows in the closest location to Corcovado National Park, extensive gardens, excellent tours and guides, and first-class service. **Pros:** unrivaled location adjoining national park; excellent tours, service, and facilities; reasonably priced. **Cons:** an adventure to get here: be prepared for a thrilling, wet landing; no air-conditioning; steep road to beach. [$] *Rooms from: $350* ✉ *Northern border of Corcovado* ☎ *2256–3181, 888/896–6097 in U.S.* 🌐 *www.casacorcovado.com* 🛏 *14 bungalows* ⏲ *Closed mid-Sept.–mid-Nov.* 🍴 *All-inclusive.*

$$$$ ALL-INCLUSIVE 🏨 **Copa de Arbol Beach & Rainforest Resort.** The newest kid on the beach block, Copa de Arbol is ultra-luxurious, ultra-cool (comes with air-conditioning), and ultra-expensive, but it is idyllically sited between crashing ocean surf and dense jungle, right on the Coastal Path walking trail that connects Drake Bay to Corcovado. **Pros:** comfort, hotel-like luxury in the jungle; idyllic location. **Cons:** accessible only by boat (with a wet landing) or on foot; boat transportation and tours not included, making price high, relative to other area lodges; lots of steps to negotiate. [$] *Rooms from: $600* ✉ *Along Coastal Path, 1 beach north of Playa Caletas* ☎ *8935-1212* 🌐 *www.copadearbol.com* 🛏 *9 luxury cabins, 2 deluxe duplex suites* 🍴 *All-inclusive.*

$$$ B&B/INN FAMILY 🏨 **Drake Bay Wilderness Resort.** Between the river and the ocean, this breezy resort has wide-open views of Drake Bay and the most kid-friendly grounds, with lots of flat, open space for romping, a saltwater swimming pool, and rocky tidal pools to explore. **Pros:** great location; family- and elderly friendly and affordable; good food; free laundry service and free kayaks. **Cons:** not a lot of privacy in cabins. [$] *Rooms from: $250* ✉ *Southern end of bay, at mouth of Río Agujitas* ☎ *2775–1716* 🌐 *www.drakebay.com* 🛏 *20 rooms, 3 tents* 🍴 *All meals.*

$$ B&B/INN 🏨 **Jinetes de Osa.** The most comfortable and reasonably priced place to stay in the village of Drake, this small bay-side hotel with a casual open-air restaurant has simple rooms with tile floors and hot-water showers. **Pros:** convenient location; affordable rates; adventuresome, active clientele. **Cons:** standard rooms are smallish with no air-conditioning; access is on foot, since the tide washes right up to the lodge steps. [$] *Rooms from: $100* ✉ *West side of bay* ☎ *2231–5806 in San José, 2775–3232 lodge* 🌐 *www.jinetesdeosa.com* 🛏 *12 rooms* 🍴 *Breakfast.*

8

$$$$
B&B/INN
Fodor's Choice
★

La Paloma Lodge. Sweeping ocean views, impeccably appointed accommodations, and lots of tropical-foliage privacy make this lodge the area's most romantic. **Pros:** idyllic tropical setting with ocean views and easy access to beach; privacy; great service; interesting guests from all over the world. **Cons:** steepish climbs to some ranchos; no air-conditioning or screens in ranchos, but mosquito nets available on request. $ *Rooms from: $600* ⊠ *On Drake Bay, near Drake Bay Wilderness Resort* ☎ *2239–0954 office in San José, 2775–1684 lodge* ⊕ *www.lapalomalodge.com* ⬋ *4 rooms, 7 ranchos* ☉ *Closed mid-Sept.– mid-Nov.* ❚◎❚ *All meals.*

$$
ALL-INCLUSIVE

Punta Marenco Lodge. This rustic lodge has the best location on the Pacific side of the Osa Peninsula, with South Seas island–style thatch-roof cabins perched on the spine of a ridge overlooking the sea. **Pros:** castaway-island remoteness; trails are as good as those in Corcovado National Park; reasonable all-inclusive price. **Cons:** very rustic; steep climb uphill to lodge; limited electricity and contact with outside world. $ *Rooms from: $130* ⊠ *Beachfront directly east of Caño Island, 6 km (4 miles) south of Drake village* ☎ *2292–2775 for reservations, 2294–8947* ⊕ *www.lodgepuntamarenco.com* ⬋ *19 cabinas* ❚◎❚ *All-inclusive.*

TORTUGUERO AND THE CARIBBEAN COAST

WELCOME TO TORTUGUERO AND THE CARIBBEAN COAST

TOP REASONS TO GO

★ **Dolphin-watching:** Bottlenose, tucuxi, and Atlantic spotted dolphins ply the southern Caribbean coast.

★ **Food and flavors:** Leave *gallo pinto* (rice and beans) behind in favor of mouthwatering *rondón* (meat or fish stew) or *caribeño* (Caribbean) rice and beans, stewed in coconut milk.

★ **Music:** Mix reggae and calypso with your salsa. Rhythms waft in from the far-off Caribbean islands; and homegrown musicians are making names for themselves, too.

★ **Sportfishing:** World-class tarpon and snook attract serious anglers to the shores off Tortuguero National Park.

★ **Turtles:** People from around the world flock to the northern Caribbean for the annual nesting of four species.

1 The Sarapiquí Loop. The Sarapiquí Loop circles Braulio Carrillo National Park, rare for its easy-to-access primary rain forest.

2 Northern Lowlands. The Northern Lowlands have little to offer tourists in their own right, but are close to Braulio Carrillo Park and rafting-trip put-in points. The region can be done as a long day trip from San José as well.

3 Tortuguero. The northern Caribbean coast encompasses the coastal jungles and canals leading to and through Tortuguero National Park. Boat and air travel are the only ways to reach this roadless region.

4 **Southern Caribbean Coast.** The southern Caribbean coast stretches south from port-of-call Limón to Panama. Towns along the coast have an Afro-Caribbean vibe—some are more backpackerish than others. Beaches are fringed with forest, and waters are rough. Surfers make the trip for Salsa Brava.

GETTING ORIENTED

Costa Rica's Caribbean coast is sometimes called its Atlantic coast, so as not to confuse tourists looking for the white sand and clear blue waters of the Caribbean Islands. This Caribbean is different, with sands in shades of brown and black, waters that are rough and murky (but ideal for surfing), dense jungle, heavy and frequent rain, and a less sophisticated, laid-back approach to tourism. It is beautiful and fascinating in its own way, but it's definitely not St. Barts.

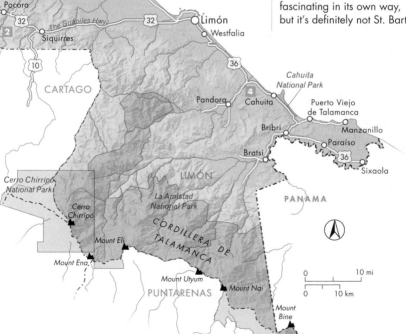

TORTUGUERO NATIONAL PARK

At various times of the year, four species of sea turtles—green, hawksbill, loggerhead, and giant leatherback—lumber up the 35 km (22 miles) of beach to deposit their eggs for safekeeping.

In 1975 the Costa Rican government established Tortuguero National Park (Parque Nacional Tortuguero) to protect the sea turtle population, which had been decimated after centuries of being aggressively hunted for its eggs and carapaces. This is the best place in Costa Rica to observe these magnificent creatures' nesting and hatching rituals. Still, despite preservation efforts, less than 1% of the hatchlings will make it to adulthood.

Turtles may be the name of the game here, but keep your eyes peeled for nonturtle species, too: tapirs, jaguars, anteaters, ocelots, howler monkeys, white-faced capuchin monkeys, three-toed sloths, collared and white-lipped peccaries, coatis, and blue morpho butterflies also populate the park. You can wander the beach independently when the turtles aren't nesting, but riptides make swimming dangerous, and shark rumors persist. *(See page 526 for more information.)*

BEST TIME TO GO

The July-through-October nesting season for the green turtle is Tortuguero's most popular time to visit. It rains here (a lot!) year-round, so expect to get wet no matter when you go. February through April and September and October are a tad drier.

FUN FACT

One of nature's mysteries is how turtles find their way back to the same beach years later. It's thought that the sand leaves a biological imprint on the turtle hatchlings during their scurry to the sea, which directs females to return here years later to nest.

BEST WAY TO EXPLORE

BIRD-WATCHING AND WILDLIFE

This is a birder's dream destination. Some of the rarer species you'll find here include the snowy cotinga, palm warbler, and yellow-tailed oriole. Waterbirds and herons abound. On a recent foray, members of the Birding Club of Costa Rica were treated to a close-up view of a wide-eyed rufescent tiger-heron chick sitting in his nest, squawking impatiently for food. You'll also see iguanas, caimans, and sloths. Bird-watching and wildlife spotting sometimes collide: while watching two beautiful agami herons feeding on a muddy bank, birders were shaken up by the sudden splash of a crocodile attacking the herons. Happily, the herons were quicker off the mark than the birders were!

BOAT RIDES

It's not quite *The African Queen,* but a boat ride along the narrow vine-draped canals here is close. Once you're off the main canal, the specially designed, narrow tour boats glide relatively quietly—using mandated electric motors—and slowly, which makes for better wildlife spotting and fewer waves that erode the lagoon banks. Another alternative is to rent a kayak and go at your own speed along the canals.

TOURS

Most visitors opt for a fully escorted tour with one of the big lodges, because you're looked after from the moment you're picked up at your San José hotel until you're dropped off a day or two or seven later. All include a couple of standard tours of the park in their package prices. It's entirely possible to stay at a smaller in-town place and make à la carte arrangements yourself. No matter which way you go, your park tour will be on foot or by boat. Remember: you'll find no four-wheeled vehicles up here.

TOP REASONS TO GO

Luxury in the Jungle
Don't let tales of Tortuguero's isolation dissuade you from making a trip. No question: the place is remote. But the lodges up here package everything (overnight lodging, meals, tours, and, best of all, guided round-trip transport) into one price in true "leave the driving to them" fashion. You won't lift a finger.

Plane or Boat Only
Whoever coined the old adage "Getting there is half the fun" might have had Tortuguero in mind. Plane and boat are the only ways to get to this no-road sector of Costa Rica. If you have the time, the fully escorted boat trips to and from the jungle give you a real Indiana Jones experience.

Turtles
Tortuguero takes its name from the Spanish word for turtle (*tortuga*), and here you'll get the chance to observe the nesting and hatching of four species of sea turtle, and to ponder one of nature's amazing rituals.

CAHUITA NATIONAL PARK

In a land known for its dark-sand beaches, the coral-based white sand of Cahuita National Park (Parque Nacional Cahuita) is a real standout.

The only Costa Rican park jointly administered by the National Parks Service and a community, it starts at the southern edge of the village of Cahuita and runs pristine mile after pristine mile southward. Whereas most of the country's protected areas tender only land-based activities, this park entices you offshore as well.

Roughly parallel to the coastline, a 7-km (4-mile) trail passes through the forest to Cahuita Point. A hike of a few hours along the trail—always easiest in the dry season—lets you spot howler and white-faced capuchin monkeys, coatimundis, armadillos, and raccoons. The coastline is encircled by a 2½-square-km (1-square-mile) coral reef. The park was first created to protect this reef. You'll find superb snorkeling off Cahuita Point, but sadly, the coral reef is slowly being killed by sediment, intensified by deforestation and the erosive effects of the 1991 earthquake that hit the coast. *(See page 546 for more information.)*

BEST TIME TO GO

As is the case on this coast, you can expect rain here no matter what the time of year. February through April and September and October are drier months, and offer the best visibility for snorkeling. (Those are the least desirable months if you're here to surf.)

FUN FACT

When Costa Rica began charging admission to national parks, residents successfully requested an exemption, fearing that such charges would harm the local economy. Your admission fee to this park is voluntary at the town entrance.

BEST WAY TO EXPLORE

BEACHING IT

The waves here are fabulous for bodysurfing along the section of beach at the Puerto Vargas entrance. This wide swath of shoreline is also great for strolling, jogging, or just basking in the Caribbean sun—be careful of riptides along this stretch of coast. The safest swimming is in front of the camping area.

CYCLING

Cycling makes a pleasant way to see the park in the dry season. Seemingly everybody in Cahuita and Puerto Viejo de Talamanca rents bicycles. (The southern entrance to the park is close enough to Puerto Viejo that it could be your starting point, too.) The park trail gets muddy at times, and you run into logs, river estuaries, and other obstacles.

HIKING

A serious 7-km (4-mile) hiking trail runs from the park entrance at Kelly Creek all the way to Puerto Vargas. Take a bus or catch a ride to Puerto Vargas and hike back around the point in the course of a day. Remember to bring plenty of water, food, and sunscreen.

SNORKELING

Tour operators in Cahuita will bring you to a selection of prime snorkeling spots offshore. If you want to swim out on your own, the best snorkeling spot is off Punta Vargas at the south end of the park. Along with the chance to see some of the 500 or so species of tropical fish that live here, you'll see some amazing coral formations, including impressive elk horn, majestic blue stag horn, and eerie yellow brain corals. When the water is clear and warm, the snorkeling is great. But that warm water also appeals to jellyfish—if you start to feel a tingling sensation on your arms or legs, make a beeline for the shore. Each little sting doesn't hurt much, but accumulated stings can result in a major allergic reaction in some people.

TOP REASONS TO GO

Easy Access
With one of its two entrances sitting in "downtown" Cahuita, access to the park is a snap. But ease of access does not mean the place is overrun with visitors. Fortunately, this is no Manuel Antonio.

Lots of Lodging
Closeness to Cahuita and Puerto Viejo de Talamanca and their spectrum of lodging options means you'll have no trouble finding a place to stay that fits your budget. You can even camp in the park if you're up for roughing it.

Snorkeling
Costa Rica's largest living coral reef just offshore means the snorkeling is phenomenal here. Watch for blue parrot fish and angelfish as they weave their way among equally colorful species of coral, sponges, and seaweeds. Visit during the Caribbean coast's two mini-dry seasons for the best visibility.

9

ECO-LODGES IN THE CARIBBEAN

Year-round rainfall begets year-round greenery on the Caribbean coast. You can count on lushness here when the rest of Costa Rica's landscape turns dusty during its dry season.

Not only does Costa Rica's Caribbean region host a different culture than the rest of the country, but its landscape is entirely different, too. Things are verdant all year, and that gives the eastern portion of the country a more tropical feel than the rest of Costa Rica. Development has been slow to come to the coast—anyone over the age of 20 well remembers the days of few roads, no phones, and no television. For you, that means far fewer visitors than along north and central Pacific coasts and a far more authentic experience since the environment is better preserved and the local culture respected. *Small* is the watchword for tourism around here—always has been and always will be. Developers do float occasional trial balloons about international megatourism projects in this region, but they get shot down quickly by the folks here who do not want their Caribbean coast to turn into the Pacific coast, thank you very much.

GOOD PRACTICES

Stay at locally owned lodgings. That's easy in the Caribbean, since the international chains are nowhere to be found here. Smaller lodgings that support the local economy are the universal norm. A stay here means that you are supporting those communities, too.

Consider taking public or semipublic transportation when visiting the Caribbean. Cahuita and Puerto Viejo de Talamanca have good bus and shuttle service; your own two feet, bicycles, and taxis make it easy to get around once you arrive. Of course, a Tortuguero visit means you leave the transportation to someone else. There's no other choice.

TOP ECO-LODGES IN THE CARIBBEAN

ALMONDS & CORALS, GANDOCA-MANZANILLO WILDLIFE REFUGE

Almonds & Corals scatters its comfortable platformed bungalows unobtrusively throughout its forest property along the coast and connects them with each other and to its restaurant, reception, and the beach by softly lighted paths. That and the myriad environmentally themed activities conducted by local guides really do give that "get away from it all" experience with a bit of rustic luxury. *(Full hotel review on page 563.)*

CASA MARBELLA, TORTUGUERO

Most visitors to Tortuguero opt for a stay at one of the big all-inclusive lodges lining the canals outside the village. Yet our favorite in-town lodging provides a far more intimate Tortuguero experience with one-on-one nature tours, rather than big groups, for just a fraction of the cost. Canadian owner and naturalist Daryl Loth is a knowledgeable and well-respected figure in the area. Though onetime outsiders, the folks at Casa Marbella have become arguably the town's biggest boosters, working closely with people here to develop sustainable, nonintrusive tourism that will benefit the entire community. We like and appreciate this "transplanted foreigner" model. *(Full hotel review on page 531.)*

RAINFOREST ADVENTURES, BRAULIO CARRILLO NATIONAL PARK

Although the site is best known for its famous aerial tram, there is accommodation here. The park is one of the Caribbean region's premier attractions, and staying here lets you enjoy the place after the day-trippers have left. The nine unobtrusive cabins are so inconspicuously tucked away that few people even know they exist. In an effort to minimize impact, food is locally grown, and electricity shuts off after 9 pm. Of course, the rates include the full complement of the site's eco-theme activities.

BIOGEM

In 2009, the nonprofit Natural Resources Defense Council (NRDC) named the entire country one of its BioGems, a designation the New York–based environmental crusader usually reserves for a single site or species. In doing so, NRDC recognizes the country's wealth of biodiversity and its fragile status. The organization has pledged to work with the Costa Rican government in areas of reforestation and development of renewable energy technology. (With approximately 99% of Costa Rica's energy coming from hydroelectric and wind power, the country already does an impressive job in that latter regard.) Caribbean residents know NRDC well. The organization worked closely with people in the region at the grassroots level to block attempts to turn the southern Caribbean coast over to offshore oil exploration. Such drilling would have damaged the coast's fragile mangroves, sand beaches, and coral reefs. After many years, the oil companies' proposals have, thankfully, been put to rest for good.

9

By Jeffrey Van Fleet

The tourist brochures tout the country's Caribbean coast as "the other Costa Rica." Everything about this part of Costa Rica seems different: different culture, different history, different climate, and different activities. Expect different prices, too. Your travel dollar goes further here than elsewhere in the country. This region was long ago discovered by European adventure seekers—you're quite likely to hear Dutch, German, and Italian spoken by the visitors here—but is much less known in North American circles.

The ethnic mix differs markedly here, as it does all along the Caribbean coast of Central America. The region was first settled by the British, and then throughout the 19th century, by the descendants of Afro-Caribbean slaves who came to work on the banana plantations and construct the Atlantic railroad. That makes the Caribbean coast the best place in the country to find English speakers, although the language is disappearing as Spanish takes over.

It is rainier here than in other parts of Costa Rica, and the rain is distributed pretty evenly year-round without a distinct dry season—though October (when the rest of Costa Rica is getting deluged with rain) is the driest month. The region will never draw the typical fun-in-the-sun crowd that frequents the drier Pacific coast, but it does offer a year-round forested lushness and just as many activities at a more reasonable price.

PLANNING

WHEN TO GO
HIGH SEASON: FEBRUARY TO APRIL
Climate is the Caribbean's bugaboo and will forever prevent it from becoming the same high-powered tourist destination that the northern Pacific coast is. (Frankly, we consider that to be a blessing.) The Caribbean lacks a true dry season, though February to April could be called

a "drier" season, with many sunny days and intermittent showers. Yet, despite weather patterns that differ from the rest of Costa Rica, places here charge high-season rates from December to April, just as they do elsewhere in the country. Prices skew a bit lower in the Caribbean, though, than elsewhere in Costa Rica.

LOW SEASON: MAY TO AUGUST AND DECEMBER TO JANUARY

The heaviest rains (and periodic road closures) come in December and January, high season elsewhere in Costa Rica. During the rainiest months visitors are fewer. May through August sees rain, too, although not quite as much. The popularity of this part of the country among European travelers means that July and August become mini–high seasons here. Tortuguero sets its own seasons, with higher prices the norm during the prime turtle-watching months of July through September.

SHOULDER SEASON: SEPTEMBER TO NOVEMBER

Want in on a little secret? When the rest of Costa Rica settles into the soggiest time of year, the sun comes out and the weather begins to dry up in this part of the country. The Caribbean coast makes the perfect refuge from the insufferably wet months of September and October elsewhere.

PLANNING YOUR TIME

Attractions near Guápiles and Siquirres lend themselves to long day trips from San José. Tour operators also have whirlwind daylong Tortuguero trips from San José. We recommend you avoid these—the area really deserves two or, ideally, three days. Choose a single Caribbean destination and stay put if you have just a few days. (Cahuita and Puerto Viejo de Talamanca are ideal for that purpose.) If you have a week, you can tackle the north and south coasts.

GETTING HERE AND AROUND

AIR TRAVEL

You can fly daily from San José to the airstrip in Tortuguero (TTQ) via Nature Air. Nature Air also flies Thursday and Saturday to the small airport in Bocas del Toro, Panama (BOC).

Contact **Nature Air** ✉ *Aeropuerto Juan Santamaría, San José* ☎ *2299–6000* ⊕ *www.natureair.com.*

BUS AND SHUTTLE TRAVEL

Grupo Caribeños buses, some snazzy double-deckers, connect San José's Gran Terminal del Caribe with Guápiles, Siquirres, and Limón. Autotransportes MEPE, which has a lock on bus service to the south Caribbean coast, has a reputation for being lackadaisical, but is really quite dependable. Its San José buses depart from the capital's Terminal Atlántico Norte. MEPE drivers and ticket sellers are accustomed to dealing with foreigners; even if their English is limited, they'll figure out what you want. MEPE occasionally runs extra buses to Cahuita and Puerto Viejo de Talamanca during the high season. Bus fares to this region are reasonable. From San José, expect to pay $2.50 to Guápiles, $6 to Limón, $10 to Cahuita, $11 to Puerto Viejo de Talamanca, and $15 to Sixaola and the Panamanian border.

If you prefer a more private form of travel, consider taking a shuttle. Gray Line Tourist Bus has daily service that departs from many San José hotels for Cahuita and Puerto Viejo de Talamanca. Tickets are $45 and must be reserved at least a day in advance. Comfortable air-conditioned Interbus vans depart from San José hotels daily for Cahuita and Puerto Viejo de Talamanca. Reserve tickets ($47) a day in advance.

Bus Contacts Autotransportes MEPE ⊠ *C. 9 and Avda. 12, Barrio La Merced, San José* ☎ *2257–8129* ⊕ *www.mepecr.com.* **Gray Line Tourist Bus** ☎ *2220– 2126* ⊕ *www.graylinecostarica.com.* **Grupo Caribeños** ⊠ *C. Ctl. and Avda. 13, Barrio Tournón, San José* ☎ *2222–0610* ⊕ *www.grupocaribenos.com.* **Interbus** ☎ *2283–5573* ⊕ *www.interbusonline.com.*

CAR TRAVEL

With the exception of Tortuguero, this region is one of the country's most accessible. The southern coast is a three- to four-hour drive from San José, over mostly decent roads (by Costa Rican standards), and public transportation is frequent and reliable. Gas stations are plentiful between Guápiles and Limón, but their numbers dwindle to two between Limón and Puerto Viejo de Talamanca. The northern Caribbean coast is another story: the total absence of roads means you have to arrive by plane or boat. Most travelers go with a tour booked through one of the large Tortuguero lodges.

If you're driving here, remember that fog often covers the mountains in Braulio Carrillo National Park, north of San José, by early afternoon. Cross this area in the morning if you can. Always exercise utmost caution on the portion of highway that twists and turns through the park. Check road conditions before you set out; occasional landslide closures through Braulio Carrillo necessitate leaving San José from the southeast, passing through Cartago, Paraíso, and Turrialba, then rejoining the Caribbean Highway at Siquirres, a route that adds an extra tiring 90 minutes onto your trip.

HEALTH AND SAFETY

All the standard tropical precautions apply when traveling in the Caribbean region. This is a very warm part of the country, so carry water, wear a hat, and use plenty of sunscreen. The undertow is dangerous along virtually the entire coast, making swimming risky. Wear mosquito repellent in low-lying coastal areas, where a few cases of dengue have been reported.

MONEY MATTERS

ATMs are becoming more common in this part of the country, although we recommend, if possible, stocking up on cash in San José. You'll find cash machines in Guápiles, Guácimo, Siquirres, and several in Limón. Puerto Viejo de Talamanca has two; Cahuita has one; Tortuguero has none. Remember: Many smaller places—there are a lot of those here in the Caribbean—do not accept credit cards.

RESTAURANTS

The many open-air dining spots out here provide you with that ultimate tropical dining experience, with Puerto Viejo de Talamanca offering one of Costa Rica's most varied dining scenes. Think seafood, chicken, coconut, and fruits in the Caribbean. Restaurateurs take advantage of the bounty of the land and sea in this part of the country.

HOTELS

The high-rise, glitzy resorts of the Pacific coast are nowhere to be found in the Caribbean. The norm here is small, independent lodgings, usually family owned and operated. Fewer visitors in this region mean plenty of decent lodging at affordable prices most of the year. But tourism *is* growing, so it's risky to show up without reservations. Surprisingly few places here have air-conditioning, but sea breezes and ceiling fans usually provide sufficient ventilation. Smaller places frequently don't take credit cards; those that do may give discounts if you pay with cash. *Hotel reviews have been shortened. For full information, visit Fodors.com.*

WHAT IT COSTS IN DOLLARS			
$	**$$**	**$$$**	**$$$$**
Restaurants	Under $10	$10–$15	$16–$25	over $25
Hotels	Under $75	$75–$150	$151–$250	over $250

Restaurant prices are the average cost of a main course at dinner or, if dinner is not served, at lunch. Hotel prices are the lowest cost of a standard double room in high season.

PACKAGE TOURS

One of Costa Rica's most remote regions is also one of its prime tourist destinations. No roads lead to Tortuguero on the northeast coast, so plane or boat is your only option. If you don't want to bother with logistics, consider booking a package tour with one of the lodges. It will include all transport from San José, overnights, meals, and guided tours. Prices look high at first, but considering all you get, they are quite reasonable. Other types of regional tours are also available: **Horizontes** (☎ 2222–2022 ⊕ *www.horizontes.com*) tours include naturalist guides and transport by 4WD vehicle.

9

THE SARAPIQUÍ LOOP

The area immediately north of the San José metro area doesn't leap to mind when discussing ecotourism in Costa Rica, but it should. The Sarapiquí River gave its name to this region at the foot of the Cordillera Central mountain range. To the west is the rain forest of Braulio Carrillo National Park, and to the east are Tortuguero National Park and Barra del Colorado National Wildlife Refuge. These splendid national parks share the region with thousands of acres of farmland, including palm, banana, and pineapple plantations, as well as cattle ranching. Cheap land and rich soil brought a wave of Ticos to this area a half century ago. Until the construction of Highway 126 in 1957; which connects the area to San José, this was one of the most isolated parts of Costa Rica, with little or no tourism. Government homesteading projects brought many residents, who cleared massive swaths of the rain forest for cattle grazing and agriculture. Now, ironically, old-growth lowland rain forest, montane cloud forest, and wetlands exist only within the borders of the national parks and several adjoining private reserves. A growing selection of nature lodges has set up shop here, and you can enjoy their offerings 60 to 90 minutes after you leave the capital. (Just try getting to the Osa Peninsula on the southern Pacific coast in that same time.)

BRAULIO CARRILLO NATIONAL PARK

30 km (19 miles) (45 mins) north of San José.

One of Central America's largest tracts of primary cloud forest looms just north of the San José metro area. The primary highway to the Caribbean coast passes right through the park, and most visitors see it from their car or van windows.

GETTING HERE AND AROUND

From San José, travel northeast on Calle 3, which becomes the Braulio Carrillo Highway (Highway 32), toward Limón. This highway winds through the park, entering at the main ranger station, Zurquí, and exiting at the Quebrada González ranger station. The Barva station is on the west side of the park, north of Zurquí, and is the easiest to access. From Heredia, drive north to Sacramento on Highway 114. The station is 4 km (2½ miles) northeast of Sacramento on a trail that's accessible on foot or by 4WD (except during heavy rains). If you're doing the driving, try to make this a morning trip, as the highway through the park begins to fog over in the afternoon.

Any bus going to Guápiles, Siquirres, and Puerto Viejo de Sarapiquí can drop you off at the Zurquí ranger station. Buses ($2) depart from San José Monday through Saturday from the Atlántico Norte bus station (for Guápiles) or the Gran Terminal del Caribe (for Siquirres or Puerto Viejo de Sarapiquí) several times daily. A cab from San José costs around $50. A number of tour companies offer one-day tours from San José, and, quite honestly, that is the easiest and safest way to visit the park.

EXPLORING

Barva Volcano. This 2,896-meter (9,500-foot) volcanic summit is the highest point in Braulio Carrillo National Park. Dormant for 300 years now, Barva is massive: its lower slopes are almost completely planted with coffee fields and hold more than a dozen small towns, nearly all of which are named after saints. On the upper slopes are pastures lined with exotic pines and the occasional native oak or cedar, giving way to the botanical diversity of the cloud forest near the top. The air is usually cool near the summit, which combines with the pines and pastures to evoke the European or North American countryside.

Barva's misty, luxuriant summit is the only part of Braulio Carrillo where camping is allowed, and it's a good place to see the rare resplendent quetzal early in the morning. Because it's somewhat hard to reach, Barva receives a mere fraction of the crowds that flock to the summits of Poás and Irazú. A two- to four-hour hike in from the Barva ranger station takes you to the main crater, which is about 162 meters (540 feet) in diameter. The almost vertical sides are covered in *sombrillas de pobre,* a plant that thrives in the highlands, and oak trees laden with

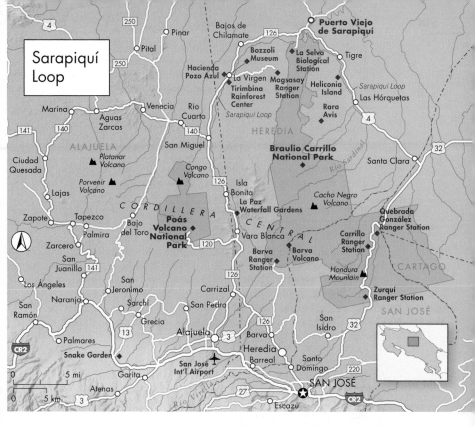

epiphytes (nonparasitic plants that grow on other plants). The crater is filled with an otherworldly black lake. Farther down the track into the forest lies a smaller crater lake. ■TIP→ **Bring rain gear, boots, and a warm shirt. Stay on the trail when hiking anywhere in Braulio Carrillo; even experienced hikers who know the area have lost their way up here, and the rugged terrain makes wandering through the woods very dangerous. In addition, muggings of hikers have been reported in the park. (This is the closest national park to San José and its attendant urban problems.) Go with a ranger.**

For access to the volcano, start from Sacramento, north of Heredia. North of Barva de Heredia the road grows narrow and steep. At Sacramento the paved road turns to dirt, growing worse as it nears the Barva ranger station. We recommend a 4WD vehicle, especially during the rainy season. From the ranger station you can take a 4WD vehicle over the extremely rocky road to the park entrance (dry season only), or hike up on foot. The walk through the cloud forest to the crater's two lakes takes two to four hours, but your efforts should be rewarded by great views (as long as you start before 8 am, to avoid the mist). ⊠ *Access via the park's Barva ranger station* ☎ *192 national parks hotline in Costa Rica* ⊠ *$10 (in addition to $12 Braulio Carrillo Park entrance)* ⊗ *Tues.–Sun. 7–4.*

Braulio Carrillo National Park. In a country where deforestation is still rife, hiking through dense, primary tropical cloud forest is an experience to be treasured. The park owes its foundation to the public outcry provoked by the construction of the highway of the same name through this region in the late 1970s—the government bowed to pressure from environmentalists, and somewhat ironically, Braulio Carrillo is the national park that is most accessible from the capital, thanks to the highway. Covering 443 square km (171 square miles), the extremely diverse terrain ranges from 55 meters (108 feet) to about 2,896 meters (9,500 feet) above sea level and extends from the central volcanic range down the Caribbean slope to La Selva research station near Puerto Viejo de Sarapiquí. The park protects a series of ecosystems ranging from the cloud forests on the upper slopes to the tropical wet forest of the Magsasay sector; it is home to 6,000 tree species, 500 bird species, and 135 mammal species.

Despite the park's immense size and proximity to the capital, visitor facilities are extremely limited. Penetrating the park's depths is a project only for the truly intrepid.

The **Zurquí ranger station** is to the right of the highway, ½ km (¼ mile) before the Zurquí Tunnel. Here a short trail loops through the cloud forest. Hikes are steep; wear hiking boots to protect yourself from mud, slippage, and snakes. The main trail through primary forest, 1½ km (1 mile) long, culminates in a *mirador* (lookout point), but alas, the highway mars the view. Monkeys, tapirs, jaguars, kinkajous, sloths, raccoons, margays, and porcupines all live in this forest, and resident birds include the resplendent quetzal and the eagle. Orchids, bromeliads, heliconias, fungi, and mushrooms live closer to the floor. Another trail leads into the forest to the right, beginning about 17 km (11 miles) after the tunnel, where it follows the Quebrada González, a stream with a cascade and swimming hole. There are no campsites in this part of the park. The **Carrillo ranger station,** 22 km (14 miles) northeast along the highway from Zurquí, marks the beginning of trails that are less steep. Farther north on this highway, near the park entrance/exit toward Guápiles, is the **Quebrada González** ranger station. To the east of Heredia, a road climbs **Barva Volcano** from San Rafael. ☎ *2290–8202 Sistemas de Areas de Conservación, 192 national parks hotline in Costa Rica* 💳 *$12* ⊙ *Daily 7–4.*

PUERTO VIEJO DE SARAPIQUÍ

80 km (48 miles) north of San José.

One of Costa Rica's lesser-known eco-destinations has been developing a growing selection of nature-themed activities in recent years. In the 19th century, Puerto Viejo de Sarapiquí was a thriving river port and the only link with the coastal lands straight east. Fortunes nose-dived with the construction of a full-fledged port in the town of Moín near Limón, and today Puerto Viejo has a slightly run-down air. The activities of the Nicaraguan Contras made this a danger zone in the 1980s, but now that the political situation has improved, boats once again ply the old route up the Sarapiquí River to the San Juan River on the Nicaraguan frontier, from where you can travel downstream to Barra del Colorado or Tortuguero. (Wars of words still occasionally flare up between Costa Rica and Nicaragua, but they need not concern you as a visitor.) A few tour companies have Sarapiquí River tours with up to Class III rapids in the section between

Chilamate and La Virgen, with plenty of wildlife to see. If you prefer to leave the driving to them, many of the lodges operate boat tours on the tamer sections of the river.

GETTING HERE AND AROUND

The Braulio Carrillo Highway runs from Calle 3 in San José and passes the Zurquí and Quebrada González sectors of Braulio Carrillo National Park. It branches at Santa Clara, north of the park, with the paved Highway 4 continuing north to Puerto Viejo de Sarapiquí. Alternatively, an older winding road connects San José with Puerto Viejo de Sarapiquí, passing through Heredia and Vara Blanca. The former route is easier, with less traffic; the latter route is more scenic but heavily trafficked. (If you are at all prone to motion sickness, take the newer road.) The roads are mostly paved, with the usual rained-out dirt and rock sections; road quality depends on the time of year, the length of time since the last visit by a road crew, and/or the amount of rain dumped by the latest tropical storm. Heavy rains sometimes cause landslides that block the highway near the Zurquí Tunnel inside the park, in which case you have to go via Vara Blanca. Check conditions before you set out. Get an early start; fog begins to settle in on both routes by mid-afternoon. ■ TIP→ There are gas stations on the Braulio Carrillo Highway at the turnoff to Puerto Viejo de Sarapiquí, as well as just outside town. Fill the tank when you get the chance.

Grupo Caribeños buses travel several times daily via both routes—more frequently via the newer route, though—and leave from San José's Gran Terminal del Caribe.

ESSENTIALS

Bank/ATM Banco Nacional ⊠ *Across from post office* ☎ *2766–6012.*

Medical Clinic Red Cross ⊠ *West end of town* ☎ *2766–6901.*

Post Office Correos ⊠ *Across from Banco Nacional.*

EXPLORING

Dr. María Eugenia Bozzoli Museum of Indigenous Cultures (*Museo de Culturas Indígenas Doctora María Eugenia Bozzoli*). Costa Rica's indigenous peoples don't get the visibility of those in Guatemala or Mexico, probably because they number only 40,000 out of a population of 4 million. This museum, part of the Centro Neotrópico Sarapiquís, provides a well-rounded all-under-one-roof introduction to the subject. Nearly 400 artifacts of the Boruca, Bribri, Cabécar, Guaymí, and Maleku peoples are displayed, including masks, musical instruments, and shamanic healing sticks. Start by watching a 17-minute video introduction, *Man*

Insanely steep hills and heavy rainfall make this country a mecca for white-water sports.

and Nature in Pre-Columbian Costa Rica. A botanical garden next door cultivates medicinal plants still used by many traditional groups. In 1999 researchers discovered an archaeological site on the grounds that contains pre-Columbian tombs and petroglyphs dating from the 15th century. The site is still under study. ✉ *La Virgen de Sarapiquí, 17 km (11 miles) southwest of Puerto Viejo* ☎ *2761–1004* ⊕ *www.sarapiquis. org* ✉ *$15 (includes guide)* ⊗ *Daily 9–5.*

Heliconia Island. Some 70 species of the heliconia, a relative of the banana, are among the collections that populate 5 acres of botanical gardens on this island in the Sarapiquí River. Expect to see ample bird and butterfly life, too. ✉ *La Chaves, 8 km (5 miles) south of Puerto Viejo de Sarapiquí* ☎ *2764–5220* ⊕ *www.heliconiaisland.com* ✉ *$10, $18 with guide* ⊗ *Daily 9–5.*

FAMILY **La Selva Biological Station.** At the confluence of the Puerto Viejo and Sarapiquí rivers, La Selva packs about 420 bird species, 460 tree species, and 500 butterfly species into just 15 square km (6 square miles). Spottings might include the spider monkey, poison dart frog, agouti, collared peccary, and dozens of other rare creatures. Extensive, well-marked trails and swing bridges, many of which are wheelchair accessible, connect habitats as varied as tropical wet forest, swamps, creeks, rivers, secondary regenerating forest, and pasture. The site is a project of the Organization for Tropical Studies, a research consortium of 63 U.S., Australian, and Latin American universities, and is one of three biological stations OTS operates in Costa Rica. To see the place, take an informative three-hour morning or afternoon nature walk with one of La Selva's bilingual guides, who are some of the country's best.

Walks start every day at 8 am and 1:30 pm. For a completely different view of the forest, set off on a guided two-hour walk at 5:45 am or the night tour at 6 pm. If you get a group of at least seven together, you can enroll in the daylong Bird-Watching 101 course, which can be arranged anytime for $70 per person. Or get a group of at least six together and tag along with one of the resident research scientists for a half day. Young children won't feel left out either, with a very basic nature-identification course geared to them. Even with all the offerings, La Selva can custom-design excursions to suit your own special interests, too. Advance reservations are required for the dawn and night walks as well as for any of the courses. ⊠ *6 km (4 miles) south of Puerto Viejo de Sarapiquí* ✛ *Drive south from Puerto Viejo, and look for signs on the west side of the road. La Selva is a $10 taxi ride from Puerto Viejo de Sarapiquí* ☎ *2766–6565, 2524–0607 in San José, 919/684–5774 in North America* ⊕ *www.threepaths.co.cr* ✉ *Nature walk $32, dawn or night walk $40* ☉ *Walks daily at 5:45 and 8 am, 1:30, and 6 pm.*

FAMILY **Snake Garden.** One of a growing number of Costa Rica's serpentaria, the Snake Garden shows off some 50 species of reptiles, including all the poisonous snakes (and most of the nonpoisonous ones) found in Costa Rica, as well as pythons, anacondas, and rattlesnakes from elsewhere in North and South America. You can handle a few specimens upon request and under supervision. ⊠ *La Virgen de Sarapiquí, 400 m south of Centro Neotrópico Sarapiquís* ☎ *2761–1059* ✉ *$15* ☉ *Daily 9–5.*

Standard Fruit Company. Curious about the life and times of Costa Rica's most famous yellow fruit? The company known as Dole in North America has two-hour Banana Tours to guide you through the process from plantation to processing to packing. Visits are best arranged through several San José travel agencies, who will transport you to the site here. Options include a longer tour at a plantation here in Sarapiquí or a shorter tour south of the Caribbean port of Limón, which is primarily geared toward cruise-ship passengers. ☎ *8383–4596* ⊕ *www.bananatourcostarica.com* ✉ *$10* ☉ *Tours daily at 10.*

Tirimbina Rainforest Center. This working biological research station encompasses 750 acres of primary forest and 8 km (5 miles) of trails, some of them traversing hanging bridges at canopy level. Tours introduce you to bats, frogs, and other common but often misunderstood creatures, and show off the beauty of the forest. Reservations are recommended for all activities, and required for the bat, frog, birding, and night tours. ⊠ *La Virgen de Sarapiquí, 17 km (11 miles) southwest of Puerto Viejo* ☎ *2761–0333* ⊕ *www.tirimbina.org* ✉ *$15, $25 guided nature walk, $25 night walk, $22 bat tour, $25 frog tour, $25 bird-watching tour, $27 chocolate tour* ☉ *Daily 7–5. Guided nature walks daily 8 and 10 am and 1:30 and 3 pm; bird-watching tour daily 6; bat tour daily 7:30 pm with reservation; frog tour daily 7:30 pm with reservation; chocolate tour daily 8 and 10 and 1:30 and 3; night walk at 7 pm with reservation.*

SPORTS AND THE OUTDOORS
TOUR OPERATORS
Hacienda Pozo Azul. The canopy tour ($53) at this horse ranch and dairy farm has 12 zip lines, ranging in height from 18 to 27 meters (60 to 90 feet). Pozo Azul also has riding excursions for all experience levels through the region around La Virgen. A two-hour tour is $44, a half day is $53. Check out the multiday tours, too, if you're an experienced rider. Half-day, full-day, and two-day rough-and-tumble back-roads bike tours ($45–$75) are also available, as is a guided 27-meter (90-foot) river canyon descent ($40). ✉ *La Virgen de Sarapiquí, 17 km (11 miles) southwest of Puerto Viejo* ☎ *2438–2616, 877/810–6903* ⊕ *www.pozoazul.com.*

Hotel Gavilán Río Sarapiquí. The hotel runs wildlife- and bird-watching tours from its site on the river near Puerto Viejo de Sarapiquí. ✉ *700 m north of Comando Atlántico (naval command)* ☎ *2766–6743, 2234–9507 in San José* ⊕ *www.gavilanlodge.com.*

RAFTING
The Virgen del Socorro area is one of the most popular put-in points for white-water rafters, and offers both Class II and III rapids. Trips leaving from the Chilamate put-in are more tranquil, with mostly Class I rapids. The put-in point depends on the weather and season.

Several operators lead tours on the Sarapiquí River.

Ríos Tropicales. You can raft the Class III La Virgen section of the Sarapiquí River on day excursions from San José ($90). ☎ *2233–6455, 866/722–8273 in North America* ⊕ *www.riostropicales.com.*

WHERE TO STAY
$

HOTEL
🔲 **Hotel Gavilán Río Sarapiquí.** Beautiful gardens run down to the river, and colorful tanagers and three types of toucan feast in the citrus trees on the grounds of this two-story lodge where comfortable, terra-cotta-floored rooms are nicely accented with decorative crafts. **Pros:** lovely gardens; many activities; great for birders. **Cons:** rustic rooms; need a car to stay here; no air-conditioning; patchy Wi-Fi. $ *Rooms from: $60* ✉ *700 m north of Comando Atlántico (naval command)* ☎ *2766–6743, 2234–9507 in San José* ⊕ *www.gavilanlodge.com* ⤴ *20 rooms* ⚭ *No meals.*

$$$

B&B/INN
🔲 **La Selva Biological Station Lodge.** Other lodges provide more luxury for the money, but none can match the tropical nature experience at this working biological-research station where accommodation is in dorm-style rooms with large bunk beds and lots of screened windows or family-style cabins that sleep up to four. **Pros:** many activities, ecology-minded staff; plenty of wildlife. **Cons:** bunk beds; cabins are rustic; no air-conditioning; sometimes difficult to procure overnight space. $ *Rooms from: $186* ✉ *6 km (4 miles) south of Puerto Viejo de Sarapiquí* ☎ *2766–6565, 2524–0607 in San José* ⊕ *www.threepaths.co.cr* ⤴ *60 bunk beds, 18 cabins, 1 family house* ⚭ *All meals.*

$

HOTEL
🔲 **Posada Andrea Cristina.** The Martínez family owns and operates this basic but friendly and comfortable bed-and-breakfast, offering four high-ceiling cabins with private gardens equipped with hammocks. **Pros:** good value; secluded location; attentive owners; Spanish lessons

CLOSE UP

Rainforest Aerial Tram

Just beyond the northeastern boundary of Braulio Carrillo National Park, about 15 km (9 miles) before the Caribbean-slope town of Guápiles, a 1,200-acre reserve houses a privately owned and operated engineering marvel: a series of gondolas strung together in a modified ski-lift pulley system. (To lessen the impact on the jungle, the support pylons were lowered into place by helicopter.) The Rainforest Aerial Tram gives you a way to see the rain-forest canopy and its spectacular array of epiphyte plant life and birds from above, a feat you could otherwise accomplish only by climbing the trees yourself. Purists complain that it treats the rain forest like an amusement park, but it's an entertaining way to learn the value and beauty of rain-forest ecology.

The 21 gondolas hold five people each, plus a bilingual biologist-guide equipped with a walkie-talkie to request brief stops for snapping pictures. The ride covers 2½ km (1½ miles) in 80 minutes. The $60 price includes a biologist-guided walk through the area for ground-level orientation before or after the tram ride. Several add-ons are possible, too, with frog, snake, and butterfly exhibits, a medicinal-plant garden, and a zip-line canopy tour on-site ($50), as well as a half-day birding tour ($83). You can arrange a personal pickup in San José for a fee; alternatively, there are public buses (on the Guápiles line) every half hour from the Gran Terminal del Caribe in San José. Drivers know the tram as the *teleférico*. Many San José tour operators make a daylong tour combining the tram with another half-day option; combos with the Britt Coffee Tour or INBioparque in Santo Domingo, both near Heredia, are especially popular. Ten rustic (no air-conditioning or TV) but cozy bungalows ($155 per person) are available on-site (reservations are required). Electricity shuts off after 9 pm. Cabin rates include meals, tram tours, and guided walks. A café is open to all for breakfast, lunch, and dinner. If you're traveling the Central Pacific coast, you'll find similar installations near the town of Jacó (⇨ *Chapter 7*), 3 km (2 miles) north of Supermercado Maxi Bodega, although without the accommodation, and a restaurant open for breakfast and lunch only. The admission price at the Pacific facility includes the tram ride, nature walk, snake exhibit, heliconia and medicinal-plant gardens, and transport from Jacó-area hotels. The company also operates parks in Mexico (Riviera Maya), Jamaica (Ocho Rios), and St. Lucia. ✉ *Rainforest Adventures, Avda. 7 and C. 7, San José* ☎ *2257–5961, 866/759–8726 in North America* 🌐 *www.rainforestadventure.com* 🎟 *$60; $114 includes all attractions* 🕒 *Tours: Mon. 9–4, Tues.–Sun. 6:30–4. Call for reservations 6 am–9:30 pm.*

9

available. **Cons:** rustic rooms; cash only; mosquitoes; street noise. $ *Rooms from: $55* ✉ *½ km (¼ mile) west of town* ☎ *2766–6265* 🌐 *www.andreacristina.com* 🛏 *8 rooms* 💳 *No credit cards* 🍴 *Breakfast.*

$$ ALL-INCLUSIVE 🏨 **Rara Avis Rainforest Lodge and Reserve.** Toucans, sloths, great green macaws, howler and spider monkeys, vested anteaters, and tapirs may be on hand to greet you when you arrive at the lodge and cabins in Costa Rica's most popular private reserves, open only to overnight

Rain-forest trams are a great way to experience the Braulio Carrillo National Park.

guests. **Pros:** many activities; plenty of wildlife. **Cons:** rough trip to get here; expensive for amenities provided; property in need of renovation. $ *Rooms from: $130* ☒ *11 miles south of Puerto Viejo de Sarapiqui* ☎ *2764-1111, 2200-4238* ⊕ *www.rara-avis.com* ⇗ *14 rooms, 8 with bath* ⍐*All-inclusive.*

$$ ⍨ **Sarapiquís Rainforest Lodge.** Located within the Centro Neotrópico
HOTEL   Sarapiquís, an environmental educational center, museum, and gar-
FAMILY den, you can stay the night inside indigenous-inspired circular *palenque* (huts) buildings with palm-thatch roofs. **Pros:** good value; large rooms; private terraces; buffet-style restaurant. **Cons:** no air-conditioning; sometimes difficult to find space. $ *Rooms from: $120* ☒ *Centro Neotrópico Sarapiquís, La Virgen de Sarapiquí, 17 km (11 miles) southwest of Puerto Viejo, Puerto Viejo de Sarapiquí* ☎ *2761-1004* ⊕ *www.sarapiquis.org* ⇗ *40 rooms* ⍐*Breakfast.*

$$ ⍨ **Selva Verde Lodge.** Built on stilts over the Sarapiquí River on the edge
HOTEL   of a 2-square-km (1-square-mile) private tropical-rain-forest reserve, the lodge caters primarily to those seeking natural-history tours. **Pros:** ecology-minded staff; many activities; great for birders. **Cons:** popular with tour groups; sometimes difficult to find space; steep walk to reach a few bungalows. $ *Rooms from: $134* ☒ *7 km (4 miles) west of Puerto Viejo de Sarapiquí, Puerto Viejo de Sarapiquí* ☎ *2761-1800, 800/451-7111 in North America* ⊕ *www.selvaverde.com* ⇗ *40 rooms, 5 bungalows* ⍐*Multiple meal plans.*

THE NORTHERN LOWLANDS

The lowlands begin about an hour north of San José, and, for most visitors, are a tract of land merely to get through on the way to the coast. The Caribbean does beckon, after all, but a couple of lesser sights here may tempt you to stop. If you stay on the well-maintained main Guápiles Highway, you head southeast toward Limón and the Caribbean coast. The highway passes through sultry agricultural lowlands, home to large banana and cacao plantations, but bypasses the region's three main communities: burgeoning Guápiles and the smaller towns of Guácimo and Siquirres.

GUÁPILES

60 km (38 miles) northeast of San José.

The hub towns of Guápiles and Guácimo aren't destinations in their own right, but rather the nucleus for a few on-the-way-to-the-Caribbean activities. Guápiles, one of the country's fastest-growing cities, is the hub of northeastern Costa Rica, and with all the facilities in town, residents of the region barely need to trek to San José anymore. The smaller town of Guácimo lies 12 km (7 miles) east on the Guápiles Highway.

GETTING HERE AND AROUND

Guápiles lies just north of Braulio Carrillo National Park and straddles the highway to the Caribbean. It's an easy one-hour drive from San José just 60 km (38 miles) to the southwest, or Limón 84 km (50 miles) to the east. Grupo Caribeños buses connect San José's Gran Terminal del Caribe with Guápiles every half hour from early morning until late evening, and provide service seven times daily to Guácimo. San José's bus terminals are in sketchy neighborhoods, so take care if this is your mode of transport.

ESSENTIALS

Bank/ATM BAC San José ⊠ *Across from Casa de la Cultura* ☎ *2710–7434.* **Banco Nacional** ⊠ *200 m north of Ebal Rodríguez stadium* ☎ *2713–2000.*

Hospital Hospital de Guápiles ⊠ *90 m south of fire station* ☎ *2710–6801.*

Pharmacy Farmacia Santa Marta ⊠ *Across from Banco Nacional* ☎ *2710–6253.*

Post Office Correos ⊠ *North of MUCAP.*

Visitor Information Instituto Costarricense de Turismo ⊠ *Next to Bancrédito* ☎ *2710–7516* ⊕ *www.visitcostarica.com* ⏱ *Weekdays 8–noon and 1–4.*

EXPLORING

EARTH. The nonprofit university called EARTH (Escuela de Agricultura de la Región Tropical Húmeda, or Agricultural School of the Humid Tropical Region) researches the production of less pesticide-dependent bananas and other forms of sustainable tropical agriculture, as well as medicinal plants. The university graduates some 100 students from Latin America and Africa each year. EARTH's elegant stationery, calendars, and other paper products are made from banana stems, tobacco leaves, and coffee leaves and grounds, and are sold at

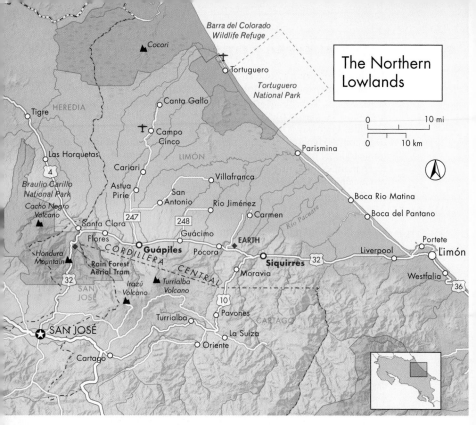

The Northern Lowlands

the on-site Oropéndola store and in many tourist shops around the country. The property encompasses a banana plantation and a forest reserve with nature trails. Half-day tours are $20; full-day, $30; and lunch is $12 for day visitors. Though priority is given to researchers and conference groups, you're welcome to stay in the school's 50-person lodging facility, with private bathrooms, hot water, and ceiling fans, for $75 a night, which includes the use of a swimming pool and exercise equipment. The site is a bird-watchers' favorite; some 250 species have been spotted here. Advance reservations are required for tours or accommodation. ⊠ *Pocora de Guácimo, 15 km (9 miles) east of Guápiles on Guápiles Hwy.* ☎ *2713–0000, 404/995–1235 in North America* ⊕ *www.earth.ac.cr.*

SIQUIRRES

28 km (17 miles) east of Guápiles.

Siquirres anchors a fertile banana- and pineapple-growing region, and marks the transition point between the agricultural lowlands and the tropical, palm-laden coast. The odd name is a corruption of the words *Si quieres* (if you want), fittingly impassive for this lackluster town. Siquirres has the unfortunate historical distinction of having once been the westernmost point to which Afro-Caribbean people could migrate.

Costa Rica implemented the law in the late 1880s—when large numbers of Afro-Caribbeans immigrated (mainly from Jamaica) to construct the Atlantic Railroad—but abolished it in the 1949 constitution.

GETTING HERE

Siquirres lies just off the main highway and is easily accessible from the east, west, or south (if you're arriving from Turrialba). Grupo Caribeños buses connect San José's Gran Terminal del Caribe with Siquirres several times daily.

ESSENTIALS

Bank/ATM Banco Nacional ⊠ *50 m south of Acón gas station* ☎ *2768–8128.*

Medical Clinic Centro de Salud de Siquirres ⊠ *West side of soccer field* ☎ *2768–6138.*

Pharmacy Farmacia Santa Lucía ⊠ *50 m east of fire station* ☎ *2768–9304.*

Post Office Correos ⊠ *Across from Guardia Rural.*

SPORTS AND THE OUTDOORS

RAFTING

Siquirres's proximity to the put-in sites of several classic rafting excursions makes it an ideal place to begin a trip.

Ríos Tropicales. Old standby Ríos Tropicales has tours on a Class III to IV section of the Pacuare River between Siquirres and San Martín, as well as the equally difficult section between Tres Equis and Siquirres. Not quite so wild, but still with Class III rapids, is the nearby Florida section of the Reventazón. Day excursions normally begin in San José, but if you're out in this part of the country, you can kick off your outing here at the company's operations center in Siquirres. ⊠ *On the highway in Siquirres* ☎ *2233–6455, 866/722–8273 in North America* ⊕ *www. riostropicales.com.*

TORTUGUERO

Some compare these dense layers of green set off by brilliantly colored flowers—a vision doubled by the jungle's reflection in mirror-smooth canals—to the Amazon. That might be stretching it, but there's still an Indiana Jones mystique to the journey up here, especially when you get off the main canals and into the narrower lagoons. The region remains one of those Costa Rican anomalies: roadless and remote, it's nevertheless one of the country's most visited places. The tourism seasons here are defined not by the rains or lack thereof (it's wet most of the year) but by the months of prime turtle hatching.

In 1970 a system of canals running parallel to the shoreline was constructed to provide safer access to the region than the dangerous journey up the seacoast. You can continue up the canals, natural and man-made, that begin in Moín, near Limón, and run all the way to Tortuguero. Or you can embark at various points north of Guápiles and Siquirres, as do public transportation and most of the package tours. (The lodges' minivans bring you from San José to the put-in point, where you continue your journey by boat.)

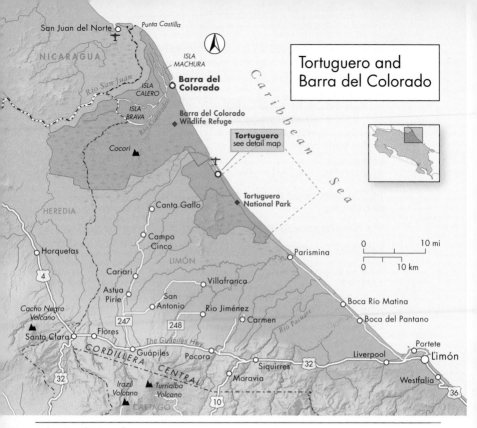

TORTUGUERO

30 mins by air and 4 hrs by road and boat northeast of San José.

Fodor's Choice
★

North of the national park of the same name, the hamlet of Tortuguero is a pleasant little place with 600 inhabitants, two churches, three bars, a handful of souvenir shops, and a small selection of inexpensive lodgings. (And one more plus: there are no motor vehicles here, a refreshing change from the traffic woes that plague the rest of Costa Rica.) You can also take a stroll on the 32-km (20-mile) beach, but avoid swimming here because of strong riptides and large numbers of bull sharks and barracuda.

The stretch of beach between the Colorado and Matina rivers was first mentioned as a nesting ground for sea turtles in a 1592 Dutch chronicle. Nearly a century earlier, Christopher Columbus compared traversing the north Caribbean coast and its swimming turtles to navigating through rocks. Because the area is so isolated—there's no road here to this day—the turtles nested undisturbed for centuries. By the mid-1900s, however, the harvesting of eggs and poaching of turtles had reached such a level that these creatures faced extinction. In 1963 an executive decree regulated the hunting of turtles and the gathering of eggs, and in 1970 the government established Tortuguero National Park; modern Tortuguero bases its economy on tourism.

NICARAGUA CANAL?

During the 1840s' California gold rush, the Río San Juan, which forms much of the border between Costa Rica and Nicaragua, became an important crossroads allowing miners and gold to move between New York and San Francisco some 70 years before the Panama Canal opened. Cornelius Vanderbilt financed the dredging of the waterway to allow ships to pass up the river to Lake Nicaragua. From here a rail line connected to the Pacific Ocean. While the Panama Canal is undergoing a much-needed expansion as it marks its centennial, plans are moving ahead to construct a full-fledged canal farther north through Nicaragua. A Chinese-backed investment group has announced plans to finance the $40 billion project, with construction predicted to begin in 2015. Stay tuned.

GETTING HERE AND AROUND

It's easier than you'd think to get to remote Tortuguero. Flying is the quickest (and most expensive) option. Nature Air provides early-morning flights to and from San José.

If you're staying at one of the lodges, its boat will meet you at the airstrip.

The big lodges all have packages that include transportation to and from San José, along with lodging, meals, and tours. Guide-staffed minivans pick you up at your San José hotel and drive you to their own put-in site, usually somewhere north of Siquirres, where you board a covered boat for the final leg on the canals to Tortuguero. The trip up entails sightseeing and animal viewing. The trip back to San José stops only for a lunch break. This is the classic "leave the driving to them" way to get to Tortuguero.

A boat from the port of Moín, near Limón, is the traditional budget method of getting to Tortuguero if you are already on the Caribbean coast. Arrive at the docks before 10 am and you should be able to find someone to take you there. The going price is $40 per person each way, and travel time is about three hours.

If you arrive in Moín in your own vehicle, JAPDEVA, Costa Rica's Atlantic port authority, operates a secure, guarded parking facility for your car while you are in Tortuguero.

It's entirely possible to make the trip independently from San José, a good option if you are staying in the village rather than at a lodge. A direct bus departs from San José's Gran Terminal del Caribe to Cariari, north of Guápiles, at 9 am. At Cariari, disembark and walk five blocks to the local terminal, where you can board a noon bus for the small crossroads of La Pavona. From here, boats leave at 1:30 pm to take you to Tortuguero, arriving around 3 pm. La Pavona has secure parking facilities. The charge is $10 per night. The Cariari–La Pavona–Tortuguero bus-boat service is provided by COOPETRACA or Viajes Clic-Clic for $10 one way. They operate jointly and honor one another's tickets.

Bus Contacts COOPETRACA ☎ 2767–7137 💳 $10 one-way.
Viajes Clic-Clic ☎ 2709–8155, 8844–0463, 8308–2006 💳 $10 one way.

■ TIP → **If you can, avoid Rubén Bananero, a company that provides bus-boat transport from Cariari.** Its aggressive agents begin to hustle you the minute you get off the bus in Cariari. (Bananero even maintains an information booth at the Gran Terminal del Caribe bus station in San José.) They'll pressure you into buying a round-trip ticket, limiting your return options, and do everything they can to steer you toward hotels that pay them a commission. Others will also try to take you to their own dedicated "information dock" in the village, steering you toward their own guides. If you've made advance reservations for guides or hotels, stand your ground and say, *"No, gracias."*

Water taxis provide transport from multiple points in the village to the lodges. Expect to pay about $3 to $5 per trip.

ESSENTIALS

Visitor Information **Kiosk**. This unstaffed booth with free brochures offers information on the town's history, the park, turtles, and other wildlife. ⊠ *Town center.* **Tortuguero Information Center** ⊠ *Across from Catholic church* ☎ *2709–8011, 8833–0827* ⊕ *www.tortuguerovillage.com.*

EXPLORING

Sea Turtle Conservancy. Florida's Sea Turtle Conservancy runs a visitor center and a museum with excellent animal photos, a video narrating local and natural history, and detailed discussions of the latest ecological goings-on and what you can do to help. There's a souvenir shop next door. For the committed ecotourist, the **John H. Phipps Biological Field Station,** which is affiliated with the conservancy and has been operating in Tortuguero for over five decades, has camping areas and dorm-style quarters with a communal kitchen. If you want to get involved in the life of the turtles, helping researchers to track turtle migration (current research, using satellite technology, has tracked turtles as far as the Florida Keys) or helping to catalog the population of neotropical migrant birds, arrange a stay in advance through the center. ⊠ *From beach at north end of village, walk north along path and watch for sign* ☎ *2709–8091, 352/373–6441 in North America* ⊕ *www.conserveturtles.org* ▣ *$1* ⊗ *Mon.–Sat. 8–4, Sun. 9–5.*

FAMILY   **Tortuguero National Park** (*Parque Nacional Tortuguero*). In 1975 the Costa
Fodor's Choice   Rican government established Tortuguero National Park to protect the
★   sea turtle population, which had been decimated after centuries of being aggressively hunted for its eggs and carapaces. This is the best place in Costa Rica to observe these magnificent creatures nesting, hatching, and scurrying to the ocean. The July-through-October nesting season for the green turtle is Tortuguero's most popular time to visit. Toss in the hawksbill, loggerhead, and leatherback—the three other species of sea turtle who nest here, although to a lesser extent—and you can expand the season from February through October. You can undertake night tours only with an authorized guide, who will be the only person in your party with a light, and that will be a light with a red covering. Photography, flash or otherwise, is strictly prohibited. The sight of a mother turtle furiously digging in the sand to bury her eggs is amazing, even from several yards away, and the spectacle of a wave of hatchlings scurrying out to sea is simply magnificent. ☎ *2710–2929* ▣ *$15* ⊗ *Daily 6–6.*

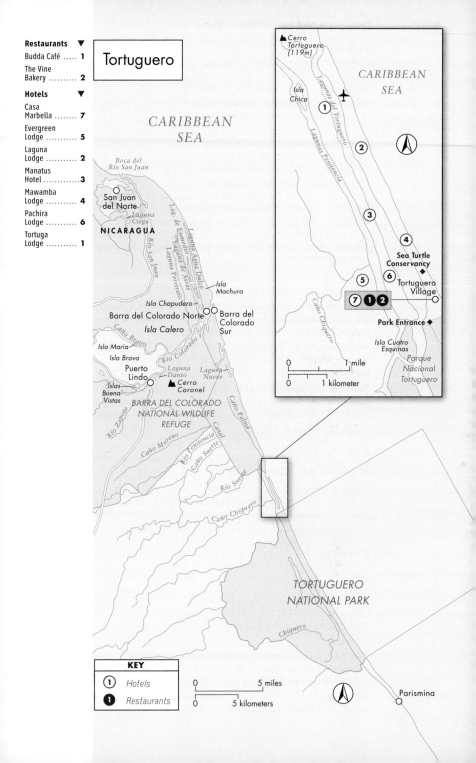

Tortuguero

CARIBBEAN
SEA

Boca del
Río San Juan

San Juan
del Norte

Laguna
Ciega

NICARAGUA

Lago de Emnedio Este

Laguna de Aglas

Laguna Agua Dulce

Laguna Pereraria

Río San Juan

Isla
Machura

Isla Chapudero

Barra del Colorado Norte

Barra del
Colorado
Sur

Isla Calero

Isla Maria

Isla Brava

Río Colorado

Caño Bravo

Puerto
Lindo

Laguna
Danto

Laguna
Nueve

Cerro
Coronel

Islas
Buena
Vistas

Río Zapote

**BARRA DEL COLORADO
NATIONAL WILDLIFE
REFUGE**

Caño Moreno

Río Penitencia

Canal

Caño Suerte

Caño Palma

Río Suerte

Caño Chiquero

TORTUGUERO
NATIONAL PARK

Chiquero

CARIBBEAN SEA

▲ Cerro
Tortuguero
(119m)

Isla
Chica

Lagunas del Tortuguero

Lagunas Penitencia

① ① ②

③

④

Sea Turtle
Conservancy ◆

⑤ ⑥ Tortuguero
Village

⑦ ❶ ❷

Park Entrance ◆

Isla Cuatro
Esquinas

Parque
Nacional
Tortuguero

0		1 mile
0		1 kilometer

Parismina

KEY

① *Hotels*

❶ *Restaurants*

0		5 miles
0		5 kilometers

BEACHES

Playa Tortuguero. The crashing waves and misty air—it rains a lot in Tortuguero—give you the unsettling feeling that you're standing at the edge of the world. Swimming and surfing are simply not possible here. (Sharks can be an issue along this stretch of coast, for one thing.) But by night, depending on the season, this beach comes alive with the age-old ritual of Tortuguero's four species of sea turtles laying and burying their eggs. They then hatch and the baby turtles scurry out to sea. (The spectacle is viewable only in the company of a licensed guide, of course.) Sunbathing? People-watching? Who needs that when this is the real show? **Amenities:** none. **Best for:** solitude; walking. ⊠ *North of Tortuguero village.*

> ### DID YOU KNOW?
>
> Some people still believe turtle eggs to be an aphrodisiacal delicacy, and some bars around Costa Rica (illegally) serve them as snacks. It's a big part of the human contribution to the turtles' disappearance.

SPORTS AND THE OUTDOORS

TOUR GUIDES AND OPERATORS

Tortuguero is one of those "everybody's a guide" places. Quality varies, but most guides are quite knowledgeable. If you stay at one of the lodges, guided tours are *usually* included in your package price (check when you book). If you hire a private guide, $10–$20 per person per hour is the going rate depending on the excursion, with most lasting three hours.

Sea Turtle Conservancy. Call or stop by the visitor center at the Sea Turtle Conservancy to get a recommendation for good local guides. ☎ *2709–8091, 352/373–6441 in San José ⊕ www.conserveturtles.org.*

Daryl Loth. Canadian-born naturalist Daryl Loth has a wealth of information about the area and conducts boat excursions on the canals and responsible turtle-watching tours in season with advance notice. ☎ *8833–0827, 2709–8011 ✍ safari@racsa.co.cr.*

Modesto Watson. Local indigenous Miskito guide Modesto Watson is legendary for his bird- and animal-spotting skills as well as for his howler-monkey imitations. The family's *Riverboat Francesca* can take you up the canals for two-day–one-night excursions to Tortuguero for $200 to $220 per person, depending on the lodge used. Trips begin at the Caribbean port of Moín, 5 km (3 miles) northwest of Limón. ☎ *2226–0986, 8843–8504, 810/433–1410 in North America ⊕ www. tortuguerocanals.com.*

Victor Barrantes. Local guide and area expert Victor Barrantes conducts hiking and boating tours around the area. ☎ *2709–8055, 8928–1169 ✍ tortuguero_info@racsa.co.cr.*

FISHING

You have your choice of mackerel, tarpon, snook, and snapper if you fish in the ocean; snook and calba if you fish in the canals. If you opt for the latter, the National Parks Service levies a $30 license fee (you are fishing in the confines of Tortuguero National Park), good for one month. Operators include the fee in your tour price.

DID YOU KNOW?

Manatees also live in Tortu-guero's canals, but they're slow moving and often hit by motorboats. Manatees are herbivores that eat up to 150 pounds of plants a day. They're also notorious for having gas, so keep your eyes peeled for bubbles in the water. Most boat pilots up here know to drive slowly.

Elvin Gutiérrez. Known as "Primo" to everyone in town, Elvin Gutiérrez takes two passengers out on the ocean for two hours or more, at $75 per hour, or for a full nine-hour day ($500). Prices include boat, motor, guide, and refreshments. ☎ *2709–8115* 🌐 *www.tortuguerosportfish.com.*

TURTLE-WATCHING

If you want to watch the *deshove* (egg laying), contact your hotel or the parks office to hire a certified local guide, required on turtle-watching excursions. The Turtle Scout Program, affiliated with the Sea Turtle Conservancy, maintains a network of knowledgeable guides and has cut out a route of less obtrusive trails that minimize long walks on the beach, all to the benefit of the turtles themselves. Note that you won't be allowed to use a camera—flash or nonflash—on the beach, and only your guide is permitted to use a flashlight (and that must be covered with red plastic), because lights can deter the turtles from nesting. Wear dark clothing if you can and avoid loud talking. Smoking is prohibited on the tours. ■ **TIP→ A few unscrupulous locals will offer to take you on a turtle-watching tour outside the allowed February-through-November season, disturbing sensitive nesting sites in the process. If it's not the season, don't go on a turtle excursion. As the signs around town admonish: "Don't become another predator."**

WHERE TO EAT

If you stay at one of the big lodges up here, your meals will be included in your package price, both in Tortuguero and on your way to and from. Usually *not* included in package prices are alcoholic beverages, soda, and bottled water. Ask to be sure.

If you're staying in town, you have a few simple, but satisfying, restaurant options to choose from.

$ ITALIAN 🍴 **Budda Café.** Pizza, crepes, pastas, and fresh fish are on the menu at this small, canal-side café in the center of town. Lattice wood over the windows, a thatched roof, and, of course, a Buddha statue make up the furnishings. Jazzy cha-cha or a Dean Martin ballad might be playing in the background. [$] *Average main: $7* ✉ *Next to ICE Bldg., Tortuguero village* ☎ *2709–8084* 💳 *No credit cards* 🕒 *Closed Mon. Nov.–Apr.*

$ CAFÉ 🍴 **The Vine Bakery.** Pastas, pizzas, and sandwiches are on the menu, but this small bakery and coffee shop is also a great place to stop for breads made with banana, carrot, and *natilla* (cream), for example. [$] *Average main: $5* ✉ *25 m north of Catholic church, Tortuguero village* ☎ *2709–8132* 💳 *No credit cards* 🕒 *No dinner.*

WHERE TO STAY

The big lodges here offer one- or two-night excursion packages. (Given the choreography it takes to get up here, opt for a more leisurely two-night stay if you can.) Rates are expensive, but prices include everything from guides, tours, meals, and snacks to minivan and boat transport, and in some cases air transport to and from San José. (The $10 entrance fee to Tortuguero National Park may or may not be included in the package price. Ask to be sure.) If you stop and calculate what you get, the price is actually quite reasonable, and the tours are undeniably great fun. Few of the lodges have phones, although all have radio contact with the outside world. All reservations must be made with their offices

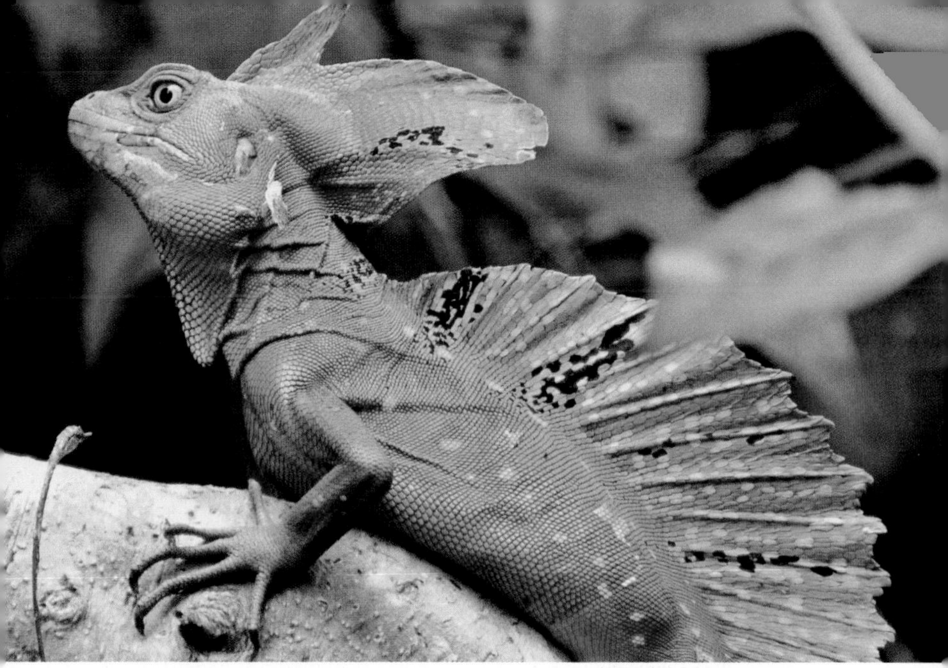

"Cruising down the canal in Tortuguero Park, we discovered this emerald basilisk, a magnificent looking creature." —Photo by Liz Stuart, Fodors.com member

in San José. Be sure to travel light; you get a baggage allowance of 25 pounds, strictly enforced. There's simply no space in the boats for you to bring more. Since you're likely returning to San José at the completion of your Tortuguero tour, your hotel in the capital may allow you to store your bigger bags there. Ask ahead of time.

$ B&B/INN Fodor's Choice ★ **Casa Marbella.** This bed-and-breakfast, the best of the in-town lodgings, is a real find, and the owner is a virtual encyclopedia of all things Tortuguero. **Pros:** knowledgeable owner; immaculate rooms. **Cons:** some pedestrian street noise; no access to lodge-package amenities of big lodges. [$] *Rooms from: $40* ✉ *Across from Catholic church, Tortuguero village* ☎ *2709–8011* 🌐 *casamarbella.tripod.com* *11 rooms* 💳 *No credit cards* 🍴 *Breakfast.*

$$$$ ALL-INCLUSIVE Fodor's Choice ★ **Evergreen Lodge.** The Evergreen offers an entirely different (and intimate) concept in Tortuguero lodging: whereas other lodges have cabins arranged around a clearing, at Evergreen they penetrate deep into the forest. **Pros:** seclusion from other lodges; lush wooded setting. **Cons:** rustic rooms; farther from town than other lodges. [$] *Rooms from: $458* ✉ *2 km (1 mile) from Tortuguero village on Canal Penitencia* ☎ *2257–2242 in San José, 800/644–7438 in North America* 🌐 *www.evergreentortuguero.com* *55 rooms* 🍴 *All-inclusive.*

$$$$ ALL-INCLUSIVE **Laguna Lodge.** Laguna is the largest of the Tortuguero lodges, and it hums with activity as befits its size; jam-packed package tours begin in San José and embark from boats at Caño Blanco, north of Siquirres. **Pros:** many activities; unique architecture. **Cons:** large numbers of guests; not for those who crave solitude. [$] *Rooms from: $472* ✉ *Between ocean and 1st canal inland* ☎ *2709–8082, 2272–4943 in San*

José, 888/259–5615 in North America 🌐 *www.lagunatortuguero.com* 🛏 *110 rooms* 🍴 *All-inclusive.*

$$$$ ALL-INCLUSIVE 🏨 **Manatus Hotel.** Amenities such as air-conditioning, television, and spa treatments are typically not found in Tortuguero, but the area's most luxurious hotel has them all. **Pros:** intimate surroundings; numerous creature comforts not ordinarily found here. **Cons:** fills up quickly in high season; degree of luxury may feel out of place in Tortuguero. [$] *Rooms from: $540* ✉ *Across river, about 1 km (½ mile) north of Tortuguero* ☎ *2709–8197, 2239–4854 in San José* 🌐 *www.manatuscostarica.com* 🛏 *12 rooms* 🍴 *All-inclusive.*

$$$$ ALL-INCLUSIVE 🏨 **Mawamba Lodge.** Nestled between the river and the ocean, Mawamba is the perfect place to kick back and relax, and it is also the only jungle lodge within walking distance (about 10 minutes) of town. **Pros:** many activities; walking distance to village. **Cons:** rustic rooms; not for those who crave solitude. [$] *Rooms from: $460* ✉ *½ km (¼ mile) north of Tortuguero on ocean side of canal* ☎ *2709–8181, 2293–8181 in San José* 🌐 *www.grupomawamba.com* 🛏 *58 cabinas* 🍴 *All-inclusive.*

$$$$ ALL-INCLUSIVE Fodor's Choice ★ 🏨 **Pachira Lodge.** This is the prettiest of Tortuguero's lodges, but not the costliest—the owners here market competitively and keep prices reasonable. **Pros:** many activities; good value; beautiful surroundings; turtle-shape pool. **Cons:** large numbers of guests; can be difficult to find space; not for those who crave solitude. [$] *Rooms from: $458* ✉ *Across river from Sea Turtle Conservancy* ☎ *2257–2242 in San José, 800/644–7438 in North America* 🌐 *www.pachiralodge.com* 🛏 *88 rooms* 🍴 *All-inclusive.*

$$$$ ALL-INCLUSIVE Fodor's Choice ★ 🏨 **Tortuga Lodge.** Lush lawns, orchids, and tropical trees surround this thatched riverside lodge owned by Costa Rica Expeditions and renowned for its nature packages and top-notch, personalized service. **Pros:** many activities; seclusion from other lodges; top-notch guides; air transfers via chartered flights; upscale clientele. **Cons:** rustic rooms; at 20 minutes away, this is farther from the park than most lodges in the area. [$] *Rooms from: $756* ✉ *Across the river from airstrip, 2 km (1 mile) from Tortuguero* ☎ *2710–8016, 2257–0766 in San José* 🌐 *www.costaricaexpeditions.com/tortuga-lodge* 🛏 *27 rooms* 🍴 *All-inclusive.*

SOUTHERN CARIBBEAN COAST

The landscape along the Guápiles Highway changes from farmland to tropics as you approach the port city of Limón. Place names change, too. You'll see signs to towns called Bristol, Stratford, and Liverpool, reflecting the region's British Caribbean heritage. At first look, tourist havens par excellence Cahuita and Puerto Viejo de Talamanca still resemble the cluttered beach towns first discovered by European backpackers over two decades ago. But both have grown up and now offer a terrific selection of fine dining and gracious lodging to complement the beaches, surfing, partying, and nature for which this area has long been known.

LIMÓN

100 km (62 miles) southeast of Guápiles, 160 km (100 miles) north and east of San José.

The colorful Afro-Caribbean flavor of one of Costa Rica's most important ports (population 90,000) is the first sign of life for seafaring visitors to Costa Rica's east coast. Limón (sometimes called "Puerto Limón") is a lively, if shabby, town with a 24-hour street life. Most travelers do not stop here, heading immediately to Cahuita and Puerto Viejo de Talamanca farther south. The wooden houses are brightly painted, but the grid-plan streets look rather worn, partly because of the damage caused by a 1991 earthquake. Street crime, including pickpocketing and nighttime mugging, is not uncommon here. Long charged with neglecting the city, the national government continually promises to turn new attention to Limón, although the results never match residents' expectations.

Limón receives thousands of visitors every year, owing in large part to its newest incarnation as a port of call. Azamara, Celebrity, Costa, Crystal, Cunard, Holland America, MSC, Oceania, Princess, and Silversea cruise ships all dock here on some of their Panama Canal or western Caribbean itineraries. The downtown Terminal de Cruceros hums with activity between October and May, with one or two boats daily during the peak season (December through March). This is the place to find telephones, Internet cafés, manicurists (they do quite a brisk business), a tourist-information booth, and tour-operator stands, too. The terminal contains souvenir stands staffed by low-key vendors who invite you to look, but don't pester you if your answer is *"No, gracias."* Much to the chagrin of local businesses, most cruise passengers exit their ships and head out on organized shore excursions, seeing the town only through the windows of their tour vans. (Unfortunately, this has become an increasingly common complaint among residents of Costa Rica's ports of call who were promised an economic boom when the ships arrived.)

GETTING HERE AND AROUND

If you're driving to the Caribbean coast, you'll pass through Limón. The Guápiles Highway that began in San José ends here at the ocean but bypasses the heart of downtown by a couple of blocks. Budget about 3½ hours for the trip. Just after the sign to "Sixaola" and the coastal highway south to Cahuita and Puerto Viejo de Talamanca is the city center. The Autotransportes Caribeños bus terminal lies at Avenida 2 and Calle 8, across from the soccer stadium, and serves routes from San José, Guápiles, and Siquirres, with buses arriving several times daily from each. Opt for the *directo* (express) service from San José rather than the *corriente* buses, which make many stops along the route. Buses to Cahuita and Puerto Viejo de Talamanca and all points on the south coast arrive and depart at the Autotransportes MEPE terminal, 200 meters east of the turnoff to the southern coastal highway.

Avenidas (avenues) run east and west, and *calles* (streets) north and south, but Limón's street-numbering system differs from that of other Costa Rican cities. "Number one" of each avenida and calle begins at the water, and numbers increase sequentially as you move inland, unlike the evens-on-one-side, odds-on-the-other scheme used in San José. But the scarcity of street signs means everyone uses landmarks anyway. Official red taxis ply the streets or wait at designated taxi stands near Parque Vargas, the Mercado Municipal, and, of course, the cruise-ship terminal.

ESSENTIALS

Bank/ATM BAC San José ⊠ *Avda. 3, Cs. 2–3* ☏ *2798–0155.*
Banco Nacional ⊠ *Avda. 2, Cs. 3–4* ☏ *2758–0094.* **Scotiabank** ⊠ *Avda. 3 and C. 2* ☏ *2798–0009.*

Hospital Hospital Dr. Tony Facio ⊠ *Hwy. to Portete* ☏ *2758–2222.*

Internet nternet Cinco Estrellas ⊠ *50 m north of Terminal de Cruceros* ☏ *2758–5752.*

Pharmacy Farmacia Británica ⊠ *East side of Maxi Bodega* ☏ *2798–1671.*

Post Office Correos ⊠ *Avda. 2 and C. 4.*

Visitor Information APDEVA *(Atlantic Port Authority).* ⊠ *Terminal de Cruceros* ⊕ *www.japdeva.go.cr* ☞ *Accessible to cruise-ship passengers only.*

EXPLORING

Cemetery. On the left side of the highway as you enter Limón is a large cemetery. (A glance as you pass by is really enough.) Notice the "Colonia China" ("Chinese colony") and corresponding sign in Chinese on the hill in the cemetery: Chinese workers made up a large part of the 1880s railroad-construction team that worked here. Thousands died of malaria and yellow fever.

Municipal Market *(Mercado Municipal).* A couple of blocks west of the north side of Parque Vargas is the lively enclosed Municipal Market, where you can buy fruit for the road ahead and experience the sights, sounds, and smells of a Central American market. ⚠ **The hustle and bustle of a crowded market always means a risk of pickpockets. Watch your things.** ⊠ *Pedestrian mall, Avda. 2, Cs. 3–4.*

Parque Vargas. The aquamarine wooden port building faces the cruise terminal, and just to the east lies the city's palm-lined seaside park, Parque Vargas. From the promenade facing the ocean you can see the raised dead coral left stranded by the 1991 earthquake. Nine or so Hoffman's two-toed sloths live in the trees of Parque Vargas; ask a passerby to point them out, as spotting them requires a trained eye.

Standard Fruit Company. The ins and outs of Costa Rica's favorite yellow fruit are on display at this banana plantation and packing plant in Bananito, just south of Limón. The hour-long tour is geared primarily toward cruise passengers. A longer tour takes place at a larger installation near Puerto Viejo de Sarapiquí in northern Costa Rica. Standard Fruit does business as "Dole" in North America. ⊠ *Bananito* ☏ *8383–4596* ⊕ *www.bananatourcostarica.com* ☉ *By appointment.*

Continued on page 539

"It was so awesome to see this huge dorado (mahi-mahi) my husband boated with help from a great first mate." —janenicole, Fodors.com member

SPORTFISHING

by Elizabeth
Goodwin

Adventurous anglers flock to Costa Rica to test their will—and patience—against an assortment of feisty fresh- and saltwater fish. Just remember: catch-and-release is sometimes expected, so the pleasure's all in the pursuit.

With so many options the hardest decision is where to go. Inshore fishing in the country's rivers and lakes yields roosterfish, snapper, barracuda, jacks, and snook. Fly-fishing afficionados love the extra-large tarpon and snook because of their sheer size and fight. The country's coasts swarm with a multitude of bigger game, including the majestic billfish that Hemingway made famous—the marlin and the sailfish.

There are many top-notch fishing outfitters up and down both coasts and around rivers and lakes, so planning a fishing trip is easy. *We list our favorites throughout the book under Sports and the Outdoors.* Charter boats range from 22 feet to 60 feet in length. With a good captain, a boat in the 22- to 26-foot range for up to three anglers can cost from $500 to $800 a day. A 28- to 32-foot boat fits four and costs from $800 to $1,400 per day. A boat for six people costs $1,400 to $1,800 and measures between 36 and 47 feet. A 60-foot boat for up to ten anglers costs about $3,000 a day. A good charter boat company employs experienced captains and offers good equipment, bait, and food and beverages.

CHOOSING A DESTINATION

Costa Rica teems with a constant supply of *pescado* (fish), some of which might seem unique to North Americans. Below are some local catches and where you'll find them.

"A local fisherman in Puerto Viejo."
xelas, fodors.com member.

Barra del Colorado (*See Chapter 9*) is a popular sportfishing hub and a great departure point for freshwater fishing on the Caribbean side of the country. Fly fishers looking for the ultimate challenge head to the **San Juan River** for its legendary tarpon. The **Colorado River** lures anglers with jack, tuna, snook, tarpon, and dorado. Transportation and tours can be arranged by the hotels listed in **Puerto Viejo de Sarapiquí** (*See Chapter 9*).

Lake Arenal and **Caño Negro Lagoon** are also great freshwater spots to snag extra-large tarpon, snook, and the ugly-but-fascinating guapote bass. Start your fishing journey in nearby **La Fortuna** (*See Chapter 5*).

On the Pacific side, **Tamarindo** is the main departure point for anglers looking to find big game, including tuna, roosterfish, and marlin. Boats also leave

from **Playas del Coco, Ocotal, Tambor,** and **Flamingo Beach,** which are best fished May through August *(see Chapter 6)*. All are close to the well-stocked northern Papagayo Gulf. If you're hunting sailfish and marlin between December and April, head to the Central Pacific coast around **Los Sueños** and **Quepos,** where up to 10 sailfish are caught per boat *(See Chapter 7)*. The southern Pacific towns, like **Puerto Jiménez, Golfito,** and **Zancudo,** are less developed than the other Pacific regions and are famous for their excellent inshore fishing for snapper and roosterfish, though offshore big game is also good in the area, especially November through January *(See Chapter 8)*.

FISHING LICENSE

Costa Rica requires that all anglers have a valid Costa Rica fishing license. You can usually pick one up at the dock entrance on the morning of your first day of fishing. Options are: one week ($15), one month ($30), and one year ($50). It's cash only. Most charters do not fold this into their rates because license enforcement is lax and it is occasionally difficult to track down people who sell fishing licenses. Ask about this before you head out.

(top) Osa Peninsula, (bottom left) *Plat de jour* is Wahoo, (bottom right) School of Tarpon

THE FISH YOU'LL FIND

By law billfish are catch-and-release only.

GASPAR (alligator gar), found in Barra del Colorado River and Lake Arenal, look like a holdover from prehistoric times and have long narrow snouts full of sharp teeth; they make great sport on light tackle. Gar meat is firm and sweet (some say shrimplike), but the eggs are toxic to humans.

Snook

MARLIN AND SAILFISH migrate northward through the year, beginning about November, when they are plentiful in the Golfito region. From December into April they spread north to Quepos, which has some of the country's best deep-sea fishing, and are present in large numbers along the Nicoya Peninsula at Carrillo and Sámara from February to April, and near Tamarindo and Flamingo from May to September. Pacific sailfish average more than 45 kilos (100 pounds), and are usually fought on a 15-pound line or less. Costa Rican laws require that all sailfish be released and bans sportsfishers from bringing them on board for photo ops.

Sailfish

GUAPOTE (rainbow bass) make their home in Lake Arenal. It's a hard-hitting catch: 5- to 6-pounders are common. Taxonomically, guapote are not related to bass, but are caught similarly, by casting or flipping plugs or spinner bait. Streams near the Cerro de la Muerte, off the Pan-American Highway leading south from San José, are stocked with guapote. The fish tend to be small, but the scenery makes a day here worthwhile.

TARPON AND SNOOK fishing are big on the Caribbean coast, centered at the mouth of the Barra del Colorado River. The acrobatic tarpon, which averages about 38 kilos (85 pounds) here, is able to swim freely between salt water and freshwater and is considered by many to be the most exciting catch on earth. Tarpon sometimes strike like a rocket, hurtling 5 meters (16 feet) into the air, flipping, and twisting left and right. Anglers say the success rate of experts is to land about 1 out of every 10 tarpon hooked. In the Colorado, schools of up to 100 tarpon following and feeding on schools of titi (small, sardinelike fish) travel for more than 160 km (100 miles) to Lake Nicaragua. The long-standing International Game Fishing Association all-tackle record was taken in this area.

WHEN TO GO

In Costa Rica, you're guaranteed a few good catches no matter what the season, as demonstrated by the cadre of sportsmen who circle the coasts year-round chasing that perfect catch. If your heart is set on an area or a type of fish, do your research ahead of time and plan accordingly.

CLOSE UP

Nicaraguan Immigration to Costa Rica

Immigration issues generate intense debate in the United States and Western Europe. Who would guess that it has become a contentious matter here in Costa Rica, too? Over the past four decades, war, poverty, dictatorship, revolution, earthquakes, and hurricanes have beset Nicaragua, Costa Rica's northern neighbor. Each new calamity has brought a wave of refugees fleeing south. Approximations vary—no one can know for sure—but high-end estimates guess that 20% of Costa Rica's population today is Nicaraguan. Speaking with a faster, more clipped accent than Costa Ricans, they do not fade into the scenery.

The refrain among Ticos is a familiar one: "They're taking our jobs!" Yet, truth be told, Nicaraguans are performing the low-end labor that Costa Ricans just won't do anymore: your hotel chambermaid may likely be Nicaraguan; the glitzy resort where you're staying was probably built with the sweat of many Nicaraguan

construction workers; and the beans that went into that delicious morning cup of Costa Rican java were likely harvested by migrant Nicaraguan coffee pickers.

Relations between Costa Rica and Nicaragua went south in 2011 with Nicaragua's occupation of the 58-square-mile Isla Calero, a Costa Rican island in the San Juan River, which forms the border between the two countries (Nicaragua based its decision to invade on a mistaken designation by Google Maps that Calero was its sovereign territory. Google Maps corrected the error, issuing a statement that its site should not be the arbiter of international boundary disputes.) The standoff continued for months, until the International Court of Justice ruled that the island does indeed belong to Costa Rica. Although relations between Costa Rica and its northern neighbor still remain chilly at this writing, the dispute need not concern you as a visitor.

9

FAMILY **Veragua Rainforest Eco-Adventure.** Limón's hottest attraction is a 4,000-acre nature theme park, about 30 minutes west of the city. It's popular with cruise-ship passengers in port for the day and is well worth a stop if you're in the area. Veragua's great strength is its small army of enthusiastic, super-informed guides who take you through a network of nature trails and exhibits of hummingbirds, snakes, frogs, butterflies, and other insects. A gondola ride overlooks the complex and transports you through the rain-forest canopy. A branch of the Original Canopy Tour, with nine platforms rising 46 meters (150 feet) above the forest floor, is here. The zip-line tour is not included in the basic admission to the park but is priced as an add-on. Packages including transportation (a minimum of two people) can be arranged from San José or Puerto Viejo de Talamanca. ⊠ *Veragua de Liverpool, 15 km (9 miles) west of Limón* ☎ *2296–5056 in San José* ⊕ *www.veraguarainforest.com* ✉ *Full-day tour $66; full-day tour with canopy tour $99; full-day tour with transportation (does not include canopy tour) from San José $149, from Puerto Viejo de Talamanca $99* ☉ *Tues.–Sun. 8–3.*

SPORTS AND THE OUTDOORS

TOUR OPERATORS

Mambo Tour. These folks can take you on three- to eight-hour excursions around the region, and even on an all-day trip to the Rainforest Aerial Tram or San José. ⊠ *Terminal de Cruceros* ☎ *8997–4198* ⊕ *www.mambotour.com.*

SHOPPING

The cruise-ship terminal contains an orderly maze of souvenir stands. Vendors are friendly; there's no pressure to buy.

Congo. The small Congo chain of gift shops has an outlet at the Veragua Rainforest Eco-Adventure park, with a good selection of crafts made by Costa Rican artisans. The shop is accessible only if you've paid admission to the park. ⊠ *Veragua de Liverpool, 15 km (9 miles) west of Limón)* ⊕ *www.costaricacongo.com* ☉ *Tues.–Sun. 9–3.*

CAHUITA

44 km (26 miles) southeast of Limón.

Dusty Cahuita, its main street flanked by wooden-slat cabins, is a backpackers' vacation town—a hippie hangout with a dash of Afro-Caribbean spice tossed in. Tucked in among the backpackers' digs are a few surprisingly nice get-away-from-it-all lodgings, and restaurants with some tasty cuisine at decent prices. After years of negative crime-related publicity, Cahuita has beefed up security—this is one of the few places in the country where you will be conscious of a visible and reassuring, though not oppressive, police presence—and has made a well-deserved comeback on the tourist circuit. No question that nearby Puerto Viejo de Talamanca has overtaken Cahuita and become the hottest spot on the southern Caribbean coast. But as Puerto Viejo grows exponentially, Cahuita's appeal is that it remains small and manageable. It's well worth a look.

GETTING HERE AND AROUND

Autotransportes MEPE buses travel from San José's Terminal Atlántico Norte four times a day, and approximately hourly throughout the day from Limón and Puerto Viejo de Talamanca. Car travel is straightforward: watch for signs in Limón and head 45 minutes south on the coastal highway. Road conditions wax and wane with the severity of the previous year's rains and with the speed at which highway crews patch the potholes. (The road's blacktop surface makes it a never-ending battle.) Cahuita has three entrances from the highway: the first takes you to the far north end of the Playa Negra road, near the Magellan Inn; the second, to the middle section of Playa Negra, near the Atlántida; and the third, to the tiny downtown.

The proximity of the Panamanian border means added police vigilance on the coastal highway. No matter what your mode of transport, expect

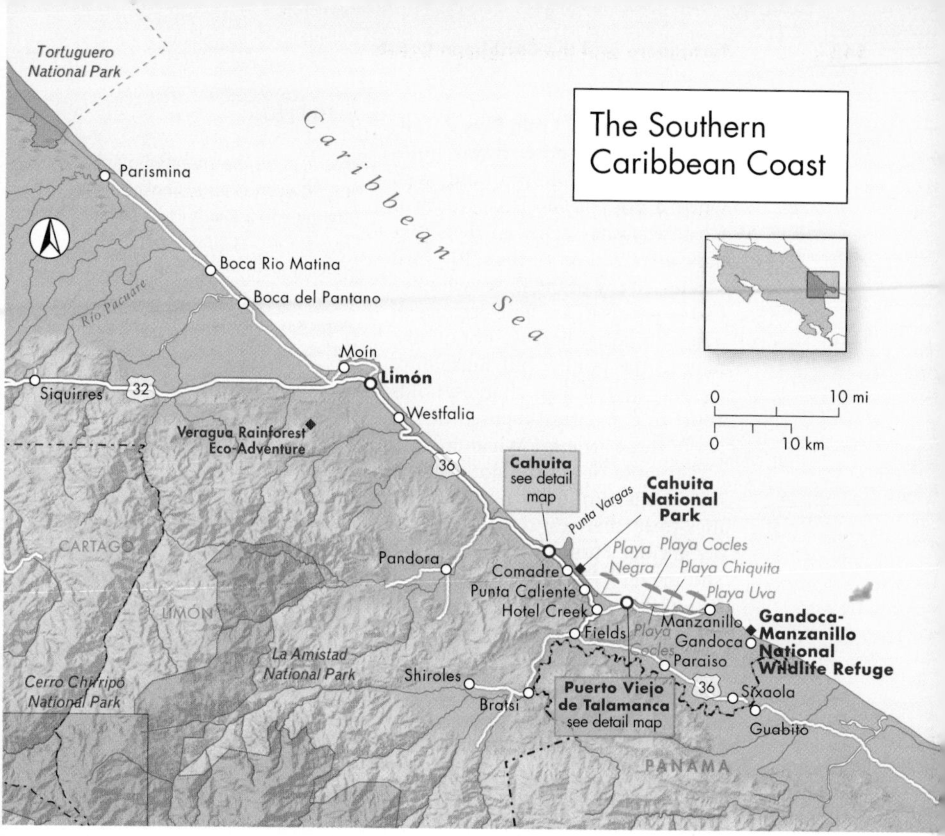
The Southern Caribbean Coast
Tortuguero National Park
Caribbean Sea
Parismina
Boca Rio Matina
Boca del Pantano
Río Pacuare
Moín
Limón
Siquirres
32
Westfalia
Veragua Rainforest Eco-Adventure
36
Cahuita see detail map
Cahuita National Park
Punta Vargas
Playa Negra
Playa Cocles
Playa Chiquita
Playa Uva
CARTAGO
LIMÓN
Pandora
Comadre
Punta Caliente
Hotel Creek
Fields
Manzanillo
Gandoca
Gandoca-Manzanillo National Wildlife Refuge
Paraiso
La Amistad National Park
Cerro Chirripó National Park
Shiroles
Bratsi
Puerto Viejo de Talamanca see detail map
Sixaola
Guabito
PANAMA
0 10 mi
0 10 km

a passport inspection and cursory vehicle search at a police checkpoint just north of Cahuita. If you're on public transportation, you may be required to disembark from the bus while it is searched.

NAVIGATING CAHUITA

Cahuita's tiny center is quite walkable, if dusty in the dry season and muddy in the wet season once you get off the few paved streets. It's about a 30-minute walk to the end of the Playa Negra road to Hotel La Diosa. Take a taxi to or from Playa Negra after dark. Cahuita has a couple of officially licensed red taxis, but most transportation is provided informally by private individuals. To be on the safe side, have your hotel or restaurant call a driver for you.

Bicycles are a popular means of utilitarian transport in Cahuita. Seemingly everyone rents basic touring bikes for $10 per day, but quality varies widely. We recommend Cabinas Brigitte.

ESSENTIALS

Bank/ATM Banco de Costa Rica ✉ *Bus terminal at entrance to town* ☎ *2755–0401.*

Internet Cabinas Palmer Internet ✉ *50 m east of Coco's* ☎ *2755–0435.*

Pharmacy Farmacia Cahuita ✉ *Bus terminal* ☎ *2755–0505.*

Post Office Correos ✉ *Bus terminal.*

EXPLORING

FAMILY

Fodor'sChoice

★

Sloth Sanctuary of Costa Rica. A full-fledged nature center a few miles northwest of Cahuita and well worth a stop, the Sloth Sanctuary of Costa Rica has dense gardens that have attracted more than 300 bird species. Many of the sloths who live on the premises are here because of illness or injury and are not on display to the public, but Buttercup, the very first of their charges, holds

court in the nature-focused gift shop. A visit is a good way to learn about these little-known animals, though numerous requests from visitors to hold or pet the sloths have to be turned down. Your admission includes a two-hour tour—no reservations are needed—and contributes to further research. Advance reservations are required for a special insider's tour that takes you behind the scenes into the sloth clinic and nursery. ✉ *9 km (5 miles) northwest of Cahuita, follow signs on Río Estrella delta* ☎ *2750–0775* ⊕ *www.slothsanctuary.com* ✉ *$25 for tours, $15 ages 5–11, free for ages 4 and under; Insider Tour $150* ☉ *Tues.–Sun. 8–2:30.*

FAMILY   **Tree of Life Wildlife Rescue Center** (*El Árbol de Vida*). Capuchin and howler monkeys, peccaries, sloths, iguanas, raccoons . . . they're all here at this wildlife sanctuary just off the Playa Negra road. As much as possible, the goal is to reintroduce these rescued animals back to nature, although the fragile condition of some means this will be their permanent home. Your admission supports the good work these folks do. ✉ *1 km (½ mile) northwest of town on Playa Negra road* ☎ *2755–0014* ⊕ *www.treeoflifecostarica.com* ✉ *$12 self-guided walk, $20 guided walk; guided walks only, July and Aug.* ☉ *Nov.–mid-Apr., Tues.–Sun. 9–3; July and Aug., Tues.–Sun. guided tour at 11am only* ☉ *Closed mid-Apr.–June, Sept., and Oct.*

BEACHES

Playa Blanca (*White Beach*). Costa Rica's Caribbean coast has no true white-sand beaches, but Cahuita's in-town beach is as close as it gets. Right at the town entrance to the national park, you're a few steps from local eateries. The park's jungle comes right up to the beach's edge, creating one of those postcard-perfect views. The undertow can be strong here; swimmers are more likely to venture out near the center of the beach. Use caution in any case. **Amenities:** food and drink. **Best for:** walking. ✉ *Town center.*

Playa Negra (*Black Beach*). Cahuita's Playa Negra—it's not the same as the beach of the same name in Puerto Viejo de Talamanca—fronts a narrow road heading north out of the town center. Depending on the stretch of sand, it puts you a few steps from eateries. Your fellow beachgoers are likely to be surfers. Remember: the waves that make for good surfing conditions cause problems for swimming. Most stretches of black-sand Playa Negra feel isolated. If there aren't visitors around, don't linger. **Amenities:** food and drink. **Best for:** surfing; walking.

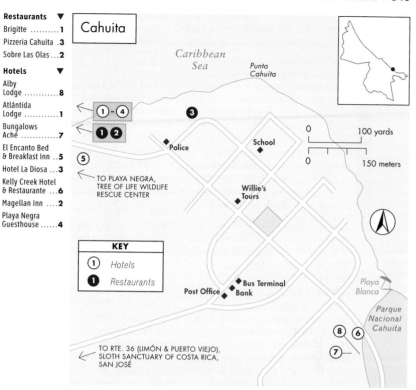

SPORTS AND THE OUTDOORS

Cahuita is small enough that its tour operators don't focus simply on the town and nearby national park, but instead line up excursions around the region, even as far away as the Tortuguero canals to the north and Bocas del Toro, Panama, to the south.

Brigitte. Here you can rent good bikes for $8 per day, as well as take part in a daylong or multiday horse-riding excursiom. ✉ *Playa Negra road, 1½ km (1 mile) from town* ☎ *2755–0053* ⊕ *www.brigittecahuita.com.*

Willie's Tours. The town's largest tour operator can set you up with a variety of adventures, including rafting, kayaking, and visiting indigenous reserves for a glimpse into traditional life. ✉ *Main street, 100 m north of Coco's Bar* ☎ *2755–1024* ⊕ *www.willietourscostarica.com.*

WHERE TO EAT

$ ✕ **Brigitte.** Fuel yourself for the morning at this informal, open-air café
CAFÉ on the Playa Negra road. A hearty breakfast of banana pancakes and fruit with honey or pineapple jam does the trick. *Gallo pinto* is on the menu, though most travelers have had their fill of that ubiquitous dish by the time they get to the Caribbean. Omelets, toast, and American-style cereals round out the offerings. **$** *Average main: $6* ✉ *Playa Negra road, 1½ km (1 mile) from town* ☎ *2755–0053* ⊕ *www.brigittecahuita. com* ⊘ *No lunch or dinner.*

9

CLOSE UP

The Old Atlantic Railroad

Christopher Columbus became the Caribbean's (and the country's) first tourist when he landed at Uvita Island near Limón during his fourth voyage to the New World in 1502. But the region was already home to thriving, if small, communities of Kekoldi, Bribri, and Cabécar indigenous peoples. If Costa Rica was an isolated backwater, its Caribbean coastal region remained even more remote from colonial times through most of the 19th century.

New York industrialist Minor Keith changed all that in 1871 with his plan to launch the British-funded Atlantic Railroad, a mode of transportation that would permit easier export of coffee and bananas to Europe. Such a project required a massive labor force, and thousands of West Indians, Asians, and Italians were brought to Costa Rica to construct the 522-km (335-mile) railroad from Limón to San José. Thousands are reputed to have died of yellow fever, malaria, and snakebite during construction of the project. Those who survived were paid relatively well, however, and by the 1930s many Afro-Caribbean residents owned their own small plots of land. When the price of cacao rose in the 1950s, they emerged as comfortable landowners. Not that they had much choice about going elsewhere: until the Civil War of 1948, black Costa Ricans were forbidden from crossing into the Central Valley lest they upset the country's racial balance, and they were thus prevented from moving when United Fruit abandoned many of its blight-ridden northern Caribbean plantations in the 1930s for green-field sites on the Pacific plain.

Costly upkeep of rail service, construction of the Braulio Carrillo Highway to the coast, declining banana production, and an earthquake that rocked the region in 1991 all sounded the death knell for the railroad. The earthquake was also a wake-up call for many here. The long lag time for aid to reach stricken areas symbolized the central government's historic neglect of the region. Development has been slow to reach this part of the country. As elsewhere in the country, communities now look to tourism to put colones in the coffers. San José has resurrected commuter-rail service within the metro area, and a few folks out here hold out faint hopes that Caribbean train service will start up once again, but that's likely a long way off.

$ PIZZA 🍴 **Pizzeria Cahuita.** Pastas and meat entrées are on the menu, but the real draw here is the 30 varieties of thin-crust pizza whipped up and served with style by a gregarious Italian family from Ravenna. The Cuatro Quesos ("four cheeses") with mozzarella, Gorgonzola, Parmesan, and fontina is the most popular. (Pizza is available only after 4 pm.) These folks do a brisk delivery business to Cahuita hotels, too. [$] *Average main: $9* ✉ *50 m east of police station* ☎ *2755–0179* 💳 *No credit cards* 🕒 *No lunch Mon.–Wed.*

$$ SEAFOOD 🍴 **Sobre Las Olas.** The name means "over the waves," and this is one of the few dining spots in Cahuita perched this close to the shore. Set along the less busy stretch of Playa Negra (as you head out of town), the dining area features terrific ocean views that perfectly complement the house specialty, red snapper, as well as a variety of other seafood and

pasta dishes. Lunch includes sandwiches and lighter fare. The menu includes a good selection of wine and natural fruit juices. [$] *Average main: $11* ✉ *Playa Negra road, just north of El Encanto* ☎ *2755–0109* 🕓 *Closed Tues.*

A TOWN THAT WON'T LET YOU DOWN

Cahuita's first tourist of note was Costa Rican president Alfredo González, whose boat shipwrecked on this stretch of coast in 1915. The president was so grateful for the aid settlers gave him that he purchased a tract of land here and donated it to them to construct a town.

WHERE TO STAY

$ B&B/INN 🏨 **Alby Lodge.** You're right in town but you'd never know it at this friendly lodging, which has cabins propped up on stilts, with hardwood floors, hot-water baths, log tables, mosquito nets, and a hammock on the front porch. **Pros:** central location; friendly staff. **Cons:** spartan rooms; large dogs onsite. [$] *Rooms from: $60* ✉ *180 m west of national park entrance* ☎ *2755–0031* 🌐 *www.albylodge.com* 🛏 *4 cabins* 💳 *No credit cards* 🍴 *No meals.*

$ HOTEL 🏨 **Atlántida Lodge.** Attractively landscaped grounds, the beach across the road, and a large pool are Atlántida's main assets. **Pros:** good value; decent pool. **Cons:** some dark rooms; lackluster staff. [$] *Rooms from: $60* ✉ *Next to soccer field at Playa Negra* ☎ *2755–0115* 🌐 *www.atlantida.cr* 🛏 *32 rooms, 2 suites* 💳 *No credit cards* 🍴 *No meals.*

$ B&B/INN 🏨 **Bungalows Aché.** Like Alby Lodge next door, Aché scatters wooden bungalows—three octagonal structures in this case—around wooded grounds that make the close-by town center seem far away. **Pros:** central location; friendly staff. **Cons:** small rooms; spartan rooms. [$] *Rooms from: $50* ✉ *180 m west of national park entrance* ☎ *2755–0119* 🌐 *www.bungalowsache.com* 🛏 *3 bungalows* 💳 *No credit cards* 🍴 *No meals.*

$$ B&B/INN Fodor's Choice ★ 🏨 **El Encanto Bed & Breakfast Inn.** Cahuita doesn't get more serene than these bungalows scattered around a garden with an extensive bromeliad collection and Buddha figures. **Pros:** friendly owners; good value; central location without being right in the heart of things. **Cons:** not for young travelers looking for a scene. [$] *Rooms from: $85* ✉ *200 m west of police station on Playa Negra road* ☎ *2755–0113* 🌐 *www.elencantocahuita.com* 🛏 *9 rooms* 🍴 *Breakfast.*

$ HOTEL 🏨 **Hotel La Diosa.** The owners' interest in Eastern religions is evidenced in the hotel's name (*La Diosa* means "goddess") and by the sign depicting a Hindu goddess, but all are welcome here at this place on the far north end of Playa Negra. **Pros:** seclusion; air-conditioning available. **Cons:** far from sights; small rooms. [$] *Rooms from: $70* ✉ *2 km (1 mile) north of town at end of Playa Negra road* ☎ *2755–0055, 800/854–7761 in North America* 🌐 *www.hotelladiosa.com* 🛏 *10 cabins* 🍴 *Breakfast.*

$ B&B/INN 🏨 **Kelly Creek Hotel & Restaurante.** Here's a wonderful budget option in a handsome wooden hotel with a terrific Spanish restaurant on the creek bank across a short pedestrian bridge from the park entrance. **Pros:** good value; terrific Spanish restaurant; friendly owners. **Cons:** dark rooms; occasional, but rare, street noise. [$] *Rooms from: $55* ✉ *Next to park entrance* ☎ *2755–0007* 🌐 *www.hotelkellycreek.com* 🛏 *4 rooms* 🍴 *No meals.*

$ ▦ **Magellan Inn.** One of Cahuita's most elegant lodgings, this group
B&B/INN of bungalows is graced with tile-floor terraces facing a pool and gardens growing on an ancient coral reef. **Pros:** seclusion; good value;
scrumptious dinners. **Cons:** far from sights; staff can be too business-
like. $ *Rooms from: $60 ⊠2 km (1 mile) north of town at end of
Playa Negra road* ☎2755–0035 ⊕ *www.magellaninn.com* ⟲6 rooms
¶⊙¶ *Breakfast.*

$ ▦ **Playa Negra Guesthouse.** This gracious, Québécois-owned lodging set
HOTEL in lush, hibiscus-strewn gardens has become our favorite place to stay
Fodor'sChoice in Cahuita. **Pros:** stylish surroundings; attentive owners; terrific rates
★ for what's offered. **Cons:** friendly dogs on-site, but not a place to stay
if you're not a canine lover. $ *Rooms from: $75 ⊠ Playa Negro road,
50 m north of soccer field* ☎2755–0127 ⊕ *www.playanegra.cr* ⟲4
rooms, 3 cottages ¶⊙¶ *Breakfast.*

NIGHTLIFE

Aside from a local bar or two, Cahuita's nightlife centers on restaurants,
all pleasant places to linger over dinner for the evening.

Chao's Paradise. If you're out this way, Chao's makes for a pleasant,
open-air space for a beer and some seafood and fries. After dark, take
a taxi to and from. ⊠ *Playa Negra road, 50 m north of soccer field*
☎2755–00284 ⊙ *Daily noon–10 pm.*

Coco's Bar. Lively reggae, soca, and samba blast weekend evenings
from the turquoise Coco's Bar. The assemblage of dogs dozing on
its veranda illustrates the rhythm of local life. ⊠ *Main road* ⊕ *www.
cocosbarcahuita.com* ⊙ *Daily noon–11 pm.*

Cocorico. Italian eatery Cocrico shows movies on DVD many evenings
at 7:30. ⊠ *Main road* ⊙ *Wed.–Mon. 4 pm–11 pm.*

Ricky's Bar. Quieter than Coco's across the street (although if Coco's
is hosting live music, you'll hear it from here, too), Ricky's is a good
place to kick back with a beer and watch the passing parade on the
main street. It's "Ricky's" or "Riki's," depending on which sign you
look at. ⊠ *Main road.*

CAHUITA NATIONAL PARK

Just south of Cahuita.

GETTING HERE AND AROUND

Choose from two park entrances: one is at the southern end of the village of Cahuita; the other is at Puerto Vargas, just off the main road,
5 km (3 miles) south of town. If you don't have a car, you can get here
easily via bike or taxi.

EXPLORING

Cahuita National Park (*Parque Nacional Cahuita*). One of Costa Rica's
most popular national parks begins at the southern edge of the town of
Cahuita. Its rain forest extends right to the edge of its curving, utterly
undeveloped 3-km (2-mile) white-sand beach. (Let's call it a "whitish-
sand beach.") The park was created to protect the 2½-square-km
(1-square-mile) coral reef that encircles the coast and offers excellent

Wildlife watching in Cahuita National Park

snorkeling off Cahuita Point. Trails into the rain forest reveal howler and white-faced capuchin monkeys, coatimundis, armadillos, and raccoons. As is the case on this coast, you can expect rain here no matter what the time of year. February through April and September and October are drier months, and offer the best visibility for snorkeling. ⊠ *Southern end of Cahuita* ☎ *2755–0461 Cahuita entrance, 2755–0302 Puerto Vargas entrance* ☒ *$5* ☉ *Daily 6–5 Cahuita entrance, daily 7–4 Puerto Vargas entrance.*

SPORTS AND THE OUTDOORS

TOUR OPERATORS

Operators in Cahuita or Puerto Viejo de Talamanca can hook you up with excursions to and in the park, or you can go on your own, especially if you use the entrance at the south edge of the village.

SNORKELING

Cahuita's reefs are just one of several high-quality snorkeling spots in the region. Rent snorkeling gear in Cahuita or Puerto Viejo de Talamanca or through your hotel; most hotels also organize trips. It's wise to work with a guide, as the number of good snorkeling spots is limited and they're not always easily accessible. Cahuita established a community lifeguard team in 2002, unusual in Costa Rica. ■ TIP→ As elsewhere up and down the Caribbean coast, the undertow poses risks for even experienced swimmers. Use extreme caution and never swim alone.

PUERTO VIEJO DE TALAMANCA

16 km (10 miles) south of Cahuita.

This muddy, colorful little town is one of the hottest spots on the international budget-travel circuit, and swarms with surfers, New Age hippies, beaded and spangled punks, would-be Rastafarians of all colors and descriptions, and wheelers and dealers—both pleasant and otherwise. Time was when most kids came here with only one thing on their mind: surfing. Today many seem to be looking for a party, with or without the surf.

But if alternative lifestyles aren't your bag, there are plenty of more "grown-up" offerings on the road heading southeast and northwest out of town. At last count, some 50 nationalities were represented in this tiny community, and most are united in concern for the environment and orderly development of tourism. (Few want to see the place become just another Costa Rican resort community.) Some locals bemoan the loss of their town's innocence, as drugs and other evils have surfaced, but this is still a fun town to visit, with a great variety of hotels, cabinas, and restaurants in every price range. Unlike some other parts of Costa Rica, no one has been priced out of the market here.

Locals use "Puerto Viejo"—British settlers called the area "Old Harbour"—to refer to the village. They drop the "de Talamanca" part; we use the complete name to avoid confusion with the other Puerto Viejo: Puerto Viejo de Sarapiquí in northern Costa Rica. (Note that you may also see this Caribbean town referred to as "Puerto Viejo de Limón.") You have access to the beach right in town, and the Salsa Brava, famed in surfers' circles for its pounding waves, is here off the coast, too. The best strands of Caribbean sand are outside the village: Playa Cocles, Playa Chiquita (technically a series of beaches), and Punta Uva, all dark-sand beaches, line the road heading southeast from town. Playa Negra—not the Playa Negra near Cahuita—is the black-sand beach northwest of town. Punta Uva, with fewer hotels and the farthest from the village, sees fewer crowds and more tranquility. Playa Negra shares that distinction, too—for now—but developers have eyed the beach as the next area for expansion.

GETTING HERE AND AROUND

The turnoff to Puerto Viejo de Talamanca is 10 km (6 miles) down the coastal highway south of Cahuita. (The highway itself continues south to Bribri and Sixaola at the Panamanian border.) The village lies another 5 km (3 miles) beyond the turnoff. The paved road passes through town and continues to Playas Cocles and Chiquita and Punta Uva before the pavement peters out at the entrance to the village of Manzanillo. "Periodically potholed" describes the condition of the road from the highway into town and as far as Playa Cocles. The newer paved sections beyond Cocles haven't disintegrated . . . yet. Autotransportes MEPE buses travel from San José's Terminal Atlántico Norte four times a day, and approximately hourly throughout the day from Limón and Cahuita. All buses from San José go into Puerto Viejo de Talamanca; most, though not all, Limón-originating buses do as well, but a couple drop you off on the highway. Check if you board in Limón.

Local buses ply the 15-km (9-mile) paved road between Puerto Viejo and Manzanillo every two hours during the day. Unless your schedule meshes exactly with theirs, you're better off biking or taking a taxi to and from the far-flung beaches along the way. Taxis charge $6 to Playa Cocles (as well as north to Playa Negra), $10 to Playa Chiquita, $12 to Punta Uva, and $18 to Manzanillo.

NAVIGATING PUERTO VIEJO DE TALAMANCA You can manage the town center quite easily on foot, though it is dusty in the dry season and muddy when it rains. (The main street is, thankfully, paved.) Everyone gets around by bike here, and seemingly everyone has one for rent. Quality varies widely, but we recommend renting from Cabinas Grant or Casa Verde Lodge. Expect to pay $10 per day for a good bike.

Cabinas Grant. Here you'll find the best selection of quality bikes in town. ✉ *100 m south of bus stop* ☎ *2750–0292.*

Casa Verde Lodge. Priority is given to guests at Casa Verde Lodge, but they usually have extra bikes nonguests can rent for a half or full day. ✉ *200 m south and 200 m east of bus stop* ☎ *2750–0015.*

Electric Bikes Costa Rica. Although its bicycles are not available to rent on your own, Electric Bikes offers two-wheeled tours around the area on battery-charged bikes. ☎ *8646–3164* ⊕ *www.ebikescr.com.*

ESSENTIALS

Bank/ATM Banco de Costa Rica ✉ *50 m south of bridge at entrance to town* ☎ *2750–0707.* **Banco Nacional** ✉ *25 m south of Correos.*

Internet ATEC (*Talamancan Association of Ecotourism and Conservation*). ✉ *Across from Restaurant Tamara* ☎ *2750–0191* ⊕ *www.ateccr.org.*
Café Internet Río Negro ✉ *Playa Cocles, 4 km (2½ miles) southeast of Puerto Viejo* ☎ *2750–0801.*

Pharmacy Farmacia Caribe ✉ *Next to Banco de Costa Rica* ☎ *2750–0698.*

Post Office Correos ✉ *Next to Banco de Costa Rica.*

Visitor Information ATEC (*Talamancan Association of Ecotourism and Conservation*). ✉ *Across from Restaurant Tamara* ☎ *2750–0191* ⊕ *www.ateccr.org.*

EXPLORING

FAMILY **Chocorart.** Cacao once ruled the Talamanca region, but few plantations are left these days. One friendly Swiss couple continues the tradition and shows you the workings of their chocolate plantation on their Chocorart chocolate tour. Follow the little-known life cycle of this

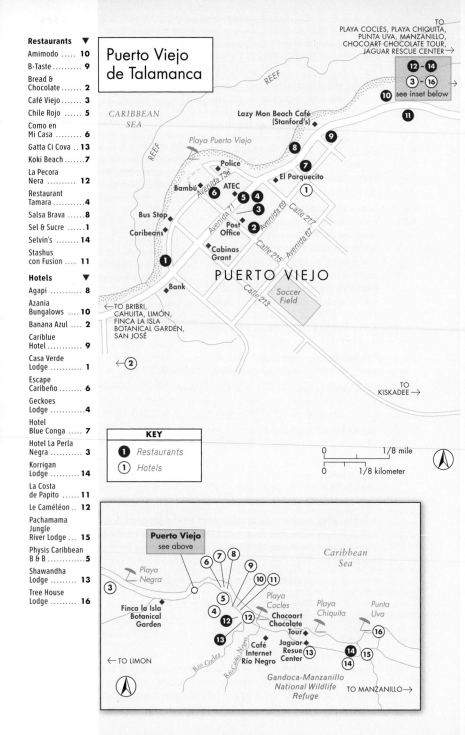

Puerto Viejo de Talamanca

TO
PLAYA COCLES, PLAYA CHIQUITA,
PUNTA UVA, MANZANILLO,
CHOCOART CHOCOLATE TOUR,
JAGUAR RESCUE CENTER →

12 – 14
3 – 16
see inset below

CARIBBEAN
SEA

REEF

REEF

Lazy Mon Beach Café
(Stanford's)

Playa Puerto Viejo

Police

Bambú

ATEC

El Parquecito

Bus Stop

Caribeans

Post
Office

Cabinas
Grant

PUERTO VIEJO

Bank

Soccer
Field

Avenida 73m
Avenida 71
Avenida 69
Avenida 67
Calle 217
Calle 215
Calle 213

← TO BRIBRI,
CAHUITA, LIMÓN,
FINCA LA ISLA
BOTANICAL GARDEN,
SAN JOSÉ

TO
KISKADEE →

KEY

① *Restaurants*
① *Hotels*

0   1/8 mile
0   1/8 kilometer

Puerto Viejo
see above

Caribbean
Sea

Playa
Negra

Finca la Isla
Botanical
Garden

Playa
Cocles

Chocoart
Chocolate
Tour

Playa
Chiquita

Punta
Uva

Café
Internet
Río Negro

Jaguar
Resue
Center

Río Cocles

Río Cocles Nuevo

Gandoca-Manzanillo
National Wildlife
Refuge

← TO LIMON

TO MANZANILLO →

crop from cultivation to processing. There's sampling at the tour's
conclusion. Call or email to reserve
a tour. Since these folks are Swiss,
they can tailor the commentary in
German, French, or Italian, in addition to English or Spanish. ⊠ *6 km
(4 miles) southeast of Puerto Viejo
at Playa Chiquita* ☎ *2750–0075*
✍ *chocorart@racsa.co.cr* ✉ *$25
per person* ⊙ *By appointment.*

Finca la Isla Botanical Garden (*Jardín
Botánico Finca La Isla*). At the
Finca la Isla Botanical Garden, you can explore a working tropical-
fruit, spice, and ornamental-plant farm. Sloths abound, and you might
see a few poison dart frogs. A $10 guided tour lasts two hours—there is
a three-person minimum, and tours must be reserved in advance—and
includes admission and a glass of the farm's homemade fruit juice. You
get the fruit juice if you wander around on your own, too—a $1 self-
guided-tour book is available in English, Spanish, French, and German.
Watch the demonstration showing how cacao beans are turned into
chocolate, and sample some of the product at the end of the tour. ⊠ *½
km (¼ mile) west of Puerto Viejo at Playa Negra* ☎ *8886–8530* ✉ *$6,
guided tour $10* ⊙ *Fri.–Mon. 10–4.*

FAMILY **Jaguar Rescue Center** (*Jaguar Centro de Rescate*). Many regard a visit to
the Jaguar Rescue Center as the highlight of their trip to Puerto Viejo.
The name is a bit misleading. The original rescued animal here was
an orphaned, injured jaguar cub that ultimately did not survive. His
memory lives on in the facility's name, even if there are no other jaguars
on-site. Primarily howler monkeys, sloths, and lots of snakes make up
the charges of the good folks here. The goal, of course, is to return the
animals to the wild, although, for some, their fragile condition means
this will end up being their permanent home. Your admission fee for
the 90-minute tour (English or Spanish) helps fund the work here. ⊠ *3
km (2 miles) southeast of Puerto Viejo between Playa Cocles and Playa
Chiquita* ☎ *2750–0710* ⊕ *www.jaguarrescue.com* ✉ *$15, free for kids
under 10* ⊙ *Mon.–Sat. tours at 9:30 and 11:30. Closed Sun.*

BEACHES

Playa Chiquita. Nothing against Puerto Viejo, but the farther you get
from town, the quieter things get. (Quite frankly, the "riff-raff" factor thins out out here.) The downside is that you'll find fewer visitors
congregating on dark-sand Chiquita and isolated stretches of beach
can spell trouble. Stay only if you see a lot of other people around. The
undertow is still a problem out here. Swim only at your risk, and don't
venture out too far. **Amenities:** none. **Best for:** surfing; walking. ⊠ *6 km
(4 miles) southeast of Puerto Viejo de Talamanca.*

Playa Cocles. The sand gets a bit lighter and the crowd slightly more
upscale—this is still Puerto Viejo, though—a couple of kilometers outside of town. Fewer vendors will pester you here than in the town itself,

9

and it'll be mostly you and other travelers. (If there's nobody around, don't linger. There's always safety in numbers.) As with all Puerto Viejo–area beaches, the undertow can be strong on Cocles. Never venture out too far. **Amenities:** food and drink. **Best for:** partiers; surfing. ⊠ *2 km (1 mile) southeast of Puerto Viejo de Talamanca.*

Playa Negra (*Black Beach*). Not to be confused with Cahuita's beach of the same name, Puerto Viejo's black-sand Playa Negra lies close to town but is relatively undeveloped. That situation is expected to change in coming years, but, for now, you'll likely have this stretch of sand north of town to yourself. Be careful about going into the water; the undertow can be strong. **Amenities:** none. **Best for:** surfing; walking. ⊠ *1 km (½ mile) north of Puerto Viejo de Talamanca.*

Playa Puerto Viejo. You can do much better than Puerto Viejo's unnamed, in-town, cluttered, dark-sand beach. Locals, friendly and occasionally a bit sketchy, gather here. The strong undertow makes swimming risky along this stretch, but surfers delight in the consistently good waves. The upside is that you're just a few steps from the in-town restaurants. **Amenities:** food and drink. **Best for:** partiers; surfing. ⊠ *In town.*

Punta Uva. The area's most beautiful beach—with dark sand like all the area strands—lies a long way from Puerto Viejo and offers splendid isolation from the commotion of town. "Uva" means "grape" in Spanish, and the beach gets its name from the sea grape trees found out here. A few nearby restaurants can take care of your culinary needs. As always here, there's the undertow to contend with. Be careful and never venture too far out into the water. **Amenities:** food and drink. **Best for:** surfing; walking. ⊠ *9 km (5½ miles) south of Puerto Viejo de Talamanca.*

SPORTS AND THE OUTDOORS

TOUR OPERATORS

As in Cahuita, tour operators and outfitters here can set up tours and activities anywhere on the south Caribbean coast.

ATEC (*Talamancan Association of Ecotourism and Conservation*). Tours with ATEC have an environmental or cultural bent, such as Afro-Caribbean or indigenous-culture walks—tours to the nearby Kekoldi indigenous reserve are especially popular—rain-forest hikes, coral-reef snorkeling trips, fishing trips, bird-watching tours, night walks, and adventure treks. Local organizations and wildlife refuges receive 15% to 20% of ATEC's proceeds. ⊠ *Across from Restaurant Tamara* ☎ 2750–0191 ⊕ *www.ateccr.org.*

Terraventuras. Well-established operator Terraventuras can lead you around Puerto Viejo de Talamanca and Cahuita, or take you on excursions to Tortuguero, the Gandoca-Manzanillo Wildlife Refuge, and Bocas del Toro in Panama. It also rents good-quality surfboards, bicycles, boogie boards, and snorkeling gear. ⊠ *100 m south of bus stop* ☎ 2750–0750 ⊕ *www.terraventuras.com.*

RAFTING

Exploradores Outdoors. Rafting excursions lie about two hours away, but one San José–based outfitter has an office here. Exploradores Outdoors is highly regarded and has one- or two-day excursions on the Pacuare River, with a pickup point here or in San José, and the option to start in one place and be dropped off at the other. The outfitter also offers sea-kayaking

CLOSE UP

Reefs at Risk

One of the most complex organisms in the marine world, a coral reef is an extraordinary and extraordinarily delicate habitat. Coral reefs are the result of the symbiotic relationship between single-cell organisms called zooxanthellae and coral polyps. The zooxanthellae grow inside the cells of the polyps, producing oxygen and nutrients that are released into the coral tissues. Corals secrete calcium carbonate (limestone) that, over time, forms the vast coral reef "superstructure." Zooxanthellae require exposure to sunlight to thrive. The healthiest coral reefs are in clear, clean, tropical seawater at a temperature of 20°C to 25°C (70°F to 80°F). Healthy coral reefs are biologically rich gardens occupied by a diverse selection of life forms, from microscopic unicellular algae and phytoplankton to a wide range of fish.

Unfortunately, coral reefs in Costa Rica are in danger. Dirt and sediment from banana plantations and logging areas, as well as runoff from pesticide use, are killing them. The dirty runoff literally clogs the pores of the zooxanthellae and smothers them. In the southern Pacific coast's Golfo Dulce, 98% of one of the oldest reefs in Costa Rica has been destroyed by this sedimentation. Many of the once-enormous reefs of Cahuita are almost entirely gone.

Human visitors, including careless snorkelers, have also damaged reefs. Simply touching a reef damages it. When exploring a coral reef, look but don't touch, and snorkel only on its outer side, preferably in calm weather. Can the reefs be saved? With commitment and time, yes. Coral is resilient, and will grow back—if the Costa Rican government makes it a priority.

---

excursions off the coast of the Gandoca-Manzanillo Wildlife Refuge. ✉ *100 m east of Lazy Mon Beach Café (aka Stanford's)* ☎ *2750–2020, 2222–6262 in San José* ⊕ *www.exploradoresoutdoors.com.*

SURFING

Surfing is the name of the game in Puerto Viejo, for everyone from newbies to Kelly Slaters. The best conditions are late December through March, but there's action all year. Longtime surfers compare the south Caribbean with Hawaii, but without the "who-do-you-think-you-are?" attitude. There are a number of breaks here, most famously **Salsa Brava**, which translates to "wild sauce." It breaks fairly far offshore and requires maneuvering past some tricky currents and a shallow reef. Hollow and primarily right breaking, Salsa Brava is one gnarly wave when it gets big. If it gets *too* big, or not big enough, check out the breaks at Punta Uva, Punta Cocles, or Playa Chiquita. Boogie boarders and bodysurfers can also dig the beach-break waves at various points along this tantalizingly beautiful coast.

Aventuras Bravas. If you've always wanted to try surfing, consider the friendly, two-hour $50 surf school at Aventuras Bravas. You start out with a small wave near the bus stop, and get a money-back guarantee that you'll be standing by the end of the lesson. (A two-hour private lesson will run you $60.) You can also rent equipment here. ✉ *Inside Rockin' J's hostel, 1 km (½ mile) southeast of Lazy Mon Beach Café (aka Stanford's)* ☎ *2750–0626* ⊕ *www.braveadventure.net.*

WHERE TO EAT

$$ ITALIAN 🍴 **Amimodo.** The name translates to "my way," and the exuberant Italian owners really do it their way, combining the cuisine of their native northern Italy with Caribbean flavors. Your antipasto might be classic bruschetta or *jamón de tiburón* (shark ham with avocado dressing), and your ravioli might be stuffed with tropical shrimp, pineapple, and curry, with avocado sauce on the side. The tropical veranda with gingerbread trim spills over onto the beach with abundant greenery, and the restaurant is a popular gathering place for Puerto Viejo's Italian community. [$] *Average main: $12* ✉ *200 m east of Lazy Mon Beach Café (aka Stanford's)* ☎ *2750–0257.*

$ BELGIAN 🍴 **B-Taste.** The "B" at this simple, open-air place with a couple of umbrella-covered tables outside stands for "Belgium," the owners' native land. They describe their offerings as "Belgian preparation with Costa Rican product." Kick off the day over a breakfast of large, thin Belgian pancakes smothered with fruit or honey. Lunch gives way to specialties such as *croque-monsieur* (grilled ham-and-cheese sandwich). If you opt for dinner here, make it an early one; the place closes at 8. [$] *Average main: $7* ✉ *Across from Lazy Mon Beach Café (aka Stanford's)* ☎ *8649–16162* 💳 *No credit cards* 🕑 *Closed Mon.*

$ CAFÉ 🍴 **Bread & Chocolate.** The takeaway line for brownies forms at the gate before this place opens at 6:30 am, but stick around and fortify yourself with a hearty breakfast of cinnamon-oatmeal pancakes, French toast, or creamy scrambled eggs, washed down with a cup of French-press coffee. Lunch brings jerk chicken, roasted red peppers, and chocolate truffles. Everything is homemade, right down to the mayonnaise. This is one of several bakery-slash-breakfast-and-lunch cafés open in town; the friendly owner gives this place the edge. [$] *Average main: $5* ✉ *50 m south of post office* ☎ *2750–0723* 💳 *No credit cards* 🕑 *Closed Tues. May–Nov. No dinner.*

$ ITALIAN 🍴 **Café Viejo.** This is the hot place to see and be seen on Puerto Viejo's main drag. The owners learned to cook at the knee of their Italian grandmother back in Rimini, and have concocted a menu, several pages long, of pizzas and handmade pastas. Recorded reggae and mambo music bops in the background. [$] *Average main: $8* ✉ *Across from ATEC* ☎ *2750–0817* 🌐 *www.cafeviejo.net* 🕑 *Closed Tues. No lunch.*

$ THAI 🍴 **Chile Rojo.** There's not a thing about the name or furnishings to reflect its Thai and Middle-Eastern offerings, but this restaurant does a brisk business. Choose from Thai grilled tuna, falafel, hummus, and samosas. Sushi is available on Saturday. The spacious, open second-floor setting catches the breezes and lets you watch the passersby down below. [$] *Average main: $9* ✉ *Across from ATEC* ☎ *2750–0319* 💳 *No credit cards* 🕑 *Closed Mon.*

$ VEGETARIAN 🍴 **Como en Mi Casa.** Everything is made on-site at this small, second-floor café. Start off the day with an order of vegan pancakes or ease into lunch with veggie burritos and a tomato-oregano-olive oil bruschetta. Bopping tunes create an upbeat atmosphere, and there is a nice balcony for dining outdoors. [$] *Average main: $5* ✉ *100 m east of bus stop* ☎ *6069–6319* 🕑 *Closed Wed. No dinner.*

$$ ✕ **Gatta Ci Cova.** Chef-owner Ilario
ITALIAN Giannoni strolls the 100 meters
over from his La Pecora Nera res-
taurant to watch over his other
baby here. The restaurant, whose
name comes from an Italian
expression meaning "things kept
secret," provides a less-formal,
less-expensive alternative to the
original, but still has all the flair
and all the fun. Lunch offerings
focus on the $10 *plato del día*, a
bargain with appetizer, salad, a

rotating selection of pastas, dessert, and a glass of wine. $ *Aver-
age main: $12* ✉ *3 km (2 miles) southeast of town at Playa Cocles*
☎ *2750–0730* ☾ *Closed Mon.*

$$ ✕ **Koki Beach.** This slightly elevated terrace restaurant with colorful fur-
ECLECTIC niture (and colorful characters) is visible to all who walk by. The trad-
eoff for being on display while you eat is the chance to watch Puerto
Viejo's parade of evening passersby and the ocean waves lapping on
the beach across the street. The mostly surf-and-turf menu means lots
of shrimp and sea bass and lots of beef and chicken, all served on or
off skewers according to your preference. A great selection of drinks
rounds out the offerings. Live music gets underway many evenings,
usually in the later hours. $ *Average main: $12* ✉ *100 m west of
Lazy Mon Beach Café (aka Stanford's)* ☎ *2750–0902* ⊕ *kokibeach.
blogspot.com* ☾ *No lunch.*

$$$ ✕ **La Pecora Nera.** Though the name means "black sheep" in Italian,
ITALIAN there's nothing shameful about this thatch-roof roadside restaurant.
Fodor's Choice There's always a lot more to choose from than you'll see on the sparse-
★ looking menu. Wait for owner/chef Ilario Giannoni to come out of the
kitchen and triumphantly announce—with flair worthy of an Italian
opera—which additional light Tuscan entrées, appetizers, and desserts
they've concocted that day. Be prepared for a long, leisurely dining
experience with attentive service. It's worth the wait; this is one of
the country's top Italian restaurants. $ *Average main: $22* ✉ *3 km
(2 miles) southeast of town at Playa Cocles* ☎ *2750–0490* ☾ *Closed
Mon. No lunch.*

$ ✕ **Restaurant Tamara.** Once upon a time, this unpretentious two-story
CARIBBEAN place was the only restaurant in town. The Caribbean food is tasty
and authentic: you can't lose with the chicken in Caribbean sauce or
virtually any of the fresh fish dishes. In the nondescript indoor seating
area you're cooled by a fan and entertained by TV; the outdoor seating
area has a palpable Jamaican motif and is a great place for people-
watching. $ *Average main: $8* ✉ *Across from ATEC* ☎ *2750–0148*
☾ *Closed Tues. May–Nov.*

$ ✕ **Salsa Brava.** The restaurant overlooking the Salsa Brava break—with
SEAFOOD sublime surf vistas—has taken the name of this famed surfing spot. Opt
for casual counter service or grab a seat at one of the colorful beach-
side tables. Lunch centers on grilled fish and meat. Try the red snapper

9

prepared in olive oil, garlic, and cayenne pepper—it's a specialty. $ *Average main: $8* ⊠ *100 m east of Lazy Mon Beach Café (aka Stanford's)* ☎ *2750–0241* ▭ *No credit cards* ☉ *Closed Mon. and Tues.*

$

FRENCH

✕ **Sel & Sucre.** The *sel* (salt) in this restaurant's name reflects the ham, chicken, spinach, goat cheese, and roasted almonds you'll find as ingredients in a huge selection of crepes. *Sucre* (sugar) shows up in the sweet versions of crepes, with the Grand Marnier a special standout. Light side salads, waffles, and cheese fondue round out the menu. Top it all off with a gourmet coffee or fruit smoothie. $ *Average main: $5* ⊠ *120 m south of bus stop* ☎ *2750–0636* ⊕ *www.seletsucrecr.com* ☉ *Closed Mon.*

$

CARIBBEAN

✕ **Selvin's.** An old standby at Punta Uva, Selvin's keeps limited, sometimes irregular, hours, especially in the off-season, so head out here if you're fortunate enough to be in town when it's open. (Always call ahead.) The owner, known to everyone in town as "Blanca," cooks up a menu of *rondón*, rice and beans, lobster, shrimp, and chicken with sweet mole sauce. $ *Average main: $7* ⊠ *7 km (4½ miles) southeast of town at Punta Uva* ☎ *2750–0664* ☉ *Closed Mon.–Wed.; may be closed other days May–June and Sept.–Nov.*

$$

ECLECTIC

Fodor's Choice

★

✕ **Stashus con Fusion.** This restaurant epitomizes Puerto Viejo: lively, organic, all the rage, but confident enough not to seek trendiness. Ordering is by sauces: Thai peanut, Indonesian-Caribbean curry, Mexican chipotle, Jamaican jerk-style, or Malaysian-guayaba curry. Then select vegetables, chicken, shrimp, or fish (marlin or tuna). Live music gets going late on Sunday evenings. $ *Average main: $11* ⊠ *200 m south of Lazy Mon Beach Café (aka Stanford's)* ☎ *2750–0530* ▭ *No credit cards* ☉ *Closed Wed. No lunch.*

WHERE TO STAY

$

HOTEL

▦ **Agapi.** Agapi means "love" in Greek, and the Costa Rican–Greek owners lovingly watch over their guests with attentive service. **Pros:** kitchens; central location. **Cons:** not for travelers who want anonymity; first-floor rooms can be dark. $ *Rooms from: $67* ⊠ *1 km (½ mile) southeast of Lazy Mon Beach Café (aka Stanford's)* ☎ *2750–0446* ⊕ *www.agapisite.com* ⤹ *5 rooms, 12 apartments* ¶◯¶ *Breakfast.*

$$

B&B/INN

▦ **Azania Bungalows.** Eight thatch-roof, A-frame bungalows are spread around Azania's ample gardens, and each sleeps four. **Pros:** good value; good Argentine restaurant. **Cons:** difficult to make reservations; bungalows are dark inside. $ *Rooms from: $95* ⊠ *1½ km (1 mile) southeast of town at Playa Cocles* ☎ *2750–0540* ⊕ *www.azania-costarica.com* ⤹ *10 bungalows* ¶◯¶ *Breakfast.*

$$

RESORT

▦ **Banana Azul.** Hardwood furnishings are abundant at this gay-friendly (but by no means exclusive) hotel at the secluded far end of Playa Negra. **Pros:** friendly management and staff; seclusion set away from hubbub of town; great ocean views. **Cons:** no kids allowed, so not an option for families. $ *Rooms from: $119* ⊠ *1½ km (1 mile) north of Puerto Viejo at end of Playa Negra* ☎ *2750–2035, 877/284–5116 in North America* ⊕ *www.bananaazul.com* ⤹ *12 rooms* ¶◯¶ *Breakfast.*

$$

HOTEL

Fodor's Choice

★

▦ **Cariblue Hotel.** The youthful Italian owners who came here to surf years ago stayed on and built a lodging that combines refinement with that hip Puerto Viejo vibe in exactly the right proportions. **Pros:** friendly owners; good restaurant. **Cons:** need a car to stay here.

Calm waters over the reef just off Punta Uva Beach near Puerto Viejo de Talamanca

[$] *Rooms from: $110* ✉ *2 km (1 mile) southeast of town at Playa Cocles* ☎ *2750–0035* 🌐 *www.cariblue.com* 🛏 *12 rooms, 8 suites, 23 bungalows* 🍴 *Breakfast.*

$ HOTEL 🏨 **Casa Verde Lodge.** If you've graduated from your backpacker days and are a bit more flush with cash but still want to be near the action, this old standby on a quiet street a couple of blocks from the center of town is ideal. **Pros:** good value; immaculate. **Cons:** difficult to find vacancies; businesslike staff. [$] *Rooms from: $54* ✉ *200 m south and 200 m east of bus stop* ☎ *2750–0015* 🌐 *www.cabinascasaverde.com* 🛏 *17 rooms, 9 with bath; 2 apartments* 🍴 *No meals.*

9

$$ B&B/INN 🏨 **Escape Caribeño.** The wonderfully friendly Italian owners are what make this place: they treat you like family. **Pros:** central location without being right in town; gregarious owners. **Cons:** some small rooms; some spartan rooms. [$] *Rooms from: $75* ✉ *400 m southeast of Lazy Mon Beach Café (aka Stanford's)* ☎ *2750–0103* 🌐 *www.escapecaribeno.com* 🛏 *18 cabins* 🍴 *No meals.*

$$$$ B&B/INN Fodor's Choice ★ 🏨 **Geckoes Lodge.** Impeccable service gives this place an edge among the area's handful of set-back-in-the-woods lodgings. **Pros:** wonderful, personalized service; lush, sumptuous surroundings; careful attention to environment. **Cons:** can be difficult to find; only two accommodations. [$] *Rooms from: $270* ✉ *3 km (2 miles) southeast of town and 1 km (½ mile) inland at Playa Cocles* ☎ *8335–5849* 🌐 *www.geckoeslodge.com* 🛏 *2 houses* 💳 *No credit cards* 🍴 *No meals.*

$$ HOTEL 🏨 **Hotel Blue Conga.** You generally have to get farther out of Puerto Viejo to enjoy the area's garden-style lodgings, but Hotel Blue Conga offers lush surroundings (and air-conditioning, a real rarity here on the coast) close to town. **Pros:** attentive owner; air-conditioning; quiet

surroundings set back from the road. **Cons:** first-floor rooms have less privacy. [$] *Rooms from: $75* ✉ *600 m south of Lazy Mon Beach Café (aka Stanford's)* ☎ *2750–0681* 🌐 *www.hotelblueconga.com* 🛏 *14 rooms* 🍴 *Breakfast.*

$$ HOTEL 🏨 **Hotel La Perla Negra.** Fine design is evident in the construction of this handsome, two-story dark-wood structure across a tiny dirt road near the end of Playa Negra. **Pros:** secluded; quality construction of buildings. **Cons:** far from sights; situated on lesser-known Playa Negra. [$] *Rooms from: $75* ✉ *Playa Negra, 1 km (½ mile) north of Puerto Viejo* ☎ *2750–0111* 🌐 *www.perlanegra-beachresort.com* 🛏 *24 rooms, 7 houses* 🍴 *Breakfast.*

$$ B&B/INN 🏨 **Korrigan Lodge.** Four octagonal wood bungalows are scattered around the secluded wooded property here with its wonderfully cool surroundings (no air-conditioning is needed). **Pros:** lush, green setting; attentive service; large, friendly dog on-site. **Cons:** can be difficult to find; dogs not for everyone. [$] *Rooms from: $105* ✉ *Punta Uva, 8 km (5 miles) south of Puerto Viejo de Talamanca* ☎ *2759–9103* 🌐 *www.korriganlodge.com* 🛏 *4 bungalows* 🍴 *Breakfast.*

$$ HOTEL 🏨 **La Costa de Papito.** Papito's raised cabins are deep in the property's wooded grounds and furnished with whimsical bright tropical blue and zebra-stripe prints. **Pros:** good value; friendly owner. **Cons:** need a car to stay here; some noise from bar area. [$] *Rooms from: $95* ✉ *2 km (1 mile) southeast of town at Playa Cocles* ☎ *2750–0080, 516/252–4509 in North America* 🌐 *www.lacostadepapito.com* 🛏 *13 cabins* 🍴 *No meals.*

$$$$ HOTEL 🏨 **Le Caméléon.** This boutique hotel fronting Playa Cocles is decidedly un–Puerto Viejo in its luxury, but if you're in the mood for a splurge here on the coast, this is the spot. **Pros:** stylish luxury; attentive staff; many amenities. **Cons:** luxury might seem out of place in Puerto Viejo. [$] *Rooms from: $250* ✉ *Playa Cocles, 200 m east of soccer field* ☎ *2750–0501, 2291–7750 in San José* 🌐 *www.lecameleonhotel.com* 🛏 *22 rooms, 1 suite* 🍴 *Breakfast.*

$$ B&B/INN 🏨 **Pachamama Jungle River Lodge.** So cool and shady is this place set within the confines of the Gandoca-Manzanillo Wildlife Refuge that the builders never bothered with the ceiling fans, as no one ever needed them. **Pros:** wonderful seclusion; friendly owners. **Cons:** far from sights; need a car to stay here. [$] *Rooms from: $75* ✉ *9 km (5½ miles) southeast of town at Punta Uva* ☎ *2759–9196* 🌐 *www.pachamamacaribe.com* 🛏 *3 bungalows, 2 houses* 🍴 *Multiple meal plans.*

$$ B&B/INN Fodor's Choice ★ 🏨 **Physis Caribbean B&B.** If you want to experience the area's well-known vibe but have outgrown Puerto Viejo's backpacker digs—we all do eventually—this lodging owned by a fun, transplanted California couple is the ticket. **Pros:** hip, knowledgeable owners; impeccable service; immaculate rooms. **Cons:** two friendly dogs on-site, so not a place to go if you dislike canines. [$] *Rooms from: $85* ✉ *1½ km (1 mile) southeast of town at Playa Cocles* ☎ *2750–0941* 🌐 *www.physiscaribbean.com* 🛏 *4 rooms* 🍴 *Breakfast.*

$$ RESORT 🏨 **Shawandha Lodge.** The service is personalized and friendly at Shawandha, whose spacious, beautifully designed bungalows are well back from the road at Playa Chiquita. **Pros:** elegant bungalows; sumptuous

restaurant; near white-sand beach. **Cons:** far from sights; easiest to stay here with a car. $ *Rooms from: $130* ⊠ *6 km (4 miles) southeast of town at Playa Chiquita* ☎ *2750–0018* ⊕ *www.shawandhalodge.com* ➷ *13 bungalows* |⊙| *Breakfast.*

$$$$ 🏠 **Tree House Lodge.** This lodging **HOTEL** complex among forested ground contains four large, stylish houses, all at ground level, one of which is built around a tree (that's the Tree House). **Pros:** attention to style in furnishings; romantic seclusion. **Cons:** far from sights; easiest to have a car to stay here. $ *Rooms from: $250* ⊠ *Punta Uva* ☎ *2750–0706, 415/878–3786 in North America* ⊕ *www.costaricatreehouse.com* ➷ *4 houses* ▭ *No credit cards* |⊙| *Breakfast.*

NEED A BREAK? **Caribeans.** At first glance, this small café could use a spelling lesson, but since Caribeans deals in coffee, the play on words is apt. Treat yourself to a latté, mocha, or coconut cappuccino, all made from organic, fair-trade coffee from the Turrialba region in the far-eastern Central Valley, and roasted here. ⊠ *2 km (1 mile) southeast of town at Playa Cocles* ☎ *8836–8930* ⊕ *www.caribeanscr.com* ⊙ *Closed Tues.*

A BAD RAP

The Caribbean has a reputation among Costa Ricans for being crime-ridden, mainly because of a few high-profile cases here years ago, the nearness of the Panamanian border, and the fact that this is an impoverished region compared with other parts of the country. In actuality, the problem is no better or worse here than elsewhere. Take the standard precautions you would when you travel anywhere and do stick to well-traveled tourist paths.

NIGHTLIFE

The distinction between dining spot and nightspot blurs as the evening progresses, as many restaurants become pleasant places to linger after dinner. Many of the bars have live music on certain nights. The town's main drag is packed with pedestrians, bicycles, and a few cars most evenings, the block between Café Viejo and El Parquecito getting the most action. Wander around; something is bound to entice you in, just be aware that some of the strictly local hangouts get a bit rough around the edges at night. ■TIP→ **When out after dark, ask a staff member at the restaurant, bar, or club to call you a taxi when you're ready to call it an evening.**

BARS

Latino's. Grab a beer and chow down on pizza or sandwiches at Latino's. A much quieter alternative to many of the nearby bars, this is a good spot to watch what's happening on the town's main drag. ⊠ *Across from ATEC* ☎ *2750–0604* ⊙ *Daily noon–10 pm.*

Tasty Waves Cantina. Tuesday is $2 taco night at the lively, sometimes rowdy, Tasty Waves Cantina. Movies get underway at 7:30 pm on Monday evening and several other nights a week as well. ⊠ *Playa Cocles, 1 km (½ mile) southeast of town* ☎ *2750–0507* ⊙ *Thurs.–Tues. noon–midnight.*

DANCE CLUBS

Café Mango. A lively mix of expats and tourists holds court at Café Mango each evening. ⊠ *20 m south of bus stop* ☏ *8691–0756* ⊘ *Daily noon–2:30 am.*

LIVE MUSIC

El Parquecito. Caribbean restaurant El Parquecito draws a very young backpacker crowd and pulls live-music duty Tuesday, Friday, and Saturday evenings. You're bound to hear "No Woman No Cry" and all the other reggae anthems. ⊠ *50 m east of ATEC* ⊘ *Daily noon–10.*

Stashus con Fusion. Organic-food restaurant Stashus con Fusion has live music Sunday evenings. ⊠ *200 m south of Lazy Mon Beach Café (aka Stanford's)* ☏ *2750–0263* ⊘ *Thurs.–Tues. 6–11.*

SHOPPING

Vendors set up stands at night on the beach road near El Parquecito, cheap jewelry being the prime fare. But the town counts a few honest-to-goodness souvenir stores, too.

Feria Agrícola. Puerto Viejo's Saturday-morning farmers' market (6 am to noon) is a good place to stock up on fresh fruits and veggies for that weekend beach picnic. It takes place in a building just south of the bus stop. ⊠ *50 m south of bus stop* ⊘ *Sat. 6–noon.*

Luluberlu. Puerto Viejo's best shop sells a wonderful selection of local indigenous carvings—balsa and *chonta* wood are especially popular—as well as jewelry, paintings, and ceramics by 30 artists from the region. ⊠ *200 m south and 50 m east of bus stop* ☏ *2750–0394* ⊘ *Daily 9–9.*

Tienda del Mar. Really two stores in one, Tienda del Mar sprawls around a street corner in the center of town and specializes in bright, colorful batik clothing of all sizes, as well as more-run-of-the-mill T-shirts, sandals, wood carvings, and postcards. ⊠ *Next to Restaurant Tamara* ⊘ *Daily 11–9.*

GANDOCA-MANZANILLO NATIONAL WILDLIFE REFUGE

15 km (9 miles) southeast of Puerto Viejo.

The boundaries of the southern Caribbean coast's preeminent wildlife refuge aren't well defined. You'll pass in and out of the forested reserve as you drive southeast from Puerto Viejo de Talamanca.

GETTING HERE AND AROUND

The paved road from Puerto Viejo de Talamanca ends at the entrance to the village of Manzanillo. Buses connect the two every two hours during the day. Taxis are a much easier proposition. Drivers in Puerto Viejo charge $18 for the trip here.

EXPLORING

Gandoca-Manzanillo National Wildlife Refuge (*Refugio Nacional de Vida Silvestre Gandoca-Manzanillo*). The refuge stretches along the southeastern coast beginning southeast of Puerto Viejo de Talamanca to the town of Manzanillo and on to the Panamanian border. Its limits are not clearly defined. Because of weak laws governing the conservation

"We found Playa Manzanillo while visiting the Caribbean side of Costa Rica. A beautiful beach and very laid-back atmosphere." —Photo by dgray, Fodors.com member

of refuges and the rising value of coastal land in this area, Gandoca-Manzanillo is less pristine than Cahuita National Park and continues to be developed. However, the refuge still has plenty of rain forest, *orey* (a dark tropical wood) and jolillo swamps, 10 km (6 miles) of beach where four species of turtles lay their eggs, and almost 3 square km (1 square mile) of *cativo* (a tropical hardwood) forest and coral reef. The Gandoca estuary is a nursery for tarpon and a wallowing spot for crocodiles and caimans.

The easiest way to explore the refuge is to hike along the coast south of Manzanillo. You can hike back out the way you came in or arrange (in Puerto Viejo de Talamanca) to have a boat pick you up at Punta Mono (Monkey Point), a three- to four-hour walk from Manzanillo, where you find secluded beaches hidden by tall cliffs of fossilized coral. The mangroves of Gandoca, with abundant caimans, iguanas, and waterfowl, lie six to eight hours away. Park administrators can tell you more and recommend a local guide; inquire when you enter Manzanillo village and the locals will point you toward them. ✉ *15 km (9 miles) southeast of Puerto Viejo de Talamanca* ☎ *2750–0398 for ATEC* 💳 *Free* ⊘ *Daily 7–4.*

Manzanillo. The village of Manzanillo maintains that "end-of-the-world" feel. Tourism is still in its infancy this far down the coast, though with the road paved all the way here, the town is a popular destination among people from Limón for weekend day trips. The rest of the week, you'll likely have the place to yourself.

BEACHES

Playa Manzanillo. Ensconced within the Gandoca-Manzanillo Wildlife Refuge, this beach comes close to being picture perfect with the lush green forest—and their resident howler monkeys—bordering the edge of the sand. The in-town stretches put you close to food and drink. A few reports of bag snatchings have occurred here when visitors weren't paying attention. As always on this stretch of coast, avoid walking on the beach alone and be careful about going into the water, the undertow can be strong. **Amenities:** food and drink. **Best for:** snorkeling; surfing; walking. ⊠ *Manzanillo village.*

> **ANOTHER GOOD BOOK**
>
> If you're headed to Panama, we'd be remiss in not recommending that you pick up a copy of *Fodor's In Focus Panama* for far more detail about Bocas del Toro and the rest of the country than we can provide here.

SPORTS AND THE OUTDOORS

TOUR OPERATORS

A guide can help you get the most out of this relatively unexplored corner of the country.

Association of Indigenous Naturalist Guides of Manzanillo. This consortium of high-quality, knowledgeable local guides knows the area well and leads a variety of half- and full-day tours. (The U.S. Agency for International Development planted the seed money to get the project going.) They can take you for a hike in the reserve or out to Monkey Point, with a return trip by boat. They also have horseback riding; bird-, dolphin-, and turtle-watching; and traditional fishing excursions. ⊠ *Main road, Manzanillo* ☎ 2759–9064 ✎ *guiasmant@yahoo.com.mx.*

DIVING AND SNORKELING

Companies in Puerto Viejo de Talamanca (⇨ *above*) can arrange boat trips to dive spots and beaches in the refuge as well.

Aquamor Talamanca Adventures. The friendly staff at Aquamor Talamanca Adventures specializes in land- and ocean-focused tours of the Gandoca-Manzanillo Wildlife Refuge, and can tend to all your water-sporting needs in these parts, with guided kayaking, snorkeling, and scuba-diving tours, as well as equipment rental. ⊠ *Main road, Manzanillo* ☎ 2759–9012 ⊕ *www.greencoast.com/aquamor.htm.*

WHERE TO EAT AND STAY

$$

CARIBBEAN

✕ **Cool & Calm Café.** A few small cafés are springing up in Manzanillo these days, including this small, semi-open-air joint with plastic chairs and tables. It isn't much to look at, but the menu satisfies with dishes such as spicy Caribbean chicken, red snapper, and curried vegetables and rice. Views of the beach (just across the road) are another plus. You can rinse off the sand at the outdoor shower next to the restaurant if you've just walked over from the beach. [$] *Average main: $12* ⊠ *50 m west of bus stop, Manzanillo* ☎ 8843–7460 ⊕ *www.coolandcalmcafe. com* ⊘ *Closed Tues. No lunch Mon.*

$

SEAFOOD

✕ **Restaurant Maxi's.** Cooled by sea breezes and shaded by tall, stately palms, this two-story, brightly painted wooden building offers weary travelers cold beer, potent cocktails, and great seafood at unbeatable prices after a day's hike in the refuge. Locals and expatriates alike come here for their lobster fix, and the fresh fish is wonderful, too. Locals tend to congregate in the rowdy but pleasant downstairs bar, where reggae beats into the wee hours. $ *Average main: $9* ⊠ *Main road, Manzanillo* ☎ *2759–9073.*

$$$$ ⬚ **Almonds & Corals** (*Almendros y Corales*). Hidden in a beachfront jun-
RESORT gle within the Gandoca-Manzanillo Wildlife Refuge, Almonds & Corals features scattered bungalows raised on stilts and linked by boardwalks lighted by kerosene lamps. **Pros:** rustic comfort; lots of activities. **Cons:** far from sights; need a car to stay here. $ *Rooms from: $250* ⊠ *Near end of road to Manzanillo* ☎ *2759–9056, 2271–3000 in San José* ⊕ *www.almondsandcorals.com* ⤳ *24 bungalows* ⦿ *Some meals.*

$ ⬚ **Cabinas Something Different.** On a quiet street, these shiny, spic-and-
B&B/INN span motel-style cabinas are a good budget option in the village of Manzanillo. **Pros:** good budget value; television unusual in a remote locale. **Cons:** small, spartan rooms. $ *Rooms from: $45* ⊠ *180 m south of Aquamor, Manzanillo* ☎ *2759–9014* ⤳ *17 cabins* ▭ *No credit cards* ⦿ *No meals.*

CROSSING INTO PANAMA VIA SIXAOLA

Costa Rica's sleepy border post at Sixaola fronts Guabito, Panama's equally quiet border crossing, 44 km (26 miles) south of the turnoff to Puerto Viejo de Talamanca. Both are merely collections of banana-plantation stilt houses and a few stores and bars; neither has any lodging or dining options, but this is a much more low-key crossing into Panama than the busy border post at Paso Canoas on the Pan-American Highway near the Pacific coast. If you've come this far, you're likely headed to **Bocas del Toro,** the real attraction in the northwestern part of Panama. This archipelago of 68 islands continues the Afro-Caribbean and indigenous themes seen on Costa Rica's Atlantic coast, and offers diving, snorkeling, swimming, and wildlife viewing. The larger islands are home to a growing selection of hotels and restaurants, everything from funky to fabulous. "Bocas" has acquired a cult following among long-term foreign visitors to Costa Rica, who find it a convenient place to travel when their permitted three-month status as a tourist has expired, since a quick 72-hour jaunt out of the country gets you another 90 days in Costa Rica.

■ TIP→ **Whatever your destination in Panama, come armed with dol-lars.** Panama uses U.S. currency, but refers to the dollar as the *balboa*. (It does mint its own coins, all the same size as their U.S. counterparts.) No one anywhere will accept or exchange your Costa Rican colones.

Costa Rican rental vehicles may not leave the country, so crossing into Panama as a tourist is an option only via public transportation. The public bus route from San José to Cahuita and Puerto Viejo de Talamanca terminates here at the border approximately six hours after leaving the capital. Taxis in Puerto Viejo de Talamanca charge about $75 for the jaunt to the border, a much quicker and reasonable option if you can split the fare among a group. Disembark and head for the

9

Costa Rican immigration office (☎ 2754–2044) down a flight of stairs from the west end of a former railroad bridge. Officials place an exit stamp in your passport, after which you walk across the bridge and present your passport to Panamanian immigration (☎ 507/759–7019). The bridge looks rickety but is safe for walking. Plans to construct a larger, more modern bridge are underway at this writing. U.S. visitors must also purchase a $5 tourist card for entry into the country. ■TIP→ Although some local residents here make the crossing without going through border formalities, you cannot. Make sure you exit and enter Costa Rica and Panama properly in either direction.

Consulate of Panama. The Panamanian consulate in San José can provide more information about travel in Panama. ✉ *San José* ☎ *2281–2103* ⊕ *www.embajadadepanamaencostarica.org* ⊙ *Weekdays 9–2.*

The border crossings are open 7 am to 5 pm (8 am to 6 pm Panamanian time) daily. Set your watch one hour ahead when you enter Panama.

Taxis wait on the Panamanian side to transport you to the small city of Changuinola, the first community of any size inside the country, from which there are bus and air connections for travel farther into Panama. Taxis can also take you to Almirante, where you'll find boat launches to Bocas del Toro.

A few tour operators in Puerto Viejo de Talamanca can set you up with shuttle transport to Bocas del Toro. They also offer day tours to the islands, but travel time and border formalities eat up a huge chunk of that day. Bocas is a fun destination and worth spending a couple of nights.

Caribe Shuttle. This company offers daily van/boat shuttle service between Puerto Viejo de Talamanca and Bocas del Toro for $32 one way. ✉ *Inside Rockin' J's hostel, 1 km (½ mile) southeast of Puerto Viejo de Talamanca, San José* ☎ *2750–0626* ⊕ *www.caribeshuttle.com.*

UNDERSTANDING COSTA RICA

COSTA RICA AT A GLANCE

FAST FACTS

Capital: San José

Type of government: Democratic republic

Independence: September 15, 1821 (from Spain)

Population: 4,586,353

Population density: 84 persons per square km (220 persons per square mile)

Literacy: 96%

Language: Spanish (official); English spoken by most in the tourism industry

Ethnic groups: White (including mestizo) 93%, black 2%, Amerindian 2%, Asian 2%, other 1%

Religion: Roman Catholic 72%, Evangelical Protestant 13%, none 10%, other 5%

GEOGRAPHY AND ENVIRONMENT

Land area: 51,100 square km (19,730 square miles); slightly smaller than the U.S. state of West Virginia

Coastline: 1,290 km (802 miles)

Terrain: Rugged central range with 112 volcanic craters that separates the eastern and western coastal plains

Natural resources: Hydroelectric power, forest products, fisheries products

Natural hazards: Droughts, flash floods, thunderstorms, earthquakes, hurricanes, active volcanoes, landslides

Flora: 9,000 species, including 1,200 orchid species and 800 fern species; tidal mangrove swamps, tropical rain forest, subalpine forest

Fauna: 36,518 species, including 34,000 species of insects and 2,000 species of butterflies

Environmental issues: Deforestation, rapid industrialization and urbanization, air and water pollution, soil degradation, plastic waste, fisheries protection

ECONOMY

Currency: Colón, (*pl.*) colones

GDP: $45.13 billion

Per capita income: $12,600

Unemployment: 7.9%

Major industries: Microprocessors, tourism, food processing, textiles and clothing, construction materials, fertilizer, plastic products

Agricultural products: Bananas, coffee, pineapples, sugarcane, corn, rice, beans, potatoes, beef

Exports: $11.5 billion

Major export products: Bananas, coffee, pineapples, electronic components, fertilizers, sugar, textiles, electricity, ornamental plants, medical equipment

Export partners: (in order of volume) United States, China, Netherlands, United Kingdom, Mexico

Imports: $16.8 billion

Major import products: Chemicals, consumer goods, electronic components, machinery, petroleum products, vehicles

Import partners: United States (46%), Mexico (6%), Japan (6%), China (6%)

DID YOU KNOW?

■ Tourism earns more foreign exchange than bananas and coffee combined.

■ Costa Rica did away with its military in 1949.

■ Five percent of the world's identified plant and animal species are found in this country.

■ Costa Rica is the home of five active volcanoes.

WILDLIFE AND PLANT GLOSSARY

Here is a rundown of some of the most common and attention-grabbing mammals, birds, reptiles, amphibians, plants, and even a few insects that you might encounter. We give the common Costa Rican names, so you can understand the local lingo, followed by the latest scientific terms.

Fauna

Agouti (*guatusa*; *Dasyprocta punctata*): A 20-inch, tailless rodent with small ears and a large muzzle, the agouti is reddish brown on the Pacific side, more of a tawny orange on the Caribbean slope. It sits on its haunches to eat large seeds and fruit and resembles a large rabbit without the long ears.

Anteater (*Oso hormiguero*): Three species of anteater inhabit Costa Rica—the very rare giant (*Myrmecophaga tridactyla*), the nocturnal silky (*Cyclopes didactylus*), and the collared, or vested (*Tamandua mexicana*). Only the last is commonly seen, and too often as roadkill. This medium-size anteater, 30 inches long with an 18-inch tail, laps up ants and termites with its long, sticky tongue and has long, sharp claws for ripping into insect nests.

Armadillo (*cusuco*; *Dasypus novemcinctus*): The nine-banded armadillo is widespread in Costa Rica and also found in the southern United States. This nocturnal and solitary edentate roots in soil with a long muzzle for a varied diet of insects, small animals, and plant material.

Baird's Tapir (*danta*; *Tapirus bairdii*): The largest land mammal in Costa Rica (to 6½ feet), Baird's tapir is something like a small rhinoceros without armor. Adapted to a wide range of habitats, it's nocturnal, seldom seen, but said to defecate and sometimes sleep in water. Tapirs are herbivorous and use their prehensile snouts to harvest vegetation. The best opportunities for viewing wild tapirs are in Corcovado National Park.

Bat (*murciélago*): With more than 100 species, Costa Rica's bats can be found eating fruit, insects, fish, small vertebrates, nectar, and even blood, in the case of the infamous vampire bat (*vampiro, Desmodus rotundus*), which far prefers cattle blood to that of any tourist. As a group, bats are extremely important ecologically, and are essential to seed dispersal, pollination, and controlling insect populations.

Butterfly (*mariposa*): Estimates of the number of butterfly species in Costa Rica vary, but all range in the thousands. The growing number of butterfly gardens popping up around the country is testament to their popularity among visitors. Three Costa Rican morpho species—spectacular, large butterflies—have a brilliant blue upper-wing surface, giving them their local nickname of *pedazos de ciel* (pieces of sky). The blue morpho (*Morpho peleides*), arguably the most distinctive, is common in moister areas and has an intense ultraviolet upper surface. Adults feed on fermenting fruit; they never visit flowers.

Caiman (*caimán*): The spectacled caiman (*Caiman crocodilus*) is a small crocodilian (to 7 feet) inhabiting freshwater, subsisting mainly on fish. Most active at night (it has bright red eye shine), it basks by day. It is distinguished from the American crocodile by a sloping brow and smooth back scales.

Coati (*pizote*; *Nasua narica*): This is a long-nose relative of the raccoon, its long tail often held straight up. Lone males or groups of females with young are active during the day, on the ground, or in trees. Omnivorous coatis feed on fruit, invertebrates, and small vertebrates. Unfortunately, many have learned to beg from tourists, especially in Monteverde and on the roads around Arenal.

Cougar (*puma*; *Felis concolor*): Mountain lions are the largest unspotted cats (to 8 feet, including the tail) in Costa Rica. Widespread but rare, they live in essentially all-wild habitats and feed on vertebrates ranging from snakes to deer.

Crocodile (*lagarto*; *Crocodylus acutus*): The American crocodile, up to 16 feet in length, is found in most major river systems, particularly the Tempisque and Tárcoles estuaries. It seldom attacks humans, preferring fish and birds. It's distinguished from the caiman by size, a flat head, narrow snout, and spiky scales.

Ctenosaur (*garrobo*; *Ctenosaura similis*): Also known as the black, or spiny-tailed, iguana, this is a large (up to 18 inches long with an 18-inch tail) tan lizard with four dark bands on its body and a tail ringed with sharp, curved spines, reminiscent of a dinosaur. Terrestrial and arboreal, it sleeps in burrows or tree hollows. It lives along the coast in the dry northwest and in wetter areas farther south. The fastest known reptile (clocked on land), the ctenosaur has been recorded moving at 21.7 miles per hour.

Dolphin (*delfín*): Several species, including bottlenose dolphins (*Tursiops truncatus*), frolic in Costa Rican waters. Often seen off Pacific shores are spotted dolphins (*Stenella attenuata*), which are small (up to 6 feet) with pale spots on the posterior half of the body; they commonly travel in groups of 20 or more and play around vessels and in bow wakes. Tucuxi dolphins (*Sotalia fluviatilis*) have also been spotted in small groups off the southern Caribbean coast, frequently with bottlenose dolphins.

Frog and Toad (*rana*, frog; *sapo*, toad): Some 120 species of frog exist in Costa Rica; many are nocturnal. The most colorful daytime amphibians are the tiny strawberry poison dart frog (*Dendrobates pumilio*) and green-and-black poison dart frog. The bright coloration of these two species, either red with blue or green hind legs or charcoal black with fluorescent green markings, warns potential predators of their toxicity. The red-eyed leaf frog (*Agalychnis callidryas*) is among the showiest of nocturnal species. The large, brown marine toad (*Bufo marinus*), also called cane toad or giant toad, comes out at night.

Howler Monkey (*mono congo*; *Alouatta palliata*): These dark, chunky-bodied monkeys (to 22 inches long with a 24-inch tail) with black faces travel in troops of up to 20. Lethargic mammals, they eat leaves, fruits, and flowers. The males' deep, resounding howls sound like lions roaring, but actually serve as communication among and between troops.

Hummingbird (*colibrí*, *Trochilidae*): Weighing just a fraction of an ounce, hummingbirds are nonetheless some of the most notable residents of tropical forests. At least 50 varieties can be found in Costa Rica, visiting typically red tubular flowers in their seemingly endless search for energy-rich nectar. Because of their assortment of iridescent colors and bizarre bills and tail shapes, watching them can be a spectator sport. Best bets are hummingbird feeders and anywhere with great numbers of flowers.

Iguana (*iguana*): Mostly arboreal but good at swimming, the iguana is Costa Rica's largest lizard: males can grow to 10 feet, including tail. Only young green iguanas (*Iguana iguana*) are bright green; adults are much duller, females dark grayish and males olive (with orangish heads in breeding season). All have round cheek scales and smooth tails.

Jaguar (*tigre*; *Panthera onca*): The largest New World feline (to 6 feet, with a 2-foot tail), this top-of-the-line predator is exceedingly rare but lives in a wide variety of habitats, from dry forest to cloud forest. It's most common in the vast Amistad Biosphere Reserve, but it is almost never seen in the wild.

Jesus Christ Lizard (*gallego*): Flaps of skin on long toes enable this spectacular lizard to run across water. Costa Rica has three species of this lizard, which is more properly called the basilisk: lineated (*Basiliscus basiliscus*) on the Pacific side is brown with pale lateral stripes; in the Caribbean, emerald (*Basiliscus plumifrons*) is marked with turquoise and black on a green body; and striped (*Basiliscus vittatus*), also on the Caribbean side, resembles the lineated basilisk. Adult males grow to 3 feet (mostly tail), with crests on the head, back, and base of the tail.

Leaf-Cutter Ant (*zompopas*; *Atta* spp.): Found in all lowland habitats, these are the most commonly noticed neotropical ants, and one of the country's most fascinating animal phenomena. Columns of ants carrying bits of leaves twice their size sometimes extend for several hundred yards from an underground nest to plants being harvested. The ants don't eat the leaves; their food is a fungus they cultivate on the leaves.

Macaw (*lapas*): Costa Rica's two species are the scarlet macaw (*Ara macao*), on the Pacific side (Osa Peninsula and Carara Biological Reserve), and the severely threatened great green macaw (*Ara ambigua*), on the Caribbean side. These are huge, raucous parrots with long tails; their immense bills are used to rip fruit apart to reach the seeds. They nest in hollow trees and are victimized by pet-trade poachers and deforestation.

Magnificent Frigatebird (*tijereta del mar*; *Fregata magnificens*): A large, black soaring bird with slender wings and forked tail, this is one of the most effortless and agile flyers in the avian world. More common on the Pacific coast, it doesn't dive or swim but swoops to pluck its food, often from the mouths of other birds.

Manatee (*manatí*; *Trichechus manatus*): Although endangered throughout its range, the West Indian manatee can be spotted in Tortuguero, meandering along in shallow water, browsing on submerged vegetation. The moniker "sea cow" is apt, as they spend nearly all their time resting or feeding. Their large, somewhat amorphous bodies won't win any beauty contests, but they do appear quite graceful.

Margay (*caucel*; *Felis wiedii*): Fairly small, this spotted nocturnal cat (22 inches long, with an 18-inch tail) is similar to the ocelot but has a longer tail and is far more arboreal: mobile ankle joints

allow it to climb down trunks head first. It eats small vertebrates.

Motmot (*pájaro bobo*; *Momotus momota*): These handsome, turquoise-and-rufous birds of the understory have racket-shaped tails. Nesting in burrows, they sit patiently while scanning for large insect prey or small vertebrates. Costa Rica has six species.

Northern Jacana (*gallito de agua*; *Jacana spinosa*): These birds are sometimes called "lily trotters" because their long toes allow them to walk on floating vegetation. Feeding on aquatic organisms and plants, they're found in almost any body of water. They expose yellow wing feathers in flight. Sex roles are reversed; "liberated" females are larger and compete for mates (often more than one), whereas the males tend to the nest and care for the young.

Ocelot (*manigordo*; *Felis pardalis*): Mostly terrestrial, this medium-size spotted cat (33 inches long, with a 16-inch tail) is active night and day and feeds on rodents and other vertebrates. Forepaws are rather large in relation to the body, hence the local name *manigordo*, which means "fat hand."

Opossum (*zorro pelón*; *Didelphis marsupialis*): Like the kangaroo, the common opossum belongs to that rare breed of mammal known as marsupials, distinguished by their brief gestation period and completion of development and nourishment following birth in the mother's pouch. The Costa Rican incarnation does not "play possum," and will bite if cornered rather than pretend to be dead.

Oropendola (*oropéndola*; *Psarocolius* spp.): These crow-size birds in the oriole family have a bright-yellow tail and nest in colonies in pendulous nests (up to 6 feet long) built by females in isolated trees. The Montezuma species has an orange beak and blue cheeks; the chestnut-headed has a yellow beak. Males make an unmistakable, loud, gurgling-liquid call. The bird is far more numerous on the Caribbean side.

Parakeet and Parrot (*pericos*, parakeets; *loros*, parrots): There are 15 species in Costa Rica (plus two macaws), all clad in green, most with a splash of a primary color or two on the head or wings. They travel in boisterous flocks, prey on immature seeds, and nest in cavities.

Peccary (*Tayassuidea*): Piglike animals with thin legs and thick necks, peccaries travel in small groups (larger where the population is still numerous); root in soil for fruit, seeds, and small creatures; and have a strong musk odor. You'll usually smell them before you see them. Costa Rica has two species: the collared peccary (*saíno*, *Tayassu tajacu*) and the white-lipped peccary (*chancho de monte*, *Tayassu pecari*). The latter is now nearly extinct.

Pelican (*pelícano*): Large size, a big bill, and a throat pouch make the brown pelican (*Pelecanus occidentalis*) unmistakable in coastal areas (it's far more abundant on the Pacific side). Pelicans often fly in V formations and dive for fish.

Quetzal (*Pharomachrus mocinno*): One of the world's most exquisite birds, the resplendent quetzal was revered by the Maya. Glittering green plumage and the male's long tail coverts draw thousands of people to highland cloud forests for sightings from February to April.

Roseate Spoonbill (*garza rosada*; *Ajaja ajaja*): Pink plumage and a spatulate bill set this wader apart from all other wetland birds; it feeds by swishing its bill back and forth in water while using its feet to stir up bottom-dwelling creatures. Spoonbills are most common around Palo Verde and Caño Negro.

Sloth (*perezoso*): Costa Rica is home to the brown-throated, three-toed sloth (*Bradypus variegatus*) and Hoffmann's two-toed sloth (*Choloepus hoffmanni*). Both grow to 2 feet, but two-toed (check forelegs) sloths often look bigger because of longer fur and are the only species in the highlands. Sloths are herbivorous, accustomed to a low-energy diet, and well camouflaged.

Snake (*culebra*): Costa Rica's serpents can be found in trees, above and below ground, and even in the sea on the Pacific coast. Most of the more than 125 species are harmless, but are best appreciated from a distance. Costa Rica's largest snake, the boa constrictor (*Boa constrictor*), reaches up to 15 feet. The fer-de-lance (*terciopelo*, *Bothrops asper*) is a much smaller (up to 6 feet) but far more dangerous viper.

Spider Monkey (*mono colorado*, *mono araña*): Lanky and long tailed, the black-handed spider monkey (*Ateles geoffroyi*) is the largest monkey in Costa Rica (to 24 inches, with a 32-inch tail). Moving in groups of two to four, they eat ripe fruit, leaves, and flowers. Incredible aerialists, they can swing effortlessly through branches using long arms and legs and prehensile tails. They are quite aggressive and will challenge onlookers and often throw down branches. Caribbean and southern Pacific populations are dark reddish brown; northwesterners are blond.

Squirrel Monkey (*mono tití*): The smallest of four Costa Rican monkeys (11 inches, with a 15-inch tail), the red-backed squirrel monkey (*Saimiri oerstedii*) has a distinctive facial pattern (black cap and muzzle, white mask) and gold-orange coloration on its back. It is the only Costa Rican monkey without a prehensile tail. The species travels in noisy, active groups of 20 or more, feeding on fruit and insects. Numbers of this endangered species have been estimated between 2,000 and 4,000 individuals. Most squirrel monkeys in Costa Rica are found in Manuel Antonio National Park, in parts of the Osa Peninsula, and around the Golfo Dulce.

Three-Wattled Bellbird (*pájaro campana*; *Procnias tricarunculata*): Although endangered, the bellbird can be readily identified in cloud forests (around Monteverde, for example), where it breeds by its extraordinary call, a bold and aggressive "bonk," unlike any other creature in the forest. If you spot a male calling, look for the three pendulous wattles at the base of its beak.

Toucan (*tucán, tucancillo*): The keel-billed toucan (*Ramphastos sulfuratus*) with the rainbow-colored beak is familiar to anyone who's seen a box of Froot Loops cereal. Chestnut-mandibled toucans (*Ramphastos swainsonii*) are the largest (18 inches and 22 inches); as the name implies, their lower beaks are brown. The smaller, stouter emerald toucanet (*Aulacorhynchus prasinus*) and yellow-eared toucanet (*Selenidera spectabilis*) are aptly named. Aracaris (*Pteroglossus spp.*) are similar to toucans, but colored orange and yellow with the trademark toucan bill.

Turtles (*tortuga*): Observing the nesting rituals of the five species of marine turtles here is one of those truly memorable Costa Rican experiences. Each species has its own nesting season and locale. The olive ridley (*lora; Lepidochelys olivacea*) is the smallest of the sea turtles (average carapace, or hardback shell, is 21–29 inches) and the least shy. Thousands engage in nighttime group-nesting rituals on the North Pacific's Ostional. At the other extreme, but only slightly farther north on Playa Grande, nests the leatherback (*baula; Dermochelys coriacea*) with its 5-foot-long shell. On the north Caribbean coast, Tortuguero hosts four of them: the leatherback, the hawksbill (*carey; Eretmochelys imbricata*), the loggerhead (*caguama; Caretta caretta*), and the green (*tortuga verde; Chelonia mydas*), with its long nesting season (June–October) that draws the most visitors and researchers.

Whales (*ballena*): Humpback whales (*Megaptera novaeanglia*) appear off the Pacific coast between November and February; they migrate from California and as far as Hawaii. You can also spot Sey whales, Bryde's whales, and farther out to sea, blue whales and sperm whales. On the Caribbean side, there are smaller (12 to 14 feet) Koiga whales.

White-Faced Capuchin Monkey (*mono cara blanca; Cebus capuchinus*): Medium-size and omnivorous, this monkey (to 18 inches, with a 20-inch tail) has black fur and a pink face surrounded by a whitish bib. Extremely active foragers, they move singly or in groups of up to 20, examining the environment closely and even coming to the ground. It's the most commonly seen monkey in Costa Rica. It's also the most often fed by visitors, to the point where some monkey populations now have elevated cholesterol levels.

White-Tailed Deer (*venado; Odocoileus virginianus*): Bambi would feel at home in Costa Rica, although his counterparts here are slightly smaller. As befits the name, these animals possess the distinctive white underside to their tail (and to their bellies). They are seen in drier parts of the country, especially in the northwest province of Guanacaste.

White-Throated Magpie-jay (*urraca; Calocitta formosa*): This southern relative of the blue jay, with a long tail and distinctive topknot (crest of forward-curved feathers), is found in the dry northwest. Bold and inquisitive, with amazingly varied vocalizations, these birds travel in noisy groups of four or more.

Flora

Ant-acacia (*acacia; Acacia spp.*): If you'll be in the tropical dry forest of Guanacaste, learn to avoid this plant. As if its sharp thorns weren't enough, acacias exhibit an intense symbiosis with various ant species (*Pseudomyrmex spp.*) that will attack anything—herbivores, other plants, and unaware human visitors that come in contact with the tree. The ants and the acacias have an intriguing relationship, though, so do look, but don't touch.

Bromeliad (*piña silvestre*): Members of the family *Bromeliaceae* are *epiphytes,* living on the trunk and branches of trees. They are not parasitic, however, and so have adapted to acquire all the necessary water and nutrients from what falls into the central "tank" formed by the leaf structure. Amphibians and insects also use the water held in bromeliads to reproduce, forming small aquatic communities perched atop tree branches. In especially wet areas, small bromeliads can even be found on power lines. Their spectacular, colorful efflorescences make popular—and expensive—houseplants in northern climes.

Heliconia (*heliconia; Heliconia* spp.): It's hard to miss these stunning plants, many of which have huge inflorescences of red, orange, and yellow, sometimes shaped like lobster claws, and leaves very much the size and shape of a banana plant. With luck, you'll catch a visiting hummingbird with a beak specially designed to delve into a heliconia flower—truly a visual treat.

Mangroves (*manglares*): Taken together, this handful of salt-tolerant trees with tangled, aboveground roots makes up its own distinct ecosystem. Buttressing the land against the sea, the trees serve as nurseries for countless species of fish, crab, and other marine animals and provide roosting habitat for marine birds. Mangroves are found on the coast in protected areas such as bays and estuaries.

Naked Indian Tree (*indio desnudo; Bursera simaruba*): This tree can be found in forests throughout Costa Rica, often forming living fences, and is instantly identifiable by its orange bark that continually sloughs off, giving rise to another common name, the sunburned tourist tree. One theory suggests that the shedding of its bark aids in removing parasites from the tree's exterior.

Orchid (*orquídea*): The huge Orchidaceae family has more than 1,200 representatives in Costa Rica alone, with nearly 90% living as epiphytes on other plants. The great diversity of the group includes not only examples of great beauty but exquisite adaptations between flowers and their insect pollinators. With a combination of rewards (nectar) and trickery (visual and chemical cues), orchids exhibit myriad ways of enticing insects to cooperate.

Strangler Fig (*matapalo; Ficus* spp.): Starting as seedlings high in the canopy, these aggressive plants grow both up toward the light and down to the soil, slowly taking over the host tree. Eventually they encircle and appear to "strangle" the host, actually killing it by hogging all the available sunlight, leaving a ring of fig trunk around an empty interior. Figs with ripe fruit are excellent places for wildlife spotting, as they attract monkeys, birds, and an assortment of other creatures.

MENU GUIDE

Rice and beans are the heart of Costa Rica's *comida típica* (typical food). It's possible to order everything from sushi to crepes in and around San José, but most Ticos have a simple diet built around rice, beans, and the myriad fruits and vegetables that flourish here. Costa Rican food isn't spicy, and many dishes are seasoned with the same five ingredients—onion, salt, garlic, cilantro, and red bell pepper.

SPANISH	ENGLISH
GENERAL DINING	
Almuerzo	Lunch
Bocas	Appetizers or snacks (literally "mouthfuls") served with drinks in the tradition of Spanish tapas
Casado	Heaping plate of rice, beans, fried plantains, cabbage salad, tomatoes, *macarrones* (noodles), and fish, chicken, or meat—or any variation thereof
Cena	Dinner
Desayuno	Breakfast
Plato del día	Plate of the day
Soda	An inexpensive café; casados are always found at sodas.
ESPECIALIDADES (SPECIALTIES)	
Arreglados	Sandwiches or meat and vegetable puff pastry
Arroz con mariscos	Fried rice with fish, shrimp, octopus, and clams, or whatever's fresh that day
Arroz con pollo	Chicken with rice
Camarones	Shrimp
Ceviche	Chilled, raw seafood marinated in lime juice, served with chopped onion and garlic
Chilaquiles	Meat-stuffed tortillas
Chorreados	Corn pancakes, served with *natilla* (sour cream)
Corvina	Sea bass
Empanadas	Savory or sweet pastry turnover filled with fruit or meat and vegetables
Empanaditas	Small empanadas

SPANISH	ENGLISH
Gallo pinto	Rice sautéed with black beans (literally, "spotted rooster"), often served for breakfast
Langosta	Lobster
Langostino	Prawns
Olla de carne	Soup of beef, chayote squash, corn, yuca (a tuber), and potatoes
Palmitos	Hearts of palm, served in salads or as a side dish
Pejibaye	A nutty, orange-color palm fruit eaten in salads, soups, and as a snack
Pescado ahumado	Smoked marlin
Picadillo	Chayote squash, potatoes, carrots, or other vegetables chopped into small cubes and combined with onions, garlic, and ground beef
Pozol	Corn soup
Salsa caribeño	A combination of tomatoes, onions, and spices that accompanies most fish dishes on the Caribbean coast

POSTRES (DESSERTS) AND DULCES (SWEETS)

Cajeta	Molasses-flavored fudge
Cajeta de coco	Fudge made with coconut and orange peel
Dulce de leche	Thick syrup of boiled milk and sugar
Flan	Caramel-topped egg custard
Mazamorra	Cornstarch pudding
Pan de maíz	Sweet corn bread
Torta chilena	Flaky, multilayer cake with dulce de leche filling
Tres leches	"Three milks" cake, made with condensed and evaporated milk and cream

FRUTAS (FRUITS)

Aguacate	Avocado
Anón	Sugar apple; sweet white flesh; resembles an artichoke with a thick rind
Banano	Banana

SPANISH	ENGLISH
Bilimbi	Looks like a miniature cucumber crossed with a star fruit; ground into a savory relish
Carambola	Star fruit
Cas	A smaller guava
Fresa	Strawberry
Granadilla	Passion fruit
Guanábana	Soursop; large, spiky yellow fruit with white flesh and a musky taste
Guayaba	Guava
Mamón chino	Rambutan; red spiky ball protecting a white fruit similar to a lychee
Mango	Many varieties, from sour green to succulently sweet oro (golden); March is the height of mango season
Manzana de agua	Water apple, shaped like a pear; juicy but not very sweet
Marañón	Cashew fruit; used in juices
Melón	Cantaloupe
Mora	Blackberry
Palmito	Heart of palm
Papaya	One of the most popular and ubiquitous fruits
Piña	Pineapple
Pipa	Green coconut; sold at roadside stands with ends chopped off and straws stuck inside
Sandía	Watermelon

BEBIDAS (BEVERAGES)

Agua dulce	Hot water sweetened with raw sugarcane
Batido	Fruit shake made with milk (con leche) or water (con agua)
Café con leche	Coffee with hot milk
Café negro	Black coffee

SPANISH	ENGLISH
Cerveza	Beer
Fresco natural	Fresh-squeezed juice
Gaseosa	Any carbonated beverage
Guaro	Harsh, clear spirit distilled from fermented sugarcane
Horchata	Cinnamon-flavor rice drink
Refresco	Tropical fruit smoothie with ice and sugar
Ron	Rum

VOCABULARY

ENGLISH	SPANISH	PRONUNCIATION

BASIC PHRASES

ENGLISH	SPANISH	PRONUNCIATION
Yes/no	Sí/no	see/no
OK.	De acuerdo.	de a-**kwer**-doe
Please.	Por favor.	pore fah-**vore**
May I?	¿Me permite?	may pair-**mee**-tay
Thank you (very much).	(Muchas) gracias.	(**moo**-chas) **grah**-see-as
You're welcome.	Con mucho gusto.*	con **moo**-cho **goose**-toe
Excuse me.	Con permiso.	con pair-**mee**-so
Pardon me.	¿Perdón?	pair-**dohn**
Could you tell me?	¿Podría decirme?	po-dree-ah deh-**seer**-meh
I'm sorry.	Disculpe.	dee-**skool**-peh
Good morning!	¡Buenos días!	**bway**-nohs **dee**-ahs
Good afternoon!	¡Buenas tardes!	**bway**-nahs **tar**-dess
Good evening!	¡Buenas noches!	**bway**-nahs **no**-chess
Goodbye!	¡Adiós!/¡Hasta luego!	ah-dee-**ohss**/ **ah**-stah-lwe-go
Mr./Mrs.	Señor/Señora	sen-**yor**/sen-**yohr**-ah
Miss	Señorita	sen-yo-**ree**-tah
Pleased to meet you.	Mucho gusto.	**moo**-cho **goose**-toe
How are you?	¿Cómo está usted?	**ko**-mo es-**tah** oo-**sted**
Very well, thank you.	Muy bien, gracias.	**moo**-ee bee-**en**, **grah**-see-as
And you?	¿Y usted?	ee oos-**ted**

*Other Spanish speakers use "De nada" (It's nothing) to say "You're welcome." The Costa Rican phrase translates as "With much pleasure."

DAYS OF THE WEEK

ENGLISH	SPANISH	PRONUNCIATION
Sunday	domingo	doe-**meen**-goh
Monday	lunes	**loo**-ness
Tuesday	martes	**mahr**-tess
Wednesday	miércoles	me-**air**-koh-less
Thursday	jueves	hoo-**ev**-ess

ENGLISH	SPANISH	PRONUNCIATION
Friday	viernes	vee-**air**-ness
Saturday	sábado	**sah**-bah-doh

USEFUL PHRASES

Do you speak English?	¿Habla usted inglés?	**ah**-blah oos-**ted** in-**glehs**
I don't speak Spanish.	No hablo español.	no **ah**-bloh es-pahn-**yol**
I don't understand (you).	No entiendo.	no en-tee-**en**-doh
I understand (you).	Entiendo.	en-tee-**en**-doh
I don't know.	No sé.	no seh
I am American/ British.	Soy americano (americana) / inglés(a).	soy ah-meh-ree-**kah**-no (ah-meh-ree-**kah**-nah)/ in-**glehs** (ah)
What's your name?	¿Cómo se llama usted?	koh-mo seh **yah**-mah **oos**-ted
My name is . . .	Me llamo . . .	may **yah**-moh
What time is it?	¿Qué hora es?	keh **o**-rah es
It is one, two, three . . . o'clock.	Es la una. . . . Son las dos, tres.	es la **oo**-nah/sohn lahs dohs, tress
How?	¿Cómo?	**koh**-mo
When?	¿Cuándo?	**kwahn**-doh
This/Next week	Esta semana / la semana que entra	**es**-teh seh-**mah**-nah/ lah seh-**mah**-nah keh **en**-trah
This/Next month	Este mes/el próximo mes	**es**-teh mehs/el **proke**-see-mo mehs
This/Next year	Este año/el año que viene	**es**-teh **ahn**-yo/el **ahn**-yo keh vee-**yen**-ay
Yesterday/today/ tomorrow	Ayer/hoy/mañana	ah-**yehr**/oy/ mahn- **yah**-nah
This morning/ afternoon	Esta mañana/tarde	**es**-tah mahn-**yah**-nah/ **tar**-deh
Tonight	Esta noche	**es**-tah **no**-cheh
What?	¿Qué?	keh
What is it?	¿Qué es esto?	keh es **es**-toh
Why?	¿Por qué?	pore **keh**

ENGLISH	SPANISH	PRONUNCIATION
Who?	¿Quién?	kee-**yen**
Where is . . . ?	¿Dónde está . . . ?	**dohn**-deh es-**tah**
the bus stop?	la parada del bus?	la pah-**rah**-dah del **boos**
the post office?	la oficina de correos?	la oh-fee-**see**-nah deh koh-**reh**-os
the museum?	el museo?	el moo-**seh**-oh
the hospital?	el hospital?	el ohss-pee-**tal**
the bathroom?	el baño?	el **bahn**-yoh
Here/there	Aquí/allá	ah-**key**/ah-**yah**
Open/closed	Abierto/cerrado	ah-bee-**er**-toh/ ser-**ah**-doh
Left/right	Izquierda/derecha	iss-key-**er**-dah/ dare-**eh**-chah
Straight ahead	Derecho	dare-**eh**-choh
Is it near/far?	¿Está cerca/lejos?	es-**tah** sehr-kah/ **leh**-hoss
I'd like . . .	Quisiera . . .	kee-see-ehr-ah
a room.	un cuarto/una habitación.	oon **kwahr**-toh/**oo**-nah ah-bee-tah-see-**on**
the key.	la llave.	lah **yah**-veh
a newspaper.	un periódico.	oon pehr-ee-**oh**-dee-koh
a stamp.	una estampilla.	**oo**-nah es-stahm-**pee**-yah
I'd like to buy . . .	Quisiera comprar . . .	kee-see-**ehr**-ah kohm-**prahr**
a dictionary.	un diccionario.	oon deek-see-oh- **nah**-ree-oh
soap.	jabón.	hah-**bohn**
suntan lotion.	loción bronceadora.	loh-see-**ohn** brohn- seh-ah-**do**-rah
a map.	un mapa.	oon **mah**-pah
a magazine.	una revista.	**oon**-ah reh-**veess**-tah
a postcard.	una tarjeta postal.	**oon**-ah tar-**het**-ah post-**ahl**

ENGLISH	SPANISH	PRONUNCIATION
How much is it?	¿Cuánto cuesta?	**kwahn**-toh **kwes**-tah
Telephone	Teléfono	tel-**ef**-oh-no
Help!	¡Auxilio!	owk-**see**-lee-oh
	¡Ayuda!	ah-**yoo**-dah
	¡Socorro!	soh-**kohr**-roh
Fire!	¡Incendio!	en-**sen**-dee-oo
Caution!/Look out!	¡Cuidado!	kwee-**dah**-doh

SALUD (HEALTH)

I am ill.	Estoy enfermo(a).	es-**toy** en-**fehr**-moh(mah)
Please call a doctor.	Por favor llame a un médico.	pohr fah-**vor ya**-meh ah oon **med**-ee-koh
acetaminophen	acetaminofeno	a-say-ta-**mee**-no-fen-oh
ambulance	ambulancia	ahm-boo-**lahn**-see-a
antibiotic	antibiótico	ahn-tee-bee-**oh**-tee-co
aspirin	aspirina	ah-spi-**ree**-na
capsule	cápsula	**cahp**-soo-la
clinic	clínica	**clee**-nee-ca
cold	resfriado	rays-free-**ah**-do
cough	tos	toess
diarrhea	diarrea	dee-ah-**ray**-a
fever	fiebre	fee-**ay**-bray
flu	gripe	**gree**-pay
headache	dolor de cabeza	doh-**lor** day cah- **bay**-sa
hospital	hospital	oh-spee-**tahl**
medication	medicamento	meh-dee-cah-**men**-to
pain	dolor	doh-**lor**
pharmacy	farmacia	fahr-**mah**-see-a
physician	médico	**meh**-dee-co
prescription	receta	ray-**say**-ta
stomachache	dolor de estómago	doh-**lor** day eh-**sto**-mah-go

TRAVEL SMART
COSTA RICA

GETTING HERE AND AROUND

■ AIR TRAVEL

If you are visiting several regions of the country, flying into San José, in the center of Costa Rica, is your best option. Flying into Liberia, in northwest Costa Rica, makes more sense if you are planning to spend your vacation entirely in the North Pacific. Fares are usually lower to San José than to Liberia. San José also has many more flights each day, making it easier if you miss a flight or have some other unexpected mishap.

Rarely does an international flight arrive in San José early enough to make a domestic connection, particularly in the rainy season, as the weather is typically unsuitable for flying in the afternoon. So you'll likely end up spending your first night in San José, leaving for your domestic destination the next morning.

It's rare, but afternoon and evening storms during the May-to-November rainy season occasionally cause flights coming into San José to be rerouted to Panama City, where you may be forced to spend the night. October, with its frequent evening fog, tends to be the worst month for reroutes. ■TIP➔ **In the rainy season, try to book a flight with the earliest arrival time available.**

Once you're in Costa Rica, some airlines recommend that you call them about three days before your return flight to reconfirm. Others explicitly say it's not necessary. It's always a good idea to check the day before you are scheduled to depart to make sure your flight time hasn't changed.

If you arrive in Costa Rica and your baggage doesn't, the first thing you should do is go to the baggage claims counter and file an official report. Then contact your airline to let them know where you will be staying. Bags are usually located within two days and can be sent to you just about anywhere in the country. Don't expect too much from local agents; try to get updates directly from your airline.

If your bag has been searched and contents are missing or damaged, file a claim with the Transportation Security Administration's Consumer Response Center as soon as possible. If your bags arrive damaged or fail to arrive at all, file a written report with the airline before leaving the airport.

When you fly out of Costa Rica, you'll have to pay a $29 airport departure tax in colones or dollars or with a Visa or MasterCard credit card. (Paying the tax via credit card means the transaction will be processed as a cash advance and incur additional fees.) You can pay at the Bancrédito counter in the airport—the line may look long but it moves quickly—or at any Bancrédito branch during your trip. (Lines at banks are *long*, so this may be a time-consuming option.) A few hotels will collect the tax for you as well.

Airline Security Issues Transportation Security Administration ⊕ *www.tsa.gov.*

AIRPORTS

Costa Rica has two international airports. Aeropuerto Internacional Juan Santamaría (SJO) is the country's main airport, about 17 km (10 miles), northwest of downtown San José, just outside the city of Alajuela. The drive takes about 30 minutes. Domestic airlines SANSA and Nature Air operate from here, SANSA in its own terminal and Nature Air inside the main building. The country's other international airport is Aeropuerto Internacional Daniel Oduber Quirós (LIR), a small airport near the city of Liberia in the North Pacific. It's about 13 km (8 miles) west of the city.

Other places where planes land in Costa Rica aren't exactly airports. They're more like carports with landing strips, and airline representatives arrive a few minutes before a plane is due to land or take off.

Most international flights arrive in the evening and depart early in the morning. Prepare yourself for long waits at immigration and customs. When you're departing the country, prepare for security checkpoints at both airports. Liquids and gels over 3 ounces are not permitted. Carry-on bags are searched again at the gates for flights to the United States. Get to the airport three hours before your flight.

Airport Information Aeropuerto Internacional Daniel Oduber Quirós (*LIR*). ✉ *Liberia* ☎ *2668–1010 in Costa Rica* ⊕ *www.liberiacostaricaairport.net.* **Aeropuerto Internacional Juan Santamaría** (*SJO*). ✉ *San José* ☎ *2437–2400, 2437–2626 in Costa Rica for departure and arrival info* ⊕ *www.fly2sanjose.com.*

GROUND TRANSPORTATION

At Aeropuerto Internacional Juan Santamaría, you exit the terminal into a fume-filled parking area flanked by hordes of taxis and tour vans. If you're with a tour, you need only look for a tour company representative with a sign that bears your name. If you need a taxi, a uniformed agent will escort you to one of the orange Taxis Unidos cabs (no other taxis are allowed in the arrivals area). The metered fare to most areas of San José is $25 to $35.

Transportation at Aeropuerto Internacional Daniel Oduber Quirós is also a mix of taxis and tour vans. The big Pacific-coast resorts provide transport, but always check with your lodging for recommendations on the best way to arrive.

FLIGHTS

From North America to San José: American flies from Miami and Dallas and, from November to April, from New York (JFK); United flies from Houston,

Newark, Chicago, and Washington Dulles (IAD); Delta flies from Atlanta and Los Angeles and, from December to April, from Minneapolis and New York (JFK); US Airways flies from Charlotte and, from December to April, from Philadelphia and Phoenix; Spirit Air flies from Fort Lauderdale; JetBlue flies from Orlando and Fort Lauderdale; Frontier flies from Denver; Air Canada Rouge, the leisure division of Air Canada, flies from Toronto; Avianca (formerly TACA) offers connections from several U.S. airports through its hub in San Salvador, El Salvador. Mexico's AeroMéxico does the same via its hub in Mexico City, and Panama's Copa also offers connections through its hub in Panama City.

From New York or Los Angeles, nonstop flights to San José are 5½ hours. San José is 3 hours from Miami, 3½ hours from Houston, and 4 hours from Charlotte and Dallas. In general, nonstop flights aren't that much more expensive. Ticket prices from hubs such as New York, Los Angeles, and Miami hover between $500 and $600, although the range varies widely.

Eleven commercial airlines fly to Liberia: American, from Dallas and Miami; Delta, from Atlanta, Los Angeles, Minneapolis, and New York (JFK); United, from Chicago, Houston and Newark; JetBlue, from New York (JFK); US Airways, from Charlotte, North Carolina; Frontier, from Denver; Sun Country Airlines from Minneapolis and Dallas (December through April); Air Canada Rouge, from Toronto, Air Canada, from Montreal (December to April); and WestJet, from Toronto. Avianca and Copa connect their U.S. gateways to Liberia via their hubs in San Salvador and Panama City, respectively.

Avianca and Copa connect San José with other Central American cities. Nature Air flies from Managua, Nicaragua, and from Bocas del Toro, Panama.

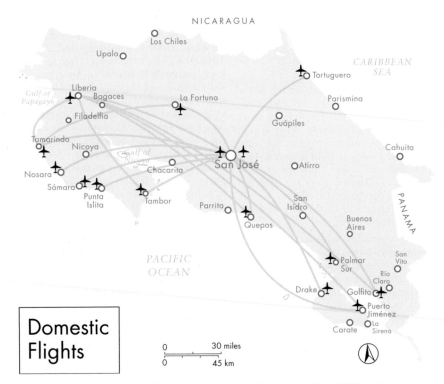

NICARAGUA

Los Chiles

Upala

CARIBBEAN
SEA

Liberia
Bagaces
La Furtuna
Parismina

Gulf of
Papagayo

Filadelfia

Guápiles

Tamarindo
Nicoya

Cahuita

Nosara
Chacarita
San José
Atirro

Sámara
Punta
Islita
Tambor
Parrita
San
Isidro

PANAMA

Quepos

Buenos
Aires

PACIFIC
OCEAN

San
Vito

Palmar
Sur

Río
Claro

Drake
Golfito

Puerto
Jiménez

Carate
La
Sirena

Domestic Flights

0   30 miles

0   45 km

Given Costa Rica's often-difficult driving conditions, domestic flights are a desirable and practical option. The informality of domestic air service—"airports" other than Liberia and San José usually consist of only an airstrip with no central building at which to buy tickets—means you might want to purchase your domestic airplane tickets in advance. You can also buy them at the international airports or at travel agencies once you're in the country. We recommend grabbing a seat as soon as you know your itinerary.

There are two major domestic commercial airlines, SANSA and Nature Air, and most of their flights leave from the San José area. You can buy tickets online, over the phone, and at most travel agencies in Costa Rica. The tiny, domestic passenger planes in Costa Rica require that you pack light. A luggage weight limit of 30 pounds is imposed by SANSA; Nature Air allows 15–40 pounds, depending on the fare. Extra luggage is sometimes allowed, but costs $1 to $3 per pound and will go standby. Neither airline can store extra baggage, but hotels and lodges may be able to store your luggage—ask ahead and bring a smaller bag for your domestic travels.

Charter flights within Costa Rica are not as expensive as you might think, and can be a good deal if you are traveling in a group. The price per person will be only slightly more than taking a regularly scheduled domestic flight, and you can set your own departure time. The country has dozens of airstrips that are accessible only by charter planes. Charter planes are most often booked through tour operators, travel agents, or remote lodges. Most charter planes are smaller than domestic commercial planes.

■TIP→ Don't book a domestic flight for the day you arrive in or leave Costa Rica; connections are extremely tight, and you'll be at the mercy of the weather.

Airline Contacts AeroMéxico ☏ 800/237–6639 in North America, 2331–6834 ⊕ www.aeromexico.com. **Air Canada/Air Canada Rouge** ☏ 888/247–2262 in North America, 0800/052–1988 in Costa Rica ⊕ www.aircanada.com. **American Airlines** ☏ 800/433–7300, 2248–2010 in Costa Rica ⊕ www.aa.com. **Avianca** ☏ 800/284–2622 in U.S., 2299–8222 in Costa Rica, 800/722–8222 in Canada ⊕ www.avianca.com. **Copa** ☏ 800/359–2672 in North America, 2223–2672 in Costa Rica ⊕ www.copaair.com. **Delta Airlines** ☏ 800/241–4141 for international reservations, 0800/056–2002 in Costa Rica ⊕ www.delta.com. **Frontier Airlines** ☏ 800/432–1359 for international reservations, 2440–4307 in Costa Rica ⊕ www.frontierairlines.com. **JetBlue** ☏ 800/538–2583 for international reservations, 2441–6851 in Costa Rica ⊕ www.jetblue.com. **Spirit Airlines** ☏ 800/772–7117, 2441–6552 in Costa Rica ⊕ www.spiritair.com. **Sun Country Airlines** ☏ 800/359–6786 in North America ⊕ www.suncountry.com. **United Airlines** ☏ 800/538–2929 for international reservations, 0800/044–0005 in Costa Rica ⊕ www.united.com. **US Airways** ☏ 800/428–4322 for international reservations, 0800/011–0793 in Costa Rica ⊕ www.usairways.com. **WestJet** ☏ 888/937–8538 in North America, 800/5381–5696 in Costa Rica ⊕ www.westjet.com.

Domestic and Charter Airlines
Aerobell Air Charter ☏ 888/359–1359 in North America, 2290–0000 in Costa Rica ⊕ www.aerobell.com. **Nature Air** ☏ 800/235–9272 in North America, 2299–6000 in Costa Rica ⊕ www.natureair.com. **SANSA** ☏ 2290–4100 in Costa Rica, 877/767–2672 in North America ⊕ www.flysansa.com.

▌BUS TRAVEL

Tica Bus has daily service to Panama and Nicaragua, with connections to Honduras, El Salvador, Guatemala, and southern Mexico. Transnica serves Nicaragua and Honduras. We recommend Tica Bus, but Transnica is acceptable in a pinch. Both companies have comfortable, air-conditioned coaches with videos and onboard toilets, and help with border procedures.

All Costa Rican towns are connected by regular bus service that's reliable, comprehensive, and inexpensive. Buses between major cities are modern, but in rural areas you may get a converted school bus without air-conditioning. On longer routes, buses stop midway at modest restaurants. Near their destinations many buses turn into large taxis, dropping passengers off one by one along the way. To save time, take a *directo* (express) bus, which still might make a few stops. Be prepared for bus-company employees and bus drivers to speak only Spanish.

The main inconvenience of long-distance buses is the time spent getting there. For example, a bus from San José to the Osa Peninsula is nine hours or more, whereas the flight is one hour. Shorter distances reduce the difference—the bus to Quepos is 3½ hours, while the flight is 30 minutes. There is no central bus station in San José; buses leave from a variety of departure points, depending on the region they serve. You usually have to return to San José to travel between outlying regions.

■TIP→ Avoid putting your belongings in the overhead bin. If you must, keep your eye on them. If anyone—even someone who looks like a bus employee—offers to put your things in the luggage compartment, politely decline. If you must put your luggage underneath the bus, get off quickly when you arrive to retrieve it.

Most bus companies don't have printed schedules, although departure times may be posted on a sign at the ticket window. Phones are usually busy or go unanswered. ■TIP→ **For the most reliable schedules, go to the bus station a day before your departure.** The official tourism board, the Instituto Costarricense de Turismo (ICT), provides bus schedules on its website, but the information is updated infrequently. Hotel employees can usually give you the information you need.

Buses usually depart and arrive on time; they may even leave a few minutes early if they are full. Tickets are sold at bus stations and on the buses themselves; reservations aren't accepted, and you must pay in person with cash. Be sure to have loose change and small bills handy; employees won't have change for a 10,000-colón bill. Buses to popular beach and mountain destinations often sell out on weekends and holidays. It's difficult to get tickets to San José on Sunday afternoon. Some companies won't sell you a round-trip ticket from the departure point; if that's the case, make sure the first thing you do on arrival in your destination is to buy a return ticket. Sometimes tickets include seat numbers, which are usually printed on the tops of the chairs or above the windows. Smoking is not permitted.

Two private bus companies, Gray Line and Interbus, travel to the most popular tourist destinations in modern, air-conditioned vans. Interbus vans usually seat 10 to 20 people, and coaches can also be reserved for large groups, Gray Line vans seat 14 to 20 people. The cost is $37 to $92 one-way, but can take hours off your trip. Gray Line offers a weekly pass ($180) good for unlimited travel; reservations are required 24 hours in advance. Interbus offers three-to seven-trip Flexipasses; they cost $125 to $275 and are good for one month. Be sure to double-check information on the websites—published prices may not be accurate and routes may be discontinued. Costa Rica Shuttle offers minivan service that's great if you're traveling in a group. Rates range from $55 to $365 for up to five people.

Bus Information Tica Bus ⊠ *Avda. 3 and C. 26, 200 m north and 100 m west of Torre Mercedes, Paseo Colón, San José* ☎ *2221–0006* ⊕ *www.ticabus.com.* **Transnica** ⊠ *C. 22, Avdas. 3–5, San José* ☎ *2223–4242* ⊕ *www.transnica.com.*

Shuttle-Van Services Costa Rica Shuttle ☎ *2289–4292, 800/849–9403 in North America* ⊕ *www.costaricashuttle.com.* **Gray Line** ☎ *2291–2222, 800/719–3905 in North America* ⊕ *www.graylinecostarica.com.* **Interbus** ☎ *4031–0888* ⊕ *www.interbusonline.com.*

■ CAR TRAVEL

Hiring a car with a driver makes the most sense for sightseeing in and around San José. You can also usually hire a taxi driver to ferry you around; most will stick to the meter, which will tick at a rate of about $15 for each hour the driver spends waiting for you. At $100 to $130 per day plus the driver's food, hiring a driver for areas outside the San José area costs almost the same as renting a four-wheel-drive vehicle, but is more expensive for multiday trips because you also have to pay for the driver's lodging. Some drivers are also knowledgeable guides; others just drive. Unless they're driving large passenger vans for established companies, it's doubtful that drivers have any special training or licensing.

Hotels can usually direct you to trusted drivers. Alamo provides professional car-and-driver services for a minimum of three days. On top of the rental fee, you pay $75 for the driver, plus food and lodging. Costa Rica Shuttle provides drivers on similar terms for $95 to $240 per day.

GASOLINE

You'll usually find 24-hour stations only in San José or along the Pan-American Highway. Most stations are open 7 to 7, although some are open until midnight. Regular unleaded gasoline is called *regular,* and high-octane unleaded, required in most modern vehicles, is called *súper.* Gas is sold by the liter.

Try to fill your tank in cities—gas is more expensive (and more likely to be dirtier) at informal fill-up places in rural areas, where gas stations can be few and far between. Major credit cards are widely accepted. There are no self-service gas stations in Costa Rica. It is not customary to tip attendants. If you want a *factura* (receipt), ask for it.

PARKING

On-street parking is scarce in downtown San José. Where you find a spot, you'll also find *guachimanes* (informal, usually self-appointed guards). They won't actually get involved if someone tries something with your car, but it's best to give them a couple of hundred colones per hour anyway. It's illegal to park in zones marked by yellow curb paint, or in front of garage doors or driveways, usually marked *no estacionar* (no parking). Downtown parking laws are strictly enforced; the fine for illegal parking is 5,000 colones (about $10). In places like San José, Alajuela, and Heredia, you'll find signs with a large E in a red circle, and the words *con boleto* (with a ticket). These tickets can be bought for ½-hour (250 colones), 1-hour (500 colones), or 2-hour (1,000 colones) increments.

Safer and ubiquitous are the public lots (*parqueos*), which average about $2 per hour. Most are open late, especially near hopping nightspots or theaters, but check beforehand. Never leave anything inside the car.

Outside San José and the surrounding communities, parking rules are far more lax. Guarded hotel or restaurant parking lots are the rule, with few public lots.

RENTAL CARS

When you reserve a car, ask about cancellation penalties, taxes, drop-off charges (if you're planning to pick up the car in one city and leave it in another), and surcharges (for being under or over a certain age, for additional drivers, or for driving beyond a specific distance). All these things can add substantially to your costs.

Request such extras as car seats and GPS devices when you book.

Rates are sometimes—but not always—better if you book in advance or reserve through a rental agency's website. Book ahead during the busier times of the year and to ensure that you get a certain type of vehicle (a van, SUV, or sports car, for instance).

■ TIP→ **If you're visiting one or two major areas, taking a shuttle van or a domestic flight is cheaper and more convenient than driving.** Renting is a good choice if you're destination hopping, staying at a hotel outside town, or going well off the beaten path. Car trips to northern Guanacaste from San José can take an entire day, so flying is a better option if you don't have a lot of time. Flying is definitely better than driving for visiting the South Pacific.

A standard vehicle is fine for most destinations, but a *doble-tracción* (four-wheel-drive vehicle) is often essential to reach the remote parts of the country, especially during the rainy season. Even in the dry season, a 4WD vehicle is necessary to reach Monteverde and some destinations in Guanacaste. The biggest 4WD vehicles can cost twice as much as an economy car, but compact 4WDs are more reasonable.

Most cars in Costa Rica have manual transmissions. ■ TIP→ **Specify when making a reservation if you want automatic transmission; it usually costs $5 more per day.** Some companies, such as Alamo and Hertz, don't charge extra. If you plan to rent a car between December 15 and January 3 or during the week leading up to Easter—when most Costa Ricans are on vacation—reserve several months ahead of time.

Costa Rica has around 30 car-rental firms. Most local firms are affiliated with international chains and offer the same guarantees and services. Tricolor, a local company, gets high marks from travelers on ⊕ *www.fodors.com*. Renting in or near San José is by far the easiest way to go. At least a dozen rental offices line San José's Paseo Colón. It's getting easier to rent outside San José, particularly on the Pacific coast. Several rental companies have set up branches in Liberia, Quepos, Manuel Antonio, Jacó, Tamarindo, and La Fortuna. In most other places across the country, it's either impossible or very difficult and expensive to rent a car.

Rental cars may not be driven across borders to Nicaragua and Panama. For a $50 fee, National and Alamo will let you drop off a Costa Rican rental car at the Nicaragua border and provide you with a Nicaraguan rental on the other side. Fuel-efficiency measures restrict cars from San José's city center between 6 am and 7 pm once a week, according to the final license-plate number (plates that end in 1 and 2 are restricted on Monday; 3 and 4, on Tuesday; 5 and 6, on Wednesday; 7 and 8, on Thursday; and 9 and 0 on Friday). This also applies to rental cars.

To rent a car, you need a driver's license, a valid passport, and a credit card. The minimum age varies; agencies such as Economy, Budget, and Alamo rent to anyone over 21; Avis sets the limit at 23, Hertz at 25. Though it's rare, some agencies have a maximum age limit.

High-season rates in San José begin at $50 a day and $200 a week for an economy car with air-conditioning, manual transmission, and unlimited mileage, along with obligatory insurance. Rates fluctuate considerably according to demand, season, and company. Rates for a 4WD vehicle during high season are $80 to $100 a day and $500 to $600 per week. Companies often require a $1,000 deposit, payable by credit card.

Cars picked up at or returned to San José's Aeropuerto Internacional Juan Santamaría incur a 12% surcharge. You can pick up cars directly at the Liberia airport, but a range of firms have offices nearby and transport you from the airport free of charge—and with no surcharge for an airport pickup. Check cars thoroughly for damage before you sign the contract. Even tough-looking 4WD vehicles should be coddled. ■ TIP➔ The charges levied by rental companies for damage—no matter how minor—are outrageous even by U.S. or European standards. One-way service surcharges are $50 to $150, depending on the drop-off point; National allows travelers free car drop-off at any of its offices with a minimum three-day rental. To avoid a hefty refueling fee, fill the tank just before you return the car. It's almost never a good deal to buy the tank of gas that's in the car when you rent it; the understanding is that you'll return it empty, but some fuel usually remains. Additional drivers can cost $10 per day. Almost all agencies have cell-phone rental; prices range between $3 and $8 per day, with national per-minute costs between 50¢ and $2.

It's wise to opt for full insurance coverage. Auto insurance in Costa Rica is a government monopoly. At a minimum, you are required to purchase third-party liability insurance through the rental agency to cover damages to other persons and vehicles. Your own credit-card coverage does not exempt you from this charge. Some rental agencies include such costs in your quoted rates. Many do not, however, and we hear numerous tales of clients shocked at the final tally when they pick up the car. Always ask what is included when you reserve.

International driving permits (IDPs), which translate your license into 10 languages, are not necessary in Costa Rica. Your own driver's license is good for the length of your initial tourist visa. You must carry your passport, or a copy of it with the entry stamp, to prove when you entered the country.

Local Agencies Economy ☎ *877/326–7368 in North America, 2299-2000 in Costa Rica* ⊕ *www.economyrentacar.com.* **Tricolor** ☎ *800/949-0234 in North America, 2440-3333 in Costa Rica* ⊕ *www.tricolorcarrental.com.*

Major Agencies Alamo ☎ *2242-7733 in Costa Rica, 877/222-9075 in North America* ⊕ *www.alamocostarica.com.* **Avis** ☎ *2293-2222 in Costa Rica, 800/331-1084 in North America* ⊕ *www.avis.co.cr.* **Budget** ☎ *2436-2000 in Costa Rica, 800/472–3325 in North America* ⊕ *www.budget.co.cr.* **Dollar** ☎ *877/767-8651 in North America, 2443-2950 in Costa Rica* ⊕ *www.dollarcostarica.com.* **Hertz** ☎ *800/654-3001 in North America, 2221-1818 in Costa Rica* ⊕ *www.hertzcostarica.com.* **National Car Rental** ☎ *877/862-8227 in North America, 2242-7878 in Costa Rica* ⊕ *www.natcar.com.*

ROAD CONDITIONS

Many travelers shy away from renting a car in Costa Rica. Indeed, this is not an ideal place to drive. In San José, traffic is bad and car theft is rampant (look for guarded lots or hotels with parking). Roads in rural areas are often unpaved or potholed—and tires usually aren't covered by the basic insurance. And Ticos are reckless drivers—with one of the highest accident rates in the world. But although driving can be a challenge, it's a great way to explore certain regions, especially the North Pacific, the Northern Plains, and the Caribbean coast (apart from roadless Tortuguero and Barra del Colorado). Keep in mind that winding roads and poor conditions make most trips longer than you'd normally expect.

The winding Pan-American Highway south of the capital is notorious for long snakes of traffic stuck behind slow-moving trucks. Look out for potholes, even in the smoothest sections of the best roads. Also watch for unmarked speed bumps where you'd least expect them, particularly on main thoroughfares in rural areas. During the rainy season, roads are in much worse shape. Check with your destination before setting out; roads, especially in Limón Province, are prone to washouts and landslides.

San José is terribly congested during weekday rush hours (7 to 9 am and 4 to 6 pm). Avoid returning to the city on Sunday evening, when traffic from the beaches can be backed up for miles. Frequent fender benders tie up traffic. Keep your windows rolled up in the center of the city, because thieves may reach into your car at stoplights and snatch purses, jewelry, and valuables.

Signage is notoriously bad, but improving. Watch carefully for *"No Hay Paso"* ("Do Not Enter") signs; one-way streets are common, and it's not unusual for a two-way to suddenly become one-way.

Highways are numbered on signs and maps, but few people use or even know the numbering system. Asking for directions to "Highway 27" will probably be met with a blank stare. Everyone calls it the "Carretera a Caldera" (highway to Caldera, on the Pacific coast) instead. Outside San José you'll run into long stretches of unpaved road. Look out for potholes, landslides during the rainy season, and cattle on the roads. Drunk drivers are a hazard on weekend nights. Driving at night is not recommended, because roads are poorly lighted and many don't have painted center lines or shoulder lines.

ROADSIDE EMERGENCIES

Costa Rica has no highway emergency service organization. In Costa Rica, 911 is the nationwide number for accidents. Traffic Police (*tránsitos*) are scattered around the country, but Costa Ricans are very good about stopping for people with car trouble. Whatever happens, don't move the car after an accident, even if a monstrous traffic jam ensues. Call 911 first if the accident is serious (nearly everyone has a cell phone), then call the emergency number of your car-rental agency.

Emergency Services Ambulance and Police ☎ *911.* **Traffic Police** (*Policía de Tránsito*). ☎ *911.*

RULES OF THE ROAD

■ TIP➜ **Obey traffic laws religiously, even if Costa Ricans don't.** Fines are frightfully high—a speeding ticket could set you back $560—and evidence exists that transit police target foreigners. Don't get too complacent if you don't see any police; cameras monitor traffic on the highways around San José. Your rental agency may charge you for a speeding ticket it receives after your return home.

Driving is on the right side of the road in Costa Rica. The highway speed limit is usually 90 kph (54 mph), which drops to 60 kph (36 mph) in residential areas. In towns, limits range from 30 to 50 kph (18 to 31 mph). Speed limits are enforced in all regions of the country. "*Alto*" means "stop" and "*ceda*" means "yield." Right turns on red are permitted except where signs indicate otherwise, but in San José this is usually not possible because of one-way streets and pedestrian crossings.

Local drunk driving laws are strict. You'll also get nailed with a $450 fine if you're caught driving in a "predrunk" state (blood alcohol levels of 0.05% to 0.075%). If your level is higher than that, the car will be confiscated, your license will be taken away, and you risk jail time. Police officers who stop drivers for speeding and drunk driving are often looking for payment on the spot— essentially a bribe. Asking for a ticket instead of paying the bribe discourages corruption and does not compromise your safety. You can generally pay the ticket at your car-rental company, which will pay it on your behalf.

Seat-belt use is mandatory. Car seats are required for children ages four and under. Children over 12 are allowed in the front seat. Drivers are prohibited from texting or using handheld cell phones.

▌ CRUISE-SHIP TRAVEL

Costa Rica is a popular cruise destination on many Panama Canal and Western Caribbean itineraries during a season that runs August–May. Most large cruises stop in the country only once. Smaller ships, including those of Windstar Cruises (capacity for 148), SeaDream Yacht Club (112 guests), Paul Gauguin Cruises (90 guests), Variety Cruises (72 guests), and highly recommended, conservation-minded Lindblad Expeditions (62 guests) offer Costa Rica–focused cruises along the Pacific coast that may include calls in neighboring Panama or Nicaragua.

Cruise Lines Azamara Club Cruises ☎ 877/999–9553 in North America ⊕ www. azamaraclubcruises.com. **Carnival** ☎ 800/764–7419 in North America ⊕ www.carnival. com. **Celebrity** ☎ 800/647–2251 in North America ⊕ www.celebritycruises.com. **Costa Cruises** ☎ 800/462–6782 ⊕ www.costacruise. com. **Crystal** ☎ 888/722–0021 in North America ⊕ www.crystalcruises.com. **Cunard** ☎ 800/728–6273 in North America ⊕ www. cunard.com. **Holland America** ☎ 800/932–4259 in North America ⊕ www.hollandamerica. com. **Lindblad Expeditions** ☎ 800/397–3348 in North America ⊕ www.expeditions.com. **MSC Cruises** ☎ 877/665–4655 in North America ⊕ www.msccruisescom. **Norwegian** ☎ 866/234–7350 in North America ⊕ www. ncl.com. **Oceania** ☎ 800/531–5619 in North America ⊕ www.oceaniacruises.com. **P&O Cruises** ☎ 877/828–4728 ⊕ www.poamericas. com. **Paul Gauguin Cruises** ☎ 800/848–6172 in North America ⊕ www.pgcruises.com. **Princess** ☎ 800/774–6237 in North America ⊕ www.princess.com. **Regent Seven Seas** ☎ 877/505–5370 in North America ⊕ www. rssc.com. **Royal Caribbean** ☎ 866/562–7625 in North America ⊕ www.royalcaribbean. com. **SeaDream Yacht Club** ☎ 800/707–4911 ⊕ www.seadream.com. **Silversea** ☎ 877/276–6816 in North America ⊕ www. silversea.com. **Star Clippers** ☎ 800/442–0551 in North America ⊕ www.starclippers.com. **Variety Cruises** ☎ 800/319–7776 ⊕ www. varietycruises.com. **Windstar Cruises** ☎ 800/258–7245 ⊕ www.windstarcruises.com.

TAXI TRAVEL

Taxis are cheap and your best bet for getting around San José. Just about every driver is friendly and eager to use a few English words to tell you about a cousin or sister in New Jersey; however, cabbies truly conversant in English are scarce. Tipping is not expected, but a good idea when you've had some extra help, especially with your bags.

Cabs are red, usually with a yellow light on top. To hail one, extend your hand and wave it at about hip height. If it's available, the driver will often flick his headlights before pulling over. The city is dotted with *paradas de taxi,* taxi queues where you stand the best chance of grabbing one. Your hotel can usually call you a reputable taxi or private car service, and when you're out to dinner or on the town, ask the manager to call you a cab—it's much easier than hailing one on the street, and safer, too.

■TIP➜ Taxi drivers are infamous for "not having change." If it's just a few hundred colones, you may as well round up. If it's a lot, ask to go to a store or gas station where you can make change. To avoid this situation, never use a 10,000-colón bill in a taxi, and avoid paying with 5,000-colón bills unless you've run up almost that much in fares.

Outside the capital area, drivers often use their odometers to creatively calculate fares. Manuel Antonio drivers are notorious for overcharging. It's illegal, but taxis charge up to double for hotel pickups or fares that take them out of the province (such as San José to Alajuela). Ask the manager at your hotel about the going rate. Outside the capital, try to avoid taking an unofficial taxi (*pirata*), although it's sometimes the only option. It's better to ask your hotel for recommendations.

It's always a good idea to make a note of the cab number (painted in a yellow triangle on the door), and sit in the backseat for safety.

ESSENTIALS

▮ ACCOMMODATIONS

Costa Rica excels in its selection of boutique hotels, tasteful bungalows, and bed-and-breakfasts, which offer a high degree of personalized service. Because they're generally small, you may have to book one or two months ahead, and up to six months in the high season. Reserving through an association or agency can significantly reduce the time you spend scanning the Internet, but you can often get a better deal and negotiate longer-stay or low-season discounts. The Costa Rican Hotels Association has online search and booking capabilities. ICT provides hotel lists searchable by star category.

High-end accommodations range from luxury tents to exquisite hotels to villa rentals. You'll find all the amenities you expect at such areas, with one notable exception: the roads and routes to even five-star villas can be atrocious. Resorts are generally one of two kinds: luxurious privileged gateways to the best of the country (such as Punta Islita) or generic medium-budget all-inclusives (such as the Spanish hotel chain Barceló). Several chain hotels have franchises in Costa Rica, and they are rarely booked solid.

Nature lodges in the South Pacific may be less expensive than they initially appear, as the nightly rate usually includes three hearty meals and sometimes even guided hikes. Internet access isn't a given, even if a place has a website. Many have an eco-friendly approach (even to luxury), so air-conditioning might not be included. Consider how isolated you want to be; some lodges are miles from neighbors and have few rainy-day diversions. The ICT's voluntary "green leaf" rating system evaluates eco-friendly lodgings. A listing can be found at ⊕ *www.turismo-sostenible.co.cr.*

Be sure to reserve well in advance for the dry season (mid-December to April everywhere except the Caribbean coast, which has a short September to October "dry" season). ▮TIP➜ **If you're having trouble finding accommodations, consider contacting a tour operator. Because they reserve blocks of rooms, you might have better luck.** During the rainy season (May to mid-November except on the Caribbean coast, where it's almost always rainy) most hotels drop their rates considerably, which sometimes sends them into a lower price category than the one we indicate.

Most hotels and other lodgings require you to give your credit-card details before confirming your reservation. Get confirmation in writing and have a copy of it handy when you check in.

Be sure you understand the hotel's cancellation policy. Some places allow you to cancel without any kind of penalty—even if you prepaid to secure a discounted rate—if you cancel at least 24 hours in advance. Others require you to cancel a week in advance or penalize you the cost of one night. Small inns and bed-and-breakfasts are most likely to require you to cancel far in advance. Most hotels allow children under a certain age to stay in their parents' room at no extra charge, but others charge for them as extra adults; find out the cutoff age for discounts.

The lodgings we list are Costa Rica's cream of the crop in each price category. When pricing accommodations, always ask what's included and what costs extra. Keep in mind that prices don't include 16.4% service and tax. Smoking is prohibited in all hotels, both in rooms and public areas. *Our local writers vet every hotel to recommend the best overnights in each price category, from budget to expensive. Unless otherwise specified, you can expect private bath, phone, and TV in your room. Hotel reviews have been shortened. For full information, visit Fodors.com.*

Lodging Resources Costa Rican Hotels Association (*Cámara Costarricense de Hoteles*). ☎ 2220-0575 ⊕ *www.costaricanhotels.com*. **Instituto Costarricense de Turismo** (*ICT*). ☎ 866/267-8274 *in North America, 2299-5800 in Costa Rica* ⊕ *www.visitcostarica.com*.

APARTMENT AND HOUSE RENTALS

Rental houses are common all over Costa Rica, particularly in the Pacific coast destinations of Manuel Antonio, Tamarindo, Ocotal, and Jacó. Homes can accommodate whole families, often for less money and at a higher comfort level. Properties are often owned by foreigners, most of them based in the United States, with property managers in Costa Rica.

Resort communities with villa-style lodgings are also growing. Nosara Beach Rentals lists apartments and villas on the Nicoya Peninsula. Escape Villas Costa Rica lists rentals in Manuel Antonio, Dominical, Jacó, Playa Flamingo, and Tamarindo. Villas International has an extensive list of properties in the Central Valley, Quepos, Jacó, and Dominical. Villas Caribe offers a variety of rentals on the North and Central Pacific coasts. For the southern Nicoya Peninsula, check Costa Rica Beach Rentals.

Contacts Costa Rica Beach Rentals
☎ 8340-3842, 973/917-8046 *in North America* ⊕ *www.costarica-beachrentals.com*.
Escape Villas Costa Rica ☎ 2203-2158, 888/771-2976 *in North America* ⊕ *www.villascostarica.com*. **Nosara Beach Rentals** ☎ 2682-0153 ⊕ *www.nosarabeachrentals.com*. **Villas & Apartments Abroad** ✉ *183 Madison Ave., Suite 1111, New York, New York, USA* ☎ 212/213-6435 *in North America* ⊕ *www.vaanyc.com*. **Villas Caribe** ☎ 800/645-7498 ⊕ *www.villascaribe.com*. **Villas International** ✉ *17 Fox La., San Anselmo, California, USA* ☎ 415/499-9490 *in North America, 800/221-2260* ⊕ *www.villasintl.com*.

BED-AND-BREAKFASTS

A number of quintessential bed-and-breakfasts—small and homey—are clustered in the Central Valley, generally offering hearty breakfasts and friendly inside information for $50 to $75 per night. You'll also find them scattered through the rest of the country, mixed in with other self-titled bed-and-breakfasts that range from small cabins in the mountains to luxurious boutique hotel–style digs in the North Pacific region.

Reservation Services Bed and Breakfast. com. Bed and Breakfast.com also sends out an online newsletter. ☎ 512/322-2710, 800/462-2632 ⊕ *www.bedandbreakfast.com*.

HOME EXCHANGES

With a direct home exchange you stay in someone else's home while they stay in yours. Some outfits also deal with vacation homes, so you're not actually staying in someone's full-time residence, just their vacant weekend place.

Home exchanges are an excellent way to immerse yourself in the true Costa Rica, particularly if you've been here before. Drawbacks include restricted options and dates. Many companies list home exchanges, but we've found Home Exchange, which lists a handful of jazzy houses around Costa Rica, to be the most reliable.

Exchange Clubs Home Exchange. $119 for a one-year online listing. ☎ 800/877-8723 ⊕ *www.homeexchange.com*.

ADDRESSES

In Costa Rica addresses are usually given in terms of how many meters the place is from a landmark. Street names and building numbers are not commonly used. Churches, stores, even large trees that no longer exist—almost anything can be a landmark, as long as everyone knows where it is, or where it used to be. A typical address in San José is *100 metros este y 100 metros sur del supermercado* (100 meters east and 100 meters south from the supermarket). ■TIP→ **In Costa Rica, each block is assumed to be 100 meters, although some blocks may be much longer and some may be shorter.**

Ticos, as Costa Ricans call themselves, are generally happy to help lost visitors, and they spend a lot of time describing where things are. But be warned—even if they don't know where something is, Ticos will often give uncertain or even wrong information rather than seem unhelpful. Ask at least two people in quick succession to avoid getting hopelessly lost. Key direction terms are *lugar* (place), *calle* (street), *avenida* (avenue), *puente* (bridge), *piso* (floor), *edificio* (building), *cruce* (intersection), *semáforo* (traffic light), *rotonda* (traffic circle), and *cuadra* (block).

COMMUNICATIONS

INTERNET

With the advent of smartphones, Internet cafés are dwindling in number. Downtown San José still has a few with high-speed connections; prices are usually less than $1 per hour. As you move away from the capital, prices rise to $2 to $4 per hour and connections become less reliable. Wildly expensive satellite Internet is available at some exclusive hotels in remote areas. Most major hotels have free wireless access or use of a wired computer. Denny's, Bagelmen's, and a number of upscale cafés are Wi-Fi–friendly, although a few travelers have been robbed of their laptops and tablets in restaurants. (Smartphones are generally safe.)

Internet access via your smartphone should work in most cities of any size, but we recommend always looking for a Wi-Fi signal to avoid surprises on your bill after you return home. Data charges are high.

Contacts Cybercafes. Cybercafes lists more than 4,000 Internet cafés worldwide. ⊕ *www.cybercafes.com.*

PHONES

The good news is that you can now make a direct-dial telephone call from virtually any point on Earth. The bad news? You can't always do so cheaply. Calling from a hotel is almost always the most expensive option; hotels usually add huge surcharges to all calls, particularly international ones. In some countries you can phone from call centers or even the post office. Calling cards usually keep costs to a minimum, but only if you purchase them locally. And then there are mobile phones, which are sometimes more prevalent—particularly in the developing world—than landlines; as expensive as mobile phone calls can be, they are still usually a much cheaper option than calling from your hotel.

CALLING WITHIN COSTA RICA

All phone numbers have eight digits. Landline numbers begin with 2; mobile numbers begin with 4, 5, 6, 7, or 8. There are no area codes in Costa Rica, so you only need dial the eight-digit number, without the 506 country code. Coin-operated phones are disappearing rapidly.

CALLING OUTSIDE COSTA RICA

The country code for the United States is 1.

Internet phone services such as Skype are by far the cheapest way to call home; it is a viable option in the Central Valley and major tourist hubs. For other regions or for more privacy, a pay phone using an international phone card is the next step up; you can also call from a pay phone using your own long-distance calling card. Dialing directly from a hotel room is very expensive, as is recruiting an international operator to connect you. ■TIP→ **Watch out for pay phones marked "Call USA/ Canada with a credit card." They are wildly expensive.**

To call overseas directly, dial 00, then the country code (dial 1 for the United States and Canada), the area code, and the number. You can make international calls from almost any phone with an international calling card purchased in Costa Rica. First dial 1199, then the PIN on the back of your card (revealed after scratching off a protective coating), then dial the phone number as you would a direct long-distance call.

AT&T, MCI, and Sprint access codes make calling long distance relatively convenient but can be very expensive. When requesting a calling card from your phone provider, ask specifically about calls from Costa Rica. Most don't work in Costa Rica. Callingcards.com is a great resource for prepaid international calling cards. It lists a calling-card company with a rate of 29¢ per minute for calls from Costa Rica to the United States.

You may find your phone company's local access number blocked in many hotel rooms. If the hotel balks, ask for an international operator, or dial the international operator yourself. One way to improve your odds of getting connected to your long-distance carrier is to sign up with more than one company: a hotel may block Sprint, for example, but not MCI. If all else fails, call from a pay phone.

Phone Resources Callingcards.com ☎ *866/299–3937* ⊕ *www.callingcards.com.* **International information** ☎ *1124.* **International operator** ☎ *1175, 1116.* **Skype** ⊕ *www.skype.com.*

CALLING CARDS
Phone cards can be used from any telephone in Costa Rica, including residential phones, cell phones, and hotel phones. It's rare to be charged a per-minute rate for the mere use of the phone in a hotel. Phone cards are sold in any business displaying the gold-and-blue *"tarjetas telefónicas"* sign. International cards tend to be easier to find in downtown San José and in popular tourist areas.

Tarjetas para llamadas nacionales (domestic calling cards) are available in denominations of 500 colones and 1,000 colones. Phone-card rates are standard throughout the country, about 1¢ per minute, half that at night; a 500-colón card provides about 125 minutes of daytime landline calls. *Tarjetas para llamadas internacionales* (international calling cards) are sold in $10, $20, 2,500-colón, 5,000-colón, and 10,000-colón amounts (denominations are inexplicably split between dollars and colones). In busy spots, roaming card-hawkers abound; feel free to take advantage of the convenience—they're legit.

Some public phones accept *tarjetas chip* ("chip" cards), which record what you spend. ■TIP→ **Avoid buying chip cards, as they frequently malfunction, can be used at few phones, and come in denominations that are insufficient for international calls.**

MOBILE PHONES
If you have an unblocked phone (some countries use different frequencies than what's used in the United States) and your service provider uses the world-standard GSM network (as do T-Mobile, Cingular, and Verizon), you can probably use your phone abroad. ■TIP→ **If you travel internationally frequently, save one of your old mobile phones or buy a cheap one on the Internet; ask your cell-phone company to unlock it for you, and take it with you as a travel phone, buying a new SIM card with pay-as-you-go service in each destination.**

If your cell-phone company has service to Costa Rica, theoretically you can use it here, but expect reception to be impossibly bad in many areas of this mountainous country. Costa Rica works on an 1,800 MHz system—a tri- or quad-band cell phone is your best bet. Note that roaming fees can be steep.

Most car-rental agencies have good deals on cell phones, often better than the companies that specialize in cell-phone rental. Rates range from $5 to $15 per day, plus varying rates for local or international coverage and minimum usage charges. Local calls average 70¢ per minute, international $1 to $1.50. You'll need your passport, a credit card, and a deposit, which varies per phone and service but averages $300 to $400; some rent only to those over 21.

Friendly and professional, Cell Service Costa Rica will get you hooked up and provides door-to-door service. Why Not Phones? has higher daily rates but free local calls, and will set you up with a card for your phone.

Contacts Cell Service Costa Rica ☎ 2296–5553 ⊕ www.cellservicecr.com. **Why Not Phones?** ☎ 2231–3500 in Costa Rica ⊕ www.whynotphones.com.

■ CUSTOMS AND DUTIES

You're always allowed to bring goods of a certain value back home without having to pay any duty or import tax. But there's a limit on the amount of tobacco and liquor you can bring back duty free, and some countries have separate limits for perfumes; for exact figures, check with your customs department. The values of so-called duty-free goods are included in these amounts. When you shop abroad, save all your receipts, as customs inspectors may ask to see them as well as the items you purchased. If the total value of your goods is more than the duty-free limit, you'll have to pay a tax (most often a flat percentage) on the value of everything beyond that limit.

When shopping in Costa Rica, keep receipts for all purchases. Be ready to show customs (*aduanas*) officials what you've bought. Pack purchases together in an easily accessible place. The only orchids you can take home are packaged in a tube and come with an export permit.

If you think a duty is incorrect, appeal the assessment. If you object to the way your clearance was handled, note the inspector's badge number. In either case, first ask to see a supervisor. If the problem isn't resolved, write to the appropriate authorities, beginning with the port director at your point of entry.

Visitors entering Costa Rica may bring in 500 grams of tobacco, 5 liters of wine or spirits, 2 kilograms of sweets and chocolates, and the equivalent of $500 worth of merchandise. One camera and one video camera, six rolls of film, binoculars, and electrical items for personal use only, including laptops and other electronics. Make sure you have personalized prescriptions for any medication you are taking. Customs officials at San José's international airport rarely examine tourists' luggage by hand, although all incoming bags are x-rayed. If you enter by land, they'll probably look through your bags. Officers at the airport generally speak English and are generally your best (only, really) option for resolving any problem. It usually takes about 30 minutes to clear immigration and customs when arriving in Costa Rica.

Pets (cats or dogs only) with updated health and vaccination certificates are welcome in Costa Rica; no prior authorization is required if bringing a dog or cat that has up-to-date (within two weeks of departure) health and vaccination cards. The Servicio Nacional de Salud Animal can provide more info.

Information in Costa Rica Costa Rica Customs (*Dirección General de Aduanas*). ☎ 2522–9000 in Costa Rica ⊕ www.hacienda.go.cr. **Servicio Nacional de Salud Animal** (*SENASA*). ☎ 2587–1600 in Costa Rica ⊕ www.senasa.go.cr.

U.S. Information U.S. Customs and Border Protection ⊕ www.cbp.gov.

▌ EATING OUT

Dining options around Costa Rica run the spectrum from elegant and formal to beachy and casual. San José and popular tourist centers, especially Manuel Antonio, offer a wide variety of cuisine types. Farther off the beaten track, expect hearty, filling local cuisine. Increasingly common as you move away from San José are the thatched conical roofs of the round, open *rancho* restaurants that serve a combination of traditional staples with simple international fare.

Every town has at least one *soda*—that's Costa Rican Spanish for a small, family-run restaurant frequented by locals. Don't expect anything as fancy as a menu. A board usually lists specials of the day. The lunchtime *casado* (literally, "married")—a "marriage" of chicken, pork, or beef with rice, beans, cabbage salad, and natural fruit drink—sets you back about $3. No one will bring you a bill; just pay the cashier when you're finished. A meal at your local soda is always a good place to practice your Spanish.

MEALS AND MEALTIMES

In San José and surrounding cities, most sodas are open daily 7 am to early evening, though some close Sunday. Other restaurants are usually open 11 am to 9 pm, and in resort areas some restaurants may stay open later. Normal dining hours in Costa Rica are noon to 3 and 6 to 9. *Desayuno* (breakfast) is served at most sodas and hotels. The traditional breakfast is *gallo pinto*, which includes eggs, plantains, and fried cheese; hotel breakfasts vary widely and generally offer lighter international options in addition to the local stick-to-your-ribs plate. *Almuerzo* (lunch) is the biggest meal of the day for Costa Ricans, and savvy travelers know that lunch specials are often a great bargain. *Cena* (dinner or supper) runs the gamut.

Except for those in hotels, many restaurants close between Christmas and New Year's Day and during Holy Week (Palm Sunday to Easter Sunday). Unless otherwise noted, the restaurants listed in this guide are open daily for lunch and dinner. Credit cards are not accepted at many rural restaurants. Always ask before you order to find out if your credit card will be accepted. Visa and Master-Card are the most commonly accepted cards; American Express and Diners Club are less widely accepted. The Discover card is increasingly accepted. ▌TIP→ Remember that 23% is added to all menu prices: 13% for tax and 10% for tip. Legally, menus are required to show after-tax, after-tip prices in colones; in practice, many tourist-oriented places do not. Because a gratuity (*propina*) is included, there's no need to tip, but if your service is good, it's nice to add a little money to the obligatory 10%.

RESERVATIONS AND DRESS

Costa Ricans generally dress more formally than North Americans. For dinner at an upscale restaurant, long pants and closed-toe shoes are standard for men except for beach locations, and women tend to wear high heels and dressy clothes that show off their figures. Shorts, flip-flops, and tank tops are not acceptable, except at inexpensive restaurants in beach towns.

VEGETARIAN OPTIONS

Vegetarians sticking to lower-budget establishments won't go hungry, but may develop a love-hate relationship with rice, beans, and fried cheese. A simple *sin carne* (no meat) request is often interpreted as "no beef," so specify *solo vegetales* (only vegetables), and for good measure, *nada de cerdo, pollo, o pescado* (no pork, chicken, or fish). More cosmopolitan restaurants are more conscious of vegetarians—upscale Asian restaurants often offer vegetarian options.

WINES, BEER, AND SPIRITS

The ubiquitous sodas generally don't have liquor licenses, but getting a drink in any other eatery isn't usually a problem. Don't let Holy Thursday and Good

Friday catch you off guard; both are legally dry days. In general, restaurant prices for imported alcohol—which includes just about everything except local beer, rum, and *guaro,* the local sugarcane firewater—may be more than what you'd like to pay.

ELECTRICITY

North American appliances are compatible with Costa Rica's electrical system (110 volts) and outlets (parallel two-prong). Australian and European appliances require a two-prong adapter and a 220-volt to 110-volt transformer. Never use an outlet that specifically warns against using higher-voltage appliances without a transformer. Dual-voltage appliances (i.e., they operate equally well on 110 and 220 volts) such as most laptops, phone chargers, and hair dryers, need only a two-prong adapter, but you should bring a surge protector for your computer.

Contacts Global Electric & Phone Directory. This website has information on electrical and telephone plugs around the world. ⊕ *www.kropla.com.* **Walkabout Travel Gear.** See "Solving the Riddle of Global Electricity" under "Shop Walkabout Travel Gear" for answers to power questions. ☏ 800/852–7085 ⊕ *www.walkabouttravelgear.com.*

EMERGENCIES

Dial 911 for an ambulance, the fire department, or the police. Costa Ricans are usually quick to respond to emergencies. In a hotel or restaurant, the staff will usually offer immediate assistance, and in a public area passersby can be counted on to stop and help.

For emergencies ranging from health problems to lost passports, contact your embassy.

U.S. Embassy United States Embassy (*Embajada de los Estados Unidos*). ⊠ *C. 120 and Avda. 0, Pavas, San José* ☏ *2519–2000* ⊕ *costarica.usembassy.gov* ⊗ *Weekdays 8–4:30.*

HEALTH

Most travelers to Costa Rica do not get any vaccinations or take any special medications. However, according to the U.S. Centers for Disease Control, travel to Costa Rica poses some risk of malaria, hepatitis A and B, dengue fever, typhoid fever, and rabies. The CDC recommends getting vaccines for hepatitis A and B and typhoid fever, especially if you are going to be in remote areas or plan to stay for more than six weeks. Children traveling to Costa Rica should be up to date on all routine immunizations.

SPECIFIC ISSUES IN COSTA RICA

Poisonous snakes, scorpions, and other pests pose a small threat in Costa Rica. Small pockets of malaria exist near the Nicaraguan border on the Caribbean coast. You probably won't need to take malaria pills before your trip, but discuss the option with your doctor. The CDC marks Costa Rica as an area infested by the *Aedes aegypti* (dengue-carrier) mosquito, but not as an epidemic region. The highest-risk area is the Caribbean, especially in the rainy season. In areas with malaria and dengue, use mosquito nets, wear clothing that covers your whole body, and use *repelente* (insect repellent) and *espirales* (mosquito coils), sold in supermarkets, pharmacies, and, sometimes, small country stores. ■TIP→ Repellents made with DEET or picaridin are most effective. Perfume and aftershave can actually attract mosquitoes.

It's unlikely that you will contract malaria or dengue, but if you start suffering from high fever, the shakes, or joint pain, make sure you ask to be tested for these diseases at a local clinic. Your embassy can provide you with a list of recommended doctors and dentists. Such symptoms in the weeks following your return should also spark concern.

Water is generally safe to drink, especially around San José, but the quality can vary; to be safe, drink bottled water. In rural areas you run a mild risk of encountering drinking water, fresh fruit, and vegetables contaminated by fecal matter, which in most cases causes a bit of traveler's diarrhea but can cause leptospirosis (which can be treated by antibiotics if detected early). Stay on the safe side by avoiding uncooked food, unpasteurized milk, and ice—ask for drinks *sin hielo* (without ice). Ceviche, raw fish cured in lemon juice—a favorite appetizer, especially at seaside resorts—is generally safe to eat.

Mild cases of diarrhea may respond to Imodium (known generically as loperamide) or Pepto-Bismol, both of which can be purchased over the counter. Drink plenty of purified water or tea; chamomile (*manzanilla* in Spanish) is a good folk remedy. In severe cases, rehydrate yourself with a salt-sugar solution (½ teaspoon salt and 4 tablespoons sugar per quart of water).

Heatstroke and dehydration are real dangers, especially for hikers, so drink lots of water. Take at least 1 liter per person for every hour you plan to be on the trail. Sunburn is the most common traveler's health problem. Use sunscreen with SPF 30 or higher. Most pharmacies and supermarkets carry sunscreen in a wide range of SPFs, though it is relatively pricey.

The greatest danger to your person actually lies off Costa Rica's popular beaches—riptides are common wherever there are waves, and tourists run into serious difficulties in them every year. If you see waves, ask the locals where it's safe to swim; and if you're uncertain, don't go in deeper than your waist. If you get caught in a rip current, swim parallel to the beach until you're free of it, and then swim back to shore. ■ TIP→ **Avoid swimming where a town's main river opens up to the sea. Septic tanks aren't common.** Do not fly within 24 hours of scuba diving.

OVER-THE-COUNTER REMEDIES

Farmacia is Spanish for pharmacy, and the names for common drugs like *aspirina, ibuprofen, and acetaminofina* (Tylenol) are basically the same as they are in English. Many drugs for which you need a prescription back home are sold over the counter in Costa Rica. Pharmacies throughout the country are generally open from 8 to 8. Some pharmacies in San José stay open 24 hours.

Government facilities—the so-called Caja hospitals (short for Caja Costarricense de Seguro Social, or Costa Rican Social Security System)—and clinics are of acceptable quality, but notoriously overburdened. Private hospitals are more accustomed to serving foreigners.

■ HOURS OF OPERATION

Like the rest of the world, Costa Rica's business hours have been expanding. Megamalls are usually open seven days a week, opening around 10 am and closing around 9 pm. Some government offices and smaller businesses close for lunch, especially in rural areas, but *jornada continúa* (without the lunch break) is becoming more common in San José. Larger museums usually keep a Monday-to-Sunday schedule, and smaller ones are open weekdays. National parks often close one day a week; for example, Manuel Antonio is closed Monday. Eateries in beach towns and other tourist areas often stay open seven days a week, while those in the cities close Sunday, and sometimes Monday. Bars and nightclubs are generally open until 1 or 2 am. Last calls vary from place to place.

Three public holidays (April 11, July 25, and October 12) are usually observed on the following Monday. Government offices and commercial establishments observe all the holidays. The only days the country truly shuts down are Holy Thursday and Good Friday; some buses still run, but no alcohol can be purchased, and most restaurants and all stores are closed.

January 1: New Year (*Año Nuevo*)

April 11: Juan Santamaría Day (*Día de Juan Santamaría*)

Easter Week: Holy Thursday and Good Friday, religious activities (*Semana Santa*)

May 1: International Labor Day (*Día del Trabajador*)

July 25: Annexation of Guanacaste Province (*Anexión de Guanacaste*)

August 2: Day of the Virgin of Los Angeles (*Virgen de los Ángeles*), patron saint of Costa Rica

August 15: Mother's Day (*Día de la Madre*)

September 15: Independence Day (*Día de Independencia*)

October 12: Culture Day (*Día de la Cultura*)

December 25: Christmas (*Navidad*)

▌MAIL

The Spanish word for post office is *correo*. Mail from the United States can take up to two to three weeks to arrive in Costa Rica (occasionally it never arrives at all). Within the country, mail service is even less reliable. Outgoing mail is marginally quicker, with delivery to North America in 5 to 10 days, especially when sent from San José. It's worth registering mail; prices are only slightly higher. All overseas cards and letters will automatically be sent airmail. Mail theft is a chronic problem, so do not mail checks, cash, or anything else of value.

Minimum postage for postcards and letters from Costa Rica to the United States and Canada costs the equivalent of U.S. 75¢.

You can have mail sent *poste restante* (*lista de correos*) to any Costa Rican post office (specify Correo Central to make sure it goes to the main downtown office). In written addresses, *apartado,* abbreviated *apdo.,* indicates a post-office box.

Post offices are generally open weekdays 7:30 to 5:30 and Saturday 8 to noon. Stamps can be purchased at post offices and some hotels and souvenir shops. These vendors will also accept the mail you wish to send; don't bother looking for a mailbox, as there are only a handful (usually in rural areas with no post office). Always check with your hotel, which may sell stamps and post your letters for you.

Shipping parcels through the post office is not for those in a hurry because packages to the United States and Canada can take weeks. Also, packages may be pilfered. However, post-office shipping is the cheapest way to go, with rates starting at $5 per kilogram.

Some stores offer shipping, but it is usually quite expensive. If you can, carry your packages home with you.

UPS has offices in San José, Tamarindo, Jacó, Manuel Antonio, Sarchí, Nuevo Arenal, La Fortuna, and Limón. DHL has drop-offs in San José (Rohrmoser, Paseo Colón), Curridabat, Escazú, Heredia, Liberia, Limón, Ciudad Quesada, Jacó, Quepos, and San Isidro de El General. FedEx has offices in San José and Heredia; it offers package pickup service in San José and other centers, such as Limón. All three have central information numbers with English-speaking staff. Prices are about 10 times what you'd pay at the post office, but packages arrive in a matter of days. "Overnight" is usually a misnomer—shipments to most North American cities take two business days.

Express Services Main Offices **DHL** ✉ *Paseo Colón, next to Budget car rental, Paseo Colón, San José* ☎ *2209–0000 in Costa Rica* ⊕ *www. dhl.co.cr.* **FedEx** ✉ *Paseo Colón and C. 40, 100 m east of León Cortés statue, San José* ☎ *800/463–3339 in Costa Rica* ⊕ *www.fedex. com* ☞ *Call for other locations.* **UPS** ✉ *Pavas Hwy., 50 m east of Pizza Hut, Pavas, San José* ☎ *2290–2828 in Costa Rica* ⊕ *www.ups.com* ☞ *Call for other locations.*

■ MONEY

In general, Costa Rica is cheaper than North America or Europe, but travelers looking for dirt-cheap developing-nation deals may find it's more expensive than they bargained for—and prices are rising as more foreigners visit.

Food in modest restaurants and public transportation are inexpensive. A 2-km (1-mile) taxi ride costs about $2.

ATMS AND BANKS

Lines at San José banks would try the patience of a saint; instead, get your spending money at a *cajero automático* (automatic teller machine). If you do use the bank, remember that Monday, Friday, and the first and last days of the month are the busiest days.

Although they are springing up at a healthy rate, don't count on using an ATM outside San José. Though not exhaustive, the A Toda Hora website lists locations of its ATH cash machines, and notes which ones offer colones (usually in increments of 10,000 colones), dollars (in increments of $20), or both; choose your region or city in the box on the homepage called *Búsqueda de Cajeros.*

For reasons of security, a growing number of ATMs shut down at 10 pm and begin working again at 6 am. In addition to banks, you'll find them in major grocery stores, some hotels, gas-station convenience stores, and even a few McDonald's. ATH, Red Total, and Scotiabank machines supposedly accept both Cirrus (a partner with MasterCard) and Plus (a partner with Visa) cards, but sometimes

don't. If you'll be spending time away from major tourist centers, particularly in the Caribbean, get all the cash you need in San José and carry a few U.S. dollars in case you run out of colones. It's helpful to have both a Visa and a MasterCard—even in San José—as some machines accept only one or the other. Both companies have sites with fairly comprehensive lists of accessible ATMs around the world.

ATMs are often out of order and sometimes run out of cash on weekends. ■TIP➔ PIN codes with more than four digits are not recognized at Costa Rican ATMs. If you have a five-digit PIN, change it with your bank before you travel. Although it seems counterintuitive, try to use ATMs only during bank business hours. If an ATM "eats" your card, you can go inside to retrieve it or get cash from a teller.

The Credomatic office, housed in the BAC San José central offices on Calle Central between Avenidas 3 and 5, is the local representative for most major credit cards; get cash advances here, or at any bank (Banco Nacional and BAC San José are good for both MasterCard and Visa; Banco Popular, and Banco de Costa Rica always accept Visa).

State banks have branches with slightly staggered hours; core times are weekdays 9 to 4, and very few are open Saturday morning. A few branches of Banco Nacional are open until 6, or occasionally 7. Private banks—Scotiabank and BAC San José—tend to keep longer hours and are usually the best places to change U.S. dollars and traveler's checks; rates may be marginally better in state banks, but the long waits cancel out any benefit. Multinational banks like Citi and Scotiabank have branches here, but none has any link to your back-home account except via your ATM card. The BAC San José in the check-in area at Aeropuerto Internacional Juan Santamaría is open daily 5 am to 10 pm.

Resources A Toda Hora (*ATH*). ☎ *2211-4500* ⊕ *www.ath.com.* **MasterCard** ⊕ *www. mastercard.com/cr.* **Visa** ⊕ *www.visa.com.*

LOCAL DO'S AND TABOOS

CUSTOMS OF THE COUNTRY

Ticos tend to use formal Spanish, preferring, for example, *con mucho gusto* (with much pleasure) instead of the typical Spanish *de nada* for "you're welcome." Family is important in Costa Rica. It is considered polite to ask about your marital status and family.

Ticos can be disarmingly direct; don't be surprised (or offended) if locals pick up on a physical trait and give you a nickname: *Chino* for anyone of Asian ethnicity, or *Gordita* if you have even an extra ounce around your hips. It's meant affectionately. In almost every other situation, a circumspect approach is advised; North American straightforwardness often comes across as abrupt here. Preceding requests with a bit of small talk (even if it's a hotel employee) goes a long way. Also, be very aware of body language and other cues—Costa Ricans don't like to say no, and will often avoid answering a question or simply say *gracias* when they really mean no.

Many Costa Rican men have a habit of ogling or making gratuitous comments when young women pass on the street. To help avoid this, take a cue from local women and leave skimpy clothing for the beach.

The expression "Tico time" was coined for a reason. Transportation, theaters, government, and major businesses tend to stick to official schedules. Anything else is flexible, and best handled by building in a little buffer time and sliding into the tropical groove.

GREETINGS

Costa Ricans are extremely polite, quick to shake hands (light squeezes are the norm) and place a kiss on the right cheek (meaning you need to bear left when going in for the peck). The formal pronoun *usted* (you) is used almost exclusively; the slangier *vos* is thrown about in informal settings and among close or young friends and relatives.

SIGHTSEEING

As you would anywhere, dress and behave respectfully when visiting churches. In houses of worship men and women should not wear shorts, sleeveless shirts, or sandals; women should wear pants or skirts below the knee. Bathing suits, short shorts, and other skimpy attire are inappropriate city wear, but tend to be the uniform in beach towns; even here, however, cover up for all but the most informal restaurants.

Panhandlers are not a major problem, but if you're in San José, you'll come across a few. It's always better to give to an established organization, but the safety net for Costa Ricans with disabilities is riddled with holes, so even a couple of hundred colones will be appreciated. A few savvy panhandlers speak excellent English and will try to draw you into conversation with a sob story about a lost passport. Keep walking.

Banks and other offices allow pregnant women and the elderly to move immediately to the front of the line, and this respect is carried over to other establishments and crowded buses. If you're in a crowd and need to step in front of them, murmur *"Con permiso"* ("Excuse me").

OUT ON THE TOWN

Locals tend to dress up to go out, whatever the activity: a snazzy (but not too dressy) outfit will serve you well in San José. To catch a waiter's attention, wave discreetly or say, *"Disculpe, señor"* (or *señora* for women); best to leave the finger snapping to the locals. For the bill, ask for *"La cuenta, por favor."* (No one will bring the check to you until you ask.) Smoking is prohibited in all places of business, including inside bars and restaurants. Excessive displays of affection draw frowns, clearly lost on the gaggles of lip-locked couples. If invited to someone's home, bring a gift such as flowers or a bottle of wine or some trinket from your home country. If offered food at someone's home, it's polite to accept it and eat it (even if you aren't hungry).

LOCAL DO'S AND TABOOS

LANGUAGE

It's always a good idea to learn a little of the local language. You need not strive for fluency; even just mastering a few basic words and terms is bound to make chatting with the locals more rewarding. At the very least, learn the rudiments of polite conversation—niceties such as *por favor* (please) and *gracias* (thank you) will be warmly appreciated. *For more words and phrases, see the Spanish glossary in the back of the book.* In the Caribbean province of Limón, a Creole English called Mekatelyu is widely spoken by older generations. English is understood by many people in these parts.

An open-ended *"¿Dónde está . . .?"* ("Where is . . .?") may result in a wall of rapid-fire Spanish. Better to avoid language as much as possible when asking for directions. You're going to have to stop often anyway, so it can be helpful to make the journey in segments: in the city, say the name of the place you want to go, and point—adding a questioning *izquierda* (left), *derecha* (right), or *directo* (straight). Do this frequently, and you'll get there. On longer journeys, keep a good map handy, and use the same strategy, asking for a nearby town on your journey rather than the final destination.

And of course, you can't go wrong with an amiable "Pura vida," which serves as "hello," "good-bye," "thanks," "cool," etc.

A phrase book and language-tape set can help get you started. *Fodor's Spanish for Travelers* is excellent. We also recommend the Fodor's Travel Phrases mobile app and Living Language Spanish.

CREDIT CARDS

It's a good idea to inform your credit-card company before you travel, especially if you're going abroad and don't travel internationally very often. Record all your credit-card numbers—as well as the phone numbers to call if your cards are lost or stolen—in a safe place. Both MasterCard and Visa have general numbers you can call (collect if you're abroad) if your card is lost, but you're better off calling the number of your issuing bank, since MasterCard and Visa usually just transfer you to your bank; your bank's number is printed on your card.

Major credit cards are accepted at most hotels and restaurants in this book; Visa and MasterCard have the widest acceptance, with American Express, Discover, and Diners Club somewhat less so. As the phone system improves, many budget hotels, restaurants, and other businesses have begun to accept plastic; but plenty of places still require payment in cash.

■TIP➜ Carry enough cash to patronize the many businesses without credit-card capability, including smaller denominations. Note that some hotels, restaurants, tour companies, and other businesses add a surcharge (around 5%) to the bill if you pay with a credit card, or give you a 5% to 10% discount if you pay in cash. It's always a good idea to pay for large purchases with a major credit card so you can cancel payment or get reimbursed if there's a problem.

CURRENCY AND EXCHANGE

Costa Rica's currency is the colón. (The plural is colones.) Prices are shown with a "¢" sign in front of the number. At this writing, the colón is about 550 to the U.S. dollar and 750 to the euro. Coins come in denominations of 5, 10, 25, 50, 100, and 500 colones. Be careful not to mix up the very similar 100- and 500-colón coins. Bills come in denominations of 1,000 (red), 2,000 (blue), 5,000 (yellow), 10,000 (green), 20,000 (orange), and 50,000 (purple) colones. Avoid using larger-denomination bills in taxis, on buses, or in small stores. Many tourist-oriented businesses accept U.S. dollars, although the exchange rate might not be favorable. Make sure the dollars are in good condition—no tears or writing—and don't use anything larger than a $20.

Costa Rican colones are sold abroad at terrible rates, so wait until you arrive in Costa Rica to get local currency. U.S. dollars are still the easiest to exchange, but euros can be exchanged for colones at just about any Banco Nacional office and at the San José and Escazú branches of other banks. Private banks—Scotiabank and BAC San José—are the best places to change U.S. dollars and traveler's checks. The arrivals area of the international airports in San José and Liberia both have ATMs and are your best bet for getting cash after you land. There is a branch of the BAC San José upstairs in the check-in area of Juan Santamaría airport where you can exchange money when you arrive—it's a much better deal than the Global Exchange counter in the baggage-claim area. Airport taxi and van drivers accept U.S. dollars. Outdoor money changers are rarely seen on the street, but avoid them if they approach; you will most certainly get a bad deal, and you risk robbery by pulling out wads of cash.

■TIP→ Even if a currency-exchange booth has a sign promising no commission, rest assured that there's some kind of huge, hidden fee. (Oh . . . that's right. The sign didn't say no fee.) And as for rates, you're almost always better off getting foreign currency at an ATM or exchanging money at a bank.

▌ PACKING

Travel light, and make sure you can carry your luggage without assistance. Even if you're planning to stay only in luxury resorts, odds are that at least once you'll have to haul your stuff a distance from bus stops, the shuttle drop-off, or the airport. Another incentive to pack

light: domestic airlines have tight weight restrictions—at this writing 11 to 13 kilograms, or 25 to 30 pounds—and not all buses have luggage compartments. Frameless backpacks and duffel bags can be squeezed into tight spaces and are less conspicuous than fancier luggage.

Bring comfortable, hand-washable clothing. T-shirts and shorts are acceptable near the beach and in tourist areas; long-sleeve shirts and pants protect your skin from ferocious sun and, in coastal regions, mosquitoes. Leave your jeans behind—they take forever to dry. Pack a waterproof, lightweight jacket and a light sweater for cool nights, early mornings, and trips up volcanoes; you'll need even warmer clothes for trips to Chirripó National Park or Cerro de la Muerte and overnight stays in San Gerardo de Dota or on the slopes of Poás Volcano. Bring at least one good (and wrinkle-free) outfit for going out at night.

It's sometimes tough to find tampons, so bring your own and since septic systems here generally cannot handle them, refrain from flushing down the toilet. For almost all toiletries, including contact lens supplies, a pharmacy is your best bet. Don't forget sunblock, and expect to sweat it off and reapply regularly in the high humidity. Definitely bring batteries, because they're expensive here.

Snorkelers staying at budget hotels should consider bringing their own equipment; otherwise, you can rent gear at most beach resorts.

You have to get down and dirty—well, more like wet and muddy—to see many of the country's natural wonders. This following packing list is not comprehensive; it's a guide to some of the things you might not think to bring. For your main piece of luggage, a sturdy internal-frame backpack is great, but a duffel bag works, too. You can get by with a rolling suitcase, but then bring a smaller backpack as well.

PACKING LIST

■ Quick-drying synthetic-fiber shirts and socks

■ Hiking boots or shoes that can get muddy and wet

■ Waterproof sport sandals (especially in the Osa Peninsula, where most transportation is by boat, and often there are no docks)

■ Knee-high socks for the rubber boots that are supplied at many lodges

■ A pair of lightweight pants (fire ants, mosquitoes, and other pests make covering yourself a necessity on deep-forest hikes)

■ Pants for horseback riding (if that's on your itinerary)

■ Waterproof, lightweight jacket, windbreaker, or poncho

■ Day pack for hikes

■ Sweater for cool nights and early mornings

■ Swimsuit

■ Insect repellent (with DEET, for forested areas and especially on the northern Caribbean coast, where there are pockets of malaria)

■ Flashlight or headlamp with spare batteries (for occasional power outages or inadequately lighted walkways at lodges)

■ Sunscreen with a minimum of SPF 30 (waterproof sunscreens are best; even if you're not swimming, you might be swimming in perspiration)

■ Large, portable water bottle

■ Hat and/or bandannas (not only do they provide shade, but they prevent perspiration from dripping down your face)

■ Binoculars (with carrying strap)

■ Camera (waterproof, or with a waterproof case or dry bag, sold in outdoor-equipment stores)

■ Imodium and Pepto-Bismol (tablet form is best)

■ Swiss Army knife (and remember to pack it in your checked luggage, never your carry-on— even on domestic flights in Costa Rica)

■ Zip-style plastic bags (they always come in handy)

■ Travel alarm clock or watch with an alarm (don't count on wake-up calls)

■ Nonelectric shaving utensils

■ Toilet paper (rarely provided in public bathrooms)

▌ PASSPORTS

U.S. citizens need only a passport to enter Costa Rica and a return plane ticket home or to another country for stays of up to 90 days. Make sure it's up to date—you'll be refused entry if the passport is due to expire in less than three months. To be on the safe side, make sure it is valid for at least six months. Spending 72 hours outside the country—Nicaragua or Panama are popular options—gets you another 90 days, but don't expect to do that undetected more than a couple of times. Customs forms ask how many visits you've made to Costa Rica in the past year.

Costa Rica has one of the highest rates of U.S. passport theft in the world. Travelers in Costa Rica are not required to carry their original documents with them at all times, although you must have easy access to them. Photocopies of the data page and your entry stamp are sufficient; those, at least, must be with you at all times. Although there have been reports from around the world about security problems with in-room safes, if your hotel doesn't have a safe in reception, locking a passport in a hotel-room safe is better than leaving it in an unlocked hiding place or carrying it with you.

▌TIP→ **For easy retrieval in the event of a lost or stolen passport, before you leave home scan your passport into a portable storage device (like an iPod) that you're carrying with you or email the scanned image to yourself.**

If your passport is lost or stolen, first call the police—having the police report can make replacement easier—and then call your embassy. You'll get a temporary Emergency Travel Document that will need to be replaced once you return home. Fees vary according to how fast you need the passport; in some cases the fee covers your permanent replacement as well. The new document will not have your entry stamps; ask if your embassy takes care of this, or whether it's your responsibility to get the necessary immigration authorization.

GENERAL REQUIREMENTS FOR COSTA RICA	
Passport	Must be valid for 3 months after date of arrival
Visa	Free upon entry for Americans
Vaccinations	None required
Driving	International driver's license not required
Departure Tax	US$29

RESTROOMS

When nature calls, look for signs that say "*servicios sanitarios*" or simply "*sanitarios.*" In smaller venues, toilet paper is tossed into a trash bin rather than into the toilet. Septic systems are delicate and the paper will clog the toilet. At some public restrooms you might have to pay 50¢ or so for a few sheets of toilet paper. At others, there may not be any toilet paper at all. It's always a good idea to have some tissues at the ready. Gas stations generally have facilities, but you may decide not to be a slave to your bladder once you get a look at them. On car trips, watch for parked buses; generally this indicates some sort of better-kept public facilities.

SAFETY

Violent crime is not a serious problem in Costa Rica, but thieves can easily prey on tourists, so be alert. The government has created a Tourism Police unit whose more

WORD OF MOUTH

"We go every year and have always felt safe everywhere that we've gone. We don't wear pricey jewelry or flash iPhones, etc. around, and we use the safe in our room, don't leave things in the car unattended, etc."
—volcangirl

than 250 officers can be seen on bikes or motorcycles patrolling areas in Guanacaste, San José, and the Arenal area.

For many English-speaking tourists, standing out like a sore thumb can't be avoided. But there are some precautions you can take:

■ Don't bring anything you can't stand to lose.

■ Don't flash expensive jewelry or watches.

■ In cities, don't carry expensive cameras or lots of cash.

■ Wear backpacks on your front; thieves can slit your backpack and run away with its contents before you notice.

■ Don't wear a waist pack, because thieves can cut the strap.

■ Distribute your cash and any valuables (including credit cards and passport) between a deep front pocket, an inside jacket or vest pocket, and a hidden money belt. (If you use a money belt, have some small bills handy so you don't have to reach for it in public.)

■ Keep your hand on your wallet if you are in a crowd or on a bus.

■ Don't let your purse dangle from your shoulder; always hold on to it with your hand for added security.

■ Keep car windows rolled up and car doors locked at all times in cities.

■ Park in designated lots—car theft is common—or if that's not possible, accept the offer of the *guachimán* (a term adopted from English, pronounced "watchie man")—men or boys who watch your car while you're gone. Give them the equivalent of a dollar an hour when you return.

■ Never leave valuables in a car, even in an attended parking lot.

■ Padlock your luggage.

■ Talk with locals or your hotel staff about any areas you should avoid. Never leave a drink unattended in a club or bar: scams involving date-rape drugs have been reported, targeting both men and women.

■ Never leave your belongings unattended, including at the beach or in a tent.

■ Use your hotel room's safe, even if there's an extra charge. If your room doesn't have one, ask the manager to put your valuables in the hotel safe and ask him or her to sign a list of what you are storing.

■ If someone does try to rob you, immediately surrender your possessions and don't try to be a hero.

Scams occur in San José. A distraction artist might squirt you with something, or spill something on you, then try to clean you off while his partner steals your backpack. Pickpockets and bag slashers work buses and crowds. Beware of anyone who seems overly friendly, aggressively helpful, or disrespectful of your personal space. Be particularly vigilant around San José's Coca-Cola bus terminal, one of the dicier areas but a central tourism hub.

A few tourists have been hit with the slashed-tire scam: someone punctures the tires of your rental car (often right at the airport, when you arrive) and then comes to your "aid" when you pull off to the side of the road and robs you. Forget about the rims: always drive to the nearest open gas station or service center if you get a flat.

Lone women travelers will get a fair amount of attention from men; to minimize hassles, avoid wearing short shorts or skirts. On the bus, try to take a seat next to a woman. Women should not walk alone in San José at night. Ask at your hotel which neighborhoods to avoid. Ignore unwanted comments. If you are being harassed on a bus, at a restaurant, or in some other public place, tell the manager. In taxis, sit in the backseat. If you want to fend off an earnest but decent admirer in a bar, you can politely say, *"Por favor, necesito un tiempo a solas"* (I'd like some time on my own, please). Stronger is *"Por favor, no me moleste"* (Please, stop bothering me), and for real pests the simple *"Váyase!"* (Go away!) is usually effective.

▌ TAXES

The airport departure tax for tourists is $29, payable in cash (dollars or colones) or with Visa. (Paying the tax via credit card means the transaction will be processed as a cash advance and incur additional fees.) All Costa Rican businesses charge a 13% sales tax, called the IVA. Hotels charge a 16.4% fee covering service and tax. Restaurants add 13% tax and 10% service fee to meals. Tourists are not refunded for taxes paid in Costa Rica.

▌ TIME

Costa Rica does not observe daylight saving time, so from November to March it's the equivalent of Central Time in the United States (one hour behind New York). The rest of the year, it is the equivalent of Mountain Time in the United States (two hours behind New York).

Time Zones Timeanddate.com
⊕ *www.timeanddate.com/worldclock.*

▌ TIPPING

Costa Rica doesn't have a tipping culture, but positive reinforcement goes a long way to fostering a culture of good service; good intentions are usually there, but execution can be hit-and-miss. Tip only for good service. ■TIP→ **Tipping in colones is best. Never tip with U.S. coins, because there's no way for locals to exchange them.**

TIPPING

Bellhop	$1–$5 or 500 colones per bag, depending on the level of the hotel
Hotel Concierge	$5 or more, if he or she performs a service for you
Hotel Doorman	$1–$2 if he helps you get a cab
Hotel Maid	$1–$3 or 500 to 1,500 colones per day (either daily or at the end of your stay, in cash)
Hotel Room-Service Waiter	$1–$2 or 500 to 1,000 colones per delivery, even if a service charge has been added
Tour Guide	$10 or 5,000 colones per day
Hired Driver	10% of the rental
Waiter	10%–15%, with 15% being the norm at high-end restaurants; nothing additional if a service charge is added to the bill
Bartender	200 colones
Restroom Attendant	$1
Coat-check	$1–$2 per item checked unless there is a fee, then nothing
Taxi Driver	200–300 colones if they've helped you navigate a complicated set of directions, or 500 colones if they've helped you with luggage, otherwise nothing

▌ TOURS

BIKING

Costa Rica is mountainous and rough around the edges. It's a rare bird who attempts a road-biking tour here. But the payoff for the ungroomed, tire-munching terrain is uncrowded, wildly beautiful off-road routes. Most bike-tour operators want to make sure you're in moderately good shape and do some biking at home. Others, such as Coast to Coast Adventures, have easier one- and two-day jaunts. Bike Arenal has biking packages in the Arenal area and around the country for all skill levels, with short and long ride options for each day. Operators generally provide top-notch equipment, including bikes and helmets, but welcome serious mountain bikers who bring their own ride. Operators usually meet you at the airport and take care of all logistics.

Useful topographical maps (not biking maps per se) are generally provided as part of the tour, and include unpaved roads. If you're striking out on your own, these maps can usually be found at downtown San José's Lehmann bookstore for about $5. Some basic Spanish is highly recommended if you're going to do it yourself.

▌TIP→ **Check with individual airlines about bike-packing requirements.** Cardboard bike boxes can be found at bike shops for about $15; more secure options start at $40. International travelers often can substitute a bike for a piece of checked luggage at no charge (if the box conforms to regular baggage dimensions), but U.S. airlines will sometimes charge a $100 to $200 handling fee each way.

Contacts Bike Arenal ☎ 2479–7150, 866/465–4114 in North America ⊕ www.bikearenal.com. **Coast to Coast Adventures** ☎ 2280–8054 in Costa Rica ⊕ www.coasttocoastadventures.com.

BIRD-WATCHING

You will get more out of your time in Costa Rica by taking a tour rather than trying to find birds on your own. Bring your own binoculars, but don't worry about a spotting scope; if you go with a company that specializes in birding tours, your guide will have one. Expect to see about 300 species during a weeklong tour. Many U.S. travel companies subcontract with the Costa Rican tour operators listed here. By arranging your tour directly with local companies, you save money. Selva Mar, a tour agency specializing in the Southern Zone, runs comprehensive tours through Birdwatching Costa Rica.

Contacts Birdwatching Costa Rica
☏ *2771–4582 in Costa Rica* ⊕ *www.
birdwatchingcostarica.com.* **Horizontes Nature
Tours** ☏ *2222–2022 in Costa Rica, 888/786–
8748 in North America* ⊕ *www.horizontes.com.*

DIVING

Costa Rica's Cocos Island—one of the
world's best dive spots—can be visited only
on a 10-day scuba safari with *Aggressor*
or *Undersea Hunter.* But Guanacaste, the
South Pacific, and, to a lesser extent, the
Caribbean, offer some respectable underwater adventures. Bill Beard's Costa Rica in the
Gulf of Papagayo is a diving-tour pioneer
and offers several Pacific-coast options. Diving Safaris Costa Rica, in Playa Hermosa,
has trips to dive sites in Guanacaste. In the
South Pacific, Costa Rica Adventure Divers in Drake Bay arranges five-night trips.
In this same area, Caño Island is a good
alternative to Cocos Island, particularly in
the rainy season, when dive sites closer to
shore are clouded by river runoff.

Contacts *Aggressor* ☏ *800/348–2628 in
North America* ⊕ *www.aggressor.com.* **Bill
Beard's Costa Rica** ☏ *877/853–0538 in
North America* ⊕ *www.billbeardcostarica.com.*
Costa Rica Adventure Divers ☏ *2231–5806,
866/553–7073 in North America* ⊕ *www.
costaricadiving.com.* **Diving Safaris Costa
Rica** ☏ *2672–1259 in Costa Rica* ⊕ *www.
costaricadiving.net.* **Undersea Hunter**
☏ *2228–6613, 800/203–2120 in North
America* ⊕ *www.underseahunter.com.*

FISHING

If fishing is your primary objective in
Costa Rica, you are better off booking
a package. During peak season you may
not even be able to find a hotel room in
the hot fishing spots, let alone one of the
top boats and skippers. The major fish
populations move along the Pacific coast
through the year, and tarpon and snook
fishing on the Caribbean is subject to the
vagaries of seasonal wind and weather
but viable year-round. San José–based
Costa Rica Outdoors has been in business
arranging fishing packages since 1995;
it is one of the best bets for full service

and honest advice about where to go and
works with the widest range of operators around the country. Anglers in the
know recommend Kingfisher Sportfishing in Playa Carrillo, Guanacaste; Bluefin
Sportfishing and J.P. Sportfishing Tours in
Quepos; the Zancudo Lodge near Golfito;
and Río Colorado Lodge on the northern
Caribbean coast.

Contacts Bluefin Sportfishing ☏ *2777–0000
in Costa Rica* ⊕ *www.bluefinsportfishing.
com.* **Costa Rica Outdoors** ☏ *2231–0306,
800/308–3394 in North America* ⊕ *www.
costaricaoutdoors.com.* **J.P. Sportfishing Tours** ☏ *2777–1613, 866/620–4188 in
U.S.* ⊕ *www.jpsportfishing.com.* **Kingfisher
Sportfishing** ☏ *2656–0091 in Costa Rica*
⊕ *www.costaricabillfishing.com.* **Río Colorado
Lodge** ☏ *2232–4063, 800/243–9777 in North
America* ⊕ *www.riocoloradolodge.com.* **The
Zancudo Lodge** ☏ *2776–0008, 800/854–8791
in North America* ⊕ *www.zancudolodge.com.*

GOLF

Putting on a green against a dramatic
Pacific backdrop isn't the first image that
springs to mind for Costa Rican vacations, but the increase in luxury resorts
and upscale tourism has created a respectable, albeit small, golfing circuit in the
Central Valley and along the Pacific coast.
Most packages maximize links time with
side excursions to explore the country's
natural riches. Costa Rica Golf Adventures organizes multiday tours at four-
and five-star lodgings.

Contacts Costa Rica Golf Adventures
☏ *888/672–2057 in North America*
⊕ *www.golfcr.com.*

HIKING

Most nature-tour companies include hiking
as part of their itineraries, but these hikes
may not be strenuous enough for serious
hikers. Ask many questions about hike
lengths and difficulty levels before booking
the tour or you may be disappointed with
the amount of time you get to spend on
the trails. The following companies cater to
both moderate and serious hikers.

Contacts **G Adventures** ☎ *888/800–4100 in North America* ⊕ *www.gadventures.com.* **Serendipity Adventures** ☎ *888/226–5050 in North America, 2556–2222 in Costa Rica* ⊕ *www.serendipityadventures.com.*

SURFING

Most Costa Rican travel agencies have packages that ferry both veterans and newcomers between the country's famed bicoastal breaks. Local experts at Surf-CostaRica.com really know their stuff, and offer standard or custom packages. Del Mar Surf Camp on the Pacific specializes in women-only surf lessons and packages. Learn how to surf, camp on the beach, and delve into personal development on Outward Bound Costa Rica's weeklong adult surf journeys.

Contacts **Del Mar Surf Camp** ☎ *2643–3197 in Costa Rica, 2682–1433 in Costa Rica, 855/833–5627 in North America* ⊕ *www. delmarsurfcamp.com.* **Outward Bound Costa Rica** ☎ *800/676–2018 in North America, 2278–6062 in Costa Rica* ⊕ *www. costaricaoutwardbound.org.* **Surf-CostaRica. com** ⊕ *www.surf-costarica.com.*

SPANISH-LANGUAGE PROGRAMS

Thousands of people travel to Costa Rica every year to study Spanish. Dozens of schools in and around San José offer professional instruction and homestays, and there are several smaller schools outside the capital. Conversa has schools in San José and in Santa Ana, west of the capital, offering hourly classes as well as a "Super Intense" program (5½ hours per day). On the east side of town, ILISA provides cultural immersion in San Pedro. Mesoamérica is a low-cost language school that is part of a nonprofit organization devoted to peace and social justice. La Academia de Español d'Amore is in beautiful Manuel Antonio. Language programs at the Institute for Central American Development Studies include optional academic seminars in English about Central America's political, social, and economic conditions.

FODORS.COM CONNECTION

Before your trip, be sure to check out what other travelers are saying in Forums on ⊕ *www.fodors.com.*

Contacts **Conversa** ☎ *2203–2071, 888/669–1664 in North America* ⊕ *www.conversa. com.* **ILISA** ☎ *2280–0700, 800/454–7248 in North America* ⊕ *www.ilisa.com.* **Institute for Central American Development Studies** (*ICADS*). ☎ *2225–0508 in Costa Rica* ⊕ *www.icads.org.* **La Academia de Español d'Amore** ☎ *2777–0233, 877/434–7290 in North America* ⊕ *www.academiadamore.com.* **Mesoamérica** ☎ *2253–3195 in Costa Rica* ⊕ *www.mesoamericaonline.net.*

VOLUNTEER PROGRAMS

In recent years more and more Costa Ricans have realized the need to preserve their country's precious biodiversity. Both Ticos and far-flung environmentalists have founded volunteer and educational concerns to this end.

Volunteer opportunities span a range of diverse interests. You can tag sea turtles as part of a research project, build trails in a national park, or volunteer at an orphanage. Many of the organizations require at least rudimentary Spanish. The Sea Turtle Conservancy is devoted to the preservation of endangered turtles. Earthwatch Institute leads science-based trips studying monkeys, turtles, rain forests, or climate change. The Talamancan Association of Ecotourism and Conservation (ATEC), as well as designing short group and individual outings centered on Costa Rican wildlife and indigenous culture, keeps an updated list of up to 30 local organizations that welcome volunteers. Beach cleanups, recycling, and some wildlife projects don't require proficiency in Spanish. The Costa Rican Humanitarian Foundation has volunteer opportunities with indigenous communities, women, street kids, community-based clinics, and education centers.

The Institute for Central American Development Studies (ICADS) is a nonprofit social justice institute that runs a language school and arranges internships and field study (college credit is available); some programs are available only to college students.

Contacts Costa Rican Humanitarian Foundation (*Fundación Humanitaria*). ☏ *8390–4192 in Costa Rica* ⊕ *www.crhf.org.* **Earthwatch Institute** ☏ *800/776–0188 in North America* ⊕ *www.earthwatch.org.* **Institute for Central American Development Studies** (*ICADS*). ☏ *2225–0508 in Costa Rica* ⊕ *www.icads.org.* **Sea Turtle Conservancy** ☏ *352/373–6441 in North America* ⊕ *www. conserveturtles.org.* **Talamancan Association of Ecotourism and Conservation** (*ATEC*). ☏ *2750–0398 in Costa Rica* ⊕ *www.ateccr.org.*

▌ VISITOR INFORMATION

The official tourism board, the Instituto Costarricense de Turismo (ICT), has an office on Avenida Central in San José and a small desk in the baggage claim area at Juan Santamaría airport. The airport counter contains a few brochures but is staffed only sporadically. Visitor information is provided by the Costa Rica Tourist Board in the United States.

Contacts Instituto Costarricense de Turismo (*ICT*). ☏ *2299–5800, 866/267–8274 in North America* ⊕ *www.visitcostarica.com.*

ONLINE TRAVEL TOOLS

InfoCostaRica has a website with good cultural info and chat rooms. The REAL Costa Rica slips in a bit of attitude with its information, and is a bit lax on updating, but scores high marks for overall accuracy. Scope out detailed maps, driving distances, and pictorial guides to the locations of hotels and businesses in some communities at CostaRicaMap.com. The Association of Residents of Costa Rica online forums are some of the region's most active and informed, with topics ranging from business and pleasure trips to the real-estate market. The *Tico Times* publishes news about Costa Rica, much of it of interest to visitors.

Contacts Association of Residents of Costa Rica (*ARCR*). ⊕ *www.arcr.net.* **CostaRicaMap. com** ⊕ *www.costaricamap.com.* **InfoCostaRica** ⊕ *www.infocostarica.com.* **The REAL Costa Rica** ⊕ *www.therealcostarica.com.* **The Tico Times.** ⊕ *www.ticotimes.net.*

INDEX